C0-ARR-574

Contemporary Authors®

ISSN 0010-7468

Contemporary Authors®

A Bio-Bibliographical Guide to Current Writers in Fiction, General Nonfiction, Poetry, Journalism, Drama, Motion Pictures, Television, and Other Fields

volume 219

Detroit • New York • San Diego • San Francisco • Cleveland • New Haven, Conn. • Waterville, Maine • London • Munich

Contemporary Authors, Vol. 219

Project Editor
Jenai A. Mynatt

Editorial
Katy Balcer, Shavon Burden, Sara Constantakis, Natalie Fulkerson, Michelle Kazensky, Julie Keppen, Joshua Kondek, Lisa Kumar, Mary Ruby, Lemma Shomali, Susan Strickland, Maikue Vang, Tracey Watson

Permissions
Lori Hines

Imaging and Multimedia
Lezlie Light, Kelly A. Quin

Composition and Electronic Capture
Kathy Sauer

Manufacturing
Lori Kessler

For more information, contact
The Gale Group, Inc.
27500 Drake Rd.
Farmington Hills, MI 48331-3535
Or you can visit our internet site at
http://www.gale.com

LIBRARY OF CONGRESS CATALOG CARD NUMBER 62-52046

ISBN 0-7876-6699-8
ISSN 0010-7468

Printed in the United States of America
10 9 8 7 6 5 4 3 2 1

Contents

Preface ... vii

Product Advisory Board ... xi

International Advisory Board ... xii

CA Numbering System and
Volume Update Chart ... xiii

Authors and Media People
Featured in This Volume ... xv

Acknowledgments ... xvii

Author Listings ... 1

Indexing note: All *Contemporary Authors* entries are indexed in the *Contemporary Authors* cumulative index, which is published separately and distributed twice a year.

As always, the most recent Contemporary Authors cumulative index continues to be the user's guide to the location of an individual author's listing.

Preface

Contemporary Authors (*CA*) provides information on approximately 115,000 writers in a wide range of media, including:

- Current writers of fiction, nonfiction, poetry, and drama whose works have been issued by commercial publishers, risk publishers, or university presses (authors whose books have been published only by known vanity or author-subsidized firms are ordinarily not included)
- Prominent print and broadcast journalists, editors, photojournalists, syndicated cartoonists, graphic novelists, screenwriters, television scriptwriters, and other media people
- Notable international authors
- Literary greats of the early twentieth century whose works are popular in today's high school and college curriculums and continue to elicit critical attention

A *CA* listing entails no charge or obligation. Authors are included on the basis of the above criteria and their interest to *CA* users. Sources of potential listees include trade periodicals, publishers' catalogs, librarians, and other users of the series.

How to Get the Most out of *CA*: Use the Index

The key to locating an author's most recent entry is the *CA* cumulative index, which is published separately and distributed twice a year. It provides access to *all* entries in *CA* and *Contemporary Authors New Revision Series* (*CANR*). Always consult the latest index to find an author's most recent entry.

For the convenience of users, the *CA* cumulative index also includes references to all entries in these Gale literary series: *Authors and Artists for Young Adults, Authors in the News, Bestsellers, Black Literature Criticism, Black Literature Criticism Supplement, Black Writers, Children's Literature Review, Concise Dictionary of American Literary Biography, Concise Dictionary of British Literary Biography, Contemporary Authors Autobiography Series, Contemporary Authors Bibliographical Series, Contemporary Dramatists, Contemporary Literary Criticism, Contemporary Novelists, Contemporary Poets, Contemporary Popular Writers, Contemporary Southern Writers, Contemporary Women Poets, Dictionary of Literary Biography, Dictionary of Literary Biography Documentary Series, Dictionary of Literary Biography Yearbook, DISCovering Authors, DISCovering Authors: British, DISCovering Authors: Canadian, DISCovering Authors: Modules* (including modules for Dramatists, Most-Studied Authors, Multicultural Authors, Novelists, Poets, and Popular/Genre Authors), *DISCovering Authors 3.0, Drama Criticism, Drama for Students, Feminist Writers, Hispanic Literature Criticism, Hispanic Writers, Junior DISCovering Authors, Major Authors and Illustrators for Children and Young Adults, Major 20th-Century Writers, Native North American Literature, Novels for Students, Poetry Criticism, Poetry for Students, Short Stories for Students, Short Story Criticism, Something about the Author, Something about the Author Autobiography Series, St. James Guide to Children's Writers, St. James Guide to Crime & Mystery Writers, St. James Guide to Fantasy Writers, St. James Guide to Horror, Ghost & Gothic Writers, St. James Guide to Science Fiction Writers, St. James Guide to Young Adult Writers, Twentieth-Century Literary Criticism, 20th Century Romance and Historical Writers, World Literature Criticism,* and *Yesterday's Authors of Books for Children.*

A Sample Index Entry:

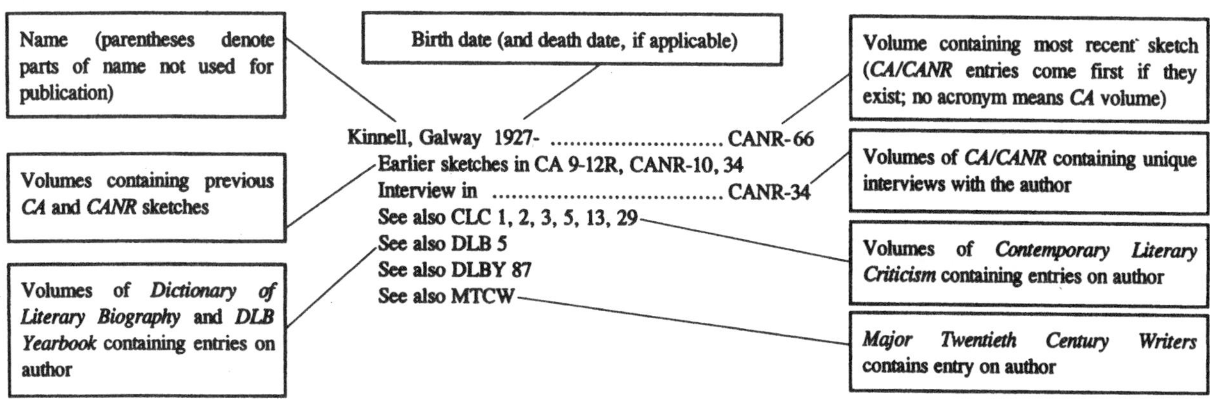

How Are Entries Compiled?

The editors make every effort to secure new information directly from the authors; listees' responses to our questionnaires and query letters provide most of the information featured in *CA*. For deceased writers, or those who fail to reply to requests for data, we consult other reliable biographical sources, such as those indexed in Gale's *Biography and Genealogy Master Index,* and bibliographical sources, including *National Union Catalog, LC MARC,* and *British National Bibliography.* Further details come from published interviews, feature stories, and book reviews, as well as information supplied by the authors' publishers and agents.

An asterisk (*) at the end of a sketch indicates that the listing has been compiled from secondary sources believed to be reliable but has not been personally verified for this edition by the author sketched.

What Kinds of Information Does An Entry Provide?

Sketches in *CA* contain the following biographical and bibliographical information:

- **Entry heading:** the most complete form of author's name, plus any pseudonyms or name variations used for writing

- **Personal information:** author's date and place of birth, family data, ethnicity, educational background, political and religious affiliations, and hobbies and leisure interests

- **Addresses:** author's home, office, or agent's addresses, plus e-mail and fax numbers, as available

- **Career summary:** name of employer, position, and dates held for each career post; resume of other vocational achievements; military service

- **Membership information:** professional, civic, and other association memberships and any official posts held

- **Awards and honors:** military and civic citations, major prizes and nominations, fellowships, grants, and honorary degrees

- **Writings:** a comprehensive, chronological list of titles, publishers, dates of original publication and revised editions, and production information for plays, television scripts, and screenplays

- **Adaptations:** a list of films, plays, and other media which have been adapted from the author's work

- **Work in progress:** current or planned projects, with dates of completion and/or publication, and expected publisher, when known

- **Sidelights:** a biographical portrait of the author's development; information about the critical reception of the author's works; revealing comments, often by the author, on personal interests, aspirations, motivations, and thoughts on writing

- **Interview:** a one-on-one discussion with authors conducted especially for *CA*, offering insight into authors' thoughts about their craft

- **Autobiographical essay:** an original essay written by noted authors for *CA*, a forum in which writers may present themselves, on their own terms, to their audience

- **Photographs:** portraits and personal photographs of notable authors

- **Biographical and critical sources:** a list of books and periodicals in which additional information on an author's life and/or writings appears

- **Obituary Notices** in *CA* provide date and place of birth as well as death information about authors whose full-length sketches appeared in the series before their deaths. The entries also summarize the authors' careers and writings and list other sources of biographical and death information.

Related Titles in the *CA* Series

Contemporary Authors Autobiography Series complements *CA* original and revised volumes with specially commissioned autobiographical essays by important current authors, illustrated with personal photographs they provide. Common topics include their motivations for writing, the people and experiences that shaped their careers, the rewards they derive from their work, and their impressions of the current literary scene.

Contemporary Authors Bibliographical Series surveys writings by and about important American authors since World War II. Each volume concentrates on a specific genre and features approximately ten writers; entries list works written by and about the author and contain a bibliographical essay discussing the merits and deficiencies of major critical and scholarly studies in detail.

Available in Electronic Formats

GaleNet. *CA* is available on a subscription basis through GaleNet, an online information resource that features an easy-to-use end-user interface, powerful search capabilities, and ease of access through the World-Wide Web. For more information, call 1-800-877-GALE.

Licensing. *CA* is available for licensing. The complete database is provided in a fielded format and is deliverable on such media as disk, CD-ROM, or tape. For more information, contact Gale's Business Development Group at 1-800-877-GALE, or visit us on our website at www.galegroup.com/bizdev.

Suggestions Are Welcome

The editors welcome comments and suggestions from users on any aspect of the *CA* series. If readers would like to recommend authors for inclusion in future volumes of the series, they are cordially invited to write the Editors at *Contemporary Authors*, Gale Group, 27500 Drake Rd., Farmington Hills, MI 48331-3535; or call at 1-248-699-4253; or fax at 1-248-699-8054.

Contemporary Authors Product Advisory Board

The editors of *Contemporary Authors* are dedicated to maintaining a high standard of excellence by publishing comprehensive, accurate, and highly readable entries on a wide array of writers. In addition to the quality of the content, the editors take pride in the graphic design of the series, which is intended to be orderly yet inviting, allowing readers to utilize the pages of *CA* easily and with efficiency. Despite the longevity of the *CA* print series, and the success of its format, we are mindful that the vitality of a literary reference product is dependent on its ability to serve its users over time. As literature, and attitudes about literature, constantly evolve, so do the reference needs of students, teachers, scholars, journalists, researchers, and book club members. To be certain that we continue to keep pace with the expectations of our customers, the editors of *CA* listen carefully to their comments regarding the value, utility, and quality of the series. Librarians, who have firsthand knowledge of the needs of library users, are a valuable resource for us. The *Contemporary Authors* Product Advisory Board, made up of school, public, and academic librarians, is a forum to promote focused feedback about *CA* on a regular basis. The six-member advisory board includes the following individuals, whom the editors wish to thank for sharing their expertise:

- **Anne M. Christensen,** Librarian II, Phoenix Public Library, Phoenix, Arizona.

- **Barbara C. Chumard,** Reference/Adult Services Librarian, Middletown Thrall Library, Middletown, New York.

- **Eva M. Davis,** Youth Department Manager, Ann Arbor District Library, Ann Arbor, Michigan.

- **Adam Janowski, Jr.,** Library Media Specialist, Naples High School Library Media Center, Naples, Florida.

- **Robert Reginald,** Head of Technical Services and Collection Development, California State University, San Bernadino, California.

- **Stephen Weiner,** Director, Maynard Public Library, Maynard, Massachusetts.

International Advisory Board

Well-represented among the 115,000 author entries published in *Contemporary Authors* are sketches on notable writers from many non-English-speaking countries. The primary criteria for inclusion of such authors has traditionally been the publication of at least one title in English, either as an original work or as a translation. However, the editors of *Contemporary Authors* came to observe that many important international writers were being overlooked due to a strict adherence to our inclusion criteria. In addition, writers who were publishing in languages other than English were not being covered in the traditional sources we used for identifying new listees. Intent on increasing our coverage of international authors, including those who write only in their native language and have not been translated into English, the editors enlisted the aid of a board of advisors, each of whom is an expert on the literature of a particular country or region. Among the countries we focused attention on are Mexico, Puerto Rico, Germany, Luxembourg, Belgium, the Netherlands, Norway, Sweden, Denmark, Finland, Taiwan, Singapore, Spain, Italy, South Africa, Israel, and Japan, as well as England, Scotland, Wales, Ireland, Australia, and New Zealand. The sixteen-member advisory board includes the following individuals, whom the editors wish to thank for sharing their expertise:

- **Lowell A. Bangerter,** Professor of German, University of Wyoming, Laramie, Wyoming.
- **Nancy E. Berg,** Associate Professor of Hebrew and Comparative Literature, Washington University, St. Louis, Missouri.
- **Frances Devlin-Glass,** Associate Professor, School of Literary and Communication Studies, Deakin University, Burwood, Victoria, Australia.
- **David William Foster,** Regent's Professor of Spanish, Interdisciplinary Humanities, and Women's Studies, Arizona State University, Tempe, Arizona.
- **Hosea Hirata,** Director of the Japanese Program, Associate Professor of Japanese, Tufts University, Medford, Massachusetts.
- **Jack Kolbert,** Professor Emeritus of French Literature, Susquehanna University, Selinsgrove, Pennsylvania.
- **Mark Libin,** Professor, University of Manitoba, Winnipeg, Manitoba, Canada.
- **C. S. Lim,** Professor, University of Malaya, Kuala Lumpur, Malaysia.
- **Eloy E. Merino,** Assistant Professor of Spanish, Northern Illinois University, DeKalb, Illinois.
- **Linda M. Rodríguez Guglielmoni,** Associate Professor, University of Puerto Rico—Mayagüez, Puerto Rico.
- **Sven Hakon Rossel,** Professor and Chair of Scandinavian Studies, University of Vienna, Vienna, Austria.
- **Steven R. Serafin,** Director, Writing Center, Hunter College of the City University of New York, New York City.
- **David Smyth,** Lecturer in Thai, School of Oriental and African Studies, University of London, England.
- **Ismail S. Talib,** Senior Lecturer, Department of English Language and Literature, National University of Singapore, Singapore.
- **Dionisio Viscarri,** Assistant Professor, Ohio State University, Columbus, Ohio.
- **Mark Williams,** Associate Professor, English Department, University of Canterbury, Christchurch, New Zealand.

CA Numbering System and Volume Update Chart

Occasionally questions arise about the *CA* numbering system and which volumes, if any, can be discarded. Despite numbers like " 29-32R," " 97-100" and "218," the entire *CA* print series consists of only 270 physical volumes with the publication of *CA* Volume 219. The following charts note changes in the numbering system and cover design, and indicate which volumes are essential for the most complete, up-to-date coverage.

CA First Revision

- 1-4R through 41-44R (11 books)
  Cover: Brown with black and gold trim.
  There will be no further First Revision volumes because revised entries are now being handled exclusively through the more efficient *New Revision Series* mentioned below.

***CA* Original Volumes**

- 45-48 through 97-100 (14 books)
  Cover: Brown with black and gold trim.
  101 through 219 (119 books)
  Cover: Blue and black with orange bands.
  The same as previous *CA* original volumes but with a new, simplified numbering system and new cover design.

***CA* Permanent Series**

- *CAP*-1 and *CAP*-2 (2 books)
  Cover: Brown with red and gold trim.
  There will be no further Permanent Series volumes because revised entries are now being handled exclusively through the more efficient *New Revision Series* mentioned below.

***CA* New Revision Series**

- CANR-1 through CANR-125 (125 books)
  Cover: Blue and black with green bands.
  Includes only sketches requiring significant changes; **sketches are taken from any previously published CA, CAP, or CANR volume.**

If You Have:	You May Discard:
CA First Revision Volumes 1-4R through 41-44R and *CA Permanent Series* Volumes 1 and 2	*CA* Original Volumes 1, 2, 3, 4 Volumes 5-6 through 41-44
CA Original Volumes 45-48 through 97-100 and 101 through 219	**NONE:** These volumes will not be superseded by corresponding revised volumes. Individual entries from these and all other volumes appearing in the left column of this chart may be revised and included in the various volumes of the *New Revision Series.*
CA New Revision Series Volumes *CANR*-1 through *CANR*-125	**NONE:** The *New Revision Series* does not replace any single volume of *CA*. Instead, volumes of *CANR* include entries from many previous *CA* series volumes. All *New Revision Series* volumes must be retained for full coverage.

A Sampling of Authors and Media People Featured in This Volume

Monica Ali
Born in Bangladesh but raised primarily in England, Ali received much critical attention before and after the 2003 publication of the novel *Brick Lane,* in which she chronicles the lives of several inhabitants of an immigrant Bangladeshi community in London's East End. Based solely on the strength of the book's unpublished manuscript, Ali was named one of *Granta*'s Best Young British Novelists. The writer went on to receive a nomination for Great Britain's Man-Booker Prize and was shortlisted for the National Book Critics Circle Award.

Robert Bausch
Bausch is a fiction writer whose novels and stories frequently revolve around the theme of family and the ways in which unforeseen events can disrupt the delicate balance of family ties. In books such as *On the Way Home,* published in 1982, and *The Gypsy Man,* released in 2002, Bausch tackles subjects related to family and community, including a soldier's readjustment to civilian life after the Vietnam War and the mystery surrounding a child's disappearance in a small town in the 1950s. An autobiographical essay by Bausch is included in this volume of *CA.*

Nalo Hopkinson
The recipient of numerous awards for her work, Hopkinson is a science-fiction author who blends African, Caribbean, and Creole folklore with the conventions of the science-fiction and fantasy genre. Born to a literary family in Jamaica, she became inspired to attempt working in the science-fiction genre after discovering that some of her favorite writers, including Samuel R. Delaney and Octavia Butler, were black. Hopkinson published her first novel, *Brown Girl in the Ring,* in 1998. *Midnight Rider,* released in 2000, was nominated for Nebula and Hugo awards. An autobiographical essay by Hopkinson is included in this volume of *CA.*

Lloyd Jones
Jones is a prolific writer and editor whose works span both fiction and nonfiction genres. His novels and stories deal with diverse subject matter, sometimes mixing fact and fiction, including the 1993 travel book *Biografi: An Albanian Quest,* in which Jones provides a narrative of his experiences while traveling through Albania in 1991. A native New Zealander, Jones received that country's 2001 Deutz Medal for Fiction for the novel *The Book of Fame,* which is a fictionalized history of a well-known New Zealand rugby team.

Bobby Knight
Known as much for his controversial style as for his accomplishments on the court, Knight spent nearly thirty years as the highly successful head basketball coach of the Indiana University Hoosiers before he was dismissed for allegedly violating the school's policy against physically abusing players. Knight went on to become head coach at Texas Tech University, and wrote the memoir *Knight: My Story* after his first season with the team. Considered one of the highest achievers in college basketball, Knight was inducted into the Basketball Hall of Fame in 1991.

Adrian Nicole LeBlanc
LeBlanc is a journalist and the author of the book *Random Family: Love, Drugs, Trouble, and Coming of Age in the Bronx,* the result of her ten-year study of the often harrowing lives of two impoverished young Latina women living in New York. Many critics praised the depth of LeBlanc's research on her subjects, as well as the novelistic quality of her writing. *Random Family* proved popular with readers, and was shortlisted for a National Book Critics Award in 2003.

Christopher Paolini
Paolini achieved publishing success while still a teen when his novel *Eragon* was released in 2003. The author, who was home-schooled, began writing the fantasy novel after earning his GED at the age of fifteen. Initially issued in 2002 by the publishing company owned by Paolini's parents, the book came to greater prominence after it was discovered by the novelist Carl Hiaasen, who connected Paolini with his publisher Alfred E. Knopf. Drawing on Old Norse mythology, the novel depicts the adventures of teen protagonist Eragon and his dragon companion Saphira as they journey through the kingdom of Alagaësua.

Ernest Shackleton
A famed Antarctic explorer, Shackleton spent the majority of his career attempting to reach the South Pole. Although he failed to meet this goal before his death in 1922, he led numerous harrowing expeditions into the Antarctic region in pursuit of his objective, and chronicled his adventures in texts such as *The Heart of the Antarctic: Being the Story of the British Antarctic Expedition 1907-1909,* originally published in1909, and *South: A Memoir of the Endurance Voyage,* which was reprinted in 1998.

Acknowledgments

Grateful acknowledgment is made to those publishers, photographers, and artists whose work appear with these authors's essays. Following is a list of the copyright holders who have granted us permission to reproduce material in this volume of *CA*. Every effort has been made to trace copyright, but if omissions have been made, please let us know.

Photographs/Art

Bausch, Robert: All photographs reproduced by permission of the author.

Hopkinson, Nalo: All photographs reproduced by permission of the author, except as noted: photo of Hopkinson with James Morrow © Beth Gwinn. Reproduced by permission of Beth Gwinn.

Whittemore, Reed: All photographs reproduced by permission of the author.

A

** Indicates that a listing has been compiled from secondary sources believed to be reliable, but has not been personally verified for this edition by the author sketched.*

ADKINS, Roy 1951-

PERSONAL: Born 1951, in Maidenhead, Berkshire, England; married August 12, 1978; wife's name, Lesley (an archeologist and writer). *Education:* University College, Cardiff, B.A. (with honors).

ADDRESSES: *Agent*—Bill Hamilton, A. M. Heath & Co., Ltd., 79 St. Martin's Lane, London WC2N 4RE, England. *E-mail*—mail@adkinsarchaeology.com.

CAREER: Archaeologist and writer.

MEMBER: Institute of Field Archaeologists, Society of Authors.

AWARDS, HONORS: London Society of Antiquaries fellow.

WRITINGS:

(With Ralph Jackson) *Neolithic Stone and Flint Axes from the River Thames,* British Museum (London, England), 1978.

WITH WIFE, LESLEY ADKINS

A Thesaurus of British Archaeology, Barnes & Noble (New York, NY), 1982, published as *The Handbook of British Archaeology,* Macmillan (London, England), 1983, reprinted, Constable (London, England), 1998.

Under the Sludge: Beddington Roman Villa: Excavations at Beddington Sewage Works 1981-1983, Beddington, Carshalton & Wallington Archaeological Society (Carshalton, England), 1986.

Archaeological Illustration, Cambridge University Press (Cambridge, England), 1989.

An Introduction to Archaeology, Apple Press (London, England), 1989.

Abandoned Places, Apple Press (London, England), 1990.

Talking Archaeology: A Handbook for Lecturers and Organizers, Council for British Archaeology (London, England), 1990.

Introduction to Romans, Apple Press (London, England), 1991.

A Field Guide to Somerset Archaeology, Dovecote (Wimborne, England), 1992.

Handbook to Life in Ancient Rome, Facts on File (New York, NY), 1994.

Dictionary of Roman Religion, Facts on File (New York, NY), 1996.

Handbook to Life in Ancient Greece, Facts on File (New York, NY), 1997.

The Keys of Egypt: The Obsession to Decipher Egyptian Hieroglyphs, HarperCollins (New York, NY), 2000, published as *The Keys of Egypt: The Race to Read the Hieroglyphs,* HarperCollins (London, England), 2000, published as *The Keys of Egypt: The Race to Crack the Hieroglyph Code,* HarperCollins (New York, NY) 2001.

The Little Book of Egyptian Hieroglyphs, Hodder & Stoughton (London, England), 2001.

The Keys of Egypt has been translated into Dutch, Spanish, Italian, German, Norwegian, Swedish, Taiwanese, and Japanese.

WORK IN PROGRESS: Trafalgar: The Biography of a Battle, for Penguin (New York, NY).

SIDELIGHTS: Husband-and-wife team of archaeologists Roy and Lesley Adkins are the authors of numerous books on archaeology and ancient history. They began their careers as field archaeologists in Great Britain, working in the town of Milton Keynes and then in South London, where they directed an excavation of a Roman villa in Beddington. Since 1985 they have also run an independent archaeological consulting firm; as consultants, they conduct both documentary research and excavation.

The Adkins' first book, *A Thesaurus of British Archaeology,* was published in 1982, and later published as *The Handbook of British Archaeology.* The couple took three years to write the book, and noted on their Web site that they decided to write it because "nothing was available giving explanations of the numerous technical terms in archaeology—the jargon that makes many people feel they are excluded from archaeology." They also commented that writing the book was such an exhausting process that "we firmly believed we would never write another book!" However, they have continued to write, producing many more volumes of archaeology and ancient history.

Introduction to the Romans is intended to provide a broad overview of this ancient culture, which still influences our own. On their Web site, the Adkins noted, "Of all our books, this is the one most often borrowed in public libraries."

Abandoned Places examines various prehistoric and historic sites worldwide, and explains the factors that led their former inhabitants to leave them—including war and natural disasters.

A Field Guide to Somerset Archaeology is a guidebook for those who wish to visit the prehistoric, Roman, and medieval sites of the county of Somerset in southwest England. The book gives directions to sites of interest, along with descriptions of the sites, information on car parking, opening times, and access for people with disabilities.

In *Under the Sludge: Beddington Roman Villa Excavations at Beddington Sewage Works 1981-1983* the Adkins describe the archaeological site of a Roman villa found in Beddington, under acres of sewage sludge once spread by the Beddington Sewage Works. Development threatened the site, so the Adkins undertook an excavation, basing their work on the fact that a Roman bath was known to exist on the site. They found the bath, but also located a villa and a prehistoric settlement. The book tells the story of the excavation, and was written largely for the people of the area, many of whom volunteered in the work.

Archaeological Illustration is a detailed manual for those interested in recording archaeological evidence through drawings. After providing a brief history of the use of illustration in archaeological work, the book covers equipment, handling, and finishing techniques, and then discusses measurement in the lab and in the field, scaling and mapping methods, and terms for recording archaeological data. The authors also discuss technical aspects of printing processes and computer graphics. In *American Antiquity,* M. Jane Kellett praised the book's "extensive source and reference lists" and wrote that it provides "many techniques and useful quick tips."

Handbook to Life in Ancient Rome and *Handbook to Life in Ancient Greece* provide concise references about these societies, with chapters on their history, economy, religion, culture, and other topics. Both books are illustrated throughout with the Adkins' own line drawings and photographs.

In *Dictionary of Roman Religion* the Adkins go beyond many existing dictionaries of classical mythology to discuss various aspects of Roman religion, including priesthoods, sacrifices, temples, altars, cult objects, burial rites, superstitions, and magic, as well as the numerous Roman gods and goddesses.

In 2000, the Adkins published *The Keys of Egypt: The Race to Read Hieroglyphics,* which examines the quest to understand ancient Egypt's beautiful and mysterious form of writing. Hieroglyphs gained widespread attention in Europe after Napoleon invaded Egypt in 1798, leading to the discovery of the famed Rosetta Stone, which contained texts in two forms of ancient Egyptian writing, as well as in Greek. The Egyptian text was finally decoded by the brilliant scholar Jean-François Champollion, who was in competition with an Englishman, Thomas Young. The coauthors describe Champollion's process of decipherment, as well as the social milieu of post-revolutionary

France, which was often not kind to intellectuals. In *Geographical,* Chris Martin praised the book's suspenseful storytelling and its description of Champollion's travails, noting, "The book is remarkably tense for a dry subject." In the London *Sunday Telegraph,* Simon Singh described the book as "a ripping tale of obsession and rivalry."

In *The Little Book of Egyptian Hieroglyphs* the Adkins present a popular manual for readers interested in hieroglyphs, particularly those who wish to visit ancient Egyptian monuments and view them with more knowledge and enjoyment. The book explains how the writing system works, provides examples of hieroglyphs and what they mean, and discusses the various types of signs used in the writing. On their Web site, the Adkins commented, "With numerous pictures of hieroglyphs and easy-to-identify pictures of gods and goddesses, this book is essential to anyone wanting to know about Egyptian writing—and will show how anyone from Adrian to Zoe can write their own name in hieroglyphs."

The Adkins have traveled in Europe, Asia Minor, and Egypt, and have led groups on archaeological tours in the United Kingdom. They frequently lecture on archaeological topics, and have taught university adult-education courses.

BIOGRAPHICAL AND CRITICAL SOURCES:

PERIODICALS

American Antiquity, April, 1993, M. Jane Kellet, review of *Archaeological Illustration,* p. 387.

Booklist, August, 1997, review of *Handbook to Life in Ancient Greece,* p. 1926.

Geographical, January, 2001, Chris Martin, review of *The Keys of Egypt: The Race to Crack the Hieroglyph Code,* p. 99.

Kirkus Reviews, September 15, 2000, review of *The Keys of Egypt.*

Publishers Weekly, October 9, 2000, review of *The Keys of Egypt,* p. 85.

Sunday Telegraph (London, England), August 27, 2000, Simon Singh, review of *The Keys of Egypt,* p. 13.

Times (London, England), October 11, 2000, Douglas Kennedy, review of *The Keys of Egypt.*

Times Higher Educational Supplement, March 30, 2001, Dr. Richard Parkinson, review of *The Keys of Egypt.*

ONLINE

Adkins Archaeology Web site, http://www.adkinsarchaeology.com (June 10, 2003).

* * *

ALEANDRI, Emelise (Francesca)

PERSONAL: Born in Riva del Garda, Italy; daughter of John Baptista (a mail carrier) and Elodia Vladimira (a teacher; maiden name, Lutterotti) Aleandri. *Education:* Hunter College, M.A. (theatre); City University of New York, Ph.D. (theatre).

ADDRESSES: *Office*—Center for Italian-American Studies, Brooklyn College, Brooklyn, NY 11210. *E-mail*—frizzilazzi@aol.com.

CAREER:

Actress, singer, dancer, choreographer, and director. Director of stage productions, including *Not Every Thief Will Bring You Grief,* off-Broadway; *Discovering Bodies,* New York Theatre Ensemble, New York, NY; *Schizzo Hey Ride,* Stage 73, New York; *Applejuice,* Joseph Jefferson Theatre Company, New York; *Duo,* Forum; *Peanuts* (children's play), Boerum Hill Children's Theatre workshop, Brooklyn, NY; *Doctor's Duty,* Brooklyn College, Brooklyn; *Superman,* Bennington College, Bennington, VT; *The Marriage Proposal,* College of New Rochelle, New Rochelle, NY; *Willpower,* New York City Community College, New York; and *The New Americans,* St. Patrick's Theatre, New York.

Also worked on other stage productions, including (as assistant to producers) *As You Like It,* Broadway production; (as assistant director) *Onward Victoria,* Broadway production; (as assistant director) *Peep,* South Street, New York; and (as assistant director) *Winning Hearts and Minds,* New York Shakespeare

Festival, Public Theatre. Choreographer of Middle Eastern dances for *The Birds,* Drama Committee Repertory, New York; and *Schizzo Hey Ride,* Stage 73, New York.

Actress in stage productions, including (as Molly, Queen of the Hoboes) *Hobo Christmas,* American Theatre of Actors (ATA), New York, 2000; (as Italian model) *96A,* Eccentric Circles Theatre; (as Princess) *The Bandit Princess,* staged reading, Kikue Tashiro; (as Good Deeds) *Everyman,* Galaxy Theatre Company; (as Maria Antonia) *Mon ami Angelique,* Provincetown Playhouse, Provincetown, MA; (as Opal Jewel) *Power,* People's Performing Company; (as Tillie) *Sweatshop,* ATA; (as Aunt Mary Masiello) *Italian Funerals and Other Festive Occasions,* Walnut Street Theatre, Philadelphia, PA; (as Antonietta) *Festa Primavera,* LaMaMa Etc., New York; (as the Good Christmas Witch) *La befana,* New York and U.S. cities; (as Suzie Merluzzi) *Perfidia,* New York and U.S. cities; (as dancer and singer) *Carnevale,* New York and U.S. cities; (as dancer) *Salute to King Tut,* Central Park Bandshell, NY; (as dancer) *Lincoln Center Gestical,* Damrosch Park, NY; (as dancer) *Gateway Showcase '80,* Gateway Community Restoration; (as dancer) *George White Ensemble,* Marymount Manhattan; *Festive Occasions; Winning Hearts and Minds,* New York Shakespeare Festival; *Show Biz Applauds Lincoln Center,* Avery Fisher Hall, New York; *La vita,* Danny's Skylight Room; and *The Gondoliers.*

Actress in films, including (as Florence) *Crooklyn,* 1994; (as Angela Patera) *West New York* (also known as *Paperblood*), 1996; (as Italian woman at murder site) *Summer of Sam,* Buena Vista, 1999; also appeared (uncredited) in *All That Jazz; Raging Bull; The World according to Garp; King of the Gypsies; The Night of the Juggler; King Kong; Defiance; Willy and Phil; Out to Lunch; This Is Videx; Snooze; Searching for Paradise; The Yards; The Frequency; Mickey Blue Eyes; Isn't She Great; 1967; Sleepers; Godfather III; My New Gun; Age of Innocence; Teenage Mutant Ninja Turtles; Hejdran; Cookie; Married to the Mob; Jerky Boys; Moonstruck; Jumping Jack Flash; Car 54; Turk 182; Fort Apache-the Bronx; John and Yoko; Danger Adrift; Regarding Henry;* and *Rooftops.*

Played Elenora Duse in television movie *Of Penguins and Peacocks,* 2000. Actress in television series, including (as Italian nurse/nun) *Loving,* American Broadcasting Companies (ABC); and (as lead) *Pirate TV Comedy Show,* Music Television (MTV). Guest star on television series, including *Nurse,* Columbia Broadcasting System (CBS); *Eischeid,* National Broadcasting Company (NBC); *All My Children,* ABC; *The Sopranos,* Home Box Office (HBO); *Our Family Honor,* ABC; *One Life to Live,* ABC; *Guiding Light,* CBS; *Internal Affairs; Tattingers,* NBC; *Donohue,* syndicated; *Another World,* NBC; *Equalizer,* CBS; *Mathnet; Law & Order,* NBC; *Law & Order: Special Victims Unit,* NBC; and *America's Most Wanted,* Fox.

Producer and host of television series *Italics Magazine Show,* CUNY-TV, New York, 1987-97. Director and producer of television specials, including *Teatro: The Legacy of Italian-American Theatre,* 1995; and *Festa: Italian Festival Traditions,* CUNY-TV, 1997.

MEMBER: Actors Equity Association, Screen Actors Guild, American Federation of Television and Radio Artists, American Guild of Variety Artists, Guild of Italian American Actors (formerly the Italian Actors Union).

AWARDS, HONORS: Elena Cornaro Award, New York State Grand Lodge Order of the Sons of Italy in America, 2001, for work in Italian-American culture.

WRITINGS:

The Italian-American Immigrant Theatre of New York City, Arcadia Publishing (Charleston, SC), 1999.

Little Italy, Arcadia Publishing (Charleston, SC), 2002.

Author of *The Legend of La Befana;* translated various plays from Italian to English; contributor of articles on theatre to journals.

BIOGRAPHICAL AND CRITICAL SOURCES:

ONLINE

Frizzi & Lazzi Web site, http://www.frizzilazzi.com/ (July 16, 2003).

Guild of Italian American Artists Web site, http://www.nygiaa.org/ (July 16, 2003).

New York State Lit Tree Web site, http://www.nyslittree.org/ (July 16, 2003), "Emelise Aleandri."*

ALI, Monica 1967-

PERSONAL: Born 1967, in Dhaka, Bangladesh; immigrated to England, 1971; daughter of Hatem (a teacher) and Joyce (a counselor) Ali; married; husband's name, Simon (a management consultant); children: Felix, Shumi (daughter). *Education:* Graduated from Wadham College, Oxford.

ADDRESSES: *Agent*—c/o Author Mail, Simon & Schuster, 1230 Avenue of the Americas, New York, NY 10020.

CAREER: Writer. Has worked in marketing for two publishing houses.

AWARDS, HONORS: Named one of *Granta*'s Best Young British Novelists, 2003; *Brick Lane* was shortlisted for Great Britain's Man-Booker Prize, the *Guardian*'s First Book Award, the National Book Critics Circle award, and was named one of the *New York Times* best books of 2003.

WRITINGS:

Brick Lane, Scribner (New York, NY), 2003.

SIDELIGHTS: Monica Ali established her reputation as one of Great Britain's most talented writers before her first novel was published. She was named one of the *Granta*'s Best Young British Novelists solely on the basis of her first manuscript, *Brick Lane,* and by the time it was published critics were eager to determine if it lived up to the hype. "Surely, *Brick Lane* can't be that good?" wrote Harriet Lane in the *Guardian,* referring to the book's pre-publication notoriety. "Actually, it's better," she answered; "Ali's novel is warm, shrewd, startling and hugely readable: the sort of book you race through greedily, dreading the last page." Ali, who was born in Bangladesh and grew up in England, chose as the subject for her novel the immigrant experience of London's Bangladeshi community, which is centered around the East End district known as Brick Lane. Critics hailed the book as a fully realized portrait of an insulated community that is as rich in detail as any novel by Dickens or Flaubert. Comparisons to other non-white British writers, such as V. S. Naipaul and Jhumpa Lahiri, and praise for her mature voice were plentiful. "Ali already has a sense of technical assurance and an inborn generosity that cannot be learned," wrote Michael Gorra in the *New York Times Book Review. Brick Lane* was named one of the *New York Times* best books of the year, with the editors deeming it "a remarkable achievement."

Brick Lane tells the story of Nazneen, a rural Bangladeshi girl who barely survives her own birth and is married off at the age of eighteen to a middle-aged, self-important man named Chanu. He whisks her away to the inhospitable East End of London with vague promises to return home as soon as he is a success. Holed up in a dingy tenement for years on end, Nazneen is isolated by culture, language, and tradition, and confined to a very limited social circle. A devout Muslim, she believes that it is her duty to passively endure her fate and submit to the will of her husband, which she does without fail through the birth and death of her first-born, a son, and the births of two more daughters. From her arrival in the mid 1980s to the days following September 11, 2001, Nazneen bears witness to her community as it is savaged by poverty, drugs, and ultimately, religious fundamentalism.

Providing contrast to Nazneen's sequestered life are letters from her sister, Hasina, who remained in Bangladesh and married for love. Hasina's letters tell a harrowing tale as her life takes a more dramatic and tragic path than Nazneen's. Following the demise of her marriage to a violent man, Hasina is forced into prostitution as the political climate changes the country beyond recognition. Though Nazneen longs to return home, her sister's letters make it clear that the world she left behind barely exists anymore. The glacial pace of Nazneen's acclimation to England occurs mainly out of necessity and because of her daughters. She learns enough English to scrape by, and when Chanu loses his job she is forced to take on piecework as a seamstress, working out of her apartment. Her work is delivered and collected by Karim, a flashy, handsome Muslim activist, who awakens a passion within Nazneen that she has never felt before. Chanu, sensing he is about to lose his wife to another man and his daughters to Western culture, prepares for the family's return to Bangladesh. Meanwhile, Nazneen, accepting the fact that she will burn in hell for her sins, embarks on an affair with Karim.

Apart from Nazneen, many critics complimented Ali on the pathos rendered in the character of Chanu, a physically repulsive man who acts superior to his wife because of his "education," but who is nothing more than a self-deluded, possessive man incapable of the intellectual growth he desires. He is "one of the novel's foremost miracles," wrote Lane. "Twice [Nazneen's] age, with a face like a frog, a tendency to quote Hume and the boundless doomed optimism of the self-improvement junkie, he is both exasperating and, to the reader at least, enormously loveable," she wrote. It's a "moving portrait," wrote *Guardian* reviewer Natasha Walter of Chanu and his relationship to Nazneen. "Ali paints a terrifically subtle portrait of how such a marriage is threatened in a culture in which a woman is encouraged to grow beyond it, how he and Nazneen build a strange relationship of simultaneous closeness and apartness, how they hurt one another and also depend on one another." "Chanu inevitably recalls V. S. Naipaul's Mr. Biswas," wrote Gorra. "That's not a limitation. Chanu doesn't stop being himself, but he also belongs to a recognizable tradition, and so does *Brick Lane.*"

Fate, specifically whether a person decides to accept or reject it, is a key theme in the book. As Ali told Benedicte Page in the *Bookseller,* "I was interested in internalised folklores—how people's memories and landscapes and the environments that surround them when they grow up inform their outlooks. So Nazneen is constantly grappling with this question of what it is about the world that she can change and what it is better to accept, or what must be accepted." In regard to how much of the novel is autobiographical, Ali stated in an essay for the *Guardian* that "I cannot draw any clear parallels with my family history. But I can feel reverberations. It is not so much a question of what inspired me. This issue is one of resonance."

Many critics reserved special praise for the novel's language. "Ali practices the self-effacement of the supremely confident writer as she subordinates her style to her protagonist's perspective," wrote Benjamin Schwarz in the *Atlantic Monthly.* James Wood of the *New Republic* similarly wrote that in "the suppression of obvious authorial style . . . the result is a lovely simplicity, as we are led to inhabit the wide-eyed ignorance of a village girl from Bangladesh, and to watch it develop itself." "One feels the enabling weight of the 19th century," wrote Gorra, in the novel's "deliberately unflamboyant and metaphorically precise" prose. Miranda France, writing in *Spectator,* exhorted Ali's "powers of observations" as "magnificent, placing Ali among Britain's greatest writers, never mind young or old."

Though nearly all of the reviews for *Brick Lane* were positive, the book did not satisfy everyone. Aparisim Ghosh of *Time International* considered the book a bland example of immigrant literature. "If you've grown up on a diet of Bengali and British-Indian literature, Ali's debut is little more than a lentil broth, warm and easily digested, but predictable and lacking in flavor," Ghosh wrote. Even more harsh was the reaction of some Bengalese residents in the very community Ali portrayed. The Greater Sylhet Welfare and Development Council, an agency that represents the country's half-million-strong Bangladeshi community, submitted an eighteen-page letter to Ali and the media, objecting to the "shameful" portrayal of the community. Comparing the novel to Salman Rushdie's *The Satanic Verses,* a book whose depiction of Islam was considered blasphemous and resulted in a decade-long *fatwa* against its author, the group called Ali's novel "a despicable insult to Bangladeshis at home and abroad."

In response to the outcry, Fareena Alam wrote in the *Guardian* that, to the contrary, the book "celebrates the humanity and complexity of a community which even Bengalis like me know so little about; a community that has been pushed to the margins of Britain's ethnic mosaic, characterised by its many economic and social troubles, filed away under the convenient label of an ethnic problem. . . . It seems that only 'ethnic' writers carry a burden of 'representation' whether they want to or not." In answering critics who wondered what right she has to write about Bengal culture when she doesn't even know the language, Ali wrote in the *Guardian,* "the answer is I can write about it because I do not truly belong. Growing up with an English mother and a Bengali father means never being an insider. Standing neither behind a closed door, nor in the thick of things, but rather in the shadow of the doorway, is a good place from which to observe. Good training, I feel, for life as a writer."

The outcry did not prevent Ali's book from staying a bestseller, nor did it detract from its critical success. *Brick Lane* was shortlisted for Great Britain's prestigious Man-Booker Prize, the *Guardian* First Book Award, and the National Book Critics Circle Award in the United States. "*Brick Lane* is a great achievement of the subtlest storytelling," wrote Wood, "the kind that proceeds illuminatingly, in units of characters rather than in wattage of 'style.'"

BIOGRAPHICAL AND CRITICAL SOURCES:

PERIODICALS

Atlantic, December, 2003, Benjamin Schwarz, review of *Brick Lane,* p. 108.

Booklist, January 1, 2004, Kathryn Leide, review of *Brick Lane* (audiobook), p. 890.

Bookseller, April 4, 2003, Benedicte Page, "An Encounter with Fate," p. 31.

Economist, June 7, 20023, review of *Brick Lane,* p. 77.

Guardian, June 1, 2003, Harriet Lane, "Ali's in Wonderland,"; June 14, 2003, Natasha Walter, "Citrus Scent of Inexorable Desire"; June 17, 2003, Monica Ali, "Where I'm Coming From"; July 13, 2003, Fareen Alam, "The Burden of Representation"; December 3, 2003, Matthew Taylor, "Brickbats Fly as Community Brands Novel 'Despicable.'"

Independent, June 1, 2003, Suzi Feay, "It's One Raita Short of a Spicy Literary Banquet"; June 20, 2003, Bonnie Greer, "The Friday Book," p. 15.

Kirkus Reviews, June 1, 2003, review of *Brick Lane,* p. 765.

Nation, Diana Abu-Jaber, *London Kills Me,* p. 25.

New Republic, September 8, 2003, James Wood, "Making It New," p. 29.

New Statesman, June 2, 2003, Francis Gilbert, "Novel of the Week," p. 53.

New York Times Book Review, September 7, 2003, Michael Gorra, "East Enders," p. 9; December 7, 2003, p. 10.

Publishers Weekly, June 23, 2003, review of *Brick Lane,* p. 43.

Spectator, June 7, 2003, Miranda France, "The Best of British," p. 37.

Time International, July 14, 2003, Aparisim Ghosh, "Flavor of the Week: Despite all the Mouthwatering Publicity, Monica Ali's Debut Novel Is a Bland Stew of Bangladeshi Cliches," p. 51.

W September, 2003, Samantha Conti, "Ali's Knockout: Britain's Newest Literary Star, Monica Ali, Takes a Trip Down Brick Lane," p. 370.*

* * *

ANANDAMURTI, Shrii Shrii 1923-1990 (Prabhat Ranjan Sarkar)

PERSONAL: Born Prabhat Ranjan Sarkar, 1923, in Jamalpur, India; name changed, 1955; died October, 1990; son of a railway accounts clerk.

CAREER: Worked as railway clerk until 1955; Ananda Marga Yoga Society, India, founder and leader, beginning 1955. Renaissance Universal, founder, leader, and teacher of Progressive Utilization Theory (Prout), under name Sarkar, 1958.

WRITINGS:

Idea and Ideology, c. 1959, 7th edition, Ananda Marga Publications (Calcutta, India), 1993.

Ananda Marga (Elementary Philosophy), Ananda Marga Yoga Society (Wichita, KS), 1967.

Baba's Grace Discourses of Shrii Shrii Anandamurti, Ananda Marga Publications (Los Altos Hills, CA), 1973.

The Great Universe: Discourses on Society, Ananda Marga Publications (Los Altos Hills, CA), 1973.

A Guide to Human Conduct (originally titled *Jiivana Veda),* Ananda Marga Publications (Denver, CO), 1980.

The Spiritual Philosophy of Shrii Shrii Anandamurti, Ananda Marga Publications (Denver, CO), 1981.

Namami Krshnasundaram, 2nd edition, Ananda Marga Pracaraka Samgha (Calcutta, India), 1981.

The Liberation of Intellect—Neo-humanism, 3rd edition, Ananda Marga Pracaraka Samgha, 1987.

Prout in a Nutshell, translated from Bengali by Acarya Vijaynanda Avadhuta and Jayanta Kumar, Ananda Marga Pracraka Samgha (Calcutta, India), 1987-1991.

Ananda Marga Ideology and Way of Life in a Nutshell, translated from Bengali by Acarya Vijayananda Avadhuta and Acrya Vishwarupababda Avadhuta, Ananda Marga Pracaraka Samgha (Calcutta, India), 1988.

Yoga Psychology, translated by Acarya Vijaynanda Avadhuta and Jayanta Kumar, Ananda Marga Publications (Calcutta, India), 1990, 3rd edition, 1998.

Sarkar's Short Stories (for children), Ananda Marga Pracaraka Samgha (Calcutta, India), 1990.

Microvitum in a Nutshell, 3rd edition, Ananda Marga Pracaraka Samgha (Calcutta, India), 1991.

Proutist Economics Discourses on Economic Liberation, Ananda Marga Pracaraka Samgha (Calcutta, India), 1992.

Prabhat sa'mgiita: Songs of the New Dawn (in Bengali and English), translated by Vijayananda Avadhuta and Ananda Mitra, Ananda Marga Pracaraka Samgha (Calcutta, India), 1993.

Discourses on Tantra, two volumes, Ananda Marga Pracaraka Samgha (Calcutta, India), 1993-94.
Narira maryada, Paribe'saka Prabhata Libreri, Ananda Marga Pracaraka Samgha (Calcutta, India), 1994.
The Awakening of Women, translated by Acarya Vijayananda Avadhuta and Avtk. Ananda Rucira Ac., Ananda Marga Publications (Calcutta, India), 1995.
Shabda cayanika (dictionary; in English and Bengali), Ananda Marga Publications (Calcutta, India), 1996.
Ananda-bacanamrtam, Paribe'saka Prabhata Laibreri, Ananda Marga Pracaraka Samgha (Calcutta, India), 1997-1998.

Some writings published under the name Prabhat Ranjan Sarkar.

BIOGRAPHICAL AND CRITICAL SOURCES:

BOOKS

Tadblavananda Avadhuta, Acharya, *Glimpses of Prout Philosophy,* Central Proutists Publications (Copenhagen, Denmark), 1981.

* * *

ANSCOMBE, Francis John 1918-2001

PERSONAL: Born May 13, 1918, in Elstree, Hertfordshire, England; immigrated to the United States, 1956; died of complications from Alzheimer's disease October 17, 2001, in New Haven, CT; son of Francis Champion and Honoria Constance (Fallowfield) Anscombe; married Phyllis Elaine Rapp, June 16, 1954; children: Francis Rossiter, Anthony John, Frederick F., Elizabeth Anscombe Valeika. *Education:* Cambridge University, B.A., 1939, M.A., 1943.

CAREER: British Ministry of Supply, staff member, 1940-45; Rothamsted Experimental Station, Harpenden, Hertfordshire, England, staff member, 1945-47; Cambridge University, Cambridge, England, lecturer in mathematics, 1948-56; Princeton University, Princeton, NJ, associate professor, 1956-60, professor of mathematics, 1960-63; Yale University, New Haven, CT, professor of statistics, 1963-88, professor emeritus, 1988-2001, founding chair of Department of Statistics. Princeton University, research associate, 1953-54; University of Chicago, visiting professor, 1959-60. National Bureau of Standards, chair of National Academy of Sciences—National Research Council advisory panel on applied mathematics, 1966-67.

WRITINGS:

Curso de aplicaciones industriales de la estadistica, 1957.
Computing in Statistical Science through APL, Springer Verlag (New York, NY), 1981.

Contributor of more than fifty articles to scientific journals.

OBITUARIES:

PERIODICALS

New York Times, October 25, 2001, obituary by Wolfgang Saxon, p. D9.

* * *

ANTHONY, Felix
See MILLUS, Donald (J.)

* * *

ANWAR, Chairil 1922-1949

PERSONAL: Born July 26, 1922 in Medan, East Sumatra, Dutch East Indies (now Indonesia); died of complications arising from cirrhosis, syphilis, and typhus April 28, 1949, in Djakarta, Indonesia; married; one daughter. *Education:* Completed elementary and two years of middle school. *Politics:* Indonesian nationalist. *Religion:* Islam.

CAREER: Poet and translator.

MEMBER: 45 Group (literary organization).

WRITINGS:

Deru tjampur debu (poetry), 1949.

Kerikil tadjam dan jang terampas dan jang putus (poetry), 1949.

(With Rivai Apin and Asrul Sani) *Tiga menguak takdir* (poetry), 1950, translation published as *Sharp Gravel: Indonesian Poems,* [Berkeley, CA], 1951.

Selected Poems, New Directions (New York, NY), 1963.

The Complete Poetry and Prose of Chairil Anwar, edited and translated by Burton Raffel, State University of New York Press (Albany, NY), 1970.

The Complete Poems of Chairil Anwar, edited and translated by Liaw Yock Fang, with H. B. Jassin, University Education Press (Singapore), 1974.

Aku ini binatang jalang, Gramedia (Djakarta, Indonesia), 1986.

Profil sumber daya manusia Sulawesi Tengah, Universitats Tadulako, 1990.

Edisi kritis puisi Chairil Anwar, Dian Rakyat, 1996.

Derai-derai cemara, Horison (Djakarta, Indonesia), 1999.

The Voice of the Night: Complete Poetry and Prose of Chairil Anwar, translated by Burton Raffel, Ohio University Center for International Studies (Athens, OH), 1993.

SIDELIGHTS: Chairil Anwar died in 1949 at age twenty-six, never living to see the publication of his works. Anwar is acknowledged as Indonesia's greatest modern poet, the first to fully utilize the Indonesian language to create unique an emotionally striking verse. "Although his total output was extremely limited, consisting of only about seventy-five poems," noted an essayist in *Twentieth-Century Literary Criticism,* "his impact upon the development of his nation's literature was enormous, a fact which is reflected in the common appellation for postwar Indonesian poets—'Chairil's Generation.'"

Very little is known about Anwar's early years, before he arrived in Djakarta, Java, in 1940 at age eighteen. He was born in the Dutch East Indies (now Indonesia). His family appears to have been financially comfortable; he enjoyed the luxury of an education at a private Dutch school, a rarity for native-born children at the time, and learned English, German, Dutch, and the Indonesian language. His educational funds were cut off prematurely when his father remarried, prompting Anwar's mother to move to Djakarta with her son. Over the next nine years, before he died, he became Indonesia's premier poet. Anwar "lived wildly, even carelessly, but he wrote with infinite care," noted Burton Raffel in the *Encyclopedia of World Literature.* Anwar had "a rare ability to absorb and transform a host of influences. His use of the Indonesian language was both magical and as close to totally new as is possible: many Indonesian writers confessed that, until his work appeared, they had no idea what Indonesian was capable of as a literary instrument," according to Raffel.

In Djakarta, Anwar was unable to support himself beyond a meagre income from his writings. Within two years of arriving in Djakarta with his mother, the Japanese invaded the island of Java. Even earning a living from his literary efforts was difficult during the occupation period, as the Japanese military overseers suppressed the publication of indigenous poetry. They deemed literary works by natives inflammatory—Anwar's early, non-nationalist writings fit that description too readily. Not until 1949 and the end of the Japanese occupation was his work published outside of small, short-lived periodicals; for most of his life, readers simply received Anwar's work through person-to-person circulation.

Anwar was an irrepressible poet, writing amid extreme difficulties—even the Japanese occupation could not still his voice. His language is intense and direct; his themes range from patriotism to love. "Penerimaan" ("Willingness") is a vivid example. "If you like I'll take you back/ With all my heart/ I'm still alone/ I know you're not what you were/Like a flower pulled into parts/ Don't crawl! Stare at me bravely/If you like, I'll take you back/For myself, but/I won't share even with a mirror." The *Twentieth-Century Literary Criticism* reviewer also noted that "Anwar's poetry represents a conscious and dramatic rejection of both the Dutch-influenced literature of his country's long colonial period and the poetry of the *Pudjangga Baru* movement which immediately preceded Anwar's era and which looked to nineteenth-century Western poetry for its models."

Perhaps this was why Anwar became a model for his fellow, up-and-coming Djakartan poets. He became a member of the "45 Group," writers who had dedicated their art and their lives to the nationalist movement. These writers had come of age through the Japanese occupation, and their writings reflected a yearning for world-class literary recognition. Although he was a model for the members of the group, Anwar never formally led, having lived in stark contrast to such a role. As James S. Holmes noted in his introduction to *Selected Poems by Chairil Anwar,* "He was too apt to disappear suddenly in the midst of the planning, deserting all the literary ado for the sailors of the harbor area, the prostitutes of downtown Djakarta or the soldiers fighting the Dutch in the mountains."

Anwar died on April 28, 1949, leaving scholars to reflect on his brief, but influential, existence. In 1967 A. Teeuw, author of *Modern Indonesian Literature,* recalled the poet as one who "gained mastery over the power of words and determined their usage. That is the magic of poetry which lends power to the ordinary word; Chairil possessed that mysterious power which is so difficult to explain. He used words in such a way that they became new and he so combined them that they illuminated each other." In this and many other ways, Teeuw concluded, Anwar "remains a living and present force in the development of Indonesia. Through his personality and his poetry he contributed to the formation of that new Indonesia, and helped to give it direction."

BIOGRAPHICAL AND CRITICAL SOURCES:

BOOKS

Anwar, Chairil, *The Complete Poetry and Prose of Chairil Anwar,* State University of New York Press (Albany, NY), 1970.

Encyclopedia of World Literature in the Twentieth Century, St. James Press (Detroit, MI), 1999.

Holmes, James, *Selected Poems,* New Directions (New York, NY), 1963.

Raffel, Burton, *The Development of Modern Indonesian Poetry,* State University of New York Press (Albany, NY), 1967.

Teeuw, A., *Modern Indonesian Literature,* Martinus Nijhoff, 1967.

Twentieth-Century Literary Criticism, Volume 22, Gale (Detroit, MI), 1987.

PERIODICALS

Literary Review, winter, 1966.*

ASCHENBRENNER, Joyce 1931-

PERSONAL: Born March 24, 1931, in Salem, OR. *Education:* Tulane University, B.A., 1954, M.A., 1956; University of Minnesota, Ph.D., 1967.

ADDRESSES: Office—Department of Anthropology, Southern Illinois University, Edwardsville, IL 62025; Dunham Museum, 1005 Pennsylvania Avenue, East St. Louis, IL 62201. *E-mail*—jaschen@siue.edu.

CAREER: Curator. Wisconsin State University, River Falls, instructor of sociology, 1965-67; Augsburg College, associate professor, 1968-70; University of Minnesota, Minneapolis, assistant professor, 1967-74; Southern Illinois University, associate professor of anthropology, 1974—; curator and education coordinator, Katherine Dunham Museum, East St. Louis, IL.

MEMBER: American Anthropological Association.

WRITINGS:

Lifelines: Black Families in Chicago, Holt, Rinehart and Winston (New York, NY), 1975.

(Editor, with Lloyd R. Collins) *Processes of Urbanism: A Multidisciplinary Approach,* Mouton (The Hague, Netherlands), 1978.

Katherine Dunham: Dancing a Life, University of Illinois Press (Urbana, IL), 2002.

Aschenbrenner has also published scholarly work in anthropology journals.

SIDELIGHTS: Joyce Aschenbrenner is curator and education coordinator at the Katherine Dunham Museum in East St. Louis, Illinois, and a professor emerita at Southern Illinois University, where she taught anthropology.

In *Lifelines: Black Families in Chicago* Aschenbrenner presents a study of African-American families in Chicago, telling their stories and exploring their values. In *American Anthropologist,* Jacqueline S. Mithun wrote that Aschenbrenner's portrayals of the families, "through rich autobiographies, stress the interactions between generations, siblings, parents and children, and males and females," and called the book "commendable" and "highly readable and enjoyable."

Processes of Urbanism: A Multidisciplinary Approach, which Aschenbrenner coedited with Lloyd R. Collins, is a collection of scholarly articles on urbanism. The articles were originally presented at a symposium held at the Ninth International Congress of Anthropological and Ethnological Sciences. Contributors to the volume come from Africa, Japan, Spain, Sweden, and the United States, and represent scholars, industry, and public services.

In *Katherine Dunham: Dancing a Life* Aschenbrenner presents a biography of Dunham, a choreographer, dancer, and dance teacher who founded the first self-supporting African-American dance company. As an anthropologist, Aschenbrenner emphasizes Dunham's views on anthropology and dance and their connection to her work as a social activist. Dunham drew on African dance movements that she learned in 1935, when she spent nine months traveling in Haiti, Trinidad, Jamaica, and Martinique, by watching local dancers and filming them with a 16-mm camera. After returning to the United States she took some of these movements and incorporated them with ballet movements and modern dance techniques in order to make them more accessible to American audiences. At the time, these techniques were revolutionary, since most African-American dancers had few opportunities and were limited to tap or acrobatics.

Aschenbrenner describes Dunham's life and work, but also tells stories of her dancers' touring experiences and discusses the community and educational programs Dunham began in East St. Louis. Aschenbrenner told Vanessa Jones in *Dance Review,* "People said, 'Katherine Dunham—she's never been political.' At that time she said, 'Well, people don't know me.'" Dunham refused to perform in front of segregated audiences, and was the choreographer of "Southland," a piece about lynching that angered the U.S. government.

While writing Dunham's biography, Aschenbrenner relied on Dunham's published memoirs *A Touch of Innocence* and *Island Possessed,* as well as information from archives, interviews with Dunham's colleagues, students, and dance company, and personal reminiscences. Aschenbrenner told Jones, "At first I was kind of scared of her. She's a very charismatic figure. I was afraid I'd make a wrong step."

BIOGRAPHICAL AND CRITICAL SOURCES:

PERIODICALS

American Anthropologist, June, 1976, p. 449.
Choice, September, 1975, p. 880; September, 1979, p. 886; March, 1980, p. 29.
Contemporary Sociology, November, 1980, p. 808.
Library Journal, September 15, 2002, p. 63.
Reviews in Anthropology, winter, 1980, p. 67.

ONLINE

University of Illinois Press Web site, http://www.press.uillinois.edu/ (January 16, 2003).
We Haitians United: We Stand for Democracy, http://www.wehaitians.com/ (January 16, 2003).*

* * *

ASHER, Jim

PERSONAL: Male. *Hobbies and other interests:* Butterfly conservation.

ADDRESSES: *Home*—24 Fettiplace Rd., Marcham, Abingdon, Oxfordshire OX13 6PL, England. *E-mail*—butterflynet@btinternet.com.

CAREER: Writer.

MEMBER: British Butterfly Conservation Society.

AWARDS, HONORS: Volunteer of the year, British Butterfly Conservation Society, 2000.

WRITINGS:

The Butterflies of Buckingham and Oxfordshire, Pisces Publications (Newbury, England), 1994.

(With Nick Greatorex-Davies, Estella Roberts, and others) *The Millennium Atlas of Butterflies in Britain and Ireland,* Oxford University Press (New York, NY), 2001.

SIDELIGHTS: Jim Asher is a coauthor of *The Millennium Atlas of Butterflies in Britain and Ireland,* a work described by some critics as an ambitious, comprehensive guide to its subject. The atlas is the result of the Butterflies for the New Millennium Project, a survey begun in 1995 to document the types and locations of butterflies in the British Isles. More than 10,000 volunteers were involved in the project, gathering data intended to provide a point of comparison with previous studies of the butterfly population and therefore guide conservation planning.

"This sumptuous work represents the fruits of this extraordinary effort," commented Gaden S. Robinson in the *Times Literary Supplement.* Robinson explained, "This beautifully produced book draws on an extraordinarily, and possibly uniquely, large data-set to give us a 'state-of-the-union' report on Britain's butterflies. The presentation is accessible, well-balanced and exemplary." Accompanying the text on the distribution of butterfly species are illustrations and detailed maps, and "each map tells its own story," Robinson noted. "The map for the Chequered Skipper comprises a tight cluster of red, orange and yellow dots in the northwest Highlands of Scotland. . . . The Essex Skipper, whose map is a solid block of colour south of a line from the Humber to Lyme Regis, has more than doubled its range in thirty years."

Several other reviewers praised the scope and execution of the atlas. John Fowles, writing in *Spectator,* called the book "a complete gazetteer . . . excellently illustrated," while a *Nature* contributor wrote that it "provides an invaluable picture" of Britain and Ireland's butterfly population. In some parts of the isles that population is endangered by loss of its habitat, although Robinson pointed out, "The widespread preconception that all our butterflies are dwindling away is wrong, however, and this book shows that the story is more that of ups and downs, albeit with many more of the latter than the former." Even so, the book's data supports a case for "active management of habitats" to assure the survival of certain species, he added. Robinson concluded that the atlas "is a mandatory addition to the library of any serious naturalist."

BIOGRAPHICAL AND CRITICAL SOURCES:

PERIODICALS

Nature, April 26, 2001, "A Passion for Butterflies," p. 1030.

Spectator, April 21, 2001, John Fowles, "Lessons of Lepidoptery," p. 40.

Times Literary Supplement, February 15, 2002, Gaden S. Robinson, "All the Ups and Downs," p. 13.*

* * *

ASHWORTH, Adele

PERSONAL: Married; two children. *Education:* University of Utah, B.A. (journalism), 1986.

ADDRESSES: *Office*—P.O. Box 270704, Flower Mound, TX 75027-0704. *E-mail*—adele@adeleashworth.com.

CAREER: Romance novelist. America West Airlines, flight attendant, 1986-93.

AWARDS, HONORS: RITA Award for best first book, Romance Writers of America, 1998, for *My Darling Caroline.*

WRITINGS:

My Darling Caroline, Jove (New York, NY), 1998.

Stolen Charms, Jove (New York, NY), 1999.

Winter Garden, Jove (New York, NY), 2000.

Someone Irresistible, Avon (New York, NY), 2001.

When It's Perfect, Avon (New York, NY), 2002.

WORK IN PROGRESS: *Duke of Sin,* the first book in a trilogy for Avon Romantic Treasures.

SIDELIGHTS: Having tried her hand at beauty pageants, singing, and working as a flight attendant, all with somewhat limited success, Adele Ashworth decided to try writing the kind of books she'd always loved to read: romance novels. As she wrote on her Web site, "her first book . . . took only three months to write and was never published because, quite frankly, it was pretty darn bad." But her next effort, *My Darling Caroline,* was not only published, it won a RITA award for best first book and established Ashworth's reputation as a solid writer of Regency and Victorian romances. Throughout it all, Ashworth has struggled with clinical depression, anxiety disorder, and obsessive-compulsive disorder, which were often misdiagnosed throughout her life, and she does what she can to raise awareness of these sometimes crippling mental illnesses.

My Darling Caroline tells the story of Caroline Grayson, a baron's daughter with more interest in science and math than clothes and dancing and the other distractions that are supposed to captivate a young lady of her position. Rejected by Oxford University as a woman, Caroline invents a male identity for herself and is accepted by Columbia University in New York. But before she departs, her wealthy father bribes attractive but penniless Brent Ravenscroft, earl of Weymerth, to marry his seemingly unmarriageable daughter. Outraged, Caroline eventually agrees to the marriage, but secretly vows to have the marriage annulled as soon as she gets to New York; a plan that will necessitate keeping her husband, eager for an heir, out of her bed until then. According to Lesley Dunlap in *Romance Reader,* "Ashworth has written some of the best sexual tension I've read in a long time. . . . Unlike many stories where the heroine refuses to succumb to the lure of the hunky hero only because the book would end at page 50 if she didn't, Caroline's resistance is the result of the lessons of a lifetime." For *Booklist* reviewer Alexandra Baker, "Ashworth's smart dialogue, complex characters, and complicated plot twists make this debut novel a joy to read."

Ashworth's *Stolen Charms* is the story of Natalie Haislett, a young lady bored by the parade of eligible, but dull, gentlemen her parents keep introducing to her. Instead, Natalie dreams of meeting the Black Knight, a notorious thief. There is one problem: to meet him she must go through Jonathan Drake, a well-known womanizer who gently, but firmly, rejected her attentions some years earlier. Overcoming her mortification, Natalie ultimately enlists Jonathan in her quest, and the two set off for the Continent to track down the Black Knight. Naturally, things turn complicated, as Natalie's feelings for Jonathan are rekindled, and his own feelings prove to be rather more ambivalent than she suspected. While finding it somewhat "difficult to make a solid connection with" Natalie, *Romance Reader* reviewer Karen Lynch found that *Stolen Charms* "is like a breath of fresh air. An intelligent story by a most talented writer."

In *Winter Garden,* Ashworth's next title, it is a hero who takes center stage. Thomas Blackwood is a government agent sent to a village in order to expose a nobly born opium dealer. A scholarly loner, Blackwood finds himself drawn into the world of Winter Garden, particularly when Madeleine DuMais, a celebrated French beauty who serves as an English spy, is sent to help Blackwood in his task. *Romance Reader* contributor Tina Engler particularly noted the strength of character development in the novel. "The author has penned a hero who, for lack of a better description, simply takes your breath away. . . . The heroine is just as intricately crafted and just as able to draw out your emotions. She's a woman readers can relate to, much more readily than the innocent doe-eyed virgins most historicals are centered around."

For her next book, Ashworth chose an unusual theme in Victorian romances: dinosaur bones. In the novel, Professor Nathan Price is set to unveil his prized fossil of a Megalosaurus jawbone appearing at the Great Exhibition of 1851, but when the actual unveiling takes place the display case is empty. Someone has stolen the rare jawbone, and a disgraced Price is laughed out of the British scientific establishment. A few years later, he devises a plan. He will have the fossil re-created as a sculpture, unveil it at an important scientific exhibit, and watch the reactions to see if he can detect the thief. To do so he enlists the services of skilled dinosaur sculptress Mimi Marsh—the very woman whose kiss had distracted him at the moment his fossil was being stolen. It is a delicate situation, with Price relying on Marsh's help, even as he begins to suspect she had a hand in the original theft. "Ashworth aptly conveys the impact that fossil discoveries had on Victorian society, but her characters lack the sympathetic dimensions and intelligence of those of her previous novels," wrote a *Publishers Weekly* reviewer. Similarly, *All about Romance* contributor Rachel Potter found that "The dinosaur angle was very interesting." However, she wrote, "The largest problem I had was that I felt that the sexual side of Nathan's and Mimi's relationship was more developed than the emotional side. . . . I never felt convinced that their love for each other was much deeper than sexual attraction." Others were more pleased. Carla Hosom, a contributor to the *Romance and Friends* Web site, wrote, "Without a doubt you MUST pick up *Someone Irresistible* by Adele Ashworth. You'll be glued to the page, completely entertained until you've turned that last page, where you'll feel disappointed the story couldn't go on forever."

In Ashworth's *When It's Perfect* Mimi Marsh's sister Mary takes center stage. A spinster who makes a living sewing undergarments for fashionable young ladies, Mary has been staying at the home of earl of Renn, preparing a trousseau for the earl's sister's upcoming wedding. Sadly, the wedding never takes place, for the story opens with the bride's death. Marcus, the earl, who has spent the last four years on archeological digs, soon returns, determined to get to the bottom of his sister's sudden death. That necessitates getting to know Mary, a woman with dark secrets of her own. Fortunately, she's not entirely averse to the attention. The book "is a little slow to build up steam," wrote *Romance Reader* reviewer Wendy Crutcher. However, "All of this groundwork pays off in spades by the second half of the story, when the sexual tension takes on plenty of heat and the couple finally succumbs." According to a *Publishers Weekly* contributor, "Mary very modernly thinks of 'working through' her guilt in regards to her own family issues. . . . Nevertheless, Mary and Marcus's feelings that they've found soul mates in each other rings true."

BIOGRAPHICAL AND CRITICAL SOURCES:

PERIODICALS

Booklist, September 15, 1998, Alexandra Baker, review of *My Darling Caroline,* p. 207.

Publishers Weekly, November 19, 2001, review of *Someone Irresistible,* p. 53; October 28, 2002, review of *When It's Perfect,* p. 57.

ONLINE

Adele Ashworth Web site, http://www.adeleashworth.com (January 20, 2003).

All about Romance, http://www.likesbooks.com/ (January 20, 2003), Rachel Potter, review of *Someone Irresistible.*

Romance and Friends, http://romanceandfriends.com (December, 2000), Carla Hosom, review of *Someone Irresistible.*

RomanceReader.com, http://www.theromancereader.com/ (September 15, 1998), Lesley Dunlap, review of *My Darling Caroline;* (September 7, 1999) Karen Lynch, review of *Stolen Charms;* (June 29, 2000) Tina Engler, review of *Winter Garden;* (May 28, 2003) Wendy Crutcher, review of *When It's Perfect.**

* * *

ATKINSON, Harley (T.) 1951-

PERSONAL: Born June 8, 1951, in Grand Prairie, Alberta, Canada; son of Walter and Ellen Marie (Lae) Atkinson; married Shirley VanAmberg (a homemaker); children: Sarah Elizabeth Dawn, Hannah May Marie. *Ethnicity:* "Caucasian." *Education:* Trinity Western College, A.A.; Canadian Bible College, B.R.E., 1980; Talbot School of Theology of Biola University, M.A., 1985, Ph.D., 1989. *Hobbies and other interests:* Sports (softball, hockey, skiing).

ADDRESSES: *Home*—359 Watson St., Toccoa, GA 30577. *Office*—Christian Education Building CEB-8, Toccoa Falls College, Toccoa Falls, GA 30598. *E-mail*—hatkins@tfc.edu.

CAREER: Minister and educator. Ordained by Christian and Missionary Alliance; worked as youth minister in Red Deer, Alberta, Canada, 1980-83; Toccoa Falls College, Toccoa Falls, GA, assistant professor, then associate professor of Christian education, 1989—, currently director of School of Christian Education.

MEMBER: North American Professors of Christian Education, Youth Ministry Educators.

WRITINGS:

(Editor and contributor) *Handbook of Young-Adult Religious Education,* Religious Education Press (Birmingham, AL), 1995.

Ministry with Youth in Crisis, Religious Education Press (Birmingham, AL), 1997.

Teaching Adolescents with Confidence, ETA, 2000.

The Power of Small Groups in Christian Education, Evangel Publishing (Nappanee, IN), 2002.

Contributor of articles to periodicals, including *Christian Education Journal;* contributor to *Baker's Encyclopedia of Christian Education,* Baker Book House, 2000.

B

BACHMAN, John (Walter) 1916-2003

OBITUARY NOTICE—See index for *CA* sketch: Born May 30, 1916, in Youngstown, OH; died of acute leukemia and stroke July 7, 2003, in Minneapolis, MN. Minister, educator, and author. Bachman was a Lutheran minister and former president of Wartburg College who was an expert in communications and was also notable for establishing an important religious radio station in Africa. He earned his undergraduate degree from Capital University in 1937, where he was also a speech instructor from 1939 to 1940. Graduating from Evangelical Lutheran Theological Seminary in 1940, he was ordained a minister the next year and served at the Emanuel Lutheran Church in Warren, Ohio, during the early 1940s. In 1944 he returned to education as a broadcasting instructor at Capital University, followed by a position as a professor of radio and chair of his department at Baylor University. In the early 1950s he established the Radio Voice of the Gospel in Ethiopia, a radio station that survived until 1974, when Emperor Haile Selassie I was overthrown by communists. By then, however, Bachman was already back in the United States. From 1956 to 1964 he was a professor of practical theology at Union Theological Seminary in New York City, and in 1964 he was hired as president of Wartburg College in Iowa. He was there for ten years before moving to Minneapolis to direct the Office of Communication and Mission Support of the American Lutheran Church, from which he retired in 1980. A strong believer in the importance of communicating the church's message to an increasingly sophisticated audience, Bachman was the author of several books about communications and the church, including *The Church in the World of Radio-Television* (1960), *Faith that Makes a Difference,* (1984), *Media: Wasteland or Wonderland* (1985), and *Together in Hope: Fifty Years of Lutheran World Relief* (1995).

OBITUARIES AND OTHER SOURCES:

PERIODICALS

Star Tribune (Minneapolis, MN), July 10, 2003, p. B6.

ONLINE

ELCA News Service, http://www.elca.org/news/ (July 14, 2003).

* * *

BAUSCH, Robert (Charles) 1945-

PERSONAL: Born April 18, 1945, in Fort Benning, GA; son of Robert Carl (in business) and Helen (Simmons) Bausch; married Geri Marrese (an accounting analyst), March 21, 1970 (divorced 1982); married Denise Natt (a college professor), August 14, 1982; children: (first marriage) Sara Hadley, Julie Ann, Suzanne; (second marriage) David Joseph. *Education:* Attended University of Illinois, 1967-68, and Northern Virginia College, 1970-72; George Mason University, B.A., 1974, M.A., 1975; M.F.A., 2001. *Politics:* Liberal—"I mistrust most institutions." *Religion:* "Lapsed Roman Catholic—I believe in people." *Hob-*

Robert Bausch

bies and other interests: "Denny, my children, books, tennis, pipes and pipe tobaccos, the Washington Redskins, music, art, Pac Man, horse racing, gambling, swimming, baseball, basketball, chess, cooking, organic gardening, movies, eating heart-attack food, Eddie Izzard, David Letterman."

ADDRESSES: Home—Stafford, VA. *Office*—Northern Virginia Community College, 15200 Neabsco Mills Rd., Woodbridge, VA 22191. *Agent*—Tim Seldes, Russell & Volkening, 50 East 19th St., New York, NY 10022.

CAREER: Has worked in a laundromat, as a cabdriver, and as a salesman of vacuum cleaners, encyclopedias, appliances, and cars; Fairfax County Public Library, Fairfax, VA, member of circulation department, 1973-74; Glebe Acres Prep School (private high school), Fairfax, teacher of English, French, and biology, 1974-76; Northern Virginia Community College, Annandale, instructor in creative writing, 1975—. *Military service:* U.S. Air Force, 1965-69, instructor in survival tactics; stationed in Illinois; became sergeant.

AWARDS, HONORS: Dictionary of Literary Biography Award for distinguished fiction, 1995, for *The White Rooster,* 2002, for *The Gypsy Man; New York Times* notable book award and *Washington Post Book World* favorite book of the year, both 2000, both for *A Hole in the Earth.*

WRITINGS:

On the Way Home, St. Martin's (New York, NY), 1982.

The Lives of Riley Chance, St. Martin's (New York, NY), 1984.

Almighty Me!, Houghton Mifflin (Boston, MA), 1991.

The White Rooster, and Other Stories, Gibbs Smith (Layton, UT), 1995.

A Hole in the Earth, Harcourt (New York, NY), 2000.

The Gypsy Man, Harcourt (New York, NY), 2002.

Contributor to magazines, including *New Virginia Review, Glimmer Train, Southern Review,* and *Atlantic.*

SIDELIGHTS: Robert Bausch is a fiction writer whose novels and stories frequently revolve around the theme of family and how unforeseen events can disrupt the delicate balance of family ties. Bausch's novels, which include *On the Way Home, A Hole in the Earth,* and *The Gypsy Man,* have all been well received by critics, some of whom consider his character-driven plots and moments of epiphany reminiscent of the fiction of Raymond Carver. Born in Georgia and raised near Washington, D.C., Bausch has long been a teacher of creative writing at North Virginia Community College. In practicing what he preaches, his novels have been lauded for their descriptive insights. In the *Denver Post,* Tom Walker wrote that Bausch "has that rare ability to see past the obvious in the human condition and has an even rarer ability to put that vision on the page in compelling fashion."

The novel *On the Way Home* examines the difficulties in adjustment the Sumner family experiences after being told that their son Michael has been killed in action in Vietnam, and then finding out that he was actually taken prisoner and has managed to escape. Between these two events, however, Dale Sumner retires from the Chicago police force and moves with his wife to Florida in an attempt to start a new life away from reminders of Michael. Just as the Sumners have begun to accept Michael's death, he returns.

The normally difficult period of readjustment to civilian life is compounded for the Sumners by the fact that Michael's new surroundings offer no positive link to his prewar existence. Withdrawn and uncommunicative, Michael angers his father, who is unable to understand why there is no hint of improvement in his son. Dale also suffers from a growing fear that his son might commit an insane act of violence, a fear that rises when one of Michael's female friends disappears.

Los Angeles Times contributor Art Seidenbaum observed that "the Bausch style is as clean and firm as a new butcher block. He does not decorate or overstate; even the mess in Michael's mind comes under the disciplined control of a storyteller who measured his sentences and trimmed his paragraphs for credibility." Ray Anello, reviewing *On the Way Home* in *Newsweek,* shared Seidenbaum's approval of the book, noting "it's not just the pain of a Vietnam vet that makes this story compelling. Robert Bausch uses Michael's homecoming to expose the discord and pain of family life as well." The story's larger, universal themes were also remarked upon by Phil DiFebo, reviewing in *Best Sellers,* who commended Bausch for having "written a novel that is suffused with that mournfulness attending the lives of those who see everywhere the reminders of some great loss. That his work speaks of Vietnam and one of its victims seems to this reader to be posterior to the book's greater themes of human love and folly."

In *A Hole in the Earth* Bausch presents the story of Henry Porter, a history teacher in the Washington, D.C., area who must cope with several overwhelming domestic crises at the same time, while failing to realize his own level of maturity has never progressed beyond late adolescence. Porter's eighteen-year-old daughter, who he has not seen in six years, shows up with her boyfriend and announces they will be spending the summer with him. Then Porter's girlfriend reveals that she is pregnant. While clumsily dealing with both situations, Porter is harassed by the belief that his father would disapprove of his lifestyle, which includes frequent visits to the racetrack and a general lack of concern for life's serious consequences. His attempts to reconcile with his daughter and settle issues with his girlfriend finally lead Porter to a painful understanding of his own failings.

Lawrence Rungren in *Library Journal* found the story to be "tender and caustic by turns, world-weary, and, ultimately, wise." A critic for *Publishers Weekly* noted that Bausch's "profound empathy for his characters, his wise understanding that the texture of life is composed of ambiguities, failures, guilt feelings—and a few successes—contributes to a flawlessly expressed novel." Other critics praised the book as well. It was named a *New York Times* Notable Book of the Year, and in a review for the *New York Times Book Review,* Will Blythe called it "original in the best sense—establishing characters so fresh yet familiar that they might be helping themselves to what's in your refrigerator even as you read about them."

The White Rooster, and Other Stories gathers together ten of Bausch's "strong, beautiful, moving stories," according to a writer for *Publishers Weekly.* Among the stories are "Vigilance," in which a policeman and a mailman burglarize homes in order to rouse their neighbors to form a crime prevention squad, "Family Lore," about a young girl witnessing her father's humiliation at the hands of his cruel brothers, and "Cougar," telling of an insomniac who withdraws to the quiet of the north woods. Linda Rodgers, in her review for the *New York Times,* found that "Bausch writes about ordinary small-town Americans caught up in the loneliness of day-to-day living." The *Publishers Weekly* critic concluded that Bausch's stories "are testaments to the human capacity to feel and connect in an emotionally alienating world." Rodgers stated that, at his best, Bausch "achieves a taut and affecting kind of poetry."

The Gypsy Man is a novel of a tight-knit community in Virginia's Blue Ridge Mountains in the 1950s. The townspeople descend into suspicion and superstition after the accidental death of a young black girl and the disappearance of a young boy who just happened to be the first black student to integrate the town's school. Some see the disappearance as evidence of the racial strife rising up across the country, but others are convinced it is the work of the legendary gypsy man, a mysterious figure who kidnaps children for no apparent reason. Penny Bone, whose husband John is in prison for killing the young girl, serves as the novel's moral center. Forced to raise her daughter, Tory, alone while her husband serves his twenty-year prison sentence, Penny is at center stage during the crisis. Penny's libidinous aunt, with whom she runs the town's grocery store, is seduced by a psychopathic murderer who escapes from the prison where John Bone has just saved the life of a guard. John expects his good deed will lead to an early release, but the discovery of the body of the missing boy on the Bones's property derails that plan.

With multiple narrators, including the psychopathic murderer himself, *The Gypsy Man* defies the conventions of most suspense novels in a way that pleased the critics. The narrators "all come alive and add richness and depth with their differences in age, gender, race, and background," wrote Michele Leber in *Library Journal,* concluding that the novel's climax is "just and satisfying." A writer for *Publishers Weekly* concurred, calling *The Gypsy Man* a "complex but utterly absorbing tale" due to its "cleverly interwoven series of narrative voices." Sarah Ferguson, writing in the *New York Times Book Review,* said the story "has all the makings of a good bluegrass song: men in trouble with the law, lonesome women, hard times, tattered dreams." Only Jabari Asim of the *Washington Post Book World* voiced reservations about the narrative technique. "Bausch apparently loved all these colorful personalities so much that he wanted to give each his moment in the spotlight, but he allows too many of them a chance at narration." Nevertheless, Asim concluded that Bausch tells his story with "consummate style."

Other critics praised the novel's realistic sense of fear. Carol Haggas in *Booklist* wrote that Bausch's writing has a "chilling intensity" and that his vivid portrayal of a community gripped by tragedy is "riveting right to the surprising end." Ferguson concluded that "it's the violent, unpredictable presence of Peach [the murderer] that transforms *The Gypsy Man* from an interesting book into a riveting one."

Though Bausch has heard tales of a supposed real-life gypsy man passed down through the oral tradition in the South, he admitted in an interview with Harcourt Books that he crafted his gypsy man purely from his imagination in an effort to tell a story about fear. "All fear is real," he said. "No matter what or who produces it." And even though the story is set in the 1950s, Bausch intended the fear it evokes to be as vivid to contemporary readers as it is to his fictional mid-century characters. "Circumstances change, the facts might be markedly different," he told the Harcourt interviewer, "but the inner life of human beings is pretty much the same and has been since we first stopped dragging our knuckles along the ground."

Bausch once told *CA:* "I didn't think I'd ever write a novel. Now that I have I don't think I'll ever write anything else. I began writing when I was in the eighth grade, wrote steadily (and loved it best—I've not since felt as excited about writing as I did then) until my high school English teachers (who meant well, I'm sure) convinced me (by correcting my writing instead of responding to it) that I had nothing of any importance to say.

"I started writing again in the service—when I went to funerals three to five times a month (and more frequently as the war in Vietnam unraveled)—and have continued to write ever since.

"I am more a teacher than a writer, since I derive as much satisfaction out of a good job there, and since I devote more of my time to teaching than writing. Writing is totally separate and by itself and doesn't seem to be influenced by things—crises, horrors, games, shows, or picnics—in my life. When the writing is going easily it is not related to anything that I can figure out. The same applies for when it's not going at all.

"I don't believe the saying 'writers are born, not made.' I also don't believe in any spirit or muse or any other Romantic notion about what drives a writer to write. I could stop writing tomorrow, increase my tennis time, and live quite contentedly for the rest of my life. I *like* it, however, that everybody *thinks* a writer is driven to his work by some demon inside him. I'm not sure *why* I like that, but I'm glad I like it. It may keep me writing."

Robert Bausch contributed the following autobiographical essay to *CA:*

AUTOBIOGRAPHICAL ESSAY:

LIFE THUS FAR

My parents grew up during the depression and spent their early youth watching the world blow up and fall apart. My father was wounded twice overseas. He got hit in Africa, was nursed back to health in a hospital in Tunisia, then got wounded again in Sicily, and was returned to the front lines in time for action in Anzio. My sister Barbara was two years old before he ever saw her. My brother Richard and I were born in 1945, at Fort Benning, Georgia, where my father was stationed after they were done with him in Italy.

My father made up his mind that if he survived the war he would have a good life. The war taught him things. He knew what mattered. In spite of the fact that his generation painted pinup girls on bombers and believed that a woman's place was in the home, he was and still is a kind and loving man. Privately he was very religious, although he wasn't ever very evangelical about it. We were Catholic, and every Wednesday night we would all sit together and my father would lead us in the rosary. I can still hear his deep, reverent voice reciting the Hail Mary.

The heroes of my father's time were silent, stoic fellows who never said how they felt. People like Gary Cooper, John Garfield, John Wayne, William Holden. Only women (and very weak men, or strong men in weak moments) expressed emotions, and when they did it was because they couldn't control them. Controlling your emotions meant not expressing them. So my father didn't use the word *love* a lot. But he knew it mattered, and all our lives we were taught the responsibility of love, what Richard sometimes calls "love's province." Not a feeling, but a way of behaving.

My childhood was full of the usual books of childhood—even now, I can hear my mother's voice saying the words of books I now read my own children. I remember my father's voice, too, although I am not sure they both read to me every night. Stories were important to my family. So were songs, and jokes, and laughter. My father was the best storyteller I've ever seen, and I've seen lots of them. He could be so many different people when he told a story. He'd include every gesture and nuance of a person's character. It didn't matter how many times we'd heard him tell a particular story, we always wanted to hear it again. After a while each story had a name. We would say, "Tell the one about Stabile," or "the one about Shucker," or "the one about Louie Marr and Toley Miller on KP."

When I was six years old we got our first television. It was a box bigger than I was, with a round screen not much larger than my face. We were living in a small three-bedroom house on Kenross Avenue in Silver Spring, Maryland. I remember tall trees and the yard cluttered with leaves. A screen door that shook as though it might come apart when you slammed it. The wind in the fall hissing through the trees, and leaves flying high around the dark eaves of our house.

We were not the first people in our neighborhood to get a television, but still I had never seen one until that day my father brought it home. I think it might have been something he saved a long time to get. He may have been proud of it.

Some of the early television shows became family gatherings. I remember nights when all six of us children sat across the living-room couch, every light out, my father and mother sitting together in a huge chair next to us, popcorn bags rattling, and *The Wizard of Oz* unfolding in front of us like a small, black-and-white dream. (I was a young man before I knew the movie turns to color in Oz. I must have been as shocked as the first movie audience to see the film.) My children can watch that movie anytime they want now, but we couldn't see it any more than once a year. So it was an event and a ritual. It marked the beginning of spring, since that was when the networks saw fit to run it on TV. Sometimes now, when I put my five-year-old son to bed and smell his fragrant washed hair, I remember all of my brothers and sisters, freshly washed and ready for bed, hair wet and combed, teeth brushed, soft and moist white feet lined up on the coffee table, waiting for the first sign of the big tornado that we knew would sweep Dorothy into Oz.

Television was so new back then, people didn't trust it or rely on it as much as they do now. We were never allowed to just occupy ourselves by watching it. In fact my memory of it includes long hours when it was off each day, a blank circle of glass that looked back at me.

We watched *I Love Lucy.* My mother reminded us all of Lucy. She looked like her, sang better and more beautifully, and was sometimes just as wildly funny. We never missed *Father Knows Best* or the old *Steve Allen* show. When I was ten years old, my heroes were people who could make my father laugh: Jackie Gleason, Art Carney, Gary Moore, Milton Berle, Jack Benny, Phil Silvers, Martha Raye, Burns and Allen. My father's laugh, even after all these years, still pleases me. I hear it in all laughter, and remember those lazy summer nights, back in the mid-fifties, lying next to my brother on the floor, watching Bilko outsmart the colonel and feeling really good because my father was laughing.

My mother's singing moved me in the same way. She could have been a nightclub singer. Her voice soothed me. I know she sang to me when I was a baby, and

"My mother and father, Helen and Robert Bausch," about 1941

something of that memory haunted me when she'd stand in front of the sink every night and sing a Glenn Miller or Tommy Dorsey song while she rinsed the dishes. All of us children had to help in the kitchen. My father wanted us to "honor" our mother. I thought "honor" was his word.

I think I understand now why *I Remember Mama* was another one of our favorite TV programs. That was about a family of six, struggling week to week, getting along, working at caring for one another in the inevitable confusion and competition of big families. I don't know that we learned anything from watching that show. I doubt it, knowing the quality of TV. Still we developed a sense of our own kinship. Ours was a large family and this show seemed to be about people like us. I don't think it was a situation comedy. It was drama. I remember how safe it made me feel to see a family like that, like ours, offered up to the whole world by TV, facing its troubles and overcoming them. Or, in the better episodes, learning to live with them.

*

There were eight of us including my parents. Six children always seemed to be the number, although I remember very clearly when my two younger brothers were born. My sister Barbara was the oldest, my parent's first child, born while my father was fighting in Italy. Then came Richard and me, and two years after that my sister Elizabeth. It did not strike me until much later, when I had only two children under five years old clattering around in my peaceful, small house, that my mother managed in a one-room apartment with four of us—Barbara at five, Richard and I running everywhere and getting into everything at three, and my little sister, Betty, one year old, learning to walk in what little space was left.

I don't know if I could identify my earliest memory—or if I'd want to. But there are two images that I have never forgotten which might have happened in the same year, even the same season. One is of me crossing a street I was not allowed to cross so I could play in a tempting forest, and the other is of a little girl, not much older than me, lying under a gray blanket in that street. People standing over her don't seem to move normally. I don't know if she was killed, but I think she must have been. In my memory, the blanket is draped over her up to her chin. Her hair is brown and her eyes are closed. She lies close to the street, as though she is a part of it.

I was four years old. My twin brother was with me. We watched through a screen from the second floor of a two-room town house my parents rented on Geranium Street in Washington, D.C. An ambulance came down the street. The image I have of it includes silence—as though it approached out of a spiritual place. It may have been loud with sirens—the old kind that sounded like human wailing—but I don't remember that.

I crossed that street sometime that year. My father told me not to go into the street at all. He was on his way to church, and I was playing with my brother in the front yard. I watched him walk up the sidewalk, wearing a gray fedora, a brown suit. I don't know why my mother was not going with him that day. Perhaps Betty was sick. Or maybe she went when my father came back, because there was no one to stay with us children.

My father had to walk to church because we did not yet own a car. I remember the sound of his shoes crunching the small stones on the sidewalk. As soon as he was out of sight, I walked across the street. Richard said, "You're going to be in trouble."

I don't know how long I stood there on the other side. My memory tricks me and I am handed this image of my father coming back almost instantly. Perhaps I was so excited and amused I forgot the time, but I don't think so. My brother thinks some neighbor named Ruth saw me as she drove to church and that she stopped and told my father and he came back. At any rate, that may have been the first time my father spanked me.

Both of these events come back to me when I try to identify the first things I remember. They don't haunt me, but perhaps something in the danger of crossing that forbidden street and the tragedy of that little girl under the gray blanket colors my vision of things when I am unconscious of my motivations and just writing.

In fact, I rarely write about things that haunt me. If I have guilt over some failure, or terrible fear of losing one of my children, those are things I learn to repress by writing about something else. I purposely think of other trouble and address that. Still, I know we are often moved by things of which we are not even remotely aware. Like most people, I am conscious of almost nothing before the age of three, but the most important influence in my life may have been the reaction of virtually everyone to the fact that I am a twin. From infancy I have been treated as though I were special. People ooh and ahh over twins. Pleased and joyous faces spend a lot of time in front of twins, looking first at one, then the other. In crowds of children, twins are singled out.

I think all those eyes looking with wonder and affection upon me, even during all the days and weeks lost to infant memory, gave me a strong sense of my own value. I am not talking about ego, mind you. I believe I am as flawed as anyone, better than some and no worse than most. I do not think I have any special talent beyond the average salesman's ability to tell a good joke, keep conversation lively, and entertain with a few funny stories. I can draw fairly well, but have no sense of color whatsoever. Words do not come easily to me, but I love them anyway. I think I have a better-than average memory, but I clutter it with things no one cares about.

When I say I developed a strong sense of my own value, I am talking more about confidence, and a willingness to offer what talent I have to the world without fear. It isn't brazenness as much as it is belief. People will pay attention to me because they have always paid attention to me.

When I was fourteen I wrote my first novel. I filled 414 legal-pad pages before I gave up and started to rewrite. I got 60 pages into the rewrite and quit. I was in the eighth grade. By that time we lived in Wheaton, Maryland, and I was attending Belt Junior High School—which, by the way, no longer exists. My English teacher showed no interest in my work, and when I turned it in for a term paper that year—to save myself from certain failure—she gave me a D because it did not have footnotes. I am sure she did not read it. My history teacher—a kind, inspiring man named Mr. Hickman—did read it. He gave me an A and encouraged me to try and publish it. My book was a Civil War story, and this was the beginning of the Civil War centennial.

I have never been as excited about writing, or enjoyed it more, than I did that year. My grades went deeper and deeper into the alphabet, but my parents didn't seem to mind. (My schoolwork never did recover.) The whole family paid attention to what I was doing. I'd come home from school and my mother would clear the dining-room table and I'd sit down and write until dinner. She'd bring me a glass of chocolate milk or ice water and ask me how it was going. I would work nonstop until dinner—usually 5:30 or 6:00. Sometimes I'd work after dinner. My father would come home late and sit down to eat across from me. My sister Barbara was taking typing that year and volunteered to type what I had written. As my handwritten pages piled up, she'd peck on her portable typewriter, trying to catch up to me.

I remember that small house now, the quiet afternoons of work, and I don't see how it was possible. When I was fourteen, all the children had been born. There were six of us. Steve was seven years old. Tim was four. Betty was twelve. Dick was my age, and Barbara was sixteen years old. The house was a small, three-bedroom Cape Cod, with a combination dining area and living room, and a very narrow kitchen. There was no basement. A washing machine was parked by the back door next to the hot-water heater. There was one bathroom. You could not sneeze anywhere in that house without being blessed from some other room. And yet I remember the house pausing for me. Letting me work on my book.

I would occupy all my time in school dreaming of what I would write each day in the silence of those long afternoons. I think I became a writer that year, but I didn't let it stick with me. That summer I got back into baseball and forgot my novel. Perhaps, but for the changes we go through at that time in our lives, I might have finished it and begun another. By the time I was fifteen, the boy who wrote the novel was some other kid way back in junior high. In any case, the experience of high school was so bad I did very well just to keep my interest in reading.

Let me tell you something about public education. As I write this, people are debating whether or not to increase the school year an extra month. Some are advocating going the year round. The objection is, of course, that this will cost lots of money. That would not be my objection. My problem with the idea is that increasing the school year would only provide *more* of a bad thing. Education would not be improved by having more days where teachers are underpaid and classrooms are too full. If anybody really wanted to improve education they'd cut class sizes in half and keep a nine-month school year and watch what happens. Watch how much ground is covered by a teacher working with fifteen students instead of thirty.

School nearly killed my imagination. I had teachers facing too many kids, insisting on the one thing that is counter to both creativity and learning: order. Learning and creativity are chaotic and frustrating and full of passion and wonder. I am not speaking from the position of the writer who naturally tends to simplify things for a balanced rhetorical statement. I have been a teacher since my first year in the air force—more than twenty-five years—and I have observed very carefully how learning takes place. Unless you are teaching math, or some other precise science, not very much learning is achieved by insisting on neatness, correctness, and the proper order of things. I know there are pea-brained people who think learning is lockstepped and orderly—who insist that material should be presented when the teacher is ready to present it, rather than when the student is ready to have it presented—but it just isn't true. I don't know if my writing career might have been rekindled my first year in high school. But I had a teacher who could not possibly respond adequately to thirty compositions from my class, as well as the one hundred and twenty she was bound to collect from her other classes. No human being could respond to each and every one of 150 essays. All she could do was attack its grammar, insist that it be neat, and give it back. Since she could. not respond to anything I said, since she could only penalize or reward me according to how correct and neat my work was, and since that seemed to indicate that it didn't matter what I said, but only how I said it, I was convinced very early in my high-school career that I had nothing of any importance to say.

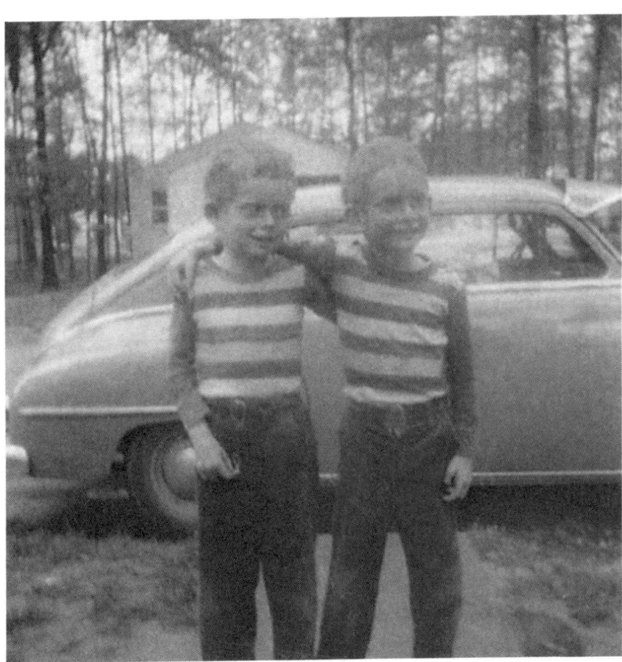

The Bausch boys at five or six years old; Robert at left

I didn't start writing again until I was in the military.

I spent most of my time in high school playing football and shooting pool, and I still don't know what providence caused me to graduate. I didn't have anything to do with it. I can't remember a single thing I learned in high school. I remember my teachers, who worked very hard I'm sure. I understand what they were up against now. Back then, I thought they were crazy. They didn't seem like people who ever had fun and they always smelled like chalk dust. I called them the "chalk people."

Although I spent no time studying I did read a lot. I loved books about the Civil War. I read them all—Shelby Foote, Bruce Catton, Henry Steele Commager, Virgil Carrington Jones, Douglas Southall Freeman, Burke Davis. My favorite was Freeman. His four-volume biography of Robert E. Lee captured me for a whole year. I loved every page of it. I loved the way those books smelled and felt in my hands, the texture of the pages and the print. I read every footnote, and when I was finished with the whole thing, I read all the source notes in the back of the last volume. I read that book three times before I was in eleventh grade. I also read all of Bruce Catton's books. In fact, I still have books on my shelf that belong to the Wheaton High School library.

Like my father, I didn't read a lot of fiction. I believed reading fiction was a waste of time because you couldn't be learning anything about history or the world from somebody's imagination. I believed this even though I had spent the entire eighth grade writing a novel.

What fiction I did read I enjoyed. I'd think of it as a sort of break from nonfiction. My mother read almost exclusively novels, and a lot of good ones adorned the shelves in our house. I found books by Hemingway, Steinbeck, John O'Hara, and Edwin O'Connor. I read them all, but at the time my favorite was O'Connor. I loved his Frank Skeffington. When I was a senior in high school I read *The Last Hurrah* twice. Then I read O'Connor's other books at the time: *The Oracle, The Edge of Sadness, I Was Dancing.*

My brother Richard and I used to read late into the night, then drag ourselves to school in the morning. My parents did not want us to stay up so late—my two younger brothers slept in the same room with us, and we were all supposed to be in bed early on school nights—so we'd place a towel at the foot of the door and if my parents walked by they'd only see a dark slot under the door and think the light was out. I don't know if this truly fooled them, but they almost never came to check on us. If they did, we'd hear them coming, snap off the light, and pretend to be asleep. When they opened the door they'd inadvertently push the towel into the corner behind the door, so they never saw it. Once they were gone, we'd put the towel back and turn the light back on.

It occurs to me now that I've talked about them as though it was always both of them who came in to check on us. I remember it was both of them, and now that I am a parent I understand that they weren't checking on us at all. They were just coming in to look at us asleep. It is that looking, late at night, while my children sleep in a bed I've provided for them, that I discover my sense of self and fatherhood and balance and even a sort of permanence. At times like that I understand my parents and love them more and wish I had loved them better.

*

I graduated from Wheaton High School in 1963 (ranked 534th in a class of 536). I had no plans. We moved to Vienna, Virginia, within the month after I graduated. My father had taken a job managing a Ford dealership in Fairfax, and after years of driving to Virginia six days a week, and working until ten every night, we were going to be within three miles of where he worked. Most of my high-school years the only time I saw him was on Saturday nights and Sundays. The whole family was happy about the move, but I didn't want to go to Virginia. All I knew about it was that it was the South. They got out of school for snow more often than we did, which didn't seem logical to me. And one of the counties there, I think it was Staunton, had closed their school system entirely rather than admit black students.

The civil rights movement was well under way by that summer. I remember Martin Luther King's speech in Washington as though it were yesterday. I saw it on television. John F. Kennedy was president and you had this feeling that things were going to change. It wasn't a bad feeling. Things needed to change. I can remember people using the word "nigger" on radio and television. Fire hoses and dogs and bombs seemed to be the white South's response to integration.

Once I was in Virginia, though, I came to like it. Vienna was a smaller town than Wheaton and our house was a little better, a little more remote. There were trees again—a forest right next to us.

The author's mother and brothers Richard, Steve, and Tim, 1962

I was eighteen years old, hustling pool for money and not motivated to do much of anything. I didn't want to go to college—that was only more school—and I didn't really need to work. I made sixty to seventy dollars a night shooting pool.

I don't remember much of that first summer in Virginia. But in late fall, just before Thanksgiving. President Kennedy was murdered in Dallas. I remember, as most who lived through it do, exactly what I was doing that day. I was with my mother. Richard had a job at AFL-CIO in Washington, and the other kids were in school. (My sister Barbara was already married.) I was sitting in the living room in front of the picture window reading, and the telephone rang. It was early afternoon. I heard my mother pick up the phone. I didn't hear anything she said. She came calmly into the room and sat down next to me. "Turn the television on, honey," she said. "They've shot the president."

After that it was all sheathed in our black-and-white screen. The lying in state, the funeral, Jack Ruby shooting Lee Harvey Oswald. It seemed as though the whole country had gone mad.

If Kennedy's death was the end of a brief period of idealism and new promise, it also shattered a kind of stillness and lethargy. Everything appeared to speed up and get more complex—as if Kennedy's death set in motion an electronic fantasy. it was as though we were all suddenly swallowed by a television, and the world came at us through a fish-eye lens with loud music and distorted images. It was easy to see the era before Kennedy's death as a kind of happy, simpler time. But it really wasn't. The fuse for Watts and other fires had already been lit. Viet Nam was a serious problem by then.

In any case, Kennedy's death did something to my sense of the future. I made up my mind that I wanted to get into politics and work toward what I believed Kennedy worked for. I remembered the "world of diversity" speech he made at American University and I came to see myself as a convert to the idea. I was eighteen when Kennedy was assassinated, and by the time I was nineteen I had a full-time job. I was enrolled in a correspondence school to study law, and I was making plans to attend Santa Monica City College in the fall of 1965. I started writing again, but this time it was for the courses in the law. I wrote legal opinions and prepared briefs and legal arguments. These were evaluated and praised very highly by my so-called law professors. (I will not name the school, but I paid $585 for the course and I got the registration form off a matchbook cover. This will give you some idea of the quality of both the school and my naivete.) I completed the course and was awarded an "L.L.B. Degree" in the spring of 1965. I was very proud of myself. I completed a three-year course in only eighteen months. I thought I would be a lawyer without having to go to college. My aunt, who was dating a lawyer at the time, got him to have a talk with me. That conversation convinced me of two things: that I could not be a lawyer, and that I should, as Kennedy always said, cut the cards.

In August of 1965, before I could enroll in college, Richard and I were drafted into the army. My father told us to "stay out of the infantry." He'd been there, and we took his word for it. So we enlisted in the air force on the buddy system.

We were told we would be able to stay together during basic training, but most likely after that we would get orders for different parts of the world. We went through basic training together, then we were sent to Chanute Air Force Base in Rantoul, Illinois. We ended up spending our entire tour of duty at the same place and doing pretty much the same thing—teaching survival techniques and equipment.

In the service I felt cheated. We were being instructed by men who could barely speak the language. Mediocrity seemed forced on all of us. I mean true mediocrity. I am not a person with ultra-high standards, and I rarely think about competence unless I am confronted with true stupidity. I worked for a man who spent every day in an alcoholic stupor, but he always got high ratings because he was near retirement and no one wanted to deprive him of that. His superiors pretended not to notice that he couldn't stand up. The only time he got close to being sober was when he slept a little too long. He never knew what was going on, or even where he was. As far as I know, he did not work a single day in three and a half years. He was the NCO in charge of training.

When air training command announced they were going to inspect the school, we were told to have the students paint it. As long as it was clean, we passed inspection. It didn't matter at all what we were teaching.

Once we had an ice storm. A hard rain, swept by a brutal wind, crossed the pavement, cuffed the small trees, and froze solid. We marched our troops across a flight line where the wind whipped so bad the entire squadron of men seemed to slide back a few inches for each forward step. When we got them to the school, they were all soaking wet and shivering. The heat in the building didn't work. We had nothing to keep warm. Our commander called somebody to tell them of our predicament and ask permission to send the troops back to their warm barracks. A general—I won't name him—ordered the air police to send two blue air force buses to our school to transport the men back to their barracks so they could get warm showers and dry clothing. Then he ordered us to march them back to the school. It was still raining ice, but that didn't matter. The general made his decision and nobody would ask him if it wouldn't make more sense to have the buses wait around and transport them back to the school. His order read that we were to march them back to school and that is what we had to do.

Perhaps now you have some idea why I say the air force felt like enforced mediocrity. Bad orders were given all the time and then we were forced to follow them or face the consequences. Frequently my brother and I faced the consequences.

For some reason I don't remember, early in my term I was told that I had been designated our squadron's volunteer for the base honors team. That too was a consequence, although I can't remember what I did to deserve it. The honors team was really only a funeral squad. We were professional mourners who traveled on blue air force buses to every military funeral within a thousand-mile radius of Chicago. By that time in my air force career, I had begun reading fiction almost exclusively. I read J. D. Salinger, Ken Kesey, Joseph Heller, some more Hemingway, George Garrett, F. Scott Fitzgerald, William Faulkner, James Jones, and Norman Mailer. I also loved the great Russian writers: Chekhov, Dostoevsky, Turgenev, Pasternak, Tolstoy. My brother was so influenced by what he was reading that he had begun to write poetry and songs, but I wasn't doing much writing then. I kept a journal only sporadically. I wrote long letters to my mother.

The funerals began to pile up on me. In the beginning, the honors team was only attending one or two funerals a month, but by 1967, after the Tet offensive, the war sent more and more bodies home and we were going to two and three funerals a week. I've only written one story about that experience, but it is still one of the most disturbing times of my life. The grieving family almost always believed we had come there to honor one of our fallen comrades. If I am haunted by anything from that period it would be all those sorrowful afternoons pretending I was a friend to the man we were burying.

I remember standing outside a church in Chicago. The weather was freezing and the cold air made my eyes water. I felt the tears on my face turning to ice. A man came up to me, steam escaping his mouth in great gasps, and said, "That's my boy in there. That's my boy."

His face was so contorted in sorrow it was difficult to look at him. I must have given the impression that I would talk to him because he kept himself in front of me, waiting. "That's my boy," he said. He took a deep breath that turned into a cry—a lament he was not prepared for. "Oh, my boy." Then he put his hands on my shoulders. I was so embarrassed for him, and sad that I didn't know his son and could not share in his grief.

"Were you with Terry before he—" he sobbed.

"No. I wasn't." That was the first time I had heard the dead boy's name. I knew he was young and he'd not been killed by the war. He'd driven his motorcycle into a bridge abutment.

"Did you know him well?" The man said.

I lied to him. I told him I'd never known a better man than his son. He nodded, wiping away frozen tears.

He thought I was crying. I hated myself for being privy to his most helpless moment, and for pretending I wasn't a stranger who was ordered to be there.

At night the body counts on the news seemed completely unbalanced. When the newsman said, "Only one hundred and ten U.S. troops died yesterday," I felt as though I would have to bury each and every one of them. One hundred and ten funerals whirled in my mind. In places like Dubuque, Iowa, Appleton, Wisconsin, Gary, Indiana, Danville, Illinois, Niles, Michigan, burials were taking place every day. I'd been to every kind of ceremony: Polish, Jewish, Catholic, Russian, Greek Orthodox.

I couldn't stand the trips on the bus. I'd sit in the back and read while the others played pinochle or gin rummy. They joked and laughed until we arrived at the sight. Then they'd get off the bus and behave with proper decorum. I wished I could accept what we had to do with the same blithe attitude, but I couldn't. I suppose most of those men were as bothered about what we were doing as I was, but their diversion was to engage in noise and banter and dirty jokes until the last minute. I did not want to laugh. It seemed disrespectful, and when we got to the funeral, if I had been laughing with the others I would have felt like even more of a fake.

Military service wasn't all bad. In spite of how much I loathed each day, I met my closest male friend—a thoroughly contrary, droll, and highly trustworthy rogue named Dennis Metter. We have been friends now for over twenty-five years and can still laugh over some of the more bizarre episodes of mediocrity that we witnessed together. We were both on the funeral squad, too, although they knew better than to send us both out to the same funeral. I think that only happened once or twice in the three years we were on the squad together.

*

When I got out of the service I stayed in Champaign, Illinois. I thought I wanted to continue at the University of Illinois, where I had begun classes during my last two years of service. But I ended up selling new and used cars for Shelby Motors on Neil Street. I did not think of myself as a writer then. I was marking time, saving money. That's what I told myself. But I had a good job—I only had to be at work one day during the week and all day Saturdays. The other days, I was supposed to be out looking for possible customers. You could do that anywhere: in poolrooms, on the golf course, in bars and restaurants, and even in the library. I spent many days, especially in winter, shooting pool half the day and reading in the library the other half. On the days when I worked—days where the sales floor was mine and anyone who walked into the dealership was a potential sale for me—I got enough leads and sold enough cars to support myself.

I liked selling cars. People almost never do that in a bad mood. It's exciting to help somebody pick out a new car and even better to deliver one. Although I still believed I would eventually go back to school, get a real law degree, and then enter politics, my year selling cars was pleasurable enough that I was not in any special hurry. I might have continued in the job, to tell the truth, but sales got worse and worse as Christmas of 1969 approached, so I decided to return home.

My brother went to Boston in the hope of beginning a career in music with the family of his best friend. Dick had begun singing with Dave Marmorstein while we were in the service. They were very good. Dick wrote beautiful and lyrical verse, and Dave set it to music. Dave also created extraordinary harmonies. But while Dick was in Boston that first year, Dave got killed in an automobile accident. Dick came back to Vienna about the same time I did.

We both attended Northern Virginia Community College in Annandale, Virginia. By that time we were both married and beginning to take school seriously. I did not have the same attitude about school by that time. Now I really did want to be educated. I still believed I wanted to be in politics, and my declared major was political science. Later I switched to international relations. Then economics. The whole time I was taking courses in English. I wanted to get credit for much of the reading I was doing, and those were courses I always did pretty well in.

My brother already considered himself a writer by that first year at Northern Virginia. He took creative-writing courses from a writer there named Joe Maiolo, who encouraged and inspired him. I was in an English composition class with an extraordinary woman named Jill Brantley, who told me I should pursue a writing career. I was flattered, but I told her I was going into politics, that my brother was the writer in the family. And, indeed, Richard's reputation, even then, preceded him. People who came in contact with his work liked it enough to talk about it to others.

I didn't see myself as a fiction writer, but I wanted to prove I could do it if I wanted. So I wrote a story called "The Gift." I don't remember much about it now, but I know it was from personal experience, and I wanted Jill Brantley to read it. I had a line in it that went like this: "I tried to open the package without ripping the paper."

When I showed the story to Richard, he pointed to that line and said, "See, that's the fiction writer in you."

"What fiction writer?"

"The one who wrote a novel in the eighth grade."

I laughed then, but now it seems like it was a sort of turning point. I began to examine how I looked at the world. I saw everything in terms of the arch of events—a movement in time toward some palpable denouement. The more I thought about things the more I realized that I viewed my life as a kind of developing story. What happened to me was plot. However adolescent that may sound, it afforded me the luxury of trusting myself to go ahead and begin writing again. It seemed like the sort of development that would best serve the "plot" of my life.

I wrote another story almost immediately. This one was the only truly autobiographical story I've ever written. It was the story I spoke of earlier about my experiences on the military honors team. I called it "Funerals" and in it I told the story of two funerals, one in summer and the other in winter. The summer funeral is for a young man killed in Viet Nam, and the winter one is for an old man, a World War I veteran. In the story, a young man on a military honors team is remembering an earlier winter funeral, waiting for the summer one to begin. The winter funeral was a disaster: ill attended, the honors team ill prepared, nothing went right; the firing squad misunderstood the commands of the new squad leader and some of them fired their guns at the wrong time. The effect of this part of the story is supposed to be hilarious, and I suppose it is. The summer funeral is intended to be tragic. The young man is forced to present the flag to the dead man's widow, who is young and beautiful and whose tears hurt the young man so much all he wants to do is tell her that her husband is not dead. When he presents her the flag and tries to console her with the sound of his voice expressing his nation's cliches about service to country and comrades and loved ones, she throws the flag back at him.

I don't know why I structured the story the way I did. Or why it became about two funerals. I'd been to thousands of them, and these two seemed representative of certain types in my experience. But the story won creative-writing contests at both Northern Virginia Community College and George Mason University, where I later transferred, so I think it may have been what finally convinced me I should write. Ironically, now when I look at that story my principle response is embarrassment. It is so obviously the work of a fledgling writer and there are so many obvious conscious choices in it that I am fairly amazed, even now, that anybody saw anything in it to admire. Still, I consider "Funerals" my first story. It was my first published story, too. I published it in the college literary magazine at both of the colleges I attended and I still have a copy of the original manuscript.

You might say that since I wrote that story, I have been trying to get back the sense of joy, expectation, and wonder writing gave me when I was fourteen years old and dreaming in all my classrooms about what I would write each afternoon when I got home. Now it is my work and I cannot find anything magical about it. Or romantic. The notion of a muse seems a wry joke on those of us who ought to know better.

While I was in college I worked various odd jobs to keep food on the table. I drove a taxi one year, worked as a waiter for two days, sold appliances in a discount store. I worked in the public library my senior year of college. I was lucky to write one story a year during this time, and I really don't remember any of the pieces I worked on back then. I was not trying to publish, nor did I do much with those stories but enter them in the yearly literary contest in the English department. I had a beautiful daughter, Sara, by the

"The day Richard moved to Iowa," 1974. Robert at left

time I got my bachelor's degree at George Mason University. I went right into graduate school at the same college and majored in the literature of the 1920s and 1930s.

*

In the fall of that year, 1974, my sister Barbara was killed with her husband in an automobile accident. They were celebrating their twelfth wedding anniversary. They left four children, between the ages of eleven and three years old. If life is divided according to tragic events, 1974 marked the end of that big, charmed family I grew up with. Now the earth was far more threatening, indifferent, dangerous, and merciless. My mother and father took the children in and they became a new family.

My mother never did get over Barbara's death. Our family had been safe from harm, had been so lucky for so long, this was a sort of death for all of us. In some ways I still don't believe it happened, and even now I wish I could talk to Barbara. It thrilled me to make her laugh. Almost everything I wrote was for her approval. I hate it that I never told her how important she was to me. But what still breaks my heart to remember is that after Barbara's death, my sister Betty and I found a collection of manuscripts she had written. In our lives I had been the writer in the family, then Dick was, and then both of us were, and Barbara listened to us, read our stories, praised our work, and she never told us that she was writing; that she was sending her manuscripts out and getting them rejected.

I wish I had asked her, just once, if she ever tried to write anything. She never went to college. I'm sure she was afraid of what we would say about her work. She was the full-time mother of four children when she was killed. I never saw her. She was grown, a housewife, a happy woman. I could talk to her about anything. But I never really saw her. My mother and father raised her children, gave them family legends and traditions and provided all that was humanly possible of love and sane response to needless tragedy. The children are grown now, and in spite of their broken childhood, I think they are happy.

I tried for years to get Barbara's work published. I still have it somewhere. Maybe someday I'll take it out and try again. It is her voice, sure and honest and full of compassion.

Barbara's courage in sending her work to publishers inspired me to do the same, and from that day I discovered her manuscripts I have been actively trying to publish. The life of a writer is rejection, and I was learning that very quickly.

By degrees I came to realize that I wanted to be a teacher. While I was in graduate school, working toward that end, I thought I was lucky to have completed one story. I got into the habit of composing one or two stories a year, and when I began my teaching career I continued to do that. I believed that was all I was capable of. It took me a long time to write a story because I composed each sentence exactly as I wanted it before I'd go to the next sentence. It could take a month to complete one page. When I finished a story I had to do very little rewriting. Also, I see now, I was not writing the way I did when I was in the eighth grade.

To support my family while I was in graduate school I took a job teaching in a small private high school in Fairfax called Glebe Acres Prep School. The pay was not very good, but the experience was invaluable. Those kids were not allowed into the public schools. Every one of them had been expelled for one reason or another, and since I remembered my own high school experience in public schools, I didn't have any trouble understanding my students. I became a teacher in the year and a half I worked at that school. I came to love most of my students, and maybe some of them will even remember me.

In 1975 I went right from graduate school to my present position at Northern Virginia Community College. It seems a preposterous irony now that I could have hated school so perfectly when I was in high school and yet I have spent all but one of the twenty-seven years since then in a classroom, on one side of the lectern or the other.

I wrote nothing but short stories for the first few years after college. I was teaching five classes at Northern Virginia, and two classes at George Mason University. By that time my second daughter, Julie, had been born and I didn't have a lot of time to write. I was no closer to publication, although I was getting a lot of kind letters from editors at major magazines encouraging me to send them more of my work. I did not think I would ever write a novel.

It seems odd now to remember that former self who looked upon the novel as this opaque and impossible thing. I had written one. The memory did not serve me. It seemed a childhood game, like pretending to be a fireman. I had pretended to be a writer. Now that I knew what that was, there was no way I could actually sit down and devote so much of my life to a sustained effort of several hundred pages. Especially when I had two gorgeous children to play with.

When I was thirty-three, Richard had already started what would become his first novel, *Real Presence.* We talked about how hard it was to break into the market with our short stories. He had gone to the University of Iowa Writers' Workshop while I was in graduate school. While he was there he wrote a collection of short stories for his thesis. Both of us had never truly completed a novel. I came to believe that the only way I could sell my stories was if I published a novel. It didn't seem like publishing one would be very difficult. After all, there are over forty thousand new books published in America every year. All I had to do was write one.

A colleague and friend, Dr. Robert Kilmer, often challenged me to begin a novel. We were both avid organic gardeners, and we both owned small pickup trucks. Frequently we would go together to get a truckload or two of horse manure for our gardens. I figured I needed some impetus and a time limit to complete a novel. On New Year's Day of 1979, Robert and I agreed that if I didn't finish my novel in one year, I would give him one truckload of manure for each day I needed past the deadline to finish it.

I had written a short story called "War Story." It was about this man whose memory of what happened to him in Viet Nam is so terrible it terrorizes him. I sent the story to an editor at Harper's who told me I had not "confronted" the conflict in my narrator's life. I decided to make this story the first chapter of my novel—that way I wouldn't have to face the horrible task of writing a first chapter at all. I put a piece of paper into my typewriter and at the top of the page I typed "Michael." In doing so, I both named my character and began chapter two of my novel.

I called the book *Coming Home,* but shortly after I started on it that movie hit the theaters. So I changed the title to *On the Way There.* I worked pretty steadily on it for most of that year. By December, I had ninety pages. I was not happy with what I had, and I had not written a single story that year, so I felt as though my efforts were wasted. But still, I had my deadline. January first was one month away, and I had this novel to finish.

I was done with school by December fifteenth. I was free for the ten days until Christmas and for ten days after that. In a period of fourteen days over that holiday I wrote the last two hundred and forty pages of that novel. I worked from ten or eleven in the morning until five or six in the evening. Each day I did not stop until I had at least twenty pages. If I got twenty pages and it was only four o'clock, I'd keep working another hour and get a few more. I did not take time to think about how things were going as I worked. I still corrected as I went, still revised each sentence until it was the way I wanted, but I would not let myself stop working. I kept at it, even when it seemed as though the English language consisted of only three words and I knew only two of them.

I finished the first draft of the book on December 30, 1979. By that time my brother had already sold his first novel, so I was fairly confident that once I'd rewritten mine, I'd sell it too. It only took me one month to rewrite the book and clean it up. By February of 1980, I was ready to mail it to an agent.

Three different agents saw it. None of them wanted it. I was almost ready to start representing it myself when my brother suggested Nat Sobel Associates, an agency that had tried to recruit him earlier that same year. I sent it to them, and Judith Weber, who loved the book, decided to represent it for me.

Something happened to me while I was writing that first book. For most of that year I kept telling myself that I was writing a NOVEL. I had this huge, generalized vision of the NOVEL hanging over my head governing everything I did. I was unwittingly trying to write all the novels I'd ever read. While I worked I couldn't shake the sense of this fake voice; I felt almost like the eighth-grader who had pretended to be a writer all those years ago, and the memory would paralyze me. I'd let days go by before I'd get the nerve to sit down and try working on it again. Then, over that Christmas holiday when the book literally erupted, I realized I was not writing a NOVEL. I was writing *this* novel. *My* novel.

I remember the first sentence I wrote after that realization. It was on page 110 of the typed manuscript, and it began the first chapter of part two of the novel. It goes like this:

I have to get rid of the beads of water on the window.

After that, writing that book was like playing in one of those padded, air inflated rooms where you can throw yourself down or up or over in any direction, fall unhurt, and bounce back up. I was free. Free to write that particular book and let it become whatever it would.

I did not sell it right away though. Thirteen different publishers turned it down, and I was pretty discouraged about ever selling it. A year after I'd finished it, St. Martin's Press purchased it for a very modest advance. By the time my novel, which was now called *On the Way Home,* hit the bookstores, Richard's first book had been released and had gotten rave reviews. *Time* magazine compared him to Flannery O'Connor. He had already sold his second novel, *Take Me Back,* to Dial Press.

Still, I was stunned at the attention my first novel got. Although the *New York Times* ignored it, everybody else paid lots of attention to it. A few weeks after the publication date, reviews started coming in the mail every day. Newspapers large and small, obscure and very famous, raved about the book. *Newsweek* called and sent a photographer to my house to take a picture of me. They featured my book in a favorable review the following week.

*

Through it all I tried to work on my second novel.

It was a book I'd started almost immediately after finishing *On the Way Home.* In the year it took to get the first book into print, I'd gotten about seventy pages of manuscript that I was calling *The Lives and Times of Riley Chance.* Again, I started with something I'd already written, a short piece called "Hard Luck Story," about a man who has lived three lives. I don't know where the story came from, except I was bored one Christmas visiting my first wife's family; I'd had a few whiskeys and I decided to sit by myself all day and write. I would not have to face anyone, and I figured I might get something I could use. The story never worked, but I thought it was creative, and I liked the idea of a man living three lives and getting kind of worn down by his third time around. It occurred to me then, as it still does now, that all lives end tragically if you take death as the end of something wonderful and the beginning of nothing. The character in the story says at one point, "Having three lives may sound good to you, but remember you also have to have three deaths. Think about that. That's what I do all the time." That one line led me to *The Lives of Riley Chance.*

Composing that book was completely different though because I did not use the story as chapter one and then extend things from an open end. I jumped into the story and pushed out on all sides. It was the frame for the whole novel, so I felt constrained by it, trapped in it. It was the hardest thing I'd ever done up to that time. I worked on it most of the first year after *On the Way Home* was released, but there were several paralyzed months in there. I was sort of swallowed up by my first novel. In spite of its great reviews and a paperback sale to Avon Bard, which kept the book in print right up until 1989, my first novel did not make up its advance, and I never made a royalty payment on it. Somebody at Avon told me it sold thirty-five thousand copies there, but I've never seen a royalty out of them either.

Still, it had gotten so many good reviews. It was very difficult not to expect the same sort of success for my second book. I finished it while I was in the process of divorcing my first wife and marrying Denny Natt, who was and still is the best friend I've ever had. That whole two-year period seems lost to me completely. I truly don't remember writing huge sections of that book or where I composed most of it. I know I worked at a typewriter, that I started another book called *Out of Season* and wrote a hundred pages or so of that before I stalled and came back to *Riley Chance.* But in the spring of 1983 I finished it and sent it to St. Martin's. It was released in 1984, got rave reviews in about twenty or so newspapers including the *New York Times,* and then disappeared.

The Lives of Riley Chance is probably the best book I will ever write. I came to it as myself, with hope and belief. I wrote it without fear. There is not one conscious choice in it. Even now, I can read parts of that book and be surprised that I wrote it. But it got such scant treatment, and sank so fast out of sight, it nearly destroyed my will to write.

I know I was probably spoiled by the reaction to my first book. It was crazy, improbable good fortune to get such wide attention for a first novel, but I convinced myself that my work was worthy of its acclaim. Richard's novel had been reviewed in *Time,* mine in *Newsweek.* We were the fabulous Bausch brothers, embarking on our gorgeous careers.

I came to expect that sort of treatment for anything I wrote. And since *The Lives of Riley Chance* was the best that I could ever do, I couldn't wait to see the reaction to it. The silence was early and perfect. Nothing after the first month. No reviews in the mail. No phone calls from national magazines. Nothing.

It took me six years to write my next novel, *Almighty Me!* I started work on it in 1985 after a year of writing short stories. I wanted to get away from the novel after *Riley Chance.* I hated the idea of another book. I was still teaching two classes at George Mason University, and five classes at Northern Virginia Community College. I couldn't take the sheer exhaustion anymore. I'd work until two or three in the morning and when I went to bed I'd be trembling so much I couldn't sleep or even get warm. Perhaps it was a function of my age, but I just didn't have the energy for a novel.

In March of 1985, my son David was born. I saw him come into the world and when I held him in my arms for the first time, I remembered and loved all my children. I was fortunate that year to get a letter from a lost child, a young woman born in 1969 who I knew existed but had never met. I will not go into the details except to say that Suzi is my daughter; I always expected she would one day come into my life, but I never dreamed she would be so much like me, or that it would provide me with such joy to know and love her. For the first time in my life, I felt that my own family was complete.

In August 1985, my mother died. None of us were prepared for that. I remember the first time I looked into my father's eyes after I knew my mother was gone, the ache in my heart of seeing in his eyes what had drained out of his life. They had been lovers and friends for fifty years. My father still has the piece of notepaper my mother wrote on when he was a senior in high school getting ready to graduate with honors, and she was in the eleventh grade asking him to remember her.

I couldn't write for a long time after my mother's death. She was an extraordinary woman. When my brother and I were in the service, she wrote a letter to each of us every week. Richard and I would sometimes compare letters trying to see if she ever got lazy and just copied one letter over again. It didn't seem possible that she could write a separate letter each week to her twin boys who were stationed in the same place. Her letters were always different. Always. She'd write the same news, the same queries and discussions of future hopes. But not once, in four years, did she ever copy Richard's letter over to send to me, or vice versa. Not once did she send one letter addressed to both of us. Dick used to look at me and say, "Could you do that?"

My mother and father created our family and it has been terrible watching time defile it, as time always does. My father was still alive and healthy, but he was incomplete without my mother.

I worked sporadically until 1987, when I made a momentous decision concerning my life's work as a teacher. I quit my job at George Mason University, took a leave of absence from Northern Virginia Community College, and began a year teaching creative writing at American University in Washington, D.C.

For the first time in my life I was working for an institution that valued my work. I had the time to write and I was encouraged to do so. The experience at American University gradually brought me back to the idea of a novel.

*

I got the idea for my next book from one line in *The Lives of Riley Chance.* At one point in the book, Riley says, "What could make heaven so good that you'd forget someone you loved deeply?" I wanted to illustrate that idea. Create it somehow. Even as a child I could never accept the idea that being away from the people I loved would be OK if I was in heaven.

While I was thinking about this idea, I had a conversation about Christ with the poet Gregory Natt, who also happens to be my brother-in-law. We were talking about Christ the man, and I wondered if he didn't take advantage of his godliness just a little bit. It seemed to me that if he was human, and God, he might make some innocent use of his godliness just because of his humanness. Even the best human being would want to avoid, say, tartar on his teeth, gum disease, or a major toothache. It probably got pretty hot in the desert, and even though no one knew about it then, certainly God would know about what was coming a little less than two thousand years hence. Wouldn't Christ have made use of an air conditioner when there was no one around to notice? Just to relieve the discomfort of that awful heat? He was human after all. Therefore, he was not perfect. If he was perfect, he'd be God, but he wouldn't be human. I wondered if he ever trimmed his beard. Every representation we have of him shows him with a perfectly trimmed beard. Who would it harm if he could just wave his hand and have his beard coiffed?

Greg wrote a poem titled "Christ Trimming His Beard," and I spent the entire year at American University finishing the first draft of a novel I called *Spanking the World.*

I believed I was done with the book, but I wasn't. It was not a very good book and I would have been embarrassed if St. Martin's had published it. My editor advised me to "set it aside." So did my agent. I might have taken their advice—which was good advice—but I'd put almost five years into that book and I couldn't face having to give it up. So I did something I've never done before. I sat down and rewrote the entire book from the first chapter. I spent the summer of 1988 revising and reworking and cutting.

Most of what I cut out of that book was bile. I came to see that I had forgotten my character and lapsed into a bitter attempt to point out all the injustices at the center of things. I had gone after television commercials, politicians, college administrators, salesmen, women, teachers, football players, all celebrities—the list was a long one. Also, my narrator never saw beyond himself. Everything that happened in the book seemed self-absorbed and fake. I wanted to write another Swiftian tale full of irony and wit, and instead I had a narrator so selfish and narrow the irony was completely invisible.

I remember the day I figured out what my story was. I came downstairs and walked into the kitchen, hugged my wife and announced that I had saved the book. I changed the title to *For God's Sake* and sent the book to Tim Seldes at Russell and Volkening, Inc. I had decided that I didn't want to push the book at Judith Weber a second time. I believed in Judith, and loved working with her, but I knew she didn't like the premise of the book and I had not changed that. I felt a change might be best for the book, if maybe not for me.

Sending my book to Tim Seldes was the best thing I ever did. He liked it and said he would be "honored to represent it." Everybody told me I had the best agent in the Milky Way, and at first I thought that was an exaggeration. Tim sent the novel to Janet Silver at Houghton Muffin in Boston, and after a few conversations between Janet and myself, Houghton Mifflin made an offer.

With the considerable help and influence of Janet Silver, and with her guidance through a lot more editing and revising, the novel became much better than I could have ever made it by myself. It is now called *Almighty Me!* and so much has happened to it already I'm afraid to think about my next book. Before *Almighty Me!* hit the stands, Hollywood Films, a division of Disney Studios, bought the film rights. It would take me fifteen years in my present position to match

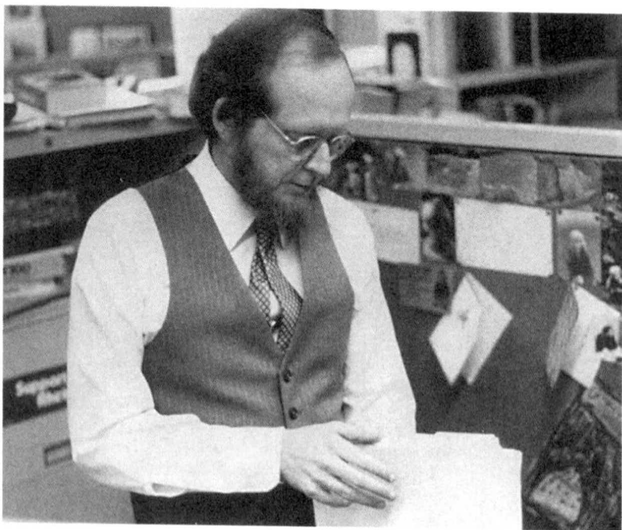

The author in 1982

the income they offered. Once again I have a book that appears as though it will get a lot of attention. I don't know that I am ready for that, but I am hopeful.

While this third novel has begun to enjoy such tremendous success, Richard recently signed on with Seymour Lawrence and will be with Houghton Mifflin now, too. For the first time in our careers we will be with the same publisher and we will both be riding high at the same time.

George Garrett calls Richard and me "the Bausch boys." It's an appellation that stuck and I like it, first because George says it with affection and I value his considerable friendship, and second because it suggests that Richard and I are in this thing together, almost as if we were a team.

Someone once asked me what it was like being a twin. I almost dismissed the question. Twins get used to the foolish line, "Am I seeing double?" And all discussions of being a twin tend to echo that line. But to tell the truth, I wouldn't want to go through life any other way. It's like having yourself and someone else with you at the same time. A person who looks, thinks, acts, and feels like you do, but who is not you. A best friend, a comrade, a competitor, a confidant. We have both pursued the same kind of life, though my writing tends toward the didactic and his is almost purely art. We joke that together we've produced nine books in the last ten years, but really Richard's work has been the most assured, the most truly beautiful, and almost certainly the most enduring. He probably feels the same way about my work, but I know better.

Still, I can't think of anything I'd rather be than one of the Bausch boys.

LIFE SINCE 1991:

A lot has happened since the publication of *Almighty Me!* I have continued my career as a teacher, working at Northern Virginia Community College. In 1994 I went back to the American University, in Washington, D.C., and while I was there, put together a collection of short stories. I got the idea for a collection after I had converted two stories that came from a novel I was working on called *A Hole in The Earth.* I had cut two chapters that I didn't think worked in the book, but that seemed to stand pretty fairly on their own, so I decided to convert them to short stories. I published one, a piece I called "Wakefulness," in *Southern Review;* and the other, a longer story called "Family Lore," in *Glimmer Train.*

I've never been much of a short story writer—not that I don't think I can do it. It's just that I've rarely wanted to do it. Publication of short stories is so very difficult to do, and the market for them is so limited, it always seems a thing I can't take the time for. I have very little time to write—given my schedule. I teach eighteen semester hours each semester during the regular school year, and twelve in the summer. I find myself working late into the night, or all day on Saturday and Sunday. When I *do* find the time to write, I don't want to work on something I know will be very difficult to publish, and will probably never see the light of day. I get to working on a novel, and that is what I spend my time on, day after day, until I am finished. But while I was at American University, I again had more time to write, so I tinkered with those two chapters, made short stories that I thought worked fairly well, and managed to publish them. I realized I had eleven stories in my filing cabinet, most of which had been published in one form or another—or had been submitted to contests, etc., and that if I put them all together, I'd have a collection. So I put them together and sent the collection to my agent. But we had little success trying to place the collection. In fact, most of the big New York houses never saw it because we decided it would be better to wait until I was finished with *A Hole in The Earth.*

Then, late that year, Gail Yngvy (pronounced Engvie), an editor at Gibbs-Smith (Peregrine Press), wrote to me and asked me if I had anything I might be willing

Robert with daughters Julie and Sara

to publish with her. Gail said she wanted to get into the "literary publishing" market and someone had mentioned me to her. I have a feeling it was Alan Cheuse, who had been publishing with Peregrine for quite some time, but I never did find out who gave her my name. I sent her the collection and told her I might be interested. In the mean time, I called my agent and asked him what he thought.

Tim's thinking was that we'd have a better shot at a major New York house if we had a novel to go with it, but I told him the novel was a long way off. I knew I had a lot more work to do on it, and that I was not near being finished with it. I realized it might be years before I was done with it, and I didn't want the collection to gather dust all that time. I am a writer, a practicing writer, and I want my work to be "out there." I asked Tim if he thought publishing the collection with Peregrine Press would hurt my chances of placing the novel when I was finished with it. He said, "Who would know you published the collection? That's such a small press, nobody will know if you go with them."

I thought it over for some time. Gail called and said she loved the stories and wanted to do the collection. She said she would have an offer in a few days, but that it wouldn't be much—"We can't compete with the major houses," she said. I knew I'd be giving the collection away. Of the eleven stories in it, she wanted ten. She had already organized them in a particular order—an order that never changed. She was very good at seeing thematic patterns in the collection that I couldn't see. Or rather, that I didn't notice—not that I looked for any. I put them in chronological order when I sent them to her, and she rearranged them into a more "logical" order. I have to say, I liked what she had done with them, and hoped we could work together on it. The offer, however, was way too small—two thousand dollars. I'd been paid six times that amount for *Almighty Me!* and I really couldn't see my way clear to let the collection go for such a small sum. Part of the problem was that a very small advance means the publisher doesn't have much to invest in your work, and if that is so, the publisher will spend very little money trying to sell your work. I wanted *some* evidence of a commitment to try and sell the book once it was published, so I said no. But Gail doubled the offer the next day, and so I agreed to having the collection done by Gibbs-Smith. I don't regret the decision, either. Gail was a good and sensitive editor with a real understanding of the connections of ideas and themes in a work of that nature. I've already said I liked the order she chose, and I liked everything else about her work as well. The cover of the book was a terrific painting of a man and woman on a blue background. The collection was called *The White Rooster, and Other Stories.*

It did not get the attention I'd hoped it would get, but *Publishers Weekly* gave it very high praise, saying that the stories "in this collection provide unalloyed pleasure." There was not a single negative line in the review—a first, for me. *The New York Times* said the stories were written with skill but that the collection overall was depressing (whatever that means). *Dictionary of Literary Biography* gave it the award for distinguished volume of short stories published in 1995. No one else reviewed the book, or paid any attention to it, and it disappeared pretty quickly off whatever shelves it might have graced—I never did see it in a bookstore. The distribution of that book was so poorly handled, people who had me in for readings couldn't get copies of it. I still don't know what the problem was, but now I have a basement full of *White Roosters*—more than a thousand copies of it, as a matter of fact. When Gibbs-Smith decided to remainder the book, I bought back ten boxes just because I thought I might be able to distribute them myself. I haven't, but maybe some day I will.

In the meantime, I continued writing *A Hole in the Earth.* I struggled mightily with that book, writing the first twenty to thirty chapters many times. I'd bog down around page 150 or so, around chapter twenty, go on for a few chapters listlessly, without hope or belief. Then I'd put the whole thing in a drawer and start over. I'd write my way up to chapter twenty-five or so, around page 200 or 220, then get stuck again. I'd go on halfheartedly for a few chapters, then quit. Put the whole thing in the drawer and start over. The next time through I'd get to page 180 and bog down, worry over what to do next, go on a bit into the next few chapters, then quit again. In the interim between false starts I'd have long periods of such heavy work—grading, and reading and preparing for classes—that I wouldn't work at all. I don't know how many times I stutter-started that book. I'm sure it was at least ten or fifteen times. For a while there, I had a file cabinet in my basement full of copies of the first part of *A Hole in The Earth.* I kept waiting for the inspiration that would help me finish it. I kept waiting to see what would happen to my character and his daughter, his girlfriend, and his father. I worried that no one would care about a thirty-nine-year-old case of arrested development, and his relationship with his family. And the character became so uninteresting to me—I'd told the beginning of his story so many times—I worried that he would be interminably uninteresting to readers. I was beginning to think whatever talent I possessed as a novelist had been used up.

Then, in the summer of 1995, my father died.

His death was totally unexpected. He was a happy man in the last year of his life. One morning in late June, he was just getting ready to take a shower, and after he turned the water on, he lay down on the towel just out of the tub and died. The doctors said there was no grimace on his face, no sign of anguish or pain. He died peacefully, waiting for the water to get hot.

The year before he died, something wonderful happened to him, and by extension, to all of us. He fell in love again.

On my desk is a picture of my father, aged seventy-two or so, in his pale blue pajamas, wearing a round-topped, one-inch-brimmed white hat, and dancing with his great grandson, Brandon. My father is really dancing, a wide grin on his face, his hand outstretched, holding onto the little boy's hand. Brandon is my niece's son, probably six or seven years old when this picture was taken. He's doing the best he can for a little guy, but mostly he's just standing there, watching my father. At least it doesn't appear that the boy is

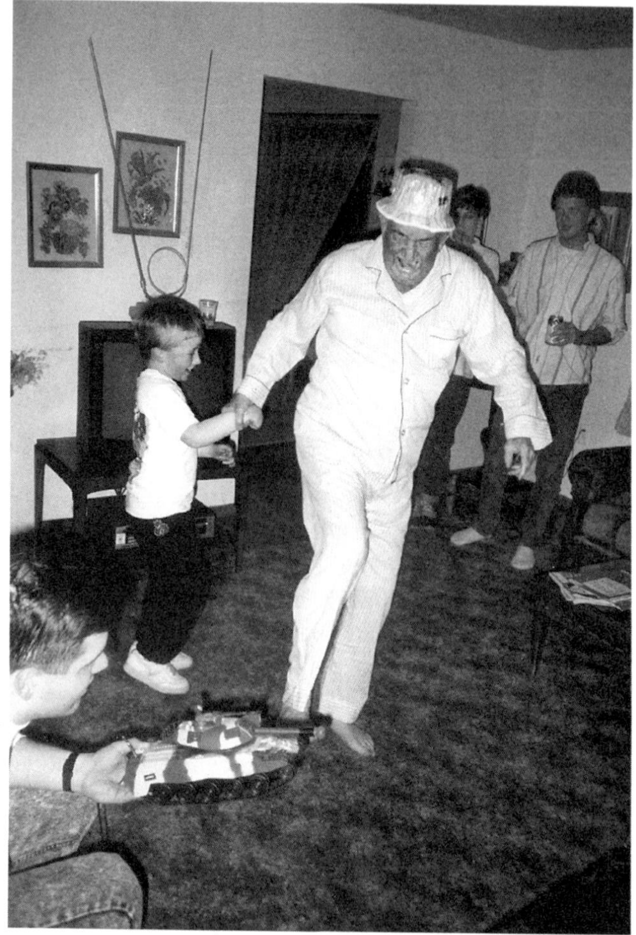

The author's father, dancing with his great grandson, Brandon

dancing. My father is in bare feet, one foot high in the air, as he kicks to the music. I know, without having been there, what song he is dancing to. It is "Two o'clock Jump," by Benny Goodman. The fact that I know that, that I can look at the picture and hear the music, and that everyone in the picture is smiling or laughing, is a measure of what I remember about my father.

The only thing missing from the picture is my mother. She had been dead for at least five years when this picture was taken, and my father was still, as we came to see later, grieving her loss. That is what we never understood about him. As he aged, he seemed less interested in life, less willing to go outside the house, to visit folks and just tell stories as he always used to. He settled into a kind of life that we all felt must have been terribly lonely. Still, he found the time to dance with Brandon, or tell stories around the table after a football game. But he wasn't himself. He seemed helpless almost, as if the earth had wounded him and left him without the strength to stand up to it anymore. As the years passed, and Brandon grew into early adolescence, and he and his mother moved into a new house and started a new family, we forgot about the changes in my father. We just got used to him as this old man who lived pretty much alone and who was very often terribly lonely. None of us truly noticed how much he wasn't himself, until my sister Betty brought her mother in law, Dee to visit one Saturday when Dad called to tell Betty he was feeling lonesome.

The house was empty, Laura and Brandon were gone and my younger brothers, Steve and Tim had just moved out, so he was truly alone. Betty piled her family in the car and went up to see him. He'd never called for help that way, never confessed to being lonely, so she was in a hurry to get to him. She brought Dee because she knew that Dad and Dee had always been good friends over the years. During that visit, Dee kissed my father. She was alone in life, too, and they were friends. But the kiss turned into something more than just friendliness, and what grew out of that encounter was the beautiful realization that Dee had been in love with my father for years, and that he, too was falling in love with her. He was seventy-seven years old. And the change in him was nothing short of extraordinary. He was in love, and young again. I mean you have to see it to believe it. I came to fully understand what people mean when they talk about "young" love. They're not talking about the age of the lovers, but the age of the love. When it is new, and young, it is as wonderful a thing as we have on earth. My father was alive again. He combed his hair, and smiled and greeted the world a strong, virile man. He wasn't helpless anymore, as he had seemed to us. And he was newly himself—my old man again. The one who laughed readily, told stories better than anyone I had ever seen, and could light up a room with just the glitter in his eyes.

*

As I said earlier, I grew up in a terrific, big, loud, happy family. We fought, bickered, laughed, teased, betrayed, cried, and screamed at each other; we also begged forgiveness and hugged each other, for all the days of my childhood. I lived in that family, then watched as my sister's four children, after her death, became a part of a new family with my mother and father—a different family. They, too, had their traditions, their joys and woes, wild crazy fun, and loud, furious fights. They, too, loved each other and still get together as much as they can as grown-ups. I was their uncle in the beginning, but now feel more like an older brother, one who left home too soon and missed out on their formidable years. I watched Laura and Brandon become yet a third family with its own traditions and remembered stories of tension and stress, laughter and joy.

But I know what it was mostly like.

I know because our family always had traditions; immutable laws of behavior based on one basic and unalterable truth: Family came first. Always. It was simply your duty to honor the people you were supposed to love.

The process of learning that was sometimes painful. My mother would say "no" when I wanted to go with my friends to a movie, or over to play pool at the local pool hall, or just to stay home and be by myself for a while, to read books and pretend I had no siblings in whose needs I had to take an interest. It all seemed so completely unfair to me. I never wanted to spend a whole day at home, squirming with my brothers and sisters, because my Aunt Florence was coming over; or because it was Barbara's birthday. Or just because, "Your father wants you here. He never sees you anymore."

Once, I was in my room, reading a book, and my father opened the door and said, "Hey, you want to go shoot some baskets?"

I was shocked that he asked me. He worked so hard, he hardly had time for things like that. And I had been running with my friends mostly. I never had time for him, and more important, never wanted time with him. I said, "No, I really don't." It was late fall, and chilly outside. I didn't want to be out in that air. I didn't want to be around anyone who had such authority over me as my father had. Mostly I tried to avoid him. That day, all I wanted was to stay home and read.

He seemed disappointed. He closed the door and went away, and I felt a pang of regret for having rejected him, but it wasn't enough to get me out of that bed. My mother did that. When my father was outside, by himself, shooting hoops, she came in and scolded me.

"What are you thinking of?" she said. "Get out there and play ball with your dad." It turned out to be one of the best times with him—one of those times you remember for the sheer fun of it, not for what it meant to you. We just had fun together. My brother Dick joined us and we played a whole afternoon under a gray sky. I never felt cold, although I remember I could see my breath.

Still, I fought with my mother at every turn whenever she said, "It's your family. What's more important?" I harbored secret enmity in my heart for my father whenever he said, "She's your mother. Honor her. Get in there and help with the dishes."

It was so unfair to me. I'd have to clean up a huge mess I didn't even make. Or I'd get thrown in with somebody who was doing that. With six of us, my mother always had plenty of help with the dishes. There was just too much noise in that small house for me. Too many people to take into account. I wanted to be out of there, running with my friends, doing things I wanted to do, without consideration of anyone else. Or that's what I believed. Mostly, I now see, I wanted to please my friends, but I would have denied it vehemently at the time. I didn't think I wanted to see to the needs of anyone but myself.

"Your sister has the flu," my mother would say. "You're going to have to help take care of her."

"I am?"

"She's very sick."

I felt nothing. I knew I didn't have it. I'd never had it. Our doctor said, "Some folks are immune, I guess." As long as I couldn't get the flu, I was happy. My mother got it all the time. If one of the children came down with it, she was almost guaranteed to be bedridden for several days if she got anywhere near the stricken party. So she decided the one who didn't get it would take care of the ones who did. (I was in my thirties the first time I knew what it felt like to get the flu. And once I knew, I understood completely why my mother wanted to avoid getting it.)

"Take your sister some soup," my mother would say, and she'd hand me a bowl of steaming chicken noodle soup. Like the soup, the noodles were homemade. She'd spend a whole morning flattening a flour, egg, and water mixture, rolling it up and very carefully cutting it into thin slices, then unrolling each one until she had these wonderful egg noodles with creases in them where they had been folded. She'd put them in the soup at the last minute, stir it until the noodles were just cooked, then she'd pour the whole thing over a pile of mashed potatoes. She called it Chicken Mash. "This will make your sister feel better." When I tell people this story, they picture an old woman leaning over a stove. But she was young then. Young and beautiful. People used to say she was a dead ringer for Maureen O'Hara.

I was always nominated to feed the sick, because as I said, I never knew what the flu felt like until I was full grown. But I hated that house when everyone had the flu. I had to stay home, watch the suffering through what seemed like a gray wall of air; I'd carry food to the stricken, add water to the cool mist humidifiers, and put cool towels on hot foreheads. This was not trauma, but it felt like it because I had such a powerful longing to escape.

The thing I remember most about my family, though, is what it was like on Christmas mornings. I think the picture of my father dancing was taken around Christmas. I'd be willing to bet on it, although I know it's possible it was in the dead of summer. He danced with Brandon a lot when he was a little boy. (Brandon is in college now, at East Carolina University.)

What I remember about Christmas mornings is a small square of space most people would call a hallway that opened into our dining room. It was right outside the bedroom doors in that small house on Valleywood Drive in Wheaton, Maryland. My two sisters, Barbara and Betty, stayed in the first room on the right as you entered the hall from the dining room. Right next to their room, on the same wall, was our room. The boys. Tim, Steve, Richard, and me. We had bunk beds. Richard and I slept on the top bunks, Steve and Tim on the bottom. Directly next to our room, the wall turned, facing the dining room entrance and forming the third side of the square. On that wall was a small linen closet, then the entrance to my parents' bedroom. On the fourth side of the square was the bathroom door, and then another long space of wall before it ended at the dining room entrance. My father would get out of bed early, walk unsteadily to that small, square space, and listen for the measured breathing of his children. I

Robert with son David

know this because I was never asleep. I don't believe any of us were.

When he was sure we couldn't hear him, he would sneak into the living room, lift the lid on top of the hi-fi set, and turn it on. He would have already placed a record on the turntable of Benny Goodman's "Two o'clock Jump." Or sometimes, he'd play Glenn Miller's "Pennsylvania 6-Five Thousand." Or "In the Mood." Whatever the selection, he would have already had it set to the highest volume. The blast of music would be intended to wake all of us up. He'd come back to the little square in front of our bedroom doors and wait for us. My mother would get out of bed and put on her robe and be standing there too, her arms folded in front of her as if to hold her robe closed, her red hair flowing down her back, her bright green eyes smiling. We all had to stay back away from the dining room entrance when we came out. We could not look through, into the living room yet. Dad would make us line up against the wall in front of Barbara and Betty's room. Steve and Tim would be so excited, whispering was impossible, but we all tried. As though we didn't want to wake up the rest of the world. It was impossible for those two boys to stand still, but we all had to line up against the wall in front of Barbara and Betty's room. From the smallest to the tallest. I was always in back with my brother Richard. Then Barbara was in front of us, Betty in front of her, Steve in front of Betty, and little Timmy first in line. We ranged in height from a little over two feet (Timmy, for a while there; he is now the tallest member of our family at six feet two) right up to five feet eleven inches.

For a few years, in the beginning, Barbara was the last in line, but Dick and I eventually outgrew her. What I remember, more than the order, was the ritual. We all had to line up first, while the music played. Then my mother and father would put their arms around each other and follow us as we walked slowly into the living room.

I have pictures too, I'm sure, of the chaos and mess we made those mornings. The piles of wrapping paper and boxes, and plastic bubble wrap. I remember those days, those Christmas days, now with so much joy and with the ache of remembered love. I don't recall a thing I got on any of those Christmases. Some years were more lean than others. It's possible that on some holiday mornings I didn't manage to get a thing I had wished for. I really don't remember. Because every one of those mornings, and all the other days and hours growing up in that family, I was given the greatest gift of all: the one that destroys meanness in you; the one that provides a sense of the beauty in people and the essence of loving and caring for others; the one that makes you aware of loveliness and the ephemeral yet lasting nature of joy; the one you take for granted all through the many years of being too busy to say what it meant to you. Only now—now when it's too late—I wish I could say to my mother and father how much I appreciate them and how fortunate I am because I was lucky enough to be in that family.

I have a family of my own now. And they're mostly grown. I'm hoping for a grandchild soon. I've tried to teach what I learned all those years in my mother and father's house, all those things I didn't realize I was learning, and that I never knew I'd be so grateful for. When you have love, and it's proffered every day in a kind of tender, yet stern, insistence and even reckless laughter; when it is given to you and you accept it in life as a thing as natural as rain or snow, or the litter of leaves in fall, you can't help but take it for granted. For a bewildered while you incorrectly understand that the world has given you this because it's there in equal measure, everywhere. You never know, until it's too late to do anything about it, how sweet the effort is: how lasting the human will to love can be in the breast of people who want to make it for *you;* who want to give it to *you,* without calculating what's in it for them; without thinking at all of what it will mean when you grow to full adulthood, see the world as it is, and forget to mention what you have been given.

Every day of my grown up life, I have wanted to do what my parents did. I have wanted to widen the province of love and weaken hate and bitterness in the hearts of my children. And I've done these things because of what I got from my family, all those lovely years when I was growing up, being loved and cherished, and unbeknownst to me, and in the best way, honored, for myself.

What greater gift is there?

*

So my father's death was very hard on all of us. We could not accept it at first. He had been so happy that last year, and we had been so lucky to see him a young man again. Dee was the best thing that could have happened to him, and so she is still this family's great gift. We are all grateful to her.

I didn't realize it, but my father's death had another, less-emotional effect on me. I was asked to write his eulogy. I didn't know how I could do that—I didn't see how I could even come close to putting into words what it meant to lose such a powerful force in all of our lives. But I managed to write something, and in the process, I saw the end of my novel. In fact, I included much of my eulogy in the book—as a kind of homage to my father. I said in the dedication that he inspired it.

He really did. I always knew what I was writing about—what Robert Hayden called "love's austere and lonely offices." In fact, I almost called the novel *Lonely Offices.* But I saw in my father's life—in the way he lived it; in how true he was always to himself and what he believed—the inspiration for my story. Writing the eulogy helped me to see what I was really up to in *A Hole in The Earth.* I was, essentially, writing everything I could remember and know about what my father believed about the world. I was including my own reaction to it—my own inability to accept it, even—but I wanted to honor what he believed as much as I could. I wanted to put it into words, for him, because he was so true to it, and because he was such a great man. He was as fallible as anyone, and he could throw anger around with the best of them, but I've never really known a more honest man in my life. He truly was just himself. That's what he offered everyone. No pretense, no dissimulation. You always knew where you stood with him. And he was a war hero. He'd won three Bronze Stars and two Purple Hearts, and several unit citations. He'd done things I could scarcely guess and none of us knew about them until he died. He told us vague stories about the war, and some of the funnier things he remembered, but other than that, he never talked about it. We found his medals after he died. I knew I could never live up to him. I wish he were alive to read *A Hole in the Earth,* because it really is written with as much as I could remember of him, and it is offered lovingly.

I finished the book in the fall of 1998, three years after my father's death. In that same year, Walter Bode at Harcourt made an offer for it. With his considerable help in the editing—especially in the arranging of chapters and episodes in my narrator's life—the book was very much improved. For one thing, Walt asked me to move a chapter about the narrator's boyhood to a place very near the beginning of the novel. It had been somewhere after the middle of the book, but I was willing to try it in the earlier stages of the story. I tried to put it somewhere after the first hundred pages, but Walt said, "No, it's got to come even earlier." I did not see what he was after, but I finally moved the chapter in the book about the narrator's boyhood trips to a place called Sylvan Dell, to around the fourth chapter or so. It was a stroke of genius to put it there. Henry, my narrator, is a fairly dysfunctional guy, and if I had left that chapter for later in the book, many of my readers would have lost interest before they got to it. Walt saw that if I included that childhood event, where Henry is seen very sympathetically as a small boy trying to please his father, that the reader would become much more attached to my narrator and therefore tolerant of his foibles and faults as the story unfolds. Many of the reviewers talked of my ability to make a character as flawed as Henry somebody the reader "cares deeply about." It's in that change, and that was Walt's idea. So you tend to want to stick with an editor like that.

I had no idea how great a success *A Hole in the Earth* would be. It was finally published in the year 2000. I didn't sell it to Hollywood, as I did with *Almighty Me!* but it was given a starred review by *Publishers Weekly,* which characterized it as a "flawlessly expressed novel." It was named a *New York Times* notable book of the year, a *Washington Post* favorite book of the year, and as I write this, it's still in print, in hardcover and paperback.

I was very glad to see the book do so well—it could not do justice to the man who inspired it, but at least I honored him in ways that I never dreamed I would. I told him the year before he died that I valued him and our big family over all other things; that what I learned in his house had served me all the days of my life. But still, I wish I could have put that book in his hands and told him once again what growing up in that family meant to me.

The same year that *A Hole in the Earth* came out, Duke University offered to buy all my papers. I started going through all my old letters, early drafts of manuscripts, and all my old false starts, and I found a book I had begun working on in 1977 or so, called *The Gypsy Man.* I'd stopped work on it for some reason and totally forgotten about it. I had about a hundred pages, so I sat down and started reading. I didn't much like what I had—which is probably why I stopped work on it—but I saw things I could do with it. The manuscript was in voices—each chapter was a different voice, telling the story. I started with an epigram that said, "Welcome to Crawford Virginia. When you finish talking to all the residents here, maybe you will know the truth about The Gypsy Man." My original plan was to construct each chapter as if it were a person speaking to the reader—maybe even answering questions. I saw, as I reread it, the problem with that concept. If the story was told by different characters in it, I found it necessary to provide exposition in each chapter about who the character was, what role they played in the story, and so on. So the story developed in a sort of start and stop way, and I quickly lost interest in it.

But looking over it, I saw that if I dropped the idea of each character "talking" to an imaginary investigator (the reader) I might be able to tell it anyway. And I liked the idea of telling a story with different narrators. So I started rewriting what I had, and let the story develop as I did without paying too much attention to who was speaking. I let different characters who'd already provided exposition about themselves, back into it—and gradually I came to see whose story it was, and how to tell it. The book ended up with thirteen different narrators, but there are 66 chapters, and many of the narrators have multiple chapters. The main characters, Penny Bone and her husband John, dominate and take center stage in the book. Minor characters like Morgan Tiller, Henry Gault and his wife Myra also tell much of the story. The whole concept of multiple narrators and different voices intrigued me and held me enthralled in that book. I worked on it longer hours and harder than any other piece of work I've ever done. I was teaching six classes again, grading papers part of the day, or reading for a creative writing workshop, or an American Literature class, and taking every spare moment to work on *The Gypsy Man.* I never knew what character I would be on any particular day, and as the story unfolded I got more and more involved in it.

So did Walt Bode. After I had about four hundred pages, I started sending what I had to him. It was his inspiration and gentle prodding and suggestions that helped me see the final shape of the book, and where it was heading. He also saw that I had an outsider, observing all these characters and frequently taking center stage. A fellow named Turnbull, who I originally conceived as a kind of "greek chorus" or investigator who would observe and comment in the King's English on all these characters and their doings. Walt believed Turnbull had to go. I agonized on it a bit, then realized what Walt was saying to me. If Turnbull were allowed to step outside the story and comment on it, as he so often did, each time he did that, he would take the reader out of the story as well. It would destroy a kind of intimacy that the multiple narrative voices created, and ruin the most powerful effect of the book.

Once I cut all of Turnbull's chapters out, I only needed to create a new "resident" of the town who could be there for the things Turnbull was there for. That gave me Ambrose, who has only one chapter, but who turns out to be an important voice in the book. Losing Turnbull was another stroke of genius on Walt Bode's part so I am doubly grateful to be working with such an editor. (He is no longer with Harcourt but we are continuing to work together on my newest novel. Harcourt agreed to let him continue to edit my work, and I am very grateful for that.)

The Gypsy Man was published in 2002, and as I write this it is still in print. The paperback is due out in November of 2003. While the reviews were very good for this novel, and it got a lot of attention—Kathleen Medwick of *O* magazine said, "being inside the minds of these characters is an experience so intimate that this becomes one of those rare books that not only sees you through unbearable losses, it almost blinds you with love," and a critic for the *New York Times Book Review* said it had "the makings of a good blue grass song"—it didn't do as well as I thought it would.

I believed *The Gypsy Man* had more commercial potential than any other book I'd written, both because of its subject matter and because of the nature of the story. It was a kind of mystery, horror tale, love story, and gothic suspense thriller all rolled into one. In fact, Harcourt had trouble putting a label on it, and toyed with all of those possible categories, before putting the book in its "mystery and suspense" section of the catalogue. In spite of the slow sales on the book, it won the award in fiction for the year 2002 of *The Dictionary of Literary Biography,* a very high honor, and perhaps that will help it a bit when it is released in paperback.

Now, I am almost finished with another novel. It is called *Out of Season.* I have a town, and more characters I care about and hope I can make a reader care about. I have been elected to the board of the Penn Faulkner Foundation, and have had the honor of working with a lot of very talented and accomplished writers over the last two years or so, and I look forward to continuing that work for at least one or two more years. I was granted a Presidential Sabbatical in the fall of 2003 to work on my novel. For the first time in my professional life at Northern Virginia Community College, I am being paid to stay at home and write. I am enjoying the time to work, and hope to finish this new novel before Christmas. I'm thinking again, of short stories.

Also, as Christmas approaches, I am thinking a lot of my mother and father. It has been almost two decades since I heard my mother laugh, and now my father has been gone almost a decade himself. Usually this time of year, I am engaged in doing things for and with my own family. Whenever I'm in my office working, and I look at this picture on my desk of my father dancing with Brandon, I remember all those years I was my father's son; I remember my mother's laugh, and the way she made me think of somebody other than myself; I think of my brothers and sisters, nieces and nephews and all of their children; I remember my own children and all the years of loving and cherishing them; and I realize that in spite of change and sadness and loss, in spite of the withering passage of time, my father is still dancing.

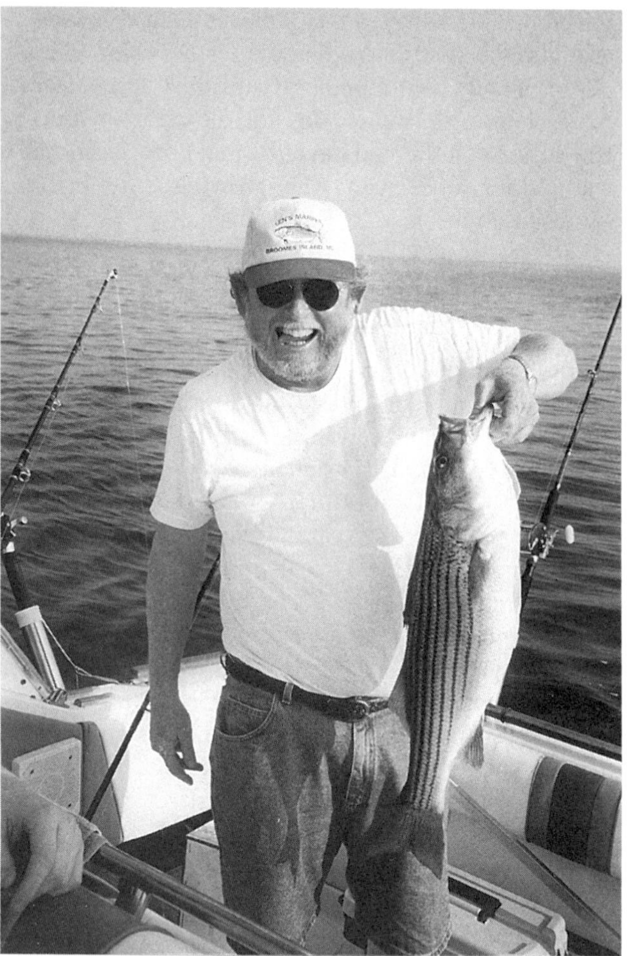

On the Petuxent River, 2002

BIOGRAPHICAL AND CRITICAL SOURCES:

BOOKS

Dictionary of Literary Biography, Volume 218: *American Short-Story Writers since World War II, Second Series,* Gale (Detroit, MI), 1999, pp. 11-19.

PERIODICALS

Best Sellers, May, 1982, Phil DiFebo, review of *On the Way Home.*

Book, November-December, 2002, Sarah Duxbury, "Brother on Brother: Double Your Reading Pleasure, Double Your Reading Fun," p. 12.

Booklist, October 1, 2002, Carol Haggas, review of *The Gypsy Man,* p. 300.

Denver Post, December 15, 2002, Tom Walker, "Convict's Plight a Treatise on Racism."

Kirkus Reviews, August 15, 2002, review of *The Gypsy Man,* p. 1156.

Library Journal, March 1, 2000, Lawrence Rungren, review of *A Hole in the Earth,* p. 123; October 2, 2002, Michele Leber, review of *The Gypsy Man,* p. 126.

Los Angeles Times, March 3, 1982, Art Seidenbaum, review of *On the Way Home;* April 5, 1984, Don Strachan, review of *The Lives of Riley Chance,* p. 34.

Newsweek, March 22, 1982, Ray Anello, review of *On the Way Home.*

New York Times, May 13, 1984, Carol Verderese, review of *The Lives of Riley Chance,* p. 22.

New York Times Book Review, May 19, 1991, David Lehman, review of *Almighty Me!,* p. 17; December 24, 1995, Linda Rodgers, a review of *The White Rooster, and Other Stories,* p. 10; August 27, 2000, Will Blythe, "Stumbling out of the Gate," p. 13; October 27, 2002, Sarah Ferguson, "The Gypsy Man: Mountain of Trouble," p. 24.

O, November, 2002, Kathleen Medick, review of *The Gypsy Man,* p. 176.

Publishers Weekly, August 14, 1995, review of *The White Rooster, and Other Stories,* p. 71; June 5, 2000, review of *A Hole in the Earth,* p. 70; September 2, 2002, review of *The Gypsy Man,* p. 53; September 16, 2002, Bridget Kinsella, "A Tale of Twin Novelists: Richard and Robert Bausch," p. 20.

Washington Post Book World, March 26, 1982; October 22, 2002, Jabari Asim, "Sociobiology as Fiction," p. C04.

ONLINE

Harcourt Books Web site, http://www.harcourtbooks.com/ (December 5, 2003), "Interview with Robert Bausch."

* * *

BELL, J(ohn) Bowyer 1931-2003

OBITUARY NOTICE—See index for *CA* sketch: Born November 15, 1931, in New York, NY; died of kidney and liver failure August 23, 2003, in New York, NY. Historian, educator, artist, critic, and author. In academic circles, Bell was renowned as an expert on wars and terrorism in Ireland, Israel, and Italy, but in other circles he was also recognized as a talented artist and art critic. A graduate of Washington and Lee University, where he earned an A.B. in 1953, he went on to receive a master's degree in 1954 and a Ph.D. in 1958, both from Duke University. It was while at Duke that he traveled to Italy on a Fulbright fellowship to study art. Here he met the artist Cy Twombly, who would prove to be a major influence on him. But although he gained praise for his art from Twombly and exhibited at the Allan Stone Gallery during his college years, Bell opted for a practical career as an academician. During the mid-1960s he was an associate professor of history at the New York Institute of Technology, and during this time he became fascinated with Ireland and the Irish Republican Army. He became a student of the IRA's struggles and interviewed many of its early leaders, work that resulted in his much-acclaimed *The Secret Army: The IRA, 1916-1970* (1971), which he continued to update, most recently as *The IRA, 1968-2000: Analysis of a Secret Army* (2000). Bell also became an expert on the struggles in other countries, including Italy, Israel, and Cyprus. After a brief stint at the Center for International Studies at the Massachusetts Institute of Technology, he joined Columbia University as a research associate at the Institute of War and Peace Studies in 1973, where he became an adjunct professor. Despite his growing expertise in other areas of the world, however, Bell repeatedly returned to Ireland to study the IRA, and often exhibited his artwork in Dublin. In the 1990s he also started a career in art criticism, contributing to magazines such as *Review.* In recent years, Bell was also president of the International Analysis Center consulting firm. His many other books about war and terrorism include *Cyprus: A Greek Tragedy* (1974), *A Time of Terror: How Democratic Societies Respond to Revolutionary Violence* (1978), *The Irish Troubles: A Generation of Violence, 1967-1992* (1993), *Dragonwars: Armed Struggle and the Conventions of Modern War* (1999), and *Murders on the Nile: The World Trade Center and Global Terror* (2003).

OBITUARIES AND OTHER SOURCES:

PERIODICALS

Independent (London, England), September 26, 2003, p. 20.

Washington Post, September 6, 2003, p. B7.

* * *

BENNETT, O. H. 1957-

PERSONAL: Born October 18, 1957, in Fort Jackson, SC; son of Oscar (in the U.S. Army) and Bettina Bennett. *Ethnicity:* "African-American." *Education:* University of Evansville, B.S. (journalism); George Mason University, M.F.A. (creative writing).

ADDRESSES: Agent—c/o Author's Mail, Laughing Owl Publishing, 12620 Hwy 90 West, Grand Bay, AL 36541. *E-mail*—bennettoh@hotmail.com.

CAREER: Technical writer and novelist. Technical writer and editor for software developer in northern Virginia, 1985—; formerly worked as an advertising copywriter. *Military service:* U.S. Marine Corps, 1982-85.

WRITINGS:

The Colored Garden (novel), Laughing Owl Publishing (Grand Bay, AL), 2000.

SIDELIGHTS: O. H. Bennett told *CA:* "I think a writer's first obligation is to communicate, and then to entertain. I aspire to tell stories that show the truth about how we are with each other and how we are with ourselves. I want them to be as truthful and as illusory as a photograph."

Bennett described his debut novel, *The Colored Garden,* as "African-American southern fiction." The story of a ten-year-old boy's summer spent on his grandparents' farm in Kentucky, the book was praised by *Booklist* contributor Ellie Barta-Moran as "beautiful and real; impossible to put down."

BIOGRAPHICAL AND CRITICAL SOURCES:

PERIODICALS

Booklist, February 15, 2000, Ellie Barta-Moran, review of *The Colored Garden,* p. 1079; November 15, 2000, Bonnie Smothers, review of *The Colored Garden,* p. 622.

Library Journal, March 15, 2000, Michele Leber, review of *The Colored Garden,* p. 124.

New York Times, June 25, 2000, Jeff Waggoner, review of *The Colored Garden.*

ONLINE

AALBC.com, http://authors.aalbc.com/ (December 9, 2003), "O. H. Bennett."

BERESFORD, Peter

See HORSLEY, (Beresford) Peter (Torrington)

* * *

BIERNAT, Len 1946-

PERSONAL: Born November 24, 1946, in Minneapolis, MN; son of Ted L. and Sophie Biernat; married Christine Jax, April 1, 1989; four children. *Education:* Mankato State College (now Minnesota State University), B.S. (English), 1968; Hamline University, J.D., 1975; University of St. Thomas, M.A. (education), 1978; New York University, LL.M., 1985.

ADDRESSES: Home—2246 Lincoln St. N.E., Minneapolis, MN 55418. *Office*—School of Law, Hamline University, 1536 Hewitt Ave., St. Paul, MN 55104. *E-mail*—lbiernat@g.w.hamline.edu; rep.len.birnat@house.mn.

CAREER: Politician, attorney, and educator. Hamline University, St. Paul, MN, professor of law, 1975—. Minnesota House of Representatives, elected member, 1996—. Member, Minneapolis School Board, 1989-96; Minnesota Academic Excellence Foundation, former board member. Formerly worked as a carpenter and union laborer; former high school teacher. Edison Youth Hockey, legal advisor, 1996. *Military service:* U.S. Army, 1969-71; became first lieutenant.

WRITINGS:

(With R. Hunter Manson) *Legal Ethics for Management and Their Counsel,* Lexis/Michie, 1996, with annual supplements, 1997-99.

* * *

BLACKWELL, Michael C. 1942-

PERSONAL: Born May 3, 1942, in Gastonia, NC; married Catherine Kanipe, August 12, 1967; children: Julie Renée, Michael C., Jr. *Education:* University of North Carolina at Chapel Hill, bachelor's degree, 1964; Southeastern Baptist Theological Seminary, M.Div., M.Th., D.Min.

ADDRESSES: Home—7449 Old Farm Rd., Thomasville, NC 27360. *Office*—Baptist Children's Homes of North Carolina, 204 Idol St., Thomasville, NC 27360; fax 336-474-7776. *E-mail*—jbcounts@bchfamily.org.

CAREER: Pastor, administrator, and author. Baptist Children's Homes of North Carolina, Thomasville, president, 1983—. Ordained Baptist minister; associate pastor of a Baptist church in Raleigh, NC, 1970; later served as pastor of Baptist churches in Richmond, VA, and Carthage, NC. *Durham Morning Herald,* journalist; also worked as news director and broadcaster for WAYS-Radio, Charlotte, NC, and for college radio stations in Chapel Hill, NC; WRAL-TV, news anchor for two years. North Carolina Institute of Political Leadership, fellow and chairperson of board of directors; Leadership North Carolina, member of executive committee; member of board of directors, North Carolina Partnership for Children, Smart Start, and Wachovia Bank.

MEMBER: National Speakers Association, North Carolina Writers Network, Rotary Club (past president).

AWARDS, HONORS: Stanley Frank Award, and L. Richardson Peryer Alumni Award, both from Leadership North Carolina; Order of the Long Leaf Pine from governor of North Carolina, 1998; Jaycee Distinguished Service Award.

WRITINGS:

New Millennium Families: How You Can Soar above the Coming Flood of Change, Parkway Publishers (Boone, NC), 2000.

A Place for Miracles: Baptist Children's Homes of North Carolina, Parkway Publishers (Boone, NC), 2002.

Upsidedown Leadership: A Dozen Big Ideas to Turn Your Nonprofit Organization Right Side Up, Parkway Publishers (Boone, NC), 2003.

Author of monthly column for *Charity and Children;* contributor to magazines and newspapers.

BIOGRAPHICAL AND CRITICAL SOURCES:

PERIODICALS

Charlotte Observer, March 18, 2000, Tony W. Cartledge, "Faith in Media."

Gaston Gazette (Gaston, NC), April 1, 2000, Neill Caldwell, "Voice of Hope," p. E1.

ONLINE

Baptist Children's Homes of North Carolina Web site, http://www.bvchfamily.org/ (December 9, 2003), "Michael C. Blackwell."

* * *

BONNERS, Susan 1947-

PERSONAL: Born April 8, 1947, in Chicago, IL; married Barry Silverman (a sculptor), December 4, 1988. *Education:* Fordham University, B.A. (English), 1970; attended New York-Phoenix School of Design, 1971-72, and National Academy of Design, 1972.

ADDRESSES: Home—Rosindale, MA. *Agent*—c/o Author Mail, Farrar, Straus & Giroux, 19 Union Square West, New York, NY 10001.

CAREER: Illustrator and author of children's books.

AWARDS, HONORS: Outstanding Science Trade Book, National Science Teachers Association/ Children's Book Council (CBC), 1976, for *Animals in Your Neighborhood,* 1977, for *Discovering What Puppies Do,* and *What Do You Want to Know about Guppies?,* 1978, for *Panda,* 1981, for *A Penguin Year,* 1982, for *A Forest Is Reborn,* 1983, for *Rain Shadow,* and 1985, for *Inside Turtle's Shell, and Other Poems of the Field;* Children's Choice citation, CBC/ International Reading Association, 1981, for *Anybody Home?;* American Book Award for children's nonfiction, 1982, for *A Penguin Year;* New Jersey Institute of Technology award, 1987, for *Sarah's Questions; Panda* and *A Penguin Year* were American Library Association Notable Books; Texas Bluebonnet Award nomination, 2001, for *Silver Balloon,* and 2003, for *Edwina Victorious.*

WRITINGS:

JUVENILE FICTION

The Wooden Doll, Lothrop, Lee & Shepard (New York, NY), 1991.

The Silver Balloon, Farrar, Straus (New York, NY), 1997.

Edwina Victorious, Farrar, Straus (New York, NY), 2000.

Above and Beyond, Farrar, Straus (New York, NY), 2001.

Making Music, Farrar, Straus (New York, NY), 2002.

SELF-ILLUSTRATED; JUVENILE NONFICTION

Panda, Delacorte (New York, NY), 1978.

A Penguin Year, Delacorte (New York, NY), 1981.

Just in Passing (wordless picture book), Lothrop, Lee & Shepard (New York, NY), 1989.

Hunter in the Snow: The Lynx, Little, Brown (Boston, MA), 1994.

Wild Ostriches of the African Savanna, Little, Brown (Boston, MA), 1997.

Why Does the Cat Do That?, Henry Holt (New York, NY), 1998.

ILLUSTRATOR

Seymour Simon, *Discovering What Garter Snakes Do,* McGraw-Hill (New York, NY), 1975.

Seymour Simon, *Animals in Your Neighborhood,* Walker & Co. (New York, NY), 1976.

Seymour Simon, *Life on Ice: How Animals Survive in the Arctic,* F. Watts (New York, NY), 1976.

Seymour Simon, *Discovering What Puppies Do,* McGraw-Hill (New York, NY), 1977.

Seymour Simon, *What Do You Want to Know about Guppies?* Four Winds Press (New York, NY), 1977.

Robert Louis Stevenson, *A Child's Garden of Verses,* Wester, 1978.

Charlene W. Billing, *Spring Peepers Are Calling,* Dodd (New York, NY), 1978.

Alan C. Elliott, *On Sunday the Wind Came,* Morrow (New York, NY), 1980.

Aileen Fisher, *Anybody Home?,* Crowell (New York, NY), 1980.

Mary Calhoun, *Audubon Cat,* Morrow (New York, NY), 1981.

James R. Newton, *A Forest Is Reborn,* Crowell (New York, NY), 1982.

Louise Fitzhugh, *I Am Four,* Delacorte (New York, NY), 1982.

James R. Newton, *Rain Shadow,* Crowell (New York, NY), 1983.

Barbara Juster Esbensen, *Cold Stars and Fireflies: Poems of the Four Seasons,* Crowell (New York, NY), 1984.

Joanne Ryder, *Inside Turtle's Shell, and Other Poems of the Field,* Macmillan (New York, NY), 1985.

Harriet Ziefert, *Sarah's Questions,* Lothrop, Lee & Shepard (New York, NY), 1986.

SIDELIGHTS: Author and illustrator Susan Bonners is well known for her fiction and nonfiction books for young people, including the award-winning novel *The Silver Balloon.* Bonners illustrated several nonfiction titles about animals written by Seymour Simon before she began penning her own texts. Her first writing venture, *Panda,* describes the living habits of this rare Chinese mammal and is accompanied by Bonners' soft blue and white watercolor illustrations. Ethel L. Heins, writing in *Horn Book,* complimented the text as "at once straightforward and poetic." Bonners uses the same combination of blue-hued illustrations and simple text to describe the life cycle of Adelie penguins in *A Penguin Year.* Praising the book's "smoothly flowing text," *Times Literary Supplement* reviewer Lucy Micklethwait added that Bonners' presentation of the subject should inspire readers' curiosity.

Bonners' first children's fiction book, *The Wooden Doll,* was published in 1991. This simple story focuses on Stephanie, a young girl who discovers that her grandmother's wooden doll has her name inscribed on the bottom of it. At first Stephanie thinks this means the doll was meant for her, but her grandparents explain that the doll once belonged to Stephanie's Polish great-grandmother, who was also named Stephanie. "Much more than a story of wanting and getting a doll, this is more about bridging the gap between generations and cultures," noted Louise L. Sherman in *School Library Journal.*

In *The Silver Balloon* a note tied to a helium balloon leads to a long-distance friendship between Gregory, a shy fourth-grader, and Pete Mayfield, a farmer. The two send each other notes and gifts revealing clues about their personalities. Through their communications, Greg overcomes his fears of communicating with others. When Mayfield sends Greg a prehistoric tooth he can not identify, Greg discovers its origin and the two become guests of honor at the natural history museum. Helen Rosenberg in *Booklist* explained that *The Silver Balloon* would appeal "to young readers on many levels—the mysteries of the gifts, the development of the friendship and the way that Greg sticks to his dreams till they come true."

In Bonners' *Edwina Victorious,* a young girl learns that she can fight city hall and win. When an injury forces Edwina's wealthy great-grandaunt and namesake to move into a senior residence, Edwina helps clean out her aunt's attic. She discovers an old typewriter and a stash of letters written by her aunt to various community leaders over forty years ago. Edwina becomes inspired by her aunt and soon begins writing letters of her own. Because she is afraid she won't be taken seriously, she forges her aunt's signature on the letters, but when the authenticity of the letters is questioned Edwina comes clean and is ultimately praised by the mayor for the positive changes resulting from her letter-writing efforts. "This charming tale is an easy fit for lessons on social activism, letter writing, and even plagiarism," concluded Kate McLean in *School Library Journal.*

In *Above and Beyond* Bonners tells of an unlikely friendship between Jerry Wheelock, a popular boy, and Danny Casey, an annoying class clown who has not seen his father in years and whose uncle is in prison for stealing cars. When Jerry researches his older cousin's rock-climbing rescue of a little girl, he discovers that his ancestors and Danny's forbears have crossed paths. He also learns that Danny's incarcerated uncle is a hero. "Never heavy-handed or trite, this is a solid story of people doing their best in sometimes morally ambiguous circumstances," remarked a critic in *Kirkus Reviews.*

Making Music is a novel about a young girl and the girl's baby brother who are forced to leave their comfortable home in the suburbs when their mother takes a job three hours away. Annie, the young girl, misses her favorite uncle, who used to give her music lessons, and she is unhappy when the movers misplace a box containing her prized horse collection. However, she discovers something good about her new neighborhood: the piano music she hears in the evenings coming from the home of an elderly neighbor, Mrs. Bergstrom. "Making music heralds a new beginning for Annie and her family and provides a warm feeling of hope for her future in her new community and for the futures of young readers who face changes in their own living arrangements," noted a reviewer in *School Library Journal.*

BIOGRAPHICAL AND CRITICAL SOURCES:

PERIODICALS

Booklist, December 15, 1994, Julie Walton, review of *Hunter in the Snow: The Lynx,* p. 755; September 15, 1997, Helen Rosenberg, review of *The Silver Balloon,* p. 234; November 1, 2002, Carolyn Phelan, review of *Making Music,* p. 489.

Bulletin of the Center for Children's Books, February, 1989, Zena Sutherland, review of *Just in Passing,* p. 142; July, 1981, p. 207.

Horn Book, April 1979, review of *Panda,* p. 181; October, 1981, pp. 548-49.

Kirkus Reviews, October 1, 2001, review of *Above and Beyond,* p. 1419; September 1, 2002, review of *Making Music,* p. 1304.

New York Times Book Review, December 10, 1978, Margaret Klee Lichtenberg, review of *Panda,* p. 82.

Publishers Weekly, October 31, 1986, review of *Sara's Questions,* p. 64; February 10, 1989, review of *Just in Passing,* p. 68; February 15, 1991, review of *The Wooden Doll,* pp. 89-90: September 1, 1997, review of *The Silver Balloon,* p. 105; November 16, 1998, review of *Why Does the Cat Do That?,* p. 75; September 13, 1999, review of *The Silver Balloon,* p. 86; November 13, 2000, review of *Edwina Victorious,* p. 104; November 4, 2002, review of *Making Music,* p. 84.

School Library Journal, February, 1979, p. 38; May, 1989, p. 77; April 1991, Louise L. Sherman, review of *The Wooden Doll,* p. 88; October, 2000, Kate McLean, review of *Edwina Victorious,* p. 112; October, 2001, Sara O'Neal, review of *Above and Beyond,* p. 148; October, 2002, Alice Casey Smith, review of *Making Music,* p. 99.

Teacher Librarian, March, 1999, Jessica Higgs, review of *Why Does the Cat Do That?,* p. 48.

Times Literary Supplement, July 23, 1982, Lucy Micklethwait, review of *A Penguin Year.**

* * *

BOON, Marcus 1963-

PERSONAL: Born 1963. *Education:* University College, London, B.A.; New York University, M.A., Ph.D.

ADDRESSES: Office—York University Department of English, 2008 Strong College, 4700 Keele St., Toronto, Ontario, Canada M3J 1P3. *E-mail*—mboon@yorku.ca.

CAREER: Journalist and educator. York University, Toronto, Ontario, Canada, assistant professor of English.

WRITINGS:

The Road of Excess: A History of Writers on Drugs, Harvard University Press (Cambridge, MA), 2002.

Contributor to periodical,s including *NME, Wire* and *21C,* among others.

SIDELIGHTS: Marcus Boon's first book, *The Road of Excess: A History of Writers on Drugs,* covers a topic steeped in controversy. In an approach that a contributor to *Kirkus Reviews* described as "impartial" and "historicized," Boon identifies basic categories of drugs—such as narcotics, anesthetics, stimulants, and psychedelics—and discusses their use by a range of writers. The author explains in his prologue that he has no wish to glorify drug use or its lifestyle. Instead, he seeks to use the tools of interdisciplinary scholarly analysis to study the literature produced by writers who used drugs. These include not only such well-known drug users as Thomas De Quincey, Samuel Taylor Coleridge, Elizabeth Barrett Browning, Charles Baudelaire, William Burroughs, Jack Kerouac, and Irvine Welsh, but also such writers as John Milton, Voltaire, Henry David Thoreau, and Jean-Paul Sartre.

Boon shows that certain types of drugs can be associated with different literary genres and styles. Stimulants, for example, would create a fragmented style aimed at achieving "microscopic levels of precision in speech and perception," while narcotics would lead to a boring and repetitive structure. *Guardian* reviewer Adam Mars-Jones found this point interesting but not consistently persuasive. The critic also detected a "worry" in the book about "whether drug experience can really be accommodated in literature." Still, Mars-Jones found *The Road of Excess,* though marred by some inconsistencies and errors, "fitfully brilliant."

Carlin Romano in *Chronicle of Higher Education* admired the book as a "phantasmagoric trip through a gallery of historic horror stories [that] provides a fine mix of sardonic aperçu and higher drug gossip despite the occasionally stuffy academic underlining." Romano appreciated the book's "vast historical sweep" and its willingness to question received ideas about the association of writers and drugs. Hailing *The Road of Excess* as an "impressive display of scholarship" and a "feast of historical surprises," *Boston Globe* contributor Rebecca Shannonhouse concluded that the book "reads more like a wide-eyed, joyous romp through a literary statesman's funhouse, where each room contains a masterfully told tale of opium or morphine, peyote or LSD, coffee or cocaine. We see a gallery of our most prized literary lions, many of them stripped bare of their pristine reputations. It is a mind-teasing exercise that is well worth the trip."

BIOGRAPHICAL AND CRITICAL SOURCES:

PERIODICALS

Boston Globe, May 4, 2003, Rebecca Shannonhouse, review of *The Road of Excess: A History of Writers on Drugs,* p. H7.

Chronicle of Higher Education, January 10, 2003, Carlin Romano, review of *The Road of Excess,* p. B13.

Denver Post, January 26, 2003, Steven Rosen, review of *The Road of Excess.*

Guardian, January 19, 2003, Adam Mars-Jones, review of *The Road of Excess.*

Kirkus Reviews, September 15, 2002, review of *The Road of Excess,* p. 1360.

Library Journal, November 15, 2002, William D. Walsh, review of *The Road of Excess,* p. 71.

New Yorker, January 6, 2003, John Lanchester, review of *The Road of Excess,* p. 80.

ONLINE

York University Web site, http://www.arts.yorku.ca/ (March 28, 2003), Marcus Boon faculty page.

* * *

BOROWSKI, Oded 1939-

PERSONAL: Born August 26, 1939, in Petakh-Tikva, Israel; dual U.S.-Israeli citizenship; son of Meir-Shalom (a businessman) and Alina Kleinman (a homemaker) Borowski; married Marcia Weil (an attorney), August 24, 1964; children: Jonathan Robert,

Orly Borowski Hardin. *Ethnicity:* "Jewish." *Education:* Attended Absalom Institute (Israel), 1964-67; Midrasha (Detroit, MI), B.H.L. (Hebrew studies), 1968; Wayne State University, B.A. (history/anthropology), 1970; University of Michigan, M.A., 1972, Ph.D. (Near Eastern studies), 1979. *Hobbies and other interests:* Hiking, nature.

ADDRESSES: Office—Emory University, Department of Near Eastern and Judaic Languages and Literature, S310 Callaway Center, Atlanta, GA 30322. *E-mail*—oborows@emory.edu.

CAREER: Educator, archeologist, and author. Emory University, Atlanta, GA, associate professor of Hebrew and biblical archeology. Excavations include Tell Gezer, Tel Dan, Ashkelon, and Beth Shemesh; codirector of Lahav Research Project, Phase III, Tel Halif, Israel.

MEMBER: National Association of Professors of Hebrew, American Schools of Oriental Research, Society for Biblical Literature, Israel Exploration Society.

WRITINGS:

Agriculture in Iron-Age Israel, Eisenbrauns (Winona Lake, IN), 1987.
Every Living Thing: Daily Use of Animals in Ancient Israel, AltaMira Press (Walnut Creek, CA), 1998.
Daily Life in Biblical Times, Brill (Boston, MA), 2003.

Contributor of articles and book reviews to periodicals; contributor to encyclopedias and books.

WORK IN PROGRESS: A book on daily life in Ancient Israel, for AltaMira Press.

SIDELIGHTS: Oded Borowski told *CA:* "I am involved with archaeological excavations at Tell Halif, Israel, where I have been digging since 1976."

BIOGRAPHICAL AND CRITICAL SOURCES:

PERIODICALS

Choice, September, 1998, E. B. Hazard, review of *Every Living Thing: Daily Use of Animals in Ancient Israel,* p. 158.
Journal of the American Oriental Society, October-December, 1989, Marvin A. Powell, review of *Agriculture in Iron-Age Israel,* p. 672.

* * *

BOUCHEZ, Colette 1960-

PERSONAL: Born 1960.

ADDRESSES: Home—New York, NY. *Agent*—c/o Author's Mail, Broadway Books, Random House, 1540 Broadway, New York, NY 10036 *E-mail*—Colette@TheVZone.net.

CAREER: Journalist and author of nonfiction. *New York Daily News,* New York, NY, staff writer and senior medical reporter, 1984-98; *HealthscoutNews.com,* medical reporter; creator of *TheVZone.net.*

MEMBER: American Medical Women's Association.

AWARDS, HONORS: Fifty-Year Anniversary Award, Multiple Sclerosis Foundation, 1996, for excellence in science writing; Emmy Award in news documentary writing and production, for reports on breast cancer; National Media Award, American Society of Rectal Surgeons, 1997; honored by American Cancer Society, American Academy of Dermatology, NBCAM, National Multiple Sclerosis Society, National Coalition of Breast Cancer Organizations, Columbia School of Journalism, and Northwestern University Medill School of Journalism for outstanding contributions in the field of medical writing.

WRITINGS:

(With Niels H. Lauersen) *Getting Pregnant: What Couples Need to Know Right Now,* Macmillan International (New York, NY), 1991, revised as *Getting Pregnant: What You Need to Know Right Now,* Fireside (New York, NY), 2000.
The V Zone: A Woman's Guide to Intimate Health Care, foreword by Elsa-Grace V. Giardina, Simon and Schuster (New York, NY), 2001.

Your Perfectly Pampered Pregnancy: Beauty, Health, and Lifestyle Advice for the Modern Mother-to-Be, Broadway Books (New York, NY), 2004.

Contributor to periodicals, including *Buffalo News, Cosmopolitan, First for Women, Fresno Bee, Globe and Mail, Los Angeles Daily News, New York Times,* and *Savvy Woman.* Syndicated columnist for Copley News Syndicate, 1978, *New York Times, Los Angeles Times,* and *Washington Post.*

SIDELIGHTS: Colette Bouchez is an internationally known journalist and author. Her career has been dedicated to health and medical writing, with a focus on women's health issues.

For fifteen years Bouchez was a medical reporter for the *New York Daily News,* earning numerous awards and honors from many prestigious medical and journalistic organizations, including the American Cancer Society, the American Academy of Dermatology, the American Society of Colon and Cancer Surgeons, and the National Coalition of Breast Cancer Organizations.

Bouchez's journalism career began in 1978 with a weekly health-and-beauty column for the Copley News Syndicate. She eventually expanded her syndicated columns through the *Los Angeles Times* and Words by Wire syndicates, the latter which regularly placed her column in the *Washington Post.*

In 1984 Bouchez joined the staff of the *New York Daily News,* where she accomplished some of her most important work. Two of her exclusive reports instigated significant women's health care legislation capable of saving hundreds of thousands of lives. In February 1997, a bill was introduced in the New York State Legislature ensuring government funding for research to help reduce unnecessary surgical procedures for women. Later that same year the Women's Health and Dioxin Act of 1997 was introduced in the 105th Congress, mandating federal testing of feminine hygiene products suspected of increasing the risk of cancer. Both legislative bodies publicly credited Bouchez's contributions to these bills and to the overall health of American women.

In 1996 Bouchez was honored with the Fifty-Year Anniversary Award for excellence in science writing by the Multiple Sclerosis Foundation. The following year she received an award from Northwestern University's Medill School of Journalism for outstanding contributions in the field of medical writing. She has also received an Emmy Award for television news documentary writing and production for her series on breast cancer for WNBC-TV and the *New York Daily News.*

Bouchez's first book, coauthored with fertility expert Dr. Niels Lauersen and titled *Getting Pregnant: What Couples Need to Know Right Now,* gives practical, specific information and advice to help couples conceive. A *Publishers Weekly* reviewer noted that the authors "offer know-how on in-vitro fertilization procedures and programs. A brief but helpful resource section lists the names of medical associations, self-help groups and physicians specializing in reproductive medicine." The book was completely revised and updated in 2000 as *Getting Pregnant: What You Need to Know Right Now.* Bouchez left the *New York Daily News* in 1998 in order to pursue further book writing projects.

In 2001 Bouchez's ground-breaking *The V Zone: A Woman's Guide to Intimate Health Care* was published. In a review on the *Exploring Womanhood Web site,* Nancy Gazzola called the book "a comprehensive and practical guide to the health and hygiene concerns regarding the vagina." Bouchez encourages women to become more familiar with their own intimate anatomy and, when health issues arise, to explore different treatment options and alternative natural solutions. She provides up-to-date information on a variety of problems, including sexually transmitted diseases, painful intercourse, recurring urinary tract infections, AIDS, and itches and rashes, along with a resource guide to personal-hygiene products that ranks their effectiveness and safety. Jodith Janes concluded in *Library Journal* that *The V Zone* is "a wonderful, easy-to-read, comprehensive guide" that is "highly recommended for all women's health collections." In 2003 Bouchez created the *V Zone Web site* to further address women's health issues.

BIOGRAPHICAL AND CRITICAL SOURCES:

PERIODICALS

Library Journal, June 15, 1991, Jodith Janes, review of *Getting Pregnant: What Couples Need to Know Right Now,* p. 95; April 15, 2001, Jodith Janes, review of *The V Zone,* p. 125.

Publishers Weekly, June 21, 1991, review of *Getting Pregnant,* p. 61.

ONLINE

Broadway Books Web site, http://www.randomhouse.com/broadway/ (July 10, 2003).

Exploring Womanhood, http://www.exploringwomanhood.com/ (July 10, 2003), Nancy Gazzola, review of *The V Zone: A Woman's Guide to Intimate Health Care.*

InterNational Council on Infertility Information Dissemination Web site, http://www.inciid.org/ (1999).

V Zone Web site, http://www.thevzone.net/ (October 3, 2003).*

* * *

BOYD, Gregory A. 1957-

PERSONAL: Born June 2, 1957, in Cleveland, OH; married; wife's name Shelley; children: four. *Education:* University of Minnesota, B.A. (philosophy), 1979; Yale University Divinity School, M.Div., 1982; Princeton Theological Seminary, Ph.D., 1988.

ADDRESSES: Home—409 Tessier Circle, Vadnais Heights, MN 55127. *Office*—Bethel College, 3900 Bethel Drive, St. Paul, MN 55112. *E-mail*—boygre@bethel.edu.

CAREER: Educator and author. Garden City Christian Church, Garden City, MN, interim pastor, 1988-89; First Baptist Church, White Bear Lake, MN, interim pastor, 1990-91; Crossroads Covenant Church, Forest Lake, MN, interim pastor, 1991-92; Church of the Open Door, Robbinsdale, MN, teaching instructor, 1989-92, interim pastor, 1992; Woodland Hills Church, St. Paul, MN, senior pastor, 1992—; Bethel College, St. Paul, professor of theology, 1986—. Speaker at church, parachurch, and college-related functions; has appeared on radio and television programs.

AWARDS, HONORS: Sears-Roebuck Foundation Teaching Excellence and Campus Leadership Award, 1992; CBA Golden Book Award, 1995, for *Letters from a Skeptic;* People's Choice Award, *Christianity Today,* 1996, for *Cynic Sage or Son of God?*

WRITINGS:

Oneness Pentecostals and the Trinity, Baker Book House (Grand Rapids, MI), 1992.

Trinity and Process: The a priori Construction of a Trinitarian Metaphysic from a Critical Evaluation of Hartshorne's Process Theism, Peter Lang Publishers (New York, NY), 1992.

Letters from a Skeptic: A Son Wrestles with His Father's Questions about Christianity, Victor Books (Wheaton, IL), 1994.

Cynic Sage or Son of God?: Recovering the Real Jesus in an Age of Revisionist Replies, BridgePoint Books, 1995.

Jesus under Siege, Victor Books (Wheaton, IL), 1995.

God at War: The Bible and Spiritual Conflict (volume I of "Satan and Evil" series), InterVarsity Press (Downers Grove, IL), 1997.

The God of the Possible: Divine Foreknowledge and the Openness of the Future, Baker Book House (Grand Rapids, MI), 2000.

(With Paul Eddy) *Evangelical Options: An Exploration of Issues in Theology,* Baker Book House (Grand Rapids, MI), 2001.

Letters from a Skeptic Study Guide, Chariot Books, 2001.

Satan and the Problem of Evil: Constructing a Warfare Theodicy (volume II of "Satan and Evil" series), InterVarsity Press (Downers Grove, IL), 2001.

The Myth of the Blueprint: Examining the Augustinian Revolution in the Theology of the Early Church, (volume III of "Satan and Evil" series), InterVarsity Press (Downers Grove, IL), 2002.

(With Paul R. Eddy) *Across the Spectrum: Understanding Issues in Evangelical Theology,* Baker Academic (Grand Rapids, MI), 2002.

Is God to Blame?: Moving beyond Pat Answers to the Problem of Evil, InterVarsity Press (Downers Grove, IL), 2003.

Contributor to magazines and journals, including *Christian Research Journal, Christian Scholars Review, Process Trinitarianism, Priscilla Papers, Journal of the Evangelical Theological Society,* and *UltraRunning.* Also author of professional papers, presentations, and published debates. Contributing scholar, *The Quest Study Bible,* Zondervan, 1994.

WORK IN PROGRESS: Experiencing Jesus: The Theology and Practice of Cataphatic Prayer.

BRAATEN, Carl E. 1929-

PERSONAL: Born January 3, 1929, in St. Paul, MN; son of Torstein F. (a missionary) and Clara A. (a missionary) Braaten; married LaVonne Gardner, September 16, 1951; children: Craig, Martha, Maria, Kristofer. *Ethnicity:* "Norwegian descent." *Education:* St. Olaf College, B.A. (philosophy, English, French; magna cum laude), 1951; Luther Seminary, B.Th., 1955; Harvard University, Th.D., 1960; studied at University of Paris, 1951-52; University of Heidelberg, 1957-58; and Oxford University, 1967-68. *Politics:* Democrat. *Religion:* "Lutheran—Evangelical Lutheran Church in America." *Hobbies and other interests:* Tennis, golf.

ADDRESSES: *Office*—Center for Catholic and Evangelical Theology, 16005 Huron Dr., Sun City West, AZ 85375. *E-mail*—Carlebraat@aol.com.

CAREER: Minister. Ordained 1958, Evangelical Lutheran Church, Minneapolis, MN; Lutheran Church of the Messiah, Minneapolis, pastor, 1958-61; Luther Seminary, St. Paul, MN, instructor in theology and church history, 1958-61; Lutheran Theological Seminary, Maywood, IL, assistant professor of theology, 1961-67; Lutheran School of Theology, Chicago, IL, professor of systematic theology, 1968-95; Center for Catholic and Evangelical Theology, Sun City West, AZ, executive director, 1991—. *Dialog: A Journal of Theology,* founding editor, 1962—; *Pro Ecclesia: A Journal of Catholic and Evangelical Theory,* founder and coeditor, 1992—.

MEMBER: American Theological Society, American Academy of Religion, North American Paul Tillich Society, Phi Beta Kappa.

AWARDS, HONORS: Fulbright scholar, 1951-52; Sinclair Kennedy fellow, Harvard University, 1957-58; Guggenheim fellow, 1967-68; Franklin Clark Fry Award, 1974-75.

WRITINGS:

AUTHOR

History and Hermeneutics, Westminster Press (Philadelphia, PA), 1966.

The Future of God: The Revolutionary Dynamics of Hope, Harper & Row (New York, NY), 1969.

Christ and Counter-Christ: Apocalyptic Themes in Theology and Culture, Fortress Press (Philadelphia, PA), 1972.

The Whole Counsel of God, Fortress Press (Philadelphia, PA), 1974.

Eschatology and Ethics: Essays on the Theology and Ethics of the Kingdom of God, Augsburg Publishing House (Minneapolis, MN), 1974.

(With wife, LaVonne Braaten) *The Living Temple: A Practical Theology of the Body and the Foods of the Earth,* Harper & Row (New York, NY), 1976.

The Flaming Center: A Theology of the Christian Mission, Fortress Press (Philadelphia, PA), 1977.

Principles of Lutheran Theology, Fortress Press (Philadelphia, PA), 1983.

Stewards of the Mysteries: Sermons for Festivals and Special Occasions, Augsburg Publishing House (Minneapolis, MN), 1983.

The Apostolic Imperative: Nature and Aim of the Church's Mission and Ministry, Augsburg Publishing House (Minneapolis, MN), 1985.

Justification: The Article by Which the Church Stands or Falls, Fortress Press (Minneapolis, MN), 1990.

No Other Gospel!: Christianity among the World's Religions, Fortress Press (Minneapolis, MN), 1992.

Mother Church: Ecclesiology and Ecumenism, Fortress Press (Minneapolis, MN), 1998.

EDITOR

(And translator, with Roy A. Harrisville) *Kerygma and History: A Symposium on the Theology of Rudolf Bultmann,* Abingdon Press (New York, NY), 1962.

(And translator, with Roy A. Harrisville) *The Historical Jesus and the Kerygmatic Christ: Essays on the New Quest of the Historical Jesus,* Abingdon Press (New York, NY), 1964.

(And translator) Martin Kähler, *The So-Called Historical Jesus and the Historic Biblical Christ,* Fortress Press (Philadelphia, PA), 1964, reprinted, 1988.

Paul Tillich, *Perspectives on Nineteenth and Twentieth-Century Protestant Theology,* Harper & Row (New York, NY), 1967.

Paul Tillich, *A History of Christian Thought,* Harper & Row (New York, NY), 1968, published as *A History of Christian Thought, from Its Judaic and Hellenistic Origins to Existentialism,* Simon & Schuster (New York, NY), 1972.

(With Avery Dulles) Wolfhart Pannenberg, *Spirit, Faith, and Church,* Westminster Press (Philadelphia, PA), 1970.

(With Robert W. Jenson) *The Futurist Option,* Newman Press (New York, NY), 1970.

The New Church Debate: Issues Facing American Lutheranism, Fortress Press (Philadelphia, PA), 1983.

(With Robert W. Jenson) *Christian Dogmatics* (two volumes), Fortress Press (Philadelphia, PA), 1984.

(With Philip Clayton) *The Theology of Wolfhart Pannenberg: Twelve American Critiques, with an Autobiographical Essay and Response,* Augsburg Publishing House (Minneapolis, MN), 1988.

Our Naming of God: Problems and Prospects of God-Talk Today, Fortress Press (Minneapolis, MN), 1989.

(With Robert W. Jenson) *Reclaiming the Bible for the Church,* W. B. Eerdmans (Grand Rapids, MI), 1995.

(With Robert W. Jenson) *A Map of Twentieth-Century Theology: Readings from Karl Barth to Radical Pluralism,* Fortress Press (Minneapolis, MN), 1995.

(With Robert W. Jenson) *Either/Or: The Gospel or Neopaganism,* W. B. Eerdmans (Grand Rapids, MI), 1995.

(With Robert W. Jenson) *The Catholicity of the Reformation,* W. B. Eerdmans (Grand Rapids, MI), 1996.

(With Robert W. Jenson) *The Two Cities of God: The Church's Responsibility for the Earthly City,* W. B. Eerdmans (Grand Rapids, MI), 1997.

(With Robert W. Jenson) *Union with Christ: The New Finnish Interpretation of Luther,* W. B. Eerdmans (Grand Rapids, MI), 1998.

(With Robert W. Jenson) *Marks of the Body of Christ,* W. B. Eerdmans (Grand Rapids, MI), 1999.

(With Robert W. Jenson) *Sin, Death, and the Devil,* W. B. Eerdmans (Grand Rapids, MI), 2000.

(With Robert W. Jenson) *Church Unity and the Papal Office: An Ecumenical Dialogue on John Paul II's Encyclical "Ut unum sint" ("That All May Be One"),* W. B. Eerdmans (Grand Rapids, MI), 2001.

(With Robert W. Jenson) *The Last Things: Biblical and Theological Perspectives on Eschatology,* W. B. Eerdmans (Grand Rapids, MI), 2002.

(With Robert W. Jenson) *The Strange New World of the Gospel: Re-evangelizing in the Postmodern World,* W. B. Eerdmans (Grand Rapids, MI), 2002.

(With Robert W. Jenson) *Jews and Christians: People of God,* W. B. Eerdmans (Grand Rapids, MI), 2003.

(With Robert W. Jenson) *Ecumenical Future: Background Papers for "In One Body through the Cross: The Princeton Proposal for Christian Unity,"* W. B. Eerdmans (Grand Rapids, MI), 2003.

Contributor to books and periodicals.

SIDELIGHTS: Carl E. Braaten was born to parents who served the Evangelical Lutheran Church as missionaries in Madagascar. Braaten himself served as a minister and an educator before becoming executive director of the Center for Catholic and Evangelical Theology.

Braaten has written or edited a long list of volumes on theology and religious thought, and several of these are collections of essays or papers that developed out of individual theological conferences. His *No Other Gospel!: Christianity among the World's Religions* is a collection of essays in which, according to Robert Cummings Neville in the *International Bulletin of Missionary Research,* "Braaten argues strongly for both missionary efforts and interfaith dialogue in which the Gospel of Jesus Christ can be proclaimed while sharing and building upon God's grace as manifested throughout many cultures and religions."

Christian Century's Donald G. Bloesch wrote that Braaten "warns of a new church conflict and the need for the church to redefine itself in the face of new heresies. A genuine reformation will not come until the church rediscovers its mission, which has now become politicized."

Braaten and Robert W. Jenson, with whom Braaten has coedited many volumes, produced *The Catholicity of the Reformation,* a collection of seven articles that came out of a lecture series and which reflects the interests of the Center for Catholic and Evangelical Theology. *Christian Century* contributor Kurt K. Hendel wrote that the volume "explores the scriptural, creedal, dogmatic, and liturgical tradition of the church and seeks to ground the community of faith in that tradition while challenging it to make a unified witness. Addressing particularly North American Lutheranism, but intentionally ecumenical, the center affirms the evangelical heritage of the Reformation while stressing the unity of the church and the catholicity of the Christian tradition."

In *Mother Church: Ecclesiology and Ecumenism,* Braaten, who views himself as an "evangelical catholic," calls for Christian unity. "This unity must be based on faith and doctrine," noted Fidon R. Mwombeki in *Interpretation,* "rather than on popular social activism which, Braaten believes, is characterized by a 'dogmatic deficit.'"

Christian Century's Michael Kinnamon noted that these essays, which Braaten wrote over a number of years, reflect "his concern that contemporary churches have allowed culture to set their agenda and thus are marked by a weakening of distinctive Christian beliefs; his call for biblical literacy and for a renewed confidence in the authority of scripture; his advocacy for a church that is evangelical and catholic; his emphasis on eschatology as the necessary framework for thinking about the church."

Braaten and Jenson coedited *Union with Christ: The New Finnish Interpretation of Luther. First Things* reviewer Ted Dorman wrote that "this brief but rich book introduces English-speaking scholars to groundbreaking research from Helsinki University that casts Martin Luther's soteriology in a new light. The 'new Finnish interpretation of Luther' finds the essence of his doctrine of salvation not in forensic justification—God declaring us just solely by virtue of Christ's sacrifice—but in something more akin to the Eastern Orthodox doctrine of theosis, or deification."

The head of the Finnish Luther project, Tuomo Mannermaa, and four colleagues, including Simo Puera, Sammeli Juntunen, Antti Raunio, and Risto Saarinen, offer seven essays. Braaten and Jenson provide the preface and responses, along with William Lazareth and Dennis Bielfeldt.

The essays in *Church Unity and the Papal Office: An Ecumenical Dialogue on John Paul II's Encyclical "Ut unum sint" ("That All May Be One")* are responses to John Paul II's invitation to a dialogue about how his office might better serve the visible unity of the Church. The essays are written by authors coming from diverse backgrounds, including Roman Catholic, Lutheran, Anglican, Methodist, and Evangelical.

George Vandervelde, commenting in *Theological Studies,* felt that the Lutheran contribution by David Yeago contains the volume's "most far-reaching and profound explorations." Vandervelde said that Yeago writes that "if Lutheran communions are to consider papal primacy seriously, they would have to recover a biblical sense of witness." Vandervelde also said that "ironically, the more 'fraternal' the relationship, the more difficult 'patient' dialogue becomes," and concluded by saying that "while even the sample of intra-Catholic polemics is illuminating, the principal value of this volume lies in the ways in which the question of primacy engenders, among and within diverse traditions, penetrating discussions concerning the interrelated issues of authority, truth, unity, and mission."

BIOGRAPHICAL AND CRITICAL SOURCES:

PERIODICALS

Christian Century, October 6, 1993, Donald G. Bloesch, review of *No Other Gospel!: Christianity among the World's Religions,* p. 950; October 15, 1997, Kurt K. Hendel, review of *The Catholicity of the Reformation,* p. 918; February 3, 1999, Michael Kinnamon, review of *Mother Church: Ecclesiology and Ecumenism,* p. 147.

First Things, December, 1999, Ted Dorman, review of *Union with Christ: The New Finnish Interpretation of Luther,* p. 49.

International Bulletin of Missionary Research, July, 1993, Robert Cummings Neville, review of *No Other Gospel!,* p. 137.

Interpretation, July, 1994, Kenneth Hamilton, review of *No Other Gospel!,* p. 317; April, 1999, Fidon R. Mwombeki, review of *Mother Church,* p. 212.

Theological Studies, September, 2002, George Vandervelde, review of *Church Unity and the Papal Office: An Ecumenical Dialogue on John Paul II's Encyclical "Ut unum sint" ("That All May Be One"),* p. 624.

ONLINE

Center for Catholic and Evangelical Theology, http://www.e-ccnet.org/ (November 10, 2003).

* * *

BRANDT, Beverly

PERSONAL: Married; three stepchildren. *Education:* Earned bachelor's degree (finance). *Hobbies and other interests:* Reading, writing.

ADDRESSES: Home—204 37th Avenue N., Box 340, St. Petersburg, FL 33704. *E-mail*—Beverly@beverlybrandt.com.

CAREER: Novelist. Formerly worked as a financial analyst for a travel agency.

AWARDS, HONORS: Dorothy Parker Award of Excellence nomination, Reviewers International, 2002, for *True North.*

WRITINGS:

NOVELS

True North, St. Martin's Press (New York, NY), 2002.
Record Time, St. Martin's Press (New York, NY), 2003.
Room Service, St. Martin's Press (New York, NY), 2003.
Dream On, St. Martin's Press (New York, NY), in press.

SIDELIGHTS: Beverly Brandt is a romance writer who has been praised for creating flawed heroines unlike the "perfume heiresses" Brandt recalled from the romance novels she read in her teens. Although she worked as a financial analyst for several years, Brandt began to question her career path in her late twenties and decided to rediscover her dream of becoming an author. She finished her first complete novel, *True North,* in 2000. "After all, there's only room for so many unfinished manuscripts in my closet," she quipped to an interviewer for *Romance Reader* online. She submitted *True North* to several agents, but they all rejected it. Brandt then sent a query letter directly to an editor at St. Martin's Press, and a few days later was asked to send the complete manuscript.

In *True North,* workaholic heroine Claire Brown books a dream vacation in the hopes of strengthening her weak relationship with her fiancee, Bryan. Nothing goes as planned, however. Bryan goes to the resort, but with someone else. Determined to enjoy herself anyway, Claire also goes the resort, but winds up sleeping in a cramped extra room located in the employee-only section. Ultimately, Claire falls in love with the resort owner, John McBride. Reviewer Heidi L. Haglin noted in *All about Romance* online that, "if you can get past certain instances of questionable behavior, especially on the heroine's part, you will find yourself drawn into a touching love story of two people who have no idea what they need in life, or in love, until they find each other." While the book was praised for its characterization, it was criticized for exploring only the motivations of female workaholics. Commented Haglin, "whether that speaks to the idea that men would feel less anxiety or regret over putting work above family or simply plot convenience, I don't know. . . . I was left with the nagging feeling that this is the book feminists warned us about." *True North* was nominated for Reviewers International's 2002 Dorothy Parker Award of Excellence in the Debut Author category.

Resilient heroines have continued to be Brandt's stock-in-trade. In her second novel, *Record Time,* unglamorous Kylie Rogers falls for David Gamble, a control freak who is the head of a record company. Said a reviewer for *Publishers Weekly,* the author creates a "delightful balance between control and confusion and pads her story with a cast of well-drawn ancillary characters" in a "fun, feel-good" novel. In *Room Service,* jet-setter Katya Morgan loses it all when her father dies and disinherits her. She then falls for Alex Sheridan, a handsome hotel manager who hires her as a housekeeper. "As Alex helps her out, Katya discovers how the rest of the world lives, and the reader enjoys a fine, funny tale," reviewer Maria Hatton explained in *Booklist.*

BIOGRAPHICAL AND CRITICAL SOURCES:

PERIODICALS

Booklist, February 15, 2003, Maria Hatton, review of *Room Service,* p. 1056.
Publishers Weekly, August 19, 2002, review of *Record Time,* p. 72.

ONLINE

All about Romance, http://www.likesbooks.com/ (June 4, 2003), Heidi L. Haglin, review of *True North.*
Beverly Brandt Web site, http://www.beverlybrandt.com (November 13, 2003).

Romance Reader, http://www.theromancereader.com/ (January 29, 2002), Cathy Sova, interview with Brandt; Karen Lynch, review of *True North.**

* * *

BRANSON, Louise

PERSONAL: Married Dusko Doder (a journalist and author); children: Thomas, Nicholas.

ADDRESSES: *Home*—Vienna, VA. *Office*—c/o *The Scotsman,* Barclay House, 108 Holyrood Road, Edinburgh EH8 8AS, Scotland.

CAREER: Journalist and author. *Sunday Times,* London, England, foreign correspondent in Moscow, USSR (now Russia), then Beijing, China; *Scotsman* (newspaper), Edinburgh, Scotland, Washington correspondent.

WRITINGS:

(With husband, Dusko Doder) *Gorbachev: Heretic in the Kremlin,* Viking (New York, NY), 1990, new edition, Penguin (New York, NY), 1991.

(With husband, Dusko Doder) *Milosevic: Portrait of a Tyrant,* Free Press (New York, NY), 1999.

SIDELIGHTS: For many years Louise Branson and her husband, Dusko Doder, have traveled the world as journalists for various media outlets. Their first two books, *Gorbachev: Heretic in the Kremlin* and *Milosevic: Portrait of a Tyrant,* sprang directly from their experiences as journalists. In his review of *Milosevic,* Zachary T. Irwin wrote in *Library Journal* that because of their backgrounds, "perhaps no two authors are better qualified for the task of such a biography." In both *Gorbachev* and *Milosevic,* the authors present profiles of men whose actions made headlines across the world but whose backgrounds are not widely known to Western readers.

Their first book, *Gorbachev,* was published as Soviet leader Mikhail Gorbachev's empire was crumbling around him. The book "was conceived as a biography of Mikhail Gorbachev," Eugene H. Methvin explained in *National Review,* but it "became an encyclopedia of his regime at home and abroad." Branson and Doder attempt to answer the question of whether Gorbachev's radical reforms of the Soviet system were part of a premeditated plan to move toward a freer political and economic system or whether they were pragmatic reactions to unforeseen circumstances that arose during Gorbachev's time in office. "Doder and Branson are less interested in the abstract analysis of historical processes and future prospects than they are in the interplay of personalities and events," Robert V. Daniels commented in *New Leader.* Daniels continued by writing that as a result, the book offers "an exciting, fast-paced narrative—week by week and sometimes day by day—of Gorbachev's first five years at the helm" of the Soviet Union.

In *Milosevic,* Branson and Doder unsympathetically profile a man who presided over his country during an era of political collapse. Slobodan Milosevic, president of the former Yugoslavia, started four wars in the Balkans during his time in office and directly or indirectly caused the deaths of tens of thousands of people. However, rather than solely concentrating on constructing a record of Milosevic's political actions, the authors attempt to uncover the motivations behind them. A reviewer explained in *Business Week* that before Branson and Doder's book, "no writer . . . truly explored what makes Milosevic tick." Branson and Doder devote twenty-five pages to Milosevic's early life, including the suicides of both of his parents and his relationship with his wife, Marjana, who is widely seen as the force behind Milosevic's seat of power; the remainder of the book is dedicated to events that occurred in the 1980s and led to the crumbling of Yugoslavia during the 1990s. "With the hardened realism that comes from years of journalism and a first-hand knowledge of the Balkan scene, Doder and Branson . . . have written a vivid and scathing biography," declared a *Publishers Weekly* contributor.

BIOGRAPHICAL AND CRITICAL SOURCES:

PERIODICALS

Booklist, November 1, 1999, Gilbert Taylor, review of *Milosevic: Portrait of a Tyrant,* p. 505.

Business Week, December 27, 1999, review of *Milosevic,* p. 32.
International Journal, spring, 2000, review of *Milosevic,* pp. 333-334.
Library Journal, January, 2000, Zachary T. Irwin, review of *Milosevic,* p. 134.
National Review, October 15, 1990, Eugene H. Methvin, review of *Gorbachev: Heretic in the Kremlin,* pp. 85-87.
New Leader, September 3, 1990, Robert V. Daniels, review of *Gorbachev,* pp. 20-21.
New Statesman, March 6, 2000, Richard Gott, review of *Milosevic,* p. 56.
New York Review of Books, January 20, 2000, Charles Simic, review of *Milosevic,* pp. 26-29.
New York Times Book Review, November 21, 1999, Charles King, review of *Milosevic,* p. 64.
Publishers Weekly, April 13, 1990, Genevieve Stuttaford, review of *Gorbachev,* p. 52; November 8, 1999, review of *Milosevic,* p. 53.
SAIS Review, summer-fall, 2000, Anna Simons, review of *Milosevic,* pp. 159-166.
Seattle Post-Intelligencer, December 29, 1999, review of *Milosevic,* p. E2.
Spectator, February 5, 2000, David Pryce-Jones, review of *Milosevic,* p. 30.
Time, July 16, 1990, Brigid O'Hara-Forster, review of *Gorbachev,* p. 82.

ONLINE

CNN Web site, http://www.cnn.com/ (March 23, 2000), transcript of web chat with Branson.*

* * *

BRUNEAU, Carol 1956-

PERSONAL: Born November 21, 1956, in Halifax, Nova Scotia, Canada; daughter of John Joseph (an accountant) and Eva Marion Williams (a registered nurse) Bruneau; married Bruce Erskine (a journalist), May 14, 1983; children: Andrew Erskine, Seamus Erskine, Angus Erskine. *Ethnicity:* "Anglo Canadian." *Education:* Dalhousie University, B.A. (English), 1977, M.A. (English), 1986; University of Western Ontario, M.A. (journalism), 1983. *Religion:* Anglican. *Hobbies and other interests:* Gardening, music, hiking, camping, spirituality.

ADDRESSES: Office—Cormorant Books Inc., R.R. No. 1, Dunvegan, Ontario K0C 1J0, Canada.

CAREER: Educator and author of fiction. Writers Federation of Nova Scotia, Halifax, Nova Scotia, Canada, guest author for writers-in-the-schools program, 1995—; Nova Scotia Community College, Halifax, part-time instructor in creative writing, 1999—. St. Paul's Home (charitable organization), board member.

MEMBER: Writers' Federation of Nova Scotia, Cancopy.

AWARDS, HONORS: Explorations grant, Canada Council for the Arts, 1994; second prize for children's writing, Atlantic Writing Awards, 1994; third prize, *Sunday Star* short-story contest, 1996; Thomas Head Raddall Atlantic Fiction Award, and Dartmouth Book Award for fiction, both 2001, both for *Purple for Sky.*

WRITINGS:

After the Angel Mill (linked short stories), Cormorant (Dunvegan, Ontario, Canada), 1995.
Depth Rapture (linked short stories), Cormorant (Dunvegan, Ontario, Canada), 1998.
Purple for Sky, Cormorant (Dunvegan, Ontario, Canada), 2000, published as *A Purple Thread for Sky: A Novel of Intertwined Lives,* Carroll & Graf (New York, NY), 2001.

Contributor to anthologies, including *Atlantica: Stories from the Maritimes and Newfoundland,* edited by Lesley Choyce, Goose Lane Editions, 2001.

WORK IN PROGRESS: Sea Bloom, "a novel about survivors of the 1917 Halifax Explosion, the largest manmade explosion before Hiroshima. It is a family saga spanning eight decades during which characters survive catastrophe, war, and sexual misdemeanors. It explores the nature of miracles, small and large."

SIDELIGHTS: Carol Bruneau told *CA:* "I've been interested in writing stories since about the age of seven. As a kid I loved the novels of Prince Edward Island-born Lucy Maud Montgomery, author of the popular *Anne of Green Gables,* and my earliest stories were childish attempts to copy her romantic tales. I couldn't help admiring her; she was really the first writer to prove that you could live and write in my part of the world—Atlantic Canada—and be successful.

"As a teenager and university student, I grew up on the work of Margaret Laurence and Alice Munro. This was my first exposure to writers who capture the truths of being female in milieus not unlike my own—small, rooted communities where connections run deep and provide tons of fodder for fiction. In a big way these writers 'legitimized' my experiences as well as my desire to write. But it wasn't until I read William Faulkner's *As I Lay Dying,* well into my B.A. in English, that the notion of assuming a narrative voice—any narrative voice you pleased—suddenly seemed possible.

"It was another fifteen years or so, however, before I did anything with this discovery. I'd enjoyed a career in journalism—mostly photojournalism—and begun raising my family of three sons before I actually got around to what I always wanted to do: write fiction. That was six years ago, and ever since, my life has been a whirlwind of beat-the-clock juggling of narrative and reality.

"From the beginning I have had to work in fits and starts, bits and pieces, whenever time and opportunity allows. Consequently, a lot of ideas, notes, and even whole scenes have gotten jotted down in check-out lines and at red lights, during soccer games and piano lessons. When it comes to the actual work, I'm a slow and disciplined writer whose most productive time is the morning. My novel *A Purple Thread for Sky* took five years to complete—three to 'cook,' another two to write. Each story or chapter takes at least five drafts, with the most significant rewriting undertaken at the second-draft stage, and subsequent drafts to hone and polish. For me the most challenging part is discovering structure and plot, which I find grows out of the characters and the narrative itself. My books are character-driven, in the sense that I believe art should imitate life. As a realist, I can't help but bristle at the imposition of plot: to me this is not just artificial but risky, and affect with the potential to compromise a story's integrity.

"For now I am mainly interested in stories that are set in the region I know best, eastern Canada—stories which are rooted in an historical context. And though history plays a role in my work, it's more as a backdrop. Mostly I'm interested in metaphor, and the universal aspects of stories that grow out of contextual experience.

"My favourite authors are presently women from the American south—from Eudora Welty to Lee Smith, Cindy Bonner, and Bobbie Ann Mason. I see parallels between my part of the world and theirs, qualities of voice and character in their work, and a sense of community and of isolation that all ring true for me in a nurturing way. Their stories lend credence to the kinds of stories I want most to tell, stories of 'ordinary' people, particularly women, their triumphs and pitfalls, and the quirks of fate that shape their lives. Humour is especially important—I suppose you could call it survivor's humour, at times quite black. For the stories of survivors, not victims, are the ones closest to my heart, and the fact that people like this abound here in this part of Canada gives me a funny sense of duty. As someone blessed with so much fodder, I feel a responsibility to write it all down."

BIOGRAPHICAL AND CRITICAL SOURCES:

PERIODICALS

Booklist, April 1, 2001, Ellie Barta-Moran, review of *A Purple Thread for Sky: A Novel of Intertwined Lives,* p. 1447.

Library Journal, June 1, 2001, Yvette Olson, review of *A Purple Thread for Sky,* p. 212.

Maclean's, June 22, 1998, review of *Depth Rapture,* p. 48.

Publishers Weekly, April 9, 2001, review of *A Purple Thread for Sky,* p. 49.

ONLINE

Writers' Federation of Nova Scotia Web site, http://www.writers.ns.ca/ (December 10, 2003), "Carol Bruneau."

BUCK, Paul H(erman) 1899-1978

PERSONAL: Born August 25, 1899, in Columbus, OH; died December 23, 1978, in Cambridge, MA; son of Henry and Adele (Kreppelt) Buck; married Sally Burwell Betts, December 21, 1927. *Education:* Ohio State University, B.A., 1921, M.A., 1922; Harvard University, Ph.D., 1935. *Religion:* Episcopalian.

CAREER: Harvard University, Cambridge, MA, instructor, then full professor of history, 1942; associate dean, Harvard Faculty of Arts and Sciences, 1939-42, dean, 1942-45, ex-officio dean, 1945-53; director of Harvard University Library, 1955-64.

MEMBER: American Historical Association, Massachusetts Historical Society.

AWARDS, HONORS: Pulitzer Prize in history, 1938, for *The Road to Reunion;* Chevalier of the Legion of Honor, 1951; LL.D., Coe College, Ohio State University and Tufts College; Litt.D., Harvard College and Princeton University.

WRITINGS:

The Road to Reunion, 1865-1900, Little, Brown (Boston, MA), 1937.

(With others) *General Education in a Free Society; Report of the Harvard Committee,* Harvard University Press (Cambridge, MA), 1945.

The Evolution of the National Park System of the United States, U.S. Government Printing Office (Washington, DC), 1946.

(With others) *Nature and Needs of Higher Education, the Report of the Commission on Financing Higher Education,* Columbia University Press (New York, NY), 1952.

(With others) *The Role of Education in American History,* Fund for the Advancement of Education (New York, NY), 1957

Social Sciences at Harvard, 1860-1920: From Inculcation to the Open Mind, Harvard University Press (Cambridge, MA), 1965.

Libraries and Universities, Harvard University Press (Cambridge, MA), 1965.

Contributed to periodical publications

SIDELIGHTS: Paul H. Buck, best known for his study of the Reconstruction period in American history, *The Road to Reunion, 1865-1900* was also a high-level instructor and administrator at Harvard University.

Buck, an Ohio native, was an enthusiastic reader and history buff who grew up "around the corner from the public library," as he put it. He attended Ohio State University before going to Harvard to earn his Ph.D. Buck became a history instructor, rising through the ranks to eventually become ex-officio dean. He was also, as Harvard's library administrator, a key figure in the 1949 opening of the Lamont Library, which was dedicated to new methods of teaching humanities.

Harvard President Nathan M. Pusey said when Buck became the head of Harvard's library system in 1954: "No one is more alert to the challenge given the library by every educational advance, or more aware of the crucial part the library has played, down though history."

The Road to Reunion emphasizes "the varied threads of reconciliation," as he wrote. "Within a generation after the close of the Civil War the particularistic aspirations of North and South had lost their bitter edge and an American nationalism existed which derived its elements indiscriminately from both the erstwhile foes."

Critics have cited his skillful analysis. "The care with which Professor Buck has composed *The Road to Reunion* is manifest on every page," N. B. Cousins wrote in *Current History.* F. L. Owsley in *Yale Review* hailed Buck's work as "a scholarly and well-balanced book" that displays "a philosophical grasp of the meaning of things." G. F. Milton in *New Republic* called it "a brilliant performance," adding that Buck "has made a real contribution to our understanding of how an America, almost riven, has become almost one again."

The Road to Reunion won the Pulitzer Prize for history in 1938. Thereafter, Buck produced a handful of other studies, including *Libraries and Universities, Social Sciences at Harvard 1860-1920: From Inculcation to the Open Mind,* and *Nature and Needs of*

Higher Education, the Report of the Commission on Financing Higher Education. One book, *General Education in a Free Society; Report of the Harvard Committee,* had a longstanding impact on Harvard policy, making study of the humanities, social science, and the natural sciences a required part of the curriculum for every student.

BIOGRAPHICAL AND CRITICAL SOURCES:

PERIODICALS

Current History, August, 1937, N. B. Cousins, review of *The Road to Reunion, 1865-1900.*

Library Journal, January 15, 1965, Richard H. Logsdon, review of *Libraries and Universities,* p. 223.

New Republic, July 7, 1937, G. F. Milton, review of *The Road to Reunion.*

Saturday Review of Literature, June 12, 1937, H. W. Odum, review of *The Road to Reunion.*

Yale Review, autumn, 1937, F. L. Owsley, review of *The Road to Reunion.**

* * *

BUMPERS, Dale L(eon) 1925-

PERSONAL: Born August 12, 1925, in Charleston, AR; son of William Rufus (a hardware store owner) and Lattie (Jones) Bumpers; married Betty Lou Flanagan (a teacher), September 4, 1949; children: Dale Brent, William Mark, Margaret Brooke. *Education:* Attended University of Arkansas; Northwestern University, J.D., 1951. *Politics:* Democrat.

ADDRESSES: Office—1779 Massachusetts Ave. NW, Washington, DC 20036-2109. *Agent*—c/o Author Mail, Random House, 201 East 50th St., New York, NY 10022.

CAREER: U.S. senator, governor, businessman, and attorney. Admitted to the Bar of the State of Arkansas, 1952; Charleston Hardware and Furniture Co., Charleston, AR, president, 1951-56; attorney in private practice, Charleston, 1952-70; cattle rancher, 1966-79; governor of State of Arkansas, 1970-74; U.S. senator, 1975-98, committees: appropriations, energy and natural resources, small business; Center for Defense Information, Washington, DC, director; Arent Fox, Washington, DC, attorney, 1998—. President, Chamber of Commerce, Charleston, AR. *Military service:* U.S. Marines, sergeant, 1943-46..

AWARDS, HONORS: All with wife, Betty Bumpers: Citizen of the Year Award, March of Dimes; Excellence in Public Service Award, American Academy of Pediatrics; Maxwell Finland Award, National Foundation for Infectious Diseases; National Institute of Allergy and Infectious Diseases named the Dale and Betty Bumpers Vaccine Research Center in honor of the couples' advocacy in the areas of public health and childhood immunization.

WRITINGS:

(With others) *Religion and Politics,* edited by W. Lawson Taitte, University of Texas Press (Dallas, TX), 1989.

The Best Lawyer in a One-Lawyer Town (memoir), Random House (New York, NY), 2002.

SIDELIGHTS: Dale Bumpers never lost an election, and he served the State of Arkansas as its governor and U.S. senator. He was succeeded as governor by William Jefferson Clinton who, when he was impeached as president, asked Bumpers to make the closing argument at his trial. Bumpers, who worked while in the U.S. Senate to increase funding for the improvement and purchase of childhood vaccines, has been honored along with his wife, Betty, for their work as health advocates.

Bumpers was a child of the Great Depression in a town with a population of fewer than a thousand people. When he was twelve years old, he saw President Franklin Roosevelt campaigning in Arkansas, being physically supported by two men at the back of the train. Bumpers's father pointed out to his children that if FDR, who was afflicted with polio, could be president, then so could any of them. The young Bumpers earned money by picking cotton, potatoes, and peas and began working in a store when he was fifteen.

During World War II he served with the U.S. Marines and was to be part of the invasion of Japan when that war ended. Upon returning to Arkansas, Bumpers completed his education and became a lawyer. He also managed the retail hardware business of his father after both of his parents were tragically killed in an automobile accident while he was in law school.

In eighteen years of practice, Bumpers lost only two jury cases. He was instrumental in Charleston's decision to become the first Southern city to integrate its schools following the 1954 Supreme Court Brown v. Board of Education decision. In 1970 Bumpers defeated segregationist Orval Faubus's comeback attempt and became, at age forty-four, the youngest governor in Arkansas history, unseating incumbent Republican governor, Winthrop Rockefeller. In 1974 Bumpers defeated J. William Fulbright for a U.S. senate seat, which he filled for twenty-four years.

Bumpers provides the opening essay of *Religion and Politics,* in which the contributors explore the relationship between the two in both an historical and a constitutional context. Stephen N. Dunning noted in *America* that Bumpers cites sources as various as James Madison and the Shah of Iran "in what is a zesty defense of the American system that protects religion from encroachment by the state and the state from domination by any religion." Bumpers was the only Southern senator to vote against the prayer in school amendment.

In an interview with a representative of the *Center for Defense Information,* Bumpers said, "I have defended the Constitution at every chance. I voted against thirty-seven constitutional amendments since I've been in the Senate and for one, and that one was a mistake. I wish I hadn't cast it. But people around here trivialize the Constitution. It's the document that's made this country great, it's made us free, the longest living organic law in the world, and yet, people around here treat it as though it's just a rough draft. So, as I look back, as I say, I cast courageous votes, I stood up for what I believed."

When Bumpers announced that he would not seek a fifth term, he added that his frustration had increased "exponentially." Commenting on Bumpers's departure, Alan Greenblatt wrote in *Congressional Quarterly Weekly* that "a stem-winding and restless orator on the Senate floor, Bumpers carried to Washington his reputation for opposing wasteful spending. The proposed space station was long a favorite target. . . . Bumpers's populism has kept him at odds with the GOP, despite his tight-fisted fiscal voting record and his efforts to look out for small-business interests in a variety of legislative arenas." Bumpers was frustrated in his attempts to reform laws governing grazing and mining on federal lands, essentially taxpayer-owned lands from which, in the case of mining, billions of dollars in minerals are extracted and no royalties paid. Another favorite cause was the preservation of wilderness through the expansion of the National Park system.

Rolling Stone's William Greider interviewed Bumpers after he left the U.S. Senate. Bumpers expressed his disgust with the state of politics in the United States and said, "I have this inordinate, probably foolish, almost childlike hope that one of these days people are going to say, 'Look, with the amount of money that we spend in this country and the amount of ignorance, environmental degradation, and problems with our health-care system we have, there's something wrong about our spending priorities.'" "If the people in this country ever wake up and realize that they can have it all for the taxes they're paying," continued Bumpers, "they'll figure out how misguided our priorities are and will demand a different caliber of leadership."

Bumpers's passion and love of country are as evident in his memoir *The Best Lawyer in a One-Lawyer Town* as are his wit and wisdom. A *Kirkus Reviews* contributor wrote that "it is the author's total candor, combined with his facility for humor spun out of rural America's plain talk, that lifts this remembrance well above the ordinary."

A *Publishers Weekly* reviewer commented that "this witty book indicates he may have a new career as a humorist on the printed page."

BIOGRAPHICAL AND CRITICAL SOURCES:

BOOKS

Bumpers, Dale, *The Best Lawyer in a One-Lawyer Town,* Random House (New York, NY), 2002.

PERIODICALS

America, January 19, 1991, Stephen N. Dunning, review of *Religion and Politics,* p. 41.

Congressional Quarterly Weekly, June 21, 1997, Alan Greenblatt, "Sen. Bumpers's Departure Dims Party Hopes of Comeback," p. 1467.

Kirkus Reviews, November 15, 2002, review of *The Best Lawyer in a One-Lawyer Town,* p. 1666.

Library Journal, November 1, 2002, Karl Helicher, review of *The Best Lawyer in a One-Lawyer Town,* p. 99.

Publishers Weekly, November 4, 2002, review of *The Best Lawyer in a One-Lawyer Town,* p. 71.

Rolling Stone, March 4, 1999, William Greider, "Checking in with Dale Bumpers," pp. 43-45, 100-101.

ONLINE

Center for Defense Information Web site, http://www.cdi.org/ (January 12, 1997), "Modern American Patriot: Senator Dale Bumpers" (interview).*

C

CARTLEDGEHAYES, Mary 1949-

PERSONAL: Born 1949, in Sandusky, OH; daughter of Douglas (a farmer and pilot) and Joanna Belle (a doll artist) Cartledge; married; divorced twice; children: two daughters. *Education:* University of South Carolina Spartanburg, B.A., 1983; Duke University, M.Div., 1994; Goucher College, M.F.A. (creative nonfiction), 2000. *Religion:* United Methodist.

ADDRESSES: Home—600 Crystal Dr., Spartanburg, SC 29302. *E-mail*—mjcsp@aol.com.

CAREER: Writer; ordained United Methodist minister, 1997; pastor of Gravely Memorial United Methodist Church, Spartanburg, SC, 1995-98. Served as director of mentoring program for Creative Nonfiction Foundation; currently writer-in-residence, World Connections for Women, Morgantown, NC.

MEMBER: Evangelical and Ecumenical Women's Caucus, Authors Guild, National Federation of Press Women.

AWARDS, HONORS: Jameson Jones Award, Duke University, for excellence in preaching; Outstanding Alumni Award, University of South Carolina Spartanburg, Arts & Sciences, 1996.

WRITINGS:

To Love Delilah: Claiming the Women of the Bible, LuraMedia (San Diego, CA), 1990.

Grace: A Memoir, Crown Publishers (New York, NY), 2003.

Contributor to *Ms., Christian Science Monitor,* and other denominational publications. Contributor to anthologies, including *The Abingdon Women's Preaching Annual* and *The Wisdom of Daughters: Two Decades of Christian Feminist Writing.*

WORK IN PROGRESS: A sequel to *Grace;* a book on preaching; a book (with co-authors) on the Church's role in peacemaking.

SIDELIGHTS: Mary Cartledgehayes is an author and ordained minister of the United Methodist Church. After divorcing twice and living in poverty, Cartledgehayes had a conversion experience that dramatically changed her life. In her book *Grace: A Memoir,* she recounts that while driving in her gold Chevette, "a shaft of gold light bathed me in luminescence, and I could see each individual ray of gold even while the rays were surrounding me and containing me." Despite the impact this experience had on her, it took Cartledgehayes ten years to discover that she was being called to a ministry in the church.

In 1992 Cartledgehayes enrolled in Duke University's Divinity School, where she gained valuable information about herself and the church, but also faced resistance for being female. Despite discrimination from some fellow seminarians, Cartledgehayes won the Jameson Jones Award for excellence in preaching. Before her time at Duke, she published her first book, *To Love Delilah: Claiming the Women of the Bible.*

The book is about seven women of the Bible, including Eve and Mary Magdalene, who were considered problematic. After graduating from Duke, Cartledgehayes began to minister at the Gravely Memorial United Methodist Church.

Many of the stories in *Grace* take place during Cartledgehayes' stay at Gravely. *Grace* also includes accounts of Cartledgehayes' childhood, education, family life, and ministry. A critic for *Publishers Weekly* extolled the book because it "demonstrates a poetic mastery over language and breaks open stereotypes about Methodists, ministers, feminists, grandmothers, musicians, and all other roles Cartledgehayes embodies."

Cartledgehayes has been praised for her preaching skills, and she recreates sermons she has delivered to her congregation in *Grace.* Marta Salij of the *Detroit Free Press* explained that "what you really need to know about Cartledgehayes is that she adores being on stage, so much that the chapters on her pastoring are literally preachy." Salij noted that the book falls short in some areas, especially when it comes to Cartledgehayes' lack of details about her congregation. Salij also said that the author's writing is "vivid and anecdotal" until she introduces the reader to her parishioners. After this, Salij noted, her writing "goes flat, as if her attention had wandered while she was mentally rewriting her next glorious oratory."

A reviewer for *Booklist* commended Cartledgehayes, saying that her personality succeeds in "making this most unusual memoir by one of the most memorable recent memoirists, funny, earthy, and poignant." In an interview with the University of South Carolina, Spartanburg's *University Review,* Cartledgehayes explained her reasons for writing *Grace:* "My life has been anything but ordinary and this book bounds together my life, theology training, and writing skills. It is more complex, beautiful and funny than anything I could have imagined writing twenty, ten, or even five years ago."

While her ministry is a central focus of her life, Cartledgehayes makes it clear that time spent with her husband and grandchildren is just as important as the time spent at the pulpit.

BIOGRAPHICAL AND CRITICAL SOURCES:

BOOKS

Cartledgehayes, Mary, *Grace: A Memoir,* Crown Publishers (New York, NY), 2003.

PERIODICALS

Booklist, February 15, 2003, June Sawyers, review of *Grace: A Memoir,* p. 1020.

Detroit Free Press, April 20, 2003, Marta Salij, "Looking Upward, but Not Inward."

Kirkus Reviews, January 15, 2003, review of *Grace: A Memoir,* p. 122.

Publishers Weekly, March 3, 2003, review of *Grace: A Memoir,* p. 70.

University Review, fall 2002, "Mary Cartledgehayes," p. 2.

* * *

CASTELLANI, Christopher 1972-

PERSONAL: Born 1972, in Wilmington, DE. *Education:* Swarthmore College, B.A.; Tufts University, M.A. (English); Boston University, M.A. (creative writing).

ADDRESSES: Agent—Mary Evans, Inc., 242 East Fifth St., New York, NY 10003. *E-mail*—chris@chriscastellani.com.

CAREER: Grub Street, Inc. (creative writing center), Boston, MA, head instructor.

AWARDS, HONORS: Stony Brook Short Fiction Prize, award, 1992, for "You'll Be Saying the Same Thing," honorable mention, 1994; Ella T. Grasso Literary Award, 1994, for short story; Glimmer Train Press Very Short Fiction Award finalist, 2000 for "Games of 1953."

WRITINGS:

A Kiss from Maddalena, Algonquin Books of Chapel Hill (Chapel Hill, NC), 2003.

SIDELIGHTS: Fiction writer Christopher Castellani won his first award, the Stony Brook Short Fiction Prize, when he was only a sophomore in college, and his talents have continued to develop. Castellani published his first novel, *A Kiss from Maddalena,* in 2003.

Castellani's debut novel is set in 1943 in the Italian village of Santa Cecilia. World War II has taken most of the men from the village, but has left behind skinny, awkward Vito Leone, who is a few months short of being eligible for the draft. Vito keeps himself occupied by taking care of his ailing mother and building a bicycle to entertain the village girls with rides while the men are away. He soon finds himself falling in love with Maddalena Piccinelli, the youngest daughter of the town's richest and most powerful family. The Piccinellis don't approve of their daughter's relationship with Vito, but the two teens continue to meet secretly, surviving their families and the war as they grow into young adults.

Critical opinion was mixed regarding *A Kiss from Maddalena.* Karen Holt in *Booklist* found the characters underdeveloped, noting that "Maddalena is often ineffectual . . . making it not easy for readers to care much whether, in this case, love conquers anything." A *Kirkus Reviews* critic expressed similar sentiments: "The beautiful final paragraph, aching with tenderness and regret, would be even more moving if . . . [Maddalena had] been a more engaging character." However, Catherine Parnell, in the *Milwaukee Journal Sentinel* online, praised Castellani's writing: "In the hands of a less talented writer, such a story might fall into the abyss of cliche. . . . Yet Castellani, writing of passion without affectation or exaggeration, deftly exposes the heart scarred by war."

BIOGRAPHICAL AND CRITICAL SOURCES:

PERIODICALS

Booklist, February 15, 2003, Karen Holt, review of *A Kiss from Maddalena,* p. 1047.
Kirkus Reviews, January 15, 2003, review of *A Kiss from Maddalena,* p. 104.
Library Journal, March 1, 2003, Judith Kicinski, review of *A Kiss from Maddalena,* p. 118.
Publishers Weekly, February 10, 2003, review of *A Kiss from Maddalena,* p. 160.

ONLINE

Christopher Castellani Web site, http://www.christophercastellani.com (November 19, 2003).
Milwaukee Journal Sentinel Online, http://www.jsonline.com/ (May 10, 2003), Catherine Parnell, "Young Love in the Shadow of War Makes for Sweet Reading."
State University of New York, Stony Brook Web site, http://naples.cc.sunysb.edu/ (November 19, 2003), "Christopher Castellani."*

* * *

CATON, Steven (Charles) 1950-

PERSONAL: Born 1950. *Education:* University of Chicago, Ph.D., 1984.

ADDRESSES: *Office*—Department of Anthropology, Harvard University, William James Hall 320, 33 Kirkland St., Cambridge, MA 02138. *E-mail*—caton@wjh.harvard.edu.

CAREER: Harvard University, Cambridge, MA, professor of anthropology. Has performed field work in Yemen and other countries in the Middle East.

WRITINGS:

"Peaks of Yemen I Summon": Poetry as Cultural Practice in a North Yemeni Tribe, University of California Press (Berkeley, CA), 1990.
Lawrence of Arabia: A Film's Anthropology, University of California Press (Berkeley, CA), 1999.
Yemen Chronicle, Hill & Wang (New York, NY), in press.

WORK IN PROGRESS: Field research in the Sana'a Basin of Yemen on water conservation.

SIDELIGHTS: Steven Caton's writings reflect his professional interest in the desert nation of Yemen, where he has studied the ritual uses of poetry, methods of mediation, and resource conservation issues. Caton's first book, *"Peaks of Yemen I Summon": Poetry as Cultural Practice in a North Yemeni Tribe* explores the connections between oral poetry and politics in local Yemeni tradition. In his *Times Literary Supplement* review of the book, Pierre Cachia noted that Caton "is . . . much to be commended for the fieldwork he has done in North Yemen. . . . Readers have cause to be grateful to Caton for his precise documentation of literary activity in a relatively inaccessible part of the world."

Not surprisingly given his interest in the Middle East, Caton has made a close study of the American film *Lawrence of Arabia.* Caton's *Lawrence of Arabia: A Film's Anthropology* offers a critique of the movie's view of colonialism, Arab "otherness," and ambivalence in morally compromising situations. *Current Anthropology* contributor Brian Keith Axel called Caton's study "insightful and far-reaching," adding that the author's analyses "elaborate a nuanced critique of visual representation, transnationalism, colonialism, Orientalism, racism, and heteronormativity." Keith concluded: "Caton's writing on this issue, reflecting critically on his own fieldwork in Yemen, is as courageous as it is insightful." In a review of the book for *Biography* magazine, Ellis Hanson observed: "Caton's largely political defense of the film is complemented with aesthetic and formal considerations of the sort that are all too rare in cultural studies of film. . . . Whatever his political qualms—and he is nothing if not a sensitive and conscientious soul—Caton is offering us an extended love letter to a film whose every frame has captivated him, perhaps even in spite of himself."

BIOGRAPHICAL AND CRITICAL SOURCES:

PERIODICALS

Biography, summer, 2000, Ellis Hanson, review of *Lawrence of Arabia: A Film's Anthropology,* p. 560.

Current Anthropology, February, 2002, Brian Keith Axel, review of *Lawrence of Arabia: A Film's Anthropology,* p. 197.

Film Quarterly, winter, 2000, Michael Bliss, review of *Lawrence of Arabia: A Film's Anthropology,* p. 58.

Journal of American Folklore, fall, 1992, Moira Killoran and Melissa Cefkin, review of *"Peaks of Yemen I Summon": Poetry as Cultural Practice in a North Yemeni Tribe,* pp. 510-511.

Times Literary Supplement, December 27, 1991, Pierre Cachia, review of *"Peaks of Yemen I Summon,"* p. 23.

ONLINE

Harvard University Anthropology Department Web site, http://140.247.102.41/AnthroCF/People/HomePages/ (October 31, 2003)"Steve Caton."

CAVANAUGH, Matt

PERSONAL: Born in Reading, England. *Education:* Oxford University, Ph.D.

ADDRESSES: *Agent*—c/o Author Mail, Clarendon Press, Oxford University Press, 198 Madison Ave., New York, NY 10016.

CAREER: St. Catherine's College, Oxford, lecturer in philosophy, 1996-2000; management consultant, 2000—.

WRITINGS:

Against Equality of Opportunity ("Oxford Philosophical Monographs" series), Clarendon Press (New York, NY), 2002.

SIDELIGHTS: Matt Cavanaugh left academia and the teaching of philosophy to become a management consultant. With *Against Equality in Opportunity,* an expansion of his postgraduate thesis on reverse discrimination, he also became the author of a controversial study of the concept of "equal opportunity."

Jeremy Waldron reviewed the volume in the *London Review of Books,* noting that "people who believe in equal opportunity veer between two incompatible propositions. The first is meritocracy: the proposition that jobs should be allocated to those who are most deserving. The second is a principle of equal chances: things should be arranged so that everyone has an equal chance of succeeding. These two propositions, he [Cavanaugh] says, are plainly in tension. If there is any ingredient of talent or natural ability in 'most deserving,' then chances of success can never be equal, at least for people as they are."

John Crace, who interviewed Cavanaugh for the London *Guardian,* commented that the author "argues that the position of most good liberals on equality of opportunity is a mixture of three principles—meritocracy, equality, and discrimination—but that if you put these under the microscope, then you discover there is little agreement over the details, leaving society with what amounts to an artificial consensus by default."

Cavanaugh does not feel it is the government's place to dictate how jobs should be allocated; it is the employer's right to make such decisions based on what benefits his or her business. An example would be a small business with a limited training budget discriminating against women of child-bearing age. Traditionally considered wrong, in Cavanaugh's view such bias is acceptable. He also feels that because individual people do not share equal traits and capabilities, the idea of affording everyone equal treatment with regard to opportunities that are scarce is unfair. With regard to an issue like the vote, which is not a scarce commodity, he is in favor of equality.

"Cavanaugh has less problem with positive discrimination," noted Crace, "arguing that it's not unfair to further desirable social needs by engineering a higher representation of some groupings in certain areas." Cavanaugh used the example of a situation that occurred in the United States. When equipment was limited, what equipment was available was used to help premature babies with greater birth weights because such babies were statistically more likely to survive. A group representing disabled children won a case preventing such decisions, and, consequently, more premature babies now die. In *Against Equality of Opportunity* Cavanaugh calls this "madness."

With regard to publicly funded education, Cavanaugh feels that making decisions based on which student is most deserving is anti-meritocratic. As to equality, he told Crace that "the government's statement that every child should have the best possible start in life is completely vacuous. With a limited amount of teachers' time, even if you were to throw twice as much money at education, it's not possible to divide things up fairly. All you can do is distribute what there is equally to a certain level, and then divide up the rest according to some other principle."

Cavanaugh questions whether it is fair that children whose parents have encouraged them to learn, and who do consequently achieve higher scores, should be discriminated against because other parents chose to busy their children by plopping them in front of a television. Cavanaugh feels that concentrating too heavily on attempting to grant equality to all is a negative idea because it creates unnecessary competition and because people question whether certain individuals are perceived to be better because they earned higher regard or if some other factor is figured into the equation.

Spectator contributor Nicholas Fearn wrote of *Against Equality of Opportunity* that "in the horse-trading of meritocracy versus equality, few have had the nerve and imagination to throw out both these ideals at once." Fearn noted that Cavanaugh feels that the idea of the government starting everyone out on an equal playing field "is a sham, for it merely seeks to give everyone an equal chance of becoming unequal, and this is a poor way of expressing the fact that we are all politically equal members of a collective enterprise." Instead, Cavanaugh feels that everyone should have enough opportunity that they can control their own lives, although the degree of that control might vary. People who need help should be helped, but there should be no master plan for distributing opportunities.

BIOGRAPHICAL AND CRITICAL SOURCES:

PERIODICALS

Guardian (London, England), March 26, 2002, John Crace, review of *Against Equality of Opportunity* and interview; April 19, 2003, Ben Rogers, review of *Against Equality of Opportunity.*

London Review of Books, September 19, 2002, Jeremy Waldron, review of *Against Equality of Opportunity,* p. 10.

Spectator, March 16, 2002, Nicholas Fearn, review of *Against Equality of Opportunity,* p. 48.*

* * *

CHAPMAN, C. Stuart 1970(?)-

PERSONAL: Born c. 1970. *Education:* Rhodes College, B.A., 1991; University of Georgia, M.A., 1994; Boston College, Ph.D. (English), 2002.

ADDRESSES: *Agent*—c/o University Press of Mississippi, 3825 Ridgewood Road, Jackson, MS 39211-6492.

CAREER: Journalist, advisor, and author. *Clarksdale Press-Register,* Clarksdale, MS, reporter; press secretary for Congresswoman Barbara Lee; Massachusetts State House, aide.

WRITINGS:

Shelby Foote: A Writer's Life, University Press of Mississippi (Jackson, MS), 2003.

Contributor to periodicals, including *Clarksdale Press-Register, Jamaica Plain Gazette, Memphis Business Journal, Memphis Commercial Appeal,* and *Modern Fiction Studies.*

SIDELIGHTS: C. Stuart Chapman's book *Shelby Foote: A Writer's Life* is an adaptation is based on Chapman's doctoral dissertation while at Boston College. In this work Chapman reveals the details of Foote's life as a southern gentleman, writer, and historian of the U.S. Civil War. He gives an intimate account of Foote's attempts to come to terms with the changing South and his place within it.

Chapman frequently corresponded with Foote while writing his book. However, some critics maintained that Chapman relies too heavily on his own deductions regarding Foote's character. "Chapman is a diligent and perceptive biographer, but he nods more than once, and his book is flawed by historical misperceptions, errors and misdatings," explained Edwin M. Yoder in the *Washington Post.* The critic went on to note: "It would also have been a better book if Chapman stepped down from the pulpit from which he feels a nagging duty to lecture 'white southerners' on their sins and defects." Other reviewers bemoaned the lack of personal information in the book. However, in the *New York Times,* reviewer Sherie Posesorski described *Shelby Foote* as "brisk" and "colorful" and praised the book for providing readers with a "a frank, full-bodied portrait of the man and an agile examination of Foote's development as a writer."

BIOGRAPHICAL AND CRITICAL SOURCES:

PERIODICALS

Charleston Post and Courier, May 18, 2003, Rosemary Michaud, "Foote Knows the Facts, Can Tell a Good Story."

Library Journal, February 15, 2003, Henry L. Carrigan, review of *Shelby Foote: A Writer's Life,* p. 138.

National Review, June 30, 2003, Michael Potemra, "Laughter and Remembering."

New York Times, April 27, 2003, Sherie Posesorski, review of *Shelby Foote.*

Washington Post, April 27, 2003, Edwin M. Yoder, Jr., review of *Shelby Foote.*

ONLINE

Charlotte Observer online, http://www.bayarea.com/ (June 16, 2003), Henry L. Carrigan, Jr., "Foote Saw Darkness before Limelight."

Go Memphis.com, http://www.gomemphis.com/ (March 16, 2003), Melissa McIntosh Brown, "Conjecture Mars Biography of Shelby Foote."

Memphis Magazine online, http://www.memphismagazine.com/ (June 16, 2003), Leonard Gill, "Foote First: The Last of the Southern Gentlemen? A Biography of Shelby Foote."

University Press of Mississippi Web site, http://www.upress.state.ms.us/ (November 15, 2003).*

* * *

CHASDI, Richard J. 1958-

PERSONAL: Born January 21, 1958, in Boston, MA; son of Simon (an educator) and Eleanor (a professor; maiden name, Hollenberg) Chasdi; married Sharon Applebaum (a teacher), October 12, 2003. *Ethnicity:* "Jewish." *Education:* Brandeis University, B.A., 1981; Boston College, M.A., 1985; Purdue University, Ph. D., 1995. *Politics:* Democrat. *Religion:* Jewish. *Hobbies and other interests:* Photography, military history.

ADDRESSES: *Office*—Center for Peace and Conflict Studies, Wayne State University, Anthony Wayne Dr., Detroit, MI 48202. *E-mail*—Rchasdi@aol.com.

CAREER: Wayne State University, Detroit, MI, member of adjunct faculty, 1996-2001, adjunct assistant professor of peace and conflict studies, 2003—; College of Wooster, Wooster, OH, visiting assistant professor of international relations, 2001-02, and history, 2002; Eastern Michigan University, Ypsilanti, scholar-in-residence, 2003. University of Michigan, faculty associate and research associate of Center for

Middle Eastern and North African Studies; University of Chicago, associate member of Center for Middle-Eastern Studies.

AWARDS, HONORS: Citation for outstanding academic title, *Choice,* 2000, for *Serenade of Suffering: A Portrait of Middle East Terrorism, 1968-1993.*

WRITINGS:

Serenade of Suffering: A Portrait of Middle East Terrorism, 1968-1993, Lexington Books (Lanham, MD), 1999.

Tapestry of Terror, Lexington Books (Lanham, MD), 2002.

Contributor to reference books. Contributor to periodicals, including *Shofar* and *Journal of Conflict Studies.*

WORK IN PROGRESS: Counter-Terror Offensives for the Ghost War World: The Rudiments of Counterterrorism Policy, for Lexington Books (Lanham, MD), completion expected in 2005; research on the al-Aqsa Intifada uprising.

SIDELIGHTS: Richard J. Chasdi told *CA:* "As a child, I spent a good deal of time in Israel during the 1960s and early 1970s."

* * *

CHECCHI, Mary Jane

PERSONAL: Married to John C. Culver (a former U.S. senator); children: John Vincent.

ADDRESSES: Home—Bethesda, MD. *Office*—c/o St. Martin's Press, 175 Fifth Ave., New York, NY 10010. *E-mail*—info@checchibooks.com.

CAREER: Writer. Former lawyer; wrote press releases, speeches, and briefing papers for politicians. Director and chief counsel to Senate majority leader Robert C. Byrd; executive director of Senate Irane-Contra investigating committee. Member, board of directors, of New Community Afterschool and Advocacy Program and Washington Psychoanalytic Foundation.

MEMBER: People Animals Love.

WRITINGS:

Are You the Pet for Me? Choosing the Right Pet for Your Family, St. Martin's Press (New York, NY), 1999.

Contributor to periodicals, including *Big Apple Parent, Delaware Pets, Dog and Kennel, Georgia Parent, Paw Print Post,* and *Pet Life.*

SIDELIGHTS: Her work as an expert on pet ownership, reflected in the book *Are You the Pet for Me? Choosing the Right Pet for Your Family,* represents a second career for Mary Jane Checchi. The first could hardly have been more different: earlier in her life, Checchi—who has described herself as a "recovering political addict" and "lapsed lawyer"—worked for Democrat senators Edmund Muskie of Maine, Birch Bayh of Indiana, and Gary Hart of Colorado. She also served as staff director and chief counsel for Robert Byrd, a Virginia Democrat who at the time was U.S. Senate majority leader. During the Iran-Contra hearings Checchi worked as executive director for the Senate investigating committee looking into the events surrounding the scandal.

In *Are You the Pet for Me?* Checchi offers advice designed to ensure a workable relationship between pets and owners. She informs the reader both of the benefits to be gained from having a pet, as well as the responsibilities and possible pitfalls associated with pet ownership. She apprises the potential pet owner of factors to consider, including the composition of the household—children or no children, for instance—as well as the prime caretaker's schedule. Obviously, someone who works at home will have different needs than someone who travels frequently on business, but one of the principles undergirding the book is the idea that most lifestyles can potentially accommodate a pet.

Checchi devotes particular attention to advising children on the many issues to consider before taking on the responsibility of a pet. For example, as noted by Anne Y. Meyers in the *Atlanta Constitution,* one of the many questions for children to consider, along with their parents, is: "Is your family stable right now? Checchi advises not to get a pet during a major adjustment in your family's lifestyle, such as divorce, moving, or pregnancy." A reviewer for *Our Children* called *Are You the Pet for Me?* "an excellent resource."

BIOGRAPHICAL AND CRITICAL SOURCES:

PERIODICALS

Atlanta Constitution, April 26, 1999, Anne Y. Meyers, "Picking the Perfect Pet," p. B4.
St. Louis Post-Dispatch, August 28, 1999, Sarah Casey Newman, "Paperback Gives Tips on Choosing a Pet," p. 43.
Washington Post, April 27, 1999, Catherine O'Neill Grace, "A Friend Like No Other," p. Z22.

ONLINE

Checchibooks Web Site, http://www.checchibooks.com/index.html (September 14, 2003).*

* * *

CHESKA, Anna
See HENLEY, Jan. (S.)

* * *

CHORAO, Ian

PERSONAL: Male; married; children: Malcolm. *Education:* Purchase College, State University of New York, B.S. (psychology), 1990.

ADDRESSES: Home—New York, NY. *Agent*—Mitchell Waters, Curtis Brown Ltd., 10 Astor Place, New York, NY 10003. *E-mail*—ensharow@aol.com.

CAREER: Novelist, author of screenplays, and art director. Jewish Association for Services for the Aged, social worker; worked for Goddard Riverside/Project Reachout. Art director for film and photo projects.

WRITINGS:

Snapped (screenplay), Illville Productions, 1998.
Bruiser (novel), Atria (New York, NY), 2003.

SIDELIGHTS: Ian Chorao is a former social worker and art director whose first novel, *Bruiser,* was published in 2003. The title character is a nine-year-old boy growing up in a troubled Manhattan household. His parents' marriage is failing and his brothers torment him mercilessly. Bruiser runs away in an attempt to escape his painful and confusing home life. Chorao's novel details Bruiser's journey of self-discovery, a trip he undertakes—accompanied by Darla, his ten-year-old neighbor—that leads him to West Virginia and North Carolina in search of answers to life's most baffling questions.

A New York native, Chorao draws on his own memories in detailing Bruiser's hometown accurately, and he composed his novel in the first person to fully capture the thoughts, feelings, dreams, and emotions of a nine-year-old boy. Reviewers applauded Chorao's precision in capturing the narrator's childhood angst. *Booklist* reviewer Donna Seaman called Chorao "an extraordinarily gifted first-time novelist," and commented that in *Bruiser* "Chorao's exquisite evocations of all the pain and wonder his young hero confronts are profoundly transporting." Jim Coan in *Library Journal* concluded that Chorao "convincingly depicts the inner landscape of children's fantasies and nightmares." A *Publishers Weekly* contributor described the novel as "starkly beautiful and unrelentingly grim," and compared it to "a roadside accident: harrowing to behold, yet impossible to ignore."

BIOGRAPHICAL AND CRITICAL SOURCES:

PERIODICALS

Booklist, February 15, 2003, Donna Seaman, review of *Bruiser,* p. 1047.
Kirkus Reviews, February 1, 2003, review of *Bruiser,* pp. 157-158.
Library Journal, February 15, 2003, Jim Coan, review of *Bruiser,* p. 167.
Publishers Weekly, March 17, 2003, review of *Bruiser,* p. 56.

ONLINE

Purchase College, S.U.N.Y. Web site, http://www.ns.purchase.edu/ (July 3, 2003), "Ian Chorao."*

* * *

CLARDY, Brian K(eith) 1967-

PERSONAL: Born August 1, 1967, in Fulton, KY; son of George T., Jr. (a physician) and Ginger R. (an elementary schoolteacher) Clardy; married Sonja Nicole Paul, September 19, 1998 (divorced November 7, 2001). *Ethnicity:* "African-American." *Education:* University of Tennessee—Martin, B.A., 1988; Murray State University, M.P.A., 1991; Southern Illinois University—Carbondale, Ph.D., 1999. *Politics:* Democrat. *Religion:* United Church of Christ. *Hobbies and other interests:* Jazz collection, attending professional sports activities, attending concerts of the Chicago Symphony Orchestra.

ADDRESSES: Home—1851 West Canal St., No. 3-B, Blue Island, IL 60406. *Office*—Triton College, 2000 Fifth Ave., River Grove, IL 60171-1995. *E-mail*—DocClardy@yahoo.com.

CAREER: University of Tennessee—Martin, instructor in political science, 1991-96; Southern Illinois University—Carbondale, lecturer in history and black American studies program, 1996-98; Triton College, River Grove, IL, professor of history and political science, 2000—. John A. Logan College, instructor, 1997. Chicago Council on Foreign Relations, member. Affiliated with Jazz Institute of Chicago and Jazz Unites.

MEMBER: American Federation of Teachers (Cook County chapter), Triton College Faculty Association, Pi Sigma Alpha, Phi Alpha Theta.

AWARDS, HONORS: Henry M. Salvatori fellow, Heritage Foundation, 1997.

WRITINGS:

The Management of Dissent: Responses to the Post-Kent State Protests at Seven Public Universities in Illinois, University Press of America (Lanham, MD), 2002.

Contributor to magazines, including *Trumpet* and *Newtopia.*

WORK IN PROGRESS: Research on U.S. foreign relations since 1900, the U.S. presidency, campaigns and elections, race in America, the black church, the U.S. Constitution, the Vietnam war era, and conflict resolution.

SIDELIGHTS: Brian K. Clardy told *CA:* "I find writing to be a joy for several reasons. It allows me to have a constructive outlet to express my own opinions and life experiences. But more importantly, it allows me to contribute to the marketplace of ideas. I love the give and take in the exchange of ideas.

"I am greatly influenced by the work of brilliant authors such as Studs Terkel, Michael Eric Dyson, and P. J. O'Rourke.

"My writing process starts with an interest in an idea, subject, or person. I simply build on my initial impressions and analyses. I give much thought to my subjects and draw from a variety of fields, including theology, history, current events, and popular culture.

"I have a lifelong passion for the liberal arts. In addition, I hold very strong views on politics, history, and religion. I am inspired to write about these vast subjects."

BIOGRAPHICAL AND CRITICAL SOURCES:

ONLINE

Brian K. Clardy Home Page, http://academics.triton.edu/faculty/bclardy (January 29, 2004).

* * *

CLARK, Glenn 1882-1956

PERSONAL: Born March 13, 1882, in Des Moines, IA; died August 16, 1956, in Minneapolis, MN; son of James S. and Fannie (Page) Clark; married Louise Miles, 1907. *Education:* Grinnell College, graduated, 1905. *Religion:* Presbyterian.

CAREER: High school principal in Des Moines, IA, 1905-08; William and Vashti College, Aledo, IL, teacher, 1908-12; Macalester College, St. Paul, MN, teacher, 1912-44. Camp Far Out (prayer movement), founder, 1930; Macalester Park Publishing Co., founder.

WRITINGS:

The Manual of the Short-Story Art, Macmillan (New York, NY), 1922.

The Soul's Sincere Desire, Atlantic Monthly Press (Boston, MA), 1925, Silver Anniversary edition, Little, Brown and Co. (Boston, MA), 1950.

Fishers of Men, Little, Brown and Co. (Boston, MA), 1928.

The Thought Farthest Out, Macalester Park Publishing (St. Paul, MN), 1930.

Water of Life, Macalester Park Publishing (St. Paul, MN), 1931.

Personality in Essay Writing, R. Long and R. R. Smith (New York, NY), 1932.

The Lord's Prayer, and Other Talks on Prayer: From the Camp Farthest Out, Macalester Park Publishing (St. Paul, MN), 1932.

(Editor) Toyohiko Kagawa, *A Grain of Wheat* (fiction), translated by Marion R. Draper, Harper and Brothers (New York, NY), 1936.

I Will Lift up Mine Eyes, Harper and Brothers (New York, NY), 1937.

The Man Who Talks with the Flowers: The Intimate Life Story of Dr. George Washington Carver, Macalester Park Publishing (St. Paul, MN), 1939.

How to Find Health through Prayer, Harper and Brothers (New York, NY), 1940.

The World's Greatest Debate, Macalester Park Publishing (St. Paul, MN), 1940.

(With Glenn Harding and Starr Daily, a pseudonym) *The Third Front through the Paths of Faith, Hope, and Love,* Macalester Park Publishing (St. Paul, MN), 1944.

The Way, the Truth, and the Life, Harper and Brothers (New York, NY), 1946.

The Man Who Walked in His Steps, [St. Paul, MN], 1946.

A Man's Reach: The Autobiography of Glenn Clark, Harper and Brothers (New York, NY), 1949.

(Editor) Jerry Gray, *The Third Strike,* Abingdon-Cokesbury Press (New York, NY), 1949.

What Would Jesus Do? Wherein a New Generation Undertakes to Walk in His Steps, Macalester Park Publishing (St. Paul, MN), 1950.

God's Reach, Macalester Park Publishing (St. Paul, MN), 1951.

"Come, Follow Me," Macalester Park Publishing (St. Paul, MN), 1952.

Be Thou Made Whole, Macalester Park Publishing (St. Paul, MN), 1953.

Windows of Heaven, photographs by Lucien Aigner, Harper (New York, NY), 1954.

On Wings of Prayer, Macalester Park Publishing (St. Paul, MN), 1955.

God's Voice in the Folklore: Nonsense Rhymes and Great Legends, Macalester Park Publishing (St. Paul, MN), 1956.

Also author of "Self-Cultivation in Extemporaneous Speaking," Minnesota Alpha Chapter, Pi Kappa Delta, Macalester College (St. Paul, MN), 1921; "Power of the Spirit on the Athletic Field," privately printed (St. Paul, MN), 1929; and "The Land We Vision," Macalester Park Publishing (St. Paul, MN), 1934. Contributor to periodicals, including *Atlantic.* Cofounder, *Clear Horizons,* 1940; also affiliated with *Fellowship Messenger* and *Manual of Prayer.*

BIOGRAPHICAL AND CRITICAL SOURCES:

BOOKS

Clark, Glenn, *A Man's Reach: The Autobiography of Glenn Clark,* Harper and Brothers (New York, NY), 1949.

Clark, Miles, *Glenn Clark: His Life and Writings,* Abingdon Press (Nashville, TN), 1975.

Religious Leaders of America, 2nd edition, Gale (Detroit, MI), 1999.*

* * *

CLARKE, Sarah 1919-2002
(Sister Sarah Clarke)

PERSONAL: Born 1919, in Eyrecourt, County Galway, Ireland; died February 5, 2002, in London, England. *Education:* Attended Chelsea School of Art, c. 1969, and University of Reading. *Religion:* Roman Catholic.

CAREER: Teacher and civil rights activist. Roman Catholic nun of order of La Sainte Union, County Kildare, Ireland, c. 1937-85; laicized, 1985. Worked as headmistress of a girls' school in Athlone, Ireland.

MEMBER: Northern Ireland Civil Rights Association (member of executive committee).

AWARDS, HONORS: Pro Ecclesia et Ponficate from the Roman Catholic Pope, 2001.

WRITINGS:

(Under name Sister Sarah Clarke) *No Faith in the System: A Search for Justice* (autobiography), Mercier Press (Cork, Ireland), 1995.

BIOGRAPHICAL AND CRITICAL SOURCES:

PERIODICALS

Guardian, February 14, 1995, Melanie McFadyean "Without Consent," p. 2.
New Statesman, March 7, 1997, Bruce Kent, review of *No Faith in the System: A Search for Justice,* p. 48.

OBITUARIES:

PERIODICALS

Times (London, England), February 12, 2002, p. 35.

ONLINE

Independent, February 6, 2002, obituary by Melanie McFadyean, p. S6.
Irish Democrat Online, http://www.irishdemocrat.co.uk/ (May 30, 2002).*

* * *

CLARKE, William Newton 1841-1912

PERSONAL: Born December 2, 1841, in Cazenovia, NY; died January 14, 1912, in Deland, FL; son of William (a Baptist minister) and Urania (Miner) Clarke; married Emily A. Smith, September 1, 1869. *Education:* Madison University (now Colgate University), B.A., 1861; Colgate Seminary, B.D., 1863.

CAREER: Ordained Baptist minister, 1856; pastor of Baptist churches in Keene, NH, 1856-69, Newton Center, MA, 1869-80, and Montreal, Quebec, Canada, 1880-83; Baptist Theological School, Toronto, Ontario, Canada, teacher of New Testament, 1883-87; Colgate Seminary (also known as Hamilton Theological Seminary), Hamilton, NY, instructor, 1887-90, J. J. Joslin Professor of Christian Theology, 1890-1908, then lecturer in Christian ethics. Pastor of Baptist church in Hamilton, NY, beginning 1887. Johns Hopkins University Levering Lecturer, 1899; Oberlin Theological Seminary lecturer, 1901; Harvard University Dudleian Lecturer, 1903; Yale University Nathaniel William Taylor Lecturer, 1905.

WRITINGS:

Commentary on Mark, 1881.
An Outline of Christian Theology: For the Use of Students in Hamilton Theological Seminary, Hamilton, N.Y., J. Wilson and Son (Cambridge, MA), 1894, published as *An Outline of Christian Theology,* Charles Scribner's Sons (New York, NY), 1898.
Can I Believe in God the Father?, Charles Scribner's Sons (New York, NY), 1899.
What Shall We Think of Christianity?, Charles Scribner's Sons (New York, NY), 1899.
A Study of Christian Missions, 1900.
Huxley and Phillips Brooks, H. R. Allenson (London, England), 1903.
The Use of the Scriptures in Theology, Charles Scribner's Sons (New York, NY), 1905.
The Christian Doctrine of God, Charles Scribner's Sons (New York, NY), 1909.
Sixty Years with the Bible: A Record of Experience, Charles Scribner's Sons (New York, NY), 1909.
The Ideal of Jesus, Charles Scribner's Sons (New York, NY), 1911.
Immortality, a Study of Belief, and Earlier Addresses, Yale University Press (New Haven, CT), 1920.

Also author of "Mystery in Religion," American Baptist Publication Society (Philadelphia, PA), 1897.

BIOGRAPHICAL AND CRITICAL SOURCES:

BOOKS

Clarke, Emily, *William Newton Clarke: A Biography, with Additional Sketches by His Friends and Colleagues,* 1916.

Religious Leaders of America, 2nd edition, Gale (Detroit, MI), 1999.

PERIODICALS

American Journal of Theology, July, 1912.
Outlook, January 27, 1912.*

* * *

CLEEVES, Ann 1954-

PERSONAL: Born October 24, 1954, in Hereford, England; married Tim Cleeves, 1977; children: two daughters. *Education:* Liverpool University, diploma (social work), 1979.

ADDRESSES: Home—19 Holywell Dene Rd., Holywell, Whitley Bay, Northumberland NE25 OLB, England. *Agent*—Murray Pollinger, 222 Old Brompton Rd., London SW5 OBZ, England.

CAREER: Writer. Camden Social Services, London, England, child care officer, 1973-75; bird observatory cook on Fair Isle, Scotland, 1975-76; in auxiliary coastguard, 1977-81; probation officer in Wirral and Cheshire, England, 1981-83.

WRITINGS:

The Sleeping and the Dead, Macmillan (London, England), 2002.
Burial of Ghosts, Macmillan (London, England), 2003.

"PALMER-JONES" SERIES; CRIME NOVELS

A Bird in the Hand, Fawcett (New York, NY), 1986.
Come Death and High Water, Fawcett (New York, NY), 1987.
Murder in Paradise, Century (London, England), 1988, Fawcett (New York, NY), 1989.
A Prey to Murder, Fawcett (New York, NY), 1989.
Sea Fever, Fawcett (New York, NY), 1991.
Another Man's Poison, Macmillan (London, England), 1992, Fawcett (New York, NY), 1993.
The Mill on the Shore, Fawcett (New York, NY), 1994.
High Island Blues, Fawcett (New York, NY), 1996.

"RAMSAY" SERIES; CRIME NOVELS

A Lesson in Dying, Century (London, England), 1990.
Murder in My Back Yard, Fawcett (New York, NY), 1991.
A Day in the Death of Dorothea Cassidy, Fawcett (New York, NY), 1992.
Killjoy, Macmillan (London, England), 1993, Fawcett (New York, NY), 1995.
The Healers, Fawcett (New York, NY), 1995.
The Baby Snatcher, Macmillan (London, England), 1997.

SIDELIGHTS: English writer Ann Cleeves has established a reputation as a significant talent in the field of the traditional detective novel. She is the creator of two series detectives: George Palmer-Jones and Stephen Ramsay. Palmer-Jones is a retired Home Office official married to a former social worker. His natural authority is augmented by his professional past and the reputation persisting from it, yet, he suffers from self-doubt and is subject to depression. He finds difficulty in adjusting to retirement and misses the structure and discipline of professional life. Eventually, he establishes an "advice agency" for the families of missing teenagers.

It is Palmer-Jones's secondary reputation as a seasoned ornithologist that involves him in crime, however. In *A Bird in the Hand* he joins a community of birdwatchers, some of whom are willing to travel any distance at a moment's notice to encounter a rare breed. Such enthusiasm amounts to obsession, a force sufficiently strong to turn a man's mind, to "alter mood, sense, even personality, like a drug." When a murder is discovered, he must consider whether it also has "the power to make a person mad enough to commit murder." The victim's influence was strong in the birding community and his complex personality takes shape as the action proceeds. Enmities surface, associations breed suspicion: one man was the victim's rival in love, another sought the same job, a third lost status by his ascendancy. A revealing slant on the victim determines a part of the truth and a rare bird contributes to the final resolution of the novel.

Come Death and High Water opens in classic style as a number of people prepare to gather at a nature reserve off the Devon coast. No sooner are they assembled than the owner of the island announces his intention to sell out: not surprisingly, he is dead by the following morning. Suspicion spreads impartially through the company and a second murder contracts the closed circle even further. *Murder in Paradise* takes Palmer-Jones to the remote island of Kinness, part of the western isles of Scotland. The closed community opens to admit a bride from the mainland and she becomes a principal witness both of life on the island and of the course of the murder investigation. Her young sister-in-law dies during the bride's wedding feast and a second murder victim is found soon enjoying Palmer-Jones's hospitality. The bride and Palmer-Jones gather such clues as an inscription on a gravestone, the dispositions of a will, and the odd maturity of a small boy.

A Prey to Murder is set in and around a Shropshire hotel where the owner, a small-scale matriarch, dies by violence. Her murder seems to be the terrible consequence of an illicit trade in birds of prey. Much of the investigation is conducted by an ebullient Welsh policeman, with Palmer-Jones rather uncomfortably in tow. Palmer-Jones's wife Molly makes her own enquiries at the hotel, and it is she who provokes the novel's violent climax. Molly's relationship with Palmer-Jones undergoes some stress during the story and is sufficient to threaten their marriage but not permanently injure it.

In in *Another Man's Poison* Palmer-Jones and Molly investigate the murder of Molly's Aunt Ursula, who is discovered dead when they arrive at her Lake District home. Other murders involve the disappearance of a birdwatcher from a Cornish boat chartered for viewing seabirds in *Sea Fever;* the supposed suicide of a celebrated naturalist at a coastal "college of the countryside" in *The Mill on the Shore;* and the murder of a birdwatcher involved in raising funds for a fake environmental group in *High Island Blues.* Of this last book featuring Palmer-Jones and his wife, a *Publishers Weekly* contributor praised Cleeves's descriptions of the "rugged countryside as spectacular birdwatching country," adding that while the "earnestness" of the birdwatchers is "interesting" and the husband-and-wife team is "convincing," the supporting characters seem "less original."

Cleeves's *A Lesson in Dying* introduces Inspector Stephen Ramsay, an impulsive, even reckless policeman who is disliked by his colleagues and prone to serious error. He investigates the murder of a blackmailer in a Northumberland village, disregarding those who had reason to wish the victim dead and arresting instead the victim's innocent wife, with disastrous consequences. Ramsay's later career is more reassuring: he stabilizes his personal life, improves his relations with his colleagues, and avoids further headstrong error. In *Murder in My Back Yard* he investigates murder close to home; the title derives from the "Not in My Back Yard" syndrome whereby politicians, supportive of destructive development elsewhere, protest when their own neighborhoods are under threat. The victim is a woman who sold the land on which new buildings are due to be constructed.

A Day in the Death of Dorothea Cassidy involves Ramsay in the reconstruction of the last day in the live of a vicar's wife, an assiduous do-gooder who was daunting in her busy benevolence. The suspects in her murder include Cassidy's stepson and his girlfriend, a dying widow, an alcoholic, and a social worker. *Killjoy* is based in a Tyneside arts centre, where the female lead in a youth theatre production is found murdered. Teenage joy-riding and ram-raiding contribute to the pattern. And *The Healers* brings Ramsay into contact with New Age travelers and a centre for alternative healing. A motive for murder arises from a therapeutic session: the ambience serves the action.

"Detail is very important in detective fiction," Cleeves once commented. "In natural history it's crucial. George Palmer-Jones is an amateur ornithologist with an eye for detail who works with his wife, Molly, to solve crimes which have a background in natural history. The series started because I was fascinated by the obsession of birdwatchers. It moved on to consider serious conservation issues like the theft of birds of prey and river pollution. The main characters have recently retired from careers in public service. Throughout their marriage they have been too busy to spend much time together. Now, in retirement, they have to adapt to being a couple again and I enjoy the tension that situation brings. *A Lesson in Dying* begins a new series set firmly in my home county of Northumberland. Like many southerners I was immediately attracted by the dramatic landscape and the tight, traditional communities. I hope to continue both series."

BIOGRAPHICAL AND CRITICAL SOURCES:

BOOKS

St. James Guide to Crime and Mystery Writers, 4th edition, St. James Press (Detroit, MI), 1996.

PERIODICALS

Publishers Weekly, September 13, 1991, review of *Sea Fever,* p. 73; February 3, 1992, review of *A Day in the Death of Dorothea Cassidy,* p. 75; May 20, 1996, review of *High Island Blues,* p. 255.*

ONLINE

Time Warner Web site, http://www.twbooks.co.uk (November 3, 2003), profile of Cleeves.*

* * *

COE, George Albert 1862-1951

PERSONAL: Born March 26, 1862, in Mendon, NY; died November 9, 1951, in Claremont, CA; son of George W. (a Methodist Episcopal minister) and Harriet (Van Voorhis) Coe; married Sadie E. Knowland (a professor of piano and music history), September 3, 1888 (died August 24, 1905). *Education:* University of Rochester, A.B., 1884; Boston University, S.T.B., 1887, A.M., 1888, Ph.D., 1891; attended University of Berlin, 1890.

CAREER: University of Southern California, Los Angeles, teacher, 1887-91, professor of philosophy, 1891-93; Northwestern University, Evanston, IL, John Evans Professor of Philosophy of Religion, 1893-1909; Union Theological Seminary, New York, NY, professor of religious education and psychology of religion, 1909-22; Columbia University Teachers College, New York, NY, professor, 1922-27.

MEMBER: Religious Education Association (founding member, 1903; president, 1909).

WRITINGS:

The Spiritual Life: Studies in the Science of Religion, Eaton & Mains (New York, NY), 1900.

The Religion of a Mature Mind, Fleming H. Revell (Chicago, IL), 1902.

Education in Religion and Morals, Fleming H. Revell (Chicago, IL), 1904.

Sadie Knowland Coe: A Chapter in a Life; October 9, 1864-August 24, 1905, privately printed (Alameda, CA), 1906.

(Editor, with Charles Foster Kent) Harold B. Hunting, *The Story of Our Bible,* Charles Scribner's Sons (New York, NY), 1915.

The Psychology of Religion, University of Chicago Press (Chicago, IL), 1916.

A Social Theory of Religious Education, Charles Scribner's Sons (New York, NY), 1917.

Law and Freedom in the School: "Can and Cannot," "Must and Must Not," "Ought and Ought Not" in Pupils' Projects, University of Chicago Press (Chicago, IL), 1924.

What Ails Our Youth, Charles Scribner's Sons (New York, NY), 1924.

The Motives of Men, Charles Scribner's Sons (New York, NY), 1928.

What Is Christian Education?, Charles Scribner's Sons (New York, NY), 1929.

Educating for Citizenship, Charles Scribner's Sons (New York, NY), 1932.

What Is Religious Education Doing to Our Conscience?, Charles Scribner's Sons (New York, NY), 1943.

Other writings include "A History of the Upsilon Chapter of the Psi Upsilon Fraternity," Upsilon Chapter, Psi Upsilon (New York), 1883; and "The Core of Good Teaching," Charles Scribner's Sons (New York, NY), 1912; coeditor of leaders' manual for *Child Study and Child Training,* by William Byron Forbush, Charles Scribner's Sons (New York, NY), 1915. Contributor to books, including *Am I Getting an Education?,* Doubleday, Doran (Garden City, NY), 1929; and *Religion in Transition,* edited by Vergilius Ferm, Allen & Unwin (London, England), 1937.

Coe's correspondence is housed in the Coe Collection, Yale Divinity School, Yale University, New Haven, CT.

BIOGRAPHICAL AND CRITICAL SOURCES:

BOOKS

Ferm, Vergilius, editor, *Religion in Transition,* Allen & Unwin (London, England), 1937.

Religious Leaders of America, 2nd edition, Gale (Detroit, MI), 1999.

PERIODICALS

Religion in Life, winter, 1952-53, H. Shelton Smith, "George Albert Coe: Revaluer of Values," pp. 46-57.

Religious Education, March-April, 1952.

OBITUARIES:

PERIODICALS

New York Times, November 10, 1951.*

* * *

COE, Marian 1931-

PERSONAL: Born March 12, 1931, in Birmingham, AL; daughter of Will (a city employee) and Susie J. (a telephone company employee) Riddle; married Paul Roman Zipperlin (an artist), July 7, 1984; children: (first marriage) Carol Coe, David McLean Coe. *Ethnicity:* "English/white." *Education:* Attended University of Alabama. *Politics:* Democrat. *Religion:* Christian. *Hobbies and other interests:* Psychology, social issues, comparative religions, metaphysics.

ADDRESSES: Home and office—SouthLore Press, 730 Grouse Moor Dr., Banner Elk, NC 28604. *E-mail*—mariancoe@skybest.com.

CAREER: Journalist, novelist, and poet. *St. Petersburg Times,* St. Petersburg, FL, features writer, 1963-83; freelance writer, 1983—. SouthLore Press, Banner Elk, NC, founder and publisher.

MEMBER: International Women's Writers Guild, Publishers Marketing Association, Florida Writers Association, North Carolina Writers Network.

AWARDS, HONORS: Fallot Literary Award, National Association of Independent Publishers, 1993, for *Legacy;* finalist in fiction category, Benjamin Franklin Award, Publishers Marketing Association, 1999, for *Eve's Mountain: A Novel of Passions and Mystery in the Blue Ridge;* Appalachian State University established the Marian Coe creative writing scholarship in her honor.

WRITINGS:

On Waking Up (verse), Valkyrie Press, 1974.

Women in Transition (verse), Miracle House, 1984.

Legacy (novel), SouthLore Press (Little Switzerland, NC), 1993.

Eve's Mountain: A Novel of Passions and Mystery in the Blue Ridge, SouthLore Press (Little Switzerland, NC), 1998.

Marvelous Secrets (stories), SouthLore Press (Little Switzerland, NC), 2000.

Key to a Cottage, SouthLore Press (Banner Elk, NC), 2003.

Contributor of short stories to periodicals.

WORK IN PROGRESS: A fictional account of two seminal leaders in spiritual healing from the 1900s.

SIDELIGHTS: Marian Coe told *CA:* "I write to communicate the inner reality of a character's life, the situation in flux, and sense of setting. Rather than being on stage myself, I choose to be the director working the lights, for the reader-audience to experience the action. The story I wish to unfold on that stage has to have underlying substance, or I have no interest in showing it.

"I leave the horror, the glitz, the tricky mystery—as well as the abstract literary expressions—to all the others who do these books so well. For me the late John Gardner's criterion expresses my personal beliefs and therefore inspiration: fiction should affirm life rather than present voyeurism or devalue meaningful ideas. Even a humorous piece can do this.

"My first short story was published in the *Birmingham News* when I was twelve years old. The next editor replied to a submission with a kind suggestion to grow up and have a life first, which I did, dealing with school, marriage, children, widowhood, then twenty years in news features at the *St. Petersburg Times*. Some stories were published elsewhere along the way. Credits now stand at five books. Writing is my focus; rewriting my time-consuming habit. *Publishers Weekly* always refers to my Southern voice and pace. Because I had a late start with my fiction, I haven't tried to knock on New York City doors, but have accepted, with no apologies, independent publishers who believe more in their books than in bottom-line profits. I have books that reviewers see as movies—if the right agent were to take a look."

BIOGRAPHICAL AND CRITICAL SOURCES:

PERIODICALS

Library Journal, January, 1993, Bettie Spivey Cormier, review of *Legacy,* p. 193; December, 1997, Rex E. Klett, review of *Eve's Mountain,* p. 158.

Publishers Weekly, January 4, 1993, review of *Legacy,* p. 70; June 12, 2000, review of *Marvelous Secrets,* p. 54

ONLINE

SouthLore Press Web site, http://www.mariancoe.com/ (December 12, 2003).*

* * *

COFFIN, Henry Sloane 1877-1954

PERSONAL: Born January 5, 1877, in New York, NY; died November 25, 1954, in Lakeville, CT; son of Edmund (a legal advisor) and Euphemia (Sloane) Coffin; married Dorothy Prentice Eells, September 6, 1906; children: two. *Education:* Yale University, graduated, 1897, B.D., 1900; attended New College, Edinburgh, Scotland, 1897-99, and University of Marburg, 1899; Union Theological Seminary, B.D., 1900.

CAREER: Ordained Presbyterian minister, 1900; pastor of Presbyterian church in Bronx, NY; Union Theological Seminary, New York, NY, teacher of practical theology, 1904-26, president, 1926-45; lecturer and public speaker, 1945-54. Madison Avenue Presbyterian Church, pastor, 1905-26; Presbyterian Church in the U.S.A., moderator of General Assembly, 1943-44. New College, Edinburgh, Scotland, Warrack Lecturer, 1926; Joseph Cook Lecturer abroad, 1946-47; Seabury-Western Theological Seminary, George Craig Stewart Lecturer on Preaching; Auburn Seminary, Russell Lecturer; Theological Seminary of the Reformed Church in the United States, Swander Lecturer; Yale University, Lyman Beecher Lecturer. Young Men's Christian Association, speaker in United States and France during World War I.

WRITINGS:

The Creed of Jesus and Other Sermons, Charles Scribner's Sons (New York, NY), 1907.

(Editor) *Hymns of the Kingdom of God with Tunes,* A. S. Barnes and Co. (New York, NY), 1910, 2nd edition (with White Vernon Ambrose) published as *Hymns of the Kingdom of God,* 1923.

Social Aspects of the Cross, Hodder & Stoughton (New York, NY), 1911.

University Sermons, Yale University Press (New Haven, CT), 1914.

Some Christian Convictions: A Practical Restatement in Terms of Present-day Thinking, Yale University Press (New Haven, CT), 1915, reprinted, Books for Libraries Press (Freeport, NY), 1972.

The Ten Commandments: With a Christian Application to Present Conditions, Hodder & Stoughton (New York, NY), 1915.

In a Day of Social Rebuilding: Lectures on the Ministry of the Church, Yale University Press (New Haven, CT), 1918.

More Christian Industrial Order, Macmillan (New York, NY), 1920.

What to Preach, George H. Doran (New York, NY), 1926.

The Portraits of Jesus Christ in the New Testament, Macmillan (New York, NY), 1926.

The Meaning of the Cross, Charles Scribner's Sons (New York, NY), 1931.

What Men Are Asking: Some Current Questions in Religion, Cokesbury Press (Nashville, TN), 1933.

God's Turn (collected sermons), Harper and Brothers (New York, NY), 1934.

Religion Yesterday and Today, Cokesbury Press (Nashville, TN), 1940.

The Public Worship of God: A Source Book, Westminster Press (Philadelphia, PA), 1946.
God Confronts Man in History, Charles Scribner's Sons (New York, NY), 1947.
Communion through Preaching: The Monstrance of the Gospel, Charles Scribner's Sons (New York, NY), 1952.
A Half Century of Union Theological Seminary, 1896-1945: An Informal History, Charles Scribner's Sons (New York, NY), 1954.
Joy in Believing: Selections from the Spoken and Written Words and the Prayers of Henry Sloane Coffin, edited by Walter Russell Bowie, Charles Scribner's Sons (New York, NY), 1956.

Contributor to books, including *Twelve Modern Apostles and Their Creeds,* edited by G. K. Chesterton and others, 1926.

BIOGRAPHICAL AND CRITICAL SOURCES:

BOOKS

Chesterton, G. K., and other editors, *Twelve Modern Apostles and Their Creeds,* 1926.
Noyes, Morgan Phelps, *Henry Sloane Coffin: The Man and His Ministry,* Charles Scribner's Sons (New York, NY), 1964.
Religious Leaders of America, 2nd edition, Gale (Detroit, MI), 1999.*

* * *

COLAIANNI, Louis 1959-

PERSONAL: Born April 29, 1959, in Paterson, NJ; son of James F. (a writer/publisher) and D. Patricia Kelly (an editor) Colaianni. *Ethnicity:* "Italian/Irish/German." *Education:* Attended Boston Conservatory of Music, 1977-79; designated Linklater Voice Teacher, 1987. *Politics:* Democrat. *Religion:* "Unity School of Practical Christianity."

ADDRESSES: Office—University of Missouri—Kansas City, Department of Theatre, PAC 404, Kansas City, MO 64110. *E-mail*—colaiannil@umkc.edu.

CAREER: University of Missouri, Kansas City, MO, associate professor, 1990—. Presenter at phonetics workshops.

MEMBER: Screen Actors Guild, Actors' Equity Association, Players Club.

WRITINGS:

The Joy of Phonetics and Accents, Drama Book (New York, NY), 1994.
Shakespeare's Names: A New Pronouncing Dictionary, Drama Book (New York, NY), 2000.
(With Cal Pritner) *How to Speak Shakespeare,* Santa Monica Press (Santa Monica, CA), 2001.

Associate editor, *Voice and Speech Review.*

WORK IN PROGRESS: Bringing Speech to Life, for Drama Publishers; *American Shakespeare: Sound and Sense;* research on language variation and on the letters of Edwin Booth.

SIDELIGHTS: Louis Colaianni told *CA:* "My primary motivation for writing is to instruct. I write text books and references for the theatre. I also have a strong interest in sociolinguistics. I have been influenced by the work of linguists and dialectologists. I was also influenced by my teacher, Kristin Linklater, author of *Freeing the Natural Voice* and *Freeing Shakespeare's Voice.*"

BIOGRAPHICAL AND CRITICAL SOURCES:

PERIODICALS

Choice, March, 2002, R. F. Falk, review of *How to Speak Shakespeare,* p. 1252.

ONLINE

Joy of Phonetics Web site, http://www.joyofphonetics.com/ (December 12, 2003).

CONNER, Walter T(homas) 1877-1952

PERSONAL: Born January 19, 1877, in Center, AR; died 1952, in the United States; son of Philip O. and Frances Jane (Monk) Conner; married Blanche Ethel Horne, 1907. *Education:* Attended Simmons College (now Hardin-Simmons University), 1896-98; Baylor University, M.A., 1908; Southwestern Baptist Theological Seminary, degree, 1908; Rochester Theological Seminary, B.D., 1910; Southern Baptist Theological Seminary, Th.D., 1916, Ph.D., 1931.

CAREER: Pastor of church in Tuscola, TX, 1898-99; Baylor University, Waco, TX, instructor in Latin; Southwestern Baptist Theological Seminary, Fort Worth, TX, teacher of systematic theology, c. 1919-1949.

WRITINGS:

A System of Christian Doctrine, Sunday School Board of the Southern Baptist Convention (Nashville, TN), 1924, published as *Christian Doctrine,* Broadman Press (Nashville, TN), 1937, enlarged revision published as *The Gospel of Redemption,* 1945.
The Epistles of John: Their Meaning and Message, Fleming H. Revell (New York, NY), 1929, revised edition published as *The Epistles of John,* Broadman Press (Nashville, TN), 1957.
Revelation and God: An Introduction to Christian Doctrine, Broadman Press (Nashville, TN), 1936.
Personal Christianity: Sermons, Zondervan Publishing House (Grand Rapids, MI), 1937.
The Christ We Need, Zondervan Publishing House (Grand Rapids, MI), 1938.
The Faith of the New Testament, Broadman Press (Nashville, TN), 1940.
What Is a Saint?, 1948.
The Work of the Holy Spirit: A Treatment of the Biblical Doctrine of the Divine Spirit, Broadman Press (Nashville, TN), 1949.
The Cross in the New Testament, edited by Jesse J. Northcutt, Broadman Press (Nashville, TN), 1954.

BIOGRAPHICAL AND CRITICAL SOURCES:

BOOKS

Newman, Stewart A., *W. T. Conner: Theologian of the Southwest,* Broadman Press (Nashville, TN), 1964.
Religious Leaders of America, 2nd edition, Gale (Detroit, MI), 1999.*

* * *

CONWAY, Sara 1962-

PERSONAL: Born 1962. *Education:* Attended University of Washington.

ADDRESSES: *Home*—Kingston, WA. *Agent*—c/o Cumberland House Publishing, 431 Harding Industrial Dr., Nashville, TN 37211.

CAREER: Edmonds Community College, Edmonds, WA, teacher of ancient and medieval history.

WRITINGS:

Murder on Good Friday, Cumberland House (Nashville, TN), 2001.
Daughters of Summer, Cumberland House (Nashville, TN), 2003.

SIDELIGHTS: Sara Conway is the author of medieval mystery novels featuring ex-Crusader and sleuth Lord Godwin, a character she introduces in her debut novel, *Murder on Good Friday.* Set in thirteenth-century England, the novel is based on actual cases of ritual murder. History reveals that in towns throughout England charges against Jews accused of complicity in the deaths of young Christian boys were usually dismissed, but a number of those arrested were found guilty and put to death. It was believed by some that a pagan ritual was held every year in which Jews crucified a Christian boy, causing hysteria not unlike that seen in connection with the Salem witch trials in Massachusetts; many of the presumed victims were considered saints or martyrs by other Christians.

In *Murder on Good Friday* Godwin, the bailiff of Hexham, investigates the Good Friday death of a little boy named Alfred, whose palms bear puncture wounds and whose side has been pierced in imitation of the crucifixion of Christ. A mob descends on the nine-member Jewish family that lives in the town, and Godwin must first protect them, then find the actual murderer. Lori Tucker, who reviewed the novel for the Monroe, Louisiana *News-Star* online, wrote that Conway "has found a theme that reminds us that some pressing current issues have been with the human race for a long, long time." Tucker called *Murder on Good Friday* "a good, thought-provoking read."

In a second novel, *Daughters of Summer,* Godwin investigates the poisoning of a wealthy merchant in the summer of 1221.

BIOGRAPHICAL AND CRITICAL SOURCES:

PERIODICALS

Publishers Weekly, February 26, 2001, review of *Murder on Good Friday,* p. 63.

ONLINE

News-Star (Monroe, LA), http://www.thenewsstar.com/ (September 30, 2001), Lori Tucker, "Medieval Mystery Helps Readers Grapple with a Few Current Issues."*

* * *

COOKE, Darwyn

PERSONAL: Born in Toronto, Ontario, Canada.

ADDRESSES: *Agent*—c/o Author Mail, DC Comics, 1700 Broadway, New York, NY 10019.

CAREER: Writer, illustrator, graphic designer, and animator. Worked in advertising; art director for magazines, including *Chatelaine.* Storyboard artist for television series *Batman* and *Superman;* designer of title sequence for *Batman Beyond;* writer/illustrator for "Catwoman" comics series.

WRITINGS:

(And illustrator) *Batman: Ego,* DC Comics (New York, NY), 2000.

(And illustrator) *Catwoman: Selina's Big Score,* DC Comics (New York, NY), 2002.

SIDELIGHTS: Darwyn Cooke was doing production design and animation for commercials when Warner Bros. placed an ad in a trade publication announcing that they were looking for people to work on the *Batman* television series. Cooke sent them a demo and was soon a storyboard artist for the show's last season; he also contributed to a number of *Superman* episodes that were being produced at the time and designed the title sequence to *Batman Beyond,* which the studio used as a trailer on their Web site. Cooke is also the writer and illustrator of the graphic novel *Batman: Ego,* which features the sinister Joker and which provides a glimpse into the psyche of Bruce Wayne through flashbacks to his childhood and career and questions what drives him to be Batman.

Emru Townsend of *Critical Eye* online asked Cooke what it is like to be working on "Batman." Cooke said, "It's certainly thrilling, but you've got to approach it with a certain amount of caution. . . . Batman is, I think, the greatest character that's ever come out of this popular medium, because he's a real guy. I could always relate to that as a kid. Actually, they asked me for my resume when I started working here, and I sent them down these drawings I did of Batman when I was six, with some crayon. It's great to be working on the character. I've gotten a big kick out of it. It's like a dream come true, from that perspective."

In addition to working on the "Catwoman" comic series, Cooke wrote and illustrated the graphic novel *Catwoman: Selina's Big Score.* Set in the 1950s, the novel reflects the feel of that period through Cooke's use of trains, gangsters, and Las Vegas. The story reveals how Selina Kyle attempts to score Mafia money that has been shipped to Canada in trade for heroin in order to bankroll her continuing fight for justice. The story features Stark, Selina's James Coburn-lookalike former lover and mentor who was double-crossed by Selina years earlier. *Gay League* online reviewer said both characters "are a complex mixture of ruthlessness and relatively noble and even selfless impulses."

Randy Lander commented on the novel for *Fourth Rail* online, noting parallels between Stark and Slam, Selina's new significant other. Lander called the book "a rocket ride, a Hollywood-style big-budget blockbuster with the smarts of *L. A. Confidential,* the style of *The Usual Suspects,* and the action and tension of *The Score.* But . . . this is no light bit of fluff; Cooke has underwritten this story of a big heist with some important character moments, and the result is a terrific read, every bit as good as I've come to expect."

BIOGRAPHICAL AND CRITICAL SOURCES:

PERIODICALS

Library Journal, November 1, 2002, Steve Raiteri, review of *Catwoman: Selina's Big Score,* p. 66.

ONLINE

Critical Eye, http://purpleplanetmedia.com/ (May 30, 1999), Emru Townsend, interview with Cooke.

Fourth Rail, http://www.thefourthrail.com/ reviews/ snapjudgments/ (August 5, 2002), Randy Lander, review of *Catwoman.*

Gay League, http://www.gayleague.com/ (January 21, 2003), Margaret, review of *Catwoman.**

* * *

COOKSHAW, Marlene 1953-

PERSONAL: Born 1953, in Lethbridge, Alberta, Canada. *Education:* Attended University of Victoria.

ADDRESSES: Home—4305 Corbett Rd., Pender Island, British Columbia, Canada V0N 2M1.

CAREER: Poet. Victoria School of Writing, faculty member and workshop presenter.

AWARDS, HONORS: First prize, poem of the year, *Arc,* 1997; first prize, national poetry contest, League of Canadian Poets, 1997; Ralph Gustafson Poetry Prize, 1999; Robinson Jeffers Tor House Prize for Poetry, 2000.

WRITINGS:

Personal Luggage, Coach House Press (Toronto, Ontario, Canada), 1984.

The Whole Elephant (poetry), Brick Books (London, Ontario, Canada), 1984.

Coupling (chapbook; prose poetry), Outlaw Editions (Victoria, British Columbia, Canada), 1994.

Bottomland: Poems (chapbook), Reference West (Victoria, British Columbia, Canada), 1995.

Double Somersaults (poetry), Brick Books (London, Ontario, Canada), 1999.

Work represented in anthologies, including *Frictions,* Second Story Press, 1989; *The Macmillan Anthology 3,* Macmillan (New York, NY), 1990; and *Meltwater,* Banff Centre Press, 1998. Contributor of poetry to literary magazines, including *Matrix, Descant, Grain, Northern Light,* and *Fiddlehead.* Editor, *Malahat Review.*

BIOGRAPHICAL AND CRITICAL SOURCES:

PERIODICALS

Canadian Literature, summer, 1991, Susan Rudy Dorscht, review of *The Whole Elephant,* p. 160.*

* * *

COOPER, Anna Julia 1856-1964

PERSONAL: Born August 10, 1856, in Raleigh, NC; died February 27, 1964, in Washington, DC; daughter of George Washington and Hannah (a slave; maiden name, Stanley) Haywood; married George A. C. Cooper (a minister), 1877.

CAREER: Oberlin Academy, teacher; Wilberforce University, head of modern languages department, c. 1884; St. Augustine's Normal and Collegiate Institute, Raleigh, NC, instructor in Latin, German, and mathematics, 1885-86; "M" Street (later Paul Laurence Dunbar) High School, Washington, DC, teacher, 1887-1930, principal, 1902-06, teacher of Latin, 1910-30; Lincoln University, Missouri, chair, department of languages, 1906-10; Frelinghuysen University (later Frelinghuysen Group of Schools for Colored Working People), Washington, DC, cofounder, 1907, president, 1930-41.

MEMBER: American Negro Academy.

WRITINGS:

A Voice from the South, by a Black Woman of the South, Aldine (Xenia, OH), 1892.

The Social Settlement: What It Is, and What It Does, Murray Brothers (Washington, DC), 1913.

L'Attitude de la France a l'égard de l'esclavage pendant la Révolution, Imprimerie de la Cour d'Appel (Paris, France), 1925, translation by Frances Richardson Keller published as *Slavery and the French Revolutionists,* Mellen (Lewiston, NY), 1988.

PRIVATELY PRINTED

Legislative Measures concerning Slavery in the United States, [Washington, DC], 1942.

Equality of Races and the Democratic Movement, [Washington, DC], 1945.

Personal Recollections of the Grimké Family and Life and Writings of Charlotte Forten Grimké, 1951.

The Third Step: An Autobiography, c. 1950.

BIOGRAPHICAL AND CRITICAL SOURCES:

PERIODICALS

Library journal, May 1, 1998, Jeris Cassel, "The Voice of Anna Julia Cooper," p. 123.

NWSA Journal, fall, 1999, Frances Richardson Keller, "An Educational Controversy: Anna Julia Cooper's Vision of Resolution," p. 49, Christina Greene, "The Voice of Anna Julia Cooper, Including: A Voice from the South and Other Important Essays, Papers, and Letters," p. 172.*

* * *

COOPER, Irving S(teiger) 1882-1935

PERSONAL: Born March 16, 1882, in Santa Barbara, CA; died January 17, 1935, in Hollywood, CA; married Susan L. Warfield, c. 1927. *Education:* University of California, graduated.

CAREER: National lecturer in theosophy; secretary to theosophist Charles Webster Leadbeater in India; lecturer in Australia, 1917; ordained priest of Liberal Catholic Church, 1918, appointed regionary bishop for United States, based in Hollywood, CA, 1919; touring lecturer, 1926. Creator of St. Alban's Cathedral, Hollywood.

WRITINGS:

Methods of Psychic Development, Theosophist Office (Adyar, Madras, India), revised edition, Theosophical Book Concern (Chicago, IL), 1912.

Ways to Perfect Health, Theosophical Book Concern (Chicago, IL), 1912.

The Secret of Happiness, Theosophical Book Concern (Chicago, IL), 1913, reprinted, Theosophical Publishing House (Wheaton, IL), 1976.

Reincarnation: The Hope of the World, Theosophical Press (Chicago, IL), 2nd edition, 1927, 5th edition, 1955, reprinted, Theosophical Publishing House (Wheaton, IL), 1979.

Ceremonies of the Liberal Catholic Rite, St. Alban Press (Los Angeles, CA), 1934, revised edition, 1964.

Theosophy Simplified, 5th edition, Theosophical Press (Wheaton, IL), 1948, reprinted, Theosophical Publishing House (Wheaton, IL), 1979.

Also affiliated with preparation of *The Liturgy of the Mass,* 1917, revised edition published as *The Liturgy of the Holy Eucharist,* 1918.

BIOGRAPHICAL AND CRITICAL SOURCES:

BOOKS

Encyclopedia of Occultism and Parapsychology, 5th edition, Gale (Detroit, MI), 2001.

Religious Leaders of America, 2nd edition, Gale (Detroit, MI), 1999.

OBITUARIES:

PERIODICALS

Ubique, March, 1935.*

COPELAND, Kenneth 1937-

PERSONAL: Born 1937, in the United States; married; wife's name, Gloria. *Education:* Attended Oral Roberts University.

ADDRESSES: *Office*—Kenneth Copeland Ministries, Inc., Fort Worth, TX 76122-0001.

CAREER: Former airplane pilot for evangelist Oral Roberts; Kenneth Copeland Ministries, Inc., Fort Worth, TX, founder and evangelist preacher. Cofounder of radio ministry, 1976, and television ministry, 1979; also affiliated with Kenneth Copeland Publications.

WRITINGS:

The Laws of Prosperity, Kenneth Copeland Publications (Fort Worth, TX), 1974.

Walking in the Realm of the Miraculous, Kenneth Copeland Publications (Fort Worth, TX), 1979.

The Miraculous Realm of God's Love, Kenneth Copeland Publications (Fort Worth, TX), 1987.

Honor: Walking in Honesty, Truth, and Integrity, Harrison House (Tulsa, OK), 1992.

(With wife, Gloria Copeland) *Healing Promises,* Kenneth Copeland Publications (Fort Worth, TX), 1994.

Dear Partner, Kenneth Copeland Publications (Fort Worth, TX), 1997.

The First Thirty Years: A Journey of Faith, Kenneth Copeland Publications (Fort Worth, TX), 1997.

Managing God's Mutual Funds—Yours and His: Understanding True Prosperity, Kenneth Copeland Productions (Fort Worth, TX), 1997.

(With Gloria Copeland) *Family Promises,* Kenneth Copeland Publications (Fort Worth, TX), 1997.

(With Gloria Copeland) *Generation Faith: The Teen Alternative,* Kenneth Copeland Publications (Fort Worth, TX), 1998.

(With Gloria Copeland) *Protection Promises,* Harrison House (Tulsa, OK), 1999.

(With Gloria Copeland) *From Faith to Faith: Devotional; A Daily Guide to Victory,* Harrison House (Tulsa, OK), 1999.

(Compiler, with Gloria Copeland) *One Word from God Can Change Your Formula for Success,* Harrison House (Tulsa, OK), 2000.

Cofounder of periodical *Believer's Voice of Victory,* 1973.

SOUND RECORDINGS

Bread upon the Water, KCP Records (Fort Worth, TX), c. 1979.

I'm a Believer, KCP Records (Fort Worth, TX), c. 1979.

Development of the Whole Man—Spirit, Soul, and Body, twelve volumes, Kenneth Copeland Ministries (Fort Worth, TX), 1982.

Love: The Way into Perfection, four volumes, Kenneth Copeland Ministries (Fort Worth, TX), 1982.

The Best of Kenneth Copeland, KCP Records (Newark, TX), 1985.

The Word, KCP Records (Newark, TX), 1989.

The Life Cycle and the Death Cycle, four volumes, Kenneth Copeland Ministries (Fort Worth, TX), 1992.

I Was on His Mind, KCP Records (Newark, TX), 1994.

It's Time to Get out of Debt: God Has a Plan, six volumes, Kenneth Copeland Ministries (Fort Worth, TX), c. 2000.

BIOGRAPHICAL AND CRITICAL SOURCES:

BOOKS

Copeland, Kenneth, *The First Thirty Years: A Journey of Faith,* Kenneth Copeland Publications (Fort Worth, TX), 1997.

Religious Leaders of America, 2nd edition, Gale (Detroit, MI), 1999.*

* * *

COPLANS, John (Rivers) 1920-2003

OBITUARY NOTICE—See index for *CA* sketch: Born June 24, 1920, in London, England; died August 21, 2003, in New York, NY. Art critic, editor, curator, educator, photographer, and author. Coplans was best known as a founder of the influential *Artforum* magazine and for his more recent career as a photographer of quirky self-portraits. The son of a physician who was interested in art, Coplans fell naturally into the art world because he was surrounded by it as a boy, leading him to draw, paint, and take photographs at an early age. With the approach of World War II, he enlisted in the Scottish Rifles, seeing action in Africa and, later, Burma; he was eventually promoted to captain in the King's African Rifles. When he returned home, he studied art in London and earned money painting houses and renting out flats that he refurbished. He earned little from his own paintings, however, although he exhibited his works at the Royal Society of British Artists and the London Group during the early 1950s. Frustrated with the art scene in England, he moved to the United States and the excitement of the Pop Art movement. He settled in San Francisco, teaching for a time at the University of California at Berkeley, where he again became restless at the state of art in academia. Partnering with businessman John Irwin, he founded *Artforum* magazine, which became an important voice in the art world. During the 1960s he served as editor-at-large and then associate editor for the magazine, and from 1971 to 1976 he was the publication's editor, also writing a great deal of criticism during this time. Coplans' rising prominence in the art world as a result of his work for *Artforum* led to curator positions at the University of California and at the Pasadena Art Museum during the 1960s, as well as a position as director of the Akron Art Institute from 1978 to 1981. While at Akron, Coplans also founded the art magazine *Dialog,* which he published from 1978 to 1980. By 1980, however, he had become disillusioned about the art world again and what he felt was its growing preoccupation with money, so he moved to New York City to begin a new career as a photographer. Coplans' photographs are mostly self-portraits, but of a very different nature. He typically took close-up pictures of sections of his naked body, an approach that drew critical praise; his photos are currently exhibited at over fifty museums around the world and collected in his books *A Self-Portrait, 1984-1997* (1997), *A Body* (2002), and *Body Parts* (2003). He was also the author of *Serial Imagery* (1968) and *Don Judd* (1971), and editor of *Roy Lichtenstein* (1972) and *Weegee: Naked New York* (1997). Although he suffered from macular degeneration that affected his vision in later years, he continued to take photographs and be involved in education, most recently as Koopman Distinguished Chair at the University of Hartford, beginning in 1991. The recipient of numerous awards and fellowships for his work, Coplans earned a National Endowment for the Humanities fellowship in 1992, and in 2001 he was named Officier de l'Ordre des Arts et des Lettres of France.

OBITUARIES AND OTHER SOURCES:

PERIODICALS

Chicago Tribune, August 23, 2003, section 2, p. 11.
Los Angeles Times, August 22, 2003, p. B13.
New York Times, August 22, 2003, p. A23.
Times (London, England), August 28, 2003.
Washington Post, August 25, 2003, p. B4.

* * *

COPPIN, Fanny (Muriel) J(ackson) 1837-1913

PERSONAL: Born Fanny Jackson, 1837, in Washington, DC; died January 21, 1913, in Philadelphia, PA; daughter of Lucy Jackson (a slave); married Levi Jenkins Coppin (a bishop), 1881. *Education:* Attended Rhode Island State Normal School, c. 1859; Oberlin College, graduated, 1865. *Religion:* African Methodist Episcopal.

CAREER: Emancipated slave and social worker. Worked as domestic servant in New Bedford, MA, and Newport, RI, and as a piano teacher and adult educator in Oberlin, OH, until 1865. Institute for Colored Youth, Philadelphia, PA, teacher and principal of female department, c. 1865-69, principal of institute, 1869-1902, also founder of industrial department, 1889; Bethel Institute, Cape Town, South Africa, teacher and missionary, 1902-03; Women's Home and Foreign Missionary Society of African Methodist Episcopal Church, president of local Women's Mite Missionary Society, then as national president. Public lecturer and fund-raiser; cofounder of home for destitute women, 1888; Women's Exchange and Girls' Home, founder, 1894.

MEMBER: National Association of Colored Women (vice president, 1897).

AWARDS, HONORS: Honors included the naming of the Fanny Jackson Coppin Girls Hall at Wilberforce Institute, Cape Town, South Africa, and Coppin State College in Baltimore, MD.

WRITINGS:

Reminiscences of School Life, and Hints on Teaching, A.M.E. Book Concern (Philadelphia, PA), 1913, reprinted, G. K. Hall (New York, NY), 1995.

Author of column "Women's Department" in *Christian Recorder,* beginning 1878. Contributor to periodicals.

BIOGRAPHICAL AND CRITICAL SOURCES:

BOOKS

Coppin, Fanny J., *Reminiscences of School Life, and Hints on Teaching,* A.M.E. Book Concern (Philadelphia, PA), 1913, reprinted, Garland Publishing (New York, NY), 1987.

Coppin, Levi J., *Unwritten History,* 1919, reprinted, Negro Universities Press (New York, NY), 1968.

Notable Black American Women, Book 1, Gale (Detroit, MI), 1992.

Perkins, Linda M., *Fanny Jackson Coppin and the Institute for Colored Youth, 1865-1902,* Garland Publishing (New York, NY), 1987.

Religious Leaders of America, 2nd edition, Gale (Detroit, MI), 1999.

PERIODICALS

New York Age, November 8, 1890.

OBITUARIES:

PERIODICALS

Tribune (Philadelphia, PA), February 1, 1913.*

* * *

COPPIN, Levi J(enkins) 1848-1924

PERSONAL: Born December 24, 1848, in Frederick, Cecil County, MD; died June 25, 1924, in Philadelphia, PA; son of John and Jane (Lilly) Coppin; married Martha Grinnage (a schoolteacher), September, 1875 (died, c. 1877); married Fanny Muriel Jackson (an educator and administrator), December 21, 1881 (died January 21, 1913); married M. Evelyn Thompson (a physician), August 14, 1914; children: (first marriage) Octavius Valentine; (third marriage) Theodosia. *Education:* Protestant Episcopal Divinity School, graduated, 1887; also attended Wilberforce University.

CAREER: African Methodist Episcopal Church, licensed preacher, 1876, ordained minister, 1880, board member (some sources say president) of Sunday School Union, 1884-88, bishop for South Africa, 1900-04, leader of district of South Carolina and Alabama, 1904-08, and district of Baltimore, Virginia, and North Carolina, based in Washington, DC, beginning 1908, president of educational board, 1908-12, president of church extension board, 1912-20, assigned to district for the Midwestern United States and parts of Canada, 1916. Teacher at church school in Maryland, c. 1865; schoolteacher in Smyrna, DE, 1870s; City Mission, Philadelphia, PA, preacher, c. 1877; Bethel Church, Philadelphia, PA, pastor, c. 1880-81; Bethel Church, Baltimore, MD, pastor, 1881-84; Allan Chapel, Philadelphia, pastor, 1884-88; *A.M.E. Review,* editor, c. 1888-96; Bethel Church (also known as Mother Bethel Church), Philadelphia, pastor, 1896-1900; Bethel Institute, Cape Town, South Africa, founder, 1901. Also worked as a brick-maker and operated a flour store in Wilmington, DE.

WRITINGS:

The Relation of Baptized Children to the Church, A.M.E. Publication Department (Philadelphia, PA), 1890.

The Key to Scriptural Interpretation, Publishing House of the A.M.E. Church (Philadelphia, PA), 1895.

Fifty-two Suggestive Sermon Syllabi, A.M.E. Book Concern (Philadelphia, PA), 1910.

Unwritten History (autobiography), A.M.E. Book Concern (Philadelphia, PA), 1919.

Author of *Observation of Persons and Things in South Africa, 1900-1904,* A.M.E. Book Concern (Philadelphia, PA); and *The Sunday School: Its Work and How to Do It.* Also author of hymns and gospel songs.

BIOGRAPHICAL AND CRITICAL SOURCES:

BOOKS

Coppin, Levi J., *Unwritten History,* A.M.E. Book Concern (Philadelphia, PA), 1919.

Notable Black American Men, Gale (Detroit, MI), 1998.

Religious Leaders of America, 2nd edition, Gale (Detroit, MI), 1999.

OBITUARIES:

PERIODICALS

New York Age, July 5, 1924.*

* * *

CORNPLANTER, Jesse J. 1889-1957

PERSONAL: Given name is sometimes spelled "Jessie"; born 1889, on Cattaraugus Reservation, NY; died 1957.

CAREER: Illustrator, painter, and carver. Long House, ritual chief; chief of village of New Town; also teacher and singer at tribal ceremonies; toured as dancer and singer. *Exhibitions:* Work represented in a traveling exhibition of the Museum of the American Indian, 1982; work collected at National Museum of the American Indian, New York State Museum, and Rochester Museum of Arts and Sciences. *Military service:* Served during World War I; received Purple Heart.

WRITINGS:

(And illustrator) *Iroquois Indian Games and Dances* (drawings), [Chicago, IL], 1913.

(And illustrator) *Legends of the Longhouse,* introduction by Carl Carmer, J. B. Lippincott (Philadelphia, PA), 1938, reprinted, I. J. Friedman (Port Washington, NY), 1963.

ILLUSTRATOR

Arthur C. Parker, *Iroquois Uses of Maize and Other Food Plants,* New York State Museum (Albany, NY), 1910.

Arthur C. Parker, *The Code of Handsome Lake, the Seneca Prophet,* New York State Museum (Albany, NY), 1910.

Charles Hamilton, editor, *Cry of the Thunderbird: The American Indian's Own Story,* Macmillan (New York, NY), 1950.

BIOGRAPHICAL AND CRITICAL SOURCES:

BOOKS

Fawcett, David M., and Lee A. Callander, *Native American Painting: Selections from the Museum of the American Indian,* Museum of the American Indian (New York, NY), 1982.

St. James Guide to Native North American Artists, St. James Press (Detroit, MI), 1998, pp. 128-130.*

* * *

CRAMER, Malinda E(lliot) 1844-1906

PERSONAL: Born February 12, 1844, in Greensboro, IN; died August 2, 1906, in San Francisco, CA; daughter of Obediah and Mary (Henshaw) Elliot; married Charles Lake Cramer (a photographer), 1872. *Education:* Studied New Thought philosophy with Emma Curtis Hopkins.

CAREER: Teacher of New Thought movement; Home College, San Francisco, CA, founder, 1888, and teacher of divine science; International Divine Science Association (now Divine Science Federation International), founder, 1892. Copublisher of *Harmony,* 1888.

WRITINGS:

Lessons in the Science of Infinite Spirit, and the Christ Method of Healing, C. W. Gordon (San Francisco, CA), 1890, revised edition published as *Divine Science and Healing,* C. L. Cramer (San Francisco, CA), 1902, published as *Divine Science and Healing: A Text-book for the Study of Divine Science, Its Application in Healing, and for the Well-being of Each Individual,* Home College of Divine Science (San Francisco, CA), 1905, published in *Divine Science: Its Principles and Practice,* Textbook of Divine Science (Denver, CO), 1957.

Basic Statements and Health Treatment of Truth: A System of Instruction in Divine Science and Its Application in Healing and for Class Training, Home and Private Use, [San Francisco, CA], 1893, 8th edition, 1905.

Malinda Cramer's Hidden Harmony, edited by Joan Cline-McCrary, Divine Science Federation International (Denver, CO), 1990.

BIOGRAPHICAL AND CRITICAL SOURCES:

BOOKS

Religious Leaders of America, 2nd edition, Gale (Detroit, MI), 1999.*

* * *

CREME, Benjamin 1922-

PERSONAL: Born 1922, in Glasgow, Scotland. *Education:* Briefly attended Glasgow School of Art. *Religion:* Theosophist.

ADDRESSES: *Agent*—c/o Author Mail, Share International Foundation, P.O. Box 41877, 1009 DB, Amsterdam, Netherlands.

CAREER: Professional artist. Share International Foundation, Amsterdam, Netherlands, founder, 1974; speaker throughout Europe and North America.

WRITINGS:

The Reappearance of the Christ and the Masters of Wisdom, Tara Press (London, England), 1980.

Messages from Maitreya the Christ, two volumes, Tara Press (London, England), 1980.

Transmission: A Meditation for the New Age, Tara Center (North Hollywood, CA), 1983, 4th edition, 1998.

Maitreya's Mission, Share International (Amsterdam, Netherlands), 1986, 3rd edition, three volumes, 1993-97.

The Ageless Wisdom Teaching, Share International Foundation (Amsterdam, Netherlands), 1996.

Contributor to periodicals, including *Share International.*

BIOGRAPHICAL AND CRITICAL SOURCES:

BOOKS

A Master Speaks, Share International Foundation (Amsterdam, Netherlands), 1985.

Encyclopedia of Occultism and Parapsychology, 5th edition, Gale (Detroit, MI), 2001.

New Age Encyclopedia, Gale (Detroit, MI), 1990.

Religious Leaders of America, 2nd edition, Gale (Detroit, MI), 1999.

ONLINE

Share International Web site, http://www.shareinternational.org/ (February 28, 2004).*

* * *

CRIDGE, Edward 1817-1913

PERSONAL: Born December 17, 1817, in Bratton-Heming, England; immigrated to Canada, 1855; died May 6, 1913, in Victoria, British Columbia, Canada; son of John Cridge; married Mary Winnell (an educator and administrator), c. 1854. *Education:* St. Peter's College, Cambridge, B.A., 1848.

CAREER: Ordained priest of Church of England, 1849; curate of Christ Church, Stratford, England, c.1849-54; Hudson's Bay Co., Vancouver Island, British Columbia, Canada, chaplain, 1854; Christ Church, Victoria, British Columbia, began as pastor, became senior minister, 1856-65, dean of Christ Church Cathedral, 1865-74; suspended from ministry, 1874; Reformed Episcopal Church in Canada, consecrated bishop for Canada and the United States west of the Rocky Mountains, 1875-1913.

WRITINGS:

As It Was in the Beginning; or, The Historic Principle Applied to the Mosaic Scriptures, Fleming H. Revell (New York, NY), 1900.

BIOGRAPHICAL AND CRITICAL SOURCES:

BOOKS

Religious Leaders of America, 2nd edition, Gale (Detroit, MI), 1999.*

* * *

CROSBY, Fanny J.
See CROSBY, Francis J(ane)

* * *

CROSBY, Frances J(ane) 1820-1915
(Fanny J. Crosby)

PERSONAL: Born March 24, 1820, in Southeast (now Brewster), Putnam County, NY; died February 12, 1915, in Bridgeport, CT; daughter of John and Mercy (Crosby) Crosby; married Alexander Van Alstyne (a teacher of the blind and a church organist), March 5, 1858; children: one child. *Education:* Attended New York Institution for the Blind. *Religion:* Methodist.

CAREER: New York Institution for the Blind, New York, NY, teacher of English and history, mid-1840s to 1858; W. B. Bradbury and Co., hymn writer, beginning 1864. Lecturer and public speaker; volunteer at rescue missions.

AWARDS, HONORS: The Fanny J. Crosby Memorial Home in Bridgeport, CT, was named for Crosby, 1925.

WRITINGS:

AS FANNY J. CROSBY

The Blind Girl and Other Poems, Wiley & Putnam (New York, NY), 1844.
Monterey and Other Poems, R. Craighead (New York, NY), 1851.
A Wreath of Columbia's Flowers (poetry), H. Dayton (New York, NY), 1858.
Crowning the Year, [New York, NY], 1881.
Bells at Evening and Other Verses, Biglow & Main (New York, NY), 1897.
Ode to the Memory of Captain John Underhill, Underhill Society of America (Brooklyn, NY) 1902.
Fanny Crosby's Life-Story, by Herself, EveryWhere Publishing (New York, NY), 1903.
Memories of Eighty Years, James H. Earle (Boston, MA), 1906.
Fanny Crosby Speaks Again: 120 Hymns, edited by Donald P. Hustad, Hope Publishing (Carol Stream, IL), 1977.
Treasures from Fanny Crosby: Blessed Assurance, Barbour Publishing (Uhrichsville, OH), 1998.

Author of thousands of hymns, cantatas, and secular songs, including "Blessed Assurance"; "Crowning the Year: Written for the Watch-night Service," 1881; "I Am Thine, O Lord"; "Jesus Is Calling"; "Jesus, Keep Me near the Cross"; "Ode to the Memory of Captain John Underhill," Underhill Society of America (Brooklyn, NY), 1902; "Pass Me Not, O Gentle Savior"; "Rescue the Perishing"; "Rosalie, the Prairie Flower"; "Safe in the Arms of Jesus"; "Savior, More than Life to Me"; "There's Music in the Air"; and "Thy Will Be Done in Me," music by Robert Nagel, Mentor Music (Albuquerque, NM), 1996. Some hymns published under pseudonyms.

BIOGRAPHICAL AND CRITICAL SOURCES:

BOOKS

Barrett, Ethel, *Fanny Crosby,* Regal Books (Ventura, CA), 1984.
Crosby, Frances J., *Fanny Crosby's Life-Story, by Herself,* EveryWhere Publishing (New York, NY), 1903.
Crosby, Frances J., *Memories of Eighty Years,* James H. Earle (Boston, MA), 1906.
Dictionary of American Biography, American Council of Learned Societies, 1928-1936, reprinted, Gale (Detroit, MI), 2002.
Jackson, Samuel Trevena, *Fanny Crosby's Story of Ninety-four Years,* Fleming H. Revell (New York, NY), 1915.
Religious Leaders of America, 2nd edition, Gale (Detroit, MI), 1999.
Ruffin, Bernard, *Fanny Crosby,* Pilgrim Press (New York, NY), 1976.

PERIODICALS

Whole Earth Review, spring, 1993, Nancy E. Hall, "And Giveth Me Songs in the Night," p. 40.

OBITUARIES:

PERIODICALS

New York Times, February 13, 1915.*

* * *

CUMMINS, Robert 1897-1982

PERSONAL: Born 1897; died April 3, 1982, in Brunswick, ME. *Education:* Miami University, Oxford, OH, B.A.; University of Cincinnati, M.A.; University of California, Th.M.

CAREER: Teacher in Thailand; pastor of Universalist churches in Ohio, early 1920s; pastor in Cincinnati, OH, 1926-32; Throop Memorial Universalist Church, Pasadena, CA, pastor, 1932-38; Universalist Church in America, general superintendent, 1938-53. Participant in planning for merger of the Universalist Church in America with American Unitarian Association.

WRITINGS:

Parish Practices in Universalist Churches: Manual of Organization and Administration, Murray Press (Boston, MA), 1946.

Excluded: The Story of the Council of Churches and the Universalists, privately printed (Boston, MA), 1964.

BIOGRAPHICAL AND CRITICAL SOURCES:

BOOKS

Religious Leaders of America, 2nd edition, Gale (Detroit, MI), 1999.*

CUNARD, (Clara) Nancy 1896-1965

PERSONAL: Born March 10, 1896, in Leicestershire, England; died March 16, 1965, in Paris, France; daughter of Sir Bache and Maud (Burke) Cunard; married Sydney Fairburn, November, 1916 (divorced 1925).

CAREER: Author, editor, publisher, and activist. Hours Press, La Chapell-Réanville, France, founder; reporter for Associated Negro Press during the Spanish Civil War.

WRITINGS:

Outlaws, Elkin Mathews (London, England), 1921.

Sublunary, Hodder & Stoughton (New York, NY), 1923.

Parallax, Hogarth (London, England), 1925.

Poems (Two) 1925, Aquila (London, England), 1930.

Black Man and White Ladyship: An Anniversary, privately printed (Toulon, France), 1931.

(Editor) *Negro Anthology, Made by Nancy Cunard, 1931-1933,* Wishart & Co. (London, England), 1934, Negro Universities Press (New York, NY), 1969.

(Editor, with Pablo Neruda) *Les poètes du monde defendant les peuple espagnols,* self-published (La Chapell-Réanville, France), 1937.

(Editor) *Authors Take Sides on the Spanish War,* Left Review (London, England), 1937.

(With George Padmore) *The White Man's Duty: An Analysis of the Colonial Question in the Light of the Atlantic Charter,* W. H. Allen (London, England), 1942.

Men-Ship-Tank-Plane, New Books (London, England), 1944.

Relève into Maquis, Grasshopper (Derby, England), 1944.

(Editor) *Poems for France, Written by Poets on France since the War, with Biographical Notes of the Authors,* La France Libre (Paris, France), 1944.

Grand Man: Memories of Norman Douglas, Secker & Warburg (London, England), 1954.

GM: Memories of George Moore, Hart-Davis (London, England), 1956.

These Were the Hours: Memories of My Hours Press, Réanville and Paris, 1928-1931, Southern Illinois University Press (Carbondale, IL), 1966.

Thoughts about Ronald Firbank, Albondocani (New York, NY), 1971.

Cunard's papers are housed in various locations: the Harry Ransom Humanities Research Center, University of Texas at Austin; the Library of Congress; and the Morris Library at Southern Illinois University at Carbondale.

SIDELIGHTS: Although she was a notorious figure during her lifetime, British poet and publisher Nancy Cunard is relatively unknown to modern readers. Once famous for her bohemian lifestyle and her association with avant-garde literary, artistic, and political circles, Cunard wrote poetry that was influenced by Georgian and emerging modernist traditions.

In addition to her own writing, Cunard, who was white, was a tremendous advocate of African and African-American culture and literature. In fact, in 1934 she compiled and published an eight-hundred-page collection of black writings called *Negro Anthology, Made by Nancy Cunard, 1931-1933.* Including many photographs, the anthology includes the writings of well-known black writers of the day such as Zora Neale Hurston, Sterling Brown, and Langston Hughes. The book contains not only works of poetry but essays and articles that address the topics and issues that were affecting blacks during the early twentieth century. Cunard herself contributed six essays and a poem titled "Southern Sheriff," which criticizes racism in the American South.

In 1916 Cunard's first published poems had appeared in an anthology series titled "Wheels," the title of which was taken from one of her poems. Other contributors to the series, which was published by Edith Sitwell, included Aldous Huxley and Cunard's longtime friend Iris Tree. Some five years later Cunard published *Outlaws,* her first book of verse, which included thirty-one new poems and five that had appeared in *Wheels.* The collection caught the attention of reviewers, including Edgell Rickword of *New Statesman,* who declared: "One can feel the pulse of an original mind beating through a rather uncongenial medium." A number of literary critics and scholars considered Cunard's third volume of verse, *Parallax,* to be her most impressive work as a poet. The book includes just a single poem that runs more than five hundred lines. The main theme of the poem is alienation and a yearning for some kind of belonging in a world that Cunard thought was unraveling. Rickword, who reviewed the book for the *Times Literary Supplement,* wrote that "it has a grasp of reality and complexity which is so frequently lacking from women's poetry."

Despite the praise she received from many of her contemporary critics, later readers have largely neglected Cunard's poetry. Some scholars, however, feel that her writings should not be forgotten because they offer a unique perspective on some of the most important issues of her time. "If her verse never quite established a secure and distinctive voice of its own, it is, nevertheless, worth reading for the insights it offers into the aesthetic and political possibilities of poetry in the period 1916 to 1940," critic Chris Hopkins wrote in the *Dictionary of Literary Biography.*

Having lived through World War I, Cunard railed against the rise of fascist political movements in Italy, Germany, and Spain. Between 1928 and 1931 she owned and operated a publishing company in La Chapelle-Réanville, France, called the Hours Press. Cunard used the press to publish high-quality small editions of prose and poetry that the commercial publishers were not interested in. Some of the better-known authors who published works with the press included Ezra Pound and Samuel Beckett. During the Spanish Civil War, Cunard worked as a news correspondent for the Associated Negro Press. She also collaborated with Chilean poet Pablo Neruda on a pamphlet that helped support the Spanish Republicans in their war against the fascist forces. Several of Cunard's books were published in the years following World War II, including three volumes of memoirs. One of these volumes, *These Were the Hours: Memories of My Hours Press, Réanville and Paris, 1928-1931,* was published posthumously in 1966.

Her bohemian lifestyle not only led Cunard into numerous romantic liaisons, both temporary and long-term, but also encouraged her excessive drinking. At the end of her life she experienced repeated bouts of drunken paranoia that led to run-ins with the police and eventually an ordered stay at a sanatorium. The drinking also took a serious toll on Cunard's health, and she died at the age of sixty-nine on March 16, 1965, in Paris, France. Some modern critics, like Hopkins, feel that Cunard's literary accomplishments will forever be entwined with her publishing activities and public life. "Her reputation is better remembered than her poetry, but her life and work are closely linked: both show a progression from a wish to shock and a rejection of old meanings to a search for new and valuable insights," concluded Hopkins.

BIOGRAPHICAL AND CRITICAL SOURCES:

BOOKS

Dictionary of Literary Biography, Volume 240: *Late Nineteeth-and Early-Twentiety-Century British Women Poets,* Gale (Detroit, MI), 2001.*

* * *

CUNHA, Euclides (Rodrigues) da 1866-1909

PERSONAL: Born January 20, 1866, in Cantagalo, Rio de Janiero, Brazil; died August 15, 1909, in Rio de Janeiro, Brazil; married Ana Solon, 1889. *Education:* Graduate of Colégio Aquino (liberal arts); attended a polytechnic school; Escola Militar, degree in mathematics and science, 1891.

CAREER: Journalist, engineer, surveyor, educator, and author. *O Estado de São Paulo,* São Paulo, Brazil, journalist; City of São Paulo, superintendent of public works; City of Santos, Brazil, head of sanitation commission, 1904; surveyor for Brazilian-Peruvian boundary expedition, 1904-06; worked at foreign ministry in Rio de Janeiro, Brazil, 1906-09; Colégio Pedro II, Rio de Janeiro, professor of logic, 1909. *Military service:* Brazilian army, 1890-96; attained rank of second lieutenant; worked as a field engineer..

AWARDS, HONORS: Elected to the Brazilian Academy of Letters and Brazilian Historical and Geographic Institute, both 1903.

WRITINGS:

Os sertões, 1902, translation with introduction and notes by Samuel Putnam published as *Rebellion in the Backlands,* University of Chicago Press (Chicago, IL), 1944.

Contrastes e confrontos (essays; title means "Contrasts and Comparisons"), 1902.

Perú versus Bolivia (history), Livraria F. Alves (Rio de Janeiro, Brazil), 1907.

Castro Alves e seu tempo (lecture), Imprensa Nacional (Rio de Janeiro, Brazil), 1907.

À margem da história (title means "On the Margin of History"), 1909.

Diário de uma expedição (autobiography), 1939.

Canudos (history), 1939.

Obra completa, second edition (two volumes), J. Aguilar (Rio de Janeiro), Brazil, 1995.

SIDELIGHTS: Euclides da Cunha, one of Brazil's greatest writers, produced the masterpiece *Os sertões* (translated into English as *Rebellion in the Backlands*), a 1902 work through which Brazil began to define itself as a country and a people.

Cunha, who was of Greek, Indian, and Celtic descent, was born in rural Rio de Janeiro to a family of modest means. His mother died when he was three, and he was raised by an aunt, older sister and grandparents. Cunha learned to love books at an early age due to his poet father. He began writing while studying at the Colégio Aquino, where he was influenced by republican factions advocating the abolition of Brazilian aristocracy in favor of a representational government. He continued his studies at a polytechnic school, then began training for an officer's command in the Brazilian army. His training ended prematurely, however, when he was expelled for insubordination: a nonviolent man, he threw down his sword in the presence of a minister of war. Cunha returned to the military academy and was commissioned a second lieutenant in 1890, the year he married. He then spent five years with the military, working as a field engineer on a border project.

Five years later, Cunha resigned his commission to become a journalist with *O Estado de São Paulo.* In 1897 he traveled to Bahia to cover the army's suppression of an uprising being led by Old Testament prophet Antonio Conselheiro (Counselor) in the Village of Canudos. The charismatic, elderly leader had drawn thousands of poor Brazilians, *sertanejos* of mixed European, African and aboriginal descent, to the commune. They rejected the Brazilian federal republic, refused to pay taxes or accept civil marriages, and believed that the end of the world was near. The sect was seen by the fledgling Brazilian government as a threat, and in February 1897, it sent more than 1,000 troops, armed with field artillery and led by its fiercest commander, to crush the peasants. But after one month, it was the villagers who were victorious, having killed most of the senior officers.

Canudos was finally overcome in a four-month siege that began in October. The government sent 8,000 troops who went house-to-house, killing approximately 15,000 people, mostly civilians, many of whom had their throats cut after they surrendered. Captured men and boys were garroted, decapitated, or disemboweled. Still Canudos never surrendered, even as the army dynamited and burned the compound. Survivors dug a common grave where those who were close to death lay with their fingers on triggers, waiting for one last chance to kill a soldier.

An *Economist* contributor noted that "though the scale of this conflict was unusual, its nature was not. The details have varied, but from the Anabaptists of Münster in 1534-35 to the Branch Davidians of Waco, Texas, in 1993, communities of religious dissidents have often suffered violent repression. What further marks out the events at Canudos is that they gave rise to a literary epic which many Brazilians still consider to be their country's greatest single book."

The battle was covered by the press, which received its information via telegraph. The news portrayed the story as a plot by the poor farmers of Canudos to overthrow the government and restore the monarchy. But Cunha had witnessed the slaughter, and although he at first supported the government's efforts to suppress the rebellion, he came to sympathize with the backlanders' cause and admire their heroism. These events provided the basis for his first book, an extraordinary analysis incorporating anthropology, philosophy, ethnology, botany, geology and geography in its account of the conflict.

Cunha wrote his book by night as he built a bridge by day. *Rebellion in the Backlands* is in three parts: "The Land," "Man," and "The Battle." *Nation* reviewer Gwyneth Cravens wrote that it "begins quietly, with a panoramic view of a desolate landscape of stark ranges, folds and buckles in the earth, ribs of quartz gleaming in the relentless sun, desiccated plains with flesh-tearing thickets of thorn trees, tortuous, boulder-strewn canyons, and rivers and swamps that vanish during the annual drought." After establishing the nature of the land, Cunha writes of the people, including Conselheiro, then the violence.

Although he had difficulty finding a publisher, *Os sertões* did prove to be popular, and its author was elected to the Brazilian Historical and Geographic Institute and to the Brazilian Academy of Letters. Cunha worked in a variety of positions over the next several years. He published *Contrastes e confrontos,* a collection of political and historical essays. He was appointed to the chair of logic of Colégio Pedro II and delivered his first address just weeks before he was shot and killed by an army officer who may have been the lover of his estranged wife. At the time, he was writing another book about the backlands. *À margem da história,* his second collection of essays, was published posthumously. Except for his first book, none of Cunha's writings, and only a few of the many books and articles that discuss him and his output, are available in English. His complete works were published in Portuguese as *Obra completa.*

BIOGRAPHICAL AND CRITICAL SOURCES:

BOOKS

Encyclopedia of World Biography, Gale (Detroit, MI), 1998, pp. 336-337.

Magill, Frank N., editor, *Cyclopedia of World Authors,* Salem Press (Pasadena, CA), 1997, pp. 486-487.

Twentieth-Century Literary Criticism, Volume 24, Gale (Detroit, MI), 1987, pp. 140-155.

PERIODICALS

Comparative Literature, summer, 1995, Thomas O. Beebee, review of *Os sertões,* p. 193.

Economist, March 1, 1997, review of *Os sertões,* p. 83.

Nation, December 7, 1992, Gwyneth Cravens, review of *Rebellion in the Backlands,* p. 706.

New York Review of Books, February 28, 1985, Michael Wood, review of *Rebellion in the Backlands,* pp. 7-8.

PMLA, May, 1993, Renata R. Mautner Wasserman, "Mario Vargas Llosa, Euclides da Cunha, and the Strategy of Intertextuality," pp. 460-469.*

CURRIE, Barbara 1942-

PERSONAL: Born 1942; married; children: two. *Education:* Trained as a nurse.

ADDRESSES: *Home*—Surrey, England. *Agent*—Knight Ayton Management, 114 St. Martin's Lane, London WC2N 4BE, England.

CAREER: Teacher of hatha yoga, 1972—, currently runs a school in Surrey, England; host of a television show; performer in yoga videotapes, including *Power of Yoga, Seven Secrets of Yoga,* and *Total Body Plan,* 2003. Worked as a nurse in a hospital in the 1960s; also worked as an airline hostess for B.O.A.C. (now British Airways) and as a model.

WRITINGS:

Fabulous Shape Forever: Yoga—the Ultimate Shape System, Andre Deutsch (London, England), 1997.

Yoga Workout: Having a Fabulous Shape Forever, Firefly Books (Buffalo, NY), 2002.

Ten-Minute Yoga Workouts: Power Tone Your Body from Top to Toe, Element Books (London, England), 2002.

Get Younger with Yoga: Lose Fifteen Years in Fifteen Minutes a Day, Thorsons (London, England), 2003.

Contributor to periodicals.

BIOGRAPHICAL AND CRITICAL SOURCES:

PERIODICALS

Library Journal, October 15, 2002, Deborah Anne Broocker, review of *Yoga Workout: Having a Fabulous Shape Forever,* p. 88.

ONLINE

Barbara Currie Unofficial Web site, http://www.barbaracurrie.ukbe.com/ (January 17, 2003).*

D

DARBY, Edwin (Wheeler) 1922-2003

OBITUARY NOTICE—See index for *CA* sketch: Born January 7, 1922, in Oakland, MD; died of heart failure August 9, 2003, in Chicago, IL. Journalist and author. Darby was a noted former financial editor for the *Chicago Sun-Times.* Educated at Ohio University, where he earned his bachelor's degree in 1942, he finished school at the beginning of World War II. He joined the U.S. Army Air Forces and spent the war teaching pilots to fly B-25s. After the war, he joined the staff at *Time* magazine as a White House correspondent and, later, Midwest correspondent. In 1958 he was hired by the *Chicago Sun-Times* to be its financial editor and columnist, a position he kept until his retirement in 1995. Darby became well known in the field of business writing, and his columns for the *Sun-Times* were eventually syndicated in about seventy newspapers nationwide. He was also the author of the book *The Fortune Builders* (1986).

OBITUARIES AND OTHER SOURCES:

PERIODICALS

Baltimore Sun, August 13, 2003, p. 5B.
Chicago Tribune, August 12, 2003, section 1, p. 11.

* * *

DAVIDSON, Donald (Herbert) 1917-2003

OBITUARY NOTICE—See index for *CA* sketch: Born March 6, 1917, in Springfield, MA; died of a heart attack September 30, 2003, in Berkeley, CA. Philosopher, educator, and author. One of the most important American philosophers of the twentieth century, Davidson was responsible for influencing philosophical thought in areas ranging from language and semantics to the concepts of meaning and belief. Educated at Harvard University, he earned his master's degree there in 1941 before enlisting in the U.S. Navy during World War II; while in the navy, he trained pilots on how to recognize enemy aircraft. He then returned to Harvard to complete his Ph.D. in philosophy in 1949, even though he had begun his studies in English and comparative literature—he had even spent a few years in the late 1930s writing radio scripts for Edward G. Robinson. Davidson eventually settled on philosophy as his main interest, and he began his academic career at Queens College of the City University of New York. During the late 1950s through the early 1970s, he taught at Stanford University, and it was here that he wrote his influential paper "Actions, Reasons, and Causes," which helped changed people's notions about how actions are taken as a result of internal beliefs rather than as a reaction to external events. Establishing himself as an important voice in areas such as ethics and semantics, Davidson moved on to teach at Princeton University, Rockefeller University, and the University of Chicago in the 1970s, and the University of California at Berkeley from 1981 until his death; he had been named Willis S. and Marion Slusser professor of philosophy in 1986. During his career, he contributed to dozens of books, as well as authoring or editing several of his own, including *Essays on Actions and Events* (1980; second edition, 2001), *Inquiries into Truth and Interpretation* (1984; second edition, 2001), *Reflecting Davidson: Donald Davidson Responding to an International Forum of Philosophers* (1993), and *Subjective, Intersubjective, Objective* (2001).

OBITUARIES AND OTHER SOURCES:

PERIODICALS

Los Angeles Times, September 8, 2003, p. B9.
New York Times, September 4, 2003, p. C14.
San Francisco Chronicle, September 5, 2003, p. A23.
Times (London, England), September 6, 2003.

ONLINE

UC Berkeley News, http://www.berkeley.edu/news/ (September 4, 2003).

* * *

DAVIS, Kenneth Culp 1908-2003

*OBITUARY NOTICE—*See index for *CA* sketch: Born December 19, 1908, in Leeton, MO; died August 30, 2003, in San Diego, CA. Attorney, educator, and author. Davis was widely credited as the creator of the field of administrative law. He completed his B.A. at Whitman College in 1931 before receiving a law degree from Harvard in 1934. After briefly practicing law in Cleveland, he joined the faculty of West Virginia University in 1935. He then worked for the Department of Justice from 1939 to 1940, before returning to academia at the University of Texas. This was followed by positions at Harvard from 1948 to 1950, the University of Minnesota from 1950 to 1961, the University of Chicago from 1961 to 1976, and, finally, the University of San Diego, where he remained until his retirement in 1994. Davis's *Administrative Law* (1951) is considered the foundation for students and practitioners of this field of law and is still referred to today. It was followed by such publications as his four-volume *Administrative Law Treatise* (1958; revised edition, 1978-84), *Administrative Law and Government* (1960; second edition, 1975), and *Administrative Law of the Eighties* (1989). He was also the author of the influential monographs *Discretionary Justice: A Preliminary Inquiry* (1969) and *Police Discretion* (1975). Significantly, his legal expertise was relied on to help write the federal Administrative Procedure Act of 1946.

OBITUARIES AND OTHER SOURCES:

PERIODICALS

Los Angeles Times, September 23, 2003, p. B11.

DAY, Michael (J.)

PERSONAL: Son of Rosemary Day (a potter and artist); married; wife's name Takako; children: Emi (daughter). *Education:* Dartmouth College, B.A. (English), 1978; University of Wyoming, M.A. (English), 1982; University of California—Berkeley, Ph.D. (rhetoric), 1996. *Hobbies and other interests:* Performing with Seventh Cavalry drum-and-bugle corps, hiking, playing piano.

*ADDRESSES: Office—*English Department, Northern Illinois University, DeKalb, IL 60115. *E-mail—*mday@niu.edu.

CAREER: Educator and author. Worked variously as a sailing instructor, cook, fishing boat deckhand, and U.S. Forestry Service timber-stand examiner. Teacher in universities in Osaka and Köbe, Japan; South Dakota School of Mines, Rapid City, associate professor of English, 1992-99; Northern Illinois University, DeKalb, assistant professor of English, 1999—. Collaboration for the Advancement of College Teaching and Learning, traveling workshop consultant, 1997—.

MEMBER: Modern Language Association, National Council of Teachers of English (member of assembly on computers in English, 1992—).

AWARDS, HONORS: Academy of American Poets Award, University of Wyoming, 1981.

WRITINGS:

A Place for Yourself, Jelm Mountain, 1982.
(Editor with Susanmarie Harrington and Rebecca Rickly) *The Online Writing Classroom,* Hampton Press (Cresskill, NJ), 2000.

Also author of numerous chapters, articles, and Web texts.

WORK IN PROGRESS: Tech/Web 2000: Technical Communications and the World Wide Web in the New Millennium; research on e-mail overload, coping strategies, rhetorical conventions and strategies in on-line discourse.

SIDELIGHTS: Michael Day told *CA:* "I write as a way to find out what I think. Beyond the familiar 'publish or perish' requirement of academia, I write out of an interest in sharing what I know with others. For relaxation and exploring the limits of the human imagination, I write poetry.

"My writings are generally on topics related to teaching writing using computers and the Internet."

BIOGRAPHICAL AND CRITICAL SOURCES:

ONLINE

Michael Day's Home Page, http://www.sdsmt.edu/online-courses/ (December 13, 2003).

* * *

del MAR, David Peterson 1957-

PERSONAL: Born 1957. *Education:* University of Oregon, B.A., M.A., and Ph.D. (history).

ADDRESSES: *Office*—University of Northern British Columbia, 3333 University Way, Prince George, British Columbia, Canada V2N 4Z9. *E-mail*—delmard@unbc.ca.

CAREER: University of Northern British Columbia, Prince George, British Columbia, Canada, professor of history. Has taught at several colleges and universities, including Portland State University, Portland, OR. Worked as a counselor, writer, curator, and historical interpreter.

WRITINGS:

What Trouble I Have Seen: A History of Violence against Wives, Harvard University Press (Cambridge, MA), 1996.

Beaten Down: A History of Interpersonal Violence in the West, University of Washington Press (Seattle, WA), 2002.

Oregon's Promise: An Interpretive History, Oregon State University Press (Corvallis, OR), 2003.

SIDELIGHTS: In his research for *What Trouble I Have Seen: A History of Violence against Wives,* historian David Peterson del Mar examined records for some 3,500 divorce cases filed in Oregon from pioneer days to the present. Del Mar also used a number of less formal sources, including popular local literature from each of the five historic eras into which his book is divided.

"This book is not bedtime reading," warned Susan Sessions Rugh in *Journal of Family History.* She went on to note that "its every page presents horrible stories that would make the reader flinch." As Rugh noted, in the book—a revision of del Mar's doctoral dissertation—he maintains that two broad cultural trends influenced the character and prevalence of wife-beating from the mid-nineteenth century to the present. On the one hand, there was a growth in self-restraint, spurred in part by the rise of feminine influence in public affairs during the latter part of the nineteenth century. This was countered, in the period from the end of World War I to the end of World War II, by the growth of a consumption and self-fulfillment ethic. Rugh further elucidated del Mar's thesis thus: "A corollary argument is that as wife beating declined, so did wives' resistance. In the twentieth century, women's resistance increased along with the incidence of abuse."

In the first two chapters, del Mar covers the settlement of the state and the end of the nineteenth century, respectively. A section of the book noted by several reviewers as its most intriguing was in the third chapter, where del Mar discusses the Whipping Post Law passed by the state legislature in 1905. The law, which remained in effect for six years before it was repealed, would have subjected wife-beaters to public beatings, but as del Mar argues, it was not a serious attempt to deal with the real issue—a fact reflected by the lack of support for it by women's reform groups. Rather, when it was applied at all, it was primarily used to punish emigrants from southern Europe, where wife-beating was more prevalent than among persons born in the United States.

The fourth chapter examines the rise of the culture of consumption, which del Mar places not in the period after World War II (as is the more traditional opinion), but rather in the era that encompassed not only the Roaring Twenties but also the Great Depression and the privations of the war itself. In the final chapter, del

Mar examines the growth of "self-realization" as a cultural theme—another trend that, in his view, helped influence a rise in spousal abuse. According to Rugh, "Each chapter follows a template: the historical setting in Oregon, a survey of gender ideologies based on secondary literature, men's goals in carrying out the abuse, then women's resistance."

According to Margaret M. R. Kellow in the *Canadian Journal of History,* del Mar's "subtle and nuanced exploration resists reductionist arguments and historicizes wife-beating, tracking change over time with exhaustive research and a perceptive eye for the impact of cultural transformations." She went on to note that "One of the strengths of Peterson del Mar's study is his portrayal of his female subjects not merely as victims, but as actors, particularly as they explain their choices and actions to the courts."

According to Deborah L. Kitchen in the *Journal of American Culture, What Trouble I Have Seen* "weaves together an extraordinary mix of contradictory threads in the histories of violence, westward expansion, race, economics, gender roles, work, attitudes about marriage and women, and changes in the economy to explain historical changes in violence against wives. . . . It is solid scholarship." "This is a fascinating book," wrote Peter N. Stearns in the *American Historical Review,* "with a bold and clear argument and a host of insights into family life and standards." "Well-written and thoroughly researched," according to Sylvia D. Hoffert in *History: Review of New Books,* "this book will be of interest to both scholars and the general reader."

BIOGRAPHICAL AND CRITICAL SOURCES:

PERIODICALS

American Historical Review, October 1997, Peter N. Stearns, review of *What Trouble I Have Seen: A History of Violence against Wives,* pp. 1236-1237.

Canadian Journal of History, August, 1997, Margaret M. R. Kellow, review of *What Trouble I Have Seen: A History of Violence against Wives,* p. 289.

History: Review of New Books, summer, 1997, Sylvia D. Hoffert, review of *What Trouble I Have Seen: A History of Violence against Wives,* p. 151.

Journal of American Culture, spring, 1998, Deborah L. Kitchen, review of *What Trouble I Have Seen: A History of Violence against Wives,* pp. 85-86.

Journal of Family History, July, 1997, Susan Sessions Rugh, review of *What Trouble I Have Seen: A History of Violence against Wives,* p. 354.

* * *

DONOVAN, Robert J(ohn) 1912-2003

OBITUARY NOTICE—See index for *CA* sketch: Born August 21, 1912, in Buffalo, NY; died of complications from a stroke August 8, 2003, in St. Petersburg, FL. Journalist and author. Donovan was a highly respected Washington, D.C. correspondent who also wrote several important presidential biographies. Originally aspiring to be a doctor, because he could not afford a medical tuition he took a job as a copy boy after high school, eventually getting himself hired as a reporter for the Buffalo *Courier Express.* He moved to the *New York Herald Tribune* in 1937, covering local government and the United Nations. With the onset of World War II, he joined the U.S. Army, serving in the 2nd Infantry and seeing action at the Battle of the Bulge. Donovan left the military as a sergeant, returning to the *Herald* and being assigned to Washington, D.C. Here, he gained the trust of President Truman and then President Eisenhower; gaining access to private information led to such books as *Eisenhower: The Inside Story* (1956). He would have similar success with President Kennedy, an association that would lead to his bestselling book *PT 109: John F. Kennedy in World War II* (1961), which was also adapted as a film starring Cliff Robertson. Donovan was next hired by the *Los Angeles Times* in 1963, and many believe that his work there did much to make it a nationally respected newspaper. After becoming an associate editor there and working as such from 1970 to 1977, Donovan left the *Los Angeles Times* to become a fellow at the Woodrow Wilson International Center for Scholars; he also taught journalism at Princeton for a year and was senior fellow at Princeton's Woodrow Wilson School of Public and International Affairs. Donovan continued to write books well into his eighties, as well as contributing to newspapers. A former president of the White House Correspondents Association, he was the author of many works, including two volumes on Truman—*Conflict and Crisis: The Presidency of Harry S. Truman, 1945-1948* (1977) and

Tumultuous Years; The Presidency of Harry S. Truman, 1949-1953 (1982)—*The Second Victory: The Marshall Plan and the Postwar Revival of Europe* (1987), and *Boxing the Kangaroo: A Reporter's Memoir* (2000).

OBITUARIES AND OTHER SOURCES:

PERIODICALS

Chicago Tribune, August 9, 2003, section 1, p. 8.
Los Angeles Times, August 9, 2003, p. B21.
New York Times, August 10, 2003, p. A24.
Times (London, England), August 27, 2003.
Washington Post, August 9, 2003, p. B7.

* * *

DOUMANI, Carol 1959-

PERSONAL: Born November 5, 1959, in Los Angeles, CA; daughter of Constantine (an importer of Oriental rugs) and Doris (Nahigian) Gertmenian; married Roy Doumani (a financier), January 1, 2980. *Ethnicity:* "Armenian." *Education:* University of Southern California, B.A., 1971.

ADDRESSES: Home—Venice, CA. *Office*—c/o Author Mail, Wave Publishing , P.O. Box 688, Venice, CA 90294. *E-mail*—carol@doumani.net.

CAREER: Novelist and photographer. Wave Publishing, Venice, CA, founder, 1994. Philanthropist and patron of the arts, with husband Roy Doumani.

AWARDS, HONORS: Brandeis University Distinguished Author award, for *Untitled, Nude.*

WRITINGS:

Untitled, Nude (novel), Wave (Venice, CA), 1995.
Chinese Checkers (novel), Wave (Venice, CA), 1996.
Good Enough to Eat: A Collection of Recipes, Wave (Venice, CA), 1999.
Indiscretions (novel), Wave (Venice, CA), 1999.
Taking Heart (novel), Wave (Venice, CA), 1999.
Putting on the Dog: Digital Photos and Canine Wisdom, Wave (Venice, CA), 2000.

ADAPTATIONS: Chinese Checkers and *Taking Heart* were both adapted as audiobooks by Books on Tape.

BIOGRAPHICAL AND CRITICAL SOURCES:

PERIODICALS

Booklist, May 1, 1996, Mary Carroll, review of *Chinese Checkers,* p. 1487; March 15, 1999, Vanessa Bush, review of *Indiscretions,* p. 1289.
Library Journal, November 1, 1996, James Dudley, review of *Chinese Checkers,* p. 120; March 1, 1999, Sheila M. Riley, review of *Indiscretions,* p. 108.
Publishers Weekly, February 6, 1995, review of *Untitled, Nude,* p. 78; May 6, 1996, review of *Chinese Checkers,* p. 71; February, 1999, review of *Indiscretions,* p. 194; November 29, 1999, review of *Taking Heart,* p. 54.

E

EBERSHOFF, David 1969-

PERSONAL: Born 1969, in Pasadena, CA. *Education:* Attended Brown University and University of Chicago.

ADDRESSES: Home—106 Suffolk St., New York, NY 10002. *Office*—Random House, 1745 Broadway, New York, NY 10019. *Agent*—Elaine Koster, 55 Central Park West, New York, NY 10023. *E-mail*—DavidEbershoff@aol.com.

CAREER: Modern Library (imprint of Random House), New York, NY, publishing director, 1998—. Princeton University, visiting lecturer. Has taught at New York University and Princeton University.

AWARDS, HONORS: Notable Book Award, *New York Times,* Rosenthal Foundation Award, American Academy of Arts, and Lambda Literary Award, all for *The Danish Girl: A Novel*; Best Books of 2001 designation, *Los Angeles Times,* for *The Rose City: Stories.*

WRITINGS:

The Danish Girl: A Novel, Viking (New York, NY), 2000.
The Rose City: Stories, Viking (New York, NY), 2001.
Pasadena: A Novel, Random House (New York, NY), 2002.

SIDELIGHTS: David Ebershoff is publishing director of Modern Library, one of Random House's most prestigious imprints. Modern Library has operated since 1917 and publishes new books and new editions of classics. Ebershoff's work at Modern Library also helps in his writing career. In a *BookPage* interview with Alden Mudge, Ebershoff reported, "I'm reading books for this list that are really helpful to me as a writer. In that way, my work feeds my writing. But there's little other overlap. I don't learn any publishing tricks that really matter in terms of writing a novel."

Ebershoff's first novel, *The Danish Girl: A Novel,* is based on a true story. It begins in Copenhagen in 1925. Greta Waud, an American portrait painter, is married to Einar Wegener, a Danish landscape painter. One day Greta's model does not show up, and she begs her husband to stand in for the model. Einar obliges and puts on the model's dress and stockings. During the sitting Greta calls Einar the woman's name Lili. Einar finds that he enjoys wearing the dress and stockings and soon begins to dress like a woman on a regular basis. Greta supports her husband's cross-dressing and his life as Lili. Einar realizes he is happiest as Lili and dreams of having a sex change. Out of love for her husband, Greta finds the only doctor who is willing to attempt the surgery. *Interview* contributor Richard Pandiscio observed that "The novel is a bold story of love and longing written as movingly and compassionately as any writer could." Jonathan Shipley in *Book Reporter* praised the novel's "lush prose and emotional insight," adding that *The Danish Girl* "is sure to create a buzz in the literary world."

Indeed, the novel attracted significant attention. *New York Times Book Review* contributor John Burnham Schwartz hailed it as an "arresting first novel" that "conjures a memorable look inside the mysterious black box of human sexuality." He further praised it as "fascinating and humane," and noted that Ebershoff proves himself "a talented writer . . . with a finely developed sense of the power of descriptive details to reveal behavior and mood." In *New Statesman,* Martyn Bedford described the novel as an "affecting and graceful debut," adding that "What Ebershoff exudes, above all, is the sense of a writer who is at one with his writing." A *Publishers Weekly* contributor declared the book a triumph with a "poignant and visionary" conclusion.

Ebershoff's *The Rose City: Stories* is a collection of seven short stories about a gay man and the challenges he faces in his life. A writer for *Publishers Weekly* described the collection as a "bouquet of vivid, hard-edged characters plagued by all-too-human frailties." *Gay & Lesbian Review Worldwide* contributor Karl Woelz hailed *The Rose City* as "one of the most beautifully written books of fiction in recent years."

Pasadena: A Novel, Ebershoff's second novel, has been widely regarded as a West-Coast version of *Wuthering Heights.* Set in the early twentieth century, the novel recounts the life and loves of Linda Stamp, who was born to poor parents in 1903 near San Diego. When her father returns from World War I he brings home with him a handsome young man named Bruder. Linda falls in love with Bruder, but he soon leaves to take a job at an orange ranch in Pasadena owned by the wealthy Willis Poore. Four years later Linda travels to Pasadena to be with Bruder. Willis is rich and that attracts Linda to him. Eventually she marries him, which she soon realizes was a mistake because she is still in love with Bruder. Several reviewers found weaknesses in the novel's plot but admired its majestic setting. As Irina Reyn remarked in the *Pittsburgh Post-Gazette,* "The historical backdrop is the [book's] star." *Los Angeles Times* writer Bettijane Levine described *Pasadena* as "a book of passions, people and places in flux, of the untamed landscape that defined those who lived in it—a force so dominant that it becomes one of the most important characters in the book."

Noting that "Ebershoff seems more in love with the landscape than with the people in it," *Boston Globe* reviewer Ann Harleman found that "the characters in *Pasadena* never quite emerge." Yet Harleman added that the book "is a novel to get lost in, caught up in the melodrama of saving a frosted orchard or a chilly heart." Finding *Pasadena* weakened by a surplus of period detail and by the "somewhat generic feel" of Ebershoff's characters, Martha Bayles in the *New York Times* nevertheless appreciated the novel as a sweeping story of grand themes. *Los Angeles Magazine* contributor Robert Ito made a similar point, describing the book as "grand reading." *Booklist* contributor Elsa Gaztambide concluded that "This is a rich blend of California history in a well-mastered plot that maintains an enduring element of surprise."

BIOGRAPHICAL AND CRITICAL SOURCES:

PERIODICALS

Advocate, March 14, 2000, Robert Plunket, review of *The Danish Girl: A Novel,* p. 64; July 3, 2001, Drew Limsky, review of *The Rose City: Stories,* p. 65.

Book, May, 2001, Chris Borris, review of *The Rose City,* p. 77.

Booklist, December 15, 1999, Neal Wyatt, review of *The Danish Girl,* p. 756; July, 2002, Elsa Gaztambide, review of *Pasadena: A Novel,* p. 1820.

Boston Globe, October 27, 2002, Ann Harleman, "The Conjunction of Fishing and Fate."

Entertainment Weekly, August 2, 2002, Troy Patterson, review of *Pasadena,* p. 68.

Esquire, March, 2000, Sven Birkerts, "Sexual Perversity in Copenhagen," p. 108.

Gay & Lesbian Review Worldwide, summer, 2000, Felice Picano, "The Art of Gender Bending," p. 60; November-December, 2001, Karl Woelz, "Tales of the Unnoticed," p. 40.

Interview, December, 1999, Richard Pandiscio, review of *The Danish Girl,* p. 72.

Lambda Book Report, March, 2000, Daniel Blue, "Changing Places," p. 15; July, 2001, Felice Picano, "Surviving the Disasters of Youth," p. 13.

Library Journal, September 1, 2001, Lisa Rohrbaugh, review of *The Rose City,* p. 237.

Los Angeles Magazine, August, 2002, Robert Ito, "Guts and Glory," p. 104.

Los Angeles Times, August 14, 2002, Bettijane Levine, "Pasadena on His Mind," p. E1.

New Statesman, April 3, 2000, Martyn Bedford, review of *The Danish Girl,* p. 57.

New York Times, July 21, 2002, Martha Bayles, "East of Eden," p. 22.

People, August 12, 2002, Allison Lynn, review of *Pasadena,* p. 49.

Publishers Weekly, November 22, 1999, review of *The Danish Girl,* p. 40; July 17, 2000, John F. Baker, "The Gender-bending Doctor," p. 78; April 16, 2001, review of *The Rose City,* p. 45.

ONLINE

Authorlink, http://www.authorlink.com/ (January 22, 2003), "An Exclusive Authorlink Interview with David Ebershoff, Publishing Director, Modern Library, Random House."

Blurb, http://www.blurb.com.au/ (January 22, 2003), Melissa Timmins, review of *The Rose City: Stories.*

BookPage, http://www.bookpage.com/ (January 22, 2003), Alden Mudge, "Insider Information: Publishing Exec Recreates the Lost World of California."

Book Reporter, http://www.bookreporter.com/ (January 22, 2003), Jonathan Shipley, review of *The Danish Girl.*

Christian Science Monitor online, http://www.csmonitor.com/ (January 22, 2003), Ron Charles, "A Day without Romance Is like a Day without Sunshine."

CNN.com, http://www.cnn.com/ (January 22, 2003), Jayne L. Bowman, "A Man Mistaken in David Ebershoff's *Danish Girl.*"

David Ebershoff Home Page, http:/www.ebershoff.com (November 2003).

Detroit Metro Times online, http://www.metrotimes.com/ (January 22, 2003), Dennis Shea, review of *The Danish Girl.*

LA Weekly online, http://www.laweekly.com/ (January 22, 2003), Michelle Huneven, "David Ebershoff's *Pasadena.*"

MPR Books, http://www.mpr.org/ (January 22, 2003), review of *Pasadena.*

New York Times on the Web, http://www.nytimes.com/ (January 20, 2003), John Burnham Schwartz, review of *The Danish Girl;* Charles Wilson, review of *The Rose City.*

Pittsburgh Post-Gazette, http://www.post-gazette.com/ (January 22, 2003), Irina Reyn, "*Pasadena* by David Ebershoff."

Queer Theory, http://www.queertheory.com/ (January 22, 2003), Sheila Bright, review of *The Danish Girl.*

Random House Web site, http://www.randomhouse.com/ (January 22, 2003), Anson Lang, "David Ebershoff."

EDELMAN, Rob 1949-

PERSONAL: Born March 25, 1949, in New York, NY; son of Sam (a tailor) and Anne (a homemaker; maiden name, Greenberg) Edelman; married Audrey Kupferberg (a film consultant, archivist, lecturer, and writer). *Ethnicity:* "Eastern European-American Jew." *Education:* State University of New York, B.S., 1976. *Politics:* Democrat. *Religion:* Jewish. *Hobbies and other interests:* Playing racquetball, attending baseball games, collecting baseball memorabilia.

ADDRESSES: Home—Amsterdam, NY. *Office*—378 Division St., Amsterdam, NY 12010. *E-mail*—akupferb@nycap.rr.com.

CAREER: Writer and film historian. University at Albany, State University of New York, Albany, lecturer in the history of cinema. WAMC (Northeast) Public Radio, film critic/commentator, 1996—.

MEMBER: Society for American Baseball Research.

AWARDS, HONORS: Top-Ten Internet Book designation, Amazon.com, 1998, for *Baseball on the Web.*

WRITINGS:

WITH WIFE, AUDREY KUPFERBERG

Angela Lansbury: A Life on Stage and Screen, Birch Lane Press (Secaucus, NJ), 1996.

The John Travolta Scrapbook, Citadel Press (Secaucus, NJ), 1997.

Meet the Mertzes: The Life Stories of "I Love Lucy's" Other Couple, Renaissance Books (Los Angeles, CA), 1999.

Matthau: A Life, Taylor Trade Press (Lanham, MD), 2002.

The Vietnam War, (children's book; part of "People at the Center of" series) Blackbirch Press (San Diego, CA), 2004.

OTHER

The Great Baseball Films: From "Right off the Bat" to "A League of Their Own," Citadel Press (Secaucus, NJ), 1994.

Baseball on the Web, MIS Press (New York, NY), 1997.

Associate editor/contributing editor of *Leonard Maltin's Movie and Video Guide,* 1981—. Contributor to books on films, filmmaking, and popular culture, including *Leonard Maltin's Movie Encyclopedia; Leonard Maltin's Family Film Guide; St. James Film Directors Encyclopedia,* edited by Andrew Sarris; *Political Companion to American Film,* edited by Gary Crowdus; *Total Baseball,* edited by John Thorn and others; *International Film Guide,* edited by Peter Cowie; *Total Baseball Catalog,* edited by David Pietrusza and others; *International Dictionary of Films and Filmmakers; Women Filmmakers and Their Films; The Stars Appear,* edited by Richard Dyer MacCann; *The Whole Film Sourcebook,* edited by Leonard Maltin; *Dictionary of Literary Biography: American Sportswriters; St. James Women Filmmakers Encyclopedia; St. James Encyclopedia of Popular Culture; Essays on Baseball and American Culture: Across the Diamond; Bowling, Beatniks, and Bell-Bottoms: Pop Culture of Twentieth-Century America; Scribner Encyclopedia of American Lives;* and *Fashion Costume and Culture.* Contributor of articles to numerous magazines and newspapers, including *New York Times, New York Post, Washington Post, American Film, Baseball America, National Pastime: A Review of Baseball History, Baseball Research Journal, Cineaste, Ballet News, Forward, American Movie Classics, Chaplin, Independent, Culturefront, Sightlines, Filmmaker,* and *American Arts.*

WORK IN PROGRESS: A memoir of Ida Lupino by Bridget Duff, daughter of Lupino and Howard Duff, cowritten with Audrey Kupferberg.

SIDELIGHTS: Rob Edelman is a film and television historian whose works include biographies of such celebrities as Angela Lansbury and Walter Matthau. A lecturer on film history at the State University of New York, Edelman is also a contributor to numerous books on film. He often collaborates with his wife, film archivist Audrey Kupferberg.

Edelman's first book was *The Great Baseball Films: From "Right off the Bat" to "A League of Their Own,"* which chronicles baseball films from the silent era to the present. Each chapter emphasizes a different aspect of baseball films, including sections on drama and comedy, race and gender, biographies of sports legends, and themes such as "the triumph of the underdog" and "loss and redemption."

In *Meet the Mertzes: The Life Stories of "I Love Lucy's" Other Couple,* Edelman and Kupferberg delve into the private lives of Vivian Vance and William Frawley, who played the Ricardos' neighbors Fred and Ethel on the classic television comedy. In addition to anecdotes about their years on the "Lucy" show, *Meet the Mertzes* examines the actors' early careers and discusses their legendary off-camera animosity.

In two additional biographies, Edelman and Kupferberg offer extended discussions of film actors Walter Matthau and Angela Lansbury. In *Angela Lansbury: A Life on Stage and Screen,* the pair trace the award-winning actress's career through more than fifty films and the long-running television mystery series *Murder She Wrote.* In *Matthau: A Life,* which a *Washington Post* reviewer called "an affectionate, celebratory new biography," the authors discuss Matthau's triumphs as an actor, his unstoppable addictions to gambling and smoking, his bitter relationship with fellow actor Barbra Streisand, and his decades-long friendship with Jack Lemmon.

Edelman told *CA:* "I have always been fascinated by the written word and the power of the written word to educate, inform, and influence. It never has been enough for me to observe an event, read a book or newspaper, or see a film. I have always been compelled to describe the event and put forth my feelings and opinions about what I have read or seen. I wrote for and edited my high school newspaper, and began my career working on a weekly paper in Brooklyn, New York. Here, and in my subsequent work as a journalist, film critic/commentator, and biographer, I have been able to express myself and my love of the written word. Along the way, I have also had the opportunity to meet and interview hundreds of fascinating people.

"More than anything else, I enjoy writing about film. From my childhood on, I have always had a passion for film. After a lifetime of watching, studying, reviewing—and being endlessly captivated by—films, I have come to believe that motion pictures play essential roles in forming our perceptions and impacting on our world views. Movies can make us think and feel. They can teach us lessons about life and history. They can reflect on our changing culture: what American and world culture was like in 1920, 1940, 1960, 1980, and today.

"In recent years, I have also been writing about various aspects of baseball. I have always been a baseball fan-atic; now, I feel extremely lucky to be able to write about the sport.

"When I write, I try to express myself simply and directly. I have no one favorite author and can cite no specific writer who has influenced me. I am at my best in the very early morning. When I am involved in a lengthy project, I will begin work at 6 a.m. or so and research or write non-stop well into the afternoon.

"The books I have written that I like best are *The Great Baseball Films* and *Matthau: A Life.* Because baseball and film are my great passions, it was an honor and a treat to be able to research and write about the manner in which the sport has been portrayed on the screen across the decades. I loved researching and writing about Walter Matthau. In particular, I relished exploring his childhood on New York's Lower East Side during the 1920s and 1930s and his involvement, however peripheral, in the Yiddish theater. Putting together the Matthau book allowed me to be in touch with my ethnicity and my roots as a child/grandchild of immigrants."

BIOGRAPHICAL AND CRITICAL SOURCES:

PERIODICALS

Bergen County Record (Bergen, NJ), November 3, 2002, Bill Ervolino, review of *Matthau: A Life.*

Entertainment Weekly, November 12, 1999, Charles Winecoff, review of *Meet the Mertzes: The Life Stories of "I Love Lucy's" Other Couple,* p. 74.

Library Journal, May 1, 1994, John Maxymuk, review of *The Great Baseball Films from "Right off the Bat" to "A League of Their Own,"* p. 105.

Palm Beach Post, October 20, 2002, Scott Eyman, review of *Matthau: A Life.*

Publishers Weekly, September 23, 2002, review of *Matthau: A Life,* p. 61.

St. Petersburg Times, October 20, 2002, Lorrie P. Lykins, review of *Matthau: A Life.*

Washington Post Book World, April 23, 1995, review of *The Great Baseball Films,* p. 12, December 22, 2002, John DiLeo, review of *Matthau: A Life,* p. 9.

* * *

EDWARDS, Kim 1958-

PERSONAL: Born May 4, 1958, in Killeen, TX; married Thomas Clayton, 1987; children: two daughters. *Education:* Attended Auburn Community College; Colgate University, B.A., 1981; University of Iowa, M.F.A., 1983, M.A. (linguistics), 1987.

ADDRESSES: Home—Lexington, KY. *Office*—Department of English, University of Kentucky, 1355 Patterson Office Tower 0027, Lexington, KY 40506. *E-mail*—Edwards@uky.edu.

CAREER: Fiction writer and educator. Visiting professor, University of Kentucky, 2003. Taught in M.F.A. programs at Washington University and Warren Wilson College; spent five years teaching in Malaysia, Japan, and Cambodia.

AWARDS, HONORS: Pushcart Prize, for short story "The Way It Felt to Be Falling"; PEN/Hemingway Award finalist, for *The Secrets of a Fire King;* National Magazine Award for Fiction; Nelson Algren Award, 1990, for short story "Sky Juice"; grants from National Endowment for the Arts, Pennsylvania Council on the Arts, Seaside Institute, Kentucky Arts Council, and Kentucky Foundation for Women; Whiting Writer's Award, 2002.

WRITINGS:

The Secrets of a Fire King: Stories, W. W. Norton (New York, NY), 1997.

Stories have appeared in periodicals, including *Paris Review, Redbook, Michigan Quarterly Review, North American Review, Iowa Woman, Threepenny Review, Chicago Tribune, Ploughshares,* and *Zoetrope.*

WORK IN PROGRESS: A novel, *Capturing Light.*

SIDELIGHTS: Kim Edwards has published many short stories in journals that include the *Paris Review, Redbook, Chicago Tribune,* and *Ploughshares.* She wrote her first short story in a fiction workshop while a student at Colgate University. "The Way It Felt to Be Falling," originally published in *Threepenny Review,* won the Pushcart Prize and is included in Edwards's first book, *The Secrets of a Fire King: Stories.*

The Secrets of a Fire King, which Nina Sonenberg in the *New York Times Book Review* deemed an "accomplished" debut, presents stories that deal with a wide range of themes and settings. Many refer to Asia, where Edwards spent five years traveling and teaching. In "Spring, Mountain, Sea," for example, a U.S. soldier's Asian bride learns about American foods and customs from the couple's neighbors, but their response to her gift of gratitude turns her away from the American culture. In "Gold," a young man's life is affected when gold is discovered in his Malaysian village, while "The Way It Felt to Be Falling" tells how a young woman learns about her inner strength when she suddenly decides to attempt a sky dive with a friend. *Chicago Tribune Books* contributor Patricia Lear described this story as sophisticated and brilliantly constructed. "The stories are impeccable, a treasure," wrote Lear, who observed that each piece "possesses the breadth of a novel." In the *Hudson Review* critic Tom Wilhelmus wrote tha,t "Rich in detail and at home with abstract ideas, Kim Edwards' stories mark an impressive beginning for a talented new storyteller."

BIOGRAPHICAL AND CRITICAL SOURCES:

PERIODICALS

Hudson Review, autumn, 1997, Tom Wilhelmus, review of *The Secrets of a Fire King: Stories,* p. 527.

Library Journal, April 15, 1997, Ellen R. Cohen, review of *The Secrets of a Fire King,* p. 122.

New York Times Book Review, April 20, 1997, Nina Sonenberg, review of *The Secrets of a Fire King,* p. 20.

Publishers Weekly, February 24, 1997, review of *The Secrets of a Fire King,* p. 64.

Tribune Books (Chicago, IL), June 1, 1997, Patricia Lear, "Getting it Right," p. 4.

ONLINE

W.W. Norton Web site, http://www.wwnorton.com/ (January 22, 2003), review of *The Secrets of a Fire King.*

Zoetrope Web site, http://www.all-story.com/ (April 3, 2003), "Kim Edwards."

* * *

ELDER, Larry (A.) 1952-

PERSONAL: Born 1952, in Los Angeles, CA; son of Randolph and Viola Elder. *Education:* Brown University, B.S. (political science), 1974; University of Michigan Law School, J.D., 1977. *Politics:* Independent.

ADDRESSES: *Office*—KABC, 3321 South LaCienega Blvd., Los Angeles, CA 90016. *E-mail*—sage@larryelder.com.

CAREER: Laurence A. Elder and Associates, founder, 1980—; Public Broadcasting System affiliate, Cleveland, OH, host of *Fabric* (monthly program) and *Larry Elder Show* (weekly talk show); KABC Radio, Los Angeles, CA, host of *The Larry Elder Show,* 1994—; *Moral Court* (television show), host. Regularly appears as a commentator on national news networks such as CNN, MSNBC, and Fox News Channel. Worked as a lawyer at a large law firm in Cleveland, OH.

AWARDS, HONORS: Marconi Award nomination, National Association of Broadcasters, 2002.

WRITINGS:

The Ten Things You Can't Say in America, St. Martin's Press (New York, NY), 2000.

Showdown: Confronting Bias, Lies, and the Special Interests That Divide America, St. Martin's (New York, NY), 2002.

Contributor to journals, including *Miami Herald, Tampa Tribune, Chicago Tribune* and *Akron Beacon Journal.*

SIDELIGHTS: Larry Elder is a nationally syndicated radio talk-show host known for his controversial views on political and social issues. His broadcasting career began when Elder was a guest on Los Angeles-based KABC Radio in 1992. The station management liked what they heard and offered Elder a job. In 1994 Elder began his talk show with KABC and within a year his show was moved to the afternoon drive slot, where he has been a ratings leader since. In addition to contributing numerous articles to major newspapers, Elder has written two books about issues facing African Americans.

In *The Ten Things You Can't Say in America* Elder takes on ten different political beliefs that Americans, he claims, are afraid to admit. He argues, for example, that blacks are more racist than whites, that there is no glass ceiling, that America is losing the war on drugs, that Republicans are no different than Democrats, and more. *Dartmouth Review* contributor Stella Baer commented, "His pellucid prose, witty sarcasm, and brave ratiocinations make *The Ten Things You Can't Say in America* engaging and informative." In *U.S. News and World Report* John Leo gave Elder "full credit for courage and candor," pointing out that, despite intense criticism from the "academic and media establishments," his views actually "seem close to those of many black Americans." A *Publishers Weekly* reviewer described the book as a "bluntly candid manifesto," adding that, despite prescriptions that may be considered "simplistic," the book is refreshingly honest and direct.

Explaining the background for his thinking in a *Reason* interview, Elder noted that his own father, who worked three jobs while attending night school to complete his high-school equivalency certificate, was his most important role model. His father voted Republican, but his mother was a liberal Democrat. "Over the dinner table, I would hear both sides," he said. "I think Republicans and Democrats essentially have to very simple philosophies. Republicans believe hard work wins. Democrats believe the system is rigged." Asked about affirmative action, which he has criticized, Elder responded that "America owes a debt to black people" that was never paid. Instead, he explained, America used affirmative action to compensate blacks. Though this was historically necessary, the practice has major flaws. "I am prepared to admit that I benefited from affirmative action," he added. "I am not prepared to admit that I would have been jobless, homeless, and illiterate had affirmative action not been in effect."

Elder again courts controversy in *Showdown: Confronting Bias, Lies, and the Special Interests That Divide America.* In this book he voices his opinion that the September 11th attacks happened because the government was too busy with domestic issues to concentrate adequately on national defense. He criticizes programs intended to combat such problems as sexism and racism, and argues for less government intervention in private affairs. "Many readers will agree with some points on government intrusion, but only readers with similar political views will appreciate his arguments," concluded *Booklist* contributor Vanessa Bush. A *Publishers Weekly* contributor, warning that the book is "not for the timid and weak of mind," found Elder's voice "refreshing" despite the controversy of his views.

BIOGRAPHICAL AND CRITICAL SOURCES:

PERIODICALS

Booklist, August, 2000, Ray Olson, review of *The Ten Things You Can't Say in America,* p. 2085; October 15, 2002, Vanessa Bush, review of *Showdown: Confronting Bias, Lies, and the Special Interests That Divide America,* p. 367.

Insight on the News, January 1, 2001, Julia Duin, review of *The Ten Things You Can't Say in America,* p. 27.

Publishers Weekly, July 24, 2000, review of *The Ten Things You Can't Say in America,* p. 76; September 9, 2002, review of *Showdown,* p. 57.

Reason, April, 1996, Nick Gillespie, Steve Kurtz, "Elder Statesman," p. 44; May, 2001, Steve Kurtz, "Inside Outsiders: Three Media Mavericks Come to Term with Success," p. 62.

U.S. News & World Report, October 16, 2000, Mike Tharp, "This Elder Gets Respect," p. 16; January 15, 2001, John Leo, "The Black Dissent," p. 11.

ONLINE

Capitalism online, http://capmag.com/ (January 22, 2003), "About Larry Elder."

Dartmouth Review online, http://www.dartreview.com/ (January 22, 2003), Stella Baer, review of *The Ten Things You Can't Say in America.*

Jefferson Review online, http://www.jeffersonreview.com/ (January 22, 2003), Mark Webster, review of *The Ten Things You Can't Say in America.*

Larry Elder Web site, http://www.larryelder.com/ (January 22, 2003), "About the Sage."

TownHall.com, http://www.townhall.com/ (January 22, 2003), "Larry Elder."*

* * *

ELDERKIN, Susan 1968-

PERSONAL: Born 1968. *Education:* Cambridge University, B.A., 1991; University of East Anglia, M.A., 1994. *Hobbies and other interests:* Yoga, running, traveling, hiking, camping.

ADDRESSES: *Home*—London, England. *Agent*—Clare Alexander, Gillon Aitken Assoc., 29 Fernshaw Rd., London SW10 0TG, England.

CAREER: Novelist, freelance journalist, and teacher of creative writing. Worked variously as an ice-cream seller and as an English teacher in a Slovakian shoe factory.

MEMBER: Society of Authors, PEN.

AWARDS, HONORS: Betty Trask Award for first novel, 2000, for *Sunset over Chocolate Mountains;* named one of *Granta* magazine's Twenty Best Young British Novelists of the decade, 2003.

WRITINGS:

Sunset over Chocolate Mountains, Atlantic Monthly Press (New York, NY), 2000.

The Voices, Grove Press (New York, NY), 2003.

WORK IN PROGRESS: A screenplay of *Sunset over Chocolate Mountains;* a third novel.

SIDELIGHTS: British writer Susan Elderkin wanted to tell stories since before she could write. A freelance journalist-turned-novelist, her first novel, *Sunset over Chocolate Mountains,* is set in the Arizona desert, where obese, retiring Theobald Moon has escaped after the death of his mother. Exploring themes of love and pain, it is a dark story filled with eccentric characters. According to reviewers, the most notable aspects of the book are Elderkin's richly descriptive writing and acute sense of place.

Theobald Moon leaves his native Great Britain to live in a mobile home, plant a cactus garden, eat candy, and practice yoga in the desert. He also drinks a glass of his own urine every morning. Despite his hermetic habits, Moon finds new friends, including the cowboy Jersey, who teaches him how to survive in the desert. A young couple from Slovakia, a shoemaker named Eva and her fugitive-murderer lover Tibor, are traveling through the area when their ice-cream truck breaks down, and they become Theobald's new neighbors. Jumping forward in time, we find Theobald bringing up a young daughter, Josie. As the girl grows up, her—and our—need to know about her origins creates the dramatic tension.

Reviewers hailed the novel as the work of a skilled new writer, although critics commented on the bleakness of much of the tale. Cheryl L. Conway commented in *Library Journal* that the novel "contains elements of mystery and beauty as well as cruelty and death." She concluded, "while well written, it is a relentlessly grim tale, and the ending does not satisfy." In the London *Observer,* Anna Shapiro observed that *Sunset over Chocolate Mountain* is "excellently written, but not exactly literature" and credited the author with "entertaining and moving" readers with a combination of "sticky love and harsh callousness." A *Publishers Weekly* reviewer called the book a "beguiling and unsettling tale" and compared Moon to the hero of *A Confederacy of Dunces* by John Kennedy Toole. *Booklist*'s Grace Fill felt the "captivating" story is "well written with memorable characters" and warned of "an unexpected chilling conclusion."

Critics with special praise for the book's imaginative descriptions included a *Kirkus Reviews* writer, who remarked that the novel is "impressive if overly self-conscious . . . rife with imagery and eccentricity." And in *Visage online,* Umbereen Beg Mirza enjoyed the book as "a breath of fresh air." Mirza concluded, "Elderkin's forte is not her plot . . . but her prose. This is some of the best new writing around."

Elderkin's second novel, *The Voices,* is also set in a remote desert location—this time the blood-red landscape of the Australian bush. It tells the story of a thirteen-year-old boy, Billy Saint, growing up in a harsh outback community. Alienated from his mother Crystal, a woman who considers herself "too sexy" to be living in such a remote location, and his father, Stan, who is more interested in the underbellies of his classic cars than his son, Billy looks to the landscape, and the local Aborigines for the meaning he senses is missing from his life. One day he hears the haunting song of an Aboriginal girl which tugs at something deep inside him—something larger and more powerful than himself. She has "sung Billy up," and he is destined to love her forever.

In an Alice Springs hospital ten years later, we find Billy recovering from gruesome wounds of a mysterious origin. Only Cecily, the Aboriginal nurse, understands the significance of these wounds, and what Billy means by the 'voices' he hears in his head. What unravels is a mesmerising account of the relationship between a man, the land he loves, and the spirits of the land that are struggling to be heard before it is too late. Stevie Davies, in an *Independent* review, called *The Voices* "a page-turner partly because we are never sure where we are, but we want to know, or what she is going to do next. For sheer narrative invention and wanton brio, [Elderkin] is without an equal."

Elderkin told *CA:* "Both my novels so far have started with place. In my early twenties I lived for a while in Los Angeles, and from there I discovered the deserts of the American southwest. One day I lay on my back on a granite boulder in Joshua Tree National [Park], looking up and the extraordinary expanse of clear blue sky that unravelled down to the horizon in every direction, and knew that the desert had got under my skin. I promised myself I would come back one day and write about it.

"The story of *The Voices* came to me while on the legendary Australian train, the Ghan express, which goes from Adelaide in the south right into the heart of Australia at Alice Springs. I had heard about the Aboriginal tradition whereby women sang up the man they wanted, casting a sort of spell on him that hooked him forever. Later, during the same trip, I travelled around the Kimberley—harsh, remote cattle station country right up in the northwest of Australia, where not even many Australians go. Here the heat in the dry season builds and builds toward a wet season, when torrential rains come down so fast that the rivers flood and cut communities off for months. The population of the Kimberley is fifty percent Aboriginal, but I found that even here Aboriginal traditions were no longer passed down any more—the younger generations were often not interested, wanting to live like the white Australians, and shunning the old ways.

"I find myself drawn to these remote landscapes because they are places where you become very aware of the thin line between life and death, which fine-tunes your sensibilities and makes every decision you make vital. The human inhabitants of these places tend to have adapted to the difficult climactic conditions in much the same way as plants do—they are tough-skinned, they are loners, they are sometimes prickly and distorted, and above all they are acutely tuned in to the natural elements around them. This sensitivity gives rise to a heightened spiritual sense, opening up a world where other forces operate. City people have lost their connection with this sense of the spiritual—by which I mean being in touch with our instinctive, animal natures rather than any ritualised, formal religion. This is the landscape within which I like to work. It gives me room to let my imagination go, and to make occasional forays into the realm of the fantastic."

BIOGRAPHICAL AND CRITICAL SOURCES:

PERIODICALS

Booklist, May 1, 2000, Grace Fill, review of *Sunset over Chocolate Mountains,* p. 1650.

Independent (London, England), 31 May 2003, Stevie Davies, review of *The Voices.*

Kirkus Reviews, May 1, 2000, review of *Sunset over Chocolate Mountains,* p. 580; September 1, 2003, review of *The Voices,* p. 1089.

Library Journal, June 1, 2000, Cheryl L. Conway, review of *Sunset over Chocolate Mountains,* p. 196.

Observer, March 12, 2000, Anna Shapiro, review of *Sunset over Chocolate Mountains.*

Publishers Weekly, May 29, 2000, review of *Sunset over Chocolate Mountains,* p. 49.

Spectator, June 7, 2003, Miranda France, review of *The Voices,* p. 37.

Times Literary Supplement, June 20, 2003, review of *The Voices,* p. 26.

ONLINE

Visage, http://visagepk.com/ (April 29, 2003), Umbereen Beg Mirza, review of *Sunset over Chocolate Mountains.*

ELINWOOD, Ellae

PERSONAL: Female.

ADDRESSES: *Home*—Ashland, OR. *Agent*—c/o Transformation through Reflection, 875 Oak St., Ashland, OR 97520. *E-mail*—elinwood@aol.com.

CAREER: Author, speaker, and educator.

WRITINGS:

Timeless Face: Free Your Face from the Signs of Stress and Time in Thirty Days, St. Martin's Griffin (New York, NY), 1997, published as *Timeless Face: Thirty Days to a Younger You through Face Reading, Acupressure, and Toning,* 1999.

(With Gregge Tiffen) *The Everything Numerology Book: Discover Your Potential for Love, Success, and Health through the Science of Numbers,* Adams Media Corporation (Avon, MA), 2003.

The Everything Tai Chi and Qi Gong Book: Enjoy Good Health, Longevity, and a Stress-free Life, Adams Media Corporation (Avon, MA), 2003.

Stay Young with Tai Chi, Charles E. Tuttle Co. (Boston, MA), in press.

Also author, with Gregge Tiffen, of *Seven Virtues: Daily Affirmations for Body and Soul.*

SIDELIGHTS: Ellae Elinwood has spent many years as a hatha yoga instructor teaching privately as well as at colleges, universities, and fitness spas. She pioneered a yoga program specifically designed for elderly men and women, and has been a teacher of Japanese shiatsu massage, *Touch for Health,* applied kinesiology, and stress management. Elinwood draws upon these varied experiences as well as her years of study in authoring several instructional books on caring for both the body and the mind.

Elinwood developed a comprehensive facial toning program called Timeless Face after years of study in yoga and Chinese face reading. The daily program, which consists of a series of exercises that can be performed in only five minutes, is outlined in *Timeless Face: Thirty Days to a Younger You through Face Reading, Acupressure, and Toning.* On her Web site, Elinwood claimed: "If the eyes are the window to the soul then the face is the expression of a lifetime."

Timeless Face was followed by Elinwood's second book, *The Everything Numerology Book: Discover Your Potential for Love, Success, and Health through the Science of Numbers.* The book, coauthored by Gregge Tiffen, is a guide to help readers tap into the "science" of numbers to improve many aspects of their personal and professional life.

Drawing upon her experience as a student and teacher of Chinese wisdom and martial arts, Elinwood has also authored *The Everything Tai Chi and Qi Gong Book: Enjoy Good Health, Longevity, and a Stress-free Life.* Describing the book as an introductory source to these arts, Anton Borja stated in a review for *Acupuncture.com* that *The Everything Tai Chi and Qi Gong Book* "surprisingly has quite a lot to offer to upper level students as well." The reviewer added that "if there is a problem with this book it would have to be the lack of pictures dedicated to the practices," but concluded: "you are certain to get valuable tips to better your practice every time you open it."

BIOGRAPHICAL AND CRITICAL SOURCES:

ONLINE

Acupuncture.com, http://www.acupuncture.com/ (June 10, 2003), Anton Borja, review of *The Everything Tai Chi and Qi Gong Book: Enjoy Good Health, Longevity, and a Stress-free Life.*

Ellae Elinwood Web site, http://www.ellaeelinwood.com (July 2, 2003).

* * *

ETTELSON, Trudy (G.) 1947-

PERSONAL: Born September 23, 1947, in Cleveland, OH; daughter of Jack Gottlieb (a barrel reconditioning supervisor) and Rose Biales (a homemaker); married Richard Ettelson (a rabbi and psychologist), August 19, 1973. *Ethnicity:* "Jewish." *Education:* Case Western Reserve, B.A. (summa cum laude), 1969; Yale

Graduate School, Ph.D. (French), 1974; HUC-JIR, M.A. (Judaica), 1980. *Politics:* Independent. *Religion:* Jewish. *Hobbies and other interests:* Creative self-help, twelve steps, religion, and literature.

ADDRESSES: Home—PMB #340, 4141 Ball Rd., Cypress, CA 90630. *Office*—DeVry University—Pomona, 901 Corporate Center Dr., Pomona, CA 91768-2642. *E-mail*—trudye2@juno.com.

CAREER: DeVry University—Pomona, Pomona, CA, associate professor of communications, 1997—. Teacher at schools, including Chaminade University, University of Chicago, and Yale University. Writing and workshop consultant; affiliated with www.doctortrudy.com and the Outdoor Circle, Honolulu, HI.

MEMBER: Modern Language Association, National Council of Teachers of English, National Writers Association.

AWARDS, HONORS: America's Best awards, for teleplay, 1996, screenplay, 1998, and short story, 1999.

WRITINGS:

Soul Stories and Steps, Alef Design Group (Los Angeles, CA), 1994.

By Golly (children's play), produced by Lakewood Theater Guild, 1996.

Adventures in Writing: From Glitches to Glories, Coctrubooks (Cypress, CA), 2001.

Also author of screenplays *Lovesick,* 1992, *Felicity* (based on Gustav Flaubert's *Un coeur simple*), 1994, and *J. J.,* 1995; author of novel *Seven Nights from Death,* 1995, and of children's book *Golly and Me,* 1996.

WORK IN PROGRESS: Research on narrative self-therapy, writing as healing, and creativity and mental health.

SIDELIGHTS: Trudy Ettelson told *CA:* "Writing is a healing, creative art that is capable of infusing all of our lives with pleasure and spirituality. *Soul Stories and Steps* explores the relationship between ancient Biblical stories and *midrash,* the retelling of those stories with a modern twist. *Adventures in Writing* explores the relationship between fiction and nonfiction in the writing process. It seeks to give a voice to the writer in all of us and to make the learning of grammar a spiritual process that is fun and entertaining.

"My students at DeVry have inspired me to give voice to the creative urges within us that long to be expressed and shared with others. A student appendix of writing glories illustrates the application of spiritual steps and stories that entertain as they teach how to write. As our Creator spins the stories of our lives, we become co-creators in the writing process. As we polish our craft, we grow through challenges that used to baffle us. Always, change within effects change without.

"The twelve Steps often provide a spiritual foundation for the writing process. Writing helps us understand the human condition and those parts of the human condition that are Divine. Whatever wounds we bear as human beings can be healed through writing, for writing is always a solution."

F

FAY, Terence J. 1932-

PERSONAL: Born June 28, 1932, in Syracuse, NY; son of Hugh (in sales) and Susan Agnes (a homemaker; maiden name, Dunne) Fay. *Ethnicity:* "Irish." *Education:* Gonzaga University, B.A. and M.A., 1961; University of Toronto—Regis College, M.A., 1967; Georgetown University, Ph.D., 1974. *Politics:* Liberal. *Religion:* Roman Catholic.

ADDRESSES: *Home*—41 Earl St., Toronto, Ontario, Canada M4Y 1M4. *Office*—508 History Office, St. Augustine's Seminary, University of Toronto, 10 St. Mary St., Toronto, Ontario, Canada M4Y 1P9. *E-mail*—terence.fay@utoronto.ca.

CAREER: Regiopolis College, Kingston, Ontario, Canada, teacher, 1950-53; University of Manitoba, Winnipeg, Manitoba, Canada, assistant professor at St. Paul's College, 1971-79; University of Winnipeg, Winnipeg, assistant professor, 1979-80; University of Manitoba, assistant professor at St. Paul's College, 1981-84; Mount Allison University, Sackville, New Brunswick, Canada, assistant professor, 1980-81; University of Toronto, Toronto, Ontario, Canada, lecturer at St. Augustine's Seminary, 1988—. Our Lady of Lourdes Church, Toronto, associate pastor; Engaged Encounter Weekends, animator. Canadian Institute of Jesuit Studies, research director for *Dictionary of Jesuit Biography: Ministry to English Canada, 1842-1987. Military service:* U.S. Navy, 1950-54.

MEMBER: Canadian Historical Association, Canadian Catholic Historical Association, Historia Ecclesiae Catholicae Canadensis, American Catholic Historical Association, Associates of Ultimate Reality and Meaning.

AWARDS, HONORS: Ching Award, Dr. Gemma Ching, 1990; Jesuit Award, Jesuit Fathers of Upper Canada, 1995; Jackman Award for public service, Jackman Foundation, 1996; Golden Alumni Award, Le Moyne College, 2003.

WRITINGS:

(Editor) *One Hundred Years: Our Lady of Lourdes Church,* Griffin House, 1991.

(Editor, with John Duggan) *Spiritual Roots: Historical Essays on the Roman Catholic Archdiocese of Toronto at 150 Years of Age,* Lourdes (Toronto, Ontario, Canada), 1991.

A History of Canadian Catholics, McGill-Queen's University Press (Kingston, Ontario, Canada), 2002.

Contributor to books, including *The Religions of Canadians,* edited by Jamie Scott, Oxford University Press (New York, NY), 2004; also contributor to dictionaries. Contributor to periodicals, including *American Review of Canadian Studies, Urban History Review, Compass: Jesuit Journal, Irish Messenger of the Sacred Heart, Studies: Irish Quarterly Review, Ultimate Reality and Meaning: Interdisciplinary Studies in the Philosophy of Understanding,* and *Historical Studies.* Editor, *CCHA Bulletin,* 1991-2002.

SIDELIGHTS: Terence J. Fay told *CA:* "I read and write history for the pleasure of doing so. As a teacher in the classroom, I find it is very important to put down in writing what I wish to talk about to the students. As French novelist André Gide once said, 'I do not know what I think until I see what I say.' Words on the page are important to me. They help me to clarify my thoughts.

"I have taught political, diplomatic, and religious history. All three fields delight me when I hear or read about them. Thomas Bokenkotter, who published *A Concise History of the Catholic Church,* inspired me greatly to do my recent book on the history of Canadian Catholics. I believe history must be vividly written to be good history and to assist the reader's memory.

"My writing method is the 'bygosh bygad' method of jumping in and doing it. It is learning by doing. Every article or book demands different methods or different models.

"By the experience of writing and editing, I have learned a more sophisticated grammar and syntax in my writing style, which makes the text more easy to read. It benefits both the author and the reader."

* * *

FINCH, Peter 1947-

PERSONAL: Born March 6, 1947, in Cardiff, Wales; son of Stanley Arthur (a DHSS inspector) and Marjorie Noele (a telephonist) Finch; married; wife's name Valerie (divorced 1995); partner of Sue Wilshere; children: two sons, one daughter. *Ethnicity:* "Welsh." *Education:* Glamorgan College of Technology, diploma (municipal administration). *Religion:* "Informal Buddhist." *Hobbies and other interests:* "Walking, history, music (specialist interest in old rock and roll, alternative country, ambient)."

ADDRESSES: Home—19 Southminster Rd., Roath, Cardiff CF23 5AT, Wales. *Office*—Mount Stuart House, Third Floor, Mount Stuart Square, Cardiff CF10 5FQ, Wales. *Agent*—Paul Beasley, 57 Productions, 57 Effingham Rd., Lea Green, London SE12 8NT, England. *E-mail*—contact@peterfinch.co.uk.

CAREER: Poet, writer, editor, and critic. Worked variously as a tent and flag maker and payroll clerk; Oriel Bookshop, Cardiff, Wales, manager, 1973-98; Yr Academi Gymreig (Welsh national literature promotion agency and society for writers), chief executive, 1998—. Founder and former editor of *Second Aeon* (journal), Cardiff, founding member of Cabaret 246, Cardiff; former member of musical trio Horse's Mouth.

MEMBER: Poetry Society, Yr Academi Gymreig (Welsh Academy; fellow), Rising Dragon Tai Chi.

AWARDS, HONORS: Welsh Arts Council grants and awards, 1968-69, for "No Walls" poetry readings, 1968, for *Second Aeon,* and 1969-70, for experimental poetry.

WRITINGS:

POETRY

(With Stephen Morris) *Wanted for Writing Poetry,* Second Aeon Publications (Cardiff, Wales), 1968.

Pieces of the Universe, Second Aeon Publications (Cardiff, Wales), 1969.

The Cycle of the Suns, Ethos Publications (Glasgow, Scotland), 1969.

Concrete Poet, Vertigo (Cardiff, Wales), 1970.

Beyond the Silence, Vertigo (Cardiff, Wales), 1970.

An Alteration in the Way I Breathe, Quickest Way Out, 1970.

(With Jeanne Rushton) *The Edge of Tomorrow,* BB Books, 1971.

The End of the Vision, John Johns Ltd., 1971.

Whitesung, Aquila, 1972.

Antarktika, Writers Forum (London, England), 1972.

Trowch Eich Radio 'Mlaen, Writers Forum (London, England), 1977.

Connecting Tubes, Writers Forum (London, England), 1980.

O Poems, Writers Forum (London, England), 1981.

Blues and Heartbreakers, Galloping Dog Press (Newcastle upon Tyne, England), 1981.

Some Music and a Little War, Rivelin Grapheme (London, England), 1984.

On Criticism, Writers Forum (London, England), 1984.

Reds in the Bed, Galloping Dog Press (Newcastle upon Tyne, England), 1985.

For Jack Kerouac: Poems on His Death, second revised edition, Writers Forum (London, England), 1987.

Selected Poems, Poetry Wales Press (Chester Springs, PA), 1987.

Make, Galloping Dog Press (Newcastle upon Tyne, England), 1990.

The Cheng Man Ch'ing Variations, Writers Forum (London, England), 1990.

Poems for Ghosts, Seren (Bridgend, Wales), 1991.

Five Hundred Cobbings, Writers Forum (London, England), 1994.

The Spell, Writers Forum (London, England), 1995.

Useful, Seren (Bridgend, Wales), 1997.

Dauber, Writers Forum (London, England), 1997.

Antibodies, Stride (Exeter, Devon, England), 1997.

Food, Seren (Bridgend, Wales), 2001.

Extrememly Useful: New and Selected Poems, Seren (Bridgend, Wales), 2003.

EDITOR

(With others), *No Walls Broadsheets,* Second Aeon Publications (Cardiff, Wales), 1970.

Typewriter Poems, Something Else Press, 1972.

How to Learn Welsh: A Guide Book for the Adult Learner, C. Davies (Swansea, Wales), 1978.

(With Meic Stephens) *Green Horse: An Anthology by Young Poets of Wales,* C. Davies (Swansea, Wales), 1978.

Small Presses and Little Magazines of the UK and Ireland: An Address List, thirteenth revised edition, Oriel (Cardiff, Wales), 1997.

OTHER

Blats, Second Aeon Publications (Cardiff, Wales), 1973.

Getting Your Poetry Published, Association of Little Presses, 1973.

Between Thirty-five and Forty-two (stories), Alun (Port Talbot, Wales), 1982.

How to Publish Your Poetry, Allison & Busby (London, England), 1985, revised edition, 1998.

How to Publish Yourself, Allison & Busby (London, England), 1987, revised edition, 1997.

Publishing Yourself: Not Too Difficult after All, Association of Little Presses, 1989.

The Poetry Business, Seren (Bridgend, Wales), 1994.

Real Cardiff, Seren (Bridgend, Wales), 2002.

Contributor to anthologies, magazines, and journals, including *PN Review, Ambit, Poetry Review, Stand, Poetry Wales,* and *Planet;* compiler of poetry section of annual *Writer's Handbook,* Macmillan, and *Black's Writers' and Artists Yearbook,* A & C Black. Recordings include *Big Band Dance Music,* Balsam Flex, 1980; *Dances Interdites,* Balsam Flex, 1982; and *The Italian Job,* Klinker Sounds, 1985; Foodball—Finch Live at the Merlin, Hungary, 2003; Finch Performances, 57 Productions, 2004.

WORK IN PROGRESS: Real Cardiff Two: The Greater City; The Big Book of Cardiff, Seren (Bridgend, Wales), 2005; additional works in the "Real Wales" series; *The Finch File,* a volume of critical analysis, University of Wales Press and Salzburg Press.

SIDELIGHTS: Best known for his poetry performances that combine wit with surrealism and humor with erudition, Peter Finch's body of work spans decades, beginning with his first volumes published in the late 1960s by Second Aeon Publications. The imprint was the publishing arm of the literary magazine Finch founded, and which rose to become the leading British poetry journal. In *Contemporary Poets,* Finch said that his first influences were the "beat" poets, and later Whitman, the surrealists, and Japanese and Chinese poets and verse forms.

Finch has written several books to help aspiring poets and writers. Martin Booth reviewed 1985's *How to Publish Your Poetry* for the *British Book News,* noting that it "covers the entire poetry business." Finch hits all the bases in counseling readers on how to prepare a manuscript, submit to magazines, copyright their work, deal with editors, self-publish, run a small press, finance, and promote their work. He advises poets on readings and competitions and also sends up the red flag in discussing the dangers of publishing through a vanity press. He lists markets, publishers, editors, and events. Booth wrote that Finch "misses not a single trick. The book is quite simply the new testament of the poetry-maker, the primary standard guide to the poetry marketplace."

Among Finch's more recent collections, *Useful* offers poems inspired by works of art, as well as by icons and situations of Welsh, and universal, culture. These include blues music, children, ex-wives, parents, blue-collar workers, old clothing, beach stones, and writing classes. In *Food,* Finch collects his poems written since 1997 that deal with food: thinking about it, preparing it, and eating it.

Real Cardiff is described by Finch at his Web site as "an alternative guidebook, history, and literary ramble." References to the Arthurian past are followed by sections on industry, tourism, and government. Finch takes the visitor, either actual or armchair, on a tour of the grand estates, old pubs, and new bars of Cardiff, as well as venues for the poetry of a city that is noted for its arts and culture scene.

Finch told *CA* that he "works at the edge where poetry turns to music and writing becomes performance art" and is "currently engaged on new translations of Welsh poets and on hypertext experiments, including the extensive 'R. S. Thomas Information,' which mixes real with imagined resources."

BIOGRAPHICAL AND CRITICAL SOURCES:

BOOKS

Brown, Tony, editor, *Welsh Writing in English: A Yearbook of Critical Essays,* volume 2, New English Review, 1996.

Murphy, Rose, editor *Contemporary Poets,* St. Martin's Press (New York, NY), 1970.

PERIODICALS

British Book News, July, 1985, Martin Booth, review of *How to Publish Your Poetry,* pp. 396-397.

ONLINE

Peter Finch Home Page, http://www.peterfinch.co.uk/ (May 16, 2003).

* * *

FLEENOR, Juliann (Evans) 1942-

PERSONAL: Born January 2, 1942, in Granite City, IL; daughter of Darwin Everas and Doris L. (Dudley) Evans; married David L. Fleenor (an accountant/software consultant), October 8, 1960; children: David L., Jr. *Ethnicity:* "White/American Indian." *Education:* Memphis State University, B.A., 1971, M.A., 1973; University of Toledo, Ph.D., 1978. *Politics:* Democrat. *Religion:* Unitarian. *Hobbies and other interests:* Herb gardens, history of herbs.

ADDRESSES: Home—20578 Primrose Ct., Palatine, IL 60010. *Office*—William Rainey Harper College, 12 West Algonquin Rd., Palatine, IL 60067. *E-mail*—jfleenor@harper.cc.il.us.

CAREER: Educator and author. Harper College, Palatine, IL, associate professor and president of faculty senate, 1992—. Illinois Community College Faculty Association, board member and curriculum chair, 1993—; Toledo United against Rape, co-founder; newspaper reporter and freelance magazine writer. Worked as a suicide and crisis intervention peer counselor.

MEMBER: National Council of Teachers of English.

WRITINGS:

(Editor) *The Female Gothic,* Edens Press (Montreal, Quebec, Canada), 1983.

Contributor to anthologies, including *New Black Mask,* 1984, and *The Longman Masters of Short Fiction,* edited by Dana Gioia and R. S. Gwynn, Longman (New York, NY), 2001. Contributor of articles to magazines and newspapers.

WORK IN PROGRESS: Research on the life of Mary Todd Lincoln.

SIDELIGHTS: Juliann Fleenor told *CA:* "My career has, as it has been in the past with other women, a pattern of beginnings and of endings, of starts, stops, and beginning again. I was motivated initially to become a writer because writing gave me the opportunity to discover myself and the world around me. When I was first in college, it was during the Vietnam War era, a period of great unrest, but also a period of great creativity. Yet I was not actually of that generation, having been born during World War II, and like others of the 1950s, being rather quiet but simmering underneath those girdles and white gloves. It is now disquieting to discover that my students, of course, do not have the memory of not only the '60s but the '70s and the '80s, and that some of them know nothing of the national turmoil we had during Watergate.

"Who influences my work? I read everything and am influenced by it all; but I particularly like the women writers living today—Alice Walker, Alice Munro, Amy Bloom, Joan Didion. The fiction I like is the fiction that speaks truth so clearly that it takes my breath away. I hate pretense.

"As for my writing process, I have several desks throughout the house and keep different projects on them, moving from desk to desk. I love quiet, although I find little right now. But I continue to struggle to find it, for it is in the silence that we hear our internal music.

"I must mention my enduring marriage to my husband. Without his presence, I am sure my life would have taken different, not necessarily better, turns. Together, we have created each other and our son, who was for so long the center of our lives. It is to that love—our shared passion for each other, my husband and I—to which I return over and over for sustenance as the world and my students and my writing changes. I have been extremely lucky to have passion for what I do—write and teach. Perhaps those are all we need—luck and passion. Without passion, luck will not come."

* * *

FLETCHER, J(oseph) S(mith) 1863-1935

PERSONAL: Born February 7, 1863, in Halifax, Yorkshire, England; died January 30, 1935, in Dorking, Surrey, England; married Rosamond Langbridge; children: one son. *Education:* Silcoates School.

CAREER: Novelist, short story writer, poet, playwright, journalist and historian. *Practical Teacher* magazine, London, England, sub-editor, 1881-83; freelance journalist in London, 1883-90; Leeds *Mercury,* staff writer, Leeds, England, 1890-1900; newspaper columnist.

MEMBER: Royal Historical Society (fellow).

WRITINGS:

NOVELS

Frank Carisbroke's Stratagem; or, Lost and Won, Jarrolds (London, England), 1888.

Andrewlina, Kegan Paul (London, England), 1889.

Mr. Spivey's Clerk, Ward & Downey (London, England), 1890.

The Winding Way, Kegan Paul (London, England), 1890.

Through Storm and Stress, Being a History of the Remarkable Adventures of Richard Fletcher of York, Chambers (London, England), 1892.

Old Lattimer's Legacy, Jarrolds (London, England), 1892, Clode (New York, NY), 1929.

The Quarry Farm, Ward & Downey (London, England), 1893.

The Remarkable Adventure of Walter Trelawney, Chambers (London, England), 1894.

The Wonderful City, Nelson (New York, NY), 1894.

Where Highways Cross, Macmillan (New York, NY), 1895.

At the Gate of the Fold, Macmillan (New York, NY), 1896.

In the Days of Drake, Blackie (London, England), 1896; Rand McNally (Chicago, IL), 1897.

Life in Arcadia, Macmillan (New York, NY), 1896.

Mistress Spitfire, Dent (London, England), 1896.

The Builders, Methuen (London, England), 1897, Mansfield (New York, NY), 1898, published as *The Furnace of Youth,* Pearson (London, England), 1914.

The Making of Matthias, John Lane (New York, NY), 1898.

The Paths of the Prudent, Methuen (London, England), 1899.

The Harvesters, Long (London, England), 1900.

Morrison's Machine, Hutchinson (London, England), 1900.

The Golden Spur, Long (London, England), 1901, Dial (New York, NY), 1928.

The Three Days' Terror, Long (London, England), 1901, Clode (New York, NY), 1927.

The Arcadians, Long (London, England), 1902.

Bonds of Steel, Digby, Long (London, England), 1902.

The Investigators, Long (London, England), 1902, Clode (New York, NY), 1930.

Anthony Everton, Chambers (London, England), 1903.

Lucian the Dreamer, Methuen (London, England), 1903.

The Secret Way, Digby, Long (London, England), 1903, Small, Maynard (Boston, MA), 1925.

David March, Methuen (London, England), 1904.

The Pigeon's Cave, Partridge (London, England), 1904.

Grand Relations, Unwin (London, England), 1905.

The Threshing-Floor, Unwin (London, England), 1905.

Highcroft Farm, Cassell (London, England), 1906.

A Maid and Her Money, Digby, Long (London, England), 1906, Doubleday, Doran (Garden City, NY), 1929.

Daniel Quayne, a Morality, Murray (London, England), 1907, Doran (New York, NY), 1926.

Grand Relations, T. Fisher Unwin (London, England), 1907.

The Harringtons of Highcroft Farm, Dodge (New York, NY), 1907.

The Queen of a Day, Unwin (London, England), 1907, Doubleday, Doran (Garden City, NY), 1929.

The Harvest Moon, Nash (London, England), 1908; McBride (New York, NY), 1909.

Mothers in Israel, Moffat, Yard (New York, NY), 1908.

Paradise Court, Unwin (London, England), 1908, Doubleday, Doran (Garden City, NY), 1929.

The Mantle of Ishmael, Nash (London, England), 1909.

Marchester Royal, Everett (London, England), 1909, Doran (New York, NY), 1926.

Hardican's Hollow, Everett (London, England), 1910, Doran (New York, NY), 1927.

The Pinfold, Everett (London, England), 1911, Doubleday, Doran (Garden City, NY), 1928.

The Fine Air of Morning, Nash (London, England), 1912, Estes (Boston, MA), 1913.

The Golden Venture, Nash (London, England), 1912.

The Bartenstein Case, Long (London, England), 1913, published as *The Bartenstein Mystery,* Dial (New York, NY), 1927.

I'd Venture All for Thee!, Nash (London, England), 1913, Doubleday, Doran (Garden City, NY), 1928.

Perris of the Cherry-Trees, Nash (London, England), 1913, Doubleday, Doran (Garden City, NY), 1930.

The Secret Cargo, Ward, Lock (London, England), 1913.

Both of This Parish, Nash (London, England), 1914.

The Marriage Lines, Nash (London, England), 1914.

The Ransom for London, Long (London, England), 1914, Dial (New York, NY), 1929.

The Shadow of Ravenscliffe, Digby, Long (London, England), 1914, Clode (New York, NY), 1928.

The Wolves and the Lamb, Ward, Lock (London, England), 1914, Knopf (New York, NY), 1925.

The King versus Wargrave, Ward, Lock (London, England), 1915, Knopf (New York, NY), 1924.

The Annexation Society, Ward, Lock (London, England), 1916, Knopf (New York, NY), 1925.

Families Repaired, Allen & Unwin (London, England), 1916.

Lynne Court Spinney, Ward, Lock (London, England), 1916, published as The *Mystery of Lynne Court,* Norman, Remington (Baltimore, MD), 1923.

Malvery Hold, Ward, Lock (London, England), 1917, published as *The Mystery of the Hushing Pool,* Hillman-Curl (New York, NY), 1938.

The Perilous Crossways, Hillman-Curl (New York, NY), 1917.

The Rayner-Slade Amalgamation, Allen & Unwin (London, England), 1917, Knopf (New York, NY), 1922.

The Amaranth Club, Ward, Lock (London, England), 1918, Knopf (New York, NY), 1926.

The Chestermark Instinct, Allen & Unwin (London, England), 1918, Knopf (New York, NY), 1921.

Heronshawe Main, Ward, Lock (London, England), 1918.

The Borough Treasurer, Ward, Lock (London, England), 1919, Knopf (New York, NY), 1921.

Droonin' Watter: A Story of Berwick and the Scottish Coast, Allen & Unwin (London, England), 1919, published as *Dead Men's Money,* Knopf (New York, NY), 1920.

The Middle Temple Murder, Knopf (New York, NY), 1919.

The Seven Days' Secret, Jarrolds (London, England), 1919, Clode (New York, NY), 1930.

The Talleyrand Maxim, Ward, Lock (London, England), 1919, Knopf (New York, NY), 1920.

The Valley of Headstrong Men, Hodder & Stoughton (London, England), 1919, Doran (New York, NY), 1924.

The Herapath Property, Ward, Lock (London, England), 1920, Knopf (New York, NY), 1921.

The Lost Mr. Linthwaite, Hodder & Stoughton (London, England), 1920, Knopf (New York, NY), 1923.

The Orange-Yellow Diamond, Newnes (London, England), 1920, Knopf (New York, NY), 1921.

The Paradise Mystery, Knopf (New York, NY), 1920, published as *Wrychester Paradise,* Ward, Lock (London, England), 1921.

Scarhaven Keep, Ward, Lock (London, England), 1920, Knopf (New York, NY), 1922.

The Root of All Evil, Hodder & Stoughton (London, England), 1921, Doran (New York, NY), 1924.

The Heaven-kissed Hill, Hodder & Stoughton (London, England), 1922, Doran (New York, NY), 1924.

In the Mayor's Parlour, John Lane (London, England), 1922, published as *Behind the Panel,* Collins (London, England), 1931.

The Markenmore Mystery, Jenkins (London, England), 1922, Knopf (New York, NY), 1923.

The Middle of Things, Knopf (New York, NY), 1922.

Ravensdene Court, Knopf (New York, NY), 1922.

The Ambitious Lady, Ward, Lock (London, England), 1923.

The Charing Cross Mystery, Putnam's (New York, NY), 1923.

The Copper Box, Hodder & Stoughton (New York, NY), 1923.

The Mazaroff Murder, Jenkins (London, England), 1923, published as *The Mazaroff Mystery,* Knopf (New York, NY), 1924.

The Million-Dollar Diamond, Jenkins (London, England), 1923, published as *The Black House in Harley Street,* Doubleday, Doran (Garden City, NY), 1928.

The Cartwright Gardens Murder, Collins (London, England), 1924, Knopf (New York, NY), 1926.

False Scent, Jenkins (London, England), 1924, Knopf (New York, NY), 1925.

The Kang-He Vase, Collins (London, England), 1924, Knopf (New York, NY), 1926.

Rippling Ruby, Putnam's (New York, NY), 1923, published as *The Mysterious Chinaman,* Jenkins (London, England), 1924.

The Safety Pin, Jenkins (London, England), 1924.

The Time-worn Town, Knopf (New York, NY), 1924.

The Bedford Row Mystery, Hodder & Stoughton (London, England), 1925, published as *The Strange Case of Mr. Henry Marchmont,* Knopf (New York, NY), 1927.

The Great Brighton Mystery, Hodder & Stoughton (London, England), 1925, Knopf (New York, NY), 1926.

The Mill of Many Windows, Doran (New York, NY), 1925.

Sea Fog, Jenkins (London, England), 1925; Knopf (New York, NY), 1926.

The Mortover Grange Mystery, Jenkins (London, England), 1926, published as *The Mortover Grange Affair,* Knopf (New York, NY), 1927.

The Stolen Budget, Hodder & Stoughton (London, England), 1926, published as *The Missing Chancellor,* Knopf (New York, NY), 1927.

The Green Rope, Knopf (New York, NY), 1927.

The Murder in the Pallant, Jenkins (London, England), 1927, Knopf (New York, NY), 1928.

The Passenger to Folkstone, Knopf (New York, NY), 1927.

Cobweb Castle, Knopf (New York, NY), 1928.

The Double Chance, Dodd, Mead (New York, NY), 1928.

The Wild Oat, Jarrolds (London, England), 1928, Doubleday, Doran (Garden City, NY), 1929.

The Wrist Mark, Knopf (New York, NY), 1928.

The Box Hill Murder, Knopf (New York, NY), 1929.

The House in Tuesday Market, Knopf (New York, NY), 1929.

The Secret of Secrets, Clode (New York, NY), 1929.

The Matheson Formula, Knopf (New York, NY), 1929.

The Borgia Cabinet, Knopf (New York, NY), 1930.

The Dressing-Room Murder, Jenkins (London, England), 1930, Knopf (New York, NY), 1931.

The South Foreland Murder, Knopf (New York, NY), 1930.

The Yorkshire Moorland Mystery, Jenkins (London, England), 1930, published as *The Yorkshire Moorland Murder,* Knopf (New York, NY), 1930.

The Guarded Room, Clode (New York, NY), 1931.

Murder at Wrides Park; Being Entry Number One in the Case-Book of Ronald Camberwell, Knopf (New York, NY), 1931.

Murder in Four Degrees; Being Entry Number Two in the Case-Book of Ronald Camberwell, Knopf (New York, NY), 1931.

The Burma Ruby, Benn (London, England), 1932, Dial (New York, NY), 1933.

Murder in the Squire's Pew; Being Entry Number Three in the Case-Book of Ronald Camberwell, Knopf (New York, NY), 1932.

Murder of the Ninth Baronet; Being Entry Number Four in the Case-Book of Ronald Camberwell, Knopf (New York, NY), 1932.

The Solution of a Mystery: Documents Relative to the Murder of Roger Maidment at Ullathwaite in the County of Yorkshire in October 1899, Doubleday (Garden City, NY), 1932.

The Grocer's Wife, Hutchinson (London, England), 1933.

Who Killed Alfred Snowe? Being Entry Number Five in the Case-Book of Ronald Camberwell, Harrap (London, England), 1933, published as *Murder of the Lawyer's Clerk,* Knopf (New York, NY), 1933.

Murder of the Only Witness; Being Entry Number Six in the Case-Book of Ronald Camberwell, Knopf (New York, NY), 1933.

Mystery of the London Banker; Being Entry Number Seven in the Case-Book of Ronald Camberwell, Harrap (London, England), 1933, published as *Murder of a Banker,* Knopf (New York, NY), 1933.

The Ebony Box; Being the First of the Further Adventures of Ronald Camberwell, Knopf (New York, NY), 1934.

Murder of the Secret Agent; Being Entry Number Eight in the Case-Book of Ronald Camberwell, Harrap (London, England), 1934; Knopf (New York, NY), 1934.

The Eleventh Hour; Being the Second of the Further Adventures of Ronald Camberwell, Knopf (New York, NY), 1935.

(With Edward Powys Mathers) *Todmanhawe Grange,* Butterworkth (London, England), 1937, published as *The Mill House Murder; Being the Last of the Adventures of Ronald Camberwell,* Knopf (New York, NY), 1937.

And Sudden Death, Hillman-Curl (New York, NY), 1938.

SHORT STORIES

One of His Little Ones, and Other Tales in Prose and Verse, Washbourne (London, England), 1888.

The Wonderful Wapentake, Lane (London, England), 1895.

God's Failures, John Lane (New York, NY), 1897.

At the Blue Bell Inn, Rand McNally (Chicago, IL), 1898.

Pasquinado, Ward, Lock (New York, NY), 1898.

The Death That Lurks Unseen, Ward, Lock (London, England), 1899.

From the Broad Acres, Richards (London, England), 1899.

The Air-Ship, and Other Stories, Digby, Long (London, England), 1903.

The Fear of the Night: A Cluster of Stories, Routledge (London, England), 1903.

The Diamonds, Digby, Long (London, England), 1904, published as *Green Ink, and Other Stories,* Jenkins (London, England), 1926.

For Those Were Stirring Times! And Other Stories, Everett (London, England), 1904.

The Ivory God, and Other Stories, Murray (London, England), 1907.

Mr. Poskitt, Nash (London, England), 1907, published as *Mr. Poskitt's Nightcaps,* Nash (London, England), 1910.

The Adventures of Archer Dawe (Sleuth-Hound), Digby, Long (London, England), 1909, published as *The Contents of the Coffin,* London Book Company (London, England), 1928.

The Wheatstack, and Other Stories, Nash (London, England), 1909.

Paul Campenhaye, Specialist in Criminology, Ward, Lock (London, England), 1918, published as *The Clue of the Artificial Eye,* Hillman-Curl (New York, NY), 1939.

Exterior to the Evidence, Hodder & Stoughton (London, England), 1920, Knopf (New York, NY), 1923.

Many Engagements, Long (London, England), 1923.

The Secret of the Barbican, and Other Stories, Hodder & Stoughton (London, England), 1924, Doran (New York, NY), 1925.

The Massingham Butterfly, and Other Stories, Small, Maynard (Boston, MA), 1926.

Safe Number Sixty-nine, and Other Stories, International Pocket Library (Boston, MA), 1926.

Behind the Monocle, and Other Stories, Jarrolds (London, England), 1928, Doubleday, Doran (Garden City, NY), 1930.

The Ravenswood Mystery, and Other Stories, Collins (London, England), 1929, published as *The Canterbury Mystery,* Collins (Glasgow, Scotland), 1933.

The Heaven-sent Witness, Doubleday (New York, NY), 1930.

The Malachite Jar, and Other Stories, Collins (London, England), 1930, published as *The Flamstock Mystery,* Collins (London, England), 1932, abridged as *The Manor House Mystery,* Collins (London, England), 1933.

The Marrendon Mystery, and Other Stories of Crime and Detection, Collins (London, England), 1930.

The Man in No. Three, and Other Stories of Crime, Love, and Mystery, Collins (London, England), 1931.

The Man in the Fur Coat, and Other Stories, Collins (London, England), 1932.

The Murder in Medora Mansions, Collins (London, England), 1933.

Find the Woman, Collins (London, England), 1933.

The Carrismore Ruby, and Other Stories, Jarrolds (London, England), 1935.

POETRY

The Bride of Venice, Poole/Dartford (London, England), 1879.

The Juvenile Poems of Joseph S. Fletcher, Snowden (Dartford, England), 1879.

Songs after Sunset, Poole/Dartford (London, England), 1881.

Early Poems, Poole (London, England), 1882.

Anima Christi, Washbourne (London, England), 1887.

Deus Homo, Washbourne (London, England), 1887.

Poems, Chiefly against Pessimism, Ward & Downey (London, England), 1893.

Ballads of Revolt, John Lane (New York, NY), 1897.

Leet Livvy: A Verse-Story in the Dialect of Osgoodcross, Simpkin, Marshall (London, England), 1915.

Verses Written in Early Youth, privately printed, 1931.

Collected Verse, 1881-1931, Harrap (London, England), 1931.

OTHER

Jesus Calls Thee! Thoughts for One in Indecision, Washbourne (London, England), 1887.

Our Lady's Month: A Manual of Devotion for the Month of May, Washbourne (London, England), 1887.

A Short Life of Cardinal Newman, Ward & Downey (London, England), 1890.

When Charles the First Was King, 3 volumes, Bentley (London, England), 1892, published in one volume, McClurg (Chicago), 1895.

Where Shall We Go for a Holiday?, Waddington (York, England), 1894.

A Picturesque History of Yorkshire, 3 volumes, Dent (London, England), 1899-1901.

Roberts of Pretoria, Methuen (London, England), 1900.

Baden-Powell of Mafeking, Methuen (London, England), 1900.

The History of the St. Leger Stakes, 1776-1901, Hutchinson (London, England), 1902, revised as *The History of the St. Leger Stakes, 1776-1926,* Hutchinson (London, England), 1927.

Owd Poskitt: His Opinions on Mr. Chamberlain in Particular and on English Trade in General, Harper (New York, NY), 1903.

A Book about Yorkshire, Methuen (London, England), 1908.

The Enchanting North, Nash (London, England), 1908.

Recollections of a Yorkshire Village, Digby, Long (London, England), 1910.

Nooks and Corners of Yorkshire, Nash (London, England), 1911.

Memories of a Spectator, Nash (London, England), 1912.

The Adventures of Turco Bullworthy, His Dog Shrimp, and His Friend Dick Wynyard, Washbourne (London, England), 1912.

The Town of Crooked Ways, Estes (Boston, MA), 1912.

Memorials of a Yorkshire Parish: A Historical Sketch of the Parish of Darrington, John Lane (New York, NY), 1917.

The Making of Modern Yorkshire 1750-1914, Allen & Unwin (London, England), 1918.

The Cistercians in Yorkshire, Macmillan (New York, NY), 1919.

Sheffield, Macmillan (New York, NY), 1919.

Leeds, Macmillan (New York, NY), 1919.

Pontefract, Macmillan (New York, NY), 1920.

Harrogate and Knaresborough, Macmillan (New York, NY), 1920.

Yorkshiremen of the Restoration, Allen & Unwin (London, England), 1921.

Halifax, Macmillan (New York, NY), 1923.

The Life and Work of St. Wilfrid of Ripon, Apostle of Sussex, Thompson (Chichester, England), 1925.

The Reformation in Northern England, Allen & Unwin (London, England), 1925.

Hearthstone Corner, (play), produced in Leeds, England, 1926.

SIDELIGHTS: A prolific writer of well over 100 books, J. S. Fletcher is best remembered for his detective novels, which were popular both in North America and in Great Britain. Born February 7, 1863, in Yorkshire, England, Fletcher reached his creative and productive peak during the 1920s and early 1930s. In the five-year period between 1920 and 1925 he published seventeen detective novels, a feat that drew the praise of a *New York Times* critic. "Each one is an ingenious, cleverly constructed tale, distinctive in plot and incidents and written with as much zest and freshness as if it were his first," the critic wrote. "The type of mental equipment that can produce each year three or more complicated plots, each dressed out with multitudinous thrilling incidents, will always be a marvel to those who do not possess it."

Fletcher tasted his first success early in his career in Great Britain, rivaling Edgar Wallace, another popular detective writer, by 1920. He remained relatively unknown in the United States, however, until President Woodrow Wilson, who was a compulsive reader of detective fiction, praised Fletcher's *The Middle Temple Murder,* which is widely considered his best work. With Wilson's endorsement, many of Fletcher's previous works were subsequently published in America, where they received a large audience and sold many copies. Despite this popularity, Fletcher's work is relatively unknown to modern readers, a fate decried by some literary critics. According to Melvyn Barnes in the *St. James Guide to Crime and Mystery Writers,* Fletcher deserves far more credit than he has received, and described him as "a writer . . . influential in popularizing detective fiction throughout two continents and possessing the innate craftsmanship of a real storyteller." Still, Barnes acknowledged that Fletcher's "best books were submerged in a torrent of mediocre work." Many commentators consider Fletcher's best novels to be The *Middle Temple Murder* and *The Charing Cross Mystery.* His short-story collections *The Adventures of Archer Dawe, Sleuth-Hound,* and *Paul Campenhaye, Specialist in Criminology* are also considered among his best work. In an essay for the *Critical Survey of Mystery and Detective Fiction,* Gerald H. Strauss discussed Fletcher's career, noting that "while he worked within the bounds of traditional English detective fiction, Fletcher's books are written in a distinctive style, feature young sleuths who are engagingly different from the typical eccentrics of his contemporaries, [and] accurately present aspects of Great Britain's landscape, both rural and urban."

Fletcher, who was orphaned in early childhood, began his career as a journalist, and was once the sub-editor for a London magazine called *Practical Teacher* (1881-1883), as well as a staff writer and columnist for the *Leeds Mercury* newspaper. By 1898, Fletcher had quit journalism so he could devote all of his time to writing books. Soon after, he published his three-volume *A Picturesque History of Yorkshire,* the first of a number of historical works that led him to become a fellow of the Royal Historical Society in 1918. As for his fiction, Fletcher had already penned a few romance novels during the 1890s. However, a keen interest in criminology led him to concentrate on creating detective and mystery novels. "I believe I got my interest in criminology right from the fact that a famous case of fraud was heard at the Quarter Sessions at a town where I was at school," Fletcher explained later in his life. "Then, when I left school, I meant to be a barrister and I read criminal law and attended a great many queer trials for some time. But turning to journalism instead, I knew of a great many queer cases and mysteries, and now and then did 'special commissions' for various big papers on famous murder trials."

While Fletcher developed a number of different sleuths during his long career writing detective fiction, many critics consider two of his most important to be Frank Spargo and Ronald Camberwell. Spargo, in particular, appeared in many of Fletcher's most successful novels, including *The Middle Temple Murder.* According to Strauss, the book is Fletcher's "major achievement and the one that has endured." Strauss noted in the *Dictionary of Literary Biography* that Spargo was one of the first characters in the mold of the journalist-detective, which later became so popular among both American and British detective writers. Spargo also appears in *The Charing Cross Mystery,* which was originally published as a magazine serial titled "Black Money." Fletcher wrote the "Ronald Camberwell" series in the 1930s. It is about a private inquiry agent in London who is in partnership with a former inspector of the Criminal Investigation Department. The two men work in cooperation with Scotland Yard to solve crimes. Fletcher was married to Rosamond Langbridge, also an author, who penned *The White Moth* (1932). The two had a son and lived for many years in Dorking, Surrey. Fletcher died there on January 30, 1935.

BIOGRAPHICAL AND CRITICAL SOURCES:

BOOKS

Critical Survey of Mystery and Detective Fiction, Salem Press (Pasadena, CA), 1988.

Dictionary of Literary Biography, Volume 70: *British Mystery Writers, 1869-1919,* Gale (Detroit, MI), 1988.

St. James Guide to Crime & Mystery Writers, 4th edition, St. James Press (Detroit, MI), 1996.*

* * *

FORD, Franklin L(ewis) 1920-2003

OBITUARY NOTICE—See index for *CA* sketch: Born December 26, 1920, in Waukegan, IL; died August 31, 2003, in Lexington, MA. Historian, educator, and author. Ford was a former professor and dean at Harvard University, and was often remembered for facing down student protestors there during Vietnam War protests. After receiving his B.A. from the University of Minnesota in 1942, he served in the Office of Strategic Services—the forerunner of the C.I.A.—during World War II. He then returned to his studies and earned his Ph.D. from Harvard University in 1950. From 1949 to 1952 he taught at Bennington College in Vermont, then he joined Harvard as an assistant professor, becoming a professor of European history in 1958, dean of the Faculty of Arts and Sciences from 1962 to 1970, and McLean Professor of Ancient and Modern History from 1968 until his retirement as professor emeritus in 1991. While serving as dean in 1969, Ford summoned police to put down a student protest that had resulted in the takeover of the university's administration building. Although this earned him some national recognition in the news, his book publications are more relevant to his career and include *Robe and Sword: The Regrouping of the French Aristocracy after Louis XIV* (1953), *Strasbourg in Transition, 1648 to 1789* (1958), *Europe, 1780-1830* (1969), and *Political Murder: From Tyrannicide to Terrorism* (1985).

OBITUARIES AND OTHER SOURCES:

PERIODICALS

Chicago Tribune, September 5, 2003, Section 1, p. 11.
Los Angeles Times, September 4, 2003, p. B13.
New York Times, September 3, 2003, p. A17.
Washington Post, September 6, 2003, p. B7.

* * *

FORISHA, Barbara L.
See KOVACH, Barbara (Ellen) L(usk)

* * *

FREEDMAN, Samuel G. 1955-

PERSONAL: Born 1955; son of a machinist; married Cynthia Sheps; children: Aaron, Sarah. *Education:* University of Wisconsin at Madison, B.A. (history and journalism). *Religion:* Jewish.

ADDRESSES: Home—New York, NY. *Agent*—c/o Barney Karpfinger, The Karpfinger Agency, 157 West 20th St., New York, NY 10011. *E-mail*—sgf1@columbia.edu.

CAREER: Journalist, author, and educator. *New York Times,* New York, NY, journalist, 1981-87; Columbia University School of Journalism, New York, NY, professor, 1991, 1993—, interim associate dean for academic affairs, 2002-03.

AWARDS, HONORS: National Book Award finalist, 1990, for *Small Victories;* Helen Bernstein Award for Excellence in Journalism, 1993, for *Upon This Rock;* Pulitzer Prize finalist, and New Jersey Humanities Council Book Award, both 1997, both for *The Inheritance;* Distinguished Teaching in Journalism award, Society of Professional Journalists, 1997; National Jewish Book Award, 2000, for *Jew vs. Jew.*

WRITINGS:

Small Victories: The Real World of a Teacher, Her Students, and Their High School, Harper and Row (New York, NY), 1990.
Upon This Rock: The Miracles of a Black Church, HarperCollins (New York, NY), 1993.
The Inheritance: How Three Families and America Moved from Roosevelt to Reagan and Beyond, Simon and Schuster (New York, NY), 1996.
Jew vs. Jew: The Struggle for the Soul of American Jewry, Simon and Schuster (New York, NY), 2000.

WORK IN PROGRESS: Who She Was: How My Mother Died and Lived, expected in 2005.

SIDELIGHTS: Samuel G. Freedman worked for several years as a journalist for the *New York Times* before he decided to expand his reportage into book-length pieces. His background as a reporter prepared him for the rigors of book authorship; as he told Wendy Smith for *Publishers Weekly:* "On most daily newspapers you're writing in present time. But at the *Times,* even if you were writing an 1100-word piece on [politics] . . . they wanted context; you had to commit some of that space to putting it in historical perspective. . . . it pushed me beyond reporting and helped prepare me for doing it at book level." Receiving acclaim for his insightful writings, in 1997 Freedman joined the faculty of Columbia University's prestigious School of Journalism.

Freedman first met high school teacher Jessica Siegel in 1987, after Siegel wrote him a candid letter responding to one of Freedman's newspaper articles. His first book, *Small Victories: The Real World of a Teacher, Her Students, and Their High School* is based upon a year spent witnessing the day-to-day trials and tribulations experienced by Siegel in her job teaching at Seward Public High School, located in a disadvantaged neighborhood of New York City. *Small Victories,* a finalist for the National Book Award in 1990, was praised by several reviewers. According to a writer for *Time,* "Considering the obstacles confronting Seward's teachers and their students, Freedman's book may be misnamed. The victories seem large indeed."

Employing a focus many reviewers have characterized as liberal, Freedman shows even more clearly how an institution can improve the lives of the poor in his second book. *Upon This Rock: The Miracles of a Black Church* is written in the same style as *Small Victories,* and again champions an underdog fighting against daunting odds. For this book Freedmen spent a year with preacher Johnny Ray Youngblood at St. Paul's Community Baptist Church in East Brooklyn, New York. He won the Helen Bernstein Award for Excellence in Journalism in 1993 for his objective reporting on St. Paul's black community. David L. Kirp, in his review for the *Nation,* wrote that "In prose whose richness and texture matches its subject, Freedman shows how a community gets created in the kind of place conventionally doomed to failure," and called *Upon This Rock* "a remarkable book."

In 1996 Freedman changed his political focus, this time examining several politically conservative New York State Republican families whose roots lay in Catholicism and the Democratic Party. *The Inheritance: How Three Families and America Moved from Roosevelt to Reagan and Beyond* shows how a group of immigrant Catholics switched political alliances in the late 1960s, and how the whole of America turned Republican. One minor criticism of the book came from James M. McPherson, who explained in the *New York Times Book Review* that Freedman's narrow focus prohibits a full examination of the topic promised by the book's subtitle. "For three-quarters of a century the South was solid for the Democrats. Now it is almost as solid for the Republicans. That is the real story of the making and unmaking of the Democratic majority," McPherson noted. In *Insight on the News,* Jeffrey Hart was more enthusiastic, praising the book for possessing "the rich texture of a great social novel" and complementing the author for shining "a clear beam of light onto the social origins of our political alignments today."

Freedman's highly acclaimed *Jew vs. Jew: The Struggle for the Soul of American Jewry* was a national bestseller when it came out in 2000. The novel also won the National Jewish Book Award in the same year. The factions of modern American Judaism—Reform, Conservative, and Orthodox—are studied, and the author concludes that despite the economic and social successes of Jews as a segment of U.S. society, their factionalism threatens to destroy them as a people. Praising the work as "beautifully written, replete with insightful and often heart-wrenching vignettes" in a review for *Society,* William B. Helmreich dubbed *Jew vs. Jew* "a clarion call to American Jewry to put its own house in order lest that house crumble into nothingness."

BIOGRAPHICAL AND CRITICAL SOURCES:

PERIODICALS

Insight on the News, October 28, 1996, Jeffrey Hart, review of *Inheritance,* p. 33.

Knight Ridder/Tribune News Service, September 13, 2000, Carlin Romano, review of *Jew vs. Jew: The Struggle for the Soul of American Jewry,* p. K7674.

Nation, July 26, 1993, Stephanie Gutman, review of *Upon This Rock,* p. 150(2).

National Review, March 15, 1993, David L. Kirp, review of *Upon This Rock,* p. 69.

New York Times, October 11, 1996, Alan Ehrenhalt, "From the New Deal to a Disgust with Government," p. B19; August 17, 2000, Jonathan Rosen, review of *Jew vs. Jew,* p. B9.

New York Times Book Review, September 22, 1996, James M. McPherson, "Grandchild of the New Deal," p. 15; September 3, 2000, Stephen J. Whitfield, review of *Jew vs. Jew,* p. B16.

Publishers Weekly, February 21, 2000, review of *Jew vs. Jew,* p. 50; September 9, 1996, Wendy Smith, "Samuel G. Freedman: History in Three Dimensions," p. 60.

Society, May/June, 2002, William B. Helmreich, review of *Jew vs. Jew,* p. 95.

Time, June 4, 1990, review of *Small Victories,* p. 84.

ONLINE

Beliefnet, http://www.beliefnet.com/ (2000), David Greenberg, review of *Jew vs. Jew.*

Columbia University Web site, http://www.columbia.edu/ (May 15, 2000), "Samuel G. Freedman."

Samuel G. Freedman Web site, http://www.samuelfreedman.com/ (July 9, 2002).

* * *

FREEMAN, Gregory A.

PERSONAL: Born in Newnan, GA; married; wife's name, Caroline. *Education:* University of Georgia, Athens, B.A.

ADDRESSES: Home—Atlanta, GA. *Office*—4880 Lower Roswell Rd., Suite 165, No. 210, Marietta, GA 30068-4385. *Agent*—Mel Berger, William Morris Agency, 1325 Avenue of the Americas, New York, NY 10019.

CAREER: Journalist and freelance writer. Worked for the Associated Press in Atlanta, GA, and as an editor with a publishing company.

AWARDS, HONORS: Sigma Delta Chi Award for Excellence, Society of Professional Journalists, 2001.

WRITINGS:

Lay This Body Down: The 1921 Murders of Eleven Plantation Slaves, Lawrence Hill Books (Chicago, IL), 1999.

Sailors to the End: The Deadly Fire on the USS Forrestal and the Heroes Who Fought It, William Morrow (New York, NY), 2002.

SIDELIGHTS: Gregory A. Freeman's first book, *Lay This Body Down: The 1921 Murders of Eleven Plantation Slaves,* is a study of the killing of poor black men who were caught up in a form of modern enslavement half a century after the U.S. Civil War. *Library Journal*'s Robert C. Jones wrote that "this moving narrative account is arguably the most complete history of this event available."

John Williams was a Georgia plantation owner who found his help in local jails where they were held for minor crimes like vagrancy, paid their fines, forced them into peonage (a form of illegal bondage), and treated them like slaves. When federal authorities began an investigation of his practices, Williams had eleven of his peons killed in order to prevent them from testifying. He ordered his black overseer, Clyde Manning, whom he had raised and exploited since childhood, to execute them. *Booklist* reviewer Vanessa Bush commented that Freeman "explores, to chilling effect, the personalities of Williams and Manning."

Some of the victims were chained together, weighted down with rocks, and thrown from bridges. Others were bludgeoned to death with an axe or shot. Many were forced to dig their own graves. The murders came to light when three corpses surfaced in a nearby river.

The murders were committed in a rural, and for the most part, bigoted community, but even in this environment, the enormity of the crimes could not be ignored. Williams was convicted of first-degree murder and received a life sentence, primarily on Manning's testimony. He was the first Southern white man to be so convicted of killing a black person since 1877. It didn't happen again for another half century. The two trials that resulted gained national attention, and it is the details of these trials that make up the study, including testimonies and FBI evidence.

A *Kirkus Reviews* contributor wrote that the book "is scrupulously researched, with an eye for the telling detail. A good true-crime story, with far-reaching implications."

Freeman drew on official U.S. Navy Files and the eyewitness accounts of twelve survivors in telling the story of the tragic events that occurred on the aircraft carrier USS *Forrestal* on July 29, 1967. In reviewing *Sailors to the End: The Deadly Fire on the USS Forrestal and the Heroes Who Fought It,* a *Publishers Weekly* reviewer wrote that Freeman "easily outclasses many military re-creations in grasping the men's varying experiences."

The disaster occurred as the ship, sailing in the Gulf of Tonkin, prepared for an air strike on North Vietnam and was driven by a series of incidents. First, an F-4 Phantom aircraft's Zuni rocket misfired, striking the fuel tank of an A-4 Skyhawk waiting on the flight deck, a craft whose pilot was John McCain, later Senator John McCain. The thousands of gallons of jet fuel that spilled onto the deck caught fire, setting off other explosions, including those of thousand-pound World War II bombs that had been loaded on aircraft. The deck was riddled with holes, through which the fuel poured below decks into crew quarters, ammunition storage areas, and plane hangars. The carrier did not go down, but before the fireballs of jet fuel were spent, and the shrapnel found its mark, 134 men lay dead and more than 150 were seriously injured. Twenty-one planes were lost, most pushed into the ocean before they could explode, and forty more were damaged, resulting in a material loss of more than $72 million.

The book is divided into three parts. In the first six chapters, Freeman describes Navy life, particularly as it is lived on a carrier, where thousands of men form the ship's crew. The second part consists of eight chapters that document the events.

James E. Hickey, who reviewed *Sailors to the End* in the *Naval War College Review,* noted that "these 150 pages are exceptionally engaging and so successful in capturing the stress and emotion of the crisis that they grab readers and leave them emotionally exhausted. In particular, the description of the death of sailor James Blaskis in a remote and inaccessible part of the ship cannot leave a reader unmoved."

The final three chapters address the investigation of the tragedy, the fates of the survivors, and the burials of the dead. Freeman notes that two groups on board the carrier had each bypassed some safety measures, and that the leaky and dangerous obsolete bombs had been transferred to the *Forrestal* and loaded on the aircraft immediately before the incident.

Captain John Beling was officially reprimanded, but the reprimand was later rescinded and he ended his career at a remote outpost in Iceland. Robert Finn pointed out in a review for *Bookreporter.com* that the U.S. Navy has also tended to blame the crew for the *Forrestal* disaster and created their 1973 training film, *Trial by Fire* based on lessons learned from that tragedy. Finn wrote that Freeman "seems to want to do two things: Praise the crew as the true heroes of the event and lay the blame on old, defective ammunition. . . . The ship's ordnance experts were enraged when they were supplied with these ancient, defective, and dangerous bombs the day before the accident—but they were told nothing else was available." Freeman writes that an escalation of the bombing campaign had been ordered by President Lyndon Johnson, even though there was not enough modern ammunition to accomplish the strikes. Finn said that "Freeman claims this factor has been swept under the rug in official assessments of what went wrong that July morning."

A *Kirkus Reviews* writer called *Sailors to the End* "a compassionate account of a dramatic incident in modern naval history, told with cinematic immediacy and narrative skill."

BIOGRAPHICAL AND CRITICAL SOURCES:

PERIODICALS

Booklist, September 15, 1999, Vanessa Bush, review of *Lay This Body Down: The 1921 Murders of Eleven Plantation Slaves,* p. 201.

Kirkus Reviews, September 15, 1999, review of *Lay This Body Down,* p. 1465; May 15, 2002, review of *Sailors to the End: The Deadly Fire on the USS Forrestal and the Heroes Who Fought It,* p. 716.

Library Journal, October 1, 1999, Robert C. Jones, review of *Lay This Body Down,* p. 108; October 1, 2002, Gerald Costa, review of *Sailors to the End,* p. 113.

Naval War College Review, autumn, 2002, James E. Hickey, review of *Sailors to the End,* p. 123.

Publishers Weekly, April 29, 2002, review of *Sailors to the End,* p. 50.

ONLINE

Bookreporter.com, http://www.bookreporter.com/ (April 29, 2003), Robert Finn, review of *Sailors to the End.*

Lay This Body Down Web site, http://www.laythisbodydown.com (April 29, 2003).

NonfictionReviews.com, http://www.nonfictionreviews.com/ (July 10, 2002), David Bloomberg, review of *Lay This Body Down.*

Sailors to the End, http://www.sailorstotheend.com (April 29, 2003).*

* * *

FREI, Terry 1955-

PERSONAL: Born 1955. *Education:* University of Colorado, Boulder, B.A., B.S., 1976.

ADDRESSES: *Office—Denver Post* Sports, 1560 Broadway, Denver, CO 80202. *Agent*—John Monteleone, Mountain Lion, Inc., P.O. Box 799, Pennington, NJ 08534. *E-mail*—freipost@hotmail.com.

CAREER: Journalist. *Denver Post,* Denver, CO, reporter, 1995—; *ESPN.com,* columnist. Previously worked for *Sporting News* and *Oregonian.*

AWARDS, HONORS: Voted Sportswriter of the Year in both Oregon and Colorado.

WRITINGS:

Horns, Hogs, and Nixon Coming: Texas vs. Arkansas in Dixie's Last Stand, Simon & Schuster (New York, NY), 2002.

WORK IN PROGRESS: Third Down and a War to Go, to be published in 2004.

SIDELIGHTS: Sportswriter Terry Frei's *Horns, Hogs, and Nixon Coming: Texas vs. Arkansas in Dixie's Last Stand* is an account of what many consider to be one of the most memorable college football games of the twentieth century. The game was played on December 6, 1969, between the top-ranked Texas Longhorns and the second-ranked Arkansas Razorbacks, both undefeated, for the Southwest Conference title. It was the last major sports event to be played by entirely white teams.

The contest was held in Fayetteville, Arkansas, amidst protests by black students who vowed to rush the field if the song "Dixie" was played to celebrate Razorback touchdowns, and by antiwar demonstrators, including veterans, who protested the Vietnam conflict outside the stadium. Fans included President Richard Nixon and Texas congressman George Bush. Frei's retelling encompasses more than the game and his studies of individual players. It also takes the pulse of the country as it experienced political and social upheaval.

Bob Holt, in the *Arkansas Democrat-Gazette,* wrote that Frei "does a masterful job of weaving in the historical significance of the turbulent times." Blackie Sherrod of the *Dallas Morning News,* who covered the game, wrote that Frei "must have worn out a dozen tape recorders in the process."

Clemson University athletic director Terry Don Phillips, a Razorback defensive lineman in 1969, noted in the *Arkansas Democrat-Gazette:* "It's sort of like that movie, *The Perfect Storm,* where you have all these things that converge at one time. It reflects a time when a lot of things were changing, not only at Arkansas, but throughout the South. I think that's the essence of the book, the many issues in America at that time, and that game probably represents the pinnacle of it." *Library Journal* critic Larry R. Little called the book "a delightful, well-researched chronicle of a turbulent era." A *San Antonio Express-News* reviewer proclaimed it "a great story, well-told, with more delicious details than a linebacker could tackle." *Denver Post* theatre critic John Moore remarked that Frei "possesses the football expertise, an uncanny ability to buttonhook diverse personal anecdotes together and an appreciation for history to tell this remarkable tale." And in *Dallas Morning News,* reviewer Si Dunn called the book a "superb blending of sports, history and politics."

BIOGRAPHICAL AND CRITICAL SOURCES:

PERIODICALS

Arkansas Democrat-Gazette, August 24, 2002, Bob Holt, review of *Horns, Hogs, and Nixon Coming: Texas vs. Arkansas in Dixie's Last Stand.*

Dallas Morning News, November 24, 2002, review of *Horns, Hogs, and Nixon Coming: Texas vs. Arkansas in Dixie's Last Stand.*

Denver Post, December 15, 2002, review of *Horns, Hogs, and Nixon Coming.*

Kirkus Reviews, September 15, 2002, review of *Horns, Hogs, and Nixon Coming,* p. 1365.

Library Journal, October 1, 2002, Larry R. Little, review of *Horns, Hogs, and Nixon Coming,* p. 105.

Publishers Weekly, October 14, 2002, review of *Horns, Hogs, and Nixon Coming,* p. 72.

San Antonio Express-News, December 1, 2002, review of *Horns, Hogs, and Nixon Coming.*

Sports Illustrated, November 18, 2002, Charles Hirshberg, review of *Horns, Hogs, and Nixon Coming,* p. R10.

ONLINE

Terry Frei Web site, http://www.terryfrei.com (June 14, 2003).

* * *

FREY, Louise I.
See IRELAND-FREY, Louise

* * *

FRIEDLANDER, Lee (Norman) 1934-

PERSONAL: Born July 14, 1934, in Aberdeen, WA; married Maria DePaoli, 1958; children: Erik, Anna. *Education:* Attended Los Angeles Art Center School; studied photography under Edward Kaminski.

ADDRESSES: Home—44 South Mountain Rd., New City, NY 10956. *Agent*—c/o Author Mail, Distributed Art Publishers, 155 Sixth Ave., 2nd Fl., New York, NY 10013.

CAREER: Photographer. Atlantic Records, photographer, 1950s; freelance photographer, 1955—; University of Minnesota, Minneapolis, artist-in-residence, 1966; University of California, Los Angeles, guest lecturer, 1970; Rice University, Houston, TX, Mellon Professor of Fine Arts, 1977. *Exhibitions:* Individual and group exhibitions in the United States, Canada, and Europe, beginning 1963; work is included in permanent collections at the Museum of Modern Art, New York, NY, Museum of Fine Arts, Boston, MA, Fogg Art Museum, Harvard University, Cambridge, MA, Smithsonian Institution, Washington, DC, New Orleans Museum of Art, LA, University of Kansas, Lawrence, National Gallery of Canada, Ottawa, Ontario, and Victoria and Albert Museum, London, England.

AWARDS, HONORS: Guggenheim fellowship, 1960, 1962, 1977; National Endowment for the Arts fellowship, 1972, 1977, 1978, 1979, 1980; Friends of Photography Peer Award, 1980; Medal of the City of Paris, 1981; Edward MacDowell Medal, 1986; John D. and Catherine T. MacArthur Foundation award, 1990.

WRITINGS:

(With Jim Dine) *Work from the Same House: Photographs and Etchings,* Trigram (London, England), 1969.

Self Portrait, Haywire Press (New York, NY), 1970.

(Editor) *E. J. Bellocq: Storyville Portraits,* [New York], 1970.

The American Monument, Eakins (New York, NY), 1976.

The Nation's Capital in Photographs, 1976 (catalogue), The Gallery (Washington, DC), 1976.

Photographs, Haywire Press (New York, NY), 1978.

Flowers and Trees, Haywire Press (New York, NY), 1981.

Factory Valleys: Ohio and Pennsylvania, Callaway Editions (New York, NY), 1982.

Lee Friedlander: Portraits, Little, Brown (Boston, MA), 1985.

Cherry Blossom Time in Japan, [New York], 1986.

Cray at Chippewa Falls, Cray Research (Minneapolis, MN), 1987.

Lee Friedlander, Pantheon Books (New York, NY), 1988.

(With Robert Cumming and Jan Groover) *Three on Technology: New Photographs,* MIT List Visual Arts Center (Cambridge, MA), 1988.

Like a One-eyed Cat: Photographs by Lee Friedlander, H. N. Abrams (New York, NY), 1989.

Nudes, Pantheon Books (New York, NY), 1991.

The Jazz People of New Orleans, Pantheon Books (New York, NY), 1992.

Maria, Smithsonian Institution Press (Washington, DC), 1992.

Letters from the People, J. Cape (London, England), 1993.

(With Robert Burley and Geoffrey James) *Viewing Olmstead,* edited by Phyllis Lambert, MIT Press (Cambridge, MA), 1996.

Bellocq: Photographs from Storyville, the Red-Light District of New Orleans, J. Cape (London, England), 1996.

The Desert Seen, Distributed Art Publishers (New York, NY), 1996.

American Musicians, Distributed Art Publishers (New York, NY), 1998.

Lee Friedlander at Work, Distributed Art Publishers (New York, NY), 2002.

Staglieno, Nazraeli (Tucson, AZ), 2002.

Lee Friedlander: Stems, Distributed Art Publishers (New York, NY), 2003.

Contributor to publications, including *Esquire, McCall's, Art in America, Current, Harper's Bazaar,* and *Camera;* contributor to books, including the introduction to *Arrivals and Departures: The Airport Pictures of Garry Winogrand,* Distributed Art Publishers (New York, NY), 2002.

SIDELIGHTS: Photographer Lee Friedlander's early work consisted of cover shots for record albums of such jazz musicians as Count Basie, Ray Charles, Miles Davis, Charles Mingus, and Billie Holiday, and these were collected decades later in *American Musicians.* As a teen, Friedlander was inspired by jazz saxophonist Charlie Parker, whose music helped him to understand the possibilities that were open to him as an artist.

Some of the people in *American Musicians* are in relaxed poses, such as Sarah Vaughan taking a nap or Art Blakey feeding his baby a bottle. Friedlander has continued to photograph musicians throughout his career, including country, gospel, and folk artists, and not of all of his subjects are stars. *American Musicians* includes photographs of singers in church choirs, New Orleans marching bands, and street musicians playing for change. Malcolm Jones, Jr., wrote in *Newsweek* that Friedlander "loves to show us the artists, famous or not, as people just getting through the day."

From the beginning, Friedlander photographed what interested him, and many of his images are of urban scenes and people, often reflected from the glass of a store display window. He briefly attended art school, then studied privately with Edward Kaminski. Hailed as one of the up-and-coming photographers of the 1960s, his first one-man show was in 1963 at the George Eastman House in Rochester, New York. In 1967 John Szarkowski, director of the photography department at the Museum of Modern in Art in New York city, exhibited Friedlander's work along with that of Diane Arbus and Friedlander's close friend Garry Winogrand in a show titled "New Documents." This exhibition was a milestone in Friedlander's career and brought him acclaim and a larger audience.

In an essay on the *University of Washington Web site,* Rod Slemmons wrote that "ultimately, Friedlander's photographs at the time of *New Documents,* and later, probably have more in common with Dadaist ideas of the 1920s than they do with the long tradition of American documentary photography. This relationship, perhaps initiated by Edward Kaminski, who had studied the work of the Surrealists and Dadaists, suggests an additional way of understanding Friedlander's work." Slemmons said that Friedlander produces "collage-like images . . . in which odd bits of conflicting information collide, some with more serious implications than others. He provides us with a new visual world in which obstruction, confusion, accident, and sometimes explosion are the driving forces. He does not provide us with a tastefully designed picture that is easy to get around in or familiar. Like the Dadaists, he is breaking some of the rules of art and reforming others to better suit his wit and intuition." Slemmons wrote that "much of Friedlander's work, especially the street photography and flowers and trees series, suggests the jazz tradition: gestural freedom of improvisation combined with highly complex, and cumulative, formal structure."

Friedlander's subjects have included other people, as well as himself. His *Self Portrait* contains photographs of Friedlander taken over ten years, either of his image or his shadow. He has restored the work of photographer E. J. Bellocq, who early in the twentieth century took pictures of women in the red-light district of New Orleans called Storyville, where prostitution was legal. Friedlander discovered eighty-nine glass negatives in a New Orleans gallery in 1958 and made prints from them. They were exhibited at the Museum of Modern Art in 1970 and collected in a book nearly forty years later.

The American Monument contains more than 200 photographs of memorialized war and civic heroes and battle sites, as well as statues of musicians and American icons, like Bill "Bojangles" Robinson and cowboy Tom Mix. *Factory Valleys: Ohio and Pennsylvania* is a collection of photographs commissioned by the Akron Art Museum that show the factory workers of the region and a bleak winter landscape.

In 1985 John Rollwagen of Cray Research, Inc. asked Friedlander to photograph the company's computer facility in Wisconsin. While there, Friedlander also took photographs of the landscape around the plant and included these in the final book, *Cray at Chippewa Falls,* which was a gift to Cray employees. "The result of this multi-layered seeing is a unique visual metaphor for what goes on at Cray," said Slemmons. "The sensuous chaos of the trees suggests the impossibly numerous wires of the super computers as well as the hair of the computer technicians."

Like a One-eyed Cat: Photographs by Lee Friedlander collects thirty years of his work in black and white. With *Nudes,* Friedlander shows young women in their stark nakedness, bumps, warts and all, alongside such inanimate objects as a door frame, desk, and flower pot. Included are four studies of the entertainer Madonna, shot before she rose to stardom, that were rejected by *Penthouse* because she was not well groomed. *Times Literary Supplement* contributor Brian Case said that "she could be an extra in some Italian Neo-realist film with her unshaven armpits, bobby pins, and hairy legs."

The Jazz People of New Orleans contains nearly 100 photographs taken between 1957 and 1974, mostly of people who were being interviewed by Tulane jazz scholars Richard Allen and William Russell for the university's archive of New Orleans Jazz. They are shown playing their instruments or relaxing as they talk about their music. The book also features Friedlander's photographs of a funeral march and life on the streets and in the neighborhoods. Teresa Wilhelm Askew wrote in *New Orleans* magazine that "this effort by Friedlander represents a nearly twenty-year odyssey of love by a great photographer."

Maria is a collection devoted to Friedlander's wife, and *Letters from the People* is a collection of Friedlander's photographs of writing in public places, including signs, numbers and letters, and graffiti.

Black-and-white photographs of the Sonoran Desert are featured in *The Desert Seen,* images filled with the thorns and branches of cacti and one self-portrait in which Friedlander's image is obscured by branches. In the book's text he recalls the lush landscape of his native Washington state, compares it to the uninviting desert, and explains why he chose to photograph the latter over ten years.

Lee Friedlander at Work is a collection of photographs taken of people at work over twenty years and reflects the period within which work shifted from industrial to technological labor. After his own retirement from everything but photography at the age of sixty-five, Friedlander focused on landscapes that included cottonwood trees. "It's something I'll probably spend the rest of my life playing with," he told a *Photo District News* writer. "I don't do lectures, I don't teach, I don't write letters. I just do what I want to do. Don't you think that's fair at sixty-five, to do what you want? It seems to work. People don't badger me about it." Friedlander ended by saying, "photography is the best thing I do. I like working. I like working all the time."

BIOGRAPHICAL AND CRITICAL SOURCES:

BOOKS

Contemporary Photographers, St. James Press (Detroit, MI), 1996.

PERIODICALS

Afterimage, January, 1993, Deborah Bright, reviews of *Nudes* and *Maria,* pp. 6-9; September-October, 1997, Stephen Longmire, review of *The Desert Seen,* p. 21.

Los Angeles Times Book Review, December 6, 1992, Fred Schruers, review of *The Jazz People of New Orleans,* pp. 2, 29.

New Orleans, November, 1992, Teresa Wilhelm Askew, review of *The Jazz People of New Orleans,* p. 34.

Newsweek, December 7, 1998, Malcolm Jones, Jr., review of *American Musicians,* p. 76.

New York Review of Books, January 9, 1997, Janet Malcolm, review of *Bellocq: Photographs from Storyville, the Red-Light District of New Orleans,* pp. 12-16.

Photo District News, January, 2002, "Catching up with . . . : A Gathering of Master Photographers, All with Gloried Pasts, Examine Their Present Work and What's Still to Come," p. 30.

Times Literary Supplement, July 12, 1991, Brian Case, reviews of *Like a One-eyed Cat: Photographs by Lee Friedlander* and *Nudes,* p. 15.

ONLINE

University of Washington Web site, http://faculty.washington.edu/ (January 22, 2003), Rod Slemmons, "A Precise Search for the Elusive."*

* * *

FRIES, Robert Francis 1911-2003

OBITUARY NOTICE—See index for *CA* sketch: Born December 16, 1911, in La Crosse, WI; died of congestive heart failure August 27, 2003, in Wilmette, IL. Historian, educator, and author. Fries was a highly respected professor emeritus at DePaul University. His first degree, from what is now the University of Wisconsin—La Crosse, was earned in education in 1933. He then taught social science at a Cashton, Wisconsin, high school for two years before attending graduate courses at the University of Wisconsin—Madison. He completed his master's degree in 1936 and his doctorate in 1939. That year he was hired as an assistant professor at DePaul University, where he rose to full professor in 1945 and chaired the department from 1945 to 1956 and from 1967 to 1976; he was also dean of University College from 1955 to 1980. When he retired in 1980, he received the university's Via Sapientiae Award for excellence in teaching. Fries was the author or editor of several history books, including *Empire in Pine: The Story of Lumbering in Wisconsin, 1830-1900* (1951; revised edition, 1989), the cowritten *Crown and Parliament in Tudor-Stuart England* (1959), and *Basic Historical Documents of European Civilization* (1972).

OBITUARIES AND OTHER SOURCES:

PERIODICALS

Chicago Tribune, August 29, 2003, section 1, p. 11.

G

GABRIEL, Gwendolyn D. 1966-

PERSONAL: Born September 18, 1966, in Dallas, TX; daughter of Joe E. (a truck driver) and Barbara J. (a nurse) Gabriel; married Richard J. Pellichet, May 18, 1997. *Ethnicity:* "African American." *Education:* Southern Methodist University, J.D., 1990; Cedar Valley College, real estate certificate, 1994; University of Texas at Austin, B.B.A., 1997. *Politics:* Democrat. *Religion:* Baptist. *Hobbies and other interests:* Crocheting, reading self-help books.

ADDRESSES: *Home*—Dallas, TX. *Office*—Brown Bag Press, P.O. Box 764585, Dallas, TX 75376. *E-mail*—gwen@brownbagpress.com.

CAREER: Attorney, entrepreneur, and author. Called to the Bar of the State of Texas; U.S. Department of Education, Dallas, TX, civil rights attorney, 1991—; in private practice of family law; volunteer attorney for low-income clients. Also works as real estate broker.

MEMBER: Alpha Kappa Alpha.

WRITINGS:

Become Totally Debt-Free in Five Years or Less: Pay off Your Mortgage, Car, Credit Cards, and More!, Brown Bag Press (Dallas, TX), 2000.

WORK IN PROGRESS: *Money Management for Young Adults;* research on more ways to save money.

SIDELIGHTS: Gwendolyn D. Gabriel told *CA:* "I am a self-proclaimed cheapskate who is also an attorney and a real estate broker. Of these titles, I believe that 'cheapskate' is the one that has had the greatest impact on my life.

"I became totally debt-free in five years by paying off all my debts, including my thirty-year mortgage loan. Being a cheapskate comes naturally to me, but I realize that it may not come as naturally to others, so I wrote my book to help others get out of debt, too. I have such a great need to help people who are struggling financially and living from paycheck to paycheck. For this reason, I am inspired to write financial books."

BIOGRAPHICAL AND CRITICAL SOURCES:

ONLINE

Brown Bag Press Web site, http://www.brownbagpress.com/ (December 12, 2003).

* * *

GALLUCCIO, Michael 1963(?)-

PERSONAL: Born c. 1963; partner of Jon Galluccio since April 16, 1982; children: Adam, Madison, Rosa.

ADDRESSES: *Home*—Maywood, NJ. *Agent*—Todd Shuster, c/o Zachary Shuster Agency, 45 Newbury St., Boston, MA 02116. *E-mail*—family@galluccio.com.

CAREER: Author, speaker, and adoption advocate.

WRITINGS:

(With Jon Galluccio and David Groff) *An American Family,* St. Martin's Press (New York, NY), 2001.

SIDELIGHTS: New Jersey couple Michael and Jon Galluccio played a pivotal role in the state court decision that allows unmarried couples to adopt children jointly. Michael and Jon had been together for sixteen years when they became foster parents to an infant boy. After a year of caring for Adam, who was born with the HIV virus and multiple drug addictions, their attempt to adopt him was blocked by a state law that prohibited unmarried couples from adopting together. A class-action lawsuit was launched, with the Galluccios as lead plaintiffs.

The couple chronicle the challenges they faced while caring for an ill infant, the court battle over Adam's adoption and the ultimate decision in their favor, and their fostering and adoption of an infant girl and her teenaged half-sister in *An American Family.* Michael and Jon alternate narration of the book, written with the help of writer David Groff. Richard J. Violette, reviewing *An American Family* for *Library Journal,* deemed the book a "heartwarming and inspiring spin on family values," while a *Publishers Weekly* reviewer called it a "moving, often funny and sometimes quite poignant memoir" exploring the many struggles that "gay couples (and unmarried heterosexual couples) often face when dealing with issues of foster care, adoption, and social intolerance."

BIOGRAPHICAL AND CRITICAL SOURCES:

PERIODICALS

Berge County Record, (Bergen County, NJ), February 11, 2001, Leslie Brody, "Two Dads, Three Adoptions," p. Y3.

Library Journal, May 1, 2001, Richard J. Violette, review of *An American Family,* p. 112.

Publishers Weekly, January 29, 2001, review of *An American Family,* p. 78.

ONLINE

Jon and Michael Galluccio Family Homepage, http://www.galluccio.com (June 17, 2003).*

* * *

GOODMAN, Celia (Mary) 1916-2002

OBITUARY NOTICE—See index for *CA* sketch: Born September 7, 1916, in Woodbridge, Suffolk, England; died October 19, 2002, in Cambridge, England. Editor and author. Goodman was a society intellectual perhaps best known for her friendships with authors George Orwell and Arthur Koestler. Educated at home and at boarding schools in England and Switzerland, she became fluent in several languages and developed a love for music (she was a talented pianist) and literature (especially German, French, and English). During World War II she worked as a nurse and afterwards became involved with magazines. She was employed as an assistant editor for the multilingual philosophical journal *Polemic* and the arts and literature magazine *Occident* in the mid-1940s. She then worked as a foreign office researcher for two years before joining the staff of the magazine *History Today* in 1951. Goodman became close friends with Arthur Koestler through her friendship with George Orwell, whose proposal of marriage she once rejected. Goodman's twin sister, Mamaine, married Koestler, and years later Goodman edited a collection of her sister's letters, *Living with Koestler: Mamaine Koestler's Letters, 1945-1951* (1985).

OBITUARIES AND OTHER SOURCES:

PERIODICALS

Guardian (London, England), November 6, 2002, p. 20.

Independent (London, England), October 25, 2002, p. 22.

Times (London, England), October 29, 2002, p. 33.

* * *

GORDON, Mordechai 1961-

PERSONAL: Born October 31, 1961, in Tel-Aviv, Israel. *Education:* Ohio University, B.A. (with honors), 1986; Duquesne University, M.A., 1987; Columbia University, M.Phil., 1993, Ph.D., 1997.

ADDRESSES: Home—325 Main St., No. 3B, White Plains, NY 10601. *E-mail*—mordechai.gordon@quinnipiac.edu.

CAREER: Educational Psychology Service Center, Lod, Israel, school psychologist, 1987-88; high school English teacher in Tel-Aviv, Israel, 1989-90; Levinski College of Education, Tel-Aviv, Israel, lecturer in education, 1993-97; Brooklyn College of the City University of New York, Brooklyn, NY, assistant professor of education, 1997-2001; Quinnipiac University, assistant professor of education, 2001—. Kibbutzim Teachers College, teacher of education courses; teacher of English as a foreign language at community centers in Tel-Aviv, Israel, 1993-95; State University of New York—College at New Paltz, adjunct assistant professor, 1998-2000; Adelphi University, adjunct assistant professor, 1999-2000.

AWARDS, HONORS: Critics Choice Award, American Educational Studies Association, 2002, for *Renewing Our Common World: Essays on Hannah Arendt and Education.*

WRITINGS:

(Editor) *Hannah Arendt and Education: Renewing Our Common World,* Westview Press (Boulder, CO), 2001.
Ten Common Misconceptions: What Many Educators Fail to See, Corwin Press, 2003.

Contributor to books, including *The Miseducation of the West,* edited by Joe Kincheloe and Shirley Steinberg, Greenwood Press (Westport, CT), 2003; and *The Academic Discourse on Colleges of Education,* edited by Alberto Bursztyn and Joe Kincheloe, Peter Lang Publishing (New York, NY). Contributor to periodicals, including *Educational Theory, Educational Philosophy and Theory, Journal of Thought, Encounter,* and *Taboo.*

* * *

GOULD, John (Thomas) 1908-2003

OBITUARY NOTICE—See index for *CA* sketch: Born October 22, 1908, in Boston, MA; died of pneumonia August 31, 2003, in Portland, ME. Journalist and author. Gould is best remembered for his many memoirs and his column "Dispatch from the Farm," which centered on his life in small-town Maine. A graduate of Bowdoin College in 1931, Gould settled on a farm in Lisbon, Maine, and began his journalism career at the *Brunswick Record.* After eight years, he was hired by the *Christian Science Monitor,* for which he began writing his column, which appeared in the paper for more than sixty years. He was also a regular contributor to the *Boston Sunday Post* until 1954 and to the *Baltimore Evening Sun;* and from 1945 to 1951 Gould ran the weekly newspaper *Lisbon Enterprise.* Gould's popular writings combined observational humor with a slightly curmudgeonly attitude that especially appealed to many New England readers. He wrote numerous books featuring New England characters, including *Farmer Takes a Wife* (1945), *The Parables of Peter Partout* (1964), *Glass Eyes by the Bottle* (1975), *No Other Place* (1984), *It Is Not Now: Tales of Maine* (1993), and *Tales from Rhapsody Home; or, What They Don't Tell You about Senior Living* (2000). Gould's writings made him a local hero, and the state of Maine declared August 17, 2002 to be John Gould Day.

OBITUARIES AND OTHER SOURCES:

PERIODICALS

Los Angeles Times, September 4, 2003, p. B12.
New York Times, September 3, 2003, p. A17.

* * *

GRAY, Wallace 1927-2001

PERSONAL: Born July 13, 1927, in Alexandria, LA; died of a heart attack December 21, 2001, in New York, NY. *Education:* Louisiana College, B.A., 1946; Louisiana State University, M.A., 1951; Columbia College, Ph.D., 1958.

CAREER: Professor and playwright. Columbia College, New York, NY, 1953-2001, began as instructor, professor of English, 1974-2001, also served as assistant dean of students. *Military service:* U.S. Navy, 1944-46.

AWARDS, HONORS: Great Teacher Award, Columbia College Alumni Association; Mark Van Doren Award, students of Columbia College, for teaching excellence; Award for Distinguished Service to the Core Curriculum, Columbia College, 1997.

WRITINGS:

The Cowboy and the Tiger (children's musical), produced in New York, NY, 1963.
Helen (play), produced off-Broadway, 1964.
Homer to Joyce (essays), Macmillan (New York, NY), 1985.

Also author of ten other plays.

SIDELIGHTS: In his *New York Times* obituary, Wallace Gray was hailed as "a favorite teacher for generations of Columbia College students." Gray spent the bulk of his teaching career at Columbia, where he began teaching in 1953. He continued teaching until the time of his death on December 21, 2001, when he died of a heart attack at the age of seventy-four.

Gray taught one of Columbia's most popular literature courses, "Eliot, Joyce, Pound" or "E.J.P" as it was known among students, for twenty years. With each new semester, he would put his students at ease with this opening line: "I know more about 'Ulysses' than anyone else in the world, and I'm going to teach it all to you." His popularity with both students and staff won him the Mark Van Doren Award as well as Columbia's Great Teacher Award and Award for Distinguished Service to the Core Curriculum. At the time of his death, Gray was the teacher with the longest service in literature humanities at Columbia.

Aside from teaching, Gray was a playwright. His *The Cowboy and the Tiger* was a long-running musical for children that was also broadcast on television. Gray also wrote and published a book titled *Homer to Joyce,* an extension of his classroom work. In it, the author examines eighteen of the most influential books of the Western World, including Homer's *Iliad,* T. S. Eliot's *The Waste Land,* James Joyce's *Ulysses,* and Virgil's *Aeneid,* among others. Gray uses these diverse titles as a basis for discussion of the human condition in Western culture. *Booklist* contributor Eric Wexler recommended the book for the connections Gray makes between the various pieces of literature. "He sees these works as speaking not only to their times but to each other in a continuous dialogue through the centuries."

Joseph Voelker, whose review was published in *Studies in Short Fiction,* said, "The book has quirks. Gray seems to indulge his interest in Athenian politics, . . . using up classroom minutes that could go towards more intrinsic matters." For instance, the critic observed, Gray "insists Antigone is just plain wrong. He scolds the principals in *Lear* for their impatience." The critic concluded that "overall, though, Gray's scholarship shows the generalist in the very best light."

BIOGRAPHICAL AND CRITICAL SOURCES:

PERIODICALS

American Spectator, December, 1987, Leonard Garment, review of *Homer to Joyce,* p. 44.
Booklist, October 1, 1985, Eric Wexler, review of *Homer to Joyce,* p. 186.
Choice, January, 1986, W. W. Waring, review of *Homer to Joyce,* p. 737.
Library Journal, October 1, 1985, Michael J. Esposito, review of *Homer to Joyce,* p. 101.
Studies in Short Fiction, summer, 1987, Joseph Voelker, review of *Homer to Joyce,* pp. 325-326.
Wall Street Journal, October 22, 1985, review of *From Homer to Joyce,* p. 26.

OBITUARIES:

PERIODICALS

New York Times, January 11, 2002, Wolfgang Saxon, "Wallace Gray, 74, Literature Teacher at Columbia," p. B8.

ONLINE

Columbia News online, http://www.columbia.edu/ (April 10, 2002), James Devitt, "English Professor and Playwright Wallace Gray Dies in NYC at 74."*

* * *

GREENE, Gloria
See JOHNSON, Doris

* * *

GREENE, Philip L(eon) 1924-1993

PERSONAL: Born December 2, 1924, in Brooklyn, NY; died September 21, 1993.

CAREER: Adelphi University, Garden City, NY, faculty member, 1959-76, professor of English and American literature, beginning 1976.

WRITINGS:

The Jane Castle Manuscript (novel), Delacorte (New York City), 1971.

Work represented in anthologies, including *Prize Stories, 1965-1966: The O. Henry Awards,* 1966. Contributor of short fiction to periodicals, including *Cavalier* and *Partisan Review.*

BIOGRAPHICAL AND CRITICAL SOURCES:

PERIODICALS

New York Times Book Review, October 3, 1971.
Transatlantic Review, autumn, 1967.

* * *

GREGERSEN, Era

PERSONAL: Born in Danzig, Germany; immigrated to United States, 1973; daughter of Heinrich and Hedwig (Gohlke) Karstens; married Erwin Gregersen (a dentist), October 21, 1944; children: Helmuth, Findtjof, Kristian, Susanna, Sabina. *Education:* Studied in Hirschberg, Germany; studied interior design in Italy, 1964-66. *Religion:* Christian. *Hobbies and other interests:* Education, human and civil rights.

ADDRESSES: *Home*—2501 South Ocean Drive, No. 536, Hollywood, FL 33019. *Agent*—c/o Pentland Press Inc., 522 Bur Oak Circle, Raleigh, NC 27612.

CAREER: Artist, sculptor, and author. Formerly worked as a schoolteacher in Germany. *Exhibitions:* Works exhibited in Sicily, Palermo, and Rome, Italy; New York, NY; Palm Beach and Miami, Fl; and Paris, France.

WRITINGS:

The Ocean—My Railroad—Diary of an Artist, 1937-1999, Pentland Press (Raleigh, NC), 1999.

Contributor of short fiction, essays, and poetry to periodicals in Germany, Italy, and the United States.

SIDELIGHTS: Era Gregersen described to *CA* her motivation for writing as a "need to communicate my thoughts and feelings. And I always use to write my diary, where and whenever I found a piece of paper and a pen.

"I never start to write with a specific subject in mind; instead I react to events and circumstances involving people who have been thrown into 'deep waters' and been forced to swim in order to survive . . . and made it long enough to get safe to shore. This includes my own life, which I love with al my passion. I never could, can, nor will give up my fight to survive, in any situation life throws me into.

"I believe all the people in this world would do the same with their life if only they could be allowed to do so—but this can only happen when there exists justice and freedom."

* * *

GRIMSLEY, Ronald 1915-2003

OBITUARY NOTICE—See index for *CA* sketch: Born October 19, 1915, in Leicester, England; died August 11, 2003, in Bristol, England. Educator and author. Grimsley was a professor of French and a noted expert on Jean-Jacques Rousseau. After completing his undergraduate work in French at University College in Leicester, he had begun graduate studies at Oxford University when World War II began. He served in the Royal Artillery and the Intelligence Corps in Europe; and with the war over, he completed a D.Phil. at Oxford in 1948 while also earning a Licence-es-Lettres from the University of Lille. The first part of his academic career was spent at University College of North Wales, where he began as a lecturer and moved his way up to university reader. In 1964 he joined Bristol University as a professor of French; he was head of the department and professor of French language and literature from 1966 until his 1981 retirement as professor emeritus. Grimsley was not only interested in literature, but also in topics ranging from philosophy to history. He was the author or editor of a dozen books, including *Existentialist Thought* (1955;

second edition, 1960), *Søren Kierkegaard and French Literature: Eight Comparative Studies* (1966), *From Montesquieu to Laclos: Studies on the French Enlightenment* (1974), and many books on Rousseau, including *Jean-Jacques Rousseau: A Study in Self-Awareness* (1961), *Rousseau and the Religious Quest* (1968), *The Philosophy of Rousseau* (1973), and *Jean-Jacques Rousseau* (1983).

OBITUARIES AND OTHER SOURCES:

PERIODICALS

Independent (London, England), August 19, 2003, p. 16.

Times (London, England), August 27, 2003.

* * *

GUI, Ming Chao 1946-

PERSONAL: Born July 1, 1946, in Kunming, Yunan, China; naturalized U.S. citizen; son of Cankun Gui (a university professor) and Mifen Guo (a university employee); divorced; children: Mason James, Marion Jane. *Ethnicity:* "Asian American." *Education:* Canton Institute of Foreign Languages, B.A., 1969; University of Texas, M.A., Ph.D., 1990. *Religion:* Christian.

ADDRESSES: *Home*—Norman, OK. *Office*—Department of Modern Languages, Literature, and Linguistics, 780 Van Vleet Oval, University of Oklahoma, Norman, OK 73019. *E-mail*—mgui@ou.edu.

CAREER: Educator and author. Provincial Broadcast Station of Guangdong, Canton, China, producer and teacher of radio course in English-as-a-second-language, 1977-82; Canton Institute of Foreign Languages, lecturer in English language and literature, 1981-83; University of Oklahoma, Norman, assistant professor of Chinese and linguistics, 1994—, and chairperson of East Asian exchange committee. Also worked as a library technician and as a bilingual translator and interpreter.

MEMBER: Linguistic Association of America and Canada, Chinese Language Teachers Association, Foreign Language Teachers Association of Oklahoma.

AWARDS, HONORS: University of Oklahoma Cecil Wood Memorial Teaching Award, 1998, and president's international travel fellowship, 2000.

WRITINGS:

The Phonological Developments of Kunming Chinese in the Past Sixty Years, Language Research (Wuhan, China), 1992.

Fronted or Nasalized? Acoustic Phonetic Analysis of Two Nasal Rhymes in Kunming Chinese, Language Research (Wuhan, China), 1997.

(Coauthor) *Report on the Field Work in Ngai Hua of Luocheng County of Guangxi Province,* Language Research (Wuhan, China), 1998.

The Influence of the Reduplication on the Semantics and Tones of Kunming Chinese, Language Research (Wuhan, China), 1999.

Phonological Analysis of Yangsan Hua of Luocheng County of Guangxi Province, Language Research (Wuhan, China), 1999.

Irregularity in English Grammar and Spelling, World of English (Beijing, China), 2000.

The Interruption of American English Intonation Patterns to the Perception of Mandarin Tones by American Students, Chinese Teaching in the World (Beijing, China), 2000.

Kunming Chinese, Lincom Europa (Munich, Germany), 2000.

Yunnanese and Kunming Chinese: A Study of the Language Communities, the Phonological Systems, and the Phonological Developments, Lincom Europa (Munich, Germany), 2002.

Contributor to periodicals, including *Fujian Foreign Language Journal.*

WORK IN PROGRESS: Research for a Kunming Chinese pronunciation dictionary; research on *Hekou Hua,* a dialect spoken in Yunan Province.

SIDELIGHTS: Ming Chao Gui told *CA:* "My father, professor Cankun Gui, a leading linguist and educator in China, is my mentor and guide. Without his inspiration and encouragement my academic achievements would not be possible. Sentimental feelings for my home town are another driving force in my research and publication. I feel the urge to do something for the place where I was given my life. "My personal experience in research and academic work can be summarized as follows. Theory is important in the way that it can be used for practical purposes. Theory for theory's sake is just like the flowers in the vase: for the look, but not for use. I would rather work on something alive than dead—living languages (synchronic linguistics investigation) rather than 'proto-languages' (diachronic linguistic investigation). To study theory does not mean to be limited or controlled by it; always be yourself. Being self-confident does not mean rejecting the experience and achievement of others. Keep reading whenever you can. When people get older, they will be wiser. Use the wisdom and try to leave something useful for the world before you leave it. Always think positively and do things in a constructive way. We have only one life; why not a better one?"

H

HALLAM, Kerry 1937-

PERSONAL: Born March 12, 1937, in England; son of Clifford (an engineer) and Ena (a seamstress) Hallam; married Cynthia Renshaw, December 2, 1989 (divorced, September, 1995); children: Karyad Brae. *Education:* Attended Central College of Art, London. *Hobbies and other interests:* Tennis, photography.

ADDRESSES: Home—P.O. Box 2188, Nantucket, MA 02584. *Agent*—Côté Literary Group, P.O. Box 1898, Mount Pleasant, SC 29465. *E-mail*—coteliterary.com.

CAREER: Landscape painter and writer. Singer and songwriter, 1966-72; recordings include the album *Autumn Harvest. Exhibitions:* Paintings exhibited in solo shows and in galleries throughout the world; work represented in private collections. *Military service:* British Army Royal Educational Corps, member of Gurkha Brigade; served in Hong Kong and Malaya.

MEMBER: American Society of Composers, Authors, and Publishers, American Writers Union, British Society of Artists, Royal Society of Artists in Watercolour.

AWARDS, HONORS: First prize, Association pour le Promotion Artistique Français, 1998.

WRITINGS:

(With Jeff Moses) *Getting to Nantucket: An Artist's Journey* (autobiography), Corinthian Books (Mount Pleasant, SC), 2000.

Kerry Hallam: Artistic Visions, Jenkintown Press (Philadelphia, PA), 2001.

Artwork included in *Far Horizons: A Celebration of Life,* Chalk & Vermillion Fine Arts (Greenwich, CT).

WORK IN PROGRESS: Kit and Kabudle.

BIOGRAPHICAL AND CRITICAL SOURCES:

ONLINE

Kerry Hallam Web site, http://www.kerryhallam.com (December 14, 2003).

* * *

HANEY, David P. 1952-

PERSONAL: Born December 17, 1952 in Minneapolis, MN; son of Joseph C. (a businessman) and Jean P. (a homemaker) Haney; married Lisa Baldwin. *Ethnicity:* "Caucasian." *Education:* Macalester College, B.A., 1974; State University of New York at Buffalo, M.A., 1979, Ph.D., 1980. *Hobbies and other interests:* Bluegrass music.

ADDRESSES: Home—911 South Minton Rd., Wilkesboro, NC 28697. *Office*—Appalachian State University, Department of English, Sanford Hall, Boone, NC 28608; fax: (828) 262-2133. *E-mail*—haneydp@appstate.edu.

CAREER: Writer, musician, and educator. Boston College, Chestnut Hill, MA, instructor, 1978-80; D'Youville College, Buffalo, NY, adjunct English instructor, 1980-81; Nichols School, Buffalo, English teacher and dean of students, 1980-81; Cambridge School, Weston, MA, English teacher, 1983-88; Swarthmore College, Swarthmore, PA, visiting assistant professor of English, 1988-89; Auburn University, Auburn, AL, assistant professor, 1989-93, Hargis associate professor, 1993-2000, Hargis professor of English literature, 2000-01; Appalachian State University, Boone, NC, professor of English and department chair, 2001—. Worked as a musician, tour manager, and booking agent, 1981-85.

MEMBER: Phi Beta Kappa.

AWARDS, HONORS: National Endowment for the Humanities summer stipend, 1990, Auburn University College of Liberal Arts summer research grant, 1991, 1997, Mortar Board Outstanding Educator, 1992; designated Panhellenic Council Outstanding Professor, 1997, Outstanding Graduate Program Officer, 2001.

WRITINGS:

William Wordsworth and the Hermeneutics of Incarnation, Pennsylvania State University Press (University Park, PA), 1993.

The Challenge of Coleridge: Ethics and Interpretation in Romanticism and Modern Philosophy, Pennsylvania State University Press (University Park, PA), 2001.

Contributor to books, including *In Proximity: Emmanuel Levinas and the Eighteenth Century,* edited by Melvin New and others, Texas Tech University Press (Lubbock, TX), 2001; *The Ethics in Literature,* edited by Andrew Hatfield and others, St. Martin's Press (New York, NY), 1999; and *Autobiography and Post-Modernism,* edited by Leigh Gilmore, et al., University of Massachusetts Press (Amherst, MA), 1994.

Contributor to periodicals, including *Studies in Romanticism, Bluegrass Unlimited, European Romantic Review,* and *Southern Humanities Review.*

Also author of numerous book reviews and conference presentations.

WORK IN PROGRESS: Essays on cognitive theory and hermeneutics; coediting (with Donald Wehrs) a volume of essays on Emmanuel Levinas and nineteenth-century literature; beginning a book on the relationship between interpretation and ethics.

SIDELIGHTS: Writer and educator David P. Haney has authored two texts on Romantic poetry in the nineteenth century. His 1993 book, *William Wordsworth and the Hermeneutics of Incarnation,* "brings considerable theological and theoretical resources to bear upon the linguistic dilemmas uncovered by post-structuralist analyses of Wordsworth," wrote John T. Netland in *Nineteenth-Century Literature.* Haney explores Wordsworth's statement that language should function as an incarnation of thought, in which "words move from the ideality of thought to become—for better and for worse—things and events in the world which are not simply separable from thought, but which must enter the realm of mortality," Haney wrote in the book's introduction.

Haney's analysis of Wordsworth's position brings him into contact with a number of important philosophers and linguists, including Derrida, De Man, and Saussure. "Haney's considerable contribution to Romantic studies is to bring the work of contemporary philosophers such as Levinas and Stanley Cavell to bear on the crucial issue of the nonrepresentational character of Wordsworth's poetics of incarnation," wrote Eric C. Walker in *ANQ.* "The book conducts throughout a sophisticated conversation with all major camps of contemporary literary theory," Walker wrote, in which Haney identifies in Wordsworth's incarnational poetics the collapse of semiotic structures such as the binary sign. Language, to Wordsworth, becomes concrete things and events rather than abstract signs.

Haney also offers new readings of portions of Wordsworth's work, such as the "Lucy" poems, and criticism of Wordsworth by a variety of sources. "One sign of the substantial contribution to Romantic studies that Haney's book offers is that, in the shadow of that imposing bulk of commentary and meta-commentary, he manages to propose important new ways to think about the violence that haunts those Lucy lyrics," Walker observed. Haney's "extended critique of Saussure, deconstruction, and representational theories of language demonstrates Haney at his best," Netland remarked. "He examines judiciously the ideological, philosophical, and linguistic implications of these views, recognizing what is at stake in these critical debates."

With *The Challenge of Coleridge: Ethics and Interpretation in Romanticism and Modern Philosophy,* Haney issues "a call to scholars in literary criticism, philosophy, and culture studies to rethink the relationship between ethics and hermeneutics in more dynamic terms than usual," wrote Regina Hewitt in *ANQ.* According to Haney, "contemporary criticism is bogged down in an either/or reductionism; it endorses either an aestheticism that disconnects art from experience or a moralism that conflates the two." The type of binary opposition in contemporary criticism limits the effectiveness of the criticism. Haney's book "offers a plan to engage us more fully in critical dialogue" by "using passages from Coleridge's works to challenge the positions of the philosophers and reciprocally using the ideas of the philosophers to sound the depths of Coleridge's works," Hewitt wrote. Christopher Strathman, writing in *Wordsworth Circle,* called the book "a thoughtful and illuminating study" that "brings Coleridge's writings into a fruitful dialogue with the work of a number of contemporary thinkers" such as Gadamer, Levinas, Ricoeur, and Nussbaum. Virgil Nemoianu, writing in *Review of Metaphysics,* called *The Challenge of Coleridge* "a good example of uninhibited common use of the whole body of Coleridge's work with the purpose of positioning him in the historical flow of European thinking."

The arguments put forth by Haney are complex, Hewitt noted, and they "can make the book daunting to read," she observed, "but the difficulties are offset by clear prose, systematic organization (including cross references among chapters) and Haney's ability to communicate his enthusiasm for intellectual inquiry. Readers who meet *The Challenge of Coleridge* will be amply rewarded for their effort."

BIOGRAPHICAL AND CRITICAL SOURCES:

PERIODICALS

ANQ, fall, 1995, Eric C. Walker, review of *William Wordsworth and the Hermeneutics of Incarnation,* pp. 56-59; summer, 2002, Regina Hewitt, review of *The Challenge of Coleridge: Ethics and Interpretation in Romanticism and Modern Philosophy,* pp. 41-44.

Criticism, winter, 2002, Paul Youngquist, review of *The Challenge of Coleridge: Ethics and Interpretation in Romanticism and Modern Philosophy,* pp. 83-86.

Nineteenth-Century Literature, December, 1994, John T. Netland, review of *William Wordsworth and the Hermeneutics of Incarnation,* pp. 375-377.

Review of Metaphysics, March, 2002, Virgil Nemoianu, review of *The Challenge of Coleridge: Ethics and Interpretation in Romanticism and Modern Philosophy,* pp. 636-638.

Wordsworth Circle, autumn, 2001, Christopher Strathman, review of *The Challenge of Coleridge: Ethics and Interpretation in Romanticism and Modern Philosophy,* pp. 181-182.

* * *

HARGROVE, (Edward Thomas) Marion (Lawton, Jr.) 1919-2003

OBITUARY NOTICE—See index for *CA* sketch: Born October 13, 1919, in Mount Olive, NC; died of complications from pneumonia August 23, 2003, in Long Beach, CA. Journalist and author. Hargrove is best remembered as the author of the humorous "Private Hargrove" books that were popular during and after World War II. He began his career as a journalist while still in high school, working part time for the *Charlotte News.* Always a rather contrary person, he was unablet to graduate from high school after refusing to take a test in geometry. Nevertheless, the *Charlotte News* hired him to work as a feature editor and columnist. Hargrove was drafted into the U.S. Army in 1941, and it was there that his unwillingness to be the perfect soldier ran him into some trouble with his sergeants; this later became material for his books. In between stints on KP (Kitchen Police) that he was assigned as punishment, Hargrove managed to write humorous articles about his life at Fort Bragg and submitted them to his old newspaper. Then Hargrove met writer Maxwell Anderson, who was at the army post doing research for a play, and showed him his articles. Anderson liked them, and helped the young army private submit them to a publisher. They were published in 1942 as *See Here, Private Hargrove,* a collection that combines humor with patriotism and which was perfect for American audiences worried about the war. It became an instant bestseller, selling over two million copies, and made Hargrove famous. The Army then assigned him to write for *Yank* in New York City, where he remained until 1945, while also publishing the sequel to his first book, *What Next, Corporal Hargrove?* (1944). Both books were adapted as movies produced by Metro-Goldwyn-Mayer and starring Robert Walker. After leaving the army as a sergeant in 1945, Hargrove started on the lecture circuit, taking up a couple of causes in particular: the need to reform the military court martial system and to improve living conditions for enlisted men. Because of these stands, he was sometimes attacked by critics who labeled him a communist, an accusation he always vehemently denied. Hargrove continued his career as a writer, too, penning scripts for the television series *Maverick* during the 1950s, writing the movie adaptation of the musical *The Music Man,* contributing to the periodical *Argosy,* and writing two novels: *Something's Got to Give* (1948) and *The Girl He Left Behind* (1956), the latter of which was also adapted to the silver screen. Later on in his career, Hargrove wrote scripts for the popular television series *I Spy* and *The Waltons.*

OBITUARIES AND OTHER SOURCES:

PERIODICALS

Chicago Tribune, August 30, 2003, section 2, p. 11.
Los Angeles Times, August 29, 2003, p. B12.
New York Times, August 28, 2003, p. A27.
Washington Post, August 29, 2003, p. B6.

* * *

HASHWAY, Robert M. 1946-

PERSONAL: Born October 28, 1946, in Pawtucket, RI. *Ethnicity:* "Syrian." *Education:* Roger Williams University, A.S., B.A.; Rhode Island College, M.A.; Boston College, Ph.D. and postdoctoral study; Harvard University, postdoctoral study, 1977-78. *Religion:* Orthodox.

ADDRESSES: *Home*—113 Greenbriar Dr., West Monroe, LA 71291. *Office*—38 Fairoaks Dr., Monroe, LA 71203. *E-mail*—hashway@msn.com.

CAREER: Roger Williams College, professor of physics, chemistry, electrical engineering, and science education, and director of media and laboratory services, 1968-72; public school mathematics teacher, 1972-75; Massachusetts State College System, director of developmental studies, faculty development, institutional enhancement, ane computer operations, 1976-84; Rhode Island College, professor of mathematics and mathematics education, 1982-86; Grambling State University, Grambling, LA, professor of education, 1986—, director of Educational Resource Center, 1986-89, chair of Analytic Studies Group, 1993—. Boston College, senior research associate at Laboratory for Social Policy Research, 1974-77, professor, 1976-78; West Warwick Public Schools, vice chair, 1980-86; Bryant College, professor, 1982-84. National Foundation for Gifted and Creative Children, research director, 1970-75; Advanced Concepts Learning Centers, president, 1982-86. Microware, Inc., president, 1982-86; RMC Corp., vice president for curriculum, 1984-86. Charles V. Hogan Mental Health Center, assistant superintendent, 1975-77.

MEMBER: Association for the Advancement of Educational Research (vice president and director of management and finance, 1997—), National Academy for Educational Research (vice president, 1997—).

AWARDS, HONORS: President's Award for Excellence in Research, Eastern Educational Research Association; Research Paper of the Year Awards, Louisiana Educational Research Association and American Educational Research Association; grants from Louisiana Board of Elementary/Secondary Education, Aerospace Corp., and Bureau of Education for the Handicapped.

WRITINGS:

Objective Mental Measurement, Praeger (Westport, CT), 1978.
Foundations of Developmental Education, Praeger (Westport, CT), 1988.
Handbook of Developmental Education, Praeger (Westport, CT), 1990.
Cognitive Styles, Mellen Research University Press, 1992.
Developmental Evaluation, Assessment, and Learning, Greenwood Press (Westport, CT), 1996.
Error-Free Mental Measurement, International Scholars Press, 1997.

Developmental Cognitive Styles, International Scholars Press, 1998.

Handbook of Support Programs for At-Risk Students in College, Praeger (Westport, CT), 1998.

(Editor and contributor) *Yearbook of Research on Developmentalism,* International Scholars Press, Volume 1: *Theoretical Foundations,* 1998, Volume 2: *Curriculum Issues,* 1999, Volume 3: *Student Personnel Issues,* 2000.

Funding Public Higher Education, International Scholars Press, 1999.

Developmental Learning Theory, Greenwood Press (Westport, CT), 2000.

Developmental Curriculum Validation, Auditing, and Evaluation, Greenwood Press (Westport, CT), 2000.

Creator of computer software programs. Contributor of more than 100 articles to professional journals, including *Journal of Social and Behavioral Sciences, Forum for Reading, College Student Journal,* and *Social Literacy Issues.* Editor, *New England Educator,* 1978-86, *Journal of Learning Improvement,* 1991—, *Newsletter of the Eastern Educational Research Association,* 1992-95, *Research for Learning Improvement, Research for Educational Reform,* and *Educational Research Quarterly.*

* * *

HAY, Elizabeth 1951-

PERSONAL: Born 1951, in Owen Sound, Ontario, Canada; married; husband's name, Mark (second marriage); children: Sochi, Ben. *Education:* Attended Victoria College and University of Toronto.

ADDRESSES: Agent—c/o Author Mail, Counterpoint, 387 Park Ave. South, 12th Floor, New York, NY 10016-8810.

CAREER: Author. CBC Radio, Canada, host, interviewer, and documentary filmmaker; taught creative writing at New York University and the University of Ottawa.

AWARDS, HONORS: National Magazine gold award for fiction, 1995; *Western* magazine award for fiction, 1995; MOSAID Technology award, Canadian Authors Association, and TORGI award, Canadian National Institute for the Blind, both for *A Student of Weather;* Marian Engel award, 2002.

WRITINGS:

Crossing the Snow Line (stories), Black Moss Press (Windsor, Ontario, Canada), 1989.

The Only Snow in Havana (nonfiction), Cormorant Books (Dunvegan, Ontario, Canada), 1992.

Captivity Tales: Canadians in New York (nonfiction), New Star Books (Vancouver, British Columbia, Canada), 1993.

Small Change (stories), Porcupine's Quill (Erin, Ontario, Canada), 1997, Counterpoint (Washington, DC), 2001.

A Student of Weather (novel), McClelland & Stewart (Toronto, Ontario, Canada), 2000, Counterpoint (Washington, DC), 2001.

Garbo Laughs (novel), Counterpoint (New York, NY), 2003.

Work represented in anthologies, including *Best Canadian Short Stories, The Journey Prize Anthology,* and *The Oxford Book of Stories by Canadian Women.*

SIDELIGHTS: Canadian author Elizabeth Hay wrote several books before her collection of short stories titled *Short Change* received rave reviews and a number of award nominations. Following the success of her first novel, *A Student of Weather, Short Change* was reprinted by Hay's U.S. publisher, Counterpoint.

The stories of *Short Change* are about relationships, including in "The Friend," one between the narrator, Beth, and Maureen, the beautiful wife of a promiscuous bisexual artist. "Hand Games" finds Beth's daughter, Annie, longing for friendship with the girl upstairs. In "Sayonara" Beth bumps into her old boss, a man who had been unable to communicate his affection for her, and so she married someone else. When the past catches up with her, she finds feelings for him may still exist.

A *Kirkus Reviews* contributor wrote that "with its masterfully crafted tonalities, this analysis of friendship has a dark urgency that's as instructive as it is unsettling."

The title character in *A Student of Weather* is Maurice Dove, a graduate student sent from Ottawa to the prairie of southwest Saskatchewan to study weather patterns during the Depression-era dust bowl. Maurice visits the farm of widower Ernest Hardy in 1938, when the farmer's daughters—the beautiful, blonde Lucinda and brazen, gangly Norma Joyce—are respectively seventeen and eight years old. The resourceful and patient Lucinda is a dedicated housekeeper, while her unpleasant younger sister avoids work and refuses to attend school. Both sisters fall in love with Maurice, who is handsome and exudes more sophistication than the girls are used to. Lucinda experiences love in her own reserved way, while Norma Joyce makes her feelings perfectly clear. After he leaves the farm, Maurice writes to Lucinda, but Norma Joyce intercepts and destroys the letters. Over time, Norma Joyce ultimately betrays her sister, and in so doing, she removes any chance of Maurice caring for Lucinda.

Robert A. Papinchak wrote in the *Milwaukee Journal Sentinel* that "the facile narrative moves from western to eastern Canada and into New York City. It illuminates distinctions between prairie life and city life. It ranges from biblical and mythological themes to painful revelations about parents and children. It lays bare the consequences of lifelong secrets and lies."

Liza Featherstone noted in the *New York Times Book Review* that Hay "deftly renders her characters' disconcerting moral ambiguities. Norma Joyce's selfishness is profoundly disturbing—yet strangely forgivable." Featherstone felt that "despite such horrifying behavior, you can't help liking Norma Joyce more than her irritatingly lovely and long-suffering sister (until in a welcome twist, Lucinda turns out not to be as virtuous as she seems)." *Booklist*'s Donna Seaman called *A Student of Weather* "painterly in its lyricism, profoundly female in its voluptuousness, and acute in its psychology." *National Post* contributor Jason Sherman commented that Norma Joyce "is not larger than life, she is life, and she comes to us fully formed in this rich, compelling, satisfying novel."

Hay's second novel, *Garbo Laughs,* is set in Ottawa, the home of writer Harriet Browning, who has been told that she resembles actress Greta Garbo. Much of the story takes place during the ice storm of 1998. Harriet is the wife of architect Lew Gold and the mother of two. Denied access to movies as a child, she is now obsessed with old films and hardly has time for her husband. She has indoctrinated her children into her world of fantasy, and Kenny, age ten, enjoys dressing up as the Frank Sinatra character in *Guys and Dolls,* while Jane is her glamorous twelve-year-old. Joining their film club is Harriet's neighbor, earthy journalist Dinah Bloom. The title of the book is a reference to the fact that Garbo almost never laughed, making it necessary to dub her laugh in films.

Into Harriet's life comes Aunt Leah, who is returning to Ottawa and needs a place to stay. Leah was once married to Lionel Frame, a friend of the Hollywood Ten and a blacklisted screenwriter. As the story continues, Lew and Dinah become attracted to each other, and Harriet resists her feelings for Leah's stepson. Illnesses are diagnosed and life goes on, except when it stops for another video of an old classic.

"It isn't a hankering for all movies but a love of old movies, with their long-dead stars, figures whose lives were at least partly shrouded in mystery, that gives Harriet's life meaning," wrote Karen Karbo in the *New York Times Book Review.* "Although she's only forty-seven, her taste in actors runs to Cary Grant and Sean Connery. Not for her Russell Crowe and Hugh Grant, with their messy dalliances and sputtering talk show appearances. Harriet doesn't just live in the movies, she lives in the past."

A *Publishers Weekly* critic called *Garbo Laughs* "a gracefully written novel, mapping out the patterns of tension and release in a family whose members are best able to express their love and disappointment through the films of the past."

BIOGRAPHICAL AND CRITICAL SOURCES:

PERIODICALS

Booklist, November 15, 2000, Donna Seaman, review of *A Student of Weather,* p. 614; October 1, 2001, Danise Hoover, review of *Small Change,* p. 299; September 1, 2003, Donna Seaman, review of *Garbo Laughs,* p. 56.

Books in Canada, September-October, 2001, review of *A Student of Weather,* p. 14.

Chatelaine, June, 2003, review of *Garbo Laughs,* p. 213.

Entertainment Weekly, October 17, 2003, Lisa Schwarzbaum, review of *Garbo Laughs,* p. 84.

Houston Chronicle, April 22, 2001, Steve Wisch, review of *A Student of Weather,* p. 15.

Kirkus Reviews, August 15, 2001, review of *Small Change,* p. 1150; August 1, 2003, review of *Garbo Laughs,* p. 978.

Library Journal, March 1, 2001, Cheryl L. Conway, review of *A Student of Weather,* p. 131; August, 2001, Lisa Nussbaum, review of *Small Change,* p. 168; September 1, 2003, Caroline M. Hallsworth, review of *Garbo Laughs,* p. 206.

Mclean's, August 21, 2000, Charles Gordon, review of *A Student of Weather,* p. 55.

Milwaukee Journal Sentinel, February 11, 2001, Robert A. Papinchak, review of *A Student of Weather,* p. 6.

National Post, May 6, 2000, Jason Sherman, review of *A Student of Weather,* p. 26.

New York Times Book Review, February 11, 2001, Liza Featherstone, review of *A Student of Weather,* p. 23; November 16, 2003, Karen Karbo, review of *Garbo Laughs,* p. L6.

Publishers Weekly, December 11, 2000, review of *A Student of Weather,* p. 63; July 28, 2003, review of *Garbo Laughs,* p. 75.

Quill and Quire, May, 2000, review of *A Student of Weather,* p. 30.

Times Literary Supplement, December 28, 2001, Lavinia Greenlaw, review of *A Student of Weather,* p. 20.

Victoria, July, 2001, Michele Slung, review of *A Student of Weather,* p. 35.

Washington Post Book World, February 20, 2001, Jabari Asim, review of *A Student of Weather,* p. C03.

ONLINE

January Magazine, http://www.januarymagazine.com/ (June, 2000), Linda Richards, interview with Hay.*

* * *

HEGWOOD, Martin 1951-

PERSONAL: Born September 23, 1951, in Pascagoula, MS; married; wife's name Linda (a teacher). *Education:* University of Mississippi, B.A.

ADDRESSES: Home—Canton, MS. *Office*—c/o Office of the Secretary of State, 401 North President St., Jackson, MS 39201. *E-mail*—mhegwood@sos.state.ms.us.

CAREER: Office of the Secretary of State of Mississippi, Jackson, senior attorney; writer.

WRITINGS:

Big Easy Backroad, St. Martin's Press (New York, NY), 1999.

The Green-eyed Hurricane, St. Martin's Minotaur (New York, NY), 2000.

Massacre Island, St. Martin's Minotaur (New York, NY), 2001.

Jackpot Bay, St. Martin's Minotaur (New York, NY), 2002.

WORK IN PROGRESS: Currently researching material for a multi-generational historical novel set in the South.

SIDELIGHTS: Martin Hegwood was raised in a four-generation household deep in the South on a Mississippi Gulf Coast bayou. His parents ran a shrimping business, and as a child he helped to haul the family's boats out of the water in order to repair them. At one time Hegwood considered becoming more involved in his parents' line of work, but he ended up going to school and becoming a lawyer. He worked as an assistant district attorney in Mississippi before taking a position as a lawyer in the office of the Mississippi secretary of state. But Hegwood also aspired to a writing career. At first he considered writing romance novels, since more novels are published in this genre than in any other. But he rejected this idea in favor of the second most popular genre, mystery novels. Since his literary debut in 1999 he has written four well-received mysteries.

Big Easy Backroad, Hegwood's first novel, introduces private investigator Jack Delmas, described by Jenny McLarin in *Booklist* as a "laid back protagonist." Jack is really most comfortable looking for white-collar criminals involved in insurance fraud, but a beautiful blonde entices him to help her find her boyfriend. She has not seen him for a while, and a local news report about a murder makes her suspect that he might be dead. After drinking a few beers at the bar where the blonde works, Jack promises to help, although the next morning he regrets it. But when the blonde also turns up dead, Jack becomes the prime suspect and the plot thickens. Trying to prove his innocence, he finds himself tangled up with a local mob, whom he suspects was also involved in killing his partner a few years ago. When Jack gets too close to the truth, the mob tries to kill him.

Big Easy Backroad earned high praise. A writer for *Kirkus Reviews* hailed it as "atmospheric and action-packed," while McLarin noted it as "a suspenseful and entertaining beginning to a promising series."

Jack Delmas makes his second appearance in *The Green-eyed Hurricane,* which is set in Biloxi in the aftermath of Hurricane Camille. Once a slow-paced seaside town, Biloxi, Mississippi was devastated by the storm; in its wake came rampant new development, including big-time gambling casinos and real estate speculation. In the novel Jack finds himself trying to defend his old buddy, shrimper Casper Perinovich, who tries singlehandedly to fight the developers who want his home and, better yet, his prime waterfront acreage. Casper refuses to give in, and one night his house explodes in fire with Casper still inside. At one point, Casper had told the investors that the only way they would get his land was over his dead body. So, Casper's niece and heir suspects foul play and pleads with Jack to investigate. A writer for *Publishers Weekly* admired the book's "kaleidoscope of action" as well as its roster of colorful characters including "lusty women, beer-swilling rednecks and snarling Vietnamese thugs." A *Kirkus Reviews* writer found this second novel "even better than Hegwood's pleasant debut."

Massacre Island, the third "Jack Delmas" mystery novel, takes place off the picturesque coast of Alabama on Dauphin Island, where Jack has gone to investigate a murder. The story soon involves white supremacists, drug smuggling, and a radical environmentalist group. In *Library Journal* Rex Klett praised the book's "unnerving action" and "atmospheric" rendering of the Gulf Coast setting. A reviewer for *Publishers Weekly* also enjoyed the setting, commenting that Hegwood paints such an attractive picture of Dauphin Island that "one feels like packing one's bags and heading south."

The fourth installment in the "Jack Delmas" series is Hegwood's *Jackpot Bay,* which takes place in what *Booklist* reviewer Jenny McLarin referred to as the "Redneck Riviera," Bay St. Louis, Mississippi. When the city's large casino starts losing money, its owners grow more and more suspicious. So they send blonde beauty Tara Stocklin, an accountant, to investigate. They also employ Delmas to make sure nothing happens to Tara while she works on the case. Tara does remain safe, but someone else gets shot. The book is filled with "wry humor, high adventure . . . and a lot of fun," wrote Rex E. Klett in *Library Journal.* "Hegwood knows his stuff," observed Jenny McLarin in *Booklist,* "and it shows."

BIOGRAPHICAL AND CRITICAL SOURCES:

PERIODICALS

Booklist, June 1, 1999, Jenny McLarin, review of *Big Easy Backroad,* p. 1800; October 15, 2002, Jenny McLarin, review of *Jackpot Bay,* p. 391.

Kirkus Reviews, June 15, 1999, review of *Big Easy Backroad,* p. 921; May 15, 2000, review of *The Green-eyed Hurricane,* p. 671; August 15, 2001, review of *Massacre Island,* p. 1167; September 15, 2002, review of *Jackpot Bay,* p. 1355.

Library Journal, October 1, 2001, Rex E. Klett, review of *Massacre Island,* p. 145; November 1, 2002, review of *Jackpot Bay,* p. 132.

Publishers Weekly, June 21, 1999, review of *Big Easy Backroad,* p. 60; May 29, 2000, review of *The Green-eyed Hurricane,* p. 55; September 10, 2001, review of *Massacre Island,* p. 64.

ONLINE

Mystery Reader, http://www.themysteryreader.com/ (September 15, 2000), Thea Davis, review of *The Green-eyed Hurricane.*

* * *

HELFAND, Jessica

PERSONAL: Female. *Education:* Yale University, B.A., 1982, M.F.A.

ADDRESSES: *Office*—P.O. Box 159, Falls Village, CT 06031; fax: 860-824-1065.

CAREER: Graphic designer and writer. Freelance writer for National Broadcasting Company, Inc. (NBC) and Columbia Broadcasting System, Inc. (CBS), 1982-85; Designers Three, New York, NY, designer, 1985-87; Roger Black Studio, senior designer, 1989-90; *Philadelphia Inquirer* (magazine), Philadelphia, PA, design director, 1990-93; Jessica Helfand Studio, Ltd., principal, 1993-97; Jessica Helfand/William Drenttel, Inc., Falls Village, CT, partner, 1997—. Visiting professor, lecturer, or critic at Yale University School of Design, New York University, Cooper Union for the Advancement of Science and Art, Columbia University School of Architecture, and North Carolina State University.

AWARDS, HONORS: Philadelphia Inquirer magazine was named the nation's best-designed Sunday magazine by the American Association of Magazine Editors, 1993; Gold Medal in New Media, New York Art Directors' Club, 1996, for Discovery Channel online; more than seventy-five awards in design excellence from the American Institute of Graphic Arts, Society of Newspaper Designers, Society of Publication Designers, American Institute of Graphic Arts, Type Directors Club, *I.D.* (magazine), *Print and Communications Arts* regional design annuals, and *American Illustration.*

WRITINGS:

Six Essays on Design and New Media, William Drenttel (New York, NY), 1995.

(Editor, with D. K. Holland and Chipp Kidd) *Graphic Design America Two: Portfolios from the Best and Brightest Design Firms from across the United States,* Rockport Publishers (New York, NY), 1997.

(Editor, with Michael Bierut, Steven Heller, and Rick Poynor) *Looking Closer 3: Classic Writings on Graphic Design,* Allworth Press (New York, NY), 2000.

Screen: Essays on Graphic Design, New Media, and Visual Culture, Princeton Architectural Press (New York, NY), 2001.

Reinventing the Wheel, Princeton Architectural Press (New York, NY), 2002.

Writer of column "Screen" for *Eye* magazine, 1996—; contributing editor to *I.D.,* 1994—, and to *Print,* 1993-95; contributor to books, including *Paul Rand,* Phaidon (London, England), 1999, and to periodicals, including *New Republic, AIGA Journal of Graphic Design,* and *Philadelphia Inquirer.*

WORK IN PROGRESS: License to Risk: The Square Revisited.

SIDELIGHTS: Graphic designer Jessica Helfand began her career writing for daytime television for several years before joining a small New York design firm. In her position as senior designer with the Roger Black Studio, she redesigned more than fifteen American and international magazines, including *Mother Earth News.* She then moved to the *Philadelphia Inquirer*'s weekly magazine and was responsible for the redesign that ultimately garnered more than five dozen awards for design, illustration, and photography during her three years there. In 1993 it was named the best-designed Sunday magazine by the American Association of Magazine Editors.

In 1993 Helfand became a freelance designer, whose projects now included Web design for a number of large clients, including the Discovery Channel and America Online. Traditional print clients included HarperCollins publishers. Helfand and William Drenttel, formed a partnership based in Connecticut in 1997.

During that year, Helfand was interviewed by Cary Murnion for *Baseline: Journal of Parsons School of Design.* Helfand said that she chose her cross-disciplinary major in resistance to being a fine arts major, "and because I was, and continue to be, interested in the theoretical foundation(s) of design as a series of smaller, complex disciplines. Lately, I am particularly interested in invoking models from other disciplines—such as architecture, music and film—as ideological templates in the development of interactive projects here in my studio."

Helfand called new media "the gold rush of the 1990s. In an environment that grows this fast, and moves this fast, it's really difficult to think, reflect, create, and design. The climate simply won't support it. For this reason, I have consciously down-sized my studio to focus on fewer projects and (hopefully) to do them better. I also find it increasingly important to concentrate on theoretical and experimental projects, to teach and to write—to extend this thinking through opportunities other than those brought in by my clients."

Helfand emphasized the importance of design history in design education and commented that she does not believe "that print is dead or will die anytime soon, nor do I think that the tenets of design as they have been taught to us traditionally are without merit in this new world. But it's a highly selective process—I would argue that while the visual manifestation of the work, and its incumbent parameters may change, the process—that is, the rigorous intellectual conceptualization and reflective form-giving—that characterizes graphic design is as important here, if not more so." Helfand noted that most new media designers are young, because older designers haven't had the software training. "But ultimately," she said, "the thinking, the idea, is always the most important thing, whether you're young or old, working in traditional or new media."

Helfand teaches design and has written a column and published several books, as either writer or editor, including *Six Essays on Design and New Media,* in which she both celebrates and questions the new technology in six articles previously published in *Print* magazine. She explores the history of design in literature and film, as well as within her own discipline. A reviewer for *I.D.* felt the volume "ought to be required reading for anyone even considering working in multimedia."

Screen: Essays on Graphic Design, New Media, and Visual Culture is a collection of twenty-three articles written by Helfand between 1994 and 2001. Most were first published as columns in *Eye,* while others come from various publications. Tim Rich said in *Print* that the opening article, titled "One, Two, Three, Faux: The Myth of Real Time," "won not just my attention but my admiration." Other sections include "Myth," "Virtuality," "Design," "Aesthetics," "Media," "Typography," "Film," "Cult of the Scratchy," and "Spin and the (Pseudo) Screen Event." A student of Paul Rand, Helfand includes two essays about him.

Rich wrote that Helfand "offers the views of an individual who experiences her subject while playing several roles—designer, writer, critic, teacher, citizen, friend, mother. This multidimensional critical perspective works well in *Screen.*" Rich called Helfand's prose "thoughtful, bright, and packed with compelling turns of thought. True, there are some exasperatingly long sentences and a trifle too much studio jargon . . . but these are far outweighed by the passion, curiosity, wit, and a rather charming impatience evident in the book. I found it refreshing to explore the essays of a critic who displays an underlying vein of common sense, a commitment to the value of clarity, and a love of reading. How unusual to see these supposedly old-fashioned values at large in the often painfully fashionable world of new media."

Reinventing the Wheel is Helfand's history of volvelles, or "information wheels." The earliest paper circles within circles were used during the Renaissance to chart celestial cycles, the tides, and the movement of heavenly bodies. Volvelles became popular during the twentieth century and were used for figuring taxes, remedies, breeding cycles, and other calculations. Helfand includes nearly 100 illustrations of the most popular, which, according to a reviewer for *Scientific American,* makes the book "visually intriguing." *Library Journal*'s Michael Dashkin wrote that "readers interested in information design will seek this out, while those interested in book and graphic design will be thrilled by the surprise."

BIOGRAPHICAL AND CRITICAL SOURCES:

PERIODICALS

Baseline: Journal of Parsons School of Design, winter, 1997, Cary Murnion, interview with Helfand, pp. 15-22.

I.D., September-October, 1996, review of *Six Essays on Design and New Media,* p. 96.

Library Journal, October 1, 2002, Michael Dashkin, review of *Reinventing the Wheel,* p. 88.

Print, January, 2000, Denise Gonzales Crisp, review of *Looking Closer 3: Classic Writings on Graphic Design,* p. 40; March-April, 2002, Tim Rich, review of *Screen: Essays on Graphic Design, New Media, and Visual Culture,* p. 32.

Scientific American, December, 2002, review of *Reinventing the Wheel,* p. 128.

ONLINE

Jessica Helfand/William Drenttel, Inc. Web site, http://www.jhwd.com/ (June 23, 2003).*

HELL, Richard 1949-
(Theresa Stern)

PERSONAL: Born Richard Meyers, October 2, 1949, in Lexington, KY; married Patty Smyth (a singer and songwriter; divorced); married second wife Sheelagh Pauline Bevan, October 5, 2002; children: (first marriage) Ruby.

ADDRESSES: *Office*—c/o CUZ Editions, P.O. Box 1599, Stuyvesant Station, New York, NY 10009-1599. *E-mail*—mail@richardhell.com.

CAREER: Writer, musician, songwriter, actor, editor, publisher, and artist. Member of rock bands, including Neon Boys, Television, Heartbreakers, and Richard Hell and the Voidoids. Publisher and editor of books and magazines under imprints Genesis: Grasp and Dot Books; editor and copublisher of CUZ Editions. *Exhibitions:* Works exhibited at Rupert Goldsworthy Gallery, New York, NY, 1998. Film appearances include *Final Reward,* directed by Rachid Kerdouche, not distributed, 1978; *The Blank Generation,* Anchor Bay, 1979; *Smithereens,* New Line, 1982; *Geek Maggot Bingo,* Monday/Wednesday/Friday, 1983; *Desperately Seeking Susan,* Columbia TriStar, 1985; *No Picnic,* Gray City, 1987; *What about Me,* Music Video Distributors, 1993; *Blind Light,* Blinding Light, 1997; *Pop Odyssee Two: House of the Rising Punk,* 3sat/ZDF, 1998; and *We're Outta Here!,* Eagle Rock 1998.

WRITINGS:

I Was a Spiral on the Floor (poems), Soyo Publishers (Amsterdam, Netherlands), 1988.
Across the Years (poems), Soyo Publishers (Amsterdam, Netherlands), 1991.
Artifact: Notebooks from Hell, 1974-80, Hanuman Books (New York, NY), 1992.
Go Now: A Novel, Scribner (New York, NY), 1996.
The Voidoid, Codex (Hove, England), 1996.
Hot and Cold: Richard Hell, PowerHouse Books (New York, NY), 2001.
(With others) *The Blank Generation* (screenplay), Anchor Bay, 1979.

Contributor to anthologies, including *The Judas Jesus,* 1988; *Am Lit: Neu Literatur aus den USA,* 1992; *Out of This World,* 1992; *Jungles d'Ameriques,* 1993; and *Aroused,* 2001. Contributor to magazines, including *Punk, Purple, Raw Periphery,* and *Rolling Stone.*

AS THERESA STERN

(With T. Verlaine) *Wanna Go Out,* (poems) Éditions Anna Polèrica (Perpignan, France), 1999.

AUTHOR OF LYRICS; SOUND RECORDINGS

Richard Hell EP, Ork, 1976.
R. I. P., ROIR (cassette), 1984; Relativity (compact disc), 1990.
(Under name Neon Boys) *Neon Boys EP,* Overground, 1991.
(Under name Dim Stars) *Dim Stars,* Caroline, 1992.
Go Now, Tim Kerr Records, 1995.
Time, Matador, 2002.

AUTHOR OF LYRICS; SOUND RECORDINGS; AS RICHARD HELL AND THE VOIDOIDS

Blank Generation, Sire, 1977.
Destiny Street, Red Star, 1982.
Funhunt, ROIR, 1989.

SIDELIGHTS: With spiked hair and his ragged shirts, often cut or torn on purpose, Richard Hell is often regarded as the progenitor of the fashion sensibility that formed an inextricable part of the mid-to late-1970s punk movement. Legend has it that British promoter Malcolm McLaren, who in many ways was the leading architect of punk as a commodity, took careful stock of Hell's dress and adapted it for the group he formed in London in the summer of 1977, the Sex Pistols. Whatever the case, there is no doubt that Hell was among the most important figures in the birth of punk, which had its roots in New York City as much as four years before the Pistols emerged on the international scene. Decades later, as the surviving members of the Sex Pistols prepared for a reunion tour, Hell returned to his past in quite a different way with the 1996 novel *Go Now.*

Born Richard Meyers and raised in Lexington, Kentucky, Hell dropped out of high school in 1966. Enamored of French surrealist literature, he found himself wildly out of place in his hometown and migrated to New York City. There he made a meager living publishing books of poetry using a second-hand printing press. Soon he was joined by Tom Verlaine, a friend from high school who had likewise left behind Kentucky for New York, and in 1973 they formed a group called the Neon Boys. Eventually this outfit became Television, a seminal band of the early punk movement, but by 1975, just before Television released its first album, Hell had quit. Johnny Thunders and Jerry Nolan had just quit the New York Dolls, a band that historically constitutes the link between the paleo-punk of the late 1960s Velvet Underground and early punk groups of mid-1970s New York. With Hell they formed the Heartbreakers. Hell remained with the Heartbreakers—not to be confused with the mainstream rock group fronted by Tom Petty—for another year before leaving to form the Voidoids in 1976.

Richard Hell and the Voidoids, as they came to be known, were featured, along with the Sex Pistols, Television, and the Talking Heads in a *Time* magazine cover story that introduced Middle America to Punk in 1978. The group released their first and most important album, *Blank Generation,* in 1977. The title of the album, was a parody of *Beat Generation,* the name of a book of poetry by Rod McKuen. Just as Hell's poetry, published in *Rolling Stone* and other magazines, contrasted sharply with McKuen's, so his chosen style of dress was a reaction to the flash and excess of the disco fashion then in vogue. In contrast to the clothing associated with discotheques such as Studio 54, Hell's style was deliberately minimalist, informed by an implicitly egalitarian ethos: the clothes were nothing if not cheap and accessible to virtually anyone.

Two more solo albums followed in the early 1980s, the era in which Hell lived the events that—to some degree at least—formed the basis for *Go Now.* In the mid-1980s he and singer Patti Smyth of the group Scandal had a daughter, Ruby. He formed the Dim Stars with members of Sonic Youth and Gumball for a 1992 album, conducted poetry readings and made videos of some, and acted in independent films. The multitalented Hell even found time to put on a show of his drawings. He continued to write and publish poetry, but his first major publication was the novel *Go Now.*

The degree to which *Go Now* is based on Hell's own life is a matter of some question, and Hell himself has offered little in the way of clarification. For starters, the protagonist and anti-hero has a name that is as clearly a pseudonym as "Richard Hell" is: Billy Mud. (In fact, Hell told the *Los Angeles Times* that he considered publishing *Go Now* under his given name, but his mother, a former English professor, was so horrified by its scenes of drug abuse, empty sex, and general degradation that she told him, "Richard, if you were at all thinking of going back to your name for my sake, don't bother.") Like Hell at the time the book takes place, in 1980 Mud is strung out on heroin. Hell also took a cross-country trip like the one on which Mud embarks with a photographer girlfriend, but the similarities end there.

The most important difference between the author and his creation is that, whereas Hell kicked the heroin habit and lived to write about it, readers of *Go Now* soon discover that Mud's future is not likely to be so fortunate. Appearing at a time when heroin use had attracted widespread public attention, *Go Now* attracted comparisons to *Trainspotting,* Irvine Welsh's novel about Scottish junkies. Asked about the similarities by a *Los Angeles Times* reporter, Hell said, "One thing we have in common is that we don't glamorize or romanticize drug use. But neither do we judge users."

Discussing the manner in which Mud squanders a great opportunity—an all-expenses-paid trip across the country with a beautiful woman, his only responsibility being to help drive and write about the road trip—Mark Hayford wrote in the *Times Literary Supplement* that "What saves *Go Now* from becoming a queasy homage to self-indulgence is the clarity and verve of Richard Hell's writing. Occasional outbursts, such as: 'A shred of nightmare blowing by gets caught on a thorn in my brain, but I can't guess its context. . . . When I reach, it disintegrates like a flake of ash on my fingertips,' suggest that Mud's proclivities may simply be a cloaking device used to usher in pockets of insight." Deirdre R. Schwiesow in *USA Today* also commented on those moments of clarity in the narrator's brain, observing that "Billy's quest leads to moments of real insight and even beauty, not to mention that there's something perversely fascinating about seeing the depths to which he sinks, resulting in a climax that is by turns thrilling and sad." Wrote Trudi Miller Rosenblum in *Billboard,* "It's a harrowing book, but compelling to read, as hope and optimism turn to doom and fatalism."

BIOGRAPHICAL AND CRITICAL SOURCES:

PERIODICALS

Billboard, June 27, 1996, Trudi Miller Rosenblum, review of *Go Now: A Novel,* p. 87.

Boston Globe, June 21, 1996, Mimi Udovitch, "Richard Hell's Journey from Punk to Junk to First Novel," p. 40.

Library Journal, May 1, 1996, Doris Lynch, review of *Go Now: A Novel,* p. 130.

Los Angeles Times, September 23, 1996, Irene Lacher, "An Ex-Punker with a Story to Tell," p. E6.

Publishers Weekly, April 29, 1996, Sybil Steinberg, review of *Go Now: A Novel,* p. 52.

Times Literary Supplement, June 28, 1996, Mark Hayford, review of *Go Now: A Novel,* p. 22.

USA Today, August 26, 1996, Deirdre R. Schwiesow, "'Go Now' Journeys down a Junkie's Ragged Road," p. 6D.

ONLINE

Richard Hell Home Page, http://www.richardhell.com/ (September 16, 2003).*

* * *

HENLEY, Jan (S.) 1956-
(Anna Cheska)

PERSONAL: Born June 30, 1956, in Worthing, West Sussex, England; daughter of Herbert (an optical glazier) and Daphne (Woodward; a secretary) Squires; married Timothy Page (divorced), Keith Henley (separated); children: Luke Page, Alexa Page, Anna Henley. *Education:* Open University, B.A. *Hobbies and other interests:* Playing tennis and badminton, pilates, listening to Italian opera, watching football, avoiding housework.

ADDRESSES: Home—13 Thorn Road, Worthington, West Sussex BN11 3ND, England. *Agent*—Teresa Chris Literary Agency, 43 Musard Road, London W6 8NR, England. *E-mail*—janhenley@hotmail.com.

CAREER: Writer. Also works as a creative writing tutor and teacher; developed manuscript appraisal service.

MEMBER: Society of Authors, Romantic Novelists Association.

WRITINGS:

Other Summers, Hodder & Stoughton (London, England), 1995.

Separate Lives, Hodder & Stoughton (London, England), 1995.

Living Lies, Hodder & Stoughton (London, England), 1996.

Somebody's Lover, Hodder & Stoughton (London, England), 1997.

Family Ties, Hodder & Stoughton (London, England), 1998.

Stepping Aside, Hodder & Stoughton (London, England), 1998.

UNDER PSEUDONYM ANNA CHESKA

Moving to the Country, Piatkus Books (London, England), 2000.

Drop Dead Gorgeous, Piatkus Books (London, England), 2001.

Love-40, Piatkus Books (London, England), 2002.

Also author of short stories in national women's magazines and articles in *New Writer* and *Writer's Forum.*

WORK IN PROGRESS: The Secret Structure of Fiction, a self-help book; *A Class Act,* a contemporary romantic comedy.

SIDELIGHTS: Jan Henley is an author of contemporary women's fiction who sometimes writes under the pseudonym Anna Cheska. She began writing short stories while at home with her young children and had her first novel published in 1995.

Henley's first novel to be published in the United States was *Moving to the Country.* In this "competent tale of marital discord," as a *Kirkus Reviews* writer described it, Jess and her husband move to the country to re-energize their tired marriage. Their daughter has just left for college and Felix's company has relocated. Even though her husband has been unfaithful for years, Jess hopes the move will bring about a change of heart. Instead, she is the one who changes, prompted by the return of both her vagabond sister who has been traveling Europe for sixteen years, and her daughter, who leaves college after a failed affair with a married man. While her husband quickly finds a new mistress, Jess discovers she has a talent for interior design and begins her own business and friendships in her new home. Danise Hoover of *Booklist* commented: "Ably portraying an assortment of neighbors and business associates, the story exudes a good deal of subtlety and genuine warmth."

In *Drop Dead Gorgeous* Henley returns to the theme of a failed marriage. Imogen and Edward West have a stable, but mundane marriage, then Edward dies suddenly. Imogen is not nearly as grieved as she expected, and she begins to uncover some secrets as she sorts through her husband's belongings. She discovers a photograph of a sexy blonde, who turns out to be Edward's grown daughter from a twenty-year affair. Imogen and her friend Jude embark on an investigative adventure that leads them to Edward's daughter and her mother. Surprisingly, Imogen begins a friendship with the very woman who had been her husband's mistress for so many years. Along the way, the two women manage to find love themselves. Margaret Hanes in *Library Journal* admired the book for "some nice touches of almost laugh-out-loud humor and interesting secondary characters." Danise Hoover of *Booklist* found *Drop Dead Gorgeous* to be "an engaging and witty tale."

Henley told *CA:* "I have written since childhood. It gives me a sense of well-being and creative release to be able to express myself on the page, but I also see myself very much as a working professional.

"I am particularity interested in how the relationships between people work and people's motivation for behaving the way they do.

"My writing has evolved over the years and I now enjoy writing comedy with a dark edge. I am always inspired by the landscape of the coast."

BIOGRAPHICAL AND CRITICAL SOURCES:

PERIODICALS

Booklist, November 15, 2001, Danise Hoover, review of *Moving to the Country,* p. 547; May 15, 2002, Danise Hoover, review of *Drop Dead Gorgeous,* p. 1574.

Kirkus Reviews, September 15, 2001, review of *Moving to the Country,* p. 1311; May 15, 2002, review of *Drop Dead Gorgeous,* p. 679.

Library Journal, November 1, 2001, Margaret Hanes Sterling, review of *Moving to the Country,* p. 132; June 1, 2002, Margaret Hanes, review of *Drop Dead Gorgeous,* p. 192.

Publishers Weekly, November 5, 2001, review of *Moving to the Country,* p. 41.

ONLINE

Anna Cheska Web site, http://www.annacheska.co.uk (April 6, 2003).

Jan Henley Web site, http://www.janhenley.co.uk (January 3, 2003).

* * *

HESSLER-KEY, Mary

PERSONAL: Born in Palmer, MA; daughter of Peter and Helen (a nurse; maiden name, Witkowski) Warakomski; married Lewis Key, November 8, 1998. *Education:* University of Massachusetts, B.S., 1974; American International College, M.A., 1976; University of Virginia, Ph.D., 1982.

ADDRESSES: Office—Mary Key and Associates, Inc., 2914 Alline Ave., Tampa, FL 33611-2802; fax: 813-832-4463. *E-mail*—marykey@tampabay.rr.com.

CAREER: Mary Key and Associates, Inc. (organizational consulting firm), Tampa, FL, principal, 1992—. Former teacher at University of Virginia, University of Tampa, and Harvard University. Also worked for consulting firms Development Dimensions International and AchieveGlobal; *Inc.* (magazine), executive director of Eagles CEO program; consultant in Europe, Asia, and Latin America. CEO Council of Tampa Bay, member of steering committee; member of Searchnet, OD Network, and Florida Council of International Development.

MEMBER: National Speakers Association, American Society for Training and Development, World Future Society, Leadership Florida.

WRITINGS:

The Entrepreneurial Cat: Thirteen Ways to Transform Your Work Life, Berrett Koehler, 2000.
What Animals Teach Us, Prima Publishing (Rocklin, CA), 2002.

WORK IN PROGRESS: Research on leadership, women in leadership, poetry, and board development.

* * *

HILGERT, Ronald J(oseph) 1934-2002

PERSONAL: Born August 5, 1934, in St. Paul, MN; died July 2, 2002, in Washington, DC; son of John Frank and Mary Katherine (Grabowenski) Hilgert; married Cecelia Helwig, November 4, 1967. *Education:* University of Minnesota, B.S., 1956; graduate study at American University, 1960-62. *Hobbies and other interests:* Magic.

CAREER: U.S. Department of Labor, Washington, DC, labor economist and statistician at Bureau of Labor Statistics in Chicago, IL, 1956, business economist, 1959-65, price economist, 1965-66; U.S. Department of Commerce, Washington, DC, program officer with Economic Development Administration, 1966; Civil Aeronautics Board, Washington, DC, economist, 1967-78, assistant chief of Routes Authority Division, Bureau of Domestic Aviation, 1978-82, chief of Monitoring and Licensing Division, beginning 1982; retired as a senior economist, 1993. Office of the Secretary of Transportation, Washington, DC, former staff member; also aviation consultant. Cathedral of St. Matthew the Apostle, volunteer. *Military service:* U.S. Army, Corps of Engineers, 1956-58; served in Germany.

MEMBER: American Economic Association, American Statistical Association.

AWARDS, HONORS: Civil Aeronautics Board, sustained meritorious performance award, 1968, special achievement awards, 1971, 1980.

WRITINGS:

Houdini Comes to America, Houdini Historical Center (Appleton, WI), 1996.

OBITUARIES:

PERIODICALS

Washington Post, July 6, 2002, p. B7.*

* * *

HILL, Sam(uel Ivey) 1953-

PERSONAL: Born August 29, 1953, in Sumter, SC; son of John H. (a manager) and Martha (a seamstress; maiden name, Stone) Hill; married Elizabeth Upsall (a horticulturalist), November 24, 1978; children: Rachel E., Michael B. *Ethnicity:* "White." *Education:* University of Georgia, B.S., 1981; University of Chicago, M.B.A., 1984. *Politics:* "Irritable." *Hobbies and other interests:* Scuba diving, bicycling.

ADDRESSES: *Home*—654 Pine St., Winnetka, IL 60093. *Office*—8120 Lawndale, Skokie, IL 60046; fax: 847-679-7122. *Agent*—Phillip Spitzer, East Hampton, NY. *E-mail*—sam_hill@heliosconsulting.com.

CAREER: U.S. Peace Corps, Washington, DC, volunteer in Sierra Leone, 1973-75; Kraft/General Foods, Chicago, IL, director of international marketing strategy, 1981-84; Booz, Allen & Hamilton, chief marketing officer in Sydney, Australia, New York, NY, and Chicago, IL, 1984-87; Kraft/General Foods, Chicago, IL, director of international marketing strategy, 1987-89; Booz, Allen & Hamilton, chief marketing officer, 1989-97; DMBB, New York, NY, vice chair for marketing strategy, 1997-98; Helios Consulting, Skokie, IL, vice chair for marketing strategy, 1998—. FTD.com, board member, 1998-2002.

WRITINGS:

(With G. Rifkin) *Radical Marketing,* Harper (New York, NY), 1998.
(With C. Lederer) *The Infinite Asset,* Harvard Business School Publishing (Boston, MA), 2001.
Sixty Trends in Sixty Minutes, Wiley (New York, NY), 2002.

Contributor to magazines and newspapers, including *Fortune, Wall Street Journal, Harvard Business Review, Financial Times, Los Angeles Times, Ad Age,* and *Journal of Business Strategy.*

WORK IN PROGRESS: Research on marketing practice for the next decade.

SIDELIGHTS: Sam Hill told *CA:* "What is my motivation for writing? I have no choice. Ideas show up, homeless, and I have to write them down to provide them a home. More seriously, I find myself compelled to write.

"My writing process has two stages. First I start assembling scraps of ideas. I arrange torn-out news items, napkin jottings, et cetera on a huge table. It is chaotic and unstructured. Then I go into disciplined mode: rewrite 2,000 words from yesterday, write 1,000 new words. I work in two two-hour blocks per day. I am impossible to live with."

* * *

HILTON, Lisa 1974-

PERSONAL: Born 1974, in Chesire, England; *Education:* Graduated from New College, Oxford University; studied art history in Florence, Italy and Paris, France.

ADDRESSES: *Home*—London, England and southern France. *Agent*—c/o Author Mail, Time Warner Books, Inc., 1271 Avenue of the Americas, New York, NY 10020.

CAREER: Writer. Has worked at Christie's Auction House, Paris, France, and as a nanny, roller-skating waitress, and model.

WRITINGS:

Athènaïs: The Life of Louis XIV's Mistress, the Queen of France, Little, Brown & (Boston, MA), 2002.

SIDELIGHTS: In her first book, Lisa Hilton examines the life of Athènaïs de Montespan, mistress of France's "Sun King," Louis XIV. A member of the royal court, the wealthy and cultured Athènaïs was already married when she began her relationship with Louis. Bold and beautiful, she drove the king's previous mistress away, manipulated her husband out of the picture, and managed to insinuate herself into the center of the king's household. Louis's wife, Marie-Therese, proved no match for the fascinating woman who held the king's affections. With Marie-Therese relegated to the background, Athènaïs lived as if she herself were the rightful queen.

Critics admired *Athènaïs: The Life of Louis XIV's Mistress, the Real Queen of France* for its expert evocation of Athènaïs's milieu. "Hilton's writing has bursts of imaginative strength," wrote Frances Wilson in the *Guardian,* adding that "the sheer strangeness and barbarism of court life in Versailles is vividly portrayed." Similarly, *USA Today* contributor Andrea Hoag observed that the book "reads more like a novel than history" and satisfies as "an intrigue-packed journey through the Great Century in France." But Wilson also noted that many biographers before Hilton have written about Athènaïs. Hilton's distinctive contribution to the subject, the critic explained, is her insight into the nature of the sexual bond between Athènaïs and the king. Indeed, as Wilson observed, Hilton suggests "that their insatiable lust—for one another but also for living—might be seen as the energy behind the seventeenth century's most splendid achievements."

Hoag also noted this theme in the book. "Hilton makes it clear," she wrote, "that satisfying Louis's insatiable sexual appetite was a full-time job for which Athènaïs was well qualified." Indeed, Athènaïs bore the king nine children—and promoted their social and economic interests with great vigor. She also advanced the careers of the country's most distinguished artists and writers, making the reign of the Sun King the most brilliant artistic era in French history.

Though critics appreciated the descriptive skill and passion that Hilton brings to her account of Athènaïs, some found her treatment of other characters less than fair. Contributors to *Publishers Weekly* and *Kirkus Reviews* were among those who faulted Hilton for focusing almost exclusively on the physical attractions—or lack thereof—of Athènaïs's rivals. Wilson, too, considered this tendency a flaw, observing that "*Athènaïs* would be a larger book if it were more generous" toward those who lacked its central figure's extraordinary beauty and charm. Nevertheless, Wilson acknowledged that Hilton's debut biography is "simply very good indeed."

BIOGRAPHICAL AND CRITICAL SOURCES:

PERIODICALS

Booklist, November 1, 2002, Margaret Flanagan, review of *Athènaïs: The Life of Louis XIV's Mistress, the Real Queen of France,* p. 472.
Contemporary Review, December, 2002, review of *Athènaïs,* p. 384.
Entertainment Weekly, January 3, 2003, Pamela Newton, review of *Athènaïs,* p. 68.
Guardian, November 2, 2002, Frances Wilson, review of *Athènaïs,*
Kirkus Reviews, September 15, 2002, review of *Athènaïs,* p. 1366.
Publishers Weekly, October 14, 2002, review of *Athènaïs,* p. 73.
USA Today, December 18, 2002, Andrea Hoag, review of *Athènaïs.*

ONLINE

FrenchCulture.org, http://www.frenchculture.org/ (April 2, 2003), review of *Athènaïs.**

* * *

HINDMAN, Hugh D.

PERSONAL: Male. *Education:* College of Wooster, B.A., 1972; Ohio State University, M.A., 1984, M.L. H.R., 1989, Ph.D., 1989.

ADDRESSES: Office—Management Dept., 406 Raley Hall, Appalachian State University, Boone, NC 28608. *E-mail*—hindmanhd@appstate.edu.

CAREER: Appalachian State University, Boone, NC, associate professor, 1988—. Worked variously as a publisher, consultant, advocate, education specialist, and unit director at a center for the developmentally disabled.

MEMBER: American Association of University Professors, Academy of Management, Society for the Promotion of Human Rights in Employment, Industrial Relations Research Association, United Auto Workers (Local 1981, National Writers Union).

WRITINGS:

Child Labor: An American History, M. E. Sharpe (Armonk, NY), 2002.

Contributor to books, including *Human Resource Management Perspectives, Context, Functions, and Outcomes,* 3rd edition, Allyn and Bacon (Boston, MA), 1995, *Human Resource Management,* 5th edition, edited by Cynthia D. Fisher and others, Houghton Mifflin (New York, NY), 2002, and *History of Childhood,* Macmillan, in press; contributor to journals, including *Journal of Labor Research, Journal of Business Ethics, Industrial Relations,* and *HR News;* reviewer for Industrial Relations Research Association and *Journal of American History;* author of technical reports and manuals.

WORK IN PROGRESS: Chapters for books and journal articles.

SIDELIGHTS: Hugh D. Hindman's courses have focused on labor relations, employment law, human resource management, and the subject of his *Child Labor: An American History.* On his Web site, Hindman notes that there are currently more than 120 million children working full-time around the world, a number equal to that of all employed adults in the United States. He also notes that twice that number of children work at least part-time. Hindman also studies the American children who once worked in coal mines and textile mills, in food processing and agriculture, often working sixty-and seventy-hour weeks to build these industries. He hopes that by investigating how the practice was discouraged, and eventually eliminated in America, solutions to help these millions of exploited children may be found. He includes links for those who would like to learn more.

Child Labor contains many of the photographs of Lewis Hine (1874-1940), a humanist who in 1904 photographed immigrants to Ellis Island, and in 1907 was assigned the task of photographing young tenement sweatshop workers by the National Child Labor Committee (NCLC). Hine traveled across the country until 1912, capturing the images of children working in factories, mills, and on the streets. Hine's work in this area was instrumental in the creation of safety laws and labor law reforms.

Hindman draws largely on the NCLC's nineteen-volume investigative reports in describing the conditions under which children worked and the actions that eventually ended child labor, including compulsory education, social reforms, and minimum wage standards. *Library Journal*'s Suzanne W. Wood called *Child Labor* a "well-structured and ably presented study."

BIOGRAPHICAL AND CRITICAL SOURCES:

PERIODICALS

Booklist, September 1, 2002, Mary Whaley, review of *Child Labor: An American History,* p. 31.
Choice, January, 2003, J. Sochen, review of *Child Labor,* p. 868.
Library Journal, September 15, 2002, Suzanne W. Wood, review of *Child Labor,* pp. 81-82.

ONLINE

Hugh D. Hindman Home Page, http://www.appstate.edu/~hindmanhd (June 6, 2003).*

* * *

HINRICHS, Bruce H. 1945-

PERSONAL: Born October 26, 1945, in Minneapolis, MN; son of William C. (a machinist) and Dorothy Kretschmar (a homemaker) Hinrichs; children: Nicole A. Hinrichs-Bideau, Danielle M. *Ethnicity:* "White." *Education:* University of Minnesota, B.A. (psychology and mathematics), 1967, M.A. (psychology). *Hobbies and other interests:* Music, guitar playing, cultural events, comedy, poetry, science.

ADDRESSES: *Home*—1913 Dupont Ave. S., No. 1, Minneapolis, MN 55403. *Office*—Century College, 3301 Century Ave. N., White Bear Lake, MN 55110. *E-mail*—b.hinrichs@cctc.cc.mn.us.

CAREER: Century College, St. Paul, MN, professor of psychology and humanities, 1988—; freelance artist. University of Illinois, artist/teacher-in-residence.

MEMBER: American Psychological Association, American Psychological Society, Phi Beta Kappa.

AWARDS, HONORS: University of Wisconsin-Madison fellowship.

WRITINGS:

Film and Art, J-Press (White Bear Lake, MN), 2000.
Mind as Mosaic: The Robot in the Machine, J-Press (White Bear Lake, MN), 2000.

Contributor of articles and essays to periodicals, including *Humanist;* and to CD-ROMs, including *Renaissance.*

WORK IN PROGRESS: *Quirks of Nature,* a book of short fiction; *Alzheimer's Disease Handbook;* research on cognitive neuroscience, Alzheimer's Disease, Modern Art and contemporary films.

SIDELIGHTS: Bruce H. Hinrichs told *CA:* "As with creating artworks, I find that writing waits on the muse, particularly good, poetic writing. There are moments when nothing works right, and at other times the sentences flow like silky cream over strawberries.

"I have been writing since college, even before, and find that it is necessary, I don't know why. It is impossible for me to name any specific influences on my writing, but I have enjoyed a wide range of works by such authors as Carl Sagan, Isaac Asimov, Franz Kafka, Gore Vidal, Italo Calvino, Milan Kundera, Jorge Luis Borges, B. F. Skinner, Joseph Heller, and lots of poets.

"I believe that today there is an antagonistic schism between the arts and the sciences that is not only unnecessary but also harmful. I believe that we should reconcile differences and encourage and appreciate both fields of endeavor.

"I love the arts and have been a professional artist for many years in a number of media, including glass-blowing, painting, and photography. My book on film takes the unique position of placing film within the domain of the arts, particularly, of course, modern and postmodern art.

"Science, too, is fascinating to me. I have spent my career teaching students about the scientific side of psychology and have researched several psychological issues, including the question of how the mind is created by the brain. My book *Mind as Mosaic: The Robot in the Machine* is the culmination of my research and thinking on this topic and I hope it is a significant contribution to the field. I also illustrated the book with my own paintings and photographs in the hopes that readers would appreciate and enjoy it."

* * *

HODGKIN, Robert Allason 1916-2003

OBITUARY NOTICE—See index for *CA* sketch: Born February 12, 1916, in Banbury, England; died August 19, 2003, in Oxford, England. Mountaineer, educator, and author. Hodgkin was a renowned mountain climber who became a well-known education theorist after suffering a serious injury. A graduate of Oxford University, where he earned a B.A. in 1937 and an M.A. in 1939, he was part of a generation of enthusiastic climbers in the Oxford University Mountaineering Club that included John Hoyland and David Cox. During the 1930s he climbed peaks in Wales, Norway, and the Caucasus. In 1938 however, he ran into trouble while climbing the Masherbrum, a 24,000-foot peak in the Himalayas. An avalanche buried the camp, and he lost several fingers and toes from frostbite, which effectively ended his climbing career. Hodgkin then began a career in education, teaching at Leighton Park in the Sudan, where he joined the civil service. From 1949 to 1955 he was principal of the Sudan Institute of Education before returning to England to be headmaster at Abbotsholme School in Uttoxeter, where he started a climbing club. He then became a freelance writer and lecturer in education studies at the Department of Educational Studies at Oxford in the 1960s, retiring in 1977; he also served as vice president of the Alpine Club from 1974 to 1975. Hodgkin was the author of several books, including *Education and Change* (1957), *Reconnaissance on an Educational Frontier* (1970), and *Playing and Exploring: Education through the Discovery of Order* (1985).

OBITUARIES AND OTHER SOURCES:

PERIODICALS

Guardian (London, England), August 30, 2003, p. 27.
Independent (London, England), August 25, 2003, p. 14.
Times (London, England), September 17, 2003.

* * *

HOLMGREN, Fredrick Carlson 1926-

PERSONAL: Born April 1, 1926, in Cadillac, MI; son of Charles Olaf and Freda Natalia (Teelander) Holmgren; married Betty Jean Margaret Carlson, June 12, 1948; children: Mark, Margaret. *Ethnicity:* "Swedish." *Education:* Calvin College, B.A., 1949; Union Theological Seminary, B.D. (magna cum laude), 1955, M.S.T. (summa cum laude), 1957, Th.D., 1963. *Religion:* Protestant. *Hobbies and other interests:* German languate, literature, culture; travel to Europe.

ADDRESSES: Home—5536 North Sawyer Ave., Chicago, IL 60625. *Office*—North Park Theological Seminary, 3225 West Foster Ave., Chicago, IL 60625-4895. *E-mail*—fholmgren@northpark.edu.

CAREER: North Park Theological Seminary, Chicago, IL, professor of Biblical literature, 1960—.

MEMBER: Society of Biblical Literature, Chicago Society of Biblical Literature.

AWARDS, HONORS: Rockefeller Foundation fellowship, 1960; Deutscher Akademischer Austauch scholar, 1991.

WRITINGS:

With Wings as Eagles: Isaiah 40/55, Biblical Scholars Press (Chappaqua, NY), 1974.

The God Who Cares: A Christian Looks at Judaism, John Knox Press (Atlanta, GA), 1979.

Israel Alive Again: A Commentary on the Books of Ezra and Nehemiah, W. B. Eerdmans (Grand Rapids, MI), 1987.

(Editor with Herman E. Schaalman) *Preaching Biblical Texts: Expositions by Jewish and Christian Scholars,* W. B. Eerdmans (Grand Rapids, MI), 1995.

The Old Testament and the Significance of Jesus: Embracing Change—Maintaining Christian Identity: The Emerging Center in Biblical Scholarship, W. B. Eerdmans (Grand Rapids, MI), 1999.

Editor, *International Theological Commentary* (28 volumes), 1982—. Contributor of articles to professional journals, including *Journal of Ecumenical Studies* and *Currents in Theology and Mission.*

SIDELIGHTS: Fredrick Carlson Holmgren's writings pay close attention to Biblical scripture as they seek to reinterpret the relationship between Christianity and Judaism. His interest in Judaism began during studies at North Park Theological Seminary in Chicago, and was further developed at Union Theological Seminary in New York City under the guidance of such well-known figures as James Muilenburg, Fredrick C. Grant, and W. D. Davies. A significant event that greatly influenced his life occurred while he was marching with the thousands accompanying civil rights leader Martin Luther King, Jr., from Selma to Montgomery, Alabama. At the front of the march, together with Dr. King, was the great Jewish tehologian Abraham Joshua Heschel. Holmgren was so impressed by Heschel's presence in this march that he began reading all of Heschel's writings.

Heschel's influence on Holmgren may be seen in almost all of Holmgren's writings. He is particularly interested in bringing about change in understanding Jewish tradition to a Christian readership—general and scholarly—in order to facilitate dialogue between two closely-related faiths.*The God Who Cares: A Christian Looks at Judaism,* which was particularly inspired by the writings of Heschel, is aimed at general readers. The work seeks to refute Christian stereotypes about Jews that persisted for centuries and caused religious intolerance and persecution. In his *America* review of the book, Jack Riemer commended Holmgren's "honest scholarship" and his attempts "to correct caricatures." Harriet L. Kaufman in *Theology Today* called the book a "reliable guide" for Christians who want a broader understanding of Judaism.

The Old Testament and the Significance of Jesus: Embracing Change—Maintaining Christian Identity: The Emerging Center in Biblical Scholarship seeks an audience of serious students and teachers who want to reexamine certain Christian readings of the Old Testament. The book uses texts from both the Old and New Testaments to explain the historical relationship between early Christians and Jews. In an *Interpretation: A Journal of Bible and Theology* review of the work, Walter Harrelson suggested that Holmgren's conclusions are "sane, temperate, and widely useful."

BIOGRAPHICAL AND CRITICAL SOURCES:

PERIODICALS

America, September 29, 1979, Jack Riemer, review of *The God Who Cares: A Christian Looks at Judaism,* pp. 218-219.

Interpretation, July, 1975, Philip B. Harner, review of *With Wings as Eagles: Isaiah 40/55,* pp. 312-313; January, 2000, Walter Harrelson, review of *The Old Testament and the Significance of Jesus: Embracing Change—Maintaining Christian Identity,* p. 86.

Theology Today, January, 1980, Harriet L. Kaufman, review of *The God Who Cares,* pp. 615-616.

* * *

HOPE, Judith Richards 1940-

PERSONAL: Born November 30, 1940, in Cincinnati, OH; daughter of Joseph Coleman and Eve Gertrude (Kemp) Richards; children: Zachary, Miranda Townes. *Education:* Wellesley College, B.A. (magna cum laude), 1961; Harvard University, J.D., 1964. *Politics:* Republican. *Religion:* Episcopalian. *Hobbies and other interests:* Music, tennis, gin rummy, mountain climbing, gourmet cooking.

ADDRESSES: Office—Paul, Hastings, Janofsky & Walker, 1299 Pennsylvania Avenue NW, Tenth Floor, Washington, DC, 20004-2400. *E-mail*—JudithRichardsHope@PaulHastings.com.

CAREER: Attorney and author. Williams & Connolly, Washington, DC, associate, 1964-67; California Rural Development Corporation, Los Angeles, CA, deputy director, 1968-69; Law Offices of Richard M. Coleman, Los Angeles, CA, counsel, 1970-75; The White House, Washington, DC, associate director for domestic counsel, 1975-77; Wald-Harkrader & Ross, Washington, DC, partner, 1977-81; Paul, Hastings, Janofsky & Walker, Washington, DC, Los Angeles, CA, New York, NY, senior partner, 1981—. Pepperdine University, Malibu, CA, adjunct professor of constitutional law, 1972; Georgetown University Law Center, Washington, DC, adjunct professor of transportation regulation, 1978-79; adjunct professor of constitutional law, 1995; Harvard Law School, lecturer on trial advocacy, 1982. Harvard Corporation board of directors, president and fellow; member of board of directors for Budd Company, Union Pacific Corporation, and General Mills.

MEMBER: Harvard Medical International (member, board of directors), Council on Foreign Relations, American Law Institute, American Bar Foundation, Sycamore Island Canoe Club, Metropolitan Club.

AWARDS, HONORS: Honorary LL.D. from Harvard University, 2000; American Law Institute, fellow.

WRITINGS:

Pinstripes and Pearls: The Women of the Harvard Law School Class of '64 Who Forged an Old-Girl Network and Paved the Way for Future Generations, Scribner (New York, NY), 2003.

SIDELIGHTS: Prior to 1961, very few women had been admitted into the Harvard School of Law, let alone graduated from it. Judith Richards Hope was one among fifteen women who entered into a class of 513 Harvard law students. She graduated in 1964, and soon became the first female partner in a well-established international corporate law firm in Washington, D.C. Since that time, Hope has served as associate director of the White House Domestic Council under President Gerald Ford and became the first woman appointed to the seven-member board of the Harvard Corporation, serving for eleven years in that capacity.

In her book *Pinstripes and Pearls: The Women of the Harvard Law School Class of '64 Who Forged an Old-Girl Network and Paved the Way for Future Generations* Hope describes what it was like to be a female member of that Harvard law class, using personal recollections and those of fellow classmates and professors. She also follows the lives and professional careers of some of her classmates, including U.S. Circuit Court justice Judith W. Rogers and Congresswoman Patricia Schroeder.

Some of the women recall that there were no women's restrooms in the law school buildings and that male students often refused to sit beside women in the classroom. Others recount tales of the "Ladies Days" that occurred during one particular professor's class. According to Joanna L. Grossman in *FindLaw,* on those specified days, all of the female students were made to sit upon a stage, facing the male students, and they were asked questions "about cases involving stolen underwear or other subjects clearly calculated to embarrass them." Another example of such antagonistic treatment of women occurred annually, when Dean Erwin Griswold invited female students to a dinner at which each one was asked to reply to the question, "Why are you at Harvard Law School, taking the place of a man?"

After graduation, these women continued to struggle against ingrained prejudices and obstacles while trying to find their niche in male-dominated career fields. Yet, despite all of the challenges of the academic and professional worlds, the women who graduated from the Harvard Law Class of 1964 became esteemed and successful professors, corporate lawyers, authors, university trustees, and entrepreneurs.

"*Pinstripes and Pearls* serves as a potent reminder of the significant changes to legal education and the legal profession," remarked Grossman. She felt that Hope's class was "notable for encountering and overcoming some extraordinary obstacles," but that "the book's claims for the impact of the women it profiles . . . may be somewhat overstated." Grossman also commented that, even forty years later, women lawyers feel frustrated by "covert discrimination and sexual harassment." A *Publishers Weekly* reviewer wrote, "She lets the memories speak for themselves." In *Kirkus Reviews,* a critic commended Hope for admitting that she had been a less-than-perfect mother, frustrated by her inability "to do it all." The same writer felt that Hope's description of her classmate's careers is "mechanical," and he would have enjoyed hearing the stories of the women who left their law careers. Mary Frances Wilkens of *Booklist* called *Pinstripes and Pearls* "a tale of true accomplishment."

BIOGRAPHICAL AND CRITICAL SOURCES:

PERIODICALS

Booklist, December 15, 2002, Mary Frances Wilkens, review of *Pinstripes and Pearls: The Women of the Harvard Law School Class of '64 Who Forged an Old-Girl Network and Paved the Way for Future Generations,* p. 712.

Kirkus Reviews, October 1, 2002, review of *Pinstripes and Pearls,* p. 1446.

New York Times, February 7, 1989, "First Woman is Appointed to Top Board at Harvard U.," p. A16.

Publishers Weekly, October 14, 2002, review of *Pinstripes and Pearls,* pp. 71-72.

ONLINE

FindLaw, http://writ.news.findlaw.com/ (March 28, 2003), Joanna L. Grossman, review of *Pinstripes and Pearls.*

New York Times on the Web, http://www.nytimes.com/ (January 12, 2003), Peter Temes, review of *Pinstripes and Pearls.*

Time online, http://www.time.com/ (February 17, 2003), Andrea Sachs, interview with Hope.

USA Today online, http://www.usatoday.com/ (April 19, 2003), Susan Page, "Class of '64: Women Who Blazed a Legal Trail."*

HOPKINSON, Nalo 1960-

PERSONAL: Born December 20, 1960, in Kingston Jamaica; immigrated to Toronto, Ontario, Canada, in 1977; daughter of Slade (a poet and actor) and Freda (a library technician) Hopkinson. *Education:* Graduated from York University; Seton Hill College, M.A., 1995.

ADDRESSES: *Home*—Toronto, Canada. *Agent*—c/o Author Mail, Warner Books, 1271 Avenue of the Americas, New York, NY 10020. *E-mail*—nalo@sff.net.

CAREER: Writer, 1997—. Has also worked in a library and as a grants officer for a local arts council. Instructor at various writing workshops.

AWARDS, HONORS: Warner Aspect first novel award, 1997, Philip K. Dick Award nominee, Philadelphia Science Fiction Society, and Ontario Arts Council Foundation award for emerging writers, both 1998, and John W. Campbell Award for best new writer, and *Locus* award for best first novel, both 1999, all for *Brown Girl in the Ring; New York Times* notable book of the year, 2000, and Nebula Award nominee, Science Fiction and Fantasy Writers of America, Philip K. Dick Award nominee, and Hugo Award nominee, World Science Fiction Society, all 2001, all for *Midnight Robber;* Sunburst Award for Canadian literature of the fantastic, 2003, for *Skin Folk.*

WRITINGS:

Brown Girl in the Ring, Warner Aspect (New York, NY), 1998.

Midnight Robber, Warner Aspect (New York, NY), 2000.

(Editor) *Whispers from the Cotton Tree Root: Caribbean Fabulist Fiction,* Invisible Cities Press, 2000.

Skin Folk (short story collection), Warner Aspect (New York, NY), 2001.

(Editor) *Mojo: Conjure Stories,* Warner Books (New York, NY).

The Salt Roads, Warner Books (New York, NY), 2003.

Nalo Hopkinson

Contributor of short stories to anthologies, including *Dark Matter,* edited by Sheree Thomas and Martin Simmons; *Women of Other Worlds,* edited by Helen Merrick and Tess Williams; *Northern Suns,* edited by David Hartwell and Glenn Grant; *Black Swan, White Raven,* edited by Ellen Datlow and Terri Windling, 1997; *Silver Birch, Blood Moon,* edited by Datlow and Windling; *Tesseracts 6,* edited by Carolyn Clink and Rob Sawyer, 1997; and *Northern Frights 5,* edited by Don Hutchinson, 1997. Author of radio plays, including *Riding the Red* and *Indicator Species,* CBC Radio. Contributor of short stories and book reviews to periodicals, including *Exile, Fireweed,* and *Science Fiction Weekly.*

ADAPTATIONS: "Greedy Choke Puppy" was adapted as a play of the same name, produced by Seeing Ear Theatre.

SIDELIGHTS: Nalo Hopkinson is an award-winning science-fiction writer whose work blends African, Caribbean, and Creole folklore with the conventions of the science-fiction and fantasy genre. Critics have responded favorably to her work, especially for its touches of magic realism and underlying themes of race and gender. Hopkinson's debut novel, *Brown Girl in the Ring,* which won the Warner Aspect First Novel contest and a major publishing deal, introduces readers to a milieu consisting of a dystopian science-fiction setting interwoven with Afro-Caribbean folklore and the patois dialect that has since come to be associated with many of her works.

The daughter of Guyanese poet, playwright, and actor Slade Hopkinson, Hopkinson grew up in a literary atmosphere. As a child she met Nobel-winning writer Derek Walcott, who founded the Trinidad Theater Workshop where her father directed plays. Though born in Jamaica, Hopkinson passed through Trinidad, Guyana, and the United States before her family settled in Toronto, Canada. Despite the family's mobility, Hopkinson grew up in a household filled with books and one that had a healthy respect for the arts.

Though she initially had no life-long dream of becoming a writer, Hopkinson—always a science fiction fan—was inspired when she discovered that some of her favorite writers, notably Samuel R. Delaney, were black. Once she discovered other science-fiction writers of color, such as Octavia Butler, Steve Barnes, and Virginia Hamilton, she began to understand that the most common trope of science fiction was one in which "white people use technology to overpower alien cultures," as she told Gregory E. Rutledge in *African American Review.* Hopkinson believes that this is a primary reason why black writers have largely avoided the genre. Instead, she began to imagine a different kind of science fiction; one told from a black woman's point of view that deals with the shibboleths of African and Caribbean society. "I think that a speculative literature from a culture that has been on the receiving end of the colonization glorified in some [SF] could be a compelling body of writing," she told Rutledge.

The title of Hopkinson's first novel, *Brown Girl in the Ring,* comes from a Caribbean schoolyard game. A dystopian story, the novel is set in the near future in the desolate neighborhoods of Toronto, which have been abandoned by the government by those who can afford to live elsewhere. Those residents who remain have been barricaded inside and left to fend for themselves. Farming and bartering have become their new way of life.

Ti-Jeanne is a single mother dealing with a new baby and her drug-addict boyfriend, Tony. When Tony gets in trouble with a gang leader, Rudy, Ti-Jeanne asks her wise grandmother for help. Gros-Jeanne, or Mami, a healer, herbalist, and a practitioner of Afro-Caribbean spiritual beliefs, helps bring Ti-Jeanne into the spirit world. But soon Ti-Jeanne finds herself battling Rudy and also coming to terms with the mother she lost long ago—the mother that is now Rudy's captive spirit. Thus, Hopkinson sets up a multi-generational novel of people coping against evil in a violent and magical world. The novel was partly inspired by Walcott's play, "Ti-Jean and His Brothers," in which three brothers battle the devil. "I wanted to acknowledge that connection to [Walcott's] work," Hopkinson told Rutledge, "so I named the three women Ti-Jeanne, Mi-Jeanne, and Gros-Jeanne," the feminine equivalents of Walcott's characters.

The novel, in which characters speak in a rich Afro-Caribbean patois, received a positive response from reviewers. A critic for *Kirkus Reviews* called the book a "splendid if gruesome debut, superbly plotted and redolent of the rhythms of Afro-Caribbean speech." *Booklist*'s Bonnie Johnston felt that Hopkinson's "exotically imaginative debut is just realistic enough," while Faren Miller of *Locus* noted that "what propels this fast-paced work is the author's gift for passionate, vivid, tale-spinning." Miller concluded that "Hopkinson is a genuine find." Writing in the *New York Times Book Review,* Gerald Jonas commented that Hopkinson "treats spirit-calling the way other science fiction writers treat nanotechnology or virtual reality."

Though David Streitfeld, writing in the *Washington Post,* felt that *Brown Girl in the Ring* "has the usual first novel faults in pacing and plotting," he praised the book's "richness of language," which "more than compensates" for any such faults. Streitfeld called *Brown Girl in the Ring* "an impressive debut." A writer for *Publishers Weekly* focused on the oral tradition in Hopkinson's work: "The musical rhythms of Caribbean voices and the earthy spirit-magic of obeah knit together this unusual fantasy." The reviewer concluded that "Hopkinson's writing is smooth and assured, and her characters lively and believable." And Carol DeAngelo, reviewing the novel in *School Library Journal,* called the book an "outstanding science-fiction novel" as well as a "page-turner that builds to an exciting conclusion."

Hopkinson's second novel, *Midnight Robber,* takes place on the planet Toussaint, which has been colonized by people from the Caribbean. Antonio Habib is the powerful mayor of Cockpit County, and his daughter Tan-Tan is the product of privilege. The planet is the picture of harmony, ministered by "Granny Nanny," an artificial intelligence which monitors everyone through aural implants. Miscreants are exiled to New Half-Way Tree, an alternate universe to Toussaint, so when Habib runs afoul of the law, killing his wife's lover, that is where he and his daughter end up. Habib remarries, but his anger gets the better of him. As her father's fortunes dwindle and he spirals into sexual excess and drunkenness, Tan-Tan struggles to find her own way. After he impregnates her, she finally kills him. At age sixteen, she is now on the run, hiding from her father's widow. In the bush she learns the secrets of the native intelligent species and transforms herself into a female version of the Midnight Robber, a Caribbean Carnival figure who dresses in black and tells stories to those he waylays. As the Robber Queen, Tan-Tan fights to survive on New Half-Way Tree. Again the story combines Caribbean and African myths and language. An allegory of displacement and diaspora, *Midnight Robber* "bears evidence that Hopkinson owns one of the more important and original voices in SF," according to a reviewer for *Publishers Weekly.*

Many critics were impressed with Hopkinson's use of language in *Midnight Robber.* Reviewing the novel for *SFSite.com,* David Soyka wrote that "Hopkinson has established herself as a unique voice in the SF and Fantasy genre, largely because that voice is grounded in the rhythms, myths, and vernacular of Caribbean and Creole cultures." *Booklist*'s Roberta Johnson called attention to Hopkinson's "exhilarating prose," which "drives an exciting story that continues with Tan-Tan befriending New Half-Way Tree's natives and coming to terms with self-hatred." A *Publishers Weekly* reviewer felt that Hopkinson's "rich and complex Carib English can be hard to follow at times, but is nonetheless quite beautiful." The reviewer also called Toussaint and New Half-Way Tree "believable, lushly detailed worlds." *School Library Journal*'s Francisca Goldsmith concluded that the book "provides an engaging nexus of science fiction and folklore."

Hopkinson is also the author of the short-story collection *Skin Folk.* Many of the stories were originally published in literary journals and anthologies, and all of them feature her trademark blend of fantasy and folklore. For the story *A Habit of Waste,* Hopkinson was inspired by her father's poem about a Jamaican bag lady. Other short stories include "Riding the Red," "Precious," "Money Tree," and "Slow Cold Chick." Gerald Jonas noted in the *New York Times Book Review* that many of her tales "are not only set in black communities, they make use of West African-derived folklore and language patterns to create fresh worlds and emotionally compelling situations." *Booklist* reviewer Roberta Johnson commented on *Skin Folk*'s "broad range of subjects," and called the stories "a delightful introduction" to Hopkinson's earlier work. A reviewer for *Publishers Weekly* praised her "strong evocation of place and her ear for dialect," concluding that "underneath [*Skin Folk*] is a sure grasp of humanity, good and bad, and the struggle to understand and to communicate."

Having edited *Whispers from the Cotton Tree Root: Caribbean Fabulist Fiction* in 2000, Hopkinson stepped into the role of editor for the second time with *Mojo: Conjure Stories,* an anthology of West African-inspired stories written by award-winning writers such as Neil Gaiman and Steven Barnes. Drag queens and Elvis impersonators populate Barth Anderson's "Lark till Dawn, Princess," while Creole cooking and zombies figure prominently in other stories. A writer for *Publishers Weekly* complimented the collection's stories, which "skillfully blend West African magic, fantasy, horror, along with plain old-fashioned readability." The theme of using "supernatural powers able to exact revenge, justice, or simple relief in the lives of Africans in the diaspora," wrote Vanessa Bush in *Booklist,* makes these "wonderful stories for fans of any genre fiction."

In *The Salt Roads* Hopkinson moves away from science fiction toward a more traditional literature, even though the hallmarks of her earlier work still are in evidence. The Afro-Caribbean goddess of love and sex, Ezili, is the common thread among three women in different eras of history: Meritet, an Egyptian prostitute in 300 A.D., Mer, an eighteenth-century slave, and Jeanne Duval, a real-life mixed-race woman who was Charles Baudelaire's lover. The far-ranging narrative encompasses Haitian folktales, all in a style reminiscent of magic realism. The story begins with three slave women summoning up Ezili as they prepare to bury a stillborn baby on the island of Saint Domingue in 1804, before it became Haiti. Ezili finds herself infused with the dead baby's vitality, which allows her to inhabit the bodies of Mer, Jeanne, and Meritet, who are linked to one another through the salt in their tears and the salt that bound them into their personal slavery.

As with Hopkinson's previous novels, critics reacted favorably to *The Salt Roads.* "The novel has a genuine vitality and generosity," wrote a reviewer for *Publishers Weekly,* though Devon Thomas of *Library Journal* said that "though the goddess connects the three women together, the women's tales themselves are much more interesting." Hopkinson told Wilda Williams of *Library Journal* that parts of the story were inspired by Angela Carter's story "The Black Venus," which is also a fictional account of Baudelaire and Jeanne Duval. The purpose of the book, Hopkinson told Williams, is "to explore the issue of biracial women and how that complicates relationships between women, especially black women." Donna Seaman, writing in *Booklist,* recognized that theme. "Like Erica Jong," Seaman wrote, "Hopkinson uses sex to entice readers into contemplating the long history of misogyny, specifically women's suffering during the African diaspora." Details of life in French-colonial Haiti, the ancient brothels of Alexandria, and nineteenth-century France lend historical authenticity to the book, according to a writer for *Kirkus Reviews,* who called *The Salt Roads* "a centuries-spanning panorama of the cultural collision between Africa and Europe."

Nalo Hopkinson contributed the following autobiographical essay to *CA:*

AUTOBIOGRAPHICAL ESSAY:

In this essay, I'm making an effort to tell you about my life.

There's this notion that when people describe things that have happened to them, they are able to tell you something called the "truth" of what actually happened. I'm not so sure. Yes, the person who had an experience is the one who's most likely to be able to tell you what really took place, but even when I'm telling the truth about myself, it feels as though I'm trying to wrap words around experience. Words are an abstraction. They can only tell part of the truth. Even telling the truth is, in a way, making up stories. Memory is not perfect, and imagination is very good at filling in the blanks, whether we know we're doing that or not.

The author with partner, writer and artist David Findlay

Hopefully I can nevertheless bring you some truths. No absolutes, but perhaps some shifting, context-dependent truths.

Probably the easiest truths to start with might be some background stuff about me.

I was born in Kingston, Jamaica, in 1960. I am of predominantly African descent, with some Jewish, European, South Asian and Taino thrown into the mix. I have lived in Jamaica, Trinidad, Guyana, the U.S. and Canada. My family moved to Canada permanently when I was sixteen. I've lived in Toronto, Canada ever since. I'm forty-two now, in 2003, as I'm writing this.

I don't remember my parents reading me stories when I was a child. They may well have, but I learned to read the words for myself very early on—by age three. My parents had taught me the Alphabet Song, and I realised that each sound in the song was intended to represent a funny mark that was a letter, and furthermore, if you strung the sounds together, you got words. I learned the sounds that the funny marks made, and it became a game to try to figure out what words they made when they were strung together, and what sense those words made when they were strung together. Reading is hard! It's an abstraction of an abstraction of an abstraction. But it was a game to me, and from then on, I was a voracious reader, and I wanted to read stories myself. When other people read them out loud, it seemed to me that they were going so slooowly, and it would take forever to learn what was happening next in the story. I could do it much quicker in my head, and get my fix of story in short order.

I remember my first day in kindergarten. I was three years old. We were living in Mount Lambert, in Trinidad. My mother would go to the bakery every day and get us fresh, hot bread with butter. At least, that's what I remember. She probably remembers it differently. But she took me to school, where the teacher gave me a book to read. I didn't understand that this was intended to last the whole term. It was one of those "see Dick run"-type primers. I read through it in a few minutes and yelled across the classroom to the teacher, "Miss, I want another book!"

That schoolroom was actually two classes, kindergarten and First Form, both taught by Miss Toby. The kindergarten took up one half of the room, and First Form the other. Again, I didn't know that. I'm told that I wandered freely between the two.

Some background information about me and my family: my father's name was Muhammed Abdur-Rahman Slade Hopkinson. He was born Clement Alan Slade Hopkinson, but changed his name in the seventies when he converted to Islam. Daddy was a writer, actor, poet, and a teacher. My brother Keita Hopkinson is a visual artist and an aspiring musician. When I give him my stories to read, he analyzes them in terms of tone, form, colour, and line. I learn more about the craft of writing from listening to him. My mother Freda Hopkinson is a semi-retired library technician. She catalogues books for a living, which is a much more entrancing occupation than it may sound.

So I always had books around me, and I always liked the weird ones; the ones with otherworldly creatures, or magic, or spaceships. The ones with talking animals.

It was probably pretty inevitable that I would find the science fiction and fantasy shelves in the adult section of the public library where my mother worked. At home, I'd been reading the copies of *Gulliver's Travels* and Homer's *Iliad* which my father taught to senior high school classes, and I'd been reading folktales collected and retold by Jamaicans Philip Sherlock and Louise Bennet Coverly. I was fascinated by tales of the unreal and the impossible. Mostly it was that they were so different from the life I was leading, and with which I was way too familiar. So yes, it was escapism, that damning word. People who read fantastical literature often get accused of reading escapist nonsense. I thought I could kiss writer Walter Mosley when he published his comments on science fiction, first in the *New York Times,* and then republished in *Dark Matter: A Century of Speculative Fiction from the African Diaspora,* edited by Sheree R. Thomas. Mosley said that escapism was the wrong way to look at it; that in order to make change, humans first had to imagine the directions in which we want to go. At last, vindication. I love that man.

There's a thing that often happens at some point when I'm being interviewed about my writing. The interviewer, whatever part of the world or whatever culture or subculture he or she comes from, will put on a curious look and say, "And why do *you* write science fiction?"—the whole of the question being, "Why are you, a black woman from the Caribbean, interested in a literature that still is largely about white people, largely men, using technology largely made by the dominant cultures to turn the world and the people in it to their desires? Where is your place in that conversation?"

It's a good question. I'm still working out the answer to why I like science fiction and fantasy so much, but I can give you a small part of it, a partial truth. Which, of course, must mean that it's also a partial untruth. My response to that question often turns on a statement made by black, gay SF writer Samuel R. Delany. He said, "We need visions of the future, and our people need them more than most." In other words, we black people need to step up to the table and start defining our futures instead of letting other people define them for us. I grew up in the days of *Star Trek,* old school, and I remember what they did to the part played by actress Nichelle Nichols, the only regular black actor in that show (the others who made brief appearances did so for one show, during which they usually died). Nichols played the part of Lt. Uhura. In those decades, Uhura was the image that television gave us of where black people would be in the future. Well, it's not a future I want. I do not fancy a career as Intergalactic Receptionist, no matter how cute the outfit and how well it shows off my thighs. (In her autobiography, Nichols says that she didn't much like how narrow her part was, either, but Dr. Martin Luther King, Jr. persuaded her to stay, because the character she played symbolised that black people would *have* a future.)

If I were to write mimetic fiction, I'd be to some extent limited by what is known of the world. If my realist character were a young, straight, fat, middle-class woman living in North America, many readers could pretty much guess at the types of struggles she might have around body image and developing as a sexual person. Readers could also probably come up with a similar list of ways in which she could try to resolve those problems. What would make the story unique would be the particular events and texture of the life that would I imagine for that character. However, in fantastical fiction, I can directly manipulate the metaphorical structure of the story. I can create a science-fictional world in which relative fatness or slimness has about the same significance as eye colour, but only persons under 5'5" are considered beautiful. I can show people desperately trying not to grow taller, and taking pills intended to cure them of the "disease" of tallness. I can show newspapers writing exposés on the "epidemic" in their society of people afflicted with surplus height disorder. I can show people who develop emotional disorders related to being tall. Another thing I might do is to create a fantastical world in which my fat protagonist magically becomes thinner the more that she can convince people to ignore her, so that at the moment when she finally would be considered beautiful, she disappears. In other words, one of the things I can do is to intervene in the readers' assumptions by creating a world in which standards are different. Or I can blatantly show what values the characters in the story are trying to live out by making them actual, by exaggerating them into the realm of the fantastical, so that the consequences conversely become so real that they are tangible.

Another example: as a black person, I have particular experiences of the world. I can use the lens of science fiction and fantasy to examine and interrogate the realities of being black in this world. As Delany has said, when it comes to envisioning our futures, black people need to get ourselves a place at the table and start directing our own paths. One of the books I read when I was a child was a fantasy in which a group of children had to endure a number of dangers and travails. At the end, they reached a beautiful land where they could have anything they wanted. They were each rewarded with immortality and their hearts' desires. The white children asked for horses, castles, jewels; in other words, property, title and money. There was one black child amongst them. There were no children of other races that I remember, and no mixed race children. And what words did the writer put in the mouth of the one black child to make the journey safely? That little darkskinned pickaninny with his big, red lips (this may be just my imagination rewriting history, but I remember the book being illustrated) asked for a small everbearing watermelon patch to lie in and all the watermelon he could eat. And he got it. That was his legacy for all of eternity. His immortal life would be spent lolling in a watermelon patch with a huge smile on his face, devouring slice after slice of watermelon the size of his head.

In one way, it was charming. That little boy had chosen the simplest, the most directly pleasurable experience he could think of. His desires were appealingly modest, and you can bet that while the other children were busy trying to cure their horses of the colic, keep people from stealing their jewels, or managing the complex intrigue of castle life, there he'd be, out in the sun, eating watermelon. But on the other hand, it was a devastating image to present to a little black girl. That little boy hadn't had the wits to ask for a home, just a patch of soil. He would only have one thing to eat forever. He would keep the same worn, torn clothing he'd started out with. I don't remember him even interacting ever with the other children. My child's brain understood his impoverished heaven as the best to which I could aspire. But you see, it seems to me that if he'd asked for some of that property and money, then he could have bought himself all the watermelon patches he wanted and still have a house and some good clothes. "We need visions of the future," said Delany, "and our people need them more than most." And how.

So I guess one of the reasons for writing in this genre is high dudgeon. Palm a measly old watermelon patch off on *me,* will you? Well, I can write myself a better ending than that! I love old folk and fairy tales, but sometimes I feel the need to rejig them a little so they suit me and people like me better.

I was a weird child. So was my brother. Nature or nurture, I'll never really be sure, because both of our parents were fairly normal folks. But you know how every nice, ordinary family always seems to breed one or two misfits? Well, I was one of those and I still am. I was a combination tomboy and egghead. I would climb trees with a book clenched between my teeth so that I'd have something to do when I got up there. I was the one who couldn't understand why lipstick always had to be some shade of red or pink, why it couldn't be green or blue or black. As I grew older, I became a teenager at a time when the feminist movement was doing a lot of agitating, and it was a boon to a young woman. I came of age knowing that I could, for instance, wear whatever I wanted, pants or skirts, that I could use fashion to express who I was, or who I was at the time. Yet I realised that when it came to clothing, men and boys didn't have the same choice. *I* can wear a fedora and a man's overcoat out in public, yet heaven help the man who decides to go out into the world wearing a leather miniskirt and a lace camisole. I was the kind of person who would ask, "But *why* can't they? What's wrong with it?" and I'd be totally dissatisfied with the answer. As I got older, I was the one asking, "But *why* am I expected to get married? And why can I have only one husband? Why not two or three? And for that matter, why do they all have to be guys?" And again, I found the answers dissatisfying. We live in a world that seems to be forever trying to limit our possibilities.

That's another reason that I was drawn to science fiction; it explores other possibilities for how we could be in the world, and how flexible human social systems are. It showed me, as a depressed, frustrated young woman, that the things in my world that were squashing my spirit and my joy didn't have to be that way.

But probably the simplest answer to why I write this literature is because I love it. It has brought me hours and days of magic when my life seemed bleak. It has taught me lessons about life that I didn't realise I was learning, because the stories themselves were so unexpected and compelling that I kept turning the page to see what was going to happen next, and before I knew it, I was a smarter person. It's probably pure arrogance for us who are writers to hope that we might be able to have that effect on someone else, but I think that that is one of the reasons we do it. We want to write stories that change people the way that good stories changed us.

My family moved to Canada from the Caribbean in 1977. My father was suffering from kidney failure and Canada was a good place to get treated for it. With the care he received there, he extended a five-year life expectancy to nineteen years, before he passed away in 1993.

I'd lived in North America as a child, and I'd lived in urban environments all my life, so getting used to Toronto was more a matter of getting used to a different flavour of urban. And that again is a partial truth. There was plenty to get used to, from Canadian accents to the fact of suddenly being in a racial and cultural minority. Though that's changing; the city's now one-third to one-half people of colour, depending on what part of it you're in. Toronto is beautiful, though I will never love the fact of having to wear a space suit eight months of the year to go outside; to me, clothing should be ornamentation, not protection. But if you want to get on my last nerve very quickly, just you cheerfully tell me that I hate the winter because I come from the tropics and I should go back there. You'd be surprised how many people think that kind of biological determinism is a caring and appropriate thing to say. People ask, "Why did you come here? The weather's so lovely where you come from! Why don't you go back there?"

But here in North America I am, and my family, and much of my extended family. And wonder of wonders, I've become a writer. My father was a writer. I thought it was a thing that fathers did, not daughters. I *am* living a fantasy. What better way to write than to write other fantasies? Maybe some of those dreams can come true, too.

Of course, those who have read my work know that many of those fantasies are nightmares. Life can be pretty harsh, and I've never been able to sugar-coat that in my writing. But even when the stories are difficult, *man* do I enjoy writing them! And that's the truth—or at least, part of it. The fact is, writing is difficult, and I don't so much enjoy writing as I enjoy *having written.* Because then I get to visit people I haven't met before and read my stories to them.

I Start Writing

I often hear other writers say that they have been obsessed with writing since they were children. I wasn't; to me, writing was what daddies did, especially poetry. I was obsessed with *reading.* The more I read, the more I thought I might want to write, but for years I didn't have the guts to try it. I'd grown up keeping many of my opinions to myself. I'd done well enough that I wasn't sure I had any. I didn't know if I'd have anything to write about.

But in 1993, feminist science-fiction author and editor Judith Merril was offering an evening class in writing science fiction and fantasy through Ryerson University (it was still Ryerson College then) in Toronto, where I live.

Judy was extremely important to the field of science fiction, as a writer, an editor, and a feminist. It was an opportunity I couldn't pass up. In order to apply to the class, you had to submit a piece of your own writing.

I had never written fiction before, other than the occasional class exercise when I was a child. With not the slightest idea what I was doing, I sat down and wrote a few pages of . . . *something* in a dead heat. It was six pages long only because I ran out of steam on page six. Didn't know what to do next. It wasn't a story yet, but I printed it up and sent it in.

I got accepted into the workshop, which never ran because there wasn't a large-enough registration. There had been only six of us, and they needed at least ten for the workshop to pay for itself. But Judy did a wonderful thing—she phoned the six of us and asked us if we wanted to learn how to run our own writing workshop with each other. "You're intelligent people," she said. "You don't need to pay someone to learn how to do this." We said yes, and a few days later, Judy had a meeting with us all in the meeting room of the co-op for retired artists where she lived. She showed us how to read and critique each others' work, Milford style, then she shooed us off to continue on our own. The resulting writing group—with a few changes in membership—continued on for about seven years. We met once a fortnight to critique each others' work. Some of us went on to be professionally published. I, slowly, began to figure out what a short story was, and how to write a whole one instead of just part of one. Eventually, my short story "Midnight Robber" tied for second place in the Short Prose Competition for Developing Writers sponsored by the Writers' Union of Canada. That story would go on to be included in my second novel of the same name. Then my short story "A Habit of Waste" was accepted for publication by Fireweed, a Toronto feminist journal.

In 1995 I was accepted into Clarion East, a short story writing workshop in science fiction, fantasy, and horror held at Michigan State University in East Lansing. The instructors were writers Joe Haldeman, Nancy Kress, Pat Murphy, Samuel R. Delany, Karen Joy Fowler, and Tim Powers. I didn't have the money to pay for it, but my writing group partner Bob Boyczuk lent it to me. Eventually I received an education grant that allowed me to repay him.

At Clarion I was one of nineteen students, and we had a different writer/instructor each week. Our job while we were there was to write, write, write, and to read and critique each others' work, and to learn all we could about the fields of science fiction, fantasy, and horror publishing.

One of the dilemmas I encountered immediately was the difficulty of trying to write science fiction and fantasy from a cultural context that isn't Graeco-European or Celtic. An example: much of SF draws on European history and folklore, to the extent that simply to mention a name—Oedipus, for instance—calls up a wealth of associations without the author needing to say another word. I liken it to "Darmok," (an episode from the fifth season of the television series *Star Trek: The Next Generation*). Actor Paul Winfield plays an alien from another planet who is trying to communicate with a human. He declaims, "Darmok and Jalad at Tanagra." In his culture, everyone would recognise the tale to which he's referring and would understand the parallels he wants to draw to his current situation. The humans, however, are just baffled. They don't know the lore of that culture. Similarly, if I wrote, "Nanny with her cheeks clenched" (referring to a piece of Jamaican folklore), only a few people would have any clue who or what I was talking about. So I found myself having to first describe the Caribbean history or the folk tale, then create my metaphors once I'd retold the existing tale. I'm still devising new strategies for doing that. I can only have so many history teachers, grad students specialising in folklore, librarians or folktale-spouting grandads conveniently show up to tell the audience what they need to know.

The Clarion writers-in-residence not only taught us about the craft of writing; they also shared their expertise about surviving as writers. They talked about the business side of signing contracts and finding agents, and told us about the tools they'd devised for organizing and juggling the many hats that a professional writer has to wear. They were generous and approachable.

What I learned about writing and being a writer at Clarion I could have learned on my own eventually; the difference is, Clarion gives it to you in six weeks, rather than in a lifetime (of course, learning to apply that knowledge does take a lifetime). It is an intense, exhilarating, exhausting environment, and it was one of the formative experiences of my writing life. I wrote more during the weeks of Clarion than I had written in the years previous. I came away more than ever with the deep desire to become a working writer. I went back to my job as a grants officer for the Toronto Arts Council, but the desire to finish a novel was eating at me. I worked away at the novel *Midnight Robber,* and got it about seventy-five percent done, and then ran out of steam. Eventually I would accept that the novel needed something different than what I was doing with it, even though I wasn't quite sure what.

Then I heard that Warner Aspect, the science fiction imprint of Warner Books in the U.S., was running a competition to choose an SF/F/H (science fiction, fantasy or horror) novel by a previously unpublished novelist. The final decision was to be made by writer C. J. Cherryh. I decided to try to write a novel with which to enter the contest. I pulled out the six unfinished pages that I had written for Judith Merril in 1993. From what I'd learned at Clarion, I suspected that what I wanted to do with that story would take a novel to complete (this is an ability I've retained; I can often tell from a brief description how long a story needs to be in order to tell itself). I began researching and writing *Brown Girl in the Ring.*

But I still had no idea of how to write a novel. I didn't write a story outline (still hate doing so), had no clue how I wanted the plot to turn out, or who all the characters would end up being. I wrote a lot of dead ends and had to backtrack. I sweated my way through three chapters of the novel, which was all I needed to have in order to enter the competition. I was so impatient! I sent those three chapters off to Warner in September of 1996. The actual competition deadline was January of 1997. By now, I was becoming used to the drill of sending short stories off to editors and getting rejection letters back. I figured that I would get a rejection letter for those three chapters of *Brown Girl in the Ring,* and then I'd decide what to do next.

Two weeks later, I received a letter from Warner Aspect. They liked the three chapters, and wanted the whole novel ("no drafts, please") so that they could send it on to the final round of judging. I had no novel. What I did have was a government writing grant that allowed me to take two months off work to concentrate on my writing, and an employer that was willing to give me those two months off. In a flop sweat, I contacted Warner and said that I would send them the novel after I'd gone over it once more to "clean it up a little." In December of 1996, I started to write in earnest.

As I wrote each new section, I workshopped it with my writing group. They thought I was crazy to hope that I, who'd never written anything longer than a few thousand words, could finish a novel in two months. I thought I was crazy, too. But one day, Brent Hayward in my writing group said, "I think you can do it, Nalo." I hung on to his faith in me. Every time I despaired, I'd remember him casually saying, "Nah, I think you can do it."

Nalo with her first editor, Betsy Mitchell, formerly of Warner Aspect

I finished the novel on January 30, 1997. I only knew that I was finished because I seemed to have tied off all the story threads. I printed it up, sent it off to Warner, and sat back to wait for the rejection letter.

Six months later I got a phone call at work from Betsy Mitchell, the then editor-in-chief of Warner Aspect. I had won the contest. Betsy estimated that there'd been over 1,000 submissions. Warner published the novel in 1998, and that's how I got my start as a novelist.

Second Novel: *Midnight Robber*

When my grant money ran out in January 1997, I went back to work. The advance from my first novel had allowed me to pay off some debts, but it wasn't enough to live on. I continued writing and submitting short stories to magazines and anthologies. Sometimes they were accepted, sometimes they were rejected. Near the end of 1998, I applied for and received two more government writing grants, and Warner Aspect said that they wanted to purchase *Midnight Robber* from me. Those three pots of money were enough to live on for a year. I gambled. I quit my job. Later, I would hear from my agent that it takes an average of five commercially successful novels before a writer can live off her writing, but at the time, I saw a chance to escape, even briefly, from the tyranny of working five days a week, fifty weeks a year, at jobs that I did because I had to in order to survive, not because I enjoyed them.

By now, I had a slightly better idea of what *Midnight Robber* needed in order to work as a novel. Over the course of a year, I rewrote the seventy-five percent I had and wrote the final twenty-five percent. I handed it in to Warner Aspect, and they accepted it. By then, it was clear that *Brown Girl in the Ring* was a success. It was getting good reviews, and people were buying it. It had gone into a second printing, and it won the Locus First Novel Award. My partner David Findlay created a Web site for me where people could read about my work and contact me via e-mail. I began to get invited to speaking engagements. This was another source of income, one I desperately needed. I live hand to mouth; still do, five years after the publication of my first novel. That's quite normal for a writer.

In the meantime, I had for the first time attended the International Conference of the Fantastic in the Arts, which happens every year in Fort Lauderdale, Florida. I gave a reading there one morning. Afterwards, two gentlemen came up to me and told me that they had just started a new publishing house, and that it had a solid financial base. The press was called Invisible Cities, after magical realist writer Italo Calvino's novel of the same name. They were interested in interstitial fiction; fiction that contained elements of the fantastic, but that couldn't be neatly fit into any genre category. They wondered whether I'd ever considered editing an anthology of other people's short fiction. I said that I had, but I hadn't figured out yet whether I wanted to collect stories around a theme, and if so, what the theme would be. "How about Caribbean fabulist fiction?" they said. Well, first they had to explain to me what the term "fabulist" meant (it means telling or inventing fables). I thought that an anthology of fabulist tales by Caribbean writers was a great idea, and since so many Caribbean writers had been colleagues of my father's, I knew that I'd probably have a fairly easy time contacting many of them. I told the people at Invisible Cities that I was interested. They submitted a contract to my agent that he said was a good one, and I began contacting Caribbean writers to tell them about *Whispers from the Cotton Tree Root: Caribbean Fabulist Fiction.* My call for submissions to the anthology went as follows:

> Bring out your duppy and jumbie tales; skin folk flights of fancy; rapsofuturist fables; your most dread of dread talks. *Whispers from the Cotton Tree Root: Caribbean Fabulist Fiction* is to be an anthology of fantastical fiction in Caribbean traditions, containing fabulist, unreal or speculative elements such as magic realism, fantasy, folklore, fable, horror or science fiction. I'm seeking well crafted and plotted fiction written from within a Caribbean or Caribbean diasporic context.

I got some wonderful stories for that anthology. A few of the writers submitting work knew me, or remembered me as a child from the Caribbean. I began to worry a bit, because I knew that there would be stories I would turn away, either because they didn't satisfy me for some reason, or because they didn't fit the anthology. How could I turn away writing by accomplished artists, some of whom had seen me in diapers as a baby? But I had to; when you're an editor, putting your name on that anthology means that you think the stories in it are strong. And in fact, those writers whose stories I didn't take responded quite well to the news. We all have to learn to deal with rejection without rancour if we're to have careers of any duration.

Whispers from the Cotton Tree Root appeared in 2000, along with my second novel, *Midnight Robber.* The stories in *Whispers* by Pamela Mordecai ("Once on the Shore of the Stream Senegambia"), Camille Hernandez-Ramdwar and myself ("The Glass Bottle Trick") were all short-listed for the James R. Tiptree, Jr. Memorial Award for speculative fiction that explores gender and gender roles. The reviews of the anthology were good. It was short-listed for the World Fantasy Award, and was named one of twelve best books of 2000 by the Vermont Book Professionals' Association.

Midnight Robber also went on to be a success; it received good reviews, was short-listed for the Tiptree and Philip K. Dick awards, the Nebula Award, the Sunburst Award (Canada), the Hugo Award; listed in the New York Public Library's "Best Books for the Teen Age 2000"; and received honourable mention in the "novels in creole" category of Cuba's Casa de las Américas prize for fiction. Like *Brown Girl in the Ring,* before it, *Midnight Robber* "earned out" beyond the initial advance that Warner Aspect had given me.

The Salt Roads (Griffonne) and *Skin Folk*

In 1999 I had won the John W. Campbell Award for Best New Writer. My agent advised me to write a proposal for another novel while there was a certain amount of buzz in the air about my work. I wrote the proposal for *Griffonne* (now called *The Salt Roads*), and in the spring of 2000, Betsy Mitchell of Warner Aspect said that she would like to buy it. Warner wanted me to turn in the new novel in less than a year, but it was more complex than anything I'd ever taken on before. It would involve research into three different historical periods and three different countries, as well as into the history of two religions. I had my work cut out for me. *The Salt Roads* would take me two-and-a-half years to complete.

While I was writing *The Salt Roads,* I decided to pursue a master's degree in creative writing. With a handful of successful books to my credit, I didn't need the degree to prove my qualifications, but I thought that having one would give me access to more short-term teaching positions, and thus help me to create a more reliable source of income for myself.

But I ran into a snag; I couldn't find a university that was willing to let me write science fiction and fantasy for my degree. In literary circles, science fiction and fantasy are generally considered to be worthless literature, usually by people who haven't read enough of it to have an informed opinion. Those professors who love those genres can sometimes convince their institutions to let them teach the occasional undergraduate reading course in science fiction and fantasy, but I couldn't find a single university that would allow me to pursue a Master of Fine Arts in writing them. One Canadian university even had the following phrase in the handbook for their M.F.A. in creative writing: "WARNING: we do not teach commercial, formulaic, non-literary writing such as science fiction, mystery and romance. Including these in your application will only hurt your chances."

I wrote the university in question, told them that I was considering taking an M.F.A. in creative writing, but that I wanted to be certain that I would have informed instruction. I referred to the above passage in their handbook and asked whether their definition of the word "formulaic" included (for example) sonnets, and whether they would turn away an applicant attempting to write along the lines of Huxley's *Brave New World* or Atwood's *A Handmaid's Tale.* They said that they would have the director of the programme get right back to me with a response. I have never heard back from them.

My writing doesn't tend to have a lot of the markers that people unfamiliar with science fiction associate with it. I don't write a lot of hard science fiction (fiction based on solving scientific problems), and I rarely have spaceships or aliens. Much of what I write is fantasy (fiction that employs supernatural phenomena). I suspected that if I didn't call my writing science fiction and if I made a point of not writing about spaceships or aliens while I was studying, I could probably get accepted into an M.F.A. programme, where they would view my work as "magical realism," or something of the sort. But frankly, I

The author with author James Morrow, her mentor at Seton Hill University

thought it was nonsense to have to closet my work that way. Spaceships and space flight are real and make very real differences in our world, and the question of alienness (of being different) has been obsessing human beings since we had minds with which to obsess. They are as valid subjects of fiction as any other human issue. If I was going to go back to school, I wanted to study with teachers who knew my genre, not with teachers who disdained it.

I eventually ended up studying at Seton Hill University in Greensburg, Pennsylvania. They had just begun a new programme, a master's degree in writing popular fiction conceived by Professor Lee McClain. It was a low-residence programme, meaning that much of the programme was conducted via e-mail, with two annual week-long residences on campus, at which time we attended various workshops on writing. My fellow students were writers of mysteries, science fiction, fantasy, horror, children's book,s and romances. My mentor was writer James Morrow, and my thesis project was *The Salt Roads.* It was an M.A. (master of arts), not the Master of Fine Arts I really wanted. An M.F.A. would have qualified me to teach creative writing at the undergraduate and graduate levels in universities. An M.A. would not. But it was the only graduate option that I could find, it would allow me to teach at the college level, and most importantly, it was a programme that was friendly toward my type of writing. I applied and was accepted. So now I had to finish the novel for two deadlines: one for my degree, and one for my publisher.

As a mentor, James Morrow was a godsend. He acted as combination goad and cheerleader. He understood what I was trying to do with this novel, and he didn't let me be lazy about any of it.

When a publisher buys a novel, common practice is to pay the writer fifty percent of the advance when the contract is signed, and another fifty percent when the writer turns in a completed (and acceptable) manuscript. I had received the first half of my advance. It was enough to live on for about six months. But because the novel was taking so long to complete (and because I was paying for my degree), that money was gone, and I was taking whatever other work I could find, which meant that I had less time and mental energy to devote to working on *The Salt Roads.* It's a pretty common dilemma for an artist; for many people, in fact. This time, however, Betsy Mitchell at Warner Aspect decided that they wanted a short story collection from me. It would give me another six months' worth of income; not enough time to finish *The Salt Roads,* but it would help a whole lot. And it would be easier for me to pull together a short story collection than to write a novel, because I could use stories that had already been published in magazines and anthologies.

I had ten short stories that Betsy agreed to use in the collection, and I wrote five new ones. I called the collection *Skin Folk,* a play on words that incorporates the idea of "kin folk" with that of the Caribbean folk tales about people who can take their skins off to transform into other creatures. The introduction to *Skin Folk* read as follows:

> Throughout the Caribbean, under different names, you'll find stories about people who aren't what they seem. Skin gives these skin folk their human shape. When the skin comes off, their true selves emerge. They may be owls. They may be vampiric balls of fire. And always, whatever the burden their skins bear, once they remove them—once they get under their own skins—they can fly. It seemed an apt metaphor for these stories collectively.

Skin Folk appeared in December of 2001, to good reviews. It would receive the World Fantasy Award and the Sunburst Award for Canadian Literature of the Fantastic.

I kept working on *The Salt Roads.* By the time I finished the manuscript for *it,* I had accumulated a few shelves of books on the history of slavery in the French Caribbean and in France, on the life of the nineteenth-century Romantic poet Charles Baudelaire, on the history and religions of Roman Egypt, and on the history and religions of Benin and other parts of West Africa. I had spoken to scholars who were experts in Egyptian history, especially the lives of women in ancient Egypt; to a woman whose specialty is sewing period clothing; to two experts in translation, one who translated a Baudelaire poem into English for me, and one who translated an excerpt of Moreau de Saint-Mery's treatise on eighteenth-century Haiti; to two scholars from Haiti; and to an expert in Roman history. I had learned what women in Ancient Egypt did for birth control, what kind of clothing a nineteenth-century French concert singer might wear, and what a brothel in fourth-century Egypt might charge for the most common sexual acts. I had learned what food you might buy from street vendors in fourth-century Aelia Capitolina (Jerusalem) and nineteenth-century Paris; and that mesmerism and ballooning were popular entertainments among rich white people in eighteenth-century Saint Domingue (Haiti). I had learned about the life of the beloved Haitian revolutionary François Makandal; about Rosa Parks's refusal to sit at the back of the bus, as black people were supposed to do; and about the black and Hispanic people who were there at the beginning of Stonewall, the historic revolt against police brutality toward queer folk.

The generosity of the people who helped me as I was writing *The Salt Roads* was astounding. So many talented people read and made detailed comments on the manuscript. People did research for me, translated for me, and otherwise gave me the benefit of their expertise. Jim Morrow managed to get me invited to Utopiales, a science-fiction festival in France, the birthplace of one of the historical figures about whom I was writing, so that I could do research on her. The festival paid my way. People gave me places to stay when I couldn't afford hotels, fed me when I was broke, suggested sources of information to me, encouraged me when I was tired and overwhelmed. Friends lent me money to pay the outstanding balance of my school fees. The acknowledgements page for *The Salt Roads* is crammed full, and I am indebted to them all.

One day, while I was still working on the novel, I got a phone call from my agent, Don Maass. He told me that my editor, Betsy Mitchell, was leaving Warner Aspect to become editor-in-chief at Del Rey Books.

When this happens to a writer, it's called being "orphaned," and it can be a disaster. Your book is under contract to the original publishing company, not the one to which your editor has moved, so even if the editor wants to take you along, you can't go, not immediately. This means that you may have no one at your existing publishing house to champion your work. It sometimes happens that writers in this position turn in their novels, only to discover that no one at their publishing house is interested in them any longer and the novels are turned away. When you lose your editor like this, you also lose the relationship that editor had built up for your work with the distributors and the bookstores. You can go to a new publishing house, but bookstore buyers looking for your work may not find you as easily, because they're looking under the publisher's name, not yours. It can be like building your name up again from scratch. Sometimes writing careers don't recover from the setback.

Betsy Mitchell is very supportive of my work, but with this move that she was making, she could not take *The Salt Roads* with her. However, Don told me that things looked hopeful. Betsy's editorial assistant Jaime Levine was going to take Betsy's place at Warner Aspect. Jaime had been working very closely with Betsy for years, knew the job and the Aspect publishing line inside out, and was also supportive of my work. In fact, Jaime would turn out to be as strong a champion of my writing as Betsy was. I breathed a sigh of relief and kept working.

I finished *The Salt Roads* in the spring of 2002, in time for my degree. The last few days had been tough going; by then, I was writing seventeen pages a day (about 4,300 words) to make my deadline. As has happened to me before, the ending of the book snuck up on me. I thought I knew which scene I was going to end with, but on the last day before I had to send the novel to Jim Morrow and to my second reader, author Nancy Springer, I wrote a scene in a way that I hadn't quite anticipated. When I was finished with that scene, I realised that I had written the ending. This has happened to me with all my novels so far; I get to a point and can go no further, and I realise that it's because I've wrapped up all the loose plot threads and resolved the protagonist's dilemma. I gave the new scene a quick rewrite, sent it off to Jim and Nancy, and waited. I already knew that Jim liked what I'd written so far, so I wasn't as worried about his assessment. But Nancy—a writer for whom I have immense respect—had not seen the novel at all before this, and she has a very different sensibility from Jim's.

But to my delight, they both passed me. Nancy had some reservations about the direction in which I'd chosen to take the plot, but thought that the novel was very well written. Jim said that I'd managed to pull off a very tough job of writing. I graduated with an M.A. from Seton Hill University in the summer of 2002.

Now it was time to see what Jaime Levine (my editor at Warner Aspect Books) thought of the novel. I sent it off to her.

Warner Aspect is an imprint of the larger outfit that is Warner Books. In effect, Aspect is a special department of Warner Books. Aspect publishes only science fiction and fantasy. When Jaime Levine read *The Salt Roads,* she thought that it might have an appeal that would include both genre fiction and mainstream fiction readers. She persuaded Jamie Raab, the editor of Warner Books, to read the novel. Raab liked it and asked Levine if she would consent to having the book published by Warner Books instead of Warner Aspect. This was exactly what my editor wanted for the book, so she happily said yes. Between the two editors, they decided to release *The Salt Roads* as a hardcover, the first of my titles to be released in hardcover format rather than as a trade paperback. They also decided that they wanted to send me on tour. When Betsy had been the head of Warner Aspect, she had sent me on a small four-city tour upon the release of *Midnight Robber.* At the time, I was aware that that was a rare thing for a second novel, and for a novel in the relatively small science fiction market, at that. Now Warner was talking about a ten-city tour: nine U.S. venues and Toronto, Canada, my home town. I was very excited, even more so when my Canadian distributor convinced Warner to add Halifax, Canada to the route. Halifax is home to one of Canada's historically black communities, and I had never been there. As of this writing, it is October of 2003. *The Salt Roads* is being released in exactly one month, and I will be off on tour. I anticipate that it will be exhausting, but I'm looking forward to it.

*

My trajectory as a writer has been an upward one so far. Despite the constant anxiety about money and the bills that sometimes go unpaid for months, this is the

The author with Jaime Levine, her current editor at Warner

job I'd rather be doing, and the rewards have been many. I've been able to meet some of my literary heroes, and to be taught by them. I've done work which has mostly made me happy. I've had the opportunity to take strong new stories by emerging and established writers and present them to the world. I have travelled to places I never thought I'd be able to visit. I'm seeing new black writers and writers of colour enter the field of science fiction and fantasy writing, and we are putting our stamp on it. It's still a trickle, but it's a start. I've had the extraordinary pleasure and honour of having people tell me how my writing has touched and helped them. I do get wary of getting typecast. The Caribbean still has an image in the rest of the world of being an "exotic" tropical paradise, so the setting and the language in some of my stories overshadow everything else in some reviewers' eyes, and that's mostly what they talk about. There are reviewers and readers who persist in interpreting all my stories as being based in Caribbean folklore, no matter what the story is about. Then they'll complain that the story was impenetrable to them because they didn't know the folk story on which it was based.

But a gratifying number of people have been able to come along with me when I try to draw them into my stories, and that is making my career as a writer a very happy one. I don't know what the future will be like. Trajectories turn downwards eventually. I can only hope that I'll have a long run at it, and if I don't, that I'll find something else to do that is also rewarding.

BIOGRAPHICAL AND CRITICAL SOURCES:

PERIODICALS

African American Review, winter, 1999, Gregory E. Rutledge, "Speaking in Tongues: An Interview with Science-Fiction Writer Nalo Hopkinson," p. 589.

Booklist, May 15, 1998, Bonnie Johnston, review of *Brown Girl in the Ring,* p. 1602; February 15, 2000, Roberta Johnson, review of *Midnight Robber,* p. 1091; November 1, 2001, Roberta Johnson, review of *Skin Folk,* p. 463; April 1, 2003, Vanessa Bush, review of *Mojo: Conjure Stories,* p. 1380; October 1, 2003, Donna Seaman, review of *The Salt Roads,* p. 299.

Emerge, July-August, 1998.

Kirkus Reviews, May 15, 1998, review of *Brown Girl in the Ring;* September 15, 2001, review of *Skin Folk,* p. 1329; October 15, 2003, review of *The Salt Roads,* p. 1242.

Library Journal, February 15, 2000, Jackie Cassada, review of *Midnight Robber,* p. 201; September 1, 2003, Wilda Williams, "Genre Fiction with a Twist," p. 36; September 1, 2003, Devon Thomas, review of *The Salt Roads,* p. 207.

Locus, May, 1998, Farren Miller, review of *Brown Girl in the Ring;* July, 1998; January, 1999, "Nalo Hopkinson: Many Perspectives."

Magazine of Science Fiction and Fantasy, July, 1998.

New York Times Book Review, July 12, 1998, Gerald Jonas, review of *Brown Girl in the Ring,* p. 26; July 30, 2000, Gerald Jonas, "Science Fiction."

Publishers Weekly, June 8, 1998, review of *Brown Girl in the Ring,* p. 51; January 3, 2000, review of *Midnight Robber,* p. 61; October 15, 2001, review of *Skin Folk,* p. 51; March 3, 2003, a review of *Mojo: Conjure Stories,* p. 58; July 21, 2003, review of *The Salt Roads,* p. 171.

School Library Journal, November, 1998, Carol DeAngelo, review of *Brown Girl in the Ring,* p. 160; June, 2000, Francisca Goldsmith, review of *Midnight Robber,* p. 173.

Starlog, February, 1999, p. 16.

Washington Post, August 30, 1998, David Streitfeld, "Science Fiction and Fantasy"; July 30, 2000.

ONLINE

Nalo Hopkinson Web site, http://www.sff.net/people/nalo (December 5, 2003).

SFFWorld.com, http://www.sffworld.com/ (March, 2000), "Interview with Nalo Hopkinson."

SFSite.com, http://www.sfsite.com/ (October 1, 2000), David Soyka, review of *Midnight Robber.*

Time Warner Web site, http://www.twbookmark.com/books/ (October 1, 2000), "Interview: Nalo Hopkinson."

* * *

HORSLEY, (Beresford) Peter (Torrington) 1921-2001
(Peter Beresford)

PERSONAL: Born March 26, 1921; died December 20, 2001; son of Arthur Beresford Horsley; married Phyllis Conrad Phinney, 1943 (marriage ended, 1976); married Ann MacKinnon Crwys-Williams, 1976; children: (first marriage) one son, one daughter; (second marriage) two stepsons, two stepdaughters. *Education:* Attended private secondary school. *Hobbies and other interests:* Skiing, stamp collecting.

CAREER: Equerry to Princess Elizabeth (now Queen Elizabeth II) and duke of Edinburgh, 1949-52; equerry to the queen, 1952-53, and to the duke of Edinburgh, 1953-56; Royal Air Force, deputy commandant of Joint Warfare Establishment at Old Sarum, England, 1966-68, assistant chief of air staff for operations, 1968-70, assistant officer in charge of bomber group, 1971-73, deputy commander in charge of Strike Command, 1973-75, also served in Cyprus, retiring in 1975 as air marshal. Robson Lowe (stamp auction house), chair; Stanley Gibbons, managing director. RCR International, director, beginning 1984; Horsley Holdings, director, beginning 1985; Yorkshire Sports, president, beginning 1986; National Printing Ink Co., chair, beginning 1987; Osprey Aviation Ltd., chair, beginning 1991. *Military service:* Served in British Merchant Navy, prior to World War II. Royal Air Force, flight instructor, bomber pilot, and air squadron commander, 1940-48; received Air Force Cross and French Croix de Guerre.

AWARDS, HONORS: Lieutenant, Royal Victorian Order, 1956; Order of the British Empire, commander, 1964, knight commander, 1974; Gold Medal, British Philatelists, 1973, for paper "The Skill and Artistry of Early British Stamp Designers"; Order of Christ of Portugal; Order of North Star of Sweden; Order of Menelik of Ethiopia.

WRITINGS:

(Under pseudonym Peter Beresford) *Journal of a Stamp Collector,* 1972.

Sounds from Another Room (autobiography), Leo Cooper (London, England), 1997.

Contributor to philately journals.

BIOGRAPHICAL AND CRITICAL SOURCES:

BOOKS

Horsley, Peter, *Sounds from Another Room,* Leo Cooper (London, England), 1997.

ONLINE

UFOMind.com, http://www.ufomind.com/ (August 14, 1997), "Close Encounter of British Air Marshal Peter Horsley."

OBITUARIES:

PERIODICALS

Daily Telegraph, December 20, 2001.

Times (London, England), February 8, 2002.*

* * *

HOYOS SALCEDO, Pedro (Pablo) 1947-

PERSONAL: Born June 22, 1947, in Versalles, Valle, Colombia; son of Efraim de J. Hoyos-Diaz (a teacher) and Gilma Adela Salcedo (a teacher); married Gloria S. Montoya, June 28, 1975; children: Juan P., Andres F., Gilma C. *Ethnicity:* "Hispanic." *Education:* Universidad Santiago de Cali, B.A., 1972; University of Massachusetts—Amherst, M.A., 1975; University of Nebraska—Lincoln, Ph.D., 1995. *Politics:* "Eclectic." *Religion:* Roman Catholic. *Hobbies and other interests:* Archaeology, numismatics, collecting graffiti.

ADDRESSES: Home—148 Ashbyrne Dr., Martinez, GA 30907. *Office*—Department of Languages, Literature, and Communication, Augusta State University, 2500 Walton Way, Augusta, GA 30904; fax 706-667-4770. *E-mail*—phoyos@aug.edu.

CAREER: Spanish teacher at schools in Darién, Colombia, 1968-71, and Tuluá, Colombia, 1971-73; University of Massachusetts—Amherst, Spanish teacher, 1973-75; Universidad de Caldas, Manizales, Colombia, Spanish teacher, 1975-92; University of Nebraska—Lincoln, Spanish teacher, 1992-95; Augusta State University, Augusta, GA, assistant professor, beginning 1995, then associate professor of Spanish language and contemporary Latin-American literature. Lecturer at colleges and universities in the United States and abroad, including Georgia Southern University, Roanoke College, and Augusta College. Active in local Hispanic community, including general coordinator of folkloric musical group Policromía Musical and Hispanic dance group Viva Panamá. *Military service:* Columbian armed forces; served one year.

MEMBER: Modern Language Association of America, Cervantes Society of America, American Association of Teachers of Spanish and Portuguese, Foreign Language Alliance for International Rapport, Southwest Council of Latin-American Studies, Foreign Language Association of Georgia, Sociedad de Profesionales Colombianos, Asociación Cultural Hispanoamericana, Alpha Mu Gamma.

AWARDS, HONORS: Named most distinguished Colombian professional in Georgia, Grupo Cultura, Inc., 2000.

WRITINGS:

De Cortés a García Márquez: ensayos de literatura hispanoamericana, Editorial Lumen (Lima, Peru), 1994.

Ejes temáticos en la obra de Ricardo Palma, Editorial Gedes (Armenia), 1998.

Ningún ser hermano es ilegal, ni el reino de dios tiene fronteras, Editorial Gedes (Armenia), 1999.

Contributor to periodicals, including *Foreign Language Notes* and *Phoenix.* Editor and director, *Hispano.*

WORK IN PROGRESS: De mio Cid a García Lorca: ensayos de literature española; research on the work of Padre de las Casas.

* * *

HUMPHREYS, J(ohn) R(ichard Adams) 1918-2003

OBITUARY NOTICE—See index for *CA* sketch: Born June 7, 1918, in Mancelona, MI; died August 25, 2003, in Santa Fe, NM. Educator and author. Humphreys was a fiction and nonfiction author and creative writing professor who founded the writers' program at Columbia University. He completed his bachelor's degree at the University of Michigan in 1940 and became a feature writer for the *Detroit Free Press* before enlisting in the Army Signal Corps during World War II. He served in England and France, returning home to publish his first book, *Vandameer's Road* (1946). He then joined the faculty at Columbia, where he taught in the English department from 1946 until 1988 and was director of the creative writing program from 1962 to 1988. Humphreys was also interested in photography, and after studying the art at the New York Institute of Photography in 1955, he became a photographer for Paddock Studios and then Dingee Studio during the late 1950s; he also tried his hand at being a disc jockey for station KTRC in 1960. After retiring from Columbia, Humphreys became an editor for Cane Hill Press in Santa Fe. Humphreys, who spent part of his time as a literary consultant for Doubleday, was the author of seven books in all, including the nonfiction works *The Last of the Middle West* (1966) and *Timeless Towns and Haunted Places* (1989), and the fiction works *Subway to Samarkand* (1977) and *Maya Red* (1989).

OBITUARIES AND OTHER SOURCES:

PERIODICALS

New York Times, September 14, 2003, p. A22.

HYDE, Mary (Morley Crapo) 1912-2003 (Mary Viscount Eccles)

OBITUARY NOTICE—See index for *CA* sketch: Born July 8, 1912, in Detroit, MI; died August 26, 2003, in Somerville, NJ. Book collector and author. Hyde, who became Lady Eccles when she married her second husband in 1984, was a noted bibliophile who specialized in the writings and records of Samuel Johnson and James Boswell. Born into a wealthy Detroit family, she earned an A.B. from Vassar in 1934, followed by graduate work at Columbia University, where she received her master's degree in 1936 and doctorate in 1947. Hyde began collecting books in earnest after marrying her first husband, an attorney who shared this passion, and together they amassed an impressive library at Four Oaks Farm in New Jersey that included rare books and papers from the sixteenth through the eighteenth centuries. As a result of her growing expertise, she also served on various advisory councils and committees for the University of Chicago, Princeton University, and Harvard University. In addition, she was a member of the advisory council for the Private Papers of Boswell and cofounded Eccles Centre for American Studies at the British Library in 1992. Hyde was the author of *Playwriting for Elizabethans, 1600-1605* (1949), *Catalogus Bibliothecae Hydeianae: The Hyde Collection of Works of Samuel Johnson* (1966), and *Four Oaks Library* (1967), as well as the coeditor of a number of scholarly works, including *The Impossible Friendship: Boswell and Mrs. Thrale* (1973) and *Bernard Shaw and Alfred Douglas: A Correspondence* (1982).

OBITUARIES AND OTHER SOURCES:

PERIODICALS

Guardian (London, England), September 16, 2003, p. 25.

Independent (London, England), September 5, 2003, p. 20.

New York Times, August 30, 2003, p. B7.

Times (London, England), September 1, 2003, p. 25.

I

IGGULDEN, Conn 1971-

PERSONAL: Born 1971, in London, England; married; wife's name Ella; children: Cameron. *Education:* London University (English).

ADDRESSES: *Home*—Hertfordshire, England. *Agent*—c/o Author Mail, Random House, 1745 Broadway, New York, NY 10019.

CAREER: Writer. St. Gregory's School, London, England, English teacher.

WRITINGS:

Emperor: The Gates of Rome, Delacorte (New York, NY), 2003.

WORK IN PROGRESS: Volumes two and three of "Emperor" trilogy.

SIDELIGHTS: While Conn Iggulden was taking over a class for a fellow teacher he picked up a history textbook that would alter his life. In it he read a passage about Julius Caesar that inspired him to write a novel about Caesar's life. As Iggulden explained to reporter Liam Rudden of the *Scotsman online,* "Most people only know of Julius Caesar in the last couple of years of his life, or from the Shakespeare play, and as I started reading up on him I soon realized that I knew none of the stories from when he was a child, or from his life as a young man. It was all good stuff." Two years later Iggulden produced his first published novel, *Emperor: The Gates of Rome,* the first in a trilogy set in the Roman Empire. Having submitted numerous novels to publishers in the past, and had all of them rejected, he was surprised when this manuscript set off a major bidding war among five large publishing houses.

Emperor relates the story of two young boys, Gaius and Marcus, as they grow to adulthood during the last years of the Roman Republic, a period of great political turmoil, chaos, and violence. Although not actually brothers, the boys are raised together and trained in the arts of war. With the brutal death of Gaius's father in a slave revolt, the boys take up residence with Gaius's uncle Marius, a consul who is a leading contender for control of the Republic. At age fourteen the boys separate. Marius joins the legions fighting in Greece and makes his fortune; Gaius remains with his uncle during a bitter civil war and learns invaluable political lessons. The story ends with Gaius, now called Julius after his dead father, departing Rome for military service. A critic for *Kirkus Reviews* called *Emperor* "an absorbing portrait of ancient Roman life and history, well written and full of suspense—even for those who know the ending." Jackie Pray of *USA Today* labeled it "dramatic historic fiction to keep adults turning pages like enthralled kids." Pray also noted that Iggulden's "writing shines in battle," adding that "Hand-to-hand combat and military clashes are Iggulden's forte." Justin Warshaw in the *Times Literary Supplement* also noted Iggulden's flair for bloody detail. His descriptions of fighting and other violence, wrote Warshaw, "are as convincing as they are horrific."

In an effort to write as authentic descriptions as possible, Iggulden spent his school breaks doing research in Rome and Pompeii trying to immerse himself in the history he was writing about. To that end, he donned battle armor, and sailed on the open seas in much the same way his characters did. A reviewer for *Publishers Weekly* recognized that "Iggulden has a solid grounding in Roman military history," but found that "anachronisms in speech and attitude roll underfoot and trip up authenticity." While Iggulden is not shy to admit that he took some liberties with the historical record, Brad Hooper of *Booklist* found that *Emperor* "casts authentically detailed light on the early years of the great Roman general and statesman Julius Caesar."

BIOGRAPHICAL AND CRITICAL SOURCES:

PERIODICALS

Booklist, November 15, 2002, Brad Hooper, review of *Emperor: The Gates of Rome,* p. 572.
Kirkus Reviews, October 15, 2002, p. 1496.
Publishers Weekly, November 4, 2002, p. 62.
Times Literary Supplement, January 24, 2003, Justin Warshaw, "The Gates of Rome."
USA Today, January 15, 2003, Jackie Pray, review of *Emperor.*

ONLINE

Decatur Daily Online, http://decaturdaily.com/ (June 5, 2003), John Davis, review of *Emperor.*
Scotsman online, http://news.scotsman.com/ (May 15, 2003), Liam Rudden, "He came, He Saw, and He Conquered."*

* * *

IRELAND-FREY, Louise 1912-
(Louise I. Frey)

PERSONAL: Born November 12, 1912, in Meridian, ID; daughter of Harry Arthur (in animal husbandry) and C. Myrtle (a homemaker; maiden name, Kahl) Ireland; married Charles T. Frey, June 10, 1939 (divorced November 12, 1971); children: Lawrence W., Robert C., William I., Stephen J. *Ethnicity:* "Caucasian." *Education:* University of Colorado—Boulder, B.A., 1934; Mount Holyoke College, M.A., 1936; Tulane University, M.D., 1940; studied hypnotherapy, 1955-57, 1978-79. *Politics:* Liberal. *Religion:* Unitarian-Universalist. *Hobbies and other interests:* Music, astronomy, metaphysics, religions.

ADDRESSES: *Home*—1322 Florida Rd., No. 4, Durango, CO 81301. *E-mail*—IrelandFrey@aol.com.

CAREER: Physician in private practice, Wichita, KS, 1942-43, and in Colorado, 1971-85; hypnotherapist and teacher of hypnosis classes, 1979-99.

MEMBER: Federation of American Scientists, Union of Concerned Scientists, Phi Beta Kappa, Sigma Xi, Alpha Omega Alpha.

AWARDS, HONORS: Gold Medallion, Colorado Centennial Essay Contest, 1976; Life Achievement Award, American Council of Hypnotist Examiners, 2001.

WRITINGS:

Freeing the Captives, Hampton Roads Publishing (Charlottesville, VA), 1999.
O Sane and Sacred Death: First-Person Accounts of Death, Blue Dolphin Publishing, 2002.

Contributor to periodicals, including *Journal of Regression Therapy.* Some writings appeared under the name Louise I. Frey.

WORK IN PROGRESS: Revising booklets for hypnosis classes; material on the metaphysical and spiritual uses of hypnosis for research and therapy; research on self-hypnosis and directive hypnosis.

SIDELIGHTS: Louise Ireland-Frey told *CA:* "From childhood I planned to write many books (and made up catchy titles for them), but writing was postponed for many decades by the Depression years, schooling, ill health, rearing four sons, et cetera. There were many things I wanted to say; some of them I wrote as letters to editors. Some were things I had learned and eagerly wanted to share.

"Kipling of the nineteenth century and Pearl Buck of the twentieth were two of my heroes, both as human beings and as writers. They wrote 'from the heart' as well as from the head, using beautiful language for their messages. They put themselves into the characters they wrote about, not standing back.

"During long years of chronic fatigue, when I was threatened by depression, as an antidote I chose a subject with a cheerful, triumphant ending, the life of Gautama Buddha, and I began by reading numerous books on the fauna, flora, and geography of northern India. This work, based on the ancient Pali scriptures, did help to counteract the horrors of World War II. Before each writing session I meditated, formally or informally, and 'lived' each episode along with the persons who actually did live it, so that the long ago became Now. The short book I had in mind became, over the next fifteen years, a trilogy: the historical novel *The Blossom of Buddha.* It has not been published.

"Aside from that I have written of events and experiences from my own life and learning, including personal experiences as hypnotic subject or facilitator. The several hundred hours of amateur experimentation with regression that a few friends and I did in the mid-fifties (largely unfettered by previous teachings) revealed that the altered state of consciousness contains amazing potential and far fewer limitations than we expected. Years later professional training qualified me for certification as a clinical hypnotherapist, and I began a new career at age sixty-seven. Results of the work with hypnosis have included a short book on the awareness of embryos and fetuses, the changes and pathways of consciousness after death of the body, and several different metaphysical aspects in between. Two books have been published so far.

"My motivation for writing? To share these fascinating experiences and knowledges that have been coming my way!"

* * *

IRWIN, Mark 1953-

PERSONAL: Born April 9, 1953, in Faribault, MN; son of William Thomas and Mary Lou (Milliron) Irwin; married Lisa Utrata; children: Heather Utrata. *Education:* Case Western Reserve University, B.A., 1974; Ph.D, 1982; University of Iowa, M.F.A., 1980. *Hobbies and other interests:* Hiking, wildlife preservation, entomology.

ADDRESSES: Home—3875 South Cherokee St., Englewood, CO 80110-3511. *E-mail*—irwin@bel-rea.com.

CAREER: Poet and educator. Cleveland Institute of Art, Cleveland, OH, associate professor, 1985-90; Fort Lewis College, Durango, CO, assistant professor, 1990-92. Visiting poet at University of Denver, 1992-93, Ohio University—Athens, 1993-94, University of Colorado—Boulder, 1997-2000, University of Nevada-Las Vegas, 2001, and Colorado College, 2001—.

MEMBER: Poetry Society of America.

AWARDS, HONORS: Wright-Plaisance traveling fellowship, 1977; Fullbright traveling fellowship to Romania, 1981; *Nation*/Discovery Award, 1984; Ohio Arts Council fellowship, 1985-86; Helene Wurlitzer Foundation fellowship, 1988; Lilly Foundation grant, 1989; National Endowment for the Arts fellowship, 1993; Pushcart Prize, 1994-95, 1997-98, 2003-04; Colorado Recognition Literary Award, 1996, 2002; Colorado Book Award, 2001.

WRITINGS:

POETRY

(Translator) *Ardis Anthology of Eastern European Poetry,* Ardis (New York, NY), 1982.
(Translator) Philippe Denis, *Notebook of Shadows: Selected Poems, 1974-1980,* Globe Press (Cleveland, OH), 1982.
(Translator) Nichita Stănescu, *Ask the Circle to Forgive You,* 1983.
Umbrellas in the Snow, 1985.
The Halo of Desire, Galileo Press (Baltimore, MD), 1987.
Against the Meanwhile (Three Elegies), Wesleyan University Press (Middletown, CT), 1988.
Quick, Now, Always, BOA Editions (Rochester, NY), 1996.
White City, BOA Editions (Rochester, NY), 2000.

(Editor) *Many Mountains Moving: A Tribute to W. S. Merwin,* Many Mountains Moving (Boulder, CO), 1999.

Bright Hunger, BOA Editions (Rochester, NY), 2004.

Contributor of poems to periodicals, including *Antaeus, American Poetry Review, Atlantic, Kenyon Review, Nation,* and *New Republic.*

SIDELIGHTS: Award-winning poet Mark Irwin is noted for collections that include *Against the Meanwhile (Three Elegies), Quick, Now, Always,* and *White City,* the last a work in which, a *Kirkus Reviews* contributor explained, the poet takes a measure of "what America, particularly the American West, has lost or left behind along the route of its forced march into the 21st century." Calling Irwin's style "beautiful and frustrating," Melissa Studdard Wiliamson characterized the poet's approach in her *American Book Review* piece on *White City:* "Irwin is a poet who looks into the world and sees more questions than answers. . . . big questions, inquiries that explore the nature of existence, meaning, and reality. They are questions that lead to meditation on transience versus permanence, tangibility versus intangibility, movement versus stasis." In the *Boston Book Review* Pamela Alexander notes that lyric poets "often set out to give us a Moment, an intensely sensory instant that stands above ordinary experince." Alexander considers Irwin a "splendid lyricist, startling us awake into such moments. . . . *White City* brims with them, rendered in flexible, inventive, sometimes mysterious language."

In the *American Book Review* Patrick Pritchett hailed *Against the Meanwhile (Three Elegies)* as "a highly accomplished volume of reflections on entropy and the rituals we use to combat it." According to a *Virginia Quarterly Review* contributor, the 1988 volume, Irwin's third collection, shows "how endings are interwoven with creation and rebirth" in the poems included: "The Wisdom of the Body," "Against the Meanwhile," and "Circling," and added that the poet "seeks, and finds . . . a certain order and beauty amid the constant change, evolution, and disorder" of a world threatened with nuclear annihilation. Pritchett noted that *Against the Meanwhile* "confirmed [Irwin] . . . as a writer of acute observational skills and lyrical limpidity." Comparing Irwin to poet Rainer Maria Rilke, *Ohio Review* contributor George Looney noted that, similar in theme to Rilke's *Duino Elegies,* Irwin's work features "an intricate noticing of the natural world, the kind of noticing that comes from the hands-on experience with perishing and renewal someone who cared for growing things acquires, the deep-rooted passion of the person who has reached under the earth and felt to cool region where life and death intertwine."

Irwin's 1996 collection *Quick, Now, Always* delves into the political with such poems as "Bucharest 1981" and "6 August 1945." Calling the verses in the collection "vibrant and alert" and "poetry to contend with," Pritchett explained in his *American Book Review* appraisal that Irwin requires readers "to reflect on the fundamental uncertainty that underlies reason itself," while in *Chelsea* critic Randall H. Watson characterized the book as "a jagged, heartbroken, and ecstatic excursus on the late twentieth century, a race through troubled paradise." Also laudatory, a *Publishers Weekly* contributor praised *Quick, Now, Always* as "brilliant" and noted that Irwin's "intellect and the urgency of his words remain traditionally steadfast."

In addition to his work as a poet, Irwin has also brought the works of European-born poets to English-speaking readers through his translation of *Notebook of Shadows: Selected Poems, 1974-1980* by French writer Philippe Denis and the verse of Eastern European poet Nichita Staescu, which Irwin translated as *Ask the Circle to Forgive You.*

BIOGRAPHICAL AND CRITICAL SOURCES:

PERIODICALS

American Book Review, August, 1996, Patrick Prichett, review of *Quick, Now, Always* p. 19; January, 2001, Melissa Studdard Williamson, review of *White City,* p. 25.

Boston Book Review, September, 2000, Pamela Alexander, review of *White City.*

Chelsea, Volume 61, 1996, Randall H. Watson, review of *Quick, Now, Always,* pp. 143-145.

Choice, April, 1988, W. J. Martz, review of *The Halo of Desire,* p. 1244.

Kirkus Reviews, January 15, 2000, review of *White City,* p. 83.

Library Journal, August, 1987, Rochelle Ratner, review of *The Halo of Desire,* p. 129.
North American Review, March, 1988, p. 72.
Ohio Review, spring, 1990, George Looney, "Keeping the World Going," pp. 116-128.
Publishers Weekly, August 26, 1988, Penny Kaganoff, review of *Against the Meanwhile,* p. 83; February 26, 1996, review of *Quick, Now, Always,* p. 101.
Virginia Quarterly Review, summer, 1989, review of *Against the Meanwhile,* p. 99.

J

JACKA, Judy 1938-

PERSONAL: Born August 1, 1938, in Melbourne, Australia; daughter of Keith (a civil engineer) and Beth (a nurse; maiden name, Cotterill) Lawrence; married David Taylor (marriage ended); married Alfred Jacka, March 13, 1972 (divorced, October, 1988); married John Garretty (an investment advisor), April 16, 2001; children: (first marriage) Milton, Matthew. *Ethnicity:* "Caucasian." *Education:* Prince Henry's Hospital, general nursing certificate, 1960; Southern School of Natural Therapies, B.H.S.; University of Melbourne, graduate diploma in human relations education, 1981. *Politics:* "Middle of the road." *Religion:* "The truth in all." *Hobbies and other interests:* Bush walking, metaphysics, meditation, philosophy, classical music.

ADDRESSES: Home and office—4 Joseph Ct., Park Orchards 3114, Victoria, Australia; fax: 03-987-64770. *E-mail*—judyjacka@bigpond.com.

CAREER: Southern School of Natural Therapies, Melbourne, Australia, began as principal, became chair, 1972-97. Self-employed natural therapist, 1971—; public speaker.

MEMBER: Australian Natural Therapists Association (life member; past chair), Medical and Scientific Network.

WRITINGS:

A Philosophy of Healing, 1977.
A-Z of Natural Therapies, Lothian, 1987.
Meditation: The Most Natural Therapy, Lothian, 1990.
Healing through Earth Energies, Lothian, 1996.
Healing Yourself Naturally, Crossing Press, 1998.
The Vivaxis Connection, Hampton Roads Publishing (Charlottesville, VA), 2000.
Synthesis in Healing, Hampton Roads Publishing (Charlottesville, VA), 2003.

WORK IN PROGRESS: Research on healing.

SIDELIGHTS: Judy Jacka told *CA:* "My writing is chiefly educational, and I have chosen to write on topics that have not already been well covered. My first book, *A Philosophy of Healing,* was published in 1977, written because, at that time, there was not any modern book covering naturopathic philosophy for my students. The next book was written as an account of how to make a synthesis of natural therapies, again because there was no such book available. The inspiration for my writing has always come from my practical experience in life, whether involving natural therapies, meditation, or healing.

"In writing and living I am eclectic so that I select information and experience from a number of sources and blend them together. This is how I practice as a natural therapist and teacher. Of particular concern is an aim to bridge science and natural therapies. Included here is the need to validate wherever possible subtle forms of healing.

"The actual practice of writing in my case is an easy discipline of two hours per day, commencing between eight and nine o'clock in the morning. I usually write nonstop during this period and edit my writing from time to time, but not every day or even weekly."

JANSEN, Erin 1967-

PERSONAL: Born May 18, 1967, in IL; daughter of Eldon (a company president) and Ellen (a travel writer; maiden name, Soret) Jansen. *Ethnicity:* "White." *Education:* Pepperdine University, B.A., 1989; London School of Economics and Political Science, M.S., 1990. *Politics:* Libertarian. *Religion:* Christian. *Hobbies and other interests:* Nature.

ADDRESSES: *Office*—NetLingo, Inc., P.O. Box 627, Ojai, CA 93024. *E-mail*—info@netlingo.com.

CAREER: Strategic Response, Los Angeles, CA, direct mail marketer, including affiliation with Rock the Vote, 1991-93; Interactive Marketing Services, New York, NY, marketing director and account manager for Virtual Yellow Pages, 1994-95; Non-Stop Internet, Inc., New York, NY, founder, president, and Web site designer, 1995-96; SiteSatellite, Internet consultant, 1996-98; NetLingo, Inc., Ojai, CA, founder, publisher, and Internet business consultant, 1998—. CareerMosaic.com, editorial and creative project manager, 1996-97; CNET Computer Network, senior online crusader, 1997; Office Depot, Inc., content manager and online editor for OfficeDepot.com, 1997-98; NetMarquee, project manager, 1998-99; Sprint, Local Services Division, e-commerce project manager for Trans-Act, 1999-2000; consultant to Winning Edge Technologies, Own America, and Upon Arrival. Guest on television and radio programs; also appeared in film *Wild@Start.*

MEMBER: National Association of Women Business Owners.

AWARDS, HONORS: Awards for *NetLingo* Web site include citation as one of top three sites of the year, *Net,* 1996, and two citations as one of the best 100 Web sites of all time, *PC* magazine.

WRITINGS:

NetLingo: The Internet Dictionary, NetLingo (Ojai, CA), 2002.

BIOGRAPHICAL AND CRITICAL SOURCES:

ONLINE

NetLingo.com, http://www.netlingo.com/ (February 10, 2003).

JASPER, Jan

PERSONAL: Female.

ADDRESSES: *Agent*—c/o St. Martin's Griffin, 175 Fifth Avenue, New York, NY 10010.

CAREER: Time management consultant, author, speaker, and educator. Conducts seminars for corporations and other groups; has appeared on television and radio.

MEMBER: American Society of Journalists and Authors, National Speakers Association.

WRITINGS:

Take Back Your Time: How to Regain Control of Work, Information, and Technology, St. Martin's Griffin (New York, NY), 1999.

Coauthor of promotional literature for IKON Office Solutions Corp. Contributor to publications, including *Investors Business Daily, Wall Street Journal, New York Daily News, Woman's Day, Redbook, Bottom Line Personal, Reader's Digest, American Way,* and *Men's Fitness;* contributor to Web sites, including *Selfgrowth.com.*

SIDELIGHTS: Jan Jasper is a productivity expert who has been training people to work smarter, not harder, since 1988. Her specialty is resolving complex time, task, and workload-management issues. Jasper streamlines her clients' systems and procedures, formulating optimum work habits and using technology to successfully manage information overload. Highly respected in her field, Jasper has appeared on both radio and television business news programs.

In addition to her seminars and consulting work, which has helped thousands of people—from *Fortune* 500 business executives to entrepreneurs—work more effectively, Jasper has also authored the book *Take Back Your Time: How to Regain Control of Work, Information, and Technology* to address the effects of technology on time management.

Writing in *Booklist,* David Rouse explained that Jasper "acknowledges that neatness may not always count, but argues that organization does; and she suggests that organization and time management are really two sides of the same coin." Jasper includes recommendations for eliminating clutter both at home and in the workplace, and even includes suggestions for time management while traveling. Rouse noted that Jasper's approach to a common problem is unique due to her "emphasis on the role that decision making plays in getting and staying organized."

BIOGRAPHICAL AND CRITICAL SOURCES:

PERIODICALS

Booklist, September 15, 1999, David Rouse, review of *Take Back Your Time: How to Regain Control of Work, Information, and Technology,* p. 207.

National Productivity Review, spring, 2000, review of *Take Back Your Time,* p. 85.

Redbook, July, 2002, review of *Take Back Your Time,* p. 144.

ONLINE

American Society of Journalists and Authors Web site, http://www.asja.org/ (July 15, 2003), Kathryn Lance, review of *Take Back Your Time: How to Regain Control of Work, Information, and Technology.*

Jan Jasper Web site, http://www.janjasper.com (July 15, 2003).*

* * *

JENKINS, Elwyn 1939-

PERSONAL: Born October 3, 1939, in Vryheid, South Africa; son of Charles (a minister) and Annie (a teacher; maiden name, Harding) Jenkins. *Education:* University of Natal, B.A., 1958, diploma of education, 1959, B.A. (with honors), 1965; University of Leeds, diploma in curricular studies, 1967; University of the Witwatersrand, M.Ed. (cum laude), 1975; University of South Africa, D.Litt. et Phil., 1980. *Hobbies and other interests:* Archaeology, rock art.

ADDRESSES: *Home*—P.O. Box 915-1157, Faerie Glen, Pretoria 0043, South Africa.

CAREER: High school teacher, 1960-70; head of English department at a college of education, 1971; Transvaal Education Department, curriculum specialist, 1972-73; head of English departments at colleges of education, 1974-80; Vista University, Pretoria, South Africa, head of English department, 1981-83, principal of Mamelodi Campus, 1982-89, senior director of student development, 1991-97, professor of English emeritus, 1998—. University of Toronto, visiting scholar, 1996; University of South Africa, research fellow at children's literature research unit, 1998—; University of London, visiting fellow at School of Advanced Study, 1999. South African Geographical Names Council, member.

MEMBER: International Research Society for Children's Literature, International Board on Books for Young People, English Academy of Southern Africa (past president; vice president, 1992—), South African Institute of Race Relations (honorary life member; past chair), South African Council for English Education (past chair), South African Scout Association (past national program commissioner).

AWARDS, HONORS: Thomas Pringle Prize for best article on English in education, English Academy of Southern Africa, 1982; Centennial Award, South African Teachers Association, 1989; award from South African Institute for Librarianship and Information Science, 1995; distinguished service award, Pretoria College of Education, 1996; Order of the Silver Protea, South African Scout Association, 1999.

WRITINGS:

Children of the Sun: Selected Writers and Themes in South African Children's Literature, Ravan, 1993.

(With P. Raper and L. Möller) *Changing Place Names,* Indicator Press (Natal, South Africa), 1996.

South Africa in English-Language Children's Literature, 1814-1912, McFarland and Co. (Jefferson, NC), 2002.

Contributor to books, including *The Cambridge Guide to Children's Books in English,* edited by Victor Watson, Cambridge University Press (New York, NY),

2001; and *Comedy, Fantasy, and Colonialism,* edited by Graeme Harper, Continuum, 2002. Contributor to periodicals, including *Lion and the Unicorn, Educational Review, Journal of Commonwealth Literature, Children's Literature in Education, Bookbird, Canadian Children's Literature, English Academy Review, Nomina Africana, English in Africa,* and *Current Writing.*

WORK IN PROGRESS: Revising *Changing Place Names;* research on nationalism in twentieth-century South African children's books in English.

* * *

JENNINGS, Kevin 1963-

PERSONAL: Born May 8, 1963, in Fort Lauderdale, FL (various sources list birthplace as Raleigh, NC, and Winston-Salem, NC); son of Chester Henry (a Baptist preacher) and Alice Verna (Johnson) Jennings; partner of Jeffrey Gerard Davis. *Education:* Harvard University, B.A. (magna cum laude), 1985; Columbia University, M.A., 1994; Stern School of Business, M.B.A. *Politics:* Democrat. *Hobbies and other interests:* Ice hockey.

ADDRESSES: Home—New York, NY. *Office*—Gay, Lesbian, and Straight Education Network, 121 West 27th St., Suite 804, New York, NY 10001-6207.

CAREER: Educator and author. Moses Brown School, Providence, RI, history teacher, 1985-87; Concord Academy, Concord, MA, history teacher, 1987-94; Gay, Lesbian, and Straight Education Network (GLSTEN), New York, NY, founder and executive director, 1994—. Point Foundation, trustee. Lecturer and commentator on radio and television.

AWARDS, HONORS: Lambda Literary Award, 1998, for *Telling Tales out of School;* Sundance Film Festival Audience Award for Best Documentary, 1998, for *Out of the Past;* Joseph Klingenstein fellow, 1993.

WRITINGS:

(Editor) *Becoming Visible: A Reader in Gay and Lesbian History for High School and College Students,* Alyson Publications (Boston, MA), 1994.

(Editor) *One Teacher in Ten: Gay and Lesbian Educators Tell Their Stories,* Alyson Publications (Boston, MA), 1994.

(Editor) *Telling Tales out of School: Gays, Lesbians, and Bisexuals Revisit Their School Days,* Alyson Books (Los Angeles, CA), 1998.

(With Pat Shapiro) *Always My Child: A Parent's Guide to Understanding Your Gay, Lesbian, Bisexual, Transgendered, or Questioning Son or Daughter,* Simon & Schuster (New York, NY), 2003.

Author and producer of documentary film *Out of the Past,* 1998.

SIDELIGHTS: Since founding the Gay, Lesbian, and Straight Education Network (GLSEN) in 1994, Kevin Jennings has been among the ranks of the leading gay rights advocates in the United States. As a speaker, writer, and commentator, he has promoted understanding and respect for people of all sexual orientations, particularly within the educational sphere. As Randal C. Archibold explained in the *New York Times,* GLSEN is staffed by fewer than twenty people, its offices located in New York's Chelsea district. With a budget comprised of foundation grants and donations, Jennings and his organization work to "raise awareness of the mistreatment of gay students as well as fight it." As Archibold reported, a 1999 GLSEN survey of almost 500 gay teens around the United States "found that 69 percent had received verbal, sexual or physical harassment in school, and 42 percent reported having been physically harassed or assaulted." Having experienced such treatment while growing up, Jennings has dedicated much of his adulthood to fighting it.

Jennings began his publishing career in 1994, the same year he founded and became executive director of GLSEN, by editing *Becoming Visible: A Reader in Gay and Lesbian History for High School and College Students.* Covering two millennia of human history, the book's thirty-nine readings describe the contributions of gays and lesbians to cultures around the world. Organized in a textbook-like format with each selection prefaced with notes by Jennings, the book allows readers "a chance to examine important events in the history of gays and lesbians," according to *Voice of Youth Advocates* reviewer Lynn Evarts, adding that it is "a chance that many of us need to take full advantage of." In the *Harvard Educational Review*

Edward J. Miech praised Jennings's introductions as "succinct and informative," and the essays selected "engaging and insightful." Noting that because it is geared for a younger readership *Becoming Visible* avoids sexually explicit material, Heather Stephenson added in the *Lambda Book Report* that in this "groundbreaking" text, Jennings "strives to combat homophobia by building empathy, focusing from the start on prejudice and oppression," and in the process "chooses apt analogies for a teen audience."

Other edited collections by Jennings include *One Teacher in Ten: Gay and Lesbian Educators Tell Their Stories* and the Lambda Literary Award-winning *Telling Tales out of School: Gays, Lesbians, and Bisexuals Revisit Their School Days.* Recounting the experiences of homosexual teachers from a variety of educational systems in locations ranging from small towns to large cities, *One Teacher in Ten* describes dealing with "homophobic parents, the cruelty of kids, unsupportive administrators, [and] concern about exacerbating cultural differences" between teacher and student as hurdles common to many of its thirty-seven contributors, according to a *Kirkus Reviews* contributor. In *Lambda Book Report* William J. Mann commended the volume as "a proud, compelling affirmation of the power of honesty, and the value of a truly honest education," while *Harvard Educational Review* critic Karen L. Mapp dubbed it "gripping, poignant, powerful, [and] emotionally charged." In a related volume, *Telling Tales out of School,* homosexual educators recall their own experiences of life as a student, creating a work that *Library Journal* contributor Debra Moore maintained will "resonate with gay and bisexual readers."

Together with coauthor Pat Shapiro, M.S.W., Jennings has also authored one of the first books to focus on the day-to-day relationship between gay or sexually questioning teens and their parents. In *Always My Child: A Parent's Guide to Understanding Your Gay, Lesbian, Bisexual, Transgendered, or Questioning Son or Daughter* he counsels confused parents attempting to understand and support children who have claimed an alternative sexual orientation. Suggestions regarding appropriate lines of communication, ways of recognizing and dealing with drug abuse or depression, and situations in which a parent's advocacy can aid a child in the world at large are all discussed. Praising the book in *Library Journal,* Linda Beck commended in particular Jennings' closing essay, in which he relates his personal story of reconciling with his mother as an adult, an essay Beck cited as being written with "the most fervor."

BIOGRAPHICAL AND CRITICAL SOURCES:

PERIODICALS

Booklist, September 15, 1994, Whitney Scott, review of *One Teacher in Ten,* p. 89.

Harvard Educational Review, summer, 1996, Edward J. Miech, review of *Becoming Visible,* pp. 408-410, and Karen L. Mapp, review of *One Teacher in Ten,* pp. 412-413.

Kirkus Reviews, July 1, 1994, review of *One Teacher in Ten,* p. 905.

Lambda Book Report, July-August, 1994, Heather Stephenson, review of *Becoming Visible,* p. 38; March-April, 1995, William J. Mann, review of *One Teacher in Ten,* p. 47.

Library Journal, May 1, 1998, David S. Azzolina, *Becoming Visible,* p. 121; November 15, 1998, Debra Moore, review of *Telling Tales out of School,* p. 82; January 2003, Linda Beck, review of *Always My Child,* p. 146.

New York Times, October 27, 1999, Randal C. Archibold, "A Gay Crusader Sees History on His Side," p. B2.

Voice of Youth Advocates, June, 1996, Lynn Evarts, review of *Becoming Visible,* p. 114.*

* * *

JIMÉNEZ LOZANO, José 1930-

PERSONAL: Born 1930.

ADDRESSES: *Agent*—c/o Author Mail, Seix Barral, Avenida Diagonal 662-664, Suite 7, Barcelona 08034, Spain.

CAREER: Writer.

AWARDS, HONORS: National critics award (Spain), 1989, for *El grano de maíz rojo;* Cervantes prize, 2002.

WRITINGS:

Meditación española sobre la libertad religiosa, Ediciones Destino (Barcelona, Spain), 1966.

Historia de un otoño, Ediciones Destino (Barcelona, Spain), 1971.

El sambenito, Ediciones Destino (Barcelona, Spain), 1972.

La salamandra, Ediciones Destino (Barcelona, Spain), 1973.

La ronquera de fray Luis y otras inquisiciones, Ediciones Destino (Barcelona, Spain), 1973.

Juan XXIII: Biografía ilustrada, Ediciones Destino (Barcelona, Spain), 1973.

El santo de mayo (short stories), Ediciones Destino (Barcelona, Spain), 1976.

Retratos y soledades, Ediciones Paulinas (Madrid, Spain), 1977.

Los cementerios civiles y la heterodoxia española, Taurus (Madrid, Spain), c. 1978.

Duelo en la casa grande, Anthropos (Barcelona, Spain), 1982.

Judíos, moriscos y conversos, Ambito (Valladolid, Spain), c. 1982, 2nd edition, 1989.

Guía espiritual de Castilla, photographs by Miguel Martín, Ambito (Valladolid, Spain), c. 1984.

Los tres cuadernos rojos, Ambito (Valladolid, Spain), 1986.

El grano de maíz rojo (short stories; title means "The Red Grain of Maize"), Anthropos (Barcelona, Spain), 1988.

(And illustrator) *Avila,* Ediciones Destino (Barcelona, Spain), 1988.

Los ojos del icono, Caja de Ahorros de Salamanca (Salamanca, Spain), 1988.

Sara de Ur, Anthropos (Barcelona, Spain), 1989.

Estampas y memorias, Incafo (Madrid, Spain), 1990.

El mudejarillo, Anthropos (Barcelona, Spain), 1992.

Segundo abecedario, Anthropos (Barcelona, Spain), 1992.

Tantas devastaciones, Fundación Jorge Guillén (Valladolid, Spain), 1992.

El cogedor de acianos, Anthropos, Editorial del Hombre (Barcelona, Spain), 1993.

La boda de Angela, Seix Barral (Barcelona, Spain), 1993.

Objetos perdidos: antología de cuentos (short stories), edited by Francisco Javier Higuero, Ayuntamiento de Valladolid Fundación Municipal de Cultura (Valladolid, Spain), 1993.

Relación topográfica, Anthropos (Barcelona, Spain), 1993.

Un fulgor tan breve (poetry), Hiperión (Madrid, Spain), 1995.

Teorema de Pitágoras, Seix Barral (Barcelona, Spain), 1995.

Un dedo en los labios, Espasa Calpe (Madrid, Spain), 1996.

Las sandalias de plata, Seix Barral (Barcelona, Spain), 1996.

Los compañeros, Seix Barral (Barcelona, Spain), 1997.

Ronda de noche, Seix Barral (Barcelona, Spain), 1998.

Maestro Huidobro, Anthropos (Barcelona, Spain), 1999.

Las señoras, Seix Barral (Barcelona, Spain), 1999.

Un hombre en la raya, Seix Barral (Barcelona, Spain), 2000.

Fray Luis de León (biography), Ediciones Omega (Barcelona, Spain), 2001.

Los lobeznos (title means "The Wolf Cubs"), Seix Barral (Barcelona, Spain), 2001.

Yo ví una vez a Ícaro (selected short stories), Castilla Ediciones (Valladolid, Spain), 2002.

Elegías menores, Editorial Pre-Textos (Madrid, Spain), 2002.

El viaje de Jonás, Ediciones del Bronce (Barcelona, Spain), 2002.

BIOGRAPHICAL AND CRITICAL SOURCES:

PERIODICALS

Symposium, winter, 1992, Francisco Javier Higuero, review of *Sara de Ur,* p. 288.*

* * *

JOHNSON, Claire M. 1956-

PERSONAL: Born December 15, 1956, in Berkeley, California; daughter of a doctor and a nurse; married; husband's name, Mark; children: Emma, Paul. *Ethnicity:* "Irish-Scots." *Education:* University of California-Berkeley, B.A.; attended California Culinary Academy. *Politics:* Democrat. *Hobbies and other interests:* Cooking, reading, gardening, quilting, sewing.

ADDRESSES: *Home*—Lafayette, CA. *Agent*—c/o Poisoned Pen Press, 6962 East First Avenue, Suite 103, Scottsdale, AZ 85251. *E-mail*—Johnson@rouxmorgue.com.

CAREER: Author and pastry chef, 1983-91; University of California-Berkeley, editor.

MEMBER: Mystery Writers of America, Sisters in Crime.

AWARDS, HONORS: Malice Domestic writers grant, 1999.

WRITINGS:

Beat until Stiff, Poisoned Pen Press (Scottsdale, AZ), 2002.

WORK IN PROGRESS: A second novel with working title *Roux Morgue.*

SIDELIGHTS: After training as a historian but being unable to find work in that crowded field, Claire M. Johnson decided to turn to her lifelong passion for cooking. She registered for an eighteen-month cooking course at the California Culinary Academy, where she acquired the skills to be a pastry chef. She then began working in some of San Francisco's best restaurants. After eight years, however, she called it quits and began a writing career. Her first book, *Beat until Stiff,* is a murder mystery set in San Francisco's restaurant district.

The novel's protagonist is Mary Ryan, a pastry chef who is recently divorced from San Francisco police detective Jim McCreary. When Mary begins prepping one day, she discovers the dead body of a co-worker hidden in the restaurant's laundry room. With Jim's partner assigned to the case, Mary herself becomes involved in the investigation. The novel presents a not-too-nice view of restaurants and their kitchens, where more than just food-making is going on. Johnson exposes the nature of philandering chefs, the demands of egotistical patrons, and the all-too-familiar practice of hiring undocumented immigrants in exchange for cheap labor.

A reviewer for *Publishers Weekly* hailed the novel as a "delicious debut," and added that it would likely appeal not only to mystery buffs but also to readers who enjoyed serious food-themed books. *Beat until Stiff* was nominated for an Agatha Award as best first novel.

BIOGRAPHICAL AND CRITICAL SOURCES:

PERIODICALS

Kirkus Reviews, October 15, 2002, review of *Beat until Stiff,* p. 1508.

Publishers Weekly, November 25, 2002, review of *Beat until Stiff,* p. 46.

ONLINE

Roux Morgue Web site, http:/www.rouxmorgue.com/ (January 16, 2003).

* * *

JOHNSON, Doris 1937-
(Gloria Greene)

PERSONAL: Born 1937.

ADDRESSES: *Home*—Queens, NY. *Agent*—c/o Author Mail, BET/Arabesque, One BET Plaza, 1900 West Place NE, Washington, DC 20036.

CAREER: Author.

WRITINGS:

Heart of Stone, BET/Arabesque (Washington, DC), 1999.

Just One Kiss, BET/Arabesque (Washington, DC), 2000.

Precious Heart, BET/Arabesque (Washington, DC), 2000.

Midsummer Moon, BET/Arabesque (Washinton, DC), 2001.

Rhythms of Love, BET/Arabesque (Washington, DC), 2002.

(With Felicia Mason and Adrianne Byrd) *Man of the House,* BET/Arabesque (Washington, DC), 2003.

Contributor, with Jacquelin Thomas and Layle Guisto to anthology *Cupid's Arrow* (contains "A Passionate Moment"), BET Publications (New York, NY), 2000.

Also contributed short story "Father at Heart" to *Man of the House,* Arabesque (Washington, DC); author of *White Lies,* Arabesque; author of *Love Unveiled* under the pseudonym Gloria Greene.

SIDELIGHTS: Doris Johnson is an author of romance novels and short stories about African Americans. Her heroines are bright, accomplished women coping with personal and professional challenges. Within this genre, her stories touch upon issues ranging from organ donation to family politics. Murder and mystery elements are part of some of her plots.

The novel *Heart of Stone* centers on Sydney Cox, a sommelier in a fancy restaurant. When her friend is sick and can not go to her job cleaning offices at night, Sydney fills in for her. Things get messy after Sidney decides to also do a little wine tasting and falls asleep. Security expert Adam Stone thinks that his drug bust has been foiled by a drunk, creating one of many obstacles to the romantic relationship that develops between them. In a review for *Romance Reader* Gwendolyn Osborne advised readers that the emotional obstacles between the two main characters makes it difficult to get close to them, but praised the elements of danger in the story.

Johnson begins *White Lies* with a prologue that shows Beatrice Vaughn killing her abusive husband after she finds him having sex with her sister. The main story is set twenty-six years later, after Beatrice's daughter Willow has returned with her aunt to the family's New York estate. Willow falls in love with Jake Rivers, a landscape architect, but their relationship is complicated by past events and family politics. Writing for *Romance Reader,* Osborne strongly recommended the book despite finding some predictable points and inconsistencies.

The central character in *Just One Kiss* is Dory Morgan, a figure introduced at the end of *White Lies.* The events of *Just One Kiss* begin when Dory is leaving a job as a journalist to pen mystery novels and do travel writing. On a cross-country train trip, she meets a mysterious man from her past, Reid Robinson, who once kissed her at party immediately before being arrested for murder. Reid still has not discovered who framed him, but his life has largely returned to normal. Reid fears disappointing Dory because he now suffers from borderline hypertension and related erectile dysfunction. In a review for *Affaire de Coeur,* Dera Williams commented that the medical issues in *Just One Kiss* are deftly treated within an entertaining novel. *Library Journal*'s Kristin Ramsdell found "a too-hectic plot" but liked the "admirable, nicely troubled protagonists."

The novel *Precious Heart* considers the effects of organ donation. Following the death of her beloved mother, Diamond Drew receives a grateful letter from the son of the woman who received her mother's heart. Diamond decides to find out if the woman is worthy of this gift. Answering the woman's ad for a live-in companion, Diamond hides her identity from the woman and gets the job, although the woman's son Steven does not approve of the arrangement. The situation becomes more complicated when Diamond and Steven find themselves attracted to each other. Osborne wrote in *Romance Reader,* "the dialogue is crisp and the secondary characters augment both the main characters and the storyline."

In *Midsummer Moon* heroine June Saxon is trying to recover from two substantial losses: an injury has ended her career as a flight attendant and a friend has stolen money June put into a business venture. She hopes to make a fresh start with a job in Paris and is paid back by her friend's ex-husband. His true identity later becomes a puzzle for June when they become romantically involved. In a review for *Booklist,* Patty Engelmann called *Midsummer Moon* "delightful" and recommended it to teens.

In *Rhythms of Love* Brynn Halsted's career as a lead dancer in a Harlem ballet troupe means everything to her and has eclipsed her personal life. She has an admirer in Simeon Storey, a composer and jazz club owner, who feels slighted by her. The two get a chance to mend their friendship, but then Brynn is hurt in an attack at the club. The career-ending incident forces her to redefine her life. In a review for *Booklist,* Engelmann deemed that "the modern Harlem renaissance is well represented" in the book, which she described as "an extraordinary romance with broad appeal."

BIOGRAPHICAL AND CRITICAL SOURCES:

PERIODICALS

Booklist, October 1, 2001, Patty Engelmann, review of *Midsummer Moon,* p. 304; September 15, 2002, Patty Engelmann, review of *Rhythms of Love,* p. 213.

Library Journal, November 15, 2000, Kristin Ramsdell, review of *Just One Kiss,* p. 56.

ONLINE

Affaire de Coeur, http://www.affairedecoeur.com/ (May 1, 2003), Dera Williams, review of *Just One Kiss.*

Romance Reader, http://www.theromancereader.com/ (March 26, 2003), Gwendolyn Osborne, review of *White Lies, Just One Kiss, Heart of Stone,* and *Precious Heart.**

* * *

JOHNSON, Pepper
See Johnson, Thomas

* * *

JOHNSON, Thomas 1964-
(Pepper Johnson)

PERSONAL: Born July 29, 1964, in Detroit, MI; son of Thomas Johnson (deceased) and Maxine Tinnon (a cleaning service worker); children: Dionte; *Ethnicity:* "Afro-American." *Education:* Ohio State University, 1985. *Religion:* Baptist. *Hobbies and other interests:* Basketball, golf, movies.

ADDRESSES: *Home*—North Providence, RI. *Agent*—Marilyn Allen, 615 Westover Rd., Stamford, CT 06902. *E-mail*—pepj52@aol.com; jparke@rawpep-52.org.

CAREER: New York Giants, linebacker, 1986-92; Cleveland Browns, linebacker, 1993-95; Detroit Lions, linebacker, 1996; New York Jets, linebacker, 1997-99; New England Patriots, inside linebacker coach, 2001—; author.

AWARDS, HONORS: High School All American, All Decade (Michigan); College All-Big Ten, 1984, 1985; named Defensive MVP, 1984, 1985; named College All-American, 1985; Pro Bowl, 1990, 1994; named All-NFL, All-Madden, and New York Jets Team MVP, 1990; Ed Block Courage Award, 1998; named to Ohio State All-Century Team, 2000; inducted into Ohio State Athletic Hall of Fame, 2001.

WRITINGS:

(With Bill Gutman) *Won for All: The Inside Story of the New England Patriots' Improbable Run to the Super Bowl,* Contemporary Books (Chicago, IL), 2003.

SIDELIGHTS: Thomas "Pepper" Johnson, who received his nickname as a young boy because he put pepper on everything he ate, received many top awards in his college and professional football career. He also played in two Super Bowls and has been inducted into his college alma mater's Athletic Hall of Fame. When he was not playing football, he found the time to create a multi-services organization for youths in Detroit and remains active in other charitable organizations. In 2000, after retiring as a football player, Johnson began his coaching career with the New England Patriots and was with the team when it made its way from last place in the National Football League to Super Bowl winners in 2001. The story of that remarkable victory is told in his book *Won for All: The Inside Story of the New England Patriots' Improbable Run to the Super Bowl.*

In this book, cowritten with Bill Gutman, Johnson takes readers behind the scenes with a surprising team. The Patriots, with their dismal beginnings of an 0-4 record, gathered very little fanfare in the early part of the season. But then the team suddenly caught on fire and fought their way to a final 11-5 winning season, good enough to land them in Super Bowl XXXVI. Even then, however, no one expected them to win.

Called one of the most exciting Super Bowl games in history, the battle between the Patriots and the St. Louis Rams surprised everyone. The Super Bowl game was close all the way, and in the last few minutes it was tied. But with just seconds remaining on the clock, the Patriots' Adam Vinatieri kicked a game-winning field goal.

The book, according to a writer for *Publishers Weekly,* "gives a first-rate account of the Patriots' transformation." Reviewers considered the book frank and honest, noting that Johnson does not shy away from dealing with unflattering material. He includes stories about how some players caused problems for the team. He also relates inspirational tales that helped the team pull together and create the Cinderella ending of one very unforgettable football season.

BIOGRAPHICAL AND CRITICAL SOURCES:

PERIODICALS

Publishers Weekly, October 28, 2002, review of *Won for All: The Inside Story of the New England Patriots' Improbably Run to the Super Bowl,* p. 64.

* * *

JOHNSTON, Carol 1951-

PERSONAL: Born May 1, 1951, in Panama Canal Zone; U.S. citizen; daughter of George W. (a clinical chemist) and Mary Elizabeth (a lobbyist; maiden name, Garner) Johnston. *Ethnicity:* "European." *Education:* Kalamazoo College, A.B., 1973; Union Theological Seminary, M.Div., 1978; Claremont Graduate School, Ph.D., 1994. *Politics:* Democrat. *Religion:* Presbyterian. *Hobbies and other interests:* Sailing, Abraham Lincoln.

ADDRESSES: Office—Christian Theological Seminary, 1000 West 42nd St., Indianapolis, IN 46208. *E-mail*—johnston@cts.edu.

CAREER: Christian Theological Seminary, Indianapolis, IN, assistant professor of theology and culture, 1991—. Lilly Endowment Fund Religion division, consultant, 1990-96, and director of Faith, Wealth, and Community Leadership Project.

MEMBER: American Academy of Religion, Society of Biblical Literature, Presbyterians for Restoring Creation.

WRITINGS:

The Wealth or Health of Nations: Transforming Capitalism from Within, Pilgrim Press (Cleveland, OH), 1998.

Also author of *And the Leaves of the Tree Are for the Healing of the Nations: Biblical and Theological Foundations for Ecojustice,* Presbyterian Church USA, 1999; and *Thinking Theologically about Faith, Wealth, and Community Leadership* (study guide).

WORK IN PROGRESS: Stewardship of the Mysteries of Faith.

BIOGRAPHICAL AND CRITICAL SOURCES:

ONLINE

Pilgrim Press Web site, http://www.pilgrimpress.com/ (December 14, 2003).

* * *

JOHNSTON, Sarah Iles 1957-

PERSONAL: Born October 25, 1957, in Bowling Green, OH; married; children: two. *Education:* University of Kansas, B.S., 1979, B.A., 1980; Cornell University, M.A., 1983, Ph.D., 1987.

ADDRESSES: Office—Department of Greek and Latin, Ohio State University, 414 University Hall, 230 North Oval Mall, Columbus, OH 43210-1319 *E-mail*—sjohnston@postbox.acs.ohio-state.edu.

CAREER: Princeton University, Princeton, NJ, lecturer, 1987-88; Ohio State University, Columbus, OH, 1988—, began as assistant professor, became professor of Greek and Latin.

MEMBER: American Philological Association, American Academy of Religion, Society for Biblical Literature, Women's Class Caucus.

AWARDS, HONORS: Mellon fellowship, Institute for Advanced Study; American Council of Learned Societies fellowship; Fondation Hardt fellowship; Den fellowship, Institute for the Advanced Study of Religion.

WRITINGS:

Hekate Soteira: A Study of Hekate's Role in the Chaldean Oracles and Related Literature, Scholars Press (Atlanta, GA), 1989.

(Editor with James J. Clauss) *Medea: Essays on Medea in Myth, Literature, Philosophy, and Art,* Princeton University Press (Princeton, NJ), 1997.

Restless Dead: Encounters between the Living and the Dead in Ancient Greece, University of California Press (Berkeley, CA), 1999.

SIDELIGHTS: Sarah Iles Johnston makes close study of ancient texts in Greek and Latin to determine religious and philosophical views of those who wrote and read the texts. Johnston has been particularly interested in the interaction between the dead and the living, the ancient concepts of soul, magic, and ghosts, and the cosmological roles of Hekate and Medea. In a *Journal of the American Academy of Religion* review of Johnston's *Hekate Soteira: A Study of Hekate's Role in the Chaldean Oracles and Related Literature,* Deborah Lyons wrote: "Johnston has performed a real service in providing a fresh interpretation of the Chaldean oracles. . . . We remain in Johnston's debt for bringing a fresh perspective to the examination of some very difficult texts." Stephen Scully in *Classical World* also felt that *Hekate Soteira* "contributes significantly to our understanding of the mysterious goddess."

Restless Dead: Encounters between the Living and the Dead in Ancient Greece explores the evolution of Greek concepts of the dead, both within their afterlife realm and through their interactions with the living. A *Choice* contributor observed that the "clearly written volume" makes "an important contribution" to the field of scholarship on ancient Greek religious beliefs.

BIOGRAPHICAL AND CRITICAL SOURCES:

PERIODICALS

Choice, November, 1999, review of *Restless Dead: Encounters between the Living and the Dead in Ancient Greece,* pp. 532-533.

Classical World, May-June, 1991, Stephen Scully, review of *Hekate Soteira: A Study of Hekate's Roles in the Chaldean Oracles and Related Literature,* p. 405.

Journal of the American Academy of Religion, fall, 1993, Deborah Lyons, review of *Hekate Soteira,* pp. 605-607.*

JOINER, Harry M(ason) 1944-

PERSONAL: Born August 30, 1944, in Paducah, KY; son of Harry B. (a hardware merchant) and Dorothy (a homemaker; maiden name, Mason) Joiner; married Suzanne Brauchli, July 10, 1968; children: Stephen A., Marianne Joiner Ledbetter, Karen Joiner Anz, David. *Ethnicity:* "White." *Education:* DePauw University, B.A., 1965; University of Kentucky, M.A., 1966, Ph. D., 1971; Graduate Institute of International Studies, Geneva, Switzerland, diploma, 1970. *Politics:* Independent. *Religion:* Methodist. *Hobbies and other interests:* Gardening, writing, guitar, walking, tennis, golf.

ADDRESSES: Home—22670 Village Lane, Athens, AL 35613. *Office*—Athens State University, Athens, AL 35611.

CAREER: Athens State University, Athens, AL, professor of political science and international commerce, 1969—.

MEMBER: Academy of International Business, Academy of International Business Educators, International Studies Association, Alabama Political Science Association.

WRITINGS:

American Foreign Policy: The Kissinger Era, Strode (Huntsville, AL), 1977.

Alabama's History: The Past and Present, Southern Textbook Publishers (Athens, AL), 1980.

Communism Today, Southern Textbook Publishers (Athens, AL), 1981.

Tennessee, Then and Now (juvenile), Southern Textbook Publishers (Athens, AL), 1983.

Alabama, Then and Now (juvenile), Southern Textbook Publishers (Athens, AL), 1986.

WORK IN PROGRESS: American Foreign Policy since 1776; research on international business, exporting and importing.

* * *

JONES, Derek

PERSONAL: Male.

ADDRESSES: Agent—c/o Author Mail, Fitzroy Dearborn, 919 North Michigan Ave., Suite 760, Chicago, IL 60611.

CAREER: Writer and editor. Channel 4, London, England, editor of programme support, 1982-95.

AWARDS, HONORS: Award for outstanding reference source, American Library Association, 2002, for *Censorship: A World Encyclopedia.*

WRITINGS:

(Editor) *Censorship: A World Encyclopedia,* four volumes, Fitzroy Dearborn (London, England), 2002.

SIDELIGHTS: Derek Jones is the editor of *Censorship: A World Encyclopedia,* a four-volume reference source that covers a broad spectrum of topics related to its subject. The book includes entries on subjects ranging from self-censorship to the proliferation of media in various nations, and it provides analysis on topics such as religious and political justifications and the social ramifications of unrestricted artistic expression. In addition, it addresses the social implications of obscenity laws and the complexities of sexual expression. Robert Potts, writing in the *Times Literary Supplement,* described *Censorship* as "a liberal publication that . . . makes no apologies for its sympathies," and he noted that "its range is tremendous, and laudable." Potts affirmed that "the emphasis in the encyclopedia . . . is heavily biased towards British and American experiences." He added, however, that "the international thrust of the encyclopedia is doubly valuable; it highlights some significant continuities, across history and across different cultures, in the reasons for censorship and the mechanisms by which it is effected."

BIOGRAPHICAL AND CRITICAL SOURCES:

PERIODICALS

Choice, June, 2002, W. L. Svitavsky, review of *Censorship: A World Encyclopedia,* p. 1731.

Library Quarterly, January, 2003, Marianna Tax Choldin, review of *Censorship,* p. 84.

Reference & User Services Quarterly, summer, 2002, Kevin Grace, review of *Censorship,* p. 385.

Times Higher Education Supplement, June 21, 2002, Judith Vidal-Hall, review of *Censorship,* p. 32.

Times Literary Supplement, February 15, 2002, Robert Potts, "Injurious to Truth?," pp. 7-8.*

* * *

JONES, Lloyd 1955-

PERSONAL: Born 1955, in Lower Hutt, New Zealand. *Education:* Graduated from Victoria University.

ADDRESSES: Home—Wellington, New Zealand. *Agent*—c/o Marketing Department, Penguin Books (NZ) Ltd., corner Rosedale and Airborne Roads, Albany, Private Bag 102902, NSMC, Auckland, New Zealand.

CAREER: Writer.

AWARDS, HONORS: Katherine Mansfield Memorial fellowship, 1988; Deutz Medal for Fiction, Montana New Zealand Book Awards, 2001, for *The Book of Fame;* Scholarship in Letters and other awards.

WRITINGS:

Gilmore's Diary (novel), Hodder and Stoughton (Auckland, New Zealand), 1985.

Splinter (novel), Hodder and Stoughton (Auckland, New Zealand), 1988.

Swimming to Australia and Other Stories, Victoria University Press (Wellington, New Zealand), 1991.

(Editor) *Into the Field of Play: New Zealand Writers on the Theme of Sport,* Tandem Press (Auckland, NZ), 1992.

Biografi: An Albanian Quest (travel book), Deutsch (London, England), 1993, published as *Biografi: A Traveller's Tale,* Harcourt (San Diego, CA), 1994.

(With Bruce Foster) *Last Saturday* (exhibition catalog), Victoria University Press (Wellington, New Zealand), 1994.

This House Has Three Walls (collection of novellas), Victoria University Press (Wellington, New Zealand), 1997.

Choo Woo (novel), Victoria University Press (Wellington, New Zealand), 1998.

The Book of Fame (novel), Penguin Books (New York, NY), 2000.

Here at the End of the World We Learn to Dance (novel), Penguin Books (Auckland, NZ), 2002.

(Author of essay) *Barefoot Kings*, photographs by John McDermott, Craig Potton Publishing (Nelson, NZ), 2002.

Series editor, Montana Estate Essay Series, for Four Winds Press, New Zealand.

ADAPTATIONS: Biografi: An Albanian Quest was adapted by Al Miller as *Matching Shadows with Homer,* music by Barbara Truex, produced in Brunswick, ME, 2002; *The Book of Fame* was adapted by Carl Nixon into a play, produced in Wellington, New Zealand, 2003.

SIDELIGHTS: Lloyd Jones's stories deal with diverse subject matter, sometimes mixing fact and fiction, sometimes telling of commonplace lives disrupted by uncommon events, either horrible or beautiful. Some reviewers have characterized his work as unusual and challenging, and he has won significant honors. An early collection of Jones's short fiction, *Swimming to Australia and Other Stories,* was shortlisted for the New Zealand Fiction Award, and his novel *The Book of Fame* received New Zealand's Deutz Medal for Fiction. *Here at the End of the World We Learn to Dance* was a finalist for that same prize. "I have no hesitation in listing Jones among the country's top 10 writers," commented Iain Sharp in a review of the latter book for Auckland, New Zealand's *Sunday Star-Times,* in which he also praised Jones's "willingness to try something different with each book."

Another landmark in Jones's body of work is *Biografi: An Albanian Quest*—published in the United States with the subtitle *A Traveller's Tale*)—which "made the literary world sit up," according to Jason Steger in the *Age.* This book finds the author walking "a fine line between fact and fiction," as Simon Garrett put it in *Lancet,* and narrates Jones's experiences while traveling in Albania in 1991, shortly after the collapse of Communism. The focal point of *Biografi* is Jones's search for Petar Shapallo, who Jones claims was the designated double of Albanian dictator Enver Hoxha, and who made numerous official appearances in Hoxha's place. According to Jones, Shapallo had given up a dental practice when he was recruited by the Albanian government because of his resemblance to Hoxha; he had plastic surgery to make the resemblance even closer. This life brought Shapallo material comfort but also isolated him. The government kept him in seclusion when he was not impersonating Hoxha; his wife and children were executed, and he was not allowed contact with his remaining family members or friends. When Hoxha died in 1985, Shapallo, well into his seventies, was left jobless and homeless. The communist government made no accommodation for him, and when it fell, Shapallo tried to join in the celebration but was jeered and assaulted by his fellow Albanians for his role in the former regime, with some even thinking him Hoxha's ghost. Jones writes of finding Shapallo in a labor camp after a journey that brought the author close encounters with the poverty and chaos of post-Communist Albania.

Jones's story found both believers and skeptics among reviewers. "If I had not myself witnessed the lengths to which regimes such as Hoxha's are prepared to go to cheat and deceive, I should have been inclined to dismiss Shapallo's story as fanciful, and Jones as naive for believing it," commented A. M. Daniels in the *Times Literary Supplement.* Hoxha's regime, though, "was surely capable of such an elaborate deception," Daniels wrote. London *Sunday Times* critic Margarette Driscoll was at first "enthralled by this tale" but later had doubts about Shapallo's authenticity, which she attempted to check, turning up no conclusive proof. Jones has since acknowledged that Shapallo is a character he created. "Defending himself," noted Sharpe in the *Sunday Star-Times,* "Jones pointed out that it was by no means uncommon for travel writers to include 'imaginative elements' in their books." Driscoll, however, maintained that "there are so many real stories of suffering in Albania and countries like it that mixing fact and fiction seems to me to devalue the trauma the country and its people have undergone." To *Washington Post* reviewer Dennis Drabelle, who also expressed doubts about Shapallo's existence, *Biografi* is "essentially a meditation on impersonation" and "a hybrid text with an unsettled relation to reality." He continued, "Yet the book has some good writing to recommend it, and Shapallo is a memorable character trapped in a plight worth exploring. Perhaps this 'tale' is best taken as neither truth nor fiction but as an odd new type of performance art." *New Statesman and Society* contributor Julian Duplain thought the ordinary Albanians whom Jones met had stories that, compared with Shapallo's, were "less grotesque but more revealing" about their country's recent developments. Dealing with the other merits of the book, Duplain wrote, "Jones chucks it all in without sufficient inquiry, confirming rather than explaining the television shorthand," although his book does provide "some strong images of a country suddenly opened up to the world." Daniels, however, called *Biografi* "travel writing as it should be: with an intellectual and emotional investment in the country which is its subject." A *Publishers Weekly* reviewer described the book as "a gem: sympathetic and informed, as enlightening as it is entertaining," and *New York Times Book Review* critic Annette Koback deemed it a work of "remarkable sublety and assurance."

As with *Biografi,* historical events figure in *The Book of Fame.* "Where *Biografi* just fits into the travel section of your local bookshop, *The Book of Fame* is deliberately subtitled 'a novel,'" reported Garrett in the *Lancet. The Book of Fame* is about a New Zealand rugby team, the All Blacks, that toured Europe and the United States in 1905, losing only one game—the Welsh Test in the United Kingdom—with that one marked by a disputed play. The team's members became heroes to New Zealanders, their performance and international fame a source of pride to a land that was still a British colony, not yet an independent nation. "Through these men," related Gilbert Wong in the *New Zealand Herald,* "New Zealanders everywhere walked a little taller, a little more confident of their place in the world." Jones tells the men's tale in first-person plural, with the team as a whole, not any individual, narrating the story.

This device allows Jones to show the players coming together "into something greater than the sum of their parts: a team," Garrett related. It also demonstrates, he noted, that they "live on in the imagination of New Zealanders still." The result is a story "about sport's place in the world . . . about what a team is, and about the relation between this team and nation-building," Garrett concluded. *Age* contributor Steger called the novel an exploration of "the origin of myth" and "the sense of self New Zealanders have both as individuals and as a nation," written in a style that is "spare and poetic." Wong offered a similar description, saying that despite the author's thorough research on the players and their tour, "What interests Jones is myth creation, what they did, not what they might have said. This is a novel, not history," composed of "terse sentences that . . . attain the intensity of poetry."

Although *Choo Woo* is wholly fictional, Jones was inspired to write it after hearing about a real case of child sexual abuse, in which a young girl was impregnated by her father, gave birth in secret, and kept the child hidden for several days. "It made me think how the hell would something like that happen?" Jones told Amy Egan for the Sydney *Daily Telegraph.* In Jones's book, the abuser of an adolescent girl, Natalie, is not her father but her mother's new boyfriend. The father, Charlie, has maintained a close relationship with Natalie during the couple of years since he and his wife, Vivienne, separated, but he becomes cut off from his daughter after the boyfriend, Ben, comes into their lives. With Vivienne in denial about her lover's true nature, Ben manipulates Natalie into a sexual affair and fathers a child whom the girl calls Choo Woo, after a sex game Ben has played with her. She hides the baby in a nearby vacant house, and it dies a few days after its birth. Natalie is left tormented by guilt, and her parents angered and bewildered at how these events could have taken place.

"Jones's novel has the conviction and untidiness of a case study, rather than the more complex emotional range it has perhaps sought," commented Peter Pierce in the *Sydney Morning Herald.* Katharine England, writing in the Adelaide *Advertiser,* thought Jones succeeded "at putting a sinister edge on the everyday, at cataloguing mental cruelty and interpreting a climate which allows abuse to flourish," but found the novel ultimately marred by a "strident, voyeuristic and oddly self-righteous tone." In Australia's *Canberra Times,* however, Frank O'Shea praised *Choo Woo* as "visceral in its authenticity" and "a book which will rivet you."

Here at the End of the World We Learn to Dance has a topic that is apparently much lighter, but the story is poignant and bittersweet. It tells of two pairs of lovers who also love the tango. In New Zealand during World War I, piano tuner Paul Schmidt begins a love affair with client Louise Cunningham by teaching her to tango. Paul, who is a target of bigotry because of his German heritage, eventually immigrates to Buenos Aires. Louise follows him, and their love endures for many years, even though he is married to another woman, who is surprised to learn, upon Paul's death, that he has asked to be buried next to Louise. In the book's other love story, set in present-day New Zealand, Paul's granddaughter Rosa, who is in her late thirties, captures the heart of naive college student Lionel, a part-time worker in her restaurant, when she teaches him the tango. He takes the relationship more seriously than she does, a circumstance that in the end forces him to grow up emotionally. Lionel narrates the story, with details of Paul and Louise's affair emerging as Rosa tells them to him. Of the two couples, Jones told *Age* writer Steger, "The only place they can achieve some sort of intimacy is on the dance floor without raising suspicion."

The novel is "ineffably sad, just like the tango itself, heartbreaking and exhilarating," commented Margie Thomson in the *New Zealand Herald.* Jones, she said, has managed "to write about music so that the words themselves express its character," using "the form and cadence of tango music" and dealing with "the wistfulness of romance, of love without possession, the poignancy of departure, of leaving and being left, that are among this music's central themes." *Sydney Morning Herald* critic James Ley praised the book's "artful construction," with a "unifying metaphor in an unspoken language of music and gesture," but he called Jones's character portrayals sometimes "lacklustre," with Paul and Louise less fully realized than Lionel and Rosa. Sharp of the *Sunday Star-Times* voiced a similar criticism of the characters, concluding, however, that though the novel is "flawed, it's still a great read." Steger thought the book "packs a powerful emotional punch," while Thomson summed it up as "very rich, but never hard work" and "a wonderful, aching tale."

BIOGRAPHICAL AND CRITICAL SOURCES:

PERIODICALS

Advertiser (Adelaide, Australia), March 13, 1999, Katharine England, "To the Dark Edges of Abuse."

Age (Melbourne, Australia), June 8, 2002, Jason Steger, "A Dance in the Margin," Saturday section, p. 7.

Canberra Times, January 31, 1999, Frank O'Shea, "Sad New Zealand Tale of Betrayal and Abuse," p. A18.

Daily Telegraph (Sydney, Australia), January 23, 1999, Amy Egan, "The Enemy Within," p. 120.

Lancet, March 9, 2002, Simon Garrett, "Nation-building and Rugby," p. 901.

New Statesman, September 10, 1993, Julian Duplain, review of *Biografi: An Albanian Quest,* p. 40.

New York Times Book Review, December 4, 1994, Annette Koback, review of *Biografi,* pp. 13, 50-51.

New Zealand Herald, August 26, 2000, Gilbert Wong, review of *The Book of Fame;* March 15, 2002, Margie Thomson, review of *Here at the End of the World We Learn to Dance.*

Publishers Weekly, September 5, 1994, review of *Biografi,* p. 105.

Sunday Star-Times (Auckland, New Zealand), September 1, 1996, Iain Sharp, "Exposing the Authors Who Wing It," p. 5; March 31, 2002, Sharp, review of *Here at the End of the World We Learn to Dance,* p. 2.

Sunday Times (London, England), September 5, 1993, Margarette Driscoll, "Double Trouble."

Sydney Morning Herald, February 20, 1999, Peter Pierce, "Against the Rules," Spectrum section, p. 9; May 4, 2002, James Ley, "Right on Detail," Spectrum section, p. 12.

Times Literary Supplement, August 6, 1993, A. M. Daniels, "Hoxha's Double," p. 12.

Washington Post, January 2, 1995, Dennis Drabelle, "Adventure in a Land of Illusion," p. D2.*

* * *

JONES, Marcus E. 1943-

PERSONAL: Born January 7, 1943, in Decatur, IL; son of George, Jr. (a laborer) and Bernetta (a licensed practical nurse) Jones; married, 1971; wife's name Diann (divorced, 1982); married Valerie Daniel (a homemaker), 1983; children: Anthony, Malik, Taisha, Samira, Malaika, Na'el, Amina, Jamia, Punch. *Ethnicity:* "African American." *Education:* Southern Illinois University, B.A., 1965, Ph.D., 1978; attended University of Ghana, 1968; Chicago State University, M.A., 1969; attended Florida State University, 1975-77, University of South Carolina, 1991-92, University of Florida, and University of Dar es Salaam, 1993. *Politics:* Independent Democrat. *Religion:* Muslim. *Hobbies and other interests:* Reading, walking, travel abroad.

ADDRESSES: *Home*—664 Stanley St. N.E., Orangeburg, SC 29115. *Office*—Claflin University, 400 College St., Orangeburg, SC 29115; fax 803-531-2860. *E-mail*—MarcusJones@claflin.edu.

CAREER: Educator and author. Geography teacher at public schools in Chicago, IL, 1965-69, 1988-89; Winston-Salem State University, Winston-Salem, NC, instructor in geography, 1969-70; Southern Illinois University, Carbondale, ombudsman, 1972-73; Florida A & M University, Tallahassee, assistant professor, 1973-76; University of South Florida, Tampa, visiting assistant professor, 1976-77; Morris Brown College, Atlanta, GA, head of Department of Social Relations, 1978-85; Clark Atlanta University, Atlanta, research coordinator, 1986-87; Valdosta State University, Valdosta, GA, visiting professor, 1986-87; Claflin University, Orangeburg, SC, associate professor, 1990—. American University in Cairo, research scholar, 1995-96; South Carolina State University, adjunct professor, 1991-2000.

MEMBER: National Association of African-American Studies (state regional coordinator, 1993-2000), Association for the Study of Classical African Civilizations, South Carolina Council for the Social Studies.

AWARDS, HONORS: Fulbright scholar in Egypt, 1995-96; Wazazi Wetu Award of Appreciation, 2000.

WRITINGS:

Black Migration in the United States with Emphasis on Selected Central Cities, Century Twenty One (Saratoga, CA), 1980.

Contributor to periodicals.

WORK IN PROGRESS: Research on African Americans and AIDS.

SIDELIGHTS: Marcus E. Jones told *CA:* "My primary motivation for writing, I believe, is to advance true knowledge through understanding human behavior. By writing and expressing my sincere thoughts, I can influence others to understand man's inhumanity to man. It is hoped that this understanding can lead to a more just and perfect society of humans on the planet Earth. I am motivated by a sense of justice and believe that the truth revealed will alone change adverse human behavior.

"My writing process involves inspiration, perspiration, and revelation. I usually have a desire of 'felt need' to write about some event which inspired my thoughts. Therefore, when I write about AIDS and black males, black unemployment, black male incarceration rates and racism, and black urbanization, I am concerned for a part of humanity in which I am a member. I believe that other members of society who read my thoughts should be motivated to behave in a positive rather than a negative manner."

* * *

JONES, Russell Celyn 1955-

PERSONAL: Born 1955, in London, England; son of Richard Eric Celyn (a customs and excise officer) and Grace Amelia Jones; married Barbara Ann Shacochis (marriage ended, 2000); children: Rebecca Grace, Rachel Amanda, Ben Richard. *Ethnicity:* "Anglo-Saxon." *Education:* University of London, B.A., University of Iowa, M.A. *Hobbies and other interests:* Sailing, surfing.

ADDRESSES: *Home*—London, England. *Office*—Department of English and Comparative Literature Studies, University of Warwick, Coventry CV4 7AL, England. *Agent*—Derek Johns, A. P. Watt, 20 John St., London SC1N 2DR, England. *E-mail*—Russell.Jones@warwick.ac.uk; Celyn.Jones@btinternet.com.

CAREER: Writer. Lecturer in writing program, University of Warwick, Coventry, England. Judge for Booker Prize, 2002. Staff reviewer, London *Times.*

AWARDS, HONORS: David Higham Prize, for *Soldiers and Innocents;* Society of Authors award, 1996, for *An Interference of Light;* Welsh Arts Council Literature Award.

WRITINGS:

Soldiers and Innocents, J. Cape (London, England), 1990.

Small Times, Viking (London, England), 1992.

An Interference of Light, Viking (London, England), 1995.

The Eros Hunter, Abacus (London, England), 1998.

Surface Tension, Abacus (London, England), 2001.

Contributor of short stories to periodicals and anthologies; contributor of reviews to periodicals, including London *Sunday Times* and *London Review of Books.* Author of screenplays and television scripts.

ADAPTATIONS: Work has been adapted for BBC Radio and BBC-TV.

SIDELIGHTS: British author Russell Celyn Jones has established a reputation for penning novels and stories that tackle difficult topics in a stylish and original way. His novels deal variously with the criminal element in London, the uneasy relationship between parents, children, and siblings, and the consequences of political strife for individuals caught up in it. *New Statesman* contributor Nicola Upson called Jones "a thoughtful writer with a sensitive approach to conflicts of love and identity." Educated at the University of London and the Iowa Writers' Workshop, Jones began publishing fiction in the early 1990s and is recognized for work that is "at once gripping and provocative," to quote Emily Melton in *Booklist.*

The heroes in Jones's novels challenge stereotypes of English civility and manners. The protagonist of his debut work, *Soldiers and Innocents,* becomes unhinged after shooting a pregnant civilian in Northern Ireland. Harry Langland in *Small Times* makes his living as a pickpocket and meets his doom when he tries to rise above his seedy lifestyle. The central character in *An Interference of Light,* Aaron Lewis, is an American spy trying to steal industry secrets from a group of Welsh slate cutters. As John Melmoth noted in the *Times Literary Supplement,* Jones is known for his "novels about men who live outside the law. The trick that he turns is to make victims of his protagonists in spite of their unloveliness."

In a *London Review of Books* critique of *Small Times,* Jonathan Coe observed that Jones "draws a convincing . . . portrait of London high and low-life, and sketches in a nimble political parable about 'the new utilitarian culture' without resorting to polemic." Bharat Tandon in the *Times Literary Supplement* credited Jones with "imagining a contemporary London that sounded neither prissy nor falsely streetwise." The same critic felt that the "sombre tone" of *An Interference of Light* "can make for some striking images." Tandon added that *An Interference of Light* "is clearly plotted with great care and intricacy."

The plot of *Surface Tension* hinges upon the unconventional relationship between siblings Mark and Geena McLuhan. Himself highly educated and reliable, Mark dotes on his older sister even though she haunts the club scene and cannot hold a steady job. When Geena begins having hallucinations, she learns an old family secret: she was adopted in South Africa during the era of apartheid. Geena travels to South Africa to find her birth parents and winds up putting herself in danger: Mark and his father must come to her rescue. *Booklist* contributor Emily Melton found the story "harrowing" and "imaginative." In his *Times Literary Supplement* review of the novel, Nick Laird wrote that the plot "moves swiftly in short episodic chapters, and is energized by the shifts from emotional issues to more conventional scenarios such as kidnapping and gun-running. The novel's themes-how history informs contemporary troubles, how reconciliation with the past is necessary to live in the present-neatly underpin both the personal and political situations."

Jones is a staff reviewer for the London *Times* and a lecturer in creative writing at several universities. He also writes screenplays and television scripts.

BIOGRAPHICAL AND CRITICAL SOURCES:

PERIODICALS

Booklist, October 15, 2002, Emily Melton, review of *Surface Tension,* p. 388.

Books, March, 1990, review of *Soldiers and Innocents,* p. 18.

London Review of Books, March 26, 1992, Jonathan Coe, review of *Small Times,* p. 21.

New Statesman, April 7, 1995, Phil Edwards, review of *An Interference of Light,* p. 53; December 4, 1998, Jonathan Coe, review of *The Eros Hunter,* p. 48; February 5, 2001, Nicola Upson, review of *Surface Tension,* p. 56.

Observer (London, England), February 16, 1992, David Buckley, review of *Small Times,* p. 59; April 26, 1998, Bill Saunders, review of *Soldiers and Innocents,* p. 18.

Times Literary Supplement, February 21, 1992, John Melmoth, "Designer-dipping," p. 18; February 4, 1995, Bharat Tandon, "Secrets in Stones," p. 20; January 19, 2001, Nick Laird, "The Sweetheart Impulse," p. 24.

ONLINE

Crime Time online, http://www.crimetime.co.uk/bookreviews/ (May 15, 2003), Ingrid Yornstrand, review of *Surface Tension.*

* * *

JOSEPH, Sheri 1967-

PERSONAL: Born November 8, 1967, in Silver Spring, MD; daughter of Leroy and Kathleen Joseph. *Education:* University of the South, B.A., 1989; University of Georgia, Ph.D., 1997.

ADDRESSES: *Home*—951 Shadowridge Dr., Atlanta, GA 30316. *Office*—Georgia State University, Department of English, 33 Gilmer Street SE, Unit 8, Atlanta, GA 30303. *E-mail*—sherijos@aol.com.

CAREER: Writer. University of Georgia, Athens, instructor; editorial and teaching assistant for *Georgia Review,* 1994-2000; Morehead State University, Morehead, KY, assistant professor of creative writing, 2000-02; Georgia State University, Atlanta, assistant professor of English and creative writing, 2002—. Member, board of directors, AIDS Coalition of NE Georgia, 1998-2000.

MEMBER: Associated Writing Programs.

AWARDS, HONORS: Sewanee Writers' Conference Tennessee Williams Scholar, 2001; Walter E. Dakin fellow, 2003.

WRITINGS:

Bear Me Safely Over, Atlantic Monthly Press (New York, NY), 2002.

Contributor of short fiction to anthologies and literary journals, including *Georgia Review, Kenyon Review,* and *Other Voices.*

WORK IN PROGRESS: An untitled novel follow-up to *Bear Me Safely Over,* which includes the same characters but in a very different context.

SIDELIGHTS: Sheri Joseph's first book of fiction, *Bear Me Safely Over,* is a cycle of short stories that can be read as a novel, the stories all involving the same characters and a continuing plot.

In what a *Publishers Weekly* reviewer called "a gutsy, realistic, and lyrical portrait of country people struggling to find meaning in their constricted lives," Joseph introduces the reader to her three main characters. Paul is a gay teenager who has been arrested for prostitution and is verbally abused and humiliated by his stepbrother, Curtis. Curtis plays in a band and is engaged to Sidra, a sympathetic young woman whose sister died of AIDS. She is drawn to Paul for complex reasons and ends up taking him in after he fights with his family, much to the disgust of her fiancée. The story gets even more complicated when Paul begins to develop a romantic relationship with Kent, a member of Curtis's band. Pam Kingsbury of *Southern Scribe* observed, "Joseph handles the book's themes—loss, homophobia, families reinventing themselves, and religious fundamentalism—with subtlety and assurance. Her characters, no longer religious but deeply spiritual, reach a kind of salvation by the book's end."

Joseph told *CA:* "*Bear Me Safely Over,* my first book, has been read by many as a novel, but it's actually a cycle of short stories. The idea was important to me in composing the book, which is multivocal and alinear, circling around various members of two Georgia families about to be joined by marriage. As I write, I try to let my characters tell me their stories and to let one story or voice rise out of another, so that they answer one another and the book builds naturally with a sort of balance of dissent like that of human communities.

"I seem to write a lot about family in various forms, especially about people who feel excluded or unsatisfied by traditional family structures, yet cannot deny a need for connection on that level, who therefore seek substitutes. And I also write about the religious impulse, again of the sort thwarted by traditional religion that nonetheless can't stop seeking something authentic to replace it. Now I may be speaking of my new novel, but all of this applies equally to both."

BIOGRAPHICAL AND CRITICAL SOURCES:

PERIODICALS

Advocate, July 23, 2002, David Bahr, "Family Feud."
Booklist, April 15, 2002, John Green, review of *Bear Me Safely Over,* p. 1382.
Cincinatti CityBeat, May 5, 2002, Brandon Brady, "Writer's Block: What a Kick!"
Kirkus Reviews, March 1, 2002, review of *Bear Me Safely Over,* p. 279.
Lambda Book Report, May, 2002, Andrew Beierle, "Handsome, Headstrong, and Sexually Precocious," p. 17.
New York Times Book Review, November 25, 2002, Ann Powers, "Sex, Death, and Rock 'n' Roll."
Publishers Weekly, March 18, 2002, review of *Bear Me Safely Over,* p. 75.
Southern Scribe, September, 2002, Pam Kingsbury, interview with Joseph.

ONLINE

Georgia State University Web site, http://www.gsu.edu/ (January 6, 2003), "Sheri Joseph."

* * *

JOSLIN, Michael (E.) 1949-

PERSONAL: Born May 20, 1949, in Philadelphia, PA; son of Charles E. (in the military) and Anne (Strauff) Joslin; married Pam Wilder, January 14, 1995; children: Blanche, Dylan, Mitchell. *Education:* Attended U.S. Military Academy, West Point, 1967-70; University of South Carolina—Columbia, B.A. (magna cum laude), 1973, Ph.D. (with distinction), 1977.

ADDRESSES: *Home*—1236 Greasy Creek Rd., Bakersville, NC 28705. *Office*—Lees-McRae College, P.O. Box 128, Banner Elk, NC 28604.

CAREER: Educator, photographer, and writer. Jacksonville University, Jacksonville, FL, assistant professor of English, 1978-82, teacher at Governor's School for the Talented and Gifted, 1981; East Tennessee State University, Johnson City, temporary English teacher, 1985-89, fellow of Center for Appalachian Studies and Services, 1987; Lees-McRae College, Banner Elk, NC, faculty member, 1989-90, associate professor, 1990-96, professor of English, 1996—. Freelance writer and photographer, 1982—, with photography represented in exhibitions, including "Mountain Epiphanies" and "Spots of Time: Life under the Black Mountains." Participant in workshops and lecture/slide presentations.

MEMBER: Appalachian Consortium, Phi Beta Kappa, Phi Kappa Phi.

AWARDS, HONORS: Havilah Babcock creative writing award; awards for best news article and best news photograph, North Carolina Soil Conservation Service, 1988; Edgar Tufts Award, Lees-McRae College, 1998, for excellence in teaching.

WRITINGS:

Mountain People, Places, and Ways: A Southern Appalachian Sampler, Overmountain Press (Johnson City, TN), 1991.
More Mountain People, Places, and Ways: Another Southern Appalachian Sampler, Overmountain Press (Johnson City, TN), 1992.
Our Living Heritage, Overmountain Press (Johnson City, TN), 1998.
Appalachian Bounty: Nature's Gifts from the Mountains, Overmountain Press (Johnson City, TN), 2000.

Work represented in anthologies, including *In Place: A Collection of Appalachian Writers,* edited by Ronald K. Giles, Center for Appalachian Studies and Services (Johnson City, TN), 1988; and *Appalachia Inside-Out: An Anthology of Appalachian Literature,* edited by Jack Higgs and Ambrose Manning, University of Tennessee Press (Knoxville, TN), 1995. Contributor of articles, photographs, and reviews to periodicals, including *Now and Then, North Carolina Arts Journal, Balsams and Hemlocks, Mountain Times, Multi-Cultural Digest,* and *Draft Horse Journal.*

SIDELIGHTS: Michael Joslin told *CA:* "My writing and photography focus on the natural and human culture of the Southern Appalachians. I work with the reality of the region, basing my articles and books on interviews, personal observation, and research. A strong regional flavor persists in the mountains, although the homogenous national culture is slowly replacing many of the old ways of thought, speech, and action under the inexorable pressure of the media, developers, and tourists. I attempt to capture the unique aspect that lingers. I relish the pleasure of the experience and create a record that perhaps will endure."

* * *

JULAVITS, Heidi

PERSONAL: Born in ME; married Manny Howard (a food writer; divorced); married Ben Marcus (a writer, editor, and professor). *Education:* Columbia University, M.F.A.

ADDRESSES: Home—21 South Portland Ave., Brooklyn, NY 11217-1378.

CAREER: Writer. *Believer* (literary magazine), New York, NY, editor. Worked variously as an English teacher, movie extra, fashion copywriter, and waitress.

AWARDS, HONORS: "Marry the One Who Gets There First" was selected for *Best American Short Stories 1999;* named a Writer on the Verge by *Village Voice Literary Supplement.*

WRITINGS:

The Mineral Palace, G. P. Putnam's Sons (New York, NY), 2000.

The Effect of Living Backwards, G. P. Putnam's Sons (New York, NY), 2003.

(With Jenny Gage) *Hotel Andromeda,* Artspace Books (San Francisco, CA), 2003.

Work represented in anthologies, including *Writers Harvest 2: A Collection of New Fiction* and *Zoetrope: All-Story: Close Your Eyes and Think of England,* Volume 2, number 3; contributor of stories to periodicals, including *McSweeney's, Story,* and *Esquire.*

SIDELIGHTS: Heidi Julavits worked at many jobs during her twenties and wrote short stories on the side. She also spent several years working on her first novel, *The Mineral Palace,* before it and a second novel were purchased by G. P. Putnam's Sons. Julavits, at age thirty, was then able to quit waitressing and concentrate on her writing.

The Mineral Palace is set in the 1930s in Pueblo, Colorado. Julavits chose the location because her own grandmother had moved there from Minnesota with her doctor husband and young son, passing up the opportunity to study at Columbia University, from which Julavits herself graduated. Like Bena Jonssen, the protagonist of the book, her grandmother hated her new home.

In a *Beatrice* interview with Ron Hogan, Julavits said she chose the 1930s "because it gave me a lot more behavioral leeway with the characters. . . . I had this sense that I wanted this dramatic act to occur, but I wanted it to be sympathetic. I wanted it to be understandable. And I felt that the climate of the 1930s enabled a certain sympathy with the characters and enabled a certain sense to be made of the act, that possibly in another time period would have been more challenging."

A *Publishers Weekly* writer who reviewed *The Mineral Palace* wrote that Julavits "can be a magician with language, spinning brilliant metaphors and investing descriptive scenes with almost palpable dimensionality." In this dark novel that is dotted with death, Bena is married to Ted, a womanizing doctor, and is the mother of a sickly newborn. Her mental state and sense of dislocation in the Depression-era dust bowl is improved only slightly when she takes a job writing the society column for the local newspaper. Through her work, she begins to meet the local characters, including cowboy Red Grissom. Bena also bumps into the woman she later learns is Bonnie Parker, who bums a cigarette and some aspirin from Bena and gives her a tarnished silver charm in return. Bonnie and Clyde are killed in Louisiana soon after.

Bena is unable to convince Ted that there is something different about their child and attempts to come to terms with her brother's death. She also tries to understand why people take the extreme actions they do in difficult times. *Library Journal* reviewer Ellen

R. Cohen felt that some readers may find the suffering—emotional, psychological, and physical—"too overwhelming. The writing, however, is superb."

Newsweek's Jeff Giles called *The Mineral Palace* "a marvelous debut novel: harrowing, poetic, and tragic," and remarked that Julavits is "such a gifted, visceral writer—dust and hailstorms a specialty—that even her most painful visions can be beautiful to behold."

Melanie Rehak wrote in a *Harper's Bazaar* review that Julavits's psychological portrait of the desperate Bena is "gorgeously rendered" and commented she has "woven an utterly convincing case for human sympathy." Just before Julavits signed the contract for her debut novel, her grandmother was diagnosed with lung cancer. Sadly, she died before the book was completed.

The Effect of Living Backwards, called a "quick-witted black comedy" by *Library Journal*'s Colleen Lougen, is Julavits's second novel. The book tells the story of sisters Alice and Edith, whose plane is hijacked as they travel to Edith's wedding in Morocco. The hijackers are led by a blind man named Bruno, and as Alice, who is multilingual, takes part in hostage negotiations, she finds herself falling for him. But Edith also turns on the charm. A *Kirkus Reviews* contributor wrote that "the story is as much about sibling love and rivalry as about the ethical issues raised by terrorism—the women's mutual devotion is balanced by their intense competitiveness for attention."

Five years after the publication of her first novel, Julavits became coeditor of the *Believer,* a literary magazine sponsored by Dave Eggers. In an article for the *New York Observer* online, Joe Hagan wrote that in her debut essay, "The Snarky, Dumbed-down World of Book Reviewing," Julavits "earnestly chides the literary-industrial complex of book reviewers for succumbing to a 'hostile, knowing, bitter tone of contempt' that is suffocating the creative lives of the literati." "As Ms. Julavits herself points out, complaining about the state of book reviewing is an old chestnut," noted Hagan, "going back to George Orwell's 1936 essay 'In Defence of the Novel.' Ms. Julavits feels, however, that the cycle of complaint has reached a moment of fresh urgency. It's not, she wants to make clear, that she's against criticism, or even negative criticism. . . . But at some point—she doesn't say when—the nastiness always lurking in the world of book reviews simply got out of hand."

BIOGRAPHICAL AND CRITICAL SOURCES:

PERIODICALS

Harper's Bazaar, September, 2000, Melanie Rehak, review of *The Mineral Palace,* p. 406.

Kirkus Reviews, May 1, 2003, review of *The Effect of Living Backwards,* p. 631.

Library Journal, August, 2000, Ellen R. Cohen, review of *The Mineral Palace,* p. 157; May 15, 2003, Colleen Lougen, review of *The Effect of Living Backwards,* p. 124.

Newsweek, September 18, 2000, Jeff Giles, review of *The Mineral Palace,* p. 82.

New York Times Book Review, September 24, 2000, Anita Gates, review of *The Mineral Palace,* p. 19.

Publishers Weekly, July 31, 2000, review of *The Mineral Palace,* p. 67.

ONLINE

Beatrice.com, http://www.beatrice.com/ (September 16, 2002), Ron Hogan, interview with Julavits.

BookPage, http://www.bookpage.com/ (September 16, 2002), Linda Stankard, review of *The Mineral Palace.*

Failbetter.com, http://www.failbetter.com/ (September 23, 2002), interview with Julavits.

iVenus, http://www.ivenus.com/ (September 16, 2002), Marius Silke, review of *The Mineral Palace.*

Lighthouse Inkwell, http://www.lighthousewriters.com/ (September 23, 2002), Jenny Vacchiano, interview with Julavits.

New York Observer online, http://www.observer.com/ (May 27, 2003), Joe Hagan, "Hunting Snark: Heidi Julavits Stomps a Virus."*

K

KAI, Tara

PERSONAL: Daughter of Khosro Karamad and Nasrin Tehrani (a homemaker). *Education:* Studied at Bonn University, Aachen University, and University of Paderborn, received B.A. and M.A.; postgraduate study, University of Paderborn. *Hobbies and other interests:* Yoga, swimming, traveling, writing.

ADDRESSES: Home—Miami, FL. *Office*—Department of English, Florida International University, University Park Campus, 11200 Southwest Eighth St., Miami, FL 33199. *E-mail*—TaraKai@yahoo.com.

CAREER: University of Paderborn, Paderborn, Germany, English literature instructor, 1994-96; Taslimi Construction Company, Santa Monica, CA, project engineer, 1998-99; Florida International University, Miami, FL, adjunct professor of English, 1999—. Project consultant and coordinator, Online Geriatric University.

WRITINGS:

Dar es Salaam: A Novel, Bridge Works (Bridgehampton, NY), 2002.

Contributor of short stories to American and German anthologies, including *About Life, the Uni, and the Rest,* Unicum Publications (Bochum, Germany), 1995; *Foreigner in a Cold Land,* Herder Publications (Munich, Germany), 1992, and *A World Between,* George Braziller (New York, NY), 1999. Contributor of articles and stories to periodicals, including *Gablers* and *A World Between.*

SIDELIGHTS: Tara Kai is a fiction writer whose work reflects her own international travels in Europe, Africa, and America. Kai's debut novel, *Dar es Salaam,* is set in the African city of that name and presents the coming-of-age tale of a precocious fourteen-year-old girl. Tatum, the novel's central character, journeys from England to Tanzania with her mother, stepfather, and two siblings. During her extended stay in Tanzania Tatum falls in love with—and finally seduces—a forty-year-old African man named Mohammed. The novel explores not only the uncertain ground of teenage passion but also the dynamic of a blended family far removed from their traditional surroundings.

Kai told a contributor to *Writers Monthly* that she received "hundreds of rejections" for *Dar es Salaam* before finally finding a publisher. Once released, the book was greeted with warm reviews. "Kai knows how a fourteen-year-old girl feels," wrote Phaedra Trethan in the *Philadelphia Inquirer.* "She knows the self-loathing, the social awkwardness, the love-hate relationship with one's parents. She also knows Africa: the beauty, the poverty and the people." To quote a *Publishers Weekly* critic, "Kai shows considerable promise, particularly in her characterizations." A correspondent for *Kirkus Reviews* called *Dar es Salaam* "an eerily honest story of adolescent obsession that conjures up Nabokov even as it offers a fresh and grounded view of East Africa."

Reflecting on her publishing debut in *Writers Monthly,* Kai said: "It's so personal and yet so revealing to have a book on the bookshelf. It's hours of sitting at home alone, creating sentences and then having it in a bookstore where anyone can read it."

BIOGRAPHICAL AND CRITICAL SOURCES:

PERIODICALS

Booklist, October 15, 2002, Kristine Huntley, review of *Dar es Salaam,* p. 386.

Kirkus Reviews, August 1, 2002, review of *Dar es Salaam,* p. 1063.

Philadelphia Inquirer, December 29, 2002, Phaedra Trethan, "Debut Novel a Descriptive Story Set in Africa."

Publishers Weekly, September 2, 2002, review of *Dar es Salaam,* p. 51.

South Florida Sun Sentinel, October 27, 2002, Chauncey Mabe, "Miami Writer an Enigma, Wrapped in a Book Jacket."

ONLINE

Writers Monthly, http://www.writersmonthly.com/ (May 25, 2003), Jessica Clark, "A Shot of Hope."

* * *

KAIN, John F(orrest) 1935-2003

OBITUARY NOTICE—See index for *CA* sketch: Born November 9, 1935, in Fort Wayne, IN; died of cancer August 4, 2003, in Dallas, TX. Economist, educator, and author. Kain was a respected professor of economics and African-American studies. He completed his undergraduate work at Bowling Green State University in 1957, and then went on to earn his doctorate at the University of California at Berkeley in 1961. For the next year, he worked as a researcher for the RAND Corp., and then taught economics at the U.S. Air Force Academy from 1962 to 1964. This was followed by a stint at the London School of Economics before he joined the faculty at Harvard University in 1967 as director of the program on regional and urban economics. Kain remained at Harvard for most of his career, becoming a full professor in 1969 and serving as chair of the department of city planning from 1975 to 1981. In 1991 he was named Henry Lee Professor of Economics, a position he held until leaving Harvard in 1997 to become professor of economics and director of the Cecil and Ida Green Center at the School of Social Sciences at the University of Texas in Dallas. He was professor emeritus there at the time of his death. During his career, Kain also served as a senior staff member for the National Bureau of Economic Research in Cambridge from 1967 to 1972, and he was an associate editor of the *Review of Economics and Statistics.* He was the author or editor of several books, including *Race and Poverty: The Economics of Discrimination* (1969), *Essays on Urban Spatial Structure* (1975), *Housing and Neighborhood Dynamics: A Simulation Study* (1985), and *Increasing the Productivity of the Nation's Urban Transportation Infrastructure* (1992).

OBITUARIES AND OTHER SOURCES:

PERIODICALS

Chronicle of Higher Education, September 5, 2003, p. A61.

* * *

KANE, Andrea

PERSONAL: Married; children: one daughter.

ADDRESSES: Home—NJ. *Office*—c/o Rainbow Connection Enterprises, Inc., 1982 Washington Valley Rd., PMB 510, P.O. Box 309, Martinsville, NJ 08836-0309. *E-mail*—WriteToMe@andreakane.com.

CAREER: Author.

WRITINGS:

ROMANCE NOVELS

My Heart's Desire ("Barretts" series), Pocket Books (New York, NY), 1991.

Dream Castle, Pocket Books (New York, NY), 1992.
Masque of Betrayal, Pocket Books (New York, NY), 1993.
Samantha ("Barretts" series), Pocket Books (New York, NY), 1994.
Echoes in the Mist ("Kingsleys" series), Pocket Books (New York, NY), 1994.
The Last Duke ("Thorntons and Bromleighs" series), Pocket Books (New York, NY), 1995.
Emerald Garden, Pocket Books (New York, NY), 1996.
Wishes in the Wind, ("Kingsleys" series), Pocket Books (New York, NY), 1996.
The Black Diamond ("Black Diamond" series), Pocket Books (New York, NY), 1997.
Legacy of the Diamond ("Black Diamond" series), Pocket Books (New York, NY), 1997.
The Music Box, Pocket Books (New York, NY), 1998.
The Theft ("Thorntons and Bromleighs" series), Pocket Books (New York, NY), 1998.
The Gold Coin ("Coin" series), Sonnet Books (New York, NY), 1999.
The Silver Coin ("Coin" series), Sonnet Books (New York, NY), 1999.
Run for Your Life, Pocket Books (New York, NY), 2000.
No Way Out, Pocket Books (New York, NY), 2001.
Scent of Danger, Pocket Books (New York, NY), 2003.

Contributed the novella "Yuletide Treasure," part of the "Thorntons and Bromleighs" series, to the anthology *A Gift of Love,* 1996. Also contributed the story "Stone Cold" to the anthology *Wait until Dark.*

SIDELIGHTS: Among the early influences on romance writer Andrea Kane were Walt Disney movies and Nancy Drew mysteries—elements that, she later wrote, would be incorporated in her writing. Her career began with historical thrillers, most set in the Regency period of early nineteenth-century England. Among these books are *The Gold Coin* and its companion work, *The Silver Coin.* Kane has since gone on to pen contemporary romantic thrillers, starting with *Run for Your Life,* a *New York Times* best-seller. Many of her novels focus on the members of a single family.

In *The Theft,* one of the Regency romances, Kane bringst back Lady Noelle Bromleigh, who first appeared as a four-year-old girl in the novella "Yuletide Treasure." Noelle is the adopted daughter of Eric, earl of Bromleigh. As *The Theft* begins, she attempts to find her biological father, Franco Baricci, who has opened an art gallery in London. Also seeking Baricci is Earl Ashford Thornton, who wants Baricci for a very different reason: Thornton is an art detective, and he suspects Baricci of selling treasures he has stolen. Meeting on the train to London, Noelle and Ashford fall in love and join forces against the man who abandoned Noelle long before.

"Kane's tale is fast-paced," wrote Deborah Rysso in *Booklist,* "and although historical, the language flows easily. The characters are likeable." According to Maria Simson in *Publishers Weekly,* "There are lots of good plot twists cleverly woven into Regency mores and styles to keep readers intrigued and entertained."

The protagonists of *The Gold Coin,* Anastasia and Breanna Colby, are identical, but not twins. As children, the two cousins recognized each other as kindred spirits, alike in soul as much as appearance, and pledged to come to one another's aid when needed. Now, fourteen years later, Anastasia desperately needs Breanna's help. Her problem is not financial: she has a sizeable inheritance, but Breanna's unscrupulous father, the Viscount George Colby, wants to get hold of it by making himself Anastasia's legal guardian. Anastasia's late father, however, entrusted Damen Lockwood, marquess of Sheldrake, as trustee over the estate. Colby's ambitions are further thwarted when he discovers a new complication: Anastasia has fallen in love with Lord Sheldrake. Now the marquess and the two ladies must work together to protect Anastasia's life and fortune.

"This tale delivers excitement and romance," according to Rysso, who added that "Kane's lyrical flair and courageous female characters ensure a satisfying and suspenseful read." Wrote Mark Rotella in *Publishers Weekly,* "Kane's engrossing plot and her quick-witted, passionate characters should make readers eagerly await this novel's companion, *The Silver Coin* . . . in which Breanna may pay the price for her bravery."

In *Run for Your Life,* Kane shifts the setting to modern-day Manhattan, where she makes use of a device employed often in her historical romances: a crime that forces heroine and hero to make common cause. In this case, the details of the crime are at first unclear to Victoria Kensington, an attorney whose mentally unstable sister Audrey runs through Central Park in a hospital gown, supposedly chased by would-be assailants. The trail leads back to the mysterious Hope Institute, but in order to go further, Victoria needs the help of Zachary Hamilton, an intelligence expert. The problem is that she and Zachary are former lovers and must overcome their past before they can solve the problem at hand. "What sets this book apart from other romantic thrillers," according to Rotella, "is Kane's deft skill in defining the actions of her lead characters: her love scenes, for example, are exceptional, neither euphemistic nor clinical."

The protagonists of *Scent of Danger* are Sabrina Radcliffe and Dylan Newport. Dylan is an attorney for Carson Brooks, a perfume magnate who has sustained a gunshot in the kidney and needs a kidney transplant if he is going to live. Brooks had no children he had ever met, but, remembering a sperm donation he made thirty years ago, instructs Newport to track down his child—who turns out to be Sabrina. Wrote Brianna Yamashita in *Publishers Weekly,* "Kane's . . . diverse cast of characters and careful balancing of romance and mystery will keep readers from dwelling on the unlikelier twists."

BIOGRAPHICAL AND CRITICAL SOURCES:

PERIODICALS

Booklist, September 15, 1998, Deborah Rysso, review of *The Theft,* p. 212; July 1999, Deborah Rysso, review of *The Gold Coin,* p. 1929.

Chicago Sun-Times, March 16, 2003, Dolores Flaherty and Roger Flaherty, "An Irish Lass in Slavery," p. 15.

Competitive Intelligence, September-October, 2001, Sarah Davis, review of *Run for Your Life,* p. 54.

Cosmopolitan, March, 2003, "A Night of Sexual Healing," p. 212.

Publishers Weekly, August 10, 1998, Maria Simson, review of *The Theft,* p. 385; July 19, 1999, Mark Rotella, review of *The Gold Coin,* p. 192; October 30, 2000, Mark Rotella, review of *Run for Your Life,* p. 53; December 16, 2002, Brianna Yamashita, review of *Scent of Danger,* p. 51.

ONLINE

Andrea Kane Web site, http://www.andreakane.com (September 16, 2003).

RomanticTimes.com, http://www.romantictimes.com/ (September 16, 2003).*

* * *

KÁNYÁDI, Sándor 1929-

PERSONAL: Born 1929, in Galambfalva, Transylvania, Romania. *Education:* Attended Bólyai University (Romania).

ADDRESSES: *Agent*—c/o Twisted Spoon Press, P.O. Box 21, Preslova 12, Prague 5 150 21, Czech Republic.

CAREER:

Poet and translator. Has worked for various publications as editor.

AWARDS, HONORS: Romanian Writers' Union poetry prize; Hungarian Kossuth prize; Austrian Herder prize; Central European Time Millennium prize, 2000.

WRITINGS:

Sirálytánc, Állami Irodalmi és Muvészeti Kiadó (Bukarest, Romania), 1957.

Kicsi legény, nagy tarisznya, Ifjúsági Könyvkiadó (Bukarest, Romania), 1961.

Harmat a csillagon: versek, Irodalmi Könyvkiadó(Bukarest, Romania), 1964.

Kikapcsolódás: versek, Irodalmi Könyvkiadó (Bukarest, Romania), 1966.

Függ oleges lovak: versek, Irodalmi Könyvkiadó (Bukarest, Romania), 1968.

A bánatos királylány kútja: versek, mesék, toörténetek, Kriterion (Bukarest, Romania), 1972.

Fától fáig: versek, 1955-1970, Kriterion (Bukarest, Romania), 1972.

Kányádi Sándor legszebb versei, Albatrosz (Bukarest, Romania), 1977.

Egy kis madárka ül vala: erdélyi száxa népköltészet, Kriterion (Bukarest, Romania), 1977.

Szürkület: versek, 1970-1977, Kriterion (Bukarest, Romania), 1978.

Fekete-piros versek, Magvet (Budapest, Hungary), 1979.

Farkas uz o furulya: mesék, versek, történetek, Móra (Budapest, Hungary), 1979.

Kenyérmadár: versek, mesëk, történetek, Kriteriion (Bukarest, Romania), 1980.

Tavaszi tarisznya, Móra (Budapest, Hungary), 1982.

Madármarasztaló: versek, Kicsiknek, nagyoknak, Kriterion (Bukarest, Romania), 1986.

Sörény és koponya: új versek, Csokonai Kiadó Vállalat (Debrecen, Hungary), 1989.

Valaki jár a fák hegyén, Magyar Könyvklub (Budapest, Hungary), 1997.

Talpas történetek és a kiváncsi hold, Pallas-Akadémia (Csikszereda, Romania), 1997.

Talpas történetek, Holnap (Budapest, Hungary), 1999.

Csipkebokor az alkonyatban, Magyar Konyvklub (Budapest, Hungary), 1999.

Szitaköt o tánca, General Press (Budapest, Hungary), 1999.

45 Poems, translated by Istvá Falusi, Maecenas (Budapest, Hungary), 1999.

Küküll o kalendárium, Pallas-Akadémia (Csikszereda, Romania), 2001.

Meddig ér a rigófütty, Cartaphilus (Budapest, Hungary), 2001.

Dancing Embers, translated by Paul Sohar, Twisted Spoon (Prague, Czech Republic), 2002.

Ambrus the Bear and the Curious Moon, Holnap (Budapest, Hungary), 2003.

SIDELIGHTS: Sándor Kányádi was born in a small Transylvanian village to a Hungarian family of farmers. He was sent to Bolyai University in Romania where he earned a degree in Hungarian philology and gained a love of poetry. His first poem was published in 1955, and in the almost fifty years that he has been writing, he has earned many prestigious awards. His relationship with poetry, however, goes beyond writing it. He also spends much of his time traveling to local schools reciting his poetry, as well as other Hungarian classics, from memory. Yet Kányádi's life has been a difficult one, and critic Ray Olson, for *Booklist,* wrote that this might be the reason that Kányádi's poetry is so "dour." Olson added that "Kányádi is as bleak as T. S. Eliot." Other critics have also made this comparison, noting in particular how similar Kányádi's poem, "All Soul's Day in Vienna" is to Eliot's "Wasteland."

Kányádi, whom many refer to as one of the greatest Hungarian poets, is the voice of the Hungarian minority in Romania, whose land was annexed to Romania after World War I and whose villages were later bulldozed by dictator Nicolai Ceausescu in an attempt at ethnic-cleansing. When Kányádi was young, despite the difficulties in his life, he was optimistic, as expressed in a review of his 1979 publication, *Fekete-piros versek.* George Dömöri for *World Literature Today* wrote: "He started out as a starry-eyed regional poet whose optimism equaled his naïveté, manifesting itself in such lines as 'We only must have faith and/ we shall reach up high to the glittering stars!'" Later in his life, Dömöri stated, Kányádi "suffered a series of setbacks which, however, helped the poet to mature." His poetry became "more elusive and allusive," and he was committed to telling the truth, "about himself and, by implication, about the difficult, often humiliating conditions in which his community has to survive."

Kányádi has remained in his homeland despite the challenges there and in spite of generous accommodations offered to him in Hungary. His goal is to preserve his language and culture in, what Travis Jeppesen, writing for *Prague Pill* online, described as an "often-hostile environment." In 2002 English-speaking readers were given a chance to explore Kányádi's work with the publication of *Dancing Embers,* the most comprehensive collection of Kányádi's works to be translated. The Eliot-like poem of "All Souls' Day in Vienna" can be found in this publication, as well as a representative body of work from the 1960s to the turn of the twenty-first century. There are poems that celebrate nature and poems that condemn the cruelties one person can inflict on another. In a selection called "Unadorned Songs," the poet reflects on the process of aging and death. In his more recent poems, written between 1990 and 2000, Kányádi offers, according to Lucy Mallows for the *Budapest Sun,* "meditations on the conflict between the violence of man and the serenity of nature."

BIOGRAPHICAL AND CRITICAL SOURCES:

PERIODICALS

Booklist October 15, 2002, Ray Olson, review of *Dancing Embers,* p. 380.

Budapest Sun, October 31, 2002, Lucy Mallows, review of *Dancing Embers.*

World Literature Today, winter, 1981, George Gömöri, review of *Feket-piros versek,* pp. 148-149.

ONLINE

Prague Pill, http://Prague.tv/pill (January 23, 2003), Travis Jeppesen, review of *Dancing Embers.**

* * *

KARAM, Jana Abrams

PERSONAL: Female. *Education:* Columbia University, M.S.

ADDRESSES: *Home*—Morris Township, NJ. *Agent*—c/o St. Martin's Press, 175 Fifth Avenue, New York, NY 10010.

CAREER: Author and emergency medical technician.

WRITINGS:

Into the Breach: A Year of Life and Death with the EMS, St. Martin's Press (New York, NY), 2002.

SIDELIGHTS: After Jana Abrams Karam witnessed the collision of a car and a bicyclist one day, she decided to register for classes in first aid. Those classes led to further education in medicine, and eventually she became an emergency medical technician (EMT). Because Karam wanted to be a writer, too, she decided to combine her interests. In 2002 she published a book about the life of an EMT titled *Into the Breach: A Year of Life and Death with the EMS.*

Karam's territory as an EMT was impoverished Newark, New Jersey, an urban area that deals with many emergencies. A writer for *Kirkus Reviews* called *Into the Breach* "a disturbing descent into the maelstrom of city life." The same writer suggested that Karam should not hold her breath for a television, or movie, documentary because audiences could not "bear so much reality." The events Karam witnessed during her two years as an EMT included decapitations and bodies riddled with gunshots or knife wounds.

Karam peoples her book with profiles of fellow medical technicians and their unflinching dedication. In his review for *Library Journal,* Tim Delaney called the EMTs "truly unsung heroes of society." Karam also provides a history of the emergency service. Before it was created, the task of cleaning up accidents and driving the injured to hospitals or the dead to mortuaries was left to funeral homes, whose employees had little or no training in medical services. Today there are well-organized emergency medical services located in every major U.S. city. Praising *Into the Breach* for its skillful prose and insightful observations, *Booklist* contributor Vanessa Bush commended it as a "fascinating" look at "how urban social trends affect medical issues."

BIOGRAPHICAL AND CRITICAL SOURCES:

PERIODICALS

Booklist, November 15, 2002, Vanessa Bush, review of *Into the Breach,* pp. 551-552.

Kirkus Reviews, October 1, 2002, review of *Into the Breach,* p. 1447.

Library Journal, November 1, 2002, Tim Delaney, review of *Into the Breach,* p. 119.*

* * *

KELLY, Brigit Pegeen 1951-

PERSONAL: Born 1951, in Palo Alto, CA.

ADDRESSES: *Home*—506 West Main St., Urbana, IL 61801-2504. *Office*—University of Illinois, Department of English, 608 South Wright, Urbana, IL 61801. *E-mail*—b-kelly3@uiuc.edu.

CAREER: University of Illinois, Urbana-Champaign, professor of English.

AWARDS, HONORS: Yale Series of Younger Poets Prize, 1987, for *To the Place of Trumpets;* Lamont Poetry Prize, Academy of American Poets, 1994, for *Song;* Whiting Writers Award, 1996; Theodore Roethke Prize, Poetry Northwest; Discovery Award, *Nation* magazine; Cecil Hemley Award, Poetry Society of America; Pushcart Prize; fellowships from National Endowment for the Arts, Illinois State Council on the

Arts, and New Jersey Council on the Arts. Work chosen for 1993 and 1994 volumes of *The Best American Poetry.*

WRITINGS:

POETRY

To the Place of Trumpets, foreword by James Merrill, Yale University Press (New Haven, CT), 1988.
Song, BOA Editions (Brockport, NY), 1995.

WORK IN PROGRESS: A volume of poetry.

SIDELIGHTS: Brigit Pegeen Kelly's poetry is rich in detail and complex in emotion. Her subjects include the glories of nature, the capacity for evil, and the doubts stirred in her by religion. Her work has won numerous prizes; acclaimed poet James Merrill selected her first collection, *To the Place of Trumpets,* for the Yale Series of Younger Poets Prize, and her subsequent volume, *Song,* was the 1994 selection for the Lamont Poetry Prize of the Academy of American Poets, given for the best second book.

To the Place of Trumpets includes several poems that reflect Kelly's Catholic upbringing. In "Imagining Their Own Hymns," she writes of angels in stained-glass windows coming to life and flying away because they are "sick of Jesus, who never stops dying." In "Those Who Wrestle with the Angel for Us," she also uses religious imagery to portray her brother's daring as a pilot. Some poems ponder death and dying, while Kelly also observes the natural world—fields, trees, animals—and wonders how changing one aspect of a life might affect all the others.

"This is a promising first book, filled with a language that is both private and transcendent," commented Judith Kitchen in *Georgia Review.* Some poems, Kitchen noted, show Kelly to be adept at taking on a child's point of view. "The Catholic Sundays of childhood are subjected to the scrutiny of a child's honest gaze," Kitchen related. "Retrieving that child in its innocence is a difficult task, and one that Kelly has mastered beautifully." Kitchen thought Kelly too vague at times, however, painting expansive word-portraits yet leaving much unexplained. "I keep wanting more of the hidden narrative," Kitchen remarked. Some other critics, though, characterized Kelly's tendency toward ambiguity as a positive aspect of her style. The poems in *To the Place of Trumpets* "exude an ambiguous wisdom," in the opinion of *Library Journal* contributor Fred Muratori. A *Kliatt* reviewer, meanwhile, called Kelly "a poet-magician" whose work "offers great challenges and great rewards."

In *Song,* Kelly frequently uses music as a motif while dealing with many of the same subjects as in her first collection. The title poem associates a haunting tune with the brutal killing of a girl's pet goat by a group of boys. This poem "appropriately introduces the reader to some of the unexpected and compelling ways the poet achieves meaning and effect through the agency of music," observed Robert Buttel in *American Book Review.* In another poem she refers to the sounds made by bats as "the peculiar lost fluting of an outcast heart" and a group of trees as "a touchy choir," and throughout the volume she juxtaposes natural beauty against human cruelty. She also, as in her first book, refers often to religion, treating it with a mix of fascination and skepticism.

"The religious imagination is part and parcel of Kelly's work," related Stephen Yenser in the *Yale Review.* "Always in touch with the so-called natural world, her poems nonetheless present it ineluctably in Christian terms, whose implicit verities she invariably calls into question." Buttel noted that in Kelly's poems, "spiritual certainty or any connection with divinity remains elusive," but still, in dealing with nature and everyday occurrences, "she experiences uncanny, fortuitous moments that have all the revelatory impact of epiphanies." Kelly has a "singular, passionate, and accomplished art," Buttel added. *Booklist* contributor Patricia Monaghan called *Song* "a glorious, wild work" with a "symphonic" quality, while Yenser summed it up by saying it "is the reason one writes reviews. It could even be the reason one writes poems."

BIOGRAPHICAL AND CRITICAL SOURCES:

PERIODICALS

American Book Review, December-January, 1995-96, Robert Buttel, "Bird Calls," p. 17.
Booklist, February 1, 1995, Patricia Monaghan, review of *Song,* p. 988.

Georgia Review, summer, 1988, Judith Kitchen, "Speaking Passions," pp. 407-422.

Kliatt, September, 1988, review of *To the Place of Trumpets,* pp. 28-29.

Library Journal, May 15, 1988, Fred Muratori, review of *To the Place of Trumpets,* p. 84.

Yale Review, January, 1996, Stephen Yenser, "Poetry in Review," pp. 166-185.*

* * *

KELLY, Eamonn

PERSONAL: Born in Scotland. *Education:* University of Glasgow, B.A.; Strathclyde University, M.B.A.

ADDRESSES: Office—Global Business Network, 5900-X Hollis St., Emeryville, CA 94662.

CAREER: Global Business Network, Emeryville, CA, chief executive officer and president. Scottish Enterprise, former head of strategy; senior-level consultant to business and industry.

WRITINGS:

The Future of the Knowledge Economy, OECD, 1999.

(With Peter Leyden) *What's Next?: Exploring the New Terrain for Business,* Perseus (Cambridge, MA), 2002.

SIDELIGHTS: Through the aegis of the Global Business Network, Eamonn Kelly is a senior-level consultant to international corporations in fields such as telecommunications, energy, health care, manufacturing, and banking. Kelly is particularly interested in the future of global enterprise and has studied the ways in which businesses can compete successfully in an era of rapidly expanding technology. His book *What's Next?: Exploring the New Terrain for Business,* coauthored with Peter Leyden, collects the thoughts of fifty individuals from all walks of life on the business climate of the future. *Miami Herald* correspondent Richard Pachter described the book as "a panoply of viewpoints from executives, academics, scientists, historians, artists and other wool gatherers. Sure, the emphasis is on business, but their global outlook seems just right for this type of exploration."

In her *Library Journal* review of *What's Next?,* Susan C. Awe observed: "Read this book to understand the current chaotic corporate world." A reviewer for *Publishers Weekly* noted that, with so many commentators ranging outside their fields of expertise, "the reflections swerve from insightful to inane." Pachter felt that the work's value lies in its "ability to stimulate and provoke. After all, the future . . . is still largely ours to invent."

BIOGRAPHICAL AND CRITICAL SOURCES:

PERIODICALS

Library Journal, November 1, 2002, Susan C. Awe, review of *What's Next?: Exploring the New Terrain for Business,* p. 102.

Miami Herald, November 11, 2002, Richard Pachter, review of *What's Next?*

Publishers Weekly, September 16, 2002, review of *What's Next?,* p. 62.

ONLINE

Economist online, http://www.economist.com/ (May 20, 2003), executive dialogue, "What's Next?"

Global Business Network, http://gbn.org/ (May 20, 2003), profile of Kelly.*

* * *

KIETH, Sam 1963-

PERSONAL: Born 1963; married.

ADDRESSES: Agent—Albert Moy Original Art, 36-07 162nd St. Flushing, NY 11358.

CAREER: Film director and comic book author and artist. Marvel Comics, artist for "Wolverine/Hulk" series; Image Comics, creator of "The Maxx" series, 1993-98; D.C. Comics, New York, NY, creator of "Zero Girl" comics and "Four Women." Director of film *Take It to the Limit,* New Horizons Home Video, 2000.

WRITINGS:

(Illustrator) William Messner-Loebs, *Epicurus the Sage,* Volume One: *Visiting Hades,* Volume Two: *The Many Loves of Zeus,* Piranha Press, 1989-1991, expanded and published in one volume, 2003.

(And illustrator) *Zero Girl,* D.C. Comics (La Jolla, CA), 2001.

Four Women (graphic novel; collection of comic-book series), D.C. Comics/Homage (New York, NY), 2002.

The Maxx, Book One (collection of numbers 1-6), Cliffhanger, 2003.

The Art of Sam Kieth, IDW Publishing (San Diego, CA), 2003.

Contributor to comic book series, including the artwork for Neil Gaiman's "Sandman," numbers 1-5, 1987, and to "Venom," "Wolverine/Hulk," and "Peter Parker"; author and artist for comic book series "Zero Girl," "Warlock," and "The Critters."

ADAPTATIONS: Kieth's "The Maxx" comic book series was adapted as a cartoon series on MTV; trading cards, toys, and figurines were adapted from his artwork.

SIDELIGHTS: Sam Kieth is a comic-book author and artist who has contributed to a number of strips in addition to creating several of his own. While freelancing for D.C. Comics in the late 1980s, he contributed artwork to author Neil Gaiman's popular "Sandman" strip, and also created several strips of his own. His popular "The Maxx" series, which was published from 1993 to 1998, features a down-and-out vagrant who soon suspects that his supposed amnesia actually is a sign that he is from an alien land. When his dreams of mysterious creatures begin to meld with a series of brutal murders near the cityscape he inhabits, Kieth's antihero teams with a social worker friend to solve the crimes. "The Maxx" was adapted as a television series that aired on MTV in the summer of 1995. Kieth, who has also directed several films, has had his artwork collected in the retrospective volume *The Art of Sam Kieth,* published in 2003.

Kieth began to draw comics as a boy, and after graduating from high school in the early 1980s began penning black-and-white strips and subsequently freelancing for Marvel and D.C., illustrating book series and comic book covers. "The Maxx," his first solo comic-book effort, captured a large following, and subsequent series, such as "Zero Girl" and "Four Women" have proved equally popular, showing Kieth to be an engaging, if offbeat, storyteller as well as a talented graphic artist. In 2002 Marvel began publishing Kieth's "Wolverine/Hulk" comic book mini-series, a unique project for Kieth because he was able to use two of his favorite comic-book characters in stories of his own creation. As a way of supporting his colleagues in the comic-book industry, Kieth donated the monies gained from the sale of his original artwork for the "Wolverine/Hulk" books to the Comic Book Legal Defense fund and ACTOR—A Commitment to Our Roots, an organization that supports retired comic-book creators in need.

Kieth's comic book miniseries "Four Women" begins as Donna sits with her psychologist, trying to fill in some blank spots in her recent past. As memories are unlocked, Donna recalls a harrowing night when she and three of her friends were assaulted by two men after their car stalled, then exacted a brutal revenge on their attackers. "Kieth makes the grim tale gripping throughout," noted *Booklist* contributor Ray Olson. Noting that author/illustrator Kieth's sometimes "photorealistic" technique balances with his more stylized renderings to effectively delineate Donna's memories from her present situation and provide the strip with "dramatic composition," Olson praised the book-length publication of all four installments in "Four Women" as "the graphic-novel equivalent of an outstanding *Twilight Zone* episode."

BIOGRAPHICAL AND CRITICAL SOURCES:

PERIODICALS

Booklist, October 15, 2002, Ray Olson, review of *Four Women,* p. 375.

ONLINE

4-Color Review, http://figma.com/4cr/ (March 27, 2002), "Sam Kieth Donates Wolverine/Hulk Art to ACTOR."

Comicon.com, http://www.commicon.com (May 15, 2003), Matt Brady, "Sam Kieth on Zero Girl, 4 Women, and Hulk/Wolvie" (interview).

Sam Kieth Web site, http://www.samkieth.com (April 21, 2003).*

* * *

KILLHAM, Nina

PERSONAL: Born in Washington, DC; married; husband's name Andrew (a senior lecturer); children: two. *Education:* College of William and Mary, graduated.

ADDRESSES: Home—London, England. *Agent*—Author Mail, Bloomsbury U.S.A., 175 Fifth Ave., New York, NY 10010.

CAREER: Novelist. *Washington Post,* Washington, DC, former food columnist; Columbia Pictures, Los Angeles, CA, worked in office of executive production.

WRITINGS:

How to Cook a Tart, Bloomsbury (New York, NY), 2002.

Contributor to *Washington Post.* Author of screenplays.

SIDELIGHTS: Former food writer Nina Killham has done what writers are counseled to do—write about what she knows—in penning her first novel, *How to Cook a Tart.* Far from being a pastry cookbook, Killham's debut work of fiction is a crime thriller featuring Jasmine March, a Washington, D.C.–based food writer whose tidy life is disrupted when murder is added to the menu. Calling *How to Cook a Tart* a "decadent debut," a *Publishers Weekly* contributor praised the novel for its "elaborate culinary descriptions and metaphors"

With her penchant for high-fat foods, the plus-sized, food-obsessed, thirty-something March is in the process of bemoaning her flagging career with a newspaper that caters to dieters; meanwhile, her husband is cheating on her with a demanding young mistress. The silver lining to the dark clouds in March's life seems to appear when she is invited to appear on television and the influence of the Atkins diet craze suddenly makes fat popular and March a local celebrity. When the body of her husband's svelte mistress winds up conveniently deceased but inconveniently stashed in March's kitchen, Killham's novel embarks on what *Booklist* contributor Mark Knoblauch dubbed "a comedy of errors" spiced by "Killham's drooling descriptions of foods and wines."

The characters in Killham's novel "don't have personalities so much as gastronomic profiles," maintained *New York Times Book Review* contributor Jennifer Reese, "and the two are unnervingly similar." March is a woman of immense appetite; in contrast, her straying husband Daniel has become obsessed over the health of his colon and survives on high-fiber cereal in an effort to maintain internal cleanliness and thereby good health. March's daughter, sixteen-year-old Careme, is eschewing all foods as a way of acting out against her mother, while mistress Tina is a minimalist whose diet of tofu and egg whites reflects the cold, calculating strategies she is using to fund her rise to the top as a famous celebrity. Familiar with the world of cookbook journalism, Killham also introduces readers to "a whole gallery of grotesques from the world of food writing"; then, as Reese noted, the novelist humorously "skewers them all."

Reviewing *How to Cook a Tart* for the *Boston Globe,* reviewer Clea Simon praised Killham's style and use of "sassy, occasionally salty language," noting that the novelist exhibits "a sure sense of plot and gives out just enough of her characters' interior monologues to ensure that we're strung along." While praising the author's prose for its "infectious zest" and Killham for portraying March with "a motherlike affection," *San Francisco Chronicle* contributor Radhika Sharma found the book's "climax . . . disappointing, and the characters seem too narrowly defined by their food ideologies." Describing the novel as a "wickedly funny" debut, Reese added that *How to Cook a Tart* "is more than a brittle send-up of the America of Atkins and Ornish; it's an expansive satire of the ways we have become preoccupied with food."

BIOGRAPHICAL AND CRITICAL SOURCES:

PERIODICALS

Booklist, October 15, 2002, Mark Knoblauch, review of *How to Cook a Tart,* p. 386.

Boston Globe, November 11, 2002, Clea Simon, "'Tart' Is an Appetizing Mystery," p. B11.

Kirkus Reviews, July 1, 2002, review of *How to Cook a Tart,* p. 906.

New York Times Book Review, December 15, 2002, Jennifer Reese, "The Joy of Cooking," p. 17.

Publishers Weekly, September 9, 2002, review of *How to Cook a Tart,* p. 42.

San Francisco Chronicle, December 22, 2002, Radhika Sharma, review of *How to Cook a Tart.*

ONLINE

Funny Tummy, http://www.funnytummy.com/ (January 23, 2003), Claire Dederer, review of *How to Cook a Tart.**

* * *

KIM, Suki 1970-

PERSONAL: Born 1970, in Seoul, Korea; immigrated to United States. *Education:* Graduated from Barnard College; attended graduate school.

ADDRESSES: *Agent*—c/o Author Mail, Farrar, Straus, and Giroux, 19 Union Square West, New York, NY 10003.

CAREER: Freelance translator and novelist. Formerly worked as a teacher and editor.

WRITINGS:

The Interpreter, Farrar, Straus, and Giroux (New York, NY), 2003.

SIDELIGHTS: Born in Korea, Suki Kim came to New York City at the age of thirteen. She graduated from Barnard College with a degree in English and a minor in East Asian literature. After an excursion to London to study Korean literature at the graduate level, she returned to New York City and a series of jobs, including editing and teaching. Eventually she realized that writing was her true calling, and she attended a number of writers' colonies, including the Ragdale Foundation, outside Chicago, MacDowell in New Hampshire, and Millay in upstate New York. What emerged from her writing experiences was an idea for a Korean-American traveling between the two cultures. The result was *The Interpreter,* Kim's debut novel.

The Interpreter tells the story of Suzy Park, a twenty-nine-year-old Korean American who discovers that her parents, supposedly killed in a robbery, may actually have been the targets of much darker, political forces. Listless, depressed, and long estranged from her family, Park is gradually drawn into the mystery of her parents' murder and the life they led before it, which involves her in an underworld of gangs, prostitution rings, and immigrant smugglers. "While time and place are well captured, the writing is so emotionally flat that one closes the book feeling aroused but ultimately unmoved," wrote *Library Journal* reviewer Eleanor Bader. Other reviewers were more pleased. A *Publishers Weekly* reviewer found that "as the novel progresses, Kim's talents become apparent: a good eye for detail, an excellent prose style and the ability to create compelling characters." A *Kirkus Reviews* contributor called the novel a "sleek, nearly hypnotic glimpse into the world of a Korean family ruptured in translation to America."

BIOGRAPHICAL AND CRITICAL SOURCES:

PERIODICALS

Booklist, November 15, 2002, Kristine Huntley, review of *The Interpreter,* p. 572.

Kirkus Reviews, October 1, 2002, review of *The Interpreter,* p. 1419.

Library Journal, November 1, 2002, Eleanor Bader, review of *The Interpreter,* p. 129.

New York Times Book Review, January 26, 2003, Katherine Dieckmann, review of *The Interpreter,* p. 22.

Publishers Weekly, October 21, 2002, review of *The Interpreter,* p. 53.

ONLINE

Suki Kim Web site, http://www.sukikim.com (October 28, 2003).*

KNIGHT, Bobby
See KNIGHT, Robert Montgomery

* * *

KNIGHT, Robert Montgomery 1940-
(Bobby Knight)

PERSONAL: Born October 25, 1940, in Massillon, OH; son of Carroll (a railroad worker) and Hazel (Henthorne) Knight; married April 17, 1963; wife's name Nancy Lou (divorced); married Karen Edgar, 1988; children: Tim, Patrick. *Education:* Ohio State University, B.S., 1962.

ADDRESSES: Office—Men's Basketball, Spirit Center, Texas Tech University, Indiana Ave., Lubbock, TX 79409.

CAREER: Basketball coach. Cuyahoga Falls High School, Cuyahoga Falls, OH, assistant coach, 1962-63; U.S. Military Academy, West Point, NY, assistant coach, 1963-65, head coach, 1965-71; Indiana University, Bloomington, head coach, 1971-2000; Texas Tech University, Lubbock, head coach, 2001—. Naismith Memorial Basketball Hall of Fame, trustee. *Military service:* Served with U.S. Army.

MEMBER: National Association of Basketball Coaches (member, board of directors).

AWARDS, HONORS: Most Valuable Player, Orrville, OH, High School, 1957; Big Ten Coach of the Year awards, 1973, 1975, 1976, 1981, 1989; National Coach of the Year awards, 1975, 1989; named National Coach of the Year, Associated Press and *Basketball Weekly,* 1976; coached 1979 U.S. gold medal Pan-American Games basketball team; coached 1984 U.S. gold-medal Olympic basketball team; coached Indiana University NCAA national championship teams, 1976, 1981, 1987; inducted into Basketball Hall of Fame, 1991.

WRITINGS:

(With Bob Hammel) *Knight: My Story* (memoir), Thomas Dunne Books (New York, NY), 2002.

SIDELIGHTS: Robert Montgomery "Bobby" Knight is one of the highest achievers in college basketball history, and certainly one of its most controversial figures. His coaching record includes many national championships, as well as Olympic and Pan American team gold medals, and he has several times been named National Coach of the Year, unanimously in 1975. Knight insisted that his players maintain their academic standings, and in the twenty-eight seasons he coached the Indiana Hoosiers, only two of his four-year players failed to complete their degrees.

Knight was born in an industrial town, and his father was with the railroad. Knight played several sports in high school and was a great admirer of Ted Williams. Baseball was his first passion, but Knight's stubbornness changed his direction when he turned to basketball in defiance of a suspension by his baseball coach for failing to follow an order. He already had leanings toward coaching and later in his career shared friendships with coaches of basketball, baseball, and football, including Vince Lombardi, Bear Bryant, and Joe Paterno.

In attending and graduating from Ohio State University, Knight prepared for a career in law, his father's hope. He majored in education and minored in government and history. On the court, he played mostly as a substitute for Buckeye coach Fred Taylor, but he picked up coaching tips that he used during the year he coached high school basketball, then the next eight at the U.S. Military Academy at West Point, where he became head coach after two years as an assistant. Knight was inspired by General George Patton and by Colonel Red Blaik, former Army football coach and author of *You Have to Pay the Price.*

Knight adapted to the strict discipline of the Academy and used it in his training, but he is also a man who plays by his own rules, often causing problems in his interactions with administrators and staff. After his only losing season with Army, he resigned and accepted the position of head coach at Indiana University.

Knight applied his strict disciplinary methods to a shocked Indiana team. He toughened practices and forbid alumni from viewing them, which he considered a distraction, and he demanded silence when he spoke with the players. It all paid off when they came in third in the regional conference. Knight began to recruit the most promising high school players, offering only his winning program to young men who were often tempted with promises of money, guaranteed grades, and other incentives. And his teams won. They ended the 1976 season undefeated and took the NCAA national championship. Knight coached players who went on to successful careers, including Quinn Buckner, Isiah Thomas, and Steve Alford.

Knight coached the 1979 U.S. team in the Pan-American Games held in San Juan, Puerto Rico. Although they won the gold medal, Knight became embroiled in controversy for swearing at a player, verbally putting down an official, and for engaging in a physical encounter with a policeman. For the last, he was fined and sentenced to jail time, which he avoided by returning to the United States. Indiana finished in the top two the next two years and won its second national championship in 1981. During the Final Four, Knight dropped a Louisiana State fan into a trash barrel.

Columbia Broadcasting System (CBS) Sports offered Knight $500,000 a year to head the telecasting of the NCAA tournament, and Knight was ready to take the job until his star player, Landon Turner, was injured in an automobile accident and paralyzed. Knight spent months raising money for Turner's care and turned his recruiting responsibilities over to his assistant coaches. The team finished in the top three over the next three years, and Knight took the U.S. team to gold in the 1984 Olympics held in Los Angeles. This team included players Michael Jordan, Patrick Ewing, and Chris Mullin.

In the following years at Indiana, he continued to collected championships and accolades. But he also continued to court controversy. In 1997 Knight was investigated for striking guard Neil Reed, and the school instituted a "zero-tolerance" policy that Knight breached continuously over the next few years—seriously in 2000, when he allegedly grabbed freshman Kent Harvey by the neck.

Sporting News reporter Mike DeCourcy wrote that, "just as the university ingenuously conceived the zero-tolerance policy to put the onus on Knight to behave, it recognized how foolish it would have appeared to terminate its legendary coach on the word of one student whose story was contradicted by other witnesses. But the administration also saw this as the latest example of Knight's refusal to change the way he operated." DeCourcy noted that Indiana University president Myles Brand "explained Knight affronted alumni by refusing to participate in several popular gatherings of Hoosiers supporters. He said there was an incident in which Knight [verbally] abused a high-ranking female official at IU. Knight declined to follow the athletic department chain of command, essentially by continuing to ignore athletic director Clarence Doninger." In spite of his difficulties with the administration, Knight remained popular with fans and students. He learned that he had been fired by phone while on a fishing trip in Canada that he had refused to postpone. Brand said he regretted dismissing Knight but felt it was in the best interest of the university. Knight ended the season with a three-game losing streak.

Knight began coaching the Texas Tech University Red Raiders in 2001. The first season yielded a record of twenty-three wins, ten losses, and the team went to the NCAA tournament. Following the season, Knight collaborated with Bob Hammel, the awarding-winning sportswriter who had been with the *Bloomington Herald-Tribune* until his retirement, to write his memoir *Knight: My Story.*

Sports Illustrated's Charles Hirshberg wrote that "the book is his [Knight's] opportunity to spit bile, as only he can, on those he considers responsible for his firing. Which would make an amusing read if one didn't have to wade through heaps of dross to get to it." Hirshberg noted Knight's expressions of gratitude, reminiscences, and the motivational quotes by Patton and Lombardi, and said that when he "finally gets down to the business at hand—shedding his enemies' blood—he's thoroughly entertaining."

"Only mildly repentant, he now insists that his dedication to winning and his tough style were his undoing," commented a *Kirkus Reviews* contributor. *Library Journal*'s John Maxymuk felt that Knight tells his story "with opinionated gusto not often seen in these politically correct times." *Booklist*'s Wes Lukowsky wrote that "Knight displays here his palpable affection for his players and his reverence for the game and the great coaches who preceded him." A *Publishers Weekly* contributor noted that "college hoops fans can learn more about the game from this book than from most instructional guides."

BIOGRAPHICAL AND CRITICAL SOURCES:

BOOKS

Feinstein, John, *A Season on the Brink: A Year with Bob Knight and the Hoosiers,* Macmillan (New York, NY), 1986.

Knight, Bob, and Bob Hammel, *Knight: My Story* (memoir), Thomas Dunne Books (New York, NY), 2002.

PERIODICALS

Booklist, January 1, 2002, Wes Lukowsky, review of *Knight: My Story,* p. 774.

Kirkus Reviews, January 15, 2002, review of *Knight,* p. 87.

Library Journal, February 15, 2002, John Maxymuk, review of *Knight,* p. 152.

New York Times, March 10, 2002, Dave Anderson, "Bob Knight puts His Rebuttal to Indiana in His Autobiography," p. SP3.

Publishers Weekly, February 18, 2002, review of *Knight,* p. 89.

Sporting News, September 18, 2000, Mike DeCourcy, "Incorrigible, Unyielding . . . Unemployed," p. 52.

Sports Illustrated, April 1, 2002, Charles Hirshberg, "No One—Except Himself—Is Spared When the General Unloads," p. R6.

Wall Street Journal, March 28, 2002, Erich Eichman, review of *Knight,* p. A18.*

* * *

KOCH, Robert 1918-2003

OBITUARY NOTICE—See index for *CA* sketch: Born April 17, 1918, in New York, NY; died August 13, 2003, in Stamford, CT. Educator, businessman, and author. Koch was an authority on the art of Louis Comfort Tiffany and is credited by many for reviving interest in Tiffany's glass artwork. He was educated at Harvard University, where he earned an A.B. in 1939. Serving in the U.S. Army Air Forces during World War II and achieving the rank of first lieutenant, Koch later returned to school at New York University, where he received an M.A. in 1953 before taking a doctorate at Yale in 1957. He began his academic career as an assistant instructor at Queen's College from 1951 to 1953, followed by three years as a graduate assistant at Yale. He joined Southern Connecticut State College in 1956 as an assistant professor, becoming an associate in 1959 and full professor in 1966; Koch retired as a professor emeritus in 1979. But it was through his work collecting Tiffany glass and writing about it that he really made a name for himself. It all started when he served as curator for a Tiffany exhibition at the Museum of Contemporary Crafts in New York City in 1958, a show that spurred on a new interest in the work of Tiffany. Together with his wife, Koch also ran an antiques dealership and spent what time he could searching through other shops to find rare treasures; Koch would sometimes donate the rarest of these to museums. Becoming a recognized authority on Tiffany, he penned several books on his favorite subject, including *Louis C. Tiffany: Rebel in Glass* (1964; third edition, 1982), *Louis C. Tiffany's Art Glass* (1977), and *Louis C. Tiffany: The Collected Works of Robert Koch* (2001). He was also the author of *Will H. Bradley—American Artist in Print* (2002).

OBITUARIES AND OTHER SOURCES:

PERIODICALS

New York Times, September 3, 2003, p. A17.

* * *

KOHL, Judith

PERSONAL: Married Herbert Kohl (an educator), 1963; children: Antonia, Erica, Joshua.

ADDRESSES: Home—40561 Eureka Hill Rd., Point Arena, CA 95468. *Agent*—c/o Author Mail, Teacher's College Press, 1234 Amsterdam Ave., New York, NY 10027.

CAREER: Educator and author.

AWARDS, HONORS: National Book Award for Children's Literature, 1978, for *The View from the Oak: The Private World of Other Creatures;* Robert F. Kennedy Book Award (with others), 1990-91, for *The Long Haul: An Autobiography.*

WRITINGS:

(With husband, Herbert Kohl) *The View from the Oak: The Private World of Other Creatures,* illustrated by Roger Bayless, Sierra Club Books (Boston, MA), 1977.
(With Herbert Kohl) *Pack, Band, and Colony: The World of Social Animals,* illustrated by Margaret La Farge, Farrar, Straus & Giroux (New York, NY), 1983.
(With Myles Horton and Herbert Kohl) *The Long Haul: An Autobiography,* Doubleday (New York, NY), 1990.

SIDELIGHTS: Judith Kohl, along with husband Herbert Kohl, writes educational and thought-provoking works for both children and adults. The couple's first book, *The View from the Oak: The Private World of Other Creatures,* introduces readers to the world of animals by discussing how they see, feel, navigate, and think. The prize-winning book fathoms what a flower looks like to a bee, why a snake tracks incremental temperature changes, and how spiders experience space. Interactive games are included. In the Kohl's second collaborative effort, *Pack, Band, and Colony: The World of Social Animals,* they deal with how three groups of social animals—wolves, lemurs, and termites—behave within their own set of social rules.

Kohl and her husband teamed with groundbreaking educator Myles Horton to write Horton's autobiography, titled *The Long Haul.* The Kohls recorded Horton recounting his life story over several years leading up to his death in January of 1990. Maurice Isserman of the *Nation* claimed "the resulting memoir preserves the flavor of Horton's speech and personality, though the reader has to be willing to put up with frequent repetition, digressions and Horton's sometimes elliptical way of making his points."

The Kohls relay the story of Horton, the son of a Tennessee farmer and a teacher. Greatly influenced by the different types of education in his life, Horton attended Tennessee's Cumberland Presbyterian College and then went on to Union Theological Seminary in New York City. In both places he became involved with socialist ideals, particularly the causes of racial equity and labor unions. Horton brought these ideas back to Tennessee and set up the Highlander Folk School in Monteagle in 1932. The school stressed labor theory, economics, and local Appalachian culture, but the main focus was on hands-on learning, the curriculum controlled by the students.

After World War II Horton struggled to keep the school open. His formerly beneficial relationship with the Congress of Industrial Organizations ended when that organization curtailed its support of the expansion of industrial unionism. Highlander also suffered as a result of its socialist leanings and its participation in the civil rights movement. Among those individuals who were involved in the school and its teachings were Rosa Parks, Martin Luther King, Jr., Eleanor Roosevelt, Pete Seeger, and Woody Guthrie. The school continued to survive, despite two location changes and a name change; in 2002 it operated as the Highlander Research and Education Center.

BIOGRAPHICAL AND CRITICAL SOURCES:

PERIODICALS

Library Journal, March 15, 1990, Annelle R. Huggins, review of *The Long Haul: An Autobiography,* p. 100.
Nation, November 12, 1990, Maurice Isserman, review of *The Long Haul,* p. 566.
New York Times, May 20, 1990, Laura Green, review of *The Long Haul,* p. 31.
Progressive, October, 1990, John Egerton, review of *The Long Haul,* p. 41.
Publishers Weekly, February 2, 1990, review of *The Long Haul: An Autobiography,* p. 73.

ONLINE

New Press Web site, http://www.thenewpress.com/ (June 14, 2003).*

* * *

KORNBLUM, William

PERSONAL: Male. *Education:* Cornell University, B.S. (biology), 1961; University of Chicago, M.A. (social science), 1965, Ph.D. (sociology), 1971.

CAREER: Sociologist. Peace Corps volunteer in Africa; University of Washington, Seattle, faculty; City University of New York graduate school, professor of sociology, 1973—, Center for Urban Research, unit chief, 1974—, chair.

AWARDS, HONORS: Merit Honor Award, U.S. Department of Interior, for work on planning urban national recreation areas; shared First Prize in Applied Research, *Progressive Architecture* (magazine).

WRITINGS:

Blue Collar Community, foreword by Morris Janowitz, University of Chicago Press (Chicago, IL), 1974.

(With Terry M. Williams) *Growing up Poor,* Lexington Books (Lexington, MA), 1985.

(With Joseph Julian and Carolyn D. Smith) *Social Problems,* fifth edition, Prentice-Hall, (Englewood Cliffs, NJ), 1986, tenth edition, 2001.

(With Carolyn D. Smith) *Sociology in a Changing World,* Holt, Rinehart, and Winston (New York, NY), 1988, sixth edition, Wadsworth/Thomson Learning (Belmont, CA), 2002.

(With Carolyn D. Smith) *In the Field: Readings on the Field Research Experience,* Praeger (Westport, CT), 1989.

(Editor with Carolyn D. Smith) *The Healing Experience: Readings on the Social Context of Health Care,* Prentice Hall (Englewood Cliffs, NJ), 1994.

(With Terry M. Williams) *The Uptown Kids: Struggle and Hope in the Projects,* Putnam (New York, NY), 1994.

(With Carolyn D. Smith) *Sociology: The Central Questions,* Harcourt Brace College Publishers (Fort Worth, TX), 1998.

At Sea in the City: New York from the Water's Edge, illustrated by Oliver Williams, foreword by Pete Hamill, Algonquin Books of Chapel Hill (Chapel Hill, NC), 2002.

SIDELIGHTS: William Kornblum is a sociologist whose research has been concentrated in the areas of urban and rural open spaces. Among his projects was a series of studies in Manhattan that were used in planning the redevelopment of lower Times Square. Other New York projects include research of Central Park in connection with the Lila Wallace-*Reader's Digest* Funds Urban Parks Initiative.

In addition to textbooks, Kornblum has written a number of works based on his sociological research, including *Blue Collar Community,* the result of a nearly three-year study conducted in the steel mill neighborhoods of South Chicago during the 1970s. Kornblum moved his family to the community in order to thoroughly understand what life was like for the many ethnic and racial groups who served that industry, and for six months, he worked as a steel mill foreman in order to achieve the intimacy with the workers necessary to the accuracy of his study.

Mirra Komarovsky wrote in *Contemporary Sociology* that Kornblum's main theme is "the emergence of solidarities that transcend ethnic groups. As leaders (in steel mills, unions, and political clubs) compete for prestige and power they form alliances across ethnic and racial cleavages. It is through such community-forming processes that successive waves of immigrant ethnic groups take their place in general community institutions, all the while maintaining some segmented social structures based upon ethnicity and race."

A. H. Raskin noted in the *New York Times* that "through close association with his neighbors . . . Kornblum saw the glacial slowness with which the success of interracial coalitions in shifting power in local union elections inside the steel plants produced any movement in the general politics of South Chicago toward closer cooperation between the entrenched ethnic groups—Poles, Serbs, Croatians, and Italians—and the newer elements seeking a toehold. Often the progress in ward politics was all backward. Racial assertiveness among Mexican-Americans and blacks tended to foster a resurgence of self-conscious ethnic identity into the third and fourth generations."

Kornblum wrote *Growing up Poor* with Terry M. Williams, with whom he managed a youth-employment demonstration project funded by the U.S. Department of Labor in 1979. The focus of the book is the plight of youth living in three New York neighborhoods, one each in Cleveland, Ohio and Louisville, Kentucky, and the neighborhoods around Meridian, Mississippi.

The project was unique, in that because there were not enough trained ethnographers to conduct the research, a large pool of young people from the areas were hired as assistants. They wrote detailed accounts of their own lives and the dynamics of their neighborhoods and conducted interviews with their parents and their peers under the supervision of field directors. Essentially, the youth filled the key roles of both subject and researcher. The study yielded data on subjects important to policymakers, including patterns of drug use, crime, and early pregnancy, as well as providing insight into the reasons why some youths are able to escape the poverty of their surroundings while others are not.

Mercer L. Sullivan wrote in *American Journal of Sociology* that "although the book sometimes seems spread thin over so many communities and social issues, the ethnographic data presented are fascinating and provide a welcome contrast to the many quantitative studies that fail to portray the ways in which the multiple problems of poor youths, along with their resources for survival, are embedded in specific community contexts." In a *Social Forces* review, Cynthia Duncan called *Growing up Poor* "an admirable, thoughtful blend of social research and action."

Kornblum and Williams collaborated again on *The Uptown Kids: Struggle and Hope in the Projects,* completed while Kornblum was teaching at City University of New York and Williams was at the New School for Social Research. The authors focused on teens in Harlem housing projects, and drew information from journal-writing by the teens and regular meetings in Williams's Harlem apartment. The volume includes excerpts from the journals of six of the participants and observations on race, education, work, sex, and family. A *Publishers Weekly* writer noted that the authors "point out how the housing projects function as a source of strength and community."

Kornblum and Carolyn D. Smith are coeditors of *In the Field: Readings on the Field Research Experience,* a collection of essays that incudes both new writing and previously published works. Most of the studies discussed were conducted in the Unites States, and the essays show how researchers gained access to communities, formed relationships, and maintained objectivity while collecting data.

At Sea in the City: New York from the Water's Edge is Kornblum's account of the history of maritime culture and the New York coastline that he follows in *Tradition,* his twenty-four-foot sailboat. A *Kirkus Reviews* contributor wrote that Kornblum "has lots of good stories and background material, conveyed in a voice just scholarly enough to let you know he has done his research. But the tone is also personal; [Kornblum] . . . makes clear he has lived much of his understanding of the area" from his home on Long Beach, Long Island.

John D. Thomas noted in the *New York Times Book Review* that one of Kornblum's goals "is to show that efforts by environmentalists and ecologists have helped improve the city's water quality." Emily Block wrote in *Ruminator Review* that Kornblum "combines his knowledge of the town's neighborhoods and history with an amateur's love of sailing in these musings on New York, its waterways, and his own history as a sailor."

BIOGRAPHICAL AND CRITICAL SOURCES:

PERIODICALS

American Journal of Sociology, May, 1987, Mercer L. Sullivan, review of *Growing up Poor,* pp. 1570-1571.

Choice, April, 1975, review of *Blue Collar Community,* p. 298.

Comparative Studies in Society and History, July, 1999, Charles Lindholm, review of *In the Field: Readings on the Field Research Experience,* pp. 601-602.

Contemporary Sociology, March, 1976, Mirra Komarovsky, review of *Blue Collar Community,* pp. 203-204.

International Journal of Comparative Sociology, September-December, 1992, Brad Bullock, review of *In the Field,* pp. 242-243.

Journal of Contemporary Ethnography, July, 1991, William Shaffir, review of *In the Field,* p. 241.

Kirkus Reviews, March 15, 2002, review of *At Sea in the City: New York from the Water's Edge,* p. 384.

Library Journal, April 15, 2002, Harry Frumerman, review of *At Sea in the City,* p. 112.

New York Times, February 15, 1975, A. H. Raskin, review of *Blue Collar Community,* p. 27.

New York Times Book Review, July 7, 2002, John D. Thomas, review of *At Sea in the City,* p. 14.

Publishers Weekly, February 14, 1994, review of *The Uptown Kids: Struggle and Hope in the Projects,* p. 76; April 8, 2002, review of *At Sea in the City,* p. 213.
Ruminator Review, summer, 2002, Emily Bloch, review of *At Sea in the City,* p. 24.
Social Casework, May, 1987, Albert S. Alissi, review of *Growing up Poor,* pp. 317-318.
Social Forces, September, 1987, Cynthia Duncan, review of *Growing up Poor,* pp. 274-275; September, 1990, Gary Alan Fine, review of *In the Field,* pp. 336-338.
Social Work, January-February, 1987, Lawrence S. Root, review of *Growing up Poor,* p. 91.*

* * *

KOSSY, Donna J. 1957-

PERSONAL: Born May 18, 1957, in Chicago, IL; daughter of Irving and Joyce Kossy; married Ken DeVries (an artist), August 17, 1993. *Education:* Hampshire College, B.A., 1979. *Hobbies and other interests:* Watching birds and wildlife.

ADDRESSES: Office—Book Happy Booksellers, P.O. Box 86663, Portland, OR 97286. *E-mail*—dkossy@book-happy.com.

CAREER: Computer programmer, 1982-88; worked for small publishers, 1988-92; freelance writer, Portland, OR, 1992—. Book Happy Booksellers, owner, 1999—.

WRITINGS:

Kooks: A Guide to the Outer Limits of Human Belief, Feral House, 1994, expanded edition, 2001.
Strange Creations: Aberrant Ideas of Human Origins from Ancient Astronauts to Aquatic Apes, Feral House, 2001.

Contributor to periodicals, including *Utne Reader, Alternative Press Review, Puncture,* and *Portland Mercury.* Editor and publisher, *Book Happy;* past editor and publisher of *False Positive* and *Kooks.*

SIDELIGHTS: Donna J. Kossy told *CA:* "I never intended to be a writer. I only began writing, out of necessity, when I was the editor and publisher of several small magazines (usually known as 'zines). I began my first, *False Positive,* as a hobby, while working as a computer programmer in downtown San Francisco in the mid-1980s. I was also a collage artist and wanted to share my punk and surrealist-influenced collages, as well as some of the weird images, publications, and flyers I was collecting at the time with my friends and correspondents. The absolute weirdest material I put into a section called 'The Kooks Pages.' These were usually flyers that some of the most disturbed or divinely inspired people in San Francisco had handed me on the street. These flyers defied all reason; they were funny, and in some cases, it was hard to believe they even existed. I just had to share them with the world.

"In no time, I became known in 'zine circles as the 'kook lady,' and all kinds of unsolicited 'kook' material began appearing in my mailbox. This included the writings of insane people, religious fanatics, and political extremists, as well as material that was much more difficult to classify. I put them all into my 'kook files' for eventual study and classification.

"A few years later, after the novelty of their existence had worn off, I became curious about what was behind all the kooks. I began researching the background and history of some of the ideas (for example, the idea that the Anglo-Saxons are the descendants of the Ten Lost Tribes of Israel) and wrote them up into articles for my new 'zine, *Kooks.* This was the first time I had ever enjoyed writing; I was doing original research and was deeply interested in the material. *Kooks* magazine went out to a select few, and I had no clue that my research or writings could appeal to a wider audience. Later Feral House offered me a book deal for what would eventually become my first book, *Kooks: A Guide to the Outer Limits of Human Belief.* I enjoyed the challenge of writing for an audience beyond my associates in the underground press, so after the first book came out, I was ready to write another.

"While *Kooks* had been a collection of short pieces, for my second book I wanted to focus more narrowly on one topic. I had written an article for a music magazine about a strange book that had been one of the inspirations for the band DEVO. That book—and my article about it—became the inspiration for my next book, *Strange Creations: Aberrant Ideas of Human Origins from Ancient Astronauts to Aquatic Apes.*

"All in all, the inspiration for my writing comes primarily from weird publications and subsequent research into related topics in history, science, religion, and psychology."

BIOGRAPHICAL AND CRITICAL SOURCES:

PERIODICALS

Booklist, August, 2001, Mike Tribby, review of *Strange Creations: Aberrant Ideas of Human Origins from Ancient Astronauts to Aquatic Apes,* p. 2060.

Utne Reader, May-June, 1995, Steve Perry, review of *Kooks: A Guide to the Outer Limits of Human Belief,* p. 103.

Whole Earth Review, winter, 1987, Jeanne Carstensen, review of *False Positive,* p. 44; summer, 1995, Paul Wintermitz, review of *Kooks,* p. 106.

* * *

KOVACH, Barbara (Ellen) L(usk) 1941-2003 (Barbara L. Forisha)

OBITUARY NOTICE—See index for *CA* sketch: Born December 28, 1941, in Ann Arbor, MI; died July 28, 2003, in Princeton, NJ. Educator and author. Kovach was a professor and cofounder of the Leadership Development Institute at Rutgers University. She graduated from Stanford University with a B.A. in 1963 and an M.A. in 1964, followed by a doctorate at the University of Maryland in 1973. After working as a high school teacher in California during the 1960s, she became an associate professor of psychology at the University of Michigan at Dearborn in 1973, where she remained until 1984. She was then hired to teach at Rutgers, where she served as dean of University College and the School of Business. A director of the Leadership Development Program there, Kovach also cofounded the Leadership Development Institute, which was designed to help business students to become corporate leaders. Interested in psychology and personal leadership skills in the business world, she wrote several books on these topics, including *Power and Love: How to Work for Success and Still Care for Others* (1982), *Survival on the Fast Track* (1988; revised edition, 1993), *Organization Gameboard* (1989), *Leaders in Place* (1994), and *More about Survival on the Fast Track* (1996). She also produced a series of videotapes on leadership called "Keys to Leadership" (1991-97). Kovach wrote on other topics in psychology besides those on business leadership, however, and some of her other books include such titles as *Sex Roles and Personal Awareness* (1978) and *The Experience of Adolescence: Development in Context* (1983).

OBITUARIES AND OTHER SOURCES:

PERIODICALS

Chronicle of Higher Education, September 5, 2003, p. A61.

* * *

KROPOTKIN, Peter (Aleksieevich) 1842-1921

PERSONAL: Born December 12 (some sources say December 9), 1842, in Moscow, Russia; died of pneumonia February 8, 1921, in Dmitrov, Russian Soviet Federated Socialist Republic. *Education:* Educated in St. Petersburg.

CAREER: Aide to Czar Alexander II; geographer and scientist; revolutionary. *Military service:* Russian Army, officer in Siberia, 1862-67; imprisoned for revolutionary activity, 1874-76.

MEMBER: First International Working Men's Association; Socialist Party.

WRITINGS:

Words of a Rebel, 1885.

In Russian and French Prisons, 1887.

Fields, Factories and Workshops, 1899.
Memoirs of a Revolutionist, 1899.
Mutual Aid, 1902.
The Conquest of Bread, 1906.
The Great French Revolution 1789-1793, 1909.

SIDELIGHTS: Peter Kropotkin is best known as a theorist and practitioner of anarchism in late-nineteenth-century Russia. Through his writings and his political activities, Kropotkin greatly influenced the anarchist movement, and though he was ultimately unsatisfied by the revolution's political changes, his work nonetheless contributed to the international literature of anarchism. Kropotkin offered an ideal of human potential. He wrote, "Man would [in anarchism] be enabled to obtain the full development of his faculties, intellectual, artistic, and moral, without being hampered by overwork for the monopolists or by the servility and inertia of mind of the great number. He would thus be able to reach full individualization."

Kropotkin's family was aristocratic, which enabled Kropotkin to study at St. Petersburg and to serve as an aid to Czar Alexander II. At age twenty he went to Siberia as an officer of the Russian Army, and for the next five years he made a study of the zoology and geography of Siberia. In 1871, Kropotkin refused an invitation to become a member of the Russian Geographical Society, and instead became a member of the anarchist movement.

In *The Making of Modern Russia* Lionel Kochan and Richard Abraham noted that Kropotkin first became involved in the "non-conspiratorial student circles" that grew up in reaction to the conspiratorial underground: "The primary purpose of these circles was self education and self-betterment through study. The next step was to extend this process to the less privileged—the urban workers and peasants." Kropotkin himself wrote of these circles: "the only way was to settle among the people and live the people's life . . . devoting themselves entirely to the poorest part of the population." Dedicating his efforts to improving society through anarchy, in 1872 Kropotkin joined the First International Working Men's Association.

Kropotkin's activities on behalf of the disenfranchised—along with his increasing support of anarchist philosophy—led to his imprisonment in 1874. Within two years he escaped from prison to western Europe, where he was buffeted from one country to another; he was expelled from Switzerland, jailed in France, and in 1886 managed to settle in England, where he lived and wrote about his hopes for Russia. In his greatest writings on anarchism, Kropotkin explains how his theory may ennoble human nature: "Anarchism, the name given to a principle or theory of life and conduct under which society is conceived without government-harmony in such a society being obtained. . . by free agreements concluded between the various groups." This concept of "free agreements" is, for Kropotkin, based on a notion of evolution among animals: "such a society would represent nothing immutable," he writes. "On the contrary—as is seen in organic life at large—harmony would (it is contended) result from an ever-changing adjustment and readjustment of equilibrium between the multitude of forces and influences." Unlike social Darwinists, Kropotkin favored cooperation over competition and argued that sociability and cooperation exist in the animal kingdom.

While promoting violence, Kropotkin never resorted to such means. In a late essay he explained his non-confrontational efforts to promote anarchy: "for many years [I] endeavored to develop the following ideas: to show the intimate, logical connection which exists between the modern philosophy of the natural science and anarchism; to put anarchism on a scientific basis by the study of the tendencies that are apparent now in society and may indicate its further evolution; and to work out the basis of anarchist ethics . . . [and] to prove that-communism—at least partial—has more chances of being established than collectivism, especially in communes taking the lead, and that free, or anarchist-communism is the only form of communism that has any chance of being accepted in civilized societies; communism and anarchism are therefore two terms of evolution which complete each other, the one rendering the other possible and acceptable."

In June of 1917, following the Bolshevik revolution in Russia, Kropotkin returned to his homeland. He was disappointed in the changes induced by the revolution; although he abhored Bolshevik brutality, he supported even less any outside efforts to stabilize Russia's new government after the fall of Czar Nicholas II. Kropotkin lived in St. Petersburg until 1921, when he died of pneumonia.

Kropotkin was, in many way, a contradictory man: he was an aristocrat and a man of the people; he was a believer in peace and tolerance and a proponent of violent insurrection. His writing, however, promotes a coherent ideal: that man, given the freedom to evolve as other animals do, will become something finer than he is.

BIOGRAPHICAL AND CRITICAL SOURCES:

BOOKS

Kochan, Lionel, and Richard Abraham, *The Making of Modern Russia,* Penguin (London, England), 1963.*

L

LABINGER, Jay A(lan) 1947-

PERSONAL: Born July 6, 1947, in Los Angeles, CA; married May 31, 1970; wife's name Andrea; children: Barbara. *Education:* Harvey Mudd College, B.S., 1968; Harvard University, Ph.D., 1974.

ADDRESSES: *Home*—2204 Villa Maria Rd., Claremont, CA 91711. *E-mail*—jal@its.caltech.edu.

CAREER: Chemist and educator. Princeton University, Princeton, NJ, research associate chemist, 1973-74, instructor, 1974-75; University of Notre Dame, Notre Dame, IN, assistant professor of chemistry, 1975-81; Occidental Research Corp, senior research chemist, 1981-83; Arco, research advisor, 1983-86; California Institute of Technology, administrator, Beckman Institute, 1986—.

MEMBER: American Chemical Society, Society for Literature and Science, American Academy of Arts and Sciences, Society for the Social Studies of Science.

WRITINGS:

(Editor and contributor, with Harry Collins) *The One Culture?: A Conversation about Science,* University of Chicago Press (Chicago, IL), 2001.

Associate editor, *Chemical Reviews,* 1979-81; editor, *Journal of Molecular Catalysis,* 1994-98. Contributor to *Inorganic and Organometallic Chemistry.*

SIDELIGHTS: Jay A. Labinger, a noted chemist and educator, joins fellow editor Harry Collins in the 2001 book *The One Culture?: A Conversation about Science.* Including writings by both editors as well as essays by twelve physicists and sociologists of science such as Alan Sokal, Michael Lynch, Steven Weinberg, Kenneth G. Wilson, and others, *The One Culture?* addresses an argument that gained prominence in academic circles focusing on science studies during the 1990s: namely, the relevancy of hard science versus the schools of thought generated by sociologists, philosophers, and historians that used social construction and relativism as frameworks for making sense out of science's role in human development and history. The argument had its genesis in a 1962 study by historian Thomas Kuhn in which he concluded that scientific knowledge is colored by the social factors that led to its discovery. *The One Culture?*—in effect a written debate, which had its genesis in a 1997 academic conference held in Southampton, England—is divided into three sections, the first containing position papers on the so-called "Science wars," the second containing a discussion of the issues addressed in the papers, and the third comprising a response and rebuttal by each of the contributors to criticisms voiced in section two.

Several of the questions addressed by Labinger's contributors focus on the role of scientists within the decision-making process: What priority should a society place upon scientific knowledge and who is justified in transmitting such knowledge? How skeptically should so-called scientific "facts" be viewed? Is the academic field of science study "antiscience," as it was labeled following a widely reported pseudoscientific article debunking quantum gravity that New

York University physics professor Alan Sokal managed to publish in a respected cultural studies journal in 1996 that was later proven to be a total hoax? Calling the tone of *The One Culture?* "serious and respectful," *American Scientist* contributor Jan Golinski praised the volume for "clarifying what science studies . . . is trying to accomplish." In a *Choice* review P. D. Skiff noted that while the contributors "have been dueling for more than four years" their "more extreme overstatements . . . have been worn down to more sensible points," and went on to praise Labinger and Collins for drawing the focus of the arguments to central rather than peripheral issues. Praising *The One Culture?* in a review for the *Times Literary Supplement,* Peter D. Smith added that the book stands as a "important book, motivated by an exemplary spirit of academic tolerance and debate, [that] shows how bridges might be built in the future" between postmodern intellectuals and working scientists.

BIOGRAPHICAL AND CRITICAL SOURCES:

PERIODICALS

American Scientist, January-February, 2002, Jan Golinski, review of *The One Culture?: A Conversation about Science,* p. 72.

Choice, January, 2002, P. D. Skiff, review of *The One Culture?,* p. 900.

Nature, September 27, 2001, John Ziman, review of *The One Culture?,* pp. 359-360.

New Scientist, October 6, 2001, Robert Matthews, review of *The One Culture?,* p. 50.

Times Literary Supplement, July 26, 2002, Peter D. Smith, review of *The One Culture?,* p. 33.

* * *

LAKIN, Patricia 1944-

PERSONAL: Born 1944.

ADDRESSES: Agent—c/o Author Mail, Simon and Schuster, 1230 Avenue of the Americas, New York, NY 10020. *E-mail*—pattylakin@earthlink.net.

CAREER: Author of children's books. Previously worked as a school teacher.

WRITINGS:

ILLUSTRATED BY PATIENCE BREWSTER

Don't Touch My Room, Little Brown (Boston, MA), 1985.

Oh, Brother!, Little Brown (Boston, MA), 1987.

Just like Me, Little Brown (Boston, MA), 1989.

ILLUSTRATED BY DOUG CUSHMAN

Aware and Alert, Raintree Steck-Vaughn (Austin, TX), 1995.

Get Ready to Read!, Raintree Steck-Vaughn (Austin, TX), 1995.

A Good Sport, Raintree Steck-Vaughn (Austin, TX), 1995.

Information, Please, Raintree Steck-Vaughn (Austin, TX), 1995.

The Mystery Illness, Raintree Steck-Vaughn (Austin, TX), 1995.

CHILDREN'S BOOKS, "AROUND THE WORLD" SERIES

Family: Around the World, Blackbirch Press (Woodbridge, CT), 1995.

Creativity: Around the World, Blackbirch Press (Woodbridge, CT), 1995.

Growing Up: Around the World, Blackbirch Press (Woodbridge, CT), 1995.

Grandparents: Around the World, Blackbirch Press (Woodbridge, CT), 1999.

Food: Around the world, Blackbirch Press (Woodbridge, CT), 1999.

OTHER

Jet Black Pickup Truck, illustrated by Rosekrans Hoffman, Orchard Books (New York, NY), 1990.

The Palace of Stars, pictures by Kimberly Bulckin Root, Tambourine Books (New York, NY), 1993.

Jennifer Capriati: Rising Star, Rourke Enterprises (Vero Beach, FL), 1993.

Dad and Me in the Morning, illustrated by Robert G. Steele, A. Whitman (Morton Grove, IL), 1994.

Don't Forget, pictures by Ted Rand, Tambourine Books (New York, NY), 1994.

Everything You Need to Know When a Parent Doesn't Speak English, Rosen Publishing Group (New York, NY), 1994.

Hurricane!, illustrated by Vanessa Lubach, Millbrook Press (Brookfield, CT), 2000.

Fat Chance Thanksgiving, illustrated by Stacey Schuett, A. Whitman (Morton Grove, IL), 2001.

Helen Keller and the Big Storm, illustrated by Diana Magnuson, Aladdin (New York, NY), 2002.

Harry Houdini: Escape Artist, Aladdin (New York, NY), 2002.

Clarence the Copy Cat, pictures by John Manders, Doubleday (New York, NY), 2002.

Snow Day!, pictures by Scott Nash, Dial Books (New York, NY), 2002.

Subway Sonata, illustrated by Heather Maione, Millbrook Press (Brookfield, CT), 2002.

Amelia Earhart: More than a Flyer, illustrated by Alan and Leah Daniel, Aladdin (New York, NY), 2003.

Beach Day!, pictures by Scott Nash, Dial Books (New York, NY), 2004.

Also author of a publication for the New York Philharmonic's "Young People's Concerts."

WORK IN PROGRESS: Clara Barton, to be published by Simon and Schuster.

SIDELIGHTS: Patricia Lakin's books for young readers include volumes on serious subjects (*Amelia Earhart: More than a Flyer*) and even more serious ones (*Aware and Alert,* in which a police officer teaches children how to keep themselves safe from strangers), but quite a few are more whimsical. *Snow Day!,* for instance, concerns four playmates—Sam, Pam, Will, and Jill—who wake up and discover, to their delight, a thick blanket of freshly fallen snow. This alone is hardly unusual, but as the reader discovers in the first of illustrator Scott Nash's drawings, the four are crocodiles.

Nor is this the only twist. Dismayed to realize that today is a school day, the four friends remember that they can do something: in what John Peters of *Booklist* called a "perfectly timed revelation," it turns out that they are actually four school principals, and they call the local radio station to inform the newscaster that school is out for the day. Reviewers expressed doubt as to whether the characters really are school principals, or children pretending to be: hence the warning from a critic in *Publishers Weekly,* "Kids, don't try this at home." Nonetheless, several reviewers praised the book's capacity to delight and amuse, as well as its ease of reading for youngsters, with few words (other than *principal*) over two syllables. The *Publishers Weekly* commentator called *Snow Day!* "A seamless work of storytelling about a classic snow job."

The title character in *Clarence the Copy Cat* is such an avowed friend of all living creatures that he cannot bring himself to kill anything—not even a mouse. His inability to perform as a mouser earns him an unceremonious eviction from the sandwich shop where he had lived and worked, and he spends several frustrated (but amusing) frames of John Manders's illustrations trying to obtain a new job before finding a home in a library. The subsequent peace is soon shattered, however, when a mouse shows up, and Clarence is forced to develop a novel means to ensure by peaceful methods that the creature will never come back.

"Readers will sympathize with poor Clarence and root for him as he battles with the rodent and finds a solution to the problem," promised Kristin de Lacoste in *School Library Journal,* and Connie Fletcher in *Booklist* called *Clarence the Copy Cat* "a well-plotted, action-packed, comically illustrated story." A critic in *Kirkus Reviews* noted the "humorous and satisfying solution to the problem," and concluded, "Librarians take note: Young customers . . . will find much to smile about here."

BIOGRAPHICAL AND CRITICAL SOURCES:

PERIODICALS

Booklist, November 1, 2002, Connie Fletcher, review of *Clarence the Copy Cat,* p. 508; November 15, 2002, John Peters, review of *Snow Day!,* p. 611.

Kirkus Reviews, October 1, 2002, review of *Clarence the Copy Cat,* p. 1473.

New York Times Book Review, August 23, 1987, review of *Oh Brother!,* p. 27.

Publishers Weekly, October 21, 2002, review of *Snow Day!,* p. 73.

School Library Journal, October, 2002, Kristin de Lacoste, review of *Clarence the Copy Cat,* p. 116; November, 2002, Harriett Fargnoli, review of *Snow Day!,* p. 128.

ONLINE

Patricia Lakin Home Page, http://www.patricialakin.com (September 18, 2003).*

* * *

LANDETA, Matilde Soto 1910-1999

PERSONAL: Born September 20, 1910, in Mexico City, Mexico; died January 26, 1999; married Martín Toscano (a colonel in the Mexican army), 1933 (divorced 1942). *Education:* Attended Colegio de las Damas del Sagrado Corazón.

CAREER: Film director. Continuity person for several film producers in Mexico, including Films Mundiales, 1933-45; assistant to film directors, including Emilio Fernández, Mauricio Magdaleno, Julio Bracho, and Alfredo Crevena, 1945-48; from 1950s through 1970s, taught screenwriting, wrote scripts, ran a movie theater, worked as a government liaison on foreign films shot in Mexico, and worked in television, including as a director of children's television programs. Directed films include *Lola Casanova,* 1948, *La negra Augustias,* 1949, *Trotacalles,* 1951, *Islas revillagigedo,* 1990, and *Noctoruno a Rosario,* 1991.

AWARDS, HONORS: Ariel Prize for best screenplay, Mexican Academy of Motion Picture Arts and Sciences, 1956, for *Los caminos de la vida;* Lifetime Achievement award, Mexican Film Institute, 1992.

WRITINGS:

Los caminos de la vida (screenplay), 1956.
Siempre estaré contigo (screenplay), 1957.

Also contributor of articles to periodicals, including *World Press Reviews.*

SIDELIGHTS: The only woman to have broken into the male-dominated Mexican film industry during its "golden age" of the 1930 through the 1950s, Matilde Soto Landeta directed three successful movies before being forced to give up her career because of male bias. Estranged from filmmaking for forty years, she was rediscovered as a pioneer woman filmmaker in the 1970s and 1980s and finally received national tributes and many international acknowledgments at festivals in such locations as Havana, London, Tokyo, Barcelona, Créteil, Buenos Aires, and San Francisco.

Born into a distinguished family the same year that the Mexican revolution broke out, Landeta was orphaned early in life, and she and her brother Eduardo were raised in the family's grand ancestral home in San Luis Potosí by their maternal grandmother. Eventually—but separately—both were sent to the United States to study, but Landeta and her brother were reunited in Mexico City in the 1930s, a time of great post-revolutionary upheaval in the arts and culture. Eduardo became a film actor, and Landeta, although still a student, decided that she also wanted a career in the movies. Despite her family's protests, she became a "script girl" (continuity person) and went on to work with some of the Mexican cinema's greatest directors and stars. After working on more than seventy-five feature films, she fought her way through the professional hierarchy of the Mexican film-workers union to become an assistant director, working on fourteen films. She eventually succeeded in becoming the first recognized woman director in the Mexican film industry—and the first female in Latin America to direct within a studio-based production system—though she had to attend a union meeting dressed as a man in order to get the promotion.

Working in a highly competitive industrial system, Landeta co-scripted, produced, and directed three feature films before hostile producers and distributors blocked her from the industry. All of her three films adopt a clear woman-centered perspective and simultaneously work within and against the predominant genres of the Mexican industry at the time. Each film invokes a distinct moment in Mexican history—the Spanish colony in *Lola Casanova,* the Mexican revolution in *La negra Augustias,* ("The Black Angustias"), and modern urbanization in *Trotacalles* ("Streetwalker")—with narratives centered upon a conflicted heroine who assumes a conflictive social position.

In *Lola Casanova,* for example, a tale of Creole gentry captured by Indians, the captured heroine does not attempt to either civilize the Indians or escape, choosing instead to remain with them and adapt to their ways.

In the revolutionary melodrama *La negra Angustias* the mulatta Angustias, an outcast in her own village, redefines the role of women in the Mexican revolution not as a *soldadera* (camp follower), but as a powerful leader of men in battle. The film addresses not only questions of gender but also the tensions produced by racial and class differences. *Trotacalles* works within the *fichera,* or prostitute, melodrama subgenre. The narrative focuses on the parallel stories of two sisters, María, a prostitute who is exploited and abused by her pimp, Rodolfo, and Elena, the pampered wife of a rich older businessman who begins an affair with Rodolfo unaware of his relationship to her sister. In a clear reversal of the prevailing bourgeois morals, Landeta positions the married woman as the real prostitute, both within and outside her marriage.

In the 1950s Landeta had a fourth film in the works, a script she had long nurtured titled *Tribunal de menores;* a duplicitous producer, however, tricked her into ceding him the rights to the script and it was filmed by Alfonso Corona Blake as *Los caminos de la vida.* Landeta had to sue to get her name included in the credits, and the Ariel prize (the Mexican equivalent of the Oscar) she won for the script was a bittersweet triumph. As a result of her confrontations with the director of the National Cinema Bank, she was effectively barred from the industry.

Although eagerly awaited, her 1990s comeback films *Islas Revillagigedo* and *Noctoruno a Rosario* were not as well received by critics as her earlier work. The evocation of end-of-the-nineteenth-century romanticism through the failed love affair between a poet and a powerful and seductive older woman in *Noctoruno a Rosario* failed to impress even Landeta's most ardent supporters.

Landeta died on January 26, 1999.

BIOGRAPHICAL AND CRITICAL SOURCES:

BOOKS

Women Filmmakers and Their Films, St. James Press (Detroit, MI), 1998.*

LANDIS, Bill 1959-

PERSONAL: Born 1959, in Landes de Busac, France; son of a career serviceman and a civil servant; married Michelle Clifford (a writer and publisher), 1986; children: Victoria. *Education:* New York University, B.S., 1978; M.B.A., 1979. *Politics:* "Democrat, with certain affiliations to other political inclinations." *Religion:* "Thelemite." *Hobbies and other interests:* Chess, mysticism, including Aleister Crowley, Masonic and Rosecrucian lore, and tarot cards.

ADDRESSES: Home and office—Sleazoid Express, P.O. Box 620, Old Chelsea Station, New York, NY 10011. *E-mail*—info@sleazoidexpress.com.

CAREER: Author, lecturer, and publisher. Has worked as a movie projectionist.

AWARDS, HONORS: Grant, Yerba Buena Center for the Arts, 1999.

WRITINGS:

Anger: The Unauthorized Biography of Kenneth Anger, HarperCollins Publishers (New York, NY), 1995.

(With Michelle Clifford) *Sleazoid Express: A Mind-twisting Tour through the Grindhouse Cinema of Times Square,* Simon & Schuster (New York, NY), 2002.

Has also written articles for the newsletter/magazine *Sleazoid Express* and the magazine *Metasex,* as well as for the periodicals *Village Voice, Soho Weekly News, Film Comment, New York Rocker, Worldly Remains, Carbon 14, Hustler,* and *Screw.*

WORK IN PROGRESS: A collaboration with wife, Michelle Clifford, on director Joe Davian; articles, continued work on *Sleazoid Express.*

SIDELIGHTS: Bill Landis completed college at the age of twenty with a master's degree in finance and worked in the corporate world for a while but became dissatisfied with that scene. Instead, he opted for a job as a projectionist at various and somewhat sleazy movie houses on Times Square, an area, during the

1970s and 1980s referred to as the Deuce. The Deuce, wrote *Library Journal*'s Barry X. Miller was a "psychosexual netherland on 42nd Street between Seventh and Eighth Avenues." And it was here that Landis saw a lot of films.

Landis grew up, according to Kurt Loder, writing for *Rolling Stone,* as an "air-force brat" in France and England. Later his family moved to Louisiana and ultimately to New York. At the age of nine, Landis saw his first ghoulish movie, *Guttertrash* by Andy Milligan, which proved to become Landis's "first intimation that there might exist a whole netherworld of extremely weird human behavior, a world of strange, brutal beauty. It was the beginning of an obsession," wrote Loder. From then on, Landis was hooked, and as an adult he has devoted himself to what are often referred to as exploitation films.

However bad some critics might have said these movies were, they caught Landis's imagination, and he decided to write reviews about them. With only a portable typewriter at his disposal, he produced a one-page theatre guide with movie reviews and handed them out for free. From its start in 1980, his newsletter eventually expanded, as did Landis's computer knowledge, and in time he created a Web site. *Sleazoid Express* caught the eye of a major New York publisher, so Landis sat down, with his wife, Michelle Clifford, and wrote a book about his experiences. This would actually be his second book. His first was about Kenneth Anger, a man who produced some of the movies that Landis wrote about.

In the beginning Landis's newsletter had covered the movies showing on Times Square. Later he incorporated more than just movie reviews, adding histories of filmmakers and in-depth stories about the films, expanding the newsletter to a four-page monthly. The majority of the movies *Sleazoid* covered were those that fit into the horror genre—often referred to as "Blood Horror" or "Europsleaze"—like *Twitch of the Death Nerve* and *The Corpse Grinders.* In the late 1980s, however, the Deuce was closed down and in its place rose theme shops and family-oriented stores; and Landis stopped publication of his newsletter. "My heart was broken when the Deuce closed," Landis told Dan Taylor at *Exploitation Retrospect* online: "I had long ties to people in Times Square, and we all didn't know what to do next. When the theaters were open it was a place you not only worked, you socialized. . . . Then all of a sudden it was just crumbling. Not just theaters, but a certain lifestyle, was ending." That is when Landis took the time to write his book on Anger.

Coauthored anonymously with Clifford, 1995's *Anger: The Unauthorized Biography of Kenneth Anger* is a biography of seminal independent film director, Kenneth Anger. Anger, a pioneer of innovative underground films, is possibly better known by the general public as the author of his best-selling 1960 book, *Hollywood Babylon,* which is filled with Hollywood gossip and scandal. Anger, who only made nine films totaling about three hours in length, is often referred to as the granddaddy of underground films. He was born in 1927 and created his films mostly in the 1960s, a period Landis gives full focus to in his book. There is "much fascinating stuff," wrote Jerry White for *City Paper* online, "for those who don't know much about Anger's career and are just interested in the swingers that floated around the seamier avant garde circles of the 1960s." White was also impressed with Landis's quite "valuable project." White found that Landis was able to take a somewhat obscure cultural figure and place him in a larger context, thus giving the book "a real chance at a broad readership." Some of Anger's works include *Fireworks, The Inauguration of the Pleasure Dome, Invocation of My Demon Brother,* and *Scorpio Rising.*

Although Anger has become a recluse and, as a *Publishers Weekly* reviewer put it, has "reinvented his life history at will," Landis was able to develop a "fairly accurate portrait" due to his "meticulous research," which included interviewing members of Anger's family. The *Publishers Weekly* reviewer found Landis's book fascinating because of Anger's relationship with some of the era's most notorious counterculture icons, such as Mick Jagger, Anaïs Nin, Jimmy Page, and Marianne Faithful. These elements led the reviewer to refer to Landis's work as "engrossing." Referring to the difficulty of finding the truth of this enigmatic film producer, a *Kirkus Reviews* writer also praised Landis's efforts, claiming that "this is probably the most accurate biography one can hope for while its subject is alive."

After years of collaborations, in 1997 Landis contributed to his wife's magazine, *Metasex,* which was about the vice aspects of the old Times Square. In 1999 he and Clifford revived *Sleazoid Express* as a full-length magazine.

In 2002 Landis and Clifford were asked to expand the magazine into a book, which was published as, *Sleazoid Express: A Mind-twisting Tour through the Grindhouse Cinema of Times Square.* Pointing out the authenticity of Landis's book, Michael Atkinson, writing for the *Village Voice,* stated: "since Landis is a self-confessed Times Square loiterer who even worked as a manager and projectionist at various porn theaters, the accounts of backstage catacombs, audience chaos, and business subterfuge are all first-hand." Mike Tribby concluded in *Booklist* that Landis's book may not be "for every film buff," but it "will draw vintage-sleaze fans from both sides of the culture-wars skirmish line."

Landis told *CA:* "I had been typing up my own [movie] reviews since I was around eleven. At age fourteen I read Hubert Selby's *Last Exit to Brooklyn,* and it opened my eyes in many ways. One was that you could write about anything, no mater how shocking, so long as it was humanly true.

"I was very influenced by the surrealist movement, as exemplified by filmmaker Luis Bunuel. And later surrealists, particularly Fernando Arrabel and Alejandro Jodorwosky, who founded the Panic Theater movement and made influential, unforgettable films. . . . I have always held a special reverence for Jodorwosky and Arrabel; they were cult figures familiar with what I was familiar with since pre-adolescence. And they had a life situation similar to me—being born in one country while your parents were citizens of another, your ethnicity has nothing to do with it, and you spend your adulthood in yet another country. It contributes to your sense of unreality. Exploitation films that I later saw seemed an extension of surrealism, but were getting absolutely no critical recognition.

"History needs to be recorded in all its human, cultural and psychological forms, with all three overlapping. And I've never written fiction because truth was always far more surreal."

BIOGRAPHICAL AND CRITICAL SOURCES:

PERIODICALS

Austin Chronicle, February 21, 2003, review of *Sleazoid Express.*

Booklist, December 1, 2002, review of *Sleazoid Express,* p. 641.

Kirkus Reviews, May 1, 1995, review of *Anger: The Unauthorized Biography,* p. 612.

Library Journal, November 15, 2002, Barry X. Miller, review of *Sleazoid Express,* p. 73.

Publishers Weekly, June 5, 1995, review of *Anger,* p. 48.

Rolling Stone, July, 1984, Kurt Loder, "Night Creatures," pp. 91-98.

Village Voice, March 12-18, 2003, Michael Atkinson, review of *Sleazoid Express.*

Washington Post Book World, June 25, 1995, review of *Anger,* p. 13.

ONLINE

City Paper, http://www.citypaper.net/ (September 28-October 5, 1995), Jerry White, review of *Anger.*

Exploitation Retrospect, http://www.dantenet.com/ (April 29, 2003), Dan Taylor "They Put the Sin Back in Sinema: An Interview with Bill Landis and Michelle Clifford of *Sleazoid Express.*"

Metasex online, http://www.geocities.com/metasex/ (November 14, 2003).

Sleazoid Express Web site, http://www.sleazoidexpress.com/ (November 14, 2003).

* * *

LANDRUM, Larry N.

PERSONAL: Male; children: two. *Education:* Purdue University, B.A., 1965, M.A., 1967; Bowling Green State University, Ph.D., 1973.

ADDRESSES: Office—Department of English, Michigan State University, 222 Morrill Hall, East Lansing, MI 48824-1036. *E-mail*—landrum@msu.edu.

CAREER: Michigan State University, East Lansing, 1973—, began as assistant professor, professor of English, 1984—.

MEMBER: Modern Language Association, Popular Culture Association, Midwest Popular Culture Association.

WRITINGS:

(Editor with Ray B. Browne and William K. Bottorff) *Challenges in American Culture,* Bowling Green University Popular Press (Bowling Green, OH), 1970.

(Editor with Pat Browne and Ray B. Browne) *Dimensions of Detective Fiction,* Popular Press (Bowling Green, OH), 1976.

American Popular Culture: A Guide to Information Sources, Gale (Detroit, MI), 1982.

American Mystery and Detective Novels: A Reference Guide, Greenwood Press (Westport, CT), 1999.

Advisory editor, *Journal of Popular Culture,* 1967-85; bibliographer, *Journal of Popular Film,* 1972—.

SIDELIGHTS: Larry N. Landrum is a specialist in American popular culture and detective fiction. He has edited and compiled several reference texts on the subjects, including *American Popular Culture: A Guide to Information Sources* and *American Mystery and Detective Novels: A Reference Guide. American Popular Culture* ranges widely through some forty odd categories, including folklore, sports, entertainment, and advertising. Its projected audience includes students of American studies, popular literature, and cultural trends. A *Choice* reviewer found the work "a useful addition for upper-level undergraduate and graduate students." D. W. Madden, also reviewing in *Choice,* called *American Mystery and Detective Novels* "an indispensable resource" containing "quite a bit that is new and rewarding."

BIOGRAPHICAL AND CRITICAL SOURCES:

PERIODICALS

Choice, March, 1983, review of *American Popular Culture: A Guide to Information Sources,* p. 958; November, 1999, D. W. Madden, review of *American Mystery and Detective Novels: A Reference Guide,* p. 537.

Library Journal, December 1, 1976, Sheila Pepper, review of *Dimensions of Detective Fiction,* p. 2490.*

* * *

LANE, Anthony 1962-

PERSONAL: Born 1962; married Allison Pearson (a columnist and TV journalist); children: two. *Education:* Educated at Cambridge, England.

ADDRESSES: Home—London, England. *Office—New Yorker,* 4 Times Square, New York, NY 10036-6592

CAREER: Film Critic. *Independent,* London, England, deputy literary editor, 1989-1993, Sunday film critic, 1991-93; *New Yorker,* New York, NY, film critic, 1993—.

WRITINGS:

Nobody's Perfect: Writings from the New Yorker, Alfred A. Knopf (New York, NY), 2002.

SIDELIGHTS: From his enviable perch at the *New Yorker,* Anthony Lane has been one of the premier movie critics since 1993. Hired by Tina Brown from the *Independent,* an English newspaper, Lane continues to live in London but makes frequent trips to New York City. *Nobody's Perfect: Writings from the New Yorker* brings together ten years of Lane's criticism, with commentary and an introduction describing his initial experiences occupying the late Pauline Kael's office at the *New Yorker.* In addition to his views on films such as *Forrest Gump* (he disliked it) and *Titanic* (he liked it), the pieces include book reviews and a few profiles of cultural figures such as Nabokov and Buster Keaton, and even a piece on the joys of playing with Legos. "Throughout, Lane upholds the sterling virtue of good writing combined with wit and emotional engagement. But he makes no claim to be right about anything," commented *Spectator* reviewer Ian Thomson. Laura Miller, reviewing the book for the *New York Times,* also noted a certain restraint, in contrast to his predecessor: "It's exactly the egotism of great film critics that Lane lacks. Kael grabbed her readers by the scruff of the neck and carried us through her experience of a movie like so much baggage. . . . Lane, on the other hand, does not insist. He cajoles."

Most reviewers noted Lane's suppleness of language, and his comic gifts. "His prose is an amalgam of humor, intelligence, discernment, and style," in the words of *Booklist* reviewer Brad Hooper. "He is intellectual, witty, entertaining, and, without a doubt, one of the finest reviewers of our time," wrote *Library Journal* contributor Ken Winter. For some, Lane's prose set just the right tone. Novelist John Banville, writing in the *Guardian,* concluded, "It is a large part of Lane's greatness as a film reviewer—yes, greatness—that he sets this popular art form at exactly the right level of seriousness. . . . *Nobody's Perfect* shimmers with positively Nabokovian elegance, wit and delicacy of expression; it is hard to recall when one was made to laugh out loud like this and at the same time shiver with aesthetic bliss."

BIOGRAPHICAL AND CRITICAL SOURCES:

PERIODICALS

Booklist, August, 2002, Brad Hooper, review of *Nobody's Perfect: Writings from the New Yorker,* p. 365.

Guardian (Manchester, England), November 16, 2002, John Banville, "The Way They Were."

Library Journal, September 15, 2002, Ken Winter, review of *Nobody's Perfect,* p. 70.

New York Times Book Review, September 1, 2002, Laura Miller, "See the Movie, Read the Book," p. 9.

Spectator (London, England), November 30, 2002, Ian Thomson, "Stooping to Conquer," p. 50.

Times Literary Supplement, February 21, 2003, John Boorman, "Do Not Hire the Fat Man," pp. 20-21.*

* * *

LaPEÑA, Frank Raymond 1937-

PERSONAL: Born October 5, 1937, in San Francisco, CA; son of Henry and Evelyn Gladys (Towndolly) LaPeña; married Catherine Alice Sell Skinner, August 19, 1966 (divorced April, 1984); children: Kari Renee, Vincent Craig; stepchildren: Ivy, Peggy, Dan, Paul, Nancy. *Education:* California State University—Chico, B.A., 1965; San Francisco State College (now University), secondary teaching certificate, 1968; California State University—Sacramento, M.A., 1978.

ADDRESSES: Office—c/o Native American Studies Program, California State University—Sacramento, 6000 J St., Sacramento, CA 95819-2605. *E-mail*—lapenaf@csus.edu.

CAREER: Shasta Junior College, Redding, CA, instructor, 1969-71; California State University—Sacramento, began as instructor, became assistant professor of art, 1971-73, professor of art and ethnic studies and director of Native American studies, beginning 1974. Maidu Dancers and Traditionalists, dancer; Peña Adobe, Vacaville, CA, instructor, 1970; University of Alberta, instructor, 1974. U.S. Department of the Interior, research associate, 1984. Certified silversmith, 1977; painter, photographer, and mixed-media artist; art represented in many solo and group shows, including exhibitions at California State Museum, Natsoulas Gallery, Davis, CA, American Indian Community House in New York, Santa Barbara Museum of Natural History, and National Museum of the American Indian, Smithsonian Institution; work collected at Crocker Museum, Heard Museum, Turtle Foundation Center for Living Arts, and Indian Arts and Crafts Board of U.S. Department of the Interior. Port of Oakland, Oakland, CA, worked in airplane construction; also worked as secondary schoolteacher.

AWARDS, HONORS: Prizes from Kingsley Show, 1961, Northern California Art Show, 1961, 1969, North Valley Art Show, 1969, 1979, and St. John's Religious Art Festival, 1969, 1976; People on the Move Award, Young Men's Christian Association, 1975; grant from Smithsonian Institution, 1976; Order of the Hornet and Distinguished Service Award, California State University Alumni Association, 1995.

WRITINGS:

The World Is a Gift, [San Francisco, CA], 1987.

(With others; and illustrator) *California Indian Shamanism,* 1992.

(And illustrator) *Singing of Earth* (poetry), 1993.

(And illustrator) *The Sound of Rattles and Clappers,* 1994.

(And illustrator) *Commemoration,* Okeanos Press (Berkeley, CA), 1995.

(With Rebecca J. Dobkins and Carey T. Caldwell) *Memory and Imagination: The Legacy of Maidu Indian Artist Frank Day,* Oakland Museum of California (Oakland, CA), 1997.

Also illustrator of book covers. Contributing editor, *News from Native California.*

BIOGRAPHICAL AND CRITICAL SOURCES:

BOOKS

Portfolio II: Eleven American Indian Artists, American Indian Contemporary Arts (San Francisco, CA), 1988.

St. James Guide to Native North American Artists, St. James Press (Detroit, MI), 1998, pp. 298-300.

PERIODICALS

Indian Artist, spring, 1997, Jeanine Gendar, "Talking: Painter Frank LaPeña."

OTHER

Frank LaPeña: Wintu Artist and Traditionalist (documentary film), Theo-Blount Media Productions (Fair Oaks, CA), 1988.

The Heard Museum Presents Frank LaPeña, Artist and Lecturer (documentary film), Heard Museum (Phoenix, AZ), 1993.*

* * *

LAPID, Haim 1948-

PERSONAL: Born 1948, in Israel.

ADDRESSES: *Agent*—c/o Author Mail, Toby Press, P.O. Box 8531, New Milford, CT 06776-8531. *E-mail*—editorial@tobypress.com.

CAREER: Teacher, social psychologist, organizational consultant, film critic, film script writer, and fiction writer. *Military service:* Israel Defense Forces, paratrooper.

WRITINGS:

Reshimotav ha-nistarot shel segani: roman, Sifriyat po'alim (Tel Aviv, Israel), 1983, published as *Secret Notes of My Deputy.*

Breznitz, Zemorah-Bitan (Tel Aviv, Israel), 1992, translated by Yael Lotan, published as *Breznitz,*, Toby Press (Milford, CT), 2000.

Ahavot rishonot: sipurim te'udiyim Yi'sre'eliyim, Zemorah-Bitan (Tel Aviv, Israel), 1993.

Meshikhah negdit, Zemorah-Bitan (Tel Aviv, Israel), 1995.

Pesha' ha-ketivah, ha-Kibuts ha-me'uhad (Tel Aviv, Israel), 1998, translation by Yael Lotan, published as *The Crime of Writing,* Toby Press (Milford, CT), 2002.

SIDELIGHTS: Haim Lapid was born near Tel Aviv, Israel. A teacher of social and behavioral psychology, he is also an organizational consultant in Israel's high tech industry. As well as writing books, he writes film scripts for the television and movie industries, and is a film critic. *Breznitz,* translated into English, French, German, and Italian, has received popular critical acclaim by reviewers in those countries.

A critic writing for the *Buffalo News* called *Breznitz* an "engrossing" story of a homicide investigator who, while recovering from an almost fatal car accident, becomes obsessed with solving the murder of an unidentified man whose body is found near Jerusalem. Although an Arabian suspect is arrested and confesses, Breznitz believes him innocent. On a personal level, Breznitz is overwhelmed by the breakup of his extramarital affair and ruminates on what the critic called his "inner hollowness." Lev Raphael commented in *Knight Ridder/Tribune News Service* that the book is a "fine police procedural," and Victoria Esposito-Shea, writing for *Hand Held Crime* online called it "an existentialist examination of life . . . by no means light fiction. It's more like reading the great Russian novelists." A reviewer for *Library Journal* wrote: "This is a disturbing, probing book, unlikely to be forgotten."

The Crime of Writing fuses reality and fantasy to explore sexual identity and the triangle created by woman, man, and child. It also explores the underlying connection between life and literature. A *Publishers Weekly* reviewer called it a "muddled" story about a young Israeli woman who meets an older Englishman, George Brown, on a trip to London. After the woman returns to Israel, Brown dies and she receives his letters, which are in fact his confessions. The woman's novelist husband—the story's narrator—publishes the correspondence, in which Brown relates his lifelong search for the mother who abandoned him in childhood. Brown's fifty-year-long obsession poisons his life. The *Publishers Weekly* reviewer wrote that *The Crime of Writing* "wanders off into a series of murky ruminations about the so-called 'crime' of writing," and commented that, while Lapid's characters are well developed, the meandering tale "makes for a difficult, tangled read." On the other hand, a reviewer for *Library Journal* described the book as "intelligent, sensitive and tense."

BIOGRAPHICAL AND CRITICAL SOURCES:

PERIODICALS

Buffalo News, May 19, 2002, review of *Breznitz,* p. F7.

Knight Ridder/Tribune News Service, August 14, 2002, Lev Raphael, review of *The Crime of Writing,* p. K5658.

Library Journal, November 15, 2002, review of *Breznitz,* p. 43; November 15, 2002, review of *The Crime of Writing,* p. 43.

Publishers Weekly, September 23, 2002, review of *The Crime of Writing,* p. 48.

ONLINE

Hand Held Crime, http://www.handheldcrime.com/ (January 27, 2003), Victoria Esposite-Shea, review of *Breznitz.*

@The Source (Israel), http://www.thesourceisrael.com/ (January 27, 2003), "Haim Lapid."*

* * *

LAPIDGE, Michael 1942-

PERSONAL: Born February 8, 1942; son of Rae H. and Catherine Mary (Carruthers) Lapidge. *Education:* University of Calgary, B.A., 1962; University of Alberta, M.A., 1965; University of Toronto, Ph.D., 1971. *Hobbies and other interests:* Mountaineering.

ADDRESSES: Agent—c/o Author Mail, Oxford University Press, 198 Madison Ave., New York, NY 10016. *E-mail*—michael.lapidge.1@nd.edu.

CAREER: Cambridge University, Cambridge, England, lecturer, 1974-88, reader in insular Latin literature, 1988-91, Elrington and Bosworth Professor of Anglo-Saxon and fellow of Clare College, 1990—. Bayerische Akademie der Wissenschaften, correspondent fellow, 1997.

WRITINGS:

(Translator with Michael Herren) *Aldhelm, the Prose Works,* Rowman & Littlefield (Towota, NJ), 1979.

(Translator with Simon Keynes) *Alfred the Great: Asser's Life of King Alfred and Other Contemporary Sources,* Penguin Books (New York, NY), 1983.

(Editor with P. Hunter Blair) *Anglo-Saxon Northumbria,* Variorum Reprints (London, England), 1984.

(Editor with David Dumville) *Gildas: New Approaches,* Boydell and Brewer (Dover, NH), 1984.

(With Richard Sharpe) *A Bibliography of Celtic-Latin Literature, 400-1200,* Royal Irish Academy (Dublin, Ireland), 1985.

(Editor with Helmut Gneuss) *Learning and Literature in Anglo-Saxon England: Studies Presented to Peter Clemoes on the Occasion of His Sixty-fifth Birthday,* Cambridge University Press (New York, NY), 1985.

(Translator with James L. Rosier) *Aldhelm, the Poetic Works,* D. S. Brewer (Dover, NH), 1985.

(Contributor) *A New Critical History of Old English Literature,* New York University Press (New York, NY), 1986.

Abbreviations for Sources and Specification of Standard Editions for Sources, Center for Medieval and Early Renaissance Studies (New York, NY), 1988.

(Editor) *Latin Learning in Mediaeval Ireland,* Variorum Reprints (London, England), 1988.

(Editor) *Irish Books and Learning in Mediaeval Europe,* Variorum Reprints (Hampshire, England), 1990.

(Editor and translator with Michael Winterbottom) *Wulfstan of Winchester: The Life of St. Aethelwold,* Clarendon Press (New York, NY), 1991.

(Editor) *Anglo-Saxon Litanies of the Saints,* Boydell Press (Rochester, NY), 1991.

Anglo-Latin Literature, 900-1066, Hambledon Press (Rio Grande, TX), 1993.

Bede the Poet, St. Paul's Church (England), 1993.

(Editor with Bernhard Bischoff) *Biblical Commentaries from the Canterbury School,* Cambridge University Press (New York, NY), 1994.

(Editor) *Archbishop Theodore: Commemorative Studies on His Life and Influence,* Cambridge University Press (New York, NY), 1995.

(Editor with Peter S. Baker) *Byrhtferth's Enchiridion,* Oxford University Press (New York, NY), 1995.

(Editor) *Studies in Early Mediaeval Latin Glossaries,* Variorum Reprints (Brookfield, CT), 1996.

Anglo-Latin Literature, 600-899, Hambledon Press (Rio Grande, TX), 1996.

(Editor) *Columbanus: Studies on the Latin Writings,* Boydell Press (Rochester, NY), 1997.

(Editor) *The Blackwell Encyclopedia of Anglo-Saxon England,* Blackwell (Oxford, England), 1999.

The Cult of St. Swithun, Oxford University Press (New York, NY), 2003.

(Editor) *Interpreters of Early Medieval Britain,* Oxford University Press (New York, NY), 2003.

SIDELIGHTS: Michael Lapidge has spent much of his career as a literary gatekeeper for medieval studies. As a professor of Anglo-Saxon literature, his primary focus is on the religious figures of medieval times and their influences gained from other civilizations. Lapidge meticulously collects and produces inventories of works from medieval times and tries to dissect not only their meanings, but also their influence on present-day authors.

Lapidge was born on February 8, 1942, the son of Rae H. Lapidge and Catherine Mary Carruthers. He attended the University of Calgary and graduated with a B.A. in 1962. He went on to receive his master's degree at the University of Alberta in 1965 and his Ph.D. from the University of Toronto in 1971. During the years from 1974 to 1988 he lectured at Cambridge University and later served as a reader of insular Latin literature from 1988 to 1991. He has been an Elrington and Bosworth Professor of Anglo-Saxon and a fellow of Clare College, Cambridge since 1990.

In his 1985 *Learning and Literature in Anglo-Saxon England,* Lapidge, along with Helmut Gneuss, presents documents from Anglo-Saxon libraries, including wills and inventories. In his essay "Surviving Booklists from Anglo-Saxon England," Lapidge provides a commentary on each piece mentioned and the significance of its place in Anglo-Saxon literary history. Critics praised this essay, calling it concise and easy to read. The book was also reviewed as an important volume. "The editors have provided students of Old English literature with a volume which contains both invaluable works of reference and significant insights into letters and the culture of the period," maintained Joseph B. Trahern, Jr. in the *Journal of English and Germanic Philosophy.* "It is a much needed book which will be used for years."

His work as a coeditor with Richard Sharpe produced *A Bibliography of Celtic-Latin Literature, 400-1200.* Authors of Roman Britain, Wales, Cornwall, Ireland, Brittany, and Scotland are divided into sections and each of their works are listed. From there, each author's works from that time are subdivided up into major works, manuscripts, and other forms of writing. Lapidge and Sharpe also provide commentary on each of the writers of the era. The work was at once praised and criticized. While the amount of work and detail that went into the book cause some critics to praise the achievement, others criticized certain editorial decisions by Lapidge and Sharpe. For example, some reviewers were upset that certain poems by Columbanos of Bobbio were reassigned by Lapidge to Columbanus of Saint-Trond. At the same time, while some expressed their concern over the assignment of certain works, most conceded that the work is concise and a valuable addition to Celtic studies.

Lapidge has focused much of his writing career on studying the works of religious figures in medieval times. *Gildas: New Approaches*, edited by Lapidge and David Dumville, explores the writings of the British author known as Gildas the Wise, who wrote during the late fifth and sixth centuries. The collection of essays by contributing writers delves into the background of Gildas and his influences, and one essay looks into the influence of Roman politics during Gildas's era. Lapidge contributed an essay to the book surveying the complexities of Gildas's education and the cultural influences that permeate his works. The problems with the chronology and geography concerning Gildas are also addressed within the book. Historians have had trouble in identifying exactly when Gildas wrote his works and have had little success in pinpointing the reigns of the kings Gildas attacks in his writings. Gildas's use of such vernacular as "dragon" and "lion" are also addressed within the book as an attempt to date his chronology and to explore the effects of the Celtic and Latin influences on his works. Lapidge's "paper unquestionably supplies the major contribution of the book, and his analysis of Gildas's style and vocabulary sheds a flood of new light on our understanding of this author," remarked Alfred P. Smyth in the *English Historical Review.*

"Lapidge is a superb tracer of sources and influences," noted Eric John in the *Catholic Historical Review,* in regards to Lapidge's 1991 translation of *Wuflstan of Winchester: The Life of St. Aethelwold.* Little is known about Wulfstan, a monk at Old Minister. He was appointed the biographer of St. Aethelwold, a move that Lapidge argues proves that Aethelwold foresaw his canonization. Lapidge delves into the way Aethelwold taught and mastered Latin. He notes that the saint's Latin study was progressive and that his writing style made him one of the greater contributors to English prose.

Lapidge studies another religious figure in his 1995 work *Archbishop Theodore: Commemorative Studies on His Life and Influence.* The consecrated archbishop of Canterbury, Theodore of Tarsus is viewed as the second founder of Augustine's mission to the English. Archbishop Theodore reorganized the English dioceses and established a Cathedral School in Canterbury. The collection of essays within the book attempt to discover what influence Archbishop Theodore had on the Anglo-Saxon church. While the book was praised for its contribution to seventh-century Anglo-Saxon ecclesiastical history, it was not without criticism. Alfred P. Smyth in the *Albion* opined, "Lapidge's account of Theodore's career reads like a summary, but it includes an incongruous digression on the 'stunning sights' of Istanbul, which entertains the reader to a Fodor-type exposition on the marvels of the Late Antique city."

Lapidge offers an examination of another religious figure's work in *Columbanus: Studies on the Latin Writings.* For this volume, Lapidge collected various essays on the studies of the writings of the Irish monk Columbanus, who lived in voluntary exile and corresponded regularly with popes as well as preaching sermons. In addition, Columbanus founded the Luxeuil and Bobbio monasteries. The collection of essays includes studies on the Irish monk's sermons as well as the authenticity of his work. In addition to essays on the Irish monk's work, the collection includes a study on the monastic rules and poetry produced by Columbanus. Arthur G. Holder of *Church History* found the essays "represent a significant contribution to the study of this important early medieval figure."

Through his literary accomplishments, Lapidge has gained recognition for his translations of works of literature by Anglo-Saxon writers and saints as well as writings on medieval authors. His books and essays have repeatedly been praised by critics as important contributions to the world of medieval history and literature.

BIOGRAPHICAL AND CRITICAL SOURCES:

PERIODICALS

Albion, fall, 1996, pp. 459-460.
American Historical Review, June, 1986, pp. 641-642.
Catholic Historical Review, July, 1994, p. 575; July, 1996, pp. 514-515.
Church History, December, 1996, pp. 671-73; March, 1998, pp. 128-129.
English Historical Review, October, 1986, pp. 927-930; January, 1988, pp. 162-163.
History Today, February, 1987, pp. 57-58.
Journal of English and Germanic Philosophy, July, 1988, pp. 433-437.
Speculum, October, 1987, p. 1030; April, 1989, pp. 461-462.
Times Literary Supplement, March 12, 1999, p. 28.*

* * *

LASAGNA, Louis (Cesare) 1923-2003

OBITUARY NOTICE—See index for *CA* sketch: Born February 22, 1923, in Queens, NY; died of lymphoma August 6, 2003, in Newton, MA. Physician, educator, and author. Lasagna, a dean emeritus of the Sackler School of Biomedical Sciences at Tufts University, was best remembered as a pharmacologist who was at the forefront of placebo research, advocated changes in drug research improvements in medical ethics, and wrote an updated version of the Hippocratic Oath. He earned his bachelor's degree at Rutgers University in 1943 and his medical degree from Columbia University in 1947. After doing his internship and residency, he was hired as an assistant professor of pharmacology at Johns Hopkins University in 1954. He remained there through the 1960s, becoming an associate professor in 1959. Lasagna next joined the University of Rochester faculty in 1970, teaching there as a professor of pharmacology and toxicology until 1986. During the early 1970s he founded the Center for the Study of Drug Development, which later became part of Tufts. While still working as a professor of medicine at the University of Rochester until 1994, Lasagna also joined Tufts University in 1984 as a professor of pharmacology and psychiatry and was dean of the Sackler School of Medicine there. Lasagna made a name for himself in the field of pharmacology at the beginning of his career when he published the paper "A Study of the Placebo Response" in 1954. Here, he showed that the psychology of a patient could be an extremely important factor in medical treatment. The paper was so influential in the medical community that in 1997 the journal *Lancet* named it one of the most important medical achievements in the history of medicine. Throughout his career, Lasagna emphasized that doctors maintain an empathy for their patients and always consider the psychological effects of their treatments; he rewrote the Hippocratic Oath in 1964 to remind doctors they are treating human beings, not diseases and injuries, thus creating the modern version of the oath that is still often used in medical schools today. Lasagna often testified before Congress, too, favoring reforms to the drug industry that would improve drug testing before new medicines went to market. The recipient of honorary degrees from Hahnemann University in 1980 and Rutgers in 1983, Lasagna was the author of *The Doctors' Dilemmas* (1962), *Life, Death and the Doctor* (1968), and *Phenylpropanolamine: A Review* (1988); he also edited *Controversies in Therapeutics* (1980).

OBITUARIES AND OTHER SOURCES:

BOOKS

American Men and Women of Science, 21st edition, Gale (Detroit, MI), 2003.

PERIODICALS

Boston Globe, August 8, 2003, p. 80.
Chicago Tribune, August 12, 2003, section 1, p. 11.
Los Angeles Times, August 9, 2003, p. B20.
New York Times, August 11, 2003, p. A13.
Washington Post, August 10, 2003, p. C11.

ONLINE

Tufts e-News, http://enews.tufts.edu/ (August 8, 2003), "Visionary Researcher, Physician Mourned."

LaSALLE, Barbara

PERSONAL: Female; children: Ben. *Education:* Earned Ph.D.

ADDRESSES: *Agent*—Geri Thoma, Elaine Markson Literary Agency, 44 Greenwich Ave., New York, NY 10011. *E-mail*—barbara@aspergerjourney.com.

CAREER: Marriage and family therapist and documentary filmmaker. Former a kindergarten teacher. Lecturer and workshop leader; advocate for people with neurobiological disorders.

WRITINGS:

(With Benjamin Levinson) *Finding Ben: A Mother's Journey through the Maze of Asperger's,* Contemporary Books (Chicago, IL), 2003.

SIDELIGHTS: Barbara LaSalle wrote her memoir of raising her son Ben, who for years suffered from an undiagnosed illness. Ben was born in 1969 and could read and speak before he could walk. Gifted in some senses, his social abilities lagged behind due to his inability to handle changes in daily routines or loud noises, his lack of coordination, and his aversion to grooming. Ben also had many physical ailments, including Crohn's disease, asthma, crossed eyes, and obesity. LaSalle strove, often unsuccessfully, to find schools and friends who would accept her son and doctors who could pinpoint what ailed him. Ben bounced through many group homes and mental institutions, and even landed in jail. LaSalle was frustrated and found herself sometimes disgusted with her own child. In *Finding Ben* she is frank about her feelings of anger that her child was not "normal," and she confronts her own failure to deal with the situation.

Ben was diagnosed at age twenty-five with Asperger's syndrome, an autistic spectrum disorder. LaSalle and her son were relieved to have a diagnosis, and the book ends shortly after they achieve this success. Corey Seeman, writing for *Library Journal,* noted that "LaSalle does a good job of showing the thin line between gifted and disabled that exists with Asperger's children." A reviewer for *Kirkus Reviews* called the book "an introspective, honest account that may offer solace, if not hope, to other families coping with challenging children."

BIOGRAPHICAL AND CRITICAL SOURCES:

PERIODICALS

Booklist, April 1, 2003, Donna Chavez, review of *Finding Ben: A Mother's Journey through the Maze of Asperger's,* p. 1362.

Kirkus Reviews, February 1, 2003, review of *Finding Ben,* p. 210.

Library Journal, February 15, 2003, Corey Seeman, review of *Finding Ben,* p. 155.

ONLINE

Aspergerjourney.com, http://www.aspergerjourney.com/ (June 1, 2003), "Barbara LaSalle."*

* * *

LaSALLE, Mick

PERSONAL: Male. Born in Brooklyn, NY; married Amy Freed. *Education:* Rutgers University, B.A. (English); University of North Carolina, M.A.

ADDRESSES: Agent—c/o Authors Mail, St. Martin's Press, 175 Fifth Avenue, New York, NY 10001. *E-mail*—mlasalle@sfchronicle.com.

CAREER: Author and movie critic for *San Francisco Chronicle.*

WRITINGS:

Complicated Women: Sex and Power in Pre-Code Hollywood, St. Martin's Press (New York, NY), 2000.

Dangerous Men: Pre-Code Hollywood and the Birth of the Modern Man, St. Martin's Press (New York, NY), 2002.

SIDELIGHTS: Mick LaSalle is a movie critic who has written about a topic he knows well: men and women in the movies. His two books focus on what is called "pre-Code Hollywood," a five-year time period between 1929 and 1934 before Hollywood moguls instituted the Promotion Code. This code, which remained in effect until the 1960s, strictly regulated the movie industry and imposed very rigid rules about film content and characters.

Complicated Women: Sex and Power in Pre-Code Hollywood focuses on female actresses such as Greta Garbo and Jean Harlow. The book asserts that everyone paid a heavy price when the sexy, independent, and powerful women these actresses portrayed were effectively banned from the screen. As Wendy Smith of *Variety* noted, "LaSalle celebrates the serious social contribution that pre-Code films made by dramatizing changing female attitudes without ever losing sight of how much sheer joy was had in smashing all those tired Victorian conventions." LaSalle argues that this time period was the best era for women's films because the female characters were in charge of their lives. The heroines in pre-Code movies took lovers, had children out of wedlock, conducted affairs, and held professional jobs, all without apologizing. After the Code, the same actresses were forced to play submissive housewives who were forced to take their husbands back after their affairs. LaSalle also contends that the depiction of women was not the only casualty of the Code era. As Steve Kurtz observed in *Reason, Complicated Women* "demonstrates that there was something lost in Hollywood films for ove three decades. Not only were issues such as race relations almost never dealt with, but when Hollywood did attempt to take on something controversial, the storytelling was usually neutered and the result frustrating."

LaSalle's second book looks at the same time period, but concentrates on male actors. *Dangerous Men: Pre-Code Hollywood and the Birth of the Modern Man* features such actors as Clark Gable, James Cagney, and Rudolph Valentino, who were called "dangerous" because they portrayed characters who resisted authority and often displayed crude and caddish behavior, but were still respectable men. Prior to these pre-Code characters, men were portrayed as either evil criminals or heroes. A *Kirkus Reviews* writer noted that this book chronicles a period that "helped foster the very ideal of the modern man, caught between his own sense of right and an increasingly mechanized, conformist society." The book is filled with vignettes and analyses of many famous films from this era.

BIOGRAPHICAL AND CRITICAL SOURCES:

PERIODICALS

Booklist, September 15, 2000, Mike Tribby, review of *Complicated Women: Sex and Power in Pre-Code Hollywood,* p. 200.
Entertainment Weekly, September 29, 2000, review of *Complicated Women,* p. 126.
Kirkus Reviews, September 1, 2002, review of *Dangerous Men: Pre-Code Hollywood and the Birth of the Modern Man,* p. 1283.
Library Journal, August, 2000, Stephen Rees, review of *Complicated Women,* p. 107.
New York Times Book Review, October 8, 2000, Andy Webster, review of *Complicated Women,* p. 22.
Publishers Weekly, July 10, 2000, review of *Complicated Women,* p. 51.
Reason, March, 2002, Steve Kurtz, *Hollywood's Second Sex: Women and the Movies,* p. 75.
Variety, August 14, 2000, Wendy Smith, review of *Complicated Women,* p. 28.

ONLINE

BrightLightsFilm.com, http://www.brightlightsfilm.com/ (January 6, 2003), Gary Morris, review of *Complicated Women.*
Greenwich Village Gazette online, http://www.gvny.com/ (January 6, 2003), Ernest Barteldes, interview with LaSalle.
San Francisco Herald online, http://www.sfherald.com/ (January 6, 2003), Gene Mahoney, interview with LaSalle.

* * *

LATTERMAN, Terry A.

PERSONAL: Born in Utica, NY; married. *Education:* Attended McDowell Dress Designing and Illustrating School; graduate of Institute of Children's Literature and Hollywood Scriptwriting Institute. *Hobbies and other interests:* Reading, movies, gardening, growing flowers.

ADDRESSES: Home—Mesa, AZ. *Agent*—c/o Author Mail, Hampton Roads Publishing Co., 1125 Stoney Ridge Rd., Charlottesville, VA 22902. *E-mail*—tlatterman@earthlink.net.

CAREER: Utica Dispatch, Utica, NY, worked in advertising; ceramist and teacher of ceramics in California; writer and illustrator. Pussywillow Publishing House, Gilbert, AZ, publisher.

MEMBER: National League of American PEN Women, American Screenwriters Association.

WRITINGS:

(And illustrator) *Little Joe, a Hopi Indian Boy,* Pussywillow Publishing House (Gilbert, AZ), 1985.
(And illustrator) *The Watermelon Treat,* Pussywillow Publishing House (Gilbert, AZ), 1986.
(With Maya Perez) *Born with a Veil: The Life of a Spiritual Mystic,* Hampton Roads Publishing (Charlottesville, VA), 1991.
(With Maya Perez) *Using the Power of the Psalms as Your Daily Guide,* James C. Winston Publishing (Nashville, TN), 1996.

Illustrator of *The Little Tin Box* by Carolyn Anderson. Author of the screenplays *Dead or Alive, Where's Papa?, A Promise to Mama, The Caliph and the Gypsies, Mama's Wayward Helpers,* and *The Good Luck Moon.* Contributor to periodicals, including *Popular Ceramics.*

* * *

LAVIN, S(tuart) R. 1945-

PERSONAL: Born April 2, 1945, in Springfield, MA; son of Fredrick Lavin (a businessman) and Selma Laboritz; married Rosemary Dredge, January, 1978; children: David, Matthew, Raechel, Abigail, Hannah, Selma. *Ethnicity:* "Jew." *Education:* American International College, B.A. (literature), 1967; Trinity College (Hartford, CT) M.A. (literature), 1970. *Religion:* "Member of the Twelve Tribes." *Hobbies and other interests:* "Establishing an international brotherhood."

ADDRESSES: Home—41 North Union St., Cambridge, NY 12816. *Office*—Common Sense Farm, Cambridge, NY 12816. *E-mail*—srlavin@hotmail.com.

CAREER: Poet and educator. Castleton State College, Castleton, VT, professor, 1987-99.

MEMBER: Poets & Writers.

AWARDS, HONORS: Leonardo D'Vinci Award for Cultural Achievement (Florence Italy), 1977.

WRITINGS:

POETRY

Rothman's Secret Love Lament, introduction by Myles Considine, Yorick Books (Boston, MA), 1969.
The Stonecutters at War with the Cliff Dwellers: Nine Poems, illustrations by Bruce Chandler, Heron Press (Williamsburgh, MA), 1971.
Cambodian Spring: Nine Poems, Heron Press (Deerfield, MA), 1973.
Let Myself Shine, Kulchur Foundation (New York, NY), 1979.
"Outermost," Chinese Poetry International, 2000.

Also author of novel *Metacomet: The Saga of King Philip* (adaptation of *I and You* by M. Buber), and of two-act play *The Night the Mouse Roared.* Editor and publisher, *Jerusalem House.* Author of poems published in limited editions.

WORK IN PROGRESS: (With Dicky Cantrell) *The Words of a Man to a Man,* for Jerusalem House; *Abenacki Sunrise,* "a broadside," for Jerusalem House; *Abiding in the Vine,* "a look into the life of the Twelve-Tribes community."

SIDELIGHTS: S. R. Lavin told *CA:* "I write to expose injustice and cry for human compassion and justice; to be truth tellers, to expose lies and stimulate consciences."

* * *

LAWRENCE, David M(eade) 1961-

PERSONAL: Born November 12, 1961, in Westover, MA; son of George Marion (a journalist) and Kathleen Marie Lee (a secretary) Lawrence; married Alison M. Sinclair (an environmental planner), October 13, 1991; children: one son, one daughter. *Ethnicity:* "Mutt: European, Chinese, Mexican." *Education:* Louisiana State University, Shreveport, B.S. (cum laude; biology), 1983; University of Oklahoma, postgraduate studies in geography, 1983-85; attended Louisiana State University Medical Center, Shreveport, 1986-87; George Mason University, M.S. (geographic and cartographic sciences), 1991; Columbia University, M.S. (journalism), 1998; University of Virginia, enrolled in Ph.D. program (environmental sciences), 1991—. *Hobbies and other interests:* Dendochronology, ecology, geography, genealogy, history.

ADDRESSES: Home—7471 Brook Way Ct., Mechanicsville, VA 23111-1965. *Agent*—Heather Schroder, International Creative Management, Inc., 40 West 57th St., New York, NY 10019-4070. *E-mail*—dave@fuzzo.com.

CAREER: Author and journalist.

MEMBER: Authors Guild, Author's League, National Association of Science Writers, Association of American Geographers, Tree-Ring Society.

AWARDS, HONORS: Moore Award, Department of Environmental Sciences, University of Virginia, 1993; Southern Festival of Books Award, Fall for the Book Award, Boats, Books, and Brushes Award, Beneath the Sea Award, and Virginia Festival of the Book Award, all 2002, all for *Upheaval from the Abyss: Ocean Floor Mapping and the Earth Science Revolution.*

WRITINGS:

Upheaval from the Abyss: Ocean Floor Mapping and the Earth Science Revolution, Rutgers University Press (New Brunswick, NJ), 2002.

SIDELIGHTS: David M. Lawrence combined his interests in biology, geography, journalism, and environmental sciences to produce his 284-page book, *Upheaval from the Abyss: Ocean Floor Mapping and the Earth Science Revolution.* In addition to his academic studies, Lawrence also worked as a research assistant at the Lamont-Doherty Earth Observatory, which was the original home of the earth science revolution that overturned the prevailing scientific ideas about the nature of the creation, destruction, and rearrangement of the earth's surface. The researchers there put forth great effort to map the ocean floor and to prove the theory of plate tectonics.

Upheaval from the Abyss begins with a study of Alfred Wegener, the pioneer of the continental drift theory who published a paper in 1912 that demonstrates how fossils on both sides of the Atlantic Ocean are remarkably similar. After Wegener's death, his work was derided and nearly discarded until earth scientists began their revolutionary work in the late 1940s.

Lawrence writes about the lives of those scientists who continued Wegener's work, including Maurice "Doc" Ewing, Bruce Heezen, and Marie Tharp. In an interview with Lawrence for the *Rutgers University Press Web site,* the author described these three personalities in greater detail: Ewing, the founder of the Lamont Geological Observatory—which later became the Lamont-Doherty Earth Observatory—was the man whose large collection of data ultimately "clinched the scientific case for continental drift and plate tectonics"; Heezen was a promising geology graduate who accepted Ewing's offer to become a research assistant with "oceanic adventure instead of pay"; and Tharp, whose drafting skills were recognized by Ewing, devoted "forty years of her life [to] preparing maps of the world's ocean floor."

Amy Ione in *Leonardo Digital Reviews* considered Lawrence's book to be a "briskly paced . . . easy-to-read survey" of the decades-long struggle to comprehend the ocean floor. Lawrence "reminds the reader that the day-to-day experience of discovery includes much more than 'Eureka' moments," she added. Patrick Toscano wrote in *Professional Surveyor* that *Upheaval from the Abyss* "is a turbulent story, surprisingly rich with personalities and conflict." He concluded, "Read Lawrence's book as much for the adventure as the science." In a *Times Literary Supplement* review, Richard Shelton noted that "Lawrence presents his material crisply and directly as a series of adventure stories . . . and unfolds his scientific theme just as vividly and with all the rigour of the professional scientist." "This is a serviceable book covering the genesis of plate tectonics in a summary fashion," Bernard Coakley noted in his *American Scientist* article. However, he also called the book "somewhat romanticized." F. T. Manheim felt that Lawrence will enter the ranks of such esteemed science writers as Jared Diamond and Stephen J. Gould; in a *Choice* review he praised Lawrence for his "breadth of interest, critical eye for unexpected details, and contagious passion for his subjects."

Lawrence told *CA:* "Despite the scientific advances of the last few centuries, the universe remains mysterious. I cannot resist the urge to solve a mystery—thus, I was called into a scientific career early in my life. But answering questions for myself was not enough. I wanted to share my fascination with our improbable world, first as a teacher, and then as a journalist.

"I knew I wanted to be a scientist early on. The call to journalism came much later. As a teenager, I had grandiose dreams of becoming a 'famous' writer. But, despite displaying what family, friends, and teachers alleged to be signs of skill with the written word, I had no inclination toward doing the work necessary to realize the dreams.

"I did not plan to follow my father into a newsroom. I could never avoid one for long, however. Circumstances—and probably some latent desire—kept me surrounded by newsies, and following a career crisis in my early thirties I realized that I could combine science and journalism into a coherent and satisfying professional life.

"The fusion of my scientific and journalistic skills gave birth to my book, *Upheaval from the Abyss.* Although published by an academic press, the book is written as a classic narrative, combining a tale of scientific discovery with elements of mystery, adventure, and even love. The narrative, a true story, features heroes and a heroine as large, and often as flawed, as any character from classical mythology.

"My primary influences have been past teachers and mentors. Roosevelt 'Critter' Crosby inspired my fascination with science while I was a student at Oak Terrace Junior High School in Shreveport, Louisiana. Laurence Hardy, a professor of biology at Louisiana State University in Shreveport, taught me the discipline required of a scientist and also exposed me to the theories of continental drift and plate tectonics, the development of which I cover in *Upheaval from the Abyss.* Lonny Lippsett, a fellow science writer, helped me believe in myself during the crisis that led to the genesis of my career as a science writer. Finally, Sam Freedman of the Graduate School of Journalism at Columbia University in New York City ran me through his boot camp of a book-writing seminar. Without Sam, my adolescent dreams of writing a book might never have been realized.

"I am a visual writer—I have to see something to write about it. I think the visual approach is evident in *Upheaval from the Abyss,* as well as in some of my other writings. What I hoped to accomplish with the book is to tell the human side of the story, to put the reader in the field or at sea alongside the scientists whose lives I chronicle. Reason, hypotheses, and experiment are fine topics for study in themselves, but science—as I know from personal experience—is and always will be an endeavor carried out by flesh-and-blood beings."

BIOGRAPHICAL AND CRITICAL SOURCES:

PERIODICALS

American Scientist, July-August, 2002, Bernard Coakley, review of *Upheaval from the Abyss: Ocean Floor Mapping and the Earth Science Revolution,* pp. 385-87.

Choice, September, 2002, F. T. Manheim, review of *Upheaval from the Abyss,* p. 133.

Times Literary Supplement, August 2, 2002, Richard Shelton, review of *Upheaval from the Abyss,* pp. 5-7.

ONLINE

David M. Lawrence Home Page, http://fuzzo.com/ (April 2, 2003).

Leonardo Digital Reviews, http://mitpress2.mit.edu/e-journals/Leonardo/ (April 2, 2003), Amy Ione, review of *Upheaval from the Abyss.*

Professional Surveyor, http://www.profsurv.com/ (April 2, 2003), Patrick Toscano, review of *Upheaval from the Abyss.*

Rutgers University Press Web site, http://rutgerspress.rutgers.edu/ (April 2, 2003), interview with Lawrence.

* * *

LeBLANC, Adrian Nicole

PERSONAL: Female. *Education:* Smith College, B.A.; Oxford University, M.A. (philosophy and modern literature); Yale Law School, M.A. (law studies).

ADDRESSES: Home—New York, NY. *Agent*—c/o Author Mail, Simon & Schuster, 1230 Avenue of the Americas, New York, NY 10020.

CAREER: Freelance journalist. Visiting scholar, New York University School of Journalism.

AWARDS, HONORS: Knight Foundation fellow; Bunting Institute fellow; McDowell Colony residency, Richard J. Margolis award, 2000; Soros media fellowship, Open Society Institute, 2001; National Book Critics Circle nomination, 2003 for *Random Family: Love, Drugs, Trouble and Coming of Age in the Bronx.*

WRITINGS:

Random Family: Love, Drugs, Trouble, and Coming of Age in the Bronx, Simon & Schuster (New York, NY), 2003.

Contributor to *Village Voice, New Yorker, Elle, Spin, Source, Esquire,* and *New York Times Sunday Magazine.* Work has been anthologized in *The New Gilded Age: The New Yorker Looks at the Culture of Affluence,* 2000.

SIDELIGHTS: Journalist Adrian Nicole LeBlanc is the author of the book *Random Family: Love, Drugs, Trouble, and Coming of Age in the Bronx,* dubbed an "intergenerational tale of drug dealing, familial dysfunction and urban criminality" by *Washington Post* contributor John L. Jackson, Jr. Based on ten years of research LeBlanc undertook in following two young Latina residents of the Bronx, the book recounts the ups and many downs in the lives of Lourdes, Lourdes's sixteen-year-old daughter Jessica, and the many people whose lives they intersect from the late 1980s through the 1990s. Within three years Jessica becomes romantically involved with a heroin dealer named Boy George, while her younger brother Cesar makes equally unsavory friends by joining a local gang. Meanwhile, Lourdes's fourteen-year-old niece Coco becomes involved with Cesar and joins Jessica in an exciting lifestyle paid for by their boyfriend's criminal activities. Ultimately, both young women wind up on the street after their boyfriends wind up behind bars, and attempt to patch together lives from the dregs of society. In addition to being sexually molested and sent to prison, Coco has five children on the way to her twenties, two by Cesar and three by men she met while Coco was in prison.

Noting that *Random Family* "reads more like a carefully crafted novel than journalism," Jackson commented in his *Washington Post* review that, in presenting such a detailed picture of even the most minute events in the lives of Lourdes, Jessica, and others, LeBlanc succeeds in "powerful, even heart-wrenching storytelling." But, Jackson added, "it also mandates that she eschew any substantive discussion" of such social forces as poverty, market forces, and other inequalities "that provide important contextual clues for making sense of places like the South Bronx." Reflecting a similar view, Margaret Talbot praised LeBlanc in the *New York Times Book Review* for her "painstaking feat of reporting and empathy," but faulted the book for having "almost nothing to say about the larger world." *Random Family*'s "very dedication to portraying the multiplicity of hurdles," Talbot added, "the bewildering entanglement of personal failure and structural inequality that marks lives like Coco's, allows a kind of exhaustion to creep in." A *Publishers Weekly* critic found much to commend in *Random Family*, dubbing the book "extraordinary" and noting that, rather than present a broad-ranging social study LeBlanc allows readers "a rare look at the world [of the urban poor] from the subject's point of view." "LeBlanc's reporting illuminates the ugly, static reality of the street," Karen Valby added in her review for *Entertainment Weekly*. Calling the author "an unflappable narrator," Valby concluded by noting that in relating the downward spiral of the lives of Lourdes, Jessica, and Coco, the author "does an impressive job of keeping her sense of horror in check."

BIOGRAPHICAL AND CRITICAL SOURCES:

PERIODICALS

Austin Chronicle, March 14, 2003, Jordan Smith, review of *Random Family*.

Boston Globe, March 2, 2003, Dick Lehr, review of *Random Family*.

Commentary, May, 2003, Kay S. Hymowitz, review of *Random Family*, p. 73.

Entertainment Weekly, February 3. 2003, Karen Valby, "*Random Family* Startling Tale."

Kirkus Reviews, November 15, 2002, review of *Random Family*, p. 1677.

New York Times Book Review, February 9, 2003, Margaret Talbot, "In the Other Country," p. 12

Publishers Weekly, November 4, 2002, review of *Random Family*, p. 71.

Washington Post, February 12, 2003, John L. Jackson, Jr., "Numb with Pain," p. C8.

ONLINE

Atlantic Unbound, http://www.theatlantic.com/ (April 24, 2003), "Bronx Story," interview with LeBlanc.

BookPage.com, http://www.bookpage.com/ (April 3, 2003), Rebecca Denton, "A Story of Hard Luck and Hope."*

* * *

LEE, Sander H. 1951-

PERSONAL: Born January 30, 1951, in Dallas, TX; son of Herbert H. (in sales) and Marilyn (Harmelin) Lee; married Wendy Smith (a writer), July 22, 1984; children: Catherine Esther. *Education:* Georgetown University, Ph.D., 1978.

ADDRESSES: *Office*—Department of Philosophy, Keene State College, Keene, NH 03435-1402. *E-mail*—slee@keene.edu.

CAREER: Keene State College, Keene, NH, professor of philosophy, 1986—.

WRITINGS:

(Editor) *Inquiries into Values*, Edwin Mellen Press (Lewiston, NY), 1988.

Woody Allen's Angst, McFarland and Co. (Jefferson, NC), 1997.

Eighteen Woody Allen Films Analyzed, McFarland and Co. (Jefferson, NC), 2002.

WORK IN PROGRESS: Research on Graham Greene and Billy Wilder; research on the Holocaust.

* * *

LEEFELDT, Ed 1946-

PERSONAL: Born May 23, 1946, in Trenton, NJ; son of Ed and Dorothy Leefeldt; divorced; children: Kristin Leefeldt Melendez, Tim, Erik, Maren Leefeldt Kravitz. *Education:* Muhlenberg College, B.A., 1968; College of New Jersey, Ewing, M.Ed., 1970; attended

University of Texas at Austin, 1971, and University of Pennsylvania, 1999. *Hobbies and other interests:* Aviation, aeronautics, history, literature, running, biking, nature.

ADDRESSES: Home—96 Florence Lane, Manahawkin, NJ 08050. *Office*—Lighter than Air, P.O. Box 2362, Princeton, NJ 08543. *E-mail*—litenair@aol.com.

CAREER: Trentonian, Trenton, NJ, staff writer, 1971-81; *Wall Street Journal,* New York, NY, reporter, 1981-91; *Bloomberg,* New York, NY, staff writer. Barnes & Noble, leader of Writers' Exchange.

MEMBER: Toastmasters International, New York Press Club, New Jersey Foster Parents.

AWARDS, HONORS: National Institute of Mental Health fellow, 1971; New Jersey Bar Association, Media Award, 1979, for "Absolute Ballot Vote Fraud," and certificate of merit, 1981, for "In Search of the Paper Children"; New Jersey Press Association, citation for meritorious reporting, 1979, and Enterprise Award, 1980, for "Convicts Cheat Social Security"; Sigma Delta Chi Award, 1980, for journalistic excellence in features; National Endowment for the Humanities fellow, 1980; New Jersey Foster Parents Association award, 1981; Edna McConnell Clark Foundation grant, 1981-82; New York Press Club, Features Award, 1995, for "A Wall Street Detective Story," Investigative Journalism Award, 1996, for "Don't Take the Bait!"; National Press Association fellow, 1999.

WRITINGS:

In Search of the Paper Children, Center for Analysis of Public Issues, 1981.

Lighter than Air: A New Report on the Aeronautical Adventures Now Taking Place over Paris, (historical novel), privately printed (Princeton, NJ), 1990, published as *The Woman Who Rode the Wind,* Lighter than Air (Princeton, NJ), 2001.

Contributor to periodicals, including *New Jersey Reporter.*

SIDELIGHTS: Ed Leefeldt told *CA:* "Originally published as *Lighter than Air, The Woman Who Rode the Wind* was my first novel, and it's a total departure from the rest of my life, which has been spent in investigative journalism and finance. But finding 'the ten best ideas to get rich' or uncovering the latest financial scam ultimately seemed hollow to me. Millions of Americans now play with their stock portfolios every day, hoping to make even *more* money, but they forget that time is the most valuable currency of all. The real question is what you will do with your life, because that's your greatest asset.

"The idea for *Lighter than Air* came to me years ago while I was lying on the floor doing sit-ups and feeling depressed about my recent divorce. I couldn't even think of a reason to get up. Looking up, I saw a book on my shelf about a man who flew through the streets of Paris in 1901—the most beautiful time and the most beautiful city in the world. Suddenly all the music of that period began to flow through my head. It made me feel 'lighter than air,' and that was the genesis of my book. I hope the book does the same thing for the reader.

"*Lighter than Air* is a story about human potential, about rising above yourself, above everything you *think* you can do, to a higher level. Aristotle said there are three regions to the sky: the region of earth, which is closest to us; the region of water, which is cold and cloudy like the mountain peaks; and the region of fire, which is where he believed heaven would be. *Lighter than Air* is about rising to heaven . . . wherever your heaven is.

"There is also an element of hell in the book. We went through hell in the twentieth century: world wars and cold wars, holocaust and extermination. People in 1900 believed that inventions like airplanes would cure our ills and make us equals in the sky. That's one of the reasons they risked their lives—and many died—learning to fly. They called it 'the winged gospel.' Of course they were wrong. Look at all the destruction the airplane has caused. But it was the innocence of that era, the belief that things could be better if we just worked harder, that I wanted to capture. The Wright brothers, for example, tried to memorize the entire encyclopedia when they were boys. That's the spirit that existed at the turn of the twentieth century.

"I have a little of that same spirit myself. My goal in writing *Lighter than Air* was to be my own hero, to build my own flying machine and fly through the streets of a city like Paris, scattering roses on the people below. Sound crazy? All these things happened a hundred years ago, and could again. This vision is in the book."

* * *

LEFF, Julian P(aul) 1938-

PERSONAL: Born July 4, 1938, in London, England; son of Samuel (a doctor) and Vera Miriam (Levy) Leff; married Joan Lillian Raphael (a professor), January 31, 1975; children: Michael, Alex, Jessa, Jonty, Adriel. *Education:* University of London, B.Sc., 1958; M.D., 1972. *Hobbies and other interests:* Squash, swimming, croquet, chess, piano.

ADDRESSES: *Office*—Institute of Psychiatry, De Crespigny Park, London SE5 8AF, England.

CAREER: Maudsley Hospital, London, England, honorary consulting physician, 1973—; London School of Hygiene, honorary senior lecturer, 1974-89; MRC Social and Community Psychiatric Unit, London, assistant director, 1974-89, director, 1989-95; Institute of Psychiatry, London, clinical sub-dean, 1974-89, professor of social and cultural psychiatry, 1987—; Team for Assessment of Psychiatric Services, London, director, 1985—.

MEMBER: Royal College of Psychiatry (fellow), Public Health Medicine, Royal College of Physicians, National Schizophrenia Fellowship, SANE, Richmond Fellowship.

AWARDS, HONORS: Burgholzli Award, 1999, for outstanding contributions to psychiatry; Starkey Prize, Royal Society of Medicine.

WRITINGS:

(With Steven R. Hirsch) *Abnormalities in Parents of Schizophrenics: A Review of the Literature and an Investigation of Communication Defects and Deviances,* Oxford University Press (New York, NY), 1975.

Psychiatric Examination in Clinical Practice, Blackwell Scientific Publications (Oxford, England), 1978.

(With Christine Vaughn) *Expressed Emotion in Families,* Guilford Press (New York, NY), 1985.

Psychiatry around the Globe: A Transcultural View, Dekker (New York, NY), 1988.

Family Work for Schizophrenia, 1992.

(Editor, with D. Bhugra) *Principles of Social Psychiatry,* Blackwell Publishing (Oxford, England), 1993.

(Editor) *Care in the Community: Illusion or Reality?,* Wiley (Chichester, England), 1997.

The Unbalanced Mind, Columbia University Press (New York, NY), 2001.

Has also contributed more than 200 articles in his field to magazines and scholarly journals.

SIDELIGHTS: Julian P. Leff has spent his entire career in the field of medicine and psychiatry, and is highly respected in international professional circles for his research. Leff's *The Unbalanced Mind* challenges current thinking by suggesting that psychiatric disorders are determined not only by genetics, but also by social environment.

Psychiatrists through the ages have debated the roles of genetics and personal experience in the development of mental disorders. Freud claimed that although heredity predisposes some people to neuroses, it could not entirely account for all the symptoms his patients displayed. Today, many experts argue that advances in genetic research will prove that disorders such as schizophrenia and bipolar depression are attributed to DNA and the brain's biochemistry. Leff disagrees, and *The Unbalanced Mind* is his discussion and assessment of the nature of psychiatric disorders.

Decades of research led Leff to the conclusion that, in addition to genetics, mental imbalance is influenced by cultural, socioeconomic, and political factors. He argues that the severity of depression, anxiety and schizophrenia can be lessened by supportive, uncritical relationships with partners and friends. In the same vein, emotional relationships with family members influence the course of a number of psychiatric conditions. His research also suggests that early separation from parents is a possible contributor to schizophrenia.

The book paints a relatively hopeful picture for those individuals who suffer from disorders such as schizophrenia and depression by making treatment more accessible and all-inclusive. In addition to providing a clear picture on the how's and why's of diagnosis and treatment, Leff examines what is at the root of psychiatric disorders.

The Unbalanced Mind is Leff's first book to analyze the environmental factors of psychiatric disorders, but it is far from being his first book concerning psychiatry. In 1997 he edited *Care in the Community: Illusion or Reality?,* a compilation of professional essays based on an eleven-year study of the history of psychiatric care in the United Kingdom and the West. The study was implemented upon the closing of Friern and Claybury hospitals, two British mental-health facilities. Leff and his colleagues studied the resettlement of these patients, and *Care in the Community* addresses issues such as patient management and outcomes, staff training, and community attitudes. The book dispelled many myths concerning community care and offered essential guidelines for the ongoing development of community services.

Whereas *The Unbalanced Mind* examines the effect of environmental factors on psychiatric disorders, 1993's *Principles of Social Psychiatry,* which Leff co-edited with D. Bhugra, assesses the social consequences of mental imbalances. The book is another compilation of essays by psychiatric experts, all but one of them from the United Kingdom. *British Medical Journal* reviewer Hugh Freeman called it "a major contribution to the literature."

BIOGRAPHICAL AND CRITICAL SOURCES:

PERIODICALS

American Journal of Psychiatry, April, 1994, Saxby Pridmore, review of *Family Work for Schizophrenia: A Practical Guide, 2nd edition,* p. 613; February, 1995, Myrna M. Weissman, review of *Principles of Social Psychiatry,* p. 290.

American Scientist, November-December, 2002, Arthur Kleinman, review of *Care in the Community: Illusion or Reality?,* p. 569.

British Journal of Social Work, April, 1998, Glenys Jones, review of *Care in the Community,* pp. 295-297.

British Medical Journal, July 17, 1993, Hugh Freeman, review of *Principles of Social Psychiatry,* p. 211; August 2, 1997, Leila Lessof, review of *Care in the Community,* p. 319.

Community Care, October 16, 1997, Jill Manthorpe, review of *Care in the Community,* pp. 29-30.

International Journal of Social Psychiatry, summer, 1993, Jerome Carson, review of *Family Work for Schizophrenia,* p. 154.

Library Journal, November 15, 2001, E. James Lieberman, review of *The Unbalanced Mind,* p. 86.

Man, December, 1990, Roland Littlewood, review of *Psychiatry around the Globe: A Transcultural View,* pp. 720-721.

Publishers Weekly, October 1, 2001, review of *The Unbalanced Mind,* p. 47.

Times Literary Supplement, January 23, 1998, Melanie Phillips, review of *Care in the Community,* p. 9.

ONLINE

Columbia University Web site, http://www.columbia.edu/ (January 13, 2002), review of *The Unbalanced Mind.*

Medirect, http://www.medirect.com/ (April 10, 2002), review of *Principles of Social Psychiatry.*

Upstream, http://www.mugu.com/pipermail/upstream/ (August 24, 2001), Robert L. Gleiser, *Psychopathology: Environment Key to Understanding?**

* * *

LEGGETT, Paul 1946-

PERSONAL: Born July 3, 1946, in Newark, NJ; son of Joseph (an aerospace engineer) and Jane (a homemaker and Bible teacher) Leggett; married Anne Smith, January 13, 1973 (marriage ended December, 1979); married Beth Petrie (a secretary), November 28, 1981; children: Elisabeth, Gwendolyn, James. *Ethnicity:* "Caucasian." *Education:* Syracuse University, B.S. (cum laude), 1968; Princeton Theological Seminary, M.Div., 1971, Th.M., 1973; Union Theological Seminary, Ph.D., 1982. *Religion:* Presbyterian. *Hobbies and other interests:* Jogging, mysteries (Sherlock Holmes), football, comic books, movies.

ADDRESSES: Home—63 Tuxedo Rd., Montclair, NJ 07042. *Office*—Grace Presbyterian Church, 153 Grove St., Montclair, NJ 07042. *E-mail*—Fan44@aol.com.

CAREER: Pastor of church in Philadelphia, PA, 1971-73; missionary in Costa Rica, 1974-80; Grace Presbyterian Church, Montclair, NJ, pastor, 1981—.

MEMBER: Rotary Club (president), Montclair Clergy Association (president).

AWARDS, HONORS: Margot Studer Award, Montclair State University, 1984; Outstanding Service Award, Newark Presbytery, 1994.

WRITINGS:

Lectura teológica, Seminario Biblico, 1979.
Christianisma y cultura, [San José, Costa Rica], 1984.
Terence Fisher: Horror, Myth, and Religion, McFarland and Co. (Jefferson, NC), 2001.

Contributor to periodicals, including *Christianity Today* and *Focus on Film.*

WORK IN PROGRESS: Sherlock Holmes: The Modern Redeemer Hero.

* * *

LENORMAND, Henri-René 1882-1951

PERSONAL: Born 1882; died 1951; son of René Lenormand (a composer); married Marie Kalff (an actor), 1911.

CAREER: Playwright and author.

WRITINGS:

Les paysages d'ame (poems and prose), Stock (Paris, France), 1905.
La folie blanche (play), Stock (Paris, France), 1906.
Fear, translation by Jean d'Augzan, 1913.
Trois dramaes: Les possédés, Terres chaudes, Les ratés, Crès (Zurich, Switzerland), 1918, translated by Doris Libetta Orna as *Three Plays* (includes *The Dream Doctor, Man and His Phantoms,* and *The Coward),* Payson and Clarke (New York, NY), 1928.
Les temps est un songe, Éditions de Paris-magazine (Paris, France), 1919.
Le penseur et la cretine, Crès (Paris, France), 1920.
Theatre complete (collected plays), four volumes, Crès (Paris, France), 1921-1925.
Le simoun (play), Crès (Paris, France), 1921.
Les ratés (play), Crès (Paris, France), 1921.
Le mangeur de rêves (play), Crès (Paris, France), 1922.
Failures: A Play in Fourteen Scenes, translation by Winifred Katzin, Knopf (New York, NY), 1923.
Crépuscule de théâtre (play) L'Illustration (Paris, France), 1924.
La dent rouge, Crès (Paris, France), 1924.
Une vie secrète, Crès (Paris, France), 1924.
L'armée secrète, Nouvelle Revue Française (Paris, France), 1925.
L'homee et ses fantômes, Crès (Paris, France), 1925.
Images, Connaissance (Paris, France), 1925.
À l'ombre du mal, Crès (Paris, France), 1925.
La lâche (four-act play), L'Illustration (Paris, France), 1926.
A l'écart, suivi de Printemps marocain, Flammarion (Paris, France), 1926.
L'innocente (play), L'Illustration (Paris, France), 1928.
L'amour magicien, Crès (Paris, France), 1931.
Asie (three-act play), Librarie Théatrale (Paris, France), 1931.
Un poète au théâtre: Saint-Georges de Bouhélier, Fasquelle (Paris, France), 1935.
In Theatre Street, translation by Ashley Dukes, Samuel French (New York, NY), 1937.
Les Pitoëff: souvenirs, O. Lieutier (Paris, France), 1943.
Déserts, nouvelles exotiques, Albin Michel (Paris, France), 1944.
Les coeurs anxieux, L'Elan (Paris, France), 1947.
Les confessions d'un auteur dramatique, Albin Michel (Paris, France), 1949.
Une fille est une fille (fiction), Flammarion (Paris, France), 1949, translation published as *Renée,* Creative Age Press (New York, NY), 1951.
L'enfant des sables (fiction), La Couronne Littéraire (Paris, France), 1949.
Marguerite Jamois, Calmann-Levy (Paris, France), 1950.
Troubles (novel), Flammarion (Paris, France), 1951.
(With others) *Portrait dans un miroir,* Stock, Delamain et Boutelleau (Paris, France), 1952.
The Rising (novel), translation by Lothian Small, Thames and Hudson (New York, NY), 1952.

Also author of several plays produced in Europe, including *Le reveil de l'instinct* 1908; *Le minoun; Mixture,* 1927; *Le temps est un songe; Pacifique;* and *Terre de Satan.*

SIDELIGHTS: In *Nottingham French Studies* Robert Posen assessed the career and influence of French dramatist Henri-Rene Lenormand. Lenormand completed the bulk of his work between the two world wars; his *Theatre Complete,* which contains eighteen of his most important plays, covers the years 1919 through 1942. At the same time, Lenormand was an accomplished short-story writer and novelist. "He was also the author of memoirs of certain of his contemporaries," Posen wrote, adding that the dramatist's 1943 work *Les Pitoëff: souvenirs* "is a revealing study of the great actor-manager Georges Pitoëff and his wife, Ludmilla, and of their relationship with the author." As Posen related, Lenormand was the son of composer René Lenormand and grew up in an environment of creativity. In 1908 Lenormand produced a controversial play, *Le reveil de l'instinct,* which explores the theme of incest and is based on the true story of a French officer whose experiences Lenormand had heard about in 1904.

Lenormand's early career was interrupted by World War I; after serving in the army he moved with his wife to Switzerland in 1915 to recuperate from illness. Those early years saw Lenormand producing what Posen called his "finest plays," *Les ratés* and *Le simoun.* The plays were produced in Geneva, giving Lenormand much-needed exposure and his wife, Marie Kalff, a career as an actor. "It was, therefore, as a mature dramatist that Lenormand returned to Paris in 1919," the essayist said. Some dramatic elements from *Reveil de l'instinct* anticipate Lenormand's later plays, including *Mixture,* a 1927 work in which a woman is abandoned by her lover and tries to earn a living as a singer to avoid prostitution. "Then there are Willem's notions, which he express when attacking religion, about the freedom which should be enjoyed by the creative," said Posen. "This freedom, so often claimed for 'artists,' is the theme of a number of Lenormand's works in which the relationship between the artist and the rest of society is examined." The playwright's universe, added Posen, is often completed by the addition of "minor characters, such as native servants or a half-witted child." An element of terror also enters the picture, as a Grand Guignol-type sensibility pervades some of Lenormand's drama.

Les ratés is "a play about players," Posen continued. "Lenormand's life was one that was centered on the theatre, as was that of his wife. The piece reflects [the author's] experiences of the theatre to a certain extent and in particular his love-affair with his wife, for it recalls the hardships undergone by her when he knew her as a young actress." *Les ratés* depicts the struggles of young performers from the provincial tours to the atmosphere of failure and desperation as a theatre goes under for lack of financing. The principals are all forced to find other means of revenue; actress Elle turns to prostitution while her lover, Lui, finally kills himself in despair. Despite the grim themes, much of *Les ratés* is "witty and satirical," Posen wrote. "The troupe of actors is modeled on Lenormand's own acquaintances. There are particularly well-observed scenes in which the manger has to contend with the artistic pride of a 'second ghost' who feels he should be promoted to 'first ghost,' or of the old actor whose chance to shine has come in the ironical closing scene."

Posen pointed out that "in almost all of Lenormand's plays someone commits suicide, that there are no strong characters and that even the apparently strong are hesitant." Posen cited the lead character Nico of *Le temps est un songe* as an example. Nico's suicide is preceded by the attempts of others "to counteract his morbid preoccupation with the marshy pools around the old Dutch house in which the play is set." But the outsiders' efforts are to no avail; "If a hero in [Lenormand's] plays can make any firm decision," wrote Posen, "it is only to kill himself." The author "does not attempt to suggest that it is metaphysical doubt which causes Nico's death," the essayist continued, "but he does attempt to show that Nico's inability to communicate is due in large part to his upbringing in the East, where he has gained an outlook which differentiates him from his compatriots."

After the successful premieres of *Les ratés* and *Le temps est un songe,* Lenormand wrote more than a dozen further plays during the years preceding World War II. Their settings ranged from Africa to Norway; their themes included the familiar—theatrical life—and the controversial. *La lâche* belongs in the latter camp, dealing "sympathetically with a man's cowardice in his attempt to escape conscription," as Posen related. The essayist also cited a group of "colonial" plays during that period, including *À l'ombre du mal, Pacifique,* and *Terre de satan* "in which the oppressiveness of a locality is an important influence on the characters." In such pieces Lenormand's focus remained on the European coping in a foreign environment. Geared toward that perspective, Posen suggested, the playwright's depiction of the "natives" tended to be one-sided. "This is not to say that Lenormand has no sympathy for them," Posen added. Like his contemporary André Gide, the playwright "regarded colonialism as exploitation, although, typically his greatest sympathies are for the just administrators and the self-sacrificing missionaries."

Though he turned to short stories in the 1930s, Lenormand remains best known for his theatrical efforts. The first and foremost theme in the dramatist's overall work was Freudianism. The work and writings of Sigmund Freud had come entered the popular culture during the early decades of the twentieth century, and Leormand was convinced "that Freud had irrevocably altered Man's view of himself," Posen wrote. The play *Le mangeur de rêves* even "has Freudian psychology as an actual theme. The question of the extent to which Freud's works influence Lenormand has occupied critics of this theatre perhaps more than any other."

In *Literature and Psychology* Posen elaborated on the Freudian theme, saying that "in any discussion of Lenormand's debt to psychoanalytical thought *Le mangeur de rêves* has a special place. It is the play which, more than any other, established [the dramatist] as the exponent on the French stage of Freudian concepts . . . .Paradoxically, it is the work which contains what Lenormand called 'a bitter criticism of Freudian theories.'" The story's central character, Luc, is a Freudian psychoanalyst; when he describes his methods of analysis "we recognise in them a metaphoric approach to the problem of describing creativity," Posen said. But in his search for the truth, Luc is presented as something of a voyeur, which Posen said is expressed "in extreme Freudian terms."

Whether reading a Lenormand play or watching it performed, Posen reported, one "cannot fail to recognize . . . a writer steeped in the theory and methods of Freudian psychology." However, "he remains a dramatist who finds the idiom of Freudianism useful as a vehicle for many of his ideas." Posen concluded that the playwright's "use of the language of psychology can sometimes give a false impression of a belief that the mind is capable of rigorous analysis and that the dramatist need only reveal and explain scientifically the mysteries of the human soul." In Lenormand's best plays, he said, the dramatist "succeeded in fusing the most ancient and the most modern ideas."

BIOGRAPHICAL AND CRITICAL SOURCES:

PERIODICALS

Comparative Literature, summer, 1967, Angela Belli, "Lenormand's *Asie* and Anderson's *The Wingless Victory,*" pp. 226-239.

Literature and Psychology, issue 4, 1975, Robert Posen, "A Freudian in the French Theatre," pp. 137-146.

Nottingham French Studies, May, 1967, Robert Posen, "Aspects of the Work of Henri-René Lenormand, Part 1," pp. 30-44; May, 1968, Posen, "Aspects of the Work of Henri-René Lenormand, Part 2," pp. 25-38.*

* * *

LEVY, Shawn 1961-

PERSONAL: Born October 22, 1961, in New York, NY; son of Jerome Sanford and Agnes Madeline (Shand) Levy; married Mary Elizabeth Bartholemy, December 30, 1985; children: Vincent, Anthony. *Education:* University of Pennsylvania, B.A., 1982; University of California-Irvine, M.F.A., 1985, M.A. 1989.

ADDRESSES: *Office*—American Film Magazine, 6671 Sunset Blvd., Suite 1514, Hollywood, CA 90028.

CAREER: *Box Office Magazine,* Los Angeles, associate editor, 1989-90; *American Film Magazine,* Los Angeles, senior editor, 1990-?; *Oregonian* newspaper, Portland, film critic.

WRITINGS:

King of Comedy: The Life and Art of Jerry Lewis, St. Martin's Press (New York, NY), 1996.

Rat Pack Confidential: Frank, Dean, Sammy, Peter, Joey, and the Last Great Showbiz Party, Doubleday (New York, NY), 1998.

Ready, Steady, Go!: The Smashing Rise and Giddy Fall of Swinging London, Doubleday (New York, NY), 2002.

Contributor of numerous articles to magazines and newspapers, including *New York Times, Los Angeles times, Guardian* (Manchester, England), *Sight and Sound, Movieline,* and *Interview.*

SIDELIGHTS: Shawn Levy's first book, *King of Comedy: The Art and Life of Jerry Lewis,* has been hailed both as a "penetrating unauthorized biography" by a critic from *Publishers Weekly,* and as a "meticulously detailed and resolutely unflattering" book by Michael A. Lipton of *People.* Jerry Lewis was abandoned by parents who were busy pursuing their own stage career, and he was often ridiculed by his peers when he was a child. Despite his grim early life, Jerry won the hearts of theatre-goers with the goofy character he created to play against the straight-man role of partner Dean Martin. Lewis went on to star in such films as *The Nutty Professor, The Bellboy, Cinderfella,* and *The Patsy.* Later he used his fame to raise funds in annual telethons for muscular dystrophy.

Despite his professional success, however, Lewis gained notoriety as an abusive husband and father and as an obnoxious personality. These darker sides of the star's life, according to many critics, receive fair treatment in *King of Comedy.* "Levy doesn't settle for rehashing commonly accepted facts," wrote Michael Sragow in the *New York Times Book Review,* adding that the author "keeps his balance" and strives to be "scrupulously fair." *Time* writer Bruce Handy noted that "Levy certainly doesn't shy away from psychobiography" but found that he is "notably restrained in providing it." The book, Handy felt, "should deepen and fix the public conception of Lewis."

Levy's second book, *Rat Pack Confidential: Frank, Dean, Sammy, Peter, Joey, and the Last Great Showbiz Party,* also explores a Hollywood subject. The term "rat pack" was coined by actress Lauren Bacall when the group—Frank Sinatra, Dean Martin, Sammy Davis, Jr., Peter Lawford, and Joey Bishop—showed up for a benefit looking rather disreputable. Bacall reportedly stated that the men looked "like a goddamn rat pack," and the nickname was born. This group, which sometimes included the actress Shirley MacLaine, was very popular in the 1950s and early 1960s, especially in Las Vegas, where some of them performed regularly and purchased real estate.

A reviewer for *Publishers Weekly* described *Rat Pack Confidential* as "commercial biography served up cool and catchy," while a writer for *Economist* considered it an example of "invisible fly-on-the-wall journalism" that "does little but list name upon name." *Booklist* critic Gordon Flagg, however, observed that the book "provides . . . insight into the pack as a cultural force and into the fascination it continues to exert." And Keith Cannon in *Journal of American Culture* wrote that the book "provides a reference point for understanding how the Rat Pack sensibility is resurfacing in current youth culture."

British culture is the focus of Levy's third book, *Ready, Steady, Go!: The Smashing Rise and Giddy Fall of Swinging London.* This book provides "an intriguing look at pop culture," according to Mark Bay in *Library Journal.* In conducting research for the book, Levy spent time in London with a British editor who gave him a tour of what had become the ghosts of that culture. In an interview posted on the *Powell's Books Web site,* Levy wrote that this editor turned out to be "a rabid devotee of the '60s" who showed Levy "around the city not as it is but as it used to be." Everything from the music to the fashions of that era are covered in Levy's book; as a result, wrote a *Publishers Weekly* reviewer, "the book reads as if he'd lived the era himself."

BIOGRAPHICAL AND CRITICAL SOURCES:

PERIODICALS

Booklist, April 15, 1996, Gordon Flagg, review of *King of Comedy: The Life and Art of Jerry Lewis,* p. 1406; April 15, 1998, Gordon Flagg, review of *Rat Pack Confidential: Frank, Dean, Sammy, Peter, Joey, and the Last Great Showbiz Party,* p. 1410.

Economist, May 23, 1998, review of *Rat Pack Confidential,* p. 80.

Journal of American Culture, winter, 1998, Keith Cannon, review of *Rat Pack Confidential,* pp. 93-95.

Kirkus Reviews, May 15, 2002, review of *Ready, Steady, Go!: The Smashing Rise and Giddy Fall of Swinging London,* p. 718.

Library Journal, June 1, 1998, Michael Colby, review of *Rat Pack Confidential,* pp. 110-111; July 2002, Mark Bay, review of *Ready, Steady, Go!,* p. 106.

New York Times, July 23, 2002, Michiko Kakutani, "Hipoisie and Chic-oisie and London Had the Mojo," review of *Ready, Steady, Go!,* p. E7.

New York Times Book Review, June 9, 1996, Michael Sragow, review of *King of Comedy,* p. 26.

People, June 10, 1996, Michael A. Lipton, review of *King of Comedy,* p. 35.

Publishers Weekly, March 23, 1998, review of *Rat Pack Confidential,* p. 87; June 3, 2002, review of *Ready, Steady, Go!,* p. 78.

Time, July 29, 1996, Bruce Handy, review of *King of Comedy,* pp. 80-81.

ONLINE

Powell's Books Web site, http://www.powells.com/ (April 21, 2003), Shawn Levy, "What's a Nice Yank Like You Doing Writing about Us Lot?; or, How I Came to Write *Ready, Steady, Go!*"*

* * *

LINDSTROM, Matthew J. 1969-

PERSONAL: Born August 28, 1969, in Willmar, MN; son of John S. (a state court judge) and Mary D. (a director of a women's shelter) Lindstrom; married Amy E. Braig (an artist), July 9, 1993; children: Isaac, Anna. *Ethnicity:* "White." *Education:* St. John's University (Collegeville, MN), B.A. (cum laude), 1992; Northern Arizona University, Ph.D. (with distinction), 1997. *Politics:* Green Party. *Hobbies and other interests:* Music, cooking, farmers' markets.

ADDRESSES: Home—68 Old Loudon Rd., Latham, NY 12110. *Office*—Department of Political Science, Siena College, 515 Loudon Rd., Loudonville, NY 12211; fax: 518-782-6548. *E-mail*—mlindstrom@siena.edu.

CAREER: Northern Arizona University, Flagstaff, instructor in political science, 1996-97; Siena College, Loudonville, NY, assistant professor of political science, 1997—, member of peace studies executive committee, 1998—, and environmental studies executive committee, 2000—, founder and director of Siena Program for Sustainable Land Use, 2001—. Hofstra University, guest speaker, 2001; Pace University, chair of panel on ecology, culture, and politics in land use planning, 2002; public lecturer, including appearances on television and radio programs. Regional Farm and Food Project, member of board of directors, 1998-2000; Honest Weight Food Cooperative, member, 1998—; Troy Waterfront Farmers' Market Association, cofounder and president of board of directors, 2000—; consultant to Turning Tide Productions (film production company).

MEMBER: American Political Science Association, Peace Studies Association, Justice Studies Association, Urban Affairs Association, Consortium for Peace Research, Education, and Development, Western Political Science Association.

AWARDS, HONORS: Grant from Arizona Department of Transportation, 1996-97; shared Volunteer of the Year Award, Regional Farm and Food Project, 2000; Best Paper Award, Undergraduate Division, American Political Science Association, 2002.

WRITINGS:

(With Zachary A. Smith) *The National Environmental Policy Act: Judicial Misconstruction, Legislative Indifference, and Executive Neglect,* Texas A & M University Press (College Station, TX), 2002.

(Editor, with Hugh Barling) *Surveying Sprawl: Culture, Ecology, and Politics,* Rowman & Littlefield, in press.

Contributor to books, including *Public Policy and Politics in Arizona,* 2nd edition, edited by Zachary A. Smith, Praeger Publishers (Westport, CT), 1996; *Environmental Policy: Cases in Managerial Role-Playing,* edited by Robert P. Watson, Dwight Conrad Kiel, and Steven Robar, Island Press (Covelo, CA), 2002; and *Redefining Suburban Studies: Searching for a New Paradigm,* edited by Daniel Rubey and Barbara Kelly, Greenwood Press (Westport, CT), 2002. Contributor of articles and reviews to periodicals, including *Alternative Perspectives.*

SIDELIGHTS: Matthew J. Lindstrom told *CA:* "Writing allows me to express my passion and conviction about various social and environmental issues. As a professor, I see writing as a natural extension of the classroom. Writing forces me to organize my thoughts and find the best ways of communicating an idea or interpretation—two skills also necessary for effective teaching. Knowing that one's writing is never perfectly finished or ever truly finished, I am constantly rethinking and reworking my pieces. As I write, I learn more about both the art and craft of writing, or, in a sense, the creative and scientific elements of writing.

"The bulk of my writing concerns environmental policies and issues primarily, but not exclusively, in the United States. I am currently working on land use planning issues related to the ever-increasing problem of suburban sprawl and the ensuing waste and inefficiencies. Fortunately, there are a great number of solutions to the multi-faceted issue of sprawl, and these will be explored in my forthcoming publications as well.

"Low-density, auto-dependent, generic development known as sprawl usually occurs on the fringe of metropolitan areas but affects everyone on the planet. Sprawl impacts so many different elements of everyone's lives, rich or poor, urban or rural, that the consequences of addressing some of the root causes are extremely beneficial. Concerns about the 'livability' of many neighborhoods and communities are sweeping across the country. I am excited to see and participate in efforts to counter the forces that propel sprawl. Adopting ecologically sustainable and family-friendly alternatives to sprawl will benefit the vast majority of people while only hurting a small but disproportionately influential group of people."

BIOGRAPHICAL AND CRITICAL SOURCES:

ONLINE

Matt Lindstrom Web site, http://www.siena.edu/lindstrom/ (February 11, 2003).

* * *

LIPINSKI, Tomas A.

PERSONAL: Male. *Education:* University of Wisconsin—Milwaukee, B.A., 1981, M.L.I.S., 1990; Marquette University, J.D., 1984; John Marshal Law School, LL.M., 1986; University of Illinois—Urbana-Champaign, Ph.D., 1998.

ADDRESSES: Office—Center for Information Policy Research, School of Information Studies, University of Wisconsin—Milwaukee, Milwaukee, WI 53202.

CAREER: Attorney at law, 1981-90; Syracuse University, Syracuse, NY, associate librarian and associate director of H. Douglas Barclay Law Library, 1990-92, adjunct professor of law, 1992; Milwaukee Public Library, Milwaukee, WI, librarian, 1992-94; University of Wisconsin—Milwaukee, adjunct instructor, 1994-98, assistant professor of information studies and codirector of Center for Information Policy Research, 1998—. American Institute for Paralegal Studies, instructor, 1989-93; University of Illinois—Urbana-Champaign, instructor, 1997, visiting assistant professor, 1998—; University of Pretoria, visiting professor, 1999—; Free University of Brussels, guest lecturer, 2000; guest speaker at Wisconsin Indianhead Technical College and Northeast Wisconsin Technical College; presenter at conferences in the United States and abroad; testifies as expert witness on copyright issues related to distance learning; guest on media programs. West Group, member of library school educators advisory board, 2000-02; consultant to Cooperative Educational Service Agency.

MEMBER: American Society for Information Science (president of Wisconsin chapter, 2000—), American Association of Law Librarians, American Society for Information Science and Technology, Education Law Association, Thomas More Lawyers Society, Institute of Electrical and Electronics Engineers (affiliate member), Wisconsin State Bar Association, Phi Alpha Theta, Beta Phi Mu.

WRITINGS:

(Editor and contributor) *Libraries, Museums, and Archives: Legal Issues and Challenges in the New Information Era,* Scarecrow Press (Lanham, MD), 2002.

(With Mary Minnow) *The Library's Legal Answer Book,* American Library Association, 2002.

Contributor to books, including *Information and Ethics in the Twenty-first Century,* edited by Lester J. Pourciau, 1999; *Web-based Communications, the Internet, and Distance Education,* edited by Michael G. Moore and Geoffrey T. Cozine, 2000; *Handbook of*

American Distance Education, edited by Michael G. Moore, Pennsylvania State University Press (University Park, PA), 2002; and *Readings in Virtual Research Ethics: Issues and Controversies,* edited by Elizabeth Buchanan, 2003. Editor of the book series "Working within the Information Infrastructure: Legal Rights and Responsibilities in the New Information Era," for Scarecrow Press (Lanham, MD). Contributor to periodicals, including *American Journal of Distance Education, Education Law into Practice, Ethics and Information Technology, Journal of Business Ethics, Libri, Richmond Journal of Law and Technology, Informing Science, Education Law Reporter, Brigham Young University Education and Law Review,* and *IEEE Technology and Society.* Guest coeditor, *Journal of Information Ethics,* 2000; contributing editor, *Technicalities,* 2000.

WORK IN PROGRESS: Copyright Issues in Distance Education, for Scarecrow Press (Lanham, MD); *Handbook of Legal Issues in Public and School Libraries,* Neal-Schuman Publishers.

* * *

LIVIO, Mario 1945-

PERSONAL: Born 1945, in Romania; married, wife's name Sofie; children: Sharon, Oren, Maya. *Education:* Hebrew University, Jerusalem, B.A. (physics and mathematics); Weizmann Institute, M.Sc. (theoretical particle physics); Tel Aviv University, Ph.D. (theoretical astrophysics). *Hobbies and other interests:* Art.

ADDRESSES: Office—3700 San Martin Drive, Space Telescope Science Institute, Baltimore, MD 21218. *E-mail*—mlivio@stsci.edu.

CAREER: Technion-Israel Institute of Technology, professor of physics, 1981-91; Space Telescope Science Institute, member of staff, 1991—, head of science division, 2000-03. *Military service:* Israel Army and military reserve service, paramedic.

AWARDS, HONORS: Carl K. Seyefert Lecturer in Astronomy, 2000; Paul H. Nitze fellow, 2001; Carnegie Centenary professorship, 2002.

WRITINGS:

(With Steven N. Shore and E. P. J. den Heuvel) *Interacting Binaries,* edited by H. Nussbaumer and A. Orr, Springer-Verlag (New York, NY), 1994.

(Editor, with Daniela Calzetti and Piero Madau) *Extragalactic Background Radiation,* Cambridge University Press (New York, NY), 1995.

(Editor, with Megan Donahue and Nino Panagia) *The Extragalactic Distance Scale,* Cambridge University Press (New York, NY), 1997.

The Accelerating Universe: Infinite Expansion, the Cosmological Constant, and the Beauty of the Cosmos, Wiley (New York, NY), 2000.

(Editor) *Unsolved Problems in Stellar Evolution,* Cambridge University Press (New York, NY), 2000.

(Editor, with Nino Panagia and Kailash Sahu) *Supernovae and Gamma-Ray Bursts: The Greatest Explosions since the Big Bang,* Cambridge University Press (New York, NY), 2001.

The Golden Ratio: The Story of Phi, the World's Most Astonishing Number, Broadway Books (New York, NY), 2002.

SIDELIGHTS: Mario Livio was born in Romania and for the first five years of his life was raised by his grandparents. His parents were forced to flee their homeland due to political pressures. In 1950, as pressure mounted on the Romanian Jewish community, Livio immigrated to Israel. He attended school there, where he eventually earned his doctorate in theoretical astrophysics. He served as a paramedic during three wars: the Six-Day War in 1967, the Yom Kippur War in 1973, and the war in Lebanon in 1982. Despite the tension of all these events, or maybe because of it, he fell in love with astrophysics, a subject he taught at the Technion-Israel Institute of Technology for ten years.

On the *Space Telescope Science Institute Web site,* where he has been the head of the Science Division, Livio wrote: "A love for astrophysics somehow emerged and persisted, with a special interest in the accretion of mass by black holes, neutron stars, and white dwarfs." He also stated that he has a more particular interest in "supernova explosions and their use in cosmology to determine the rate of expansion of the Universe, on the formation of black holes and the possibility to extract energy from them, on the formation of planets in disks around young stars, and on the emergence of intelligent life in the Universe." Livio also mentions his love of art, which is beautifully expressed through his books.

One such book is 2000's *The Accelerating Universe: Infinite Expansion, the Cosmological Constant, and the Beauty of the Cosmos.* Livio describes this book as a combination of "his passions for science and art." As reviewer James Trefil for the *Washington Post Book World* noted: "This book starts out with a very interesting proposition: that the understanding of science can be judged on aesthetic as well as practical grounds." This fact, wrote Trefil, is nothing new to the scientific world, where scientists are often "susceptible to beauty and elegance." However, the general public, to whom Livio's book is addressed, may be surprised to learn that scientists, as Trefil stated, are not always the "hardheaded rationalists" most people assume.

Trefil praised the manner in which Livio is able to "cleverly" mingle art and science, such as comparing the analysis of a work of man-made art—like a long-appreciated Renaissance painting—with the process of study of an object that astronomers are considering and trying to understand. However, in conclusion, Trefil also found that the beauty of astrological objects, as the beauty in any work of art made by human hands, is often found "in the eye of the beholder." Beauty, in other words, is elusive and subjective, in the world at hand and in space.

Apart from the discussion of beauty in the cosmos is the book's focus on the so-called New Cosmology that states that the universe, in contrast to what astronomers used to believe, is in fact not slowing down but is actually accelerating. "Something," wrote a *Publishers Weekly* reviewer, "is counteracting gravity." This action will, billions of years from now, make the universe an "even vaster, emptier realm, filled with stars and galaxies flickering out one by one until there is only darkness." Livio looks at both the old theories and the new ones and evaluates them on many different levels. While the *Publishers Weekly* reviewer did not appreciate the beginning chapters in which Livio compared the study of astronomy to the study of art as much as the reviewer Trefil did but did fully enjoy Livio's "elegant" explanations of some of astronomy's most difficult concepts, which Livio has written in a very understandable language. Although the words he chooses are cleansed of scientific jargon, the ideas he attempts to make sense of are extremely complex. For example, Bryce Christensen, in *Booklist* pointed out that Livio grapples with the question of whether the universe is indeed an orderly cosmos or chaotic. "Livio probes these questions," wrote Christensen, "with daring sufficient to satisfy the hungriest curiosity."

In 2002 Livio produced another book, *The Golden Ratio: The Story of Phi, the World's Most Astonishing Number.* A *Kirkus Reviews* writer pointed out that Phi, a lesser cousin of Pi, is a "never-ending, never-repeating, irrational, incommensurable, one of those special numbers like pi that confound and delight in the same breath." Livio's interest in this number is to find how often it occurs in nature. He looks at everything from petal and leaf arrangements to seashells to find this mysterious number. It is also duplicated in galaxies of stars and in the arrangement of seeds in a sunflower. To better understand this number, Livio studies its complete history in math and science. He writes about the efforts of architect le Corbusier, who used it in his work, as did artists Salvador Dali and Albrecht Dürer. Livio's efforts, as reported by the *Kirkus* reviewer is "a shining example of the aesthetics of mathematics." Tara Pepper, of *Newsweek International,* wrote that Livio's book is filled with quotes from Shakespeare and Keats, Galileo and Einstein. "In the process," the critic added, Livio "succeeds in the unlikely task of bringing a number to life."

BIOGRAPHICAL AND CRITICAL SOURCES:

PERIODICALS

Booklist, March 1, 2000, Bryce Christensen, review of *The Accelerating Universe: Infinite Expansion, the Cosmological Constant, and the Beauty of the Cosmos,* p. 1182; October 15, 2002, Gilbert Taylor, review of *The Golden Ratio: The Story of Phi, the World's Most Astonishing Number,* p. 369.

Kirkus Reviews, September 1, 2002, review of *The Golden Ratio,* pp. 1284-1285.

Library Journal, March 1, 2000, Nancy Curtis, review of *The Accelerating Universe,* p. 122.

Newsweek International, January 20, 2003, Tara Pepper, review of *The Golden Ratio,* p. 47.

Publishers Weekly, March 6, 2000, review of *The Accelerating Universe,* p. 95; September 16, 2002, review of *The Golden Ratio,* p. 62.

Science News, November 30, 2002, review of *The Golden Ratio,* p. 351.

Washington Post Book World, July 23, 2000, James Trefil, review of *The Accelerating Universe,* p. 13.

ONLINE

Space Telescope Science Institute Web site, http://www-int.stsci.edu/ (January 6, 2003), "Dr. Mario Livio."

* * *

LOIZEAUX, Elizabeth Bergmann 1950-

PERSONAL: Born December 16, 1950, in Mineola, NY; married, 1982. *Education:* Mt. Holyoke College, B.A., 1972; University of Michigan, Ann Arbor, M.A., 1974, Ph.D. (English), 1980.

ADDRESSES: *Home*—51 Walnut Ave., Takoma Park, MD 20912. *Office*—University of Maryland, Department of English, 3101 Susquehanna Hall, College Park, MD 20742. *E-mail*—eL18@umail.umd.edu.

CAREER: University of Maryland, College Park, assistant professor, then associate professor of English, 1980—, director of English undergraduate studies, 1990-95. University of Sheffield, Sheffield, England, visiting professor, 1985-86; teacher at Yeats International Summer School, 1996, 1998, and Tübingen University (Germany), 2002.

MEMBER: Modern Language Association, South Atlantic Modern Language Association, Modernist Studies Association, Society for Textual Scholarship, International Association of Word and Image Studies.

AWARDS, HONORS: National Endowment for the Humanities summer stipend, 1982; Lilly/CTE fellow, 1995-96.

WRITINGS:

Yeats and the Visual Arts, Rutgers University Press (New Brunswick, NJ), 1986.

(Editor, with Neil Fraistat) *Reimagining Textuality: Textual Studies in the Late Age of Print,* University of Wisconsin Press (Madison, WI), 2002.

Contributor of articles to journals, including *Yeats: An Annual of Critical and Textual Studies, Word & Image,* and *Review.*

SIDELIGHTS: English professor and William Butler Yeats scholar Elizabeth Bergmann Loizeaux is the author of *Yeats in the Visual Arts* and is coeditor of *Reimagining Textuality: Textual Studies in the Late Age of Print.*

Yeats in the Visual Arts is an in-depth study of the way pre-Raphaelite painting, William Morris's tapestry, William Blake's woodcuts, theatrical design, Byzantine art, and Renaissance sculpture influenced Yeats's poetry as he moved through various stages in his work. Stephen Gurney, in *Modern Age,* explained, "Throughout his life Yeats consciously or unconsciously expressed his sense of technical and thematic affinity with the tapestry makers, artists, and workers in wood, metal, bronze, or marble who engrossed his imagination. . . . For Yeats repetition of line and form in the visual arts was analogous to the patterning of rhythm and sound in poetry." Gurney called Loizeaux's book "readable and always engaging." He wrote, "Her thesis is a sound one and surprisingly not fully explored until the appearance of this handsome and visually sumptuous volume." Gurney concluded that Loizeaux's book "goes further in both detail and depth" than any other on the subject. "Her understanding of the ways in which Yeats altered his technique to give his verse the kind of tactile, physical presence that we associate with sculpture is especially intelligent in its sensitivity to verbal effects and poetic strategies."

However, Terence Diggory, writing in *Yeats,* found the final chapter on sculpture unconvincing because it changes methodology. Whereas Loizeaux's first argument—that Yeats was guided throughout his life by pre-Raphaelite principles which he reinterpreted over time—is pursued historically, her second—that sculpture replaced painting as Yeats's primary analogy for his poetry—is pursued theoretically. "Her speculations are provocative," Diggory claimed, "But to grow beyond the status of speculation, they need more support from the scholarship on these topics." Nevertheless, he concluded, "In some ways it is the most promising [chapter] in the directions it points for future research."

E. F. Harden, in *Choice,* viewed the book as Gurney did, as "the most closely argued study" on the subject to date. Harden was pleased by Loizeaux's use of many of Yeats's major poems to develop her thesis. Michael Hennessy, in *Library Journal,* likewise found that Loizeaux "ably demonstrates" the influence of the visual arts on Yeats's work.

Reimagining Textuality is a collection of nine essays; it is divided into three sections, with a response at the end of each section. The essayists, most from university English departments, specialize in cultural studies, textual editing, and verbal-visual studies. They write about technology and its impact on the production of texts; integrating visual elements into text; and the relationships between the spoken and written word, including the element of audience. Jennifer Burek Pierce, in a review for *American Communication Journal,* wrote that the book "suggests a conversation about the nature of text and textual studies in the contemporary information environment. This conversation, though, is a free-flowing one, and in the end, the authors do not find themselves on the same page. Rather, their views are divergent in tone, style, content, and conclusion. . . . Many of these essays are, as the book's title suggests, speculative and creative." Claire MacDonald, in the *Times Literary Supplement,* commented that Loizeaux and Fraistat "argue that technologies do not merely replace one another; instead, they shift in their relationship, and sometimes the crossroads opens to new pasts as well as new futures."

BIOGRAPHICAL AND CRITICAL SOURCES:

PERIODICALS

Choice, May, 1987, E. F. Harden, review of *Yeats and the Visual Arts,* p. 1398.

Library Journal, January, 1987, Michael Hennessy, review of *Yeats and the Visual Arts,* pp. 89-90.

Modern Age, winter, 1988, Stephen Gurney, review of *Yeats and the Visual Arts,,* pp. 81-87.

Times Literary Supplement, August 2, 2002, Claire MacDonald, review of *Reimagining Textuality: Textual Studies in the Late Age of Print,,* p. 22.

Victorian Studies, summer, 1988, Bruce Gardiner, review of *Yeats and the Visual Arts,* pp. 612-614.

Yeats (annual), 1987, Terence Diggory, review of *Yeats and the Visual Arts,* pp. 246-252.

ONLINE

American Communication Journal, http://acjournal.org/ (spring, 2002), Jennifer Burek Pierce, review of *Reimagining Textuality: Textual Studies in the Late Age of Print.*

University of Wisconsin Press Web site, http://www.wisc.edu/ (April 3, 2003).

* * *

LONG, Goldberry 1967(?)-

PERSONAL: Born c. 1967, in NM. *Education:* Attended Iowa Writers Workshop.

ADDRESSES: *Home*—East Palo Alto, CA. *Agent*—c/o Author Mail, Simon & Schuster, 1230 Avenue of the Americas, New York, NY 10020.

CAREER: Writer. Night school teacher.

AWARDS, HONORS: Glimmer Train Press Very Short Fiction Award, second place, 1998, for "Heaven"; Wallace Stegner fellowship, Stanford University; James Michener fellowship; Hackney Literary Award for the Novel, 2001, for *Juniper Tree Burning.*

WRITINGS:

Juniper Tree Burning, Simon & Schuster (New York, NY), 2001.

Contributor of short stories to periodicals.

SIDELIGHTS: A graduate of the Iowa Writers' Workshop who now lives in California, Goldberry Long published her debut novel in 2001 to generally warm acclaim. *Juniper Tree Burning* is composed of stories within stories: of relationships, communities and names. The book is a 460-page journey through the life of protagonist Jennie Braverman, born Juniper Tree Burning to hippie parents in the 1970s.

Juniper/Jennie and her younger brother, Sunny Boy Blue, spent their childhoods in the desert of New Mexico in an adobe stable with no running water.

They were dressed in used clothes and never visited doctors, but instead were "healed" with their parents' versions of Native American ceremonies. To say these children were neglected is optimistic; they were the forgotten offspring of distracted parents.

The bulk of the novel focuses on a grown-up Jennie, now married and a medical student, and how she handles her beloved brother's suicide. The reader is allowed glimpses into Jennie's past in the form of memories and recollections told from her viewpoint. What emerges is the narrative of a journey through emotional abuse and the personal victories and failures of the victims. While noting that the book contains "so much," indeed, "too much, if you haven't got the patience," Emily Baillargeon Russin wrote in *Seattle Weekly* online that "it's a rare thing for a book to feel this genuinely whole despite its many themes and variations, for language to be so breathtaking it hits all the truest emotional pitches."

Despite the novel's weighty subject, critics generally agreed that Long's treatment is realistic, and *Chatelaine* reviewer Bonnie Schiedel praised the author's "dark sense of humour." "Entertaining but unflinching, *Burning* is . . . an unsentimental song of grief and forgiveness," wrote Michelle Vellucci in *People.* Janet Maslin in the *New York Times* wrote that, "What matters most about Jennie and makes Ms. Long's debut a powerful one is the sheer brazenness and gusto with which Jennie is brought to life on the page."

BIOGRAPHICAL AND CRITICAL SOURCES:

PERIODICALS

Book, July, 2001, review of *Juniper Tree Burning,* p. 13.

Booklist, May 15, 2001, Nancy Pearl, review of *Juniper Tree Burning,* p. 1732.

Chatelaine, August, 2001, Bonnie Schiedel, review of *Juniper Tree Burning,* p. 12.

Library Journal, May 15, 2001, Susan A. Zappia, review of *Juniper Tree Burning,* p. 164.

Los Angeles Times, July 29, 2001, Mark Rozzo, review of *Juniper Tree Burning,* p. 10.

New York Times, June 18, 2001, Janet Maslin, "A Strange Name and Other Burdens," review of *Juniper Tree Burning,* p. 8.

New York Times Book Review, August 5, 2001, Louisa Kamps, review of *Juniper Tree Burning,* p. 23.

People, July 16, 2001, Michelle Vellucci, review of *Juniper Tree Burning,* p. 39.

Publishers Weekly, May 28, 2001, review of *Juniper Tree Burning,* p. 49.

Washington Post Book World, June 24, 2001, "Where Have All the Flowers Gone?," p. T07.

ONLINE

Seattle Weekly online, http://www.seattleweekly.com/ (January 13, 2002), Emily Baillargeon Russin, review of *Juniper Tree Burning.*

SFGate, http://www.sfgate.com/ (July 7, 2001), Megan Harlan, "What's in a Name? Hers Says a Lot: Child of Hippies Struggles to Escape."

Simon & Schuster UK Web site, http://www.simonsays.com/ (January 13, 2002).

The Stranger.com, http://www.thestranger.com/ (March 6, 2002), review of *Juniper Tree Burning.**

* * *

LUCAS, James (Sidney) 1923-2002

PERSONAL: Born 1923; died of prostate cancer June 19, 2002; married 1946; wife's name Edeltraude; children: Barbara. *Hobbies and other interests:* Gourmet cooking.

CAREER: Author and historian. Imperial War Museum, London, England, deputy head of department of photographs. *Military service:* Queen's Own Royal West Kent Regiment, First Battalion, North Africa, infantryman, 1942; Queens' Own Royal West Surrey Regiment, Italy, 1943-44; Occupation Army, Austria, 1945; Foreign Office, Germany.

AWARDS, HONORS: Radetzky Orden der Verdienstklasse Ehrenkreuz (Austria), 1996, in recognition of his work on behalf of Austrian war veterans.

WRITINGS:

Austro-Hungarian Infantry, Almark Publishing (London, England), 1973.

Hitler's Elite: Leibstandarte SS, 1933-45, MacDonald and Jane's (London, England), 1975.

(With Matthew Cooper) *Panzer: The Armoured Force of the Third Reich,* MacDonald and Jane's (London, England), 1976.

Panzer Army Africa, MacDonald and Jane's (London, England), 1977.

(With Matthew Cooper) *Panzer Grenadiers,* Presidio Press (San Rafael, CA), 1977.

(With James Barker) *Battle of Normandy, The Falaise Gap,* Holmes and Meier Publishing (New York, NY), 1978.

Germany's Elite Panzer Force: Grossdeutschland, MacDonald and Jane's (London, England), 1978.

Killing Ground: The Battle of the Falaise Gap, August 1944, Batsford (London, England), 1978.

Alpine Elite: German Mountain Troops of World War II, Jane's (London, England), 1980.

War on the Eastern Front, 1941-1945: The German Soldier in Russia, Stein and Day (New York, NY), 1980.

War in the Desert: The Eighth Army at El Alamein, Beaufort Books (New York, NY), 1982.

Kommando: German Special Forces of World War Two, St. Martin's Press (New York, NY), 1985.

Last Days of the Third Reich: The Collapse of Nazi Germany, May 1945, Morrow (New York, NY), 1986.

World War Two through German Eyes, Arms and Armour (London, England), 1987.

(Editor) *Command: From Alexander the Great to Zhukov, The Greatest Commanders of World History,* Bloomsbury (London, England), 1988.

Storming Eagles: German Airborne Forces in World War Two, Arms and Armour (London, England), 1988.

The British Soldier, Arms and Armour (London, England), 1989.

Third Reich, Arms and Armour (London, England), 1990.

Reich: The Military Role of 2nd SS Division, Arms and Armour (London, England), 1991.

Hitler's Mountain Troops, Arms and Armour (London, England), 1992.

Battle Group!: German Kampfgruppen Action of World War II, Arms and Armour (London, England), 1993.

Last Year of the German Army, May 1944-May 1945, Arms and Armour (London, England), 1994.

Hitler's Enforcers: Leaders of the Germany War Machine, 1939-45, Cassell (London, England), 1996.

SS-Kampfgruppe Peiper: An Episode in the War in Russia, February 1943, Shelf Books (Bradford, West Yorkshire, England), 1997.

Germany Handbook, Sutton (Gloucestershire, England), 1998.

Rommel's Year of Victory: The Wartime Illustrations of the Afrika Korps by Kurt Caesar, Greenhill Books (London, England), 1998.

Das Reich: The Military Role of the Second S.S. Division, Cassell (London, England), 1999.

Death in Normandy: The Last Battles of Michael Wittmann, Shelf Books (Halifax, England), 1999.

Hitler's Commanders: German Bravery in the Field, 1939-1945, Cassell (London, England), 2001.

SIDELIGHTS: Most of James Lucas's professional life was associated with war. First he served in the Queen's Own Royal Army as a British soldier in World War II, stationed in Africa, Italy, and later in Austria. In 1960 he joined the staff of the Imperial War Museum in London, eventually becoming the deputy head of the department of photographs. After retiring from this position, Lucas took up a third career, that of an author and historian. His favorite topic was World War II, a subject about which he became a respected authority—not only among scholars, but, through his work as an adviser on film and television productions about the war, among the general public as well. According to a London *Times* obituary, Lucas examined "almost every aspect of the Nazi war machine . . . combining technical information with first-hand testimony and so producing a body of work unequalled in its breadth. Having fought the Third Reich's best troops through North Africa and Italy, he knew their tenacity and resourcefulness."

Lucas's writing style was not considered typical of war histories. "Humour and enthusiasm, combined with rigorous attention to detail, were the hallmarks of his style," reported the *Times* obituary writer. Lucas was a prolific writer upon his topic of choice; and he covered many different aspects of the war, often concentrating on the German side of the conflicts. His *Battle Group! German Kampfgruppen Action of World War Two* describes the actions of various specially trained German groups—kampfgruppen—such as the infantry divisions or the so-called assault engineers. These groups, according to Leo J. Daugherty III in the *Marine Corps Gazette,* "saved or exploited situations during the advance on Moscow." Daugherty found that Lucas's account provides readers "with a gripping narrative that details the actions by individual German platoons and companies forced to hold out against overwhelming odds" in this particular front of the war.

One battle in which the German Army did not fare well is recounted in Lucas's *The Battle of Normandy: The Falaise Gap.* Although the details of this significant battle have been covered in many other publications, a reviewer for *Choice* found that Lucas's account has great value because it takes a unique point of view by drawing "heavily upon German primary sources (many unpublished)." This particular battle was very costly to Germany, which lost twice as many soldiers there than on the Russian front. Lucas's book explains why the Germans suffered so many losses. Had their strategies called for a temporary retreat, they might have "halted the advances of the U.S. 3rd Army toward the Seine," according to the *Choice* reviewer.

Lucas provides a more personal perspective in his *War on the Eastern Front, 1941-1945: The German Soldier in Russia.* In this book he conveys the war through the eyes of the German soldiers who had to endure, not only the fighting, but also the bitter cold of the Russian steppes, "an alternately frozen or burning plain stretching into Siberia," wrote Stanley L. Itkin in *Library Journal.* Lucas, in his research for this book, discovered that many German soldiers were more fearful in Russia than in other locations; not only was the landscape harsh, but the Russian soldier was a stubborn fighter and the Russian army was fierce. This personalized account, wrote Itkin, has no other book to compare with it.

War in the Desert: The Eight Army at El Alamein presents the story of a crucial World War II battle in North Africa. Here the territory also played a major role, with heat and sand plaguing the armies. Lucas again relies on oral accounts to tell the story. As Shelford Bidwell in the *Times Literary Supplement* related: "Lucas has good chapters on life in the desert, the work of the infantryman, the trooper in a tank, the sapper and the gunner. The one on the infantry is, not surprisingly, the best, as Lucas himself fought as a private in a rifle platoon."

Lucas once commented that, just because he went to war against the Germans, was no reason for him not to make friends with them. He was once taken prisoner during the war but talked his way out using his very basic (at that time) command of the German language. He convinced his captors, according to his obituary, that they were mistaken about the lines of battle and were in fact, themselves in enemy territory. The German soldiers eventually not only let Lucas and his fellow soldiers go, they turned their weapons over to Lucas and surrendered. Lucas eventually married an Austrian woman whose father was a captain in the German army.

Lucas finished his last book just prior to his death. *Hitler's Commanders: German Bravery in the Field, 1939-1945* examines the German masterminds of the war, people like Eduard Dietl, Werner Kempf, Kurt Meyer, and Theodor Scherer. As his *Times* obituarist declared, Lucas "saw himself as an archivist, searching for the ordinary men in the heat of battle, playing their part in the bigger picture." Lucas died on June 19, 2002, at the age of seventy-eight.

BIOGRAPHICAL AND CRITICAL SOURCES:

PERIODICALS

Booklist, November 15, 1980, review of *War on the Eastern Front, 1941-1945: The German Soldier in Russia,* p. 441; September 15, 1983, review of *War in the Desert: The Eighth Army at El Alamein,* p. 131; April 1, 1988, Roland Green, review of *World War Two through German Eyes,* p. 1308.

Choice, May, 1979, review of *The Battle of Normandy: The Falaise Gap,* p. 438; January, 1984, review of *War in the Desert,* p. 746.

Economist, November 20, 1982, review of *War in the Desert,* p. 102.

History: Review of New Books, August, 1979, Robert W. Love, review of *The Battle of Normandy,* p. 200; spring, 1997, Bruce F. Pauley, review of *Hitler's Enforcers: Leaders of the German War Machine, 1933-1945,* pp. 121-122.

Kliatt, spring, 1987, review of *Kommando: German Special Forces of World War Two,* p. 47.

Library Journal, March 1, 1979, Kenneth R. Jones, review of *The Battle of Normandy,* p. 627; October 15, 1980, Stanley L. Itkin, review of *War on the Eastern Front 1941-1945: The German Soldier in Russia,* p. 2204; April 1, 1992, Dennis L. Noble, review of *The Military Role of the Second S.S. Division,* p. 133; June 1, 1999, Michael Rogers, review of *Kommando,* p. 188.

Marine Corps Gazetter, September, 1999, Leo J. Daugherty III, review of *Battle Group! German Kamfgruppen Action of World War Two,* pp. 106-107.

Military Review, June, 1994, review of *Hitler's Mountain Troops,* p. 86.

Parameters, autumn, 1994, review of *Hitler's Mountain Troops,* p. 141; autumn, 1995, Colin F. Baxter, "Did Nazis Fight Better than Democrats? Historical Writing on the Combat Performance of the Allied Soldier in Normandy," pp. 113-114.

Publishers Weekly, July 12, 1985, review of *Kommando,* p. 42; March 2, 1992, review of *Das Reich: The Military Role of the Second S.S. Division,,* p. 57.

Queen's Quarterly, autumn, 1987, review of *Last Days of the Reich,* pp. 704-706.

School Library Journal, October, 1986, Mary Wadsworth Sucher, review of *Kommando,* p. 195.

Times Literary Supplement, December 31, 1982, Shelford Bidwell, "Back into Battle," review of *War in the Desert,* p. 1450.

Virginia Quarterly Review, summer, 1981, review of *War on the Eastern Front, 1941-1945: The German Soldier in Russia,* p. 86.

Washington Post Book World, August 27, 2000, review of *The Last Days of the Reich: The Collapse of Nazi Germany, May 1945,* p. 11.

OBITUARIES:

PERIODICALS

Times (London, England), August 15, 2002.*

* * *

LUDLOW, Ian
See PERDUE, Lewis

* * *

LUKEMAN, Noah

PERSONAL: Son of Brenda Shoshanna (a psychologist and psychotherapist). *Education:* Brandeis University, B.A. (English and creative writing, cum laude).

ADDRESSES: *Office*—Lukeman Literary Management Ltd., 101 North Seventh St., Brooklyn, NY 11211.

CAREER: Literary agent, author, and actor. Lukeman Literary Management Ltd., Brooklyn, NY, founder and president, 1996—. Creator of publishing rights Web site *Prepub.com.* Formerly manager for Artists Management Group, New York, NY; previously affiliated with book publishers, including William Morrow, Delphinium Books, and Farrar, Straus, Giroux.

WRITINGS:

The First Five Pages: A Writer's Guide to Staying out of the Rejection Pile, Simon and Schuster (New York, NY), 2000.

The Plot Thickens: Eight Ways to Bring Fiction to Life, St. Martin's Press (New York, NY), 2002.

Contributor to *The Practical Writer,* Penguin, 2004. Contributor to periodicals, including *Poets and Writers, Writers Digest,* and *Writer.*

WORK IN PROGRESS: A third guide for writers.

SIDELIGHTS: Noah Lukeman is president of a literary agency whose clients include the Dalai Lama and Gene Hackman, as well as winners of the Pulitzer Prize, American Book Award, Pushcart Prize, and O. Henry Award. He came up through the ranks of New York publishing, started one of the first and most successful publishing rights Web sites, *PrePub.com,* and in 2000 produced a best-seller of his own, *The First Five Pages: A Writer's Guide to Staying Out of the Rejection Pile.* All of this would be impressive for an individual of any age, but Lukeman was not yet thirty years old at the time his first book was published.

Despite his youth, Lukeman has a strong foundation from which to provide writers of all ages with guidelines for crafting a good story; in half a decade as an agent he reviewed some 50,000 manuscripts. Based on this experience, his *The First Five Pages*—the first part of a planned three-part writer's guide—focuses on the honing of the first five pages, which, if an author does not sharpen them, may well be the only part of the manuscript an editor will ever see.

The second part, *The Plot Thickens: Eight Ways to Bring Fiction to Life,* concerns plot, and a planned third volume will address dialogue.

In *The Plot Thickens: Eight Ways to Bring Fiction to Life* Lukeman asserts that "character is destiny," meaning that what characters do springs from who they are. Therefore, if a writer knows his or her characters intimately, plot will follow. "Lukeman's advice is practical," wrote Mark Rotella in *Publishers Weekly,* adding that the book is "without a hint of the flakiness that creeps into many writing guides." According to Chuck Leddy in *Writer,* "*The Plot Thickens* is a highly useful book that is written in an accessible style and filled with valuable examples."

BIOGRAPHICAL AND CRITICAL SOURCES:

PERIODICALS

Booklist, May 1, 2002, David Pitt, review of *The Plot Thickens: Eight Ways to Bring Fiction to Life,* p. 1499.

Publishers Weekly, June 24, 2002, review of *The Plot Thickens: Eight Ways to Bring Fiction to Life,* p. 51.

Writer, July, 2002, Chuck Leddy, "When Developing Your Plot, 'Character Is Destiny,'" p. 47.

ONLINE

BookzonePro.com, http://www.bookzonepro.com/ (September 17, 2003), interview with Lukeman.

Lukeman Literary Management Ltd. Web site, http://www.lukeman.com (September 17, 2003).

One Woman's Writing Retreat Web site, http://www.prairieden.com/ (September 17, 2003), interview with Lukeman.*

* * *

LUPACK, Barbara Tepa 1951-

PERSONAL: Born 1951; married Alan Lupack (a scholar and librarian).

ADDRESSES: *Home*—375 Oakdale Dr., Rochester, NY 14618.

CAREER: Former academic dean, State University of New York; former Fulbright professor of American Literature in Poland and France; University of Rochester Robbins Library, Rochester, NY, co-designer of The Camelot Project; writer.

WRITINGS:

Plays of Passion, Games of Chance: Jerzy Kosinski and His Fiction, Wyndham Hall Press (Bristol, IN), 1988.

(Editor) *Take Two: Adapting the Contemporary American Novel to Film,* Bowling Green State University Popular Press (Bowling Green, OH), 1994.

Insanity as Redemption in Contemporary American Fiction: Inmates Running the Asylum, University Press of Florida (Gainesville, FL), 1995.

(Editor) *Vision/Re-Vision: Adapting Contemporary American Fiction by Women to Film,* Bowling Green State University Popular Press (Bowling Green, OH), 1996.

(Editor) *Critical Essays on Jerzy Kosinski,* G. K. Hall (New York, NY), 1998.

(Editor with husband, Alan Lupack) *Arthurian Literature by Women,* Garland Publishing (New York, NY), 1999.

(Editor) *Nineteenth-Century Women at the Movies: Adapting Classic Women's Fiction to Film,* Bowling Green State University (Bowling Green, OH), 1999.

(With A. Lupack) *King Arthur in America,* D. S. Brewer (Rochester, NY), 1999.

Literary Adaptations in Black American Cinema: From Micheaux to Morrison, University of Rochester Press (Rochester, NY), 2002.

(Editor) *Adapting the Arthurian Legends for Children: Essays on Arthurian Juvenalia,* Palgrave Macmillan (New York, NY), 2004.

Contributor to scholarly periodicals.

ADAPTATIONS: Lupack and her husband are featured in the educational video *Tracing the Arthurian Tradition.*

SIDELIGHTS: Barbara Tepa Lupack is a scholar whose interests range widely through modern literature, film adaptation, the King Arthur legends, and the work of Polish author Jerzy Kosinski. Lupack has worked with her husband, Alan Lupack, on several books about King Arthur, and they also designed the Camelot Project at the University of Rochester's Robbins Library. This project is compiling a comprehensive database on all aspects of Arthurian literature, art, film, and critical studies. Lupack's contributions to Arthurian scholarship include *King Arthur in America,* an examination of how Arthurian legends have been adapted to suit American audiences, tastes, and cultural norms, and *Adapting the Arthurian Legends for Children: Essays on Arthurian Juvenalia,* a project that explores books and films about King Arthur for younger audiences.

Lupack's *Plays of Passion, Games of Chance: Jerzy Kosinski and His Fiction* includes biographical material on the writer and a critical treatment of his books. *Choice* contributor C. G. Masinton called the work "a fine example of applied criticism," and Stan Fogel in *Modern Fiction Studies* found it "a good book for anyone who wants an introduction to Kosinski and his writing." Kosinski's *Being There* is one of the novels covered in Lupack's *Insanity as Redemption in Contemporary American Fiction: Inmates Running the Asylum,* a book that *College Literature* contributor Terry Caesar commended as "lucidly written and solidly researched."

Lupack has published several volumes about film, with emphasis on adaptations of novels into movies. The essays in *Vision/Re-Vision: Adapting Contemporary American Fiction by Women to Film* look at individual books and films to form a general picture of how content is altered from the original medium to the adaptation. *Literary Adaptations in Black American Cinema: From Micheaux to Morrison* explores how African-American artists and intellectuals have sought to create an authentic cinematic experience for black viewers. *Variety* reviewer Katheline St. Fort called the work "intriguing" and described it as "full of engrossing behind-the-scenes details."

BIOGRAPHICAL AND CRITICAL SOURCES:

PERIODICALS

Choice, September, 1989, C. G. Masinton, review of *Plays of Passion, Games of Chance: Jerzy Kosinski and His Fiction,* p. 126; November, 1999, D. C. Homan, review of *King Arthur in America,* p. 538.

College Literature, Volume 24, number 2, Terry Caesar, review of *Insanity as Redemption in Contemporary American Fiction,* pp. 225-227.

Journal of American Studies, August, 1998, S. M. Grant, review of *Vision/Re-Vision: Adapting Contemporary American Fiction by Women to Film,* pp. 326-327.

Modern Fiction Studies, April 24, 1990, Stan Fogel, review of *Plays of Passion, Games of Chance,* pp. 764-766.

Variety, July 1, 2002, Katheline St. Fort, "Niche Tomes Take Polar Paths," p. 37.*

* * *

LYMAN, Howard F. 1939-

PERSONAL: Born 1939. *Education:* Montana State University, B.S. (agriculture), 1961.

ADDRESSES: *Office*—Voice for a Viable Future, 11288 Ventura Blvd., No. 202A, Studio City, CA 91604.

CAREER: Rancher and consumer advocate. Lyman Ranch and Lyman Cattle Company, owner, 1965-83; Montana Farmers Union, lobbyist, 1983-86; National Farmers Union, lobbyist, 1986-93; Eating with a Conscience Campaign, director, 1994-96; International Vegetarian Union, president, 1996-98; Earth Save, president, 1999-2001; Voice of a Sustainable Future, founder and president, 1993—. *Military service:* U.S. Army, 1961; involved in combat development, experimentation command.

AWARDS, HONORS: Courage of Conscience Award, Peace Abbey, 1997; honorary doctorate of Law, Los Angeles City University, 1997.

WRITINGS:

(With Glen Merzer) *Mad Cowboy: Plain Truth from the Cattle Rancher Who Won't Eat Meat,* Scribner (New York, NY), 1998.

SIDELIGHTS: Mad Cowboy: Plain Truth from the Cattle Rancher Who Won't Eat Meat is the result of Howard F. Lyman's transformation from a Montana cattle rancher to a vegan lobbyist for food safety. A spinal cord tumor that paralyzed him from the waist down was responsible for changing Lyman's attitude toward meat and the meat industry. He regretted turning his family's organic farm and ranch into a large, corporate farm that used fertilizers, pesticides, and growth hormones to boost production. He sold off several of his farms in 1983 and went to work for the Montana Farmers Union to support the small farmer, then became a lobbyist for the National Farmers Union based in Washington, D.C. Lyman's 1996 appearance on *The Oprah Winfrey Show* prompted a group of Texas cattlemen to bring a ten-million-dollar lawsuit against Lyman and show host Winfrey, but a jury found both innocent of disparaging the beef industry.

Lyman writes in *Mad Cowboy:* "Meat kills. It is the number one cause of death in America." He describes the high levels of toxic chemicals injected into animals and the pesticides sprayed on the food these animals eat. Lyman includes the scientific studies he accessed before concluding that eating meat and dairy products increases chances of cancer, heart disease, and diabetes. He also mentions the environmental effect of ranching, such as lost forest and vegetation, polluted waters, and soil erosion. Dan Ferber, reviewing Lyman's book for *Sierra,* wrote that "while this blanket indictment of ranching is simplistic . . . his basic arguments are well-supported."

BIOGRAPHICAL AND CRITICAL SOURCES:

PERIODICALS

Sierra, January, 1999, Dan Ferber, review of *Mad Cowboy: Plain Truth from the Cattle Rancher Who Won't Eat Meat,* p. 108.

Townsend Letter for Doctors and Patients, October, 2001, review of *Mad Cowboy,* p. 150.

Whole Earth Review, summer, 1999, review of *Mad Cowboy,* p. 101.

ONLINE

CityPaper Online, http://www.citypaper.net/ (June 18-25, 1998), interview by Vance Lehmkuhl.

MadCowboy.com, http://www.madcomboy.com (June 14, 2003).*

M

MACLAGAN, Michael 1914-2003

OBITUARY NOTICE—See index for *CA* sketch: Born April 14, 1914, in London, England; died August 13, 2003, in Oxford, England. Educator and author. Maclagan was a highly esteemed Oxford don who taught history at Trinity College, Dublin for more than four decades. Educated at Christ Church, he earned his bachelor's degree in 1935 and his master's degree in 1939, joining the faculty at Trinity as a fellow. The beginnings of his academic career were soon interrupted by the onset of World War II, however. During the war, he served in Britain's 16th/5th Lancers, mostly in military operations in Cairo, achieving the rank of major. Returning to England in 1946, he resumed his position at Trinity. He served in various posts there, including as senior proctor from 1954 to 1955 and senior librarian from 1960 to 1970. He retired as fellow emeritus in 1981 and accepted a post with the College of Arms, where he had been named Richmond Herald in 1980 and was able to indulge his interest in heraldry. An erudite historian who was fluent in Latin and Greek, Maclagan was the editor of Bede's *Ecclesiastical History of England* (1949) and Richard Aungerville's *Philobiblon* (1960). Furthermore, he was the author of several books, including *Trinity College 1555-1955* (1955), *"Clemency" Canning* (1962), which was awarded the Wheatley Medal, *The City of Constantinople* (1968), and *Heraldry of the Royal Families of Europe* (1981).

OBITUARIES AND OTHER SOURCES:

PERIODICALS

Independent (London, England), September 2, 2003, p. 16.

Times (London, England), August 21, 2003.

* * *

MAIMANE, Arthur 1932-

PERSONAL: Born October 5, 1932, in South Africa; married; children: five daughters.

ADDRESSES: *Agent*—c/o Author Mail, Kwela Books, P.O. Box 6525, Roggebaai, 8012 South Africa.

CAREER: *Drum Magazine,* journalist, 1952-56; *Golden City Post,* journalist, 1956-68; *Drum* (West Africa), journalist, 1958-60; *Ghana Radio Times,* journalist, 1960-61; Fleet Street Radio and Television, journalist; British Broadcasting Corporation, London, England, writer and producer; Independent TV News (ITN), senior writer; *Star* (newspaper), Cape Town, South Africa, managing editor, 1994-97; writer and media consultant, 1997—.

MEMBER: Society of Authors.

AWARDS, HONORS: Commonwealth Radio Play, first prize, 1964, for *The Opportunity;* Pringle Award for Creative Writing, English Academy of South Africa, 1978.

WRITINGS:

Victims: A Novel, Allison and Busby (London, England), 1976.

Hate No More (novel), Global (London, England), 2000.

Author of radio plays, including *The Opportunity* and *Where the Sun Shines,* both 1964, and stage plays, including *The Dung Heap Flower,* 1970, *The Prosecution,* 1971, and *Hang on in There, Nelson!*

WORK IN PROGRESS: A nonfiction book and a novel.

SIDELIGHTS: A premier journalist for *Drum* magazine during the 1960s, South African writer Arthur Maimane made a name for himself for his investigations of apartheid abuses. Many of his short stories and serialized detective pieces were published in *Drum* and other magazines. When his political activities made him persona non grata in his homeland, he went on to work as a writer and producer for a number of respected news organizations outside of Africa, including the British Broadcasting Corporation and Independent TV News. He also wrote several plays, such as the award-winning *The Opportunity* and *Hang on in There, Nelson!* With a hiatus of three decades between them, he published the novels *Victims* and *Hate No More.* Maimane returned to South Africa in 1994 to work as managing editor of the *Star* newspaper in Cape Town.

In 1997 Maimane became a media consultant and full-time writer, publishing his second novel three years later. Because of censorship in South Africa during the 1960s, *Hate No More* had waited thirty years to find a publisher. Set in the 1960s, the novel portrays the life of Phillip Mokone, a black man living in Sophiatown, South Africa. Consumed with rage against apartheid, Mokone finally resorts to an act of violence in a whites-only suburb.

BIOGRAPHICAL AND CRITICAL SOURCES:

ONLINE

Kwela Books Web site, http://www.kwela.com/ (May 15, 2001), review of *Hate No More.*

University of Natal Web site, http://www.und.ac.za/ (April 23, 2002), "Time of the Writer."*

* * *

MALLIE, Eamonn 1950-

PERSONAL: Born 1950, in Armagh, Northern Ireland; married; children: three. *Education:* Trinity College, Dublin, B.A. (with honors), 1974.

ADDRESSES: Home—Belfast, Northern Ireland. *Agent*—c/o Author Mail, Hodder & Stoughton, Ltd., 47 Bedford Square, London WC18 3DP, England. *E-mail*—emallie@globalgateway.co.uk.

CAREER: Journalist. British Broadcasting Corporation (BBC) Northern Ireland, radio current-affairs producer, 1975; reporter, 1976-79, political correspondent, 1979—. Eamonn Mallie News Services, founder, 1990, and producer of *Assembly in Focus* and *Global Gateway Headline News* Internet broadcasts; Radio C4, political analyst in Northern Ireland; freelance broadcaster with Independent Radio News, Republic of Ireland, Agence France Presse, and to radio stations in Australia, New Zealand, South Africa, Latin America, and the United States. Consultant to BBC documentaries.

WRITINGS:

(With David McKittrick) *The Fight for Peace: The Secret Story behind the Irish Peace Process,* Heinemann (London, England), 1996, 2nd edition, Mandarin (London, England), 1997.

Tom Carr: An Appreciation, privately published, E. Mallie (Belfast, Northern Ireland), 1989.

(With David McKittrick) *Endgame in Ireland* (based on a television series), Hodder & Stoughton (London, England), 2001.

Also author of *The Provisional IRA.*

SIDELIGHTS: Based in Belfast, Northern Ireland, journalist Eamonn Mallie reports on that region's political and social strife to news outlets throughout the English-speaking world, as well on a global scale, through his Internet news agency. Eamonn Mallie News Services. In addition to reporting on current events in Northern Ireland, Mallie has also authored several books that combine facts with more in-depth analysis, among them *Endgame in Ireland* and *The Fight for Peace: The Secret Story behind the Irish Peace Process,* both coauthored with fellow journalist David McKittrick.

In *The Fight for Peace* Mallie and McKittrick present what *Times Literary Supplement* contributor David Self dubbed a "lucid, even exciting, detective story" recounting the events leading up to the cease-fire declared in August of 1994 and subsequently rescinded in February of 1996—which rescission required the book's second edition. Recounting in detail the events leading up to the end of hostilities and including interviews with members of both the Irish and British civil service, police, and other key figures, the authors "focus on the changing perceptions of the republican movement . . . toward its traditional strategy of obtaining the goal of a united Ireland through physical force," explained M. L. R. Smith in *Studies in Conflict and Terrorism.* Although the book was criticized for not questioning the basis for the establishment of the peace talks in the first place, Smith explained that *The Fight for Peace* succeeds in its purpose: to "concentrate on the mechanics of the peace process, [thereby] producing a successful narrative of events, rather than delving into the implications of the process itself." While *Spectator* contributor C. D. C. Armstrong objected to a text composed in what he termed "the breathless style of a mediocre thriller" where "clichés abound," Smith praised *The Fight for Peace* as a "work of immense value to the historical record" that "illustrates the pre-eminence of seasoned journalists when it comes to the study of the military and paramilitary dimensions" of the Irish "troubles." Noting that Mallie and McKittrick contribute "genuine revelations" to the historical record, *International Affairs* contributor Roger MacGinty praised *The Fight for Peace* as "a fast-paced and highly accessible narrative."

Based on a multi-part British television broadcast, 2001's *Endgame in Ireland* covers ground similar to *The Fight for Peace* in its focus on the peace talks undertaken in Ireland beginning in 1981. Drawing their information from interviews with high-level politicians, leaders of the Irish Republican Army, and terrorist groups loyal to Great Britain, as well as from numerous documents, Mallie and McKittrick bring readers up to date regarding the meetings, negotiations, and other efforts to end a centuries-long conflict between traditionally Catholic and Protestant factions. While noting that the book "gets off to an uncertain start" as the authors recount the 1984 bombing of a political conference in Brighton, England, an *Economist* contributor noted that *Endgame in Ireland* gains ground when the coauthors delve into the personalities on both sides of the peace-process table. Indeed, the reviewer noted, "Northern Ireland has, at least, been fortunate in its journalists" who, like Mallie and McKittrick, "strive, often in trying circumstances, to maintain the highest professional standards."

BIOGRAPHICAL AND CRITICAL SOURCES:

PERIODICALS

Economist, November 10, 2001, review of *Endgame in Ireland.*

International Affairs, January, 1997, Roger MacGinty, review of *The Fight for Peace: The Inside Story of the Irish Peace Process,* pp. 1984-1985.

Political Studies, December, 1998, M. L. R. Smith, review of *The Fight for Peace,* pp. 982-983.

Spectator, May 25, 1996, C. D. C. Armstrong, "Judge a Book by It's Title," p. 34.

Studies in Conflict and Terrorism, October, 1998, M. L. R. Smith, "A Still-distant Prospect: Processing the Peace in Northern Ireland," pp. 363-367.

Times Educational Supplement, July 5, 1996, David Self, review of *The Fight for Peace,* p. 7.

Times Literary Supplement, July 26, 2002, Anthony McIntyre, "The Legal Fictions and the Awkward Questions," p. 25.

ONLINE

GlobalGateway, http://www.globalgateway.com/ (April 3, 2003), "Eamonn Mallie."*

* * *

MALMSTAD, John E. 1941-

PERSONAL: Born June 25, 1941, in Bismarck, ND; son of Manley Ellsworth and Joyce Evelyn (David) Malmstad. *Education:* Northwestern University, B.A. (summa cum laude), 1963; Princeton University, M.A., 1965, Ph.D., 1969; Harvard University, A.M. (honors), 1985. *Hobbies and other interests:* Fine arts, ballet, reading.

ADDRESSES: *Home*—8A Cogswell Ave., Cambridge, MA 02140-2001. *Office*—Harvard University, Department of Slavic Languages/Literature, Barker Ctr., 12 Quincy St., Cambridge, MA 02138. *E-mail*—malmstad@fas.harvard.edu.

CAREER: Educator and editor. Columbia University, New York, NY, instructor, 1968-69, assistant professor, 1969-73, associate professor, 1973-79, professor of Russian literature, 1979-85; Harvard University, Cambridge, MA, Samuel Hazzard Cross Professor of Slavic languages and literature, 1985—, associate dean, 1993-94. Served as visiting associate professor at Stanford University, beginning 1971, and at University of California—Berkeley, 1977-78.

MEMBER: Modern Language Association, American Association of Advancement of Slavic Studies, Association of Teachers of Slavic and East European Languages, Institute d'Etudes Slaves (France), Phi Beta Kappa.

AWARDS, HONORS: Woodrow Wilson fellow, 1963; NDFL fellow to Columbia University, 1963-66, Princeton University, 1967-68; Fulbright-Hays fellow, 1966-67, 1981, 1987; ACLS research fellow, 1972; International Researches and Exchange Board fellow, 1975; Russian Institute research fellow, 1977, 1979, 1983, 1984; Guggenheim fellow, 1980-81.

WRITINGS:

(With N. A. Bogmolov) *Mikhail Kuzmin: Iskusstivo Zhinzn' Epokha,* Novoe Literaturenoe Obozreine (Moscow, Russia), 1996, translated as *Mikhail Kuzmin: A Life in Art,* Harvard University Press (Cambridge, MA), 1999.

Contributor to professional journals.

EDITOR

(With Vladimir Markov) Mikhail Kuzmin, *Sobranie Stikhov* (collected works; German and Russian; introduction in English), 3 volumes, W. Fink (Munich, Germany), 1977.

K. N. Bugaeva, *Vospominaniia o Belom,* 3 volumes, Berkeley Slavic Specialties (Berkeley, CA), 1981.

(With Robert P. Hughes) V. F. Khodasevich, *Sobranie Sochinenii,* 3 volumes, Ardis (Ann Arbor, MI), 1983.

Andrey Bely, *Gibel' Senatora: Peterbug; Istoricheskaia Drama,* Berkeley Slavonic Specialties (Berkeley, CA), 1986.

Andrey Bely, *Spirit of Symbolism* (criticism), Cornell University Press (Ithaca, NY), 1987.

Studies in the Life and Works of Mixail Kusmin, Gesellschaft zur Förerung Slawistischer Studien (Vienna, Austria), 1989.

Lidiia Ivanova, *Vospominaniia: Kniga ob Ottse* (biography), RIK Kultura (Moscow, Russia), 1992.

Readings in Russian Modernism to Honor Vladimir Markov, 1993.

Andrey Bely i Ivanov Razumnik—Perepiska (correspondence), Atheneum (Saint Petersburg, Russia), 1998.

Russian book-review editor for *Slavic Review,* 1975-86; associate editor of *Russian Review,* 1986-88; member of editorial board for publishers, including Feniks, Opyty, Novoe Literaturnoe Obozrenie, Experiment, and Philologica Diaspora.

* * *

MANUEL, Fritzie Prigohzy 1910-

PERSONAL: Born 1910; married Frank Edward Manuel (a scholar and author), 1936 (deceased, 2003). *Education:* New York University, graduated, 1934.

ADDRESSES: *Agent*—c/o Author mail, American Philosophical Society, 104 South Fifth Street, Philadelphia, PA 19106-3387.

CAREER: Author of nonfiction and translator.

AWARDS, HONORS: (With husband, Frank E. Manuel) Frederick Melcher Award, and Ralph Waldo Emerson Award, both 1980, and National Book Award, 1983, all for for *Utopian Thought in the Western World.*

WRITINGS:

(And translator and editor with husband, Frank E. Manuel) *French Utopias: An Anthology of Ideal Societies,* Free Press (New York, NY), 1966.

(With Frank E. Manuel) *Utopian Thought in the Western World,* Belknap Press (Cambridge, MA), 1979.

(With Frank E. Manuel) *James Bowdoin and the Patriot Philosophers,* American Philosophical Society (Philadelphia, PA), 2003.

Contributor to several photography books.

SIDELIGHTS: Jointly with her husband, educator and historian Frank E. Manuel, Fritzie Prigohzy Manuel is a respected contributor to the history of social philosophy. The Manuels married in 1936, soon after Fritzie graduated from New York University's Washington Square College. Their collaboration extended beyond married life, as the two coauthored several books, including *French Utopias: An Anthology of Ideal Societies* and *Utopian Thought in the Western World.* The latter gained fame, winning the National Book Award, the Ralph Waldo Emerson Award, and the Frederick Melcher Award following its 1979 publication. The Manuels' final book, *James Bowdoin and the Patriot Philosophers,* was published in 2003, the year Frank Manuel passed away.

The Manuels' most widely read book, *Utopian Thought in the Western World,* chronicles the history of Western utopian thought by tracing the philosophy of such intellectuals as Francis Bacon, Jean Jacques Rousseau, Immanuel Kant, Karl Marx, and others. Praising the work as a "challenging" volume "of monumental scope, written with authority, wit and unfailing lucidity," *New York Times Book Review* contributor Leo Marx cited as particularly refreshing the couple's "unpretentiousness," a quality that "distinguishes their work from that of many latter-day 'psychohistorians.'" In the critic's opinion, the book's "success is attributable to a thoroughly assimilated Freudian anthropology. The Manuels regard utopianism as Western culture's distinctive expression of a universal propensity for creating imaginary havens of delight."

BIOGRAPHICAL AND CRITICAL SOURCES:

PERIODICALS

New York Times Book Review, October 21, 1979, Leo Marx, review of *Utopian Thought in the Western World,* p. 3; May 10, 1981, Anatole Broyard, "The Author-Scholars," p. 47.*

* * *

MARCELLO, Leo Luke 1945-

PERSONAL: Born August 6, 1945, in DeRidder, LA; son of Luke M. (a physician) and Bert DiGiglia Marcello. *Education:* Tulane University, B.A., 1967; Louisiana State University, M.A., 1970, Ph.D., 1976; postdoctoral studies, University of Dallas (philosophy), 1985-86, Catholic University of America (theology), 1986-88. *Religion:* Catholic.

ADDRESSES: *Home*—Louisiana. *Agent*—c/o Author Mail, Liguori Publishing, One Liguori Dr., Liguori, MO 63057.

CAREER: Educator, publisher, and poet. McNeese State University, Lake Charles, LA, visiting lecturer, 1981-82, assistant professor, 1989-92, associated professor, 1992-99, professor, 1998-2000, Shearman Academic Professor, 1992-93. University of Maryland Overseas Program, lecturer, 1976; Catholic University of America, lecturer, 1987-88, assistant professor, 1989; Howard University, instructor, 1988-89. Cramers Press, founder and publisher.

AWARDS, HONORS: Bennett Award for Poetry, Deep South Writers Conference, 1980, for poem "Buying Cheese"; David Lloyd Kreeger Award, Catholic University of America, 1987, for poetry manuscript *The Infinite Possibilities of Desire;* Shearman Foundation fellowships, 1989-90, for *Contending with Angels and Beasts,* 1990-91, and *Blackrobe's Love Letters;* Louisiana Letters Award of Excellence, *Louisiana Life* magazine, 1991, for short story; Louisiana Endowment for the Humanities grant, 1993; distinguished professor of the year citation, McNeese State University, 1993.

WRITINGS:

(Editor) *Everything Comes to Light: A Festschrift for Joy Scantlebury,* Cramers Press, 1993.

Blackrobe's Love Letters: Poems about Katharine Drexel, Xavier Review Press, 1994, new edition, Cramers Press, 2000.

The Secret Proximity of Everywhere, Blue Heron, 1994.

Silent Film, Mellen Poetry Press (Lewiston, ME), 1997.

Nothing Grows in One Place Forever: Poems of a Sicilian American, Time Being (St. Louis, MO), 1998.

Fifteen Days of Prayer with Saint Katharine Drexel, Liguori (Liguori, MO), 2002.

Contributor of poems, short stories, and articles to numerous periodicals, including *Alabama Literary Review, America, Arba Sicula, Black Buzzard Review,*

Burning Light, Cedar Rock, Christian Century, Commonweal, Context South, Delta, Distillery, Epos, Everyman, First Things, Forkroads, Greenfield Review, Image, Italian Americana, Journeymen, Louisiana English Journal, Louisiana Literature, Merrill Poetry Quarterly, Modern Liturgy, National Catholic Reporter, New Delta Review, Paterson Literary Review, Poetry NOW, Southern Review, Studia Mystica, Texas Observer, Tulane Literary Magazine, Visions International, Windless Orchard, and *Xavier Review.* Also contributor to anthologies, including *Chester H. Jones Foundation National Poetry Competition Winners, 1991; Experiments in Flight,* Kenan; *Gulf Coast Collection of Stories and Poems,* Texas Center for Writers Press; *Houston Poetry Fest, 1985, 1986, 1991; Immortelles: Poems of Life and Death in New Southern Writers,* Xavier Review Press; *The Maple Leaf Rag Fifteenth-Anniversary Anthology,* Portals; *Place of Passage,* Story Line; *Ordinary Time: Winning Poems and Short Stories,* edited by Martha Gies, Seattle, 1987; and *Uncommonplace,* Louisiana State University Press.

WORK IN PROGRESS: Contending with Angels and Beasts, a collaboration with visual artist Larry Schuh; *Mardi Gras in Black and White,* a collaboration with photographer Gary Porter; a collaborative project with brother, artist Chris Marcello, based on the life of Katherine Drexel.

BIOGRAPHICAL AND CRITICAL SOURCES:

PERIODICALS

Fra Noi, November, 1999, Fred L. Gardaphe, "Little Italy of the Heart."

Italian Americana, summer, 2000, Anthony Lombardy, review of *Nothing Grows in One Place Forever,* pp. 231-232.

Sicilia Parra, winter, 1999, review of *Nothing Grows in One Place Forever,* pp. 10-11.

* * *

MASON, Laura 1957-

PERSONAL: Born 1957.

ADDRESSES: Agent—c/o Author Mail, Prospect Books, Allaleigh House, Blackawton, Totnes, Devon TQ9, 7Dl, England.

CAREER: Author; historian of British food.

WRITINGS:

Singing the French Revolution: Popular Culture and Politics, 1787-1799, Cornell University Press (Ithaca, NY), 1996.

Sugar-Plums and Sherbet: The Prehistory of Sweets, Prospect Books (Totnes, Devon, England), 1998.

(Editor, with Catherine Brown) *Traditional Foods of Britain,* Prospect Books (Totnes, Devon, England), 1999.

Sweets and Sweet Shops, Shire Publications, 2000.

(Editor) *Food and the Rites of Passage,* Prospect Books (Totnes, Devon, England), 2002.

SIDELIGHTS: Laura Mason is an author and historian with a special interest in British food. Except for her first published book on the songs of the eighteenth-century revolution in France, her books focus on things people eat. Mason researches her subjects both in libraries and by visiting old cities and towns, and tracks down modern-day samples of old recipes. Helen Simpson, writing for the *Times Literary Supplement,* found Mason's *Sugar-Plums and Sherbet: The Prehistory of Sweets* so sweetly filled with candy and other confectioneries that the critic thought it necessary to state, at the end of her review, that the author made no mention "of tooth decay from start to finish."

In her first book, *Singing the French Revolution: Popular Culture and Politics, 1787-1799,* Mason describes Paris as a city that was filled with the sound of voices. Some of these voices were used to give political speeches, while others riled the masses, urging them to riot. Throughout these turbulent years, there could also be heard a lot of singing. "Mason's purpose in this lively book," wrote Robert M. Isherwood in the *Journal of Modern History,* "is to treat songs as a means of interpreting Revolutionary culture, as well as to analyze how the Revolution changed singing." Everyone was singing, Mason contends, on all sides of the revolution: rival legislators, varied political groups, and the general French citizenry. As

Isherwood explained, "The Revolution's unraveling . . . was the result in large part of its inability to generate a permanent song culture and polity."

There were three stages to the songs, Mason contends. In the earliest years of the revolution, there was a plentiful supply of songs devoted to political satire. During the second stage, the lyrics of songs became more poignant and more clearly revolutionary, containing what Michael E. McClellan, writing for *Notes* called "unambiguous political messages." It was in the second stage, after the collapse of the monarchy, that the song "Marsellaise" became popular. Songs became increasingly less political in the final, or third, stage, as the French people withdrew from their aggressive, stance. McClellan found that Mason's book offers "a remarkably clear picture of Paris in the 1790s." It is through the study of the lyrics of songs, Mason believes, that readers might best appreciate the confusion and the chaos of Paris during the years of the revolution, rather than reading details of that time and assuming that the French people acted as an organized unit. The variations in the songs expose the disparity between various factions in the population.

Sugar Plums and Sherbet: The Prehistory of Sweets focuses on the strong childhood memories of its author. According to Simpson in her review of the book, Mason grew up in a small town of only two thousand people, and yet she recalls that there were "seven shops selling sweets in the main street alone." The history of these sweets begins with Mason's brief reminiscence about her youth, then quickly broadens to include the history of confectioneries in Britain, a country Simpson described as one that "has been passionate about confectionery for centuries." One reason for this, besides a possible national sweet-tooth, is that the British used sweets to signify wealth. Another reason, as stated by Simpson, was that sweets "until recently, were thought to promote health." To satisfy this urge for candy and all things sweet, as E. S. Turner wrote in his *London Review of Books* appraisal, "the maritime powers fought over the slave islands of the Caribbean like dogs scrapping for bones."

Mason has also edited two books about food. The first is called the *Traditional Foods of Britain* and has been praised by the *Times Literary Supplement*'s Lesley Chamberlain for providing "fascinating details about more than 400 original products." The book covers a selection of food products that include dairy, fruits and vegetables, fish and poultry, wild game and snails, and meat. Each food type is then broken down into variations. For example, in the section on cheese, under the letter *B* the list begins with Bath cheese, followed by Baydon Hill Cheese, and then Beenleigh Blue Cheese. The region of production is then provided, followed by a description of the item, the history behind it, and the technique used to make it. By the end of the book, a definition of British culture, as seen through the foods that its people eat, is gathered. As Chamberlain put it, the book offers "the chance for Britain to assert its own definitive gastronomic identity."

Mason also edited the book *Food and the Rites of Passage,* which contains six essays by noted historians who explore, as Sue Shephard noted in the *Times Literary Supplement,* "the source of many common traditions which are still part of celebrating the important milestones of life—births, christenings, weddings and burials all call for exuberant ritual and lavish feasts." Typical of the kinds of food found at ritualistic celebrations are cakes, which, at one time, were broken over a bride's head during her wedding. Funerals of the past often were observed with lavishly planned dinners, with the deceased, well before the actual death, of course, making most of the arrangements. Food served at funerals was often an extravagant display of wealth, proving to those who attended that the recently deceased had been very successful, even if the funeral left the survivors penniless.

BIOGRAPHICAL AND CRITICAL SOURCES:

PERIODICALS

Choice, June, 1997, review of *Singing the French Revolution,* p. 1723.

Journal of Modern History, September, 1999, review of *Singing the French Revolution,* p. 712.

London Review of Books, October 29, 1998, E. S. Turner, review of *Sugar Plums and Sherbet,* p. 30.

Notes, December, 1997, Michael E. McClellan, review of *Singing the French Revolution,* pp. 478-479.

Times Literary Supplement, April 4, 1997, Normal Hampson, review of *Singing the French Revolution,,* p. 28; July 24, 1998, Helen Simpson, review of *Sugar Plums and Sherbet,* p. 10; May 21, 1999,

Lesley Chamberlain, review of *Traditional Foods of Britain,* p. 32; October 18, 2002, Sue Shephard, review of *Food and the Rites of Passage,* p. 35.*

* * *

MASSIE, Robert K(inloch) 1956-

PERSONAL: Born 1956. *Education:* Princeton University, A. B., 1978; Yale Divinity School, M.A., 1982; Harvard Business School, Ph.D., 1989. *Religion:* Episcopal.

ADDRESSES: *Office*—CERES, 99 Chauncy St., 6th Floor, Boston, MA 02111. *E-mail*—massie@ceres.org.

CAREER: Minister, activist, and political consultant. Grace Episcopal Church, New York, NY, assistant and chaplain, 1982-84; Harvard Divinity School, Cambridge, MA, lecturer, director for the Project on Business Values and the Economy, 1989-96; Coalition for Environmentally Responsible Economies (CERES), Boston, MA, executive director, 1996—. World Economic Forum, chair of steering committee, 1998-.

AWARDS, HONORS: Fulbright scholar, 1993; Lionel Gelber Prize for Best Book on International Relations, 1998, for *Loosing the Bonds: The United States and South African in the Apartheid Years.*

WRITINGS:

(Editor, with Mark Green) *The Big Business Reader,* Pilgrim Press (New York, NY), 1980, new edition (with Michael Waldman) published as *The Big Business Reader: On Corporate America,* Pilgrim Press (New York, NY), 1983.

The Hidden Moral Language of Organizations: Public Lecture, the University of Tulsa, October 15, 1995, University of Tulsa (Tulsa, OK), 1995.

Loosing the Bonds: The United States and South Africa in the Apartheid Years, Doubleday (New York, NY), 1997.

SIDELIGHTS: Author Robert K. Massie brought his training as an Episcopal minister and his background in business and political activism to bear on his prize-winning history of race relations in South Africa. *Loosing the Bonds: The United States and South Africa in the Apartheid Years,* published in 1997, also includes extensive consideration of the relationship between the United States and South Africa and the influence of the U.S. civil rights movement, the drive for divestment, and other official and unofficial policies on the movement toward apartheid. Massie also stresses the United States' own struggles with race relations and its indirect support of apartheid. He recounts how the Central Intelligence Agency (CIA) was responsible for the eventual arrest and imprisonment of Nelson Mandela, and observes that, as president, Ronald Reagan sold arms to South Africa knowing that they would be used to maintain policies of racial separatism.

Loosing the Bonds attempts to bring the story of race relations and the anti-apartheid movement into the personal dimension, focusing on the individuals involved—including Robert Kennedy, Martin Luther King, Jr., Nelson Mandela, and Desmond Tutu—and the impact on individual lives. Massie told Beatrice Grabish in *U.N. Chronicle* that he hoped *Loosing the Bonds* would not be a book "only a foreign-policy expert could read." Writing for *Library Journal,* Thomas Davis said that Massie's book demonstrates "that the individual makes a difference in shaping history." Though some reviewers suggested that Massie's approach is too thorough—Geoffrey Wheatcroft said in the *New York Times* that the book is among those "simply too long for their subject"—many nevertheless found it a significant contribution to the topic. Wheatcroft called *Loosing the Bonds* "indispensable for anyone interested in South Africa," and in *Foreign Affairs* Gail M. Gerhart wrote that "no work has so engagingly and authoritatively chronicled the movement" for corporate divestment in America. Hazel Rochman, a reviewer for *Booklist,* called *Loosing the Bonds* "a triumphant story" and a "compelling history."

Massie's interest in human-rights issues also extends to his work with the Global Reporting Initiative for the World Economic Forum and with the Coalition for Environmentally Responsible Economies (CERES), of which he is executive director.

BIOGRAPHICAL AND CRITICAL SOURCES:

PERIODICALS

America, August 29, 1998, John T. McCartney, review of *Loosing the Bonds: The United States and South Africa in the Apartheid Years,* p. 14.

Booklist, November 1, 1997, Hazel Rochman, review of *Loosing the Bonds,* p. 451.
Foreign Affairs, July-August, 1998, Gail M. Gerhart, review of *Loosing the Bonds,* p. 141.
Library Journal, December, 1997, Thomas Davis, review of *Loosing the Bonds,* p. 126.
New York Times, January 11, 1998, Geoffrey Wheatcroft, "Toppling Apartheid," p. 16.
Publishers Weekly December 22, 1997, review of *Loosing the Bonds,* p. 50.
UN Chronicle, spring, 1998, Beatrice Grabish, review of *Loosing the Bonds,* p. 45.

ONLINE

CERES Web site, http://www.ceres.org/ (September 19, 2002), "Robert K. Massie."
World Economic Forum Web site, https://members.weforum.org/ (September 19, 2002).*

* * *

McCLELLAND, Michael 1958-

PERSONAL: Born 1958. *Education:* Florida State University, B.A., M.A., Ph.D. *Hobbies and other interests:* Playing acoustic guitar.

ADDRESSES: Office—Wittenberg University, P.O. Box 720, Springfield, OH 45501. *E-mail*—mcclelland@Wittenberg.edu.

CAREER: United Press International, correspondent; Wittenberg University, Springfield, OH, professor of English, 2000—.

WRITINGS:

Oyster Blues, Simon & Schuster (New York, NY), 2002.
Tattoo Blues, I Books, 2004.

WORK IN PROGRESS: A coming-of-age novel set in the waning days of the hippie movement, with working title *Cedar Crazy.*

SIDELIGHTS: Michael McClelland spent ten years as a United Press International correspondent, covering Florida's political news, before he decided to go back to school and earn a doctorate in creative writing. Upon graduating, he took a job at Wittenberg University, in Ohio, as an English professor and decided to devote his free time to writing fiction. His first attempt has brought much positive response, such as the *Library Journal*'s Thomas L. Kilpatrick, who described it as a "wonderfully quirky, rib-splittingly funny, slightly preposterous crime novel."

McClelland used read constantly as a child. He preferred books to playing in the schoolyard and would have to smuggle novels in his backpack so he would have something to read during recess. It was this love of reading that pushed him into his writing career. His first book, *Oyster Blues* combines the fictitious elements that he accumulated during those years of reading about Tarzan and creatures from out of space as well as his investigations of Florida politics.

The protagonists of this story are Jane Ellen Ashley, a beautifully sexy Floridian oyster shucker, who is dirt-poor and, like the author, has an unquenchable desire to read; and "Happy" Harry Harper, an unemployed English professor who thinks he can take on the role of private eye because he has read so many detective stories. Both characters, coincidentally, think they have killed someone. Jane accidentally pushed a prominent senator's son into a lake and thinks he drowned. Harry is not so sure what he did; all he knows is that he fired a gun and someone may have been shot. So Jane and Harry are both on the run from the law, and while running, they get involved with gangsters and eventually meet one another and fall in love. Other characters include crooked politicians, fishermen, and tourists, Jane's drunken brother, and a man with a plastic throat.

BIOGRAPHICAL AND CRITICAL SOURCES:

PERIODICALS

Library Journal, October 1, 2002, Thomas L. Kilpatrick, review of *Oyster Blues,* p. 128.*

* * *

McLAVERTY, James 1947-

PERSONAL: Born November 8, 1947, in Derby, England; son of James McLaverty and Joan Smith. *Education:* Pembroke College, Oxford, B.A., M.A. (English literature). *Hobbies and other interests:* Music.

ADDRESSES: Home—231 Church Plantation, Keele, Staffordshire ST5 5AX, England. *Office*—English Department, Keele University, Keele, Staffordshire ST5 5BG, England. *E-mail*—ena00@engl.keele.ac.uk.

CAREER: Author. Keele University, Keele, England, professor of English literature, 1972—.

MEMBER: Johnson Club, Johnson Society, Bibliographic Society.

WRITINGS:

Pope's Printer, John Wright: A Preliminary Study, Oxford Bibliographical Society (Oxford, England), 1976.

(Editor and revisionist) *Pope and the Early Eighteenth-Century Book Trade,* David F. Foxon/Clarendon Press (New York, NY), 1991.

(Editor) J. D. Fleeman, *A Bibliography of the Works of Samuel Johnson, Treating His Published Works from the Beginnings to 1984,* Clarendon Press (Oxford, England), 2000.

Pope, Print, and Meaning, Oxford University Press (New York, NY), 2001.

Contributor of numerous scholarly articles to journals, including *Studies in Bibliography, Library, Shakespeare Survey, Nineteenth-Century Fiction, Philology,* and *Journal of the History of Ideas.*

WORK IN PROGRESS: Pope, Print, and Property, a follow-up to the boo on Pope; textual adviser and editor of poetry for *The Cambridge Edition of the Works of Jonathan Swift;* editing Swift's poems in that edition.

SIDELIGHTS: James McLaverty is a professor of English literature at Keele University in Great Britain and has as his chief interest the eighteenth-century book trade. On the *Keele University Web site* he wrote that he is "particularly interested in the ways in which the details of a book (illustration, layout, capitals, and italics, for example) can be used to express the author's meaning, and in the financial arrangements between authors and booksellers."

In 1991 McLaverty undertook a project his teacher, David Foxon, could not complete due to ill health. The book was *Pope and the Early Eighteenth-Century Book Trade.* This "lavish volume," wrote D. L. Patey for *Choice,* "is the fruit of years of painstaking study." The study covers the details of the book trade in Alexander Pope's time, sometimes exploring Pope's habits of editorializing his texts, such as removing some of the capitalization and italicization that were in use at the time. Researchers of Pope's works, such as McLaverty and Foxon, try to unravel these habits, displaying, especially in this work, that Pope had different ways of punctuating his texts, depending on what kind of audience his manuscripts were meant for. Patey suggested that McLaverty and Foxon's detailed work might not be appreciated by a mainstream audience, but for "18th-centuryists," the book is a must.

Pope is well known not just for his poetry but also for how he made a living from his creative endeavors. There were not many poets in his time who had managed to do so. This story of his "social and economic history," wrote Pat Rogers for *Times Literary Supplement,* "has been told many times, but never in quite the same detail or from quite the same perspective as found in Mclaverty/Foxon's book." Rogers also commented, "McLaverty has performed the main editorial tasks with discretion and self-effacing care. The entire book makes for absorbing, if also demanding, study."

The next book McLaverty was involved with was the work of his friend, the late J. D. Fleeman. McLaverty finished the text after Fleeman died, so that it might be published. The title of this volume is *A Bibliography of the Works of Samuel Johnson, Treating His Published Works from the Beginnings to 1984,* which Robert DeMaria, Jr., writing in the *Journal of English and Germanic Philology,* referred to as a title that "can only begin to suggest the richness and importance of its contents." This volume not only lists all of Johnson's publications, but also provides a record of his life as a writer, "including the continuation of that life in the press for the 200 years following his death in 1784." The reviewer praised McLaverty's "labors" in bringing this work to fruition. One of the interesting facts about the text that DeMaria noted was how Johnson's career can be traced through "his presence in the *Gentleman's Magazine.*" In 1735 only two short poems are printed, but three years later the magazine carries twenty-two of Johnson's works. DeMaria also praised the McLaverty/Fleeman book for making Johnson "more intelligible than he was before," and he states that he doubts there will be another work on Johnson that will "ever achieve more." Writing for

Review of English Studies, Allen Reddick credited the "expert" and "heroic hand of Professor James McLaverty" for his careful work and for his modesty for remaining "behind the curtain" of this book.

In 2001 McLaverty wrote his own book, *Pope, Print, and Meaning,* which, according to John Mullan in the *Times Literary Supplement,* demonstrates "how all Pope's means of publication shaped the meanings of his work for his contemporaries." McLaverty points out contradictions in Pope's life, such as in the poem "Epistle to Dr. Arbuthnot," in which Pope discusses the pain of being a poet and yet "presided painstakingly over the publication of his poetry." Thus much of his discomfort was, McLaverty concludes, self-imposed. Otherwise, why publish at all if it were so painful? Pope claimed that he wanted to be a private man, but McLaverty points out that the public that Pope often mentions as disdainful was not only his audience but also his source of income. So he could not afford not to publish. Another question that arises in the study of Pope's works is the idea of audience. For whom did Pope write? He wrote different versions of his poems depending on whom he thought might read his works. He wrote in one style for collectors; in another style for the general public. Mullan suggested that McLaverty leaves that question to be answered by literary critics "as well as the historian of publishing." D. L. Patey in *Choice* found McLaverty's "many small, extremely perceptive remarks" so informative that any serious student of Pope's "will want to consult" this work.

BIOGRAPHICAL AND CRITICAL SOURCES:

PERIODICALS

Choice, February, 1992, D. L. Patey, review of *Pope and the Early Eighteenth-Century Book Trade,* p. 893; June, 2002, D. L. Patey, review of *Pope, Print, and Meaning,* p. 1771.

Journal of English and Germanic Philology, January, 2002, Robert DeMaria, Jr., review of *A Bibliography of the Works of Samuel Johnson, Treating His Published Works from the Beginnings to 1984,* pp. 142-145.

Review of English Studies, November, 2001, Allen Reddick, review of *A Bibliography of the Works of Samuel Johnson,* pp. 588-590.

Times Literary Supplement, April 26, 1991, Pat Rogers, "The Business of Poetry," pp. 5-6; May 24, 2002, John Mullan, review of *Pope, Print, and Meaning,* p. 25.

ONLINE

Keele University Web site, http://www.keele.ac.uk/ (January 7, 2003), "Jim Mclaverty."

* * *

McNEAL, Shay 1946-

PERSONAL: Born November 5, 1946, in Sturgis, KY; daughter of John H, Earl Evans (an executive with the Red Cross) and Mary Ellen Baird; married Richard McNeal (died 1972); married Gordon K. Smith, October 24, 1975 (divorced 1982); children: (first marriage) Hethur; (second marriage) Paris. *Education:* DeKalb College. *Politics:* Democrat. *Hobbies and other interests:* Horseback riding.

ADDRESSES: Agent—c/o Author Mail, HarperCollins Publishers, 10 East 53rd Street, New York, NY 10022.

CAREER: Savannah St. Mission, Atlanta, GA, assistant director, 1968-70; Lovable Company, Atlanta, special project assistant, 1970-71; Montgomery Ward, New York, NY, associate buyer, 1971-73; Dan River Mills, New York, NY, national fashion director; Macy's, Atlanta, marketing director, 1974-78; Smith McNeal Advertising, Atlanta, president, 1978-86; William Cook Advertising, Atlanta, senior vice president, 1986-89; Preemptive Ltd., Beverly Hills, CA, president, 1989-91; Georgetown Productions, Washington, DC, 1991—; author. Contributor to BBC and Discovery Channel; consultant to political campaigns.

MEMBER: American Association of Advertising Agencies, Executive Women's Association, Atlanta Advertising Club, Delmarva Research Center for History and Culture, Educational Film Center.

AWARDS, HONORS: AdWeek Atlanta designation as one of the Top Advertising Women in the Southeast, 1987.

WRITINGS:

The Secret Plot to Save the Tsar: The Truth behind the Romanov Mystery, Morrow/HarperCollins (New York, NY), 2002.

SIDELIGHTS: Shay McNeal, a successful advertising executive with a strong interest in history, began research in 1995 for her book about the fate of Russia's imperial family, the Romanovs. The Russian tsar and his family were reportedly murdered by the Bolsheviks in 1918, but suspicious details of the family's remains and subsequent rumors about survivors kept the story of this royal family alive. As it became available following the fall of the USSR, McNeal examined newly declassified information about the case and published the results of her investigation in *The Secret Plot to Save the Tsar: The Truth behind the Romanov Mystery.*

The subject of the Romanovs' death has attracted many writers, but McNeal's book, according to *Book Page* reviewer Alan Prince, is different. She "widens the scope of the Romanov tragedy by tracing complicated relationships and complex intrigues," Prince observed. Some of the details McNeal discovered include attempted rescues of the royal family by none other than King George V of Great Britain, President Woodrow Wilson, and other powerful politicians in Japan and Europe. Apparently even Vladimir Lenin was involved, having been provided financial support from the Allies to ensure that the family would remain safe.

McNeal disputes archaeological evidence and DNA testing that supports the Bolshevik story. Why, she asks in the book, were the certified facts of DNA bone-testing of the alleged Romanov physical remains put under lock and key? Did the officials have something to hide? On her Web site McNeal has stated that her main goal was not to reach any definitive conclusions as to the fate of the Romanovs, but to act as a "conduit" for her readers. "I feel there is even more work to be done," she wrote, adding that "my readers . . . will, no doubt, add more primary source information to this historic puzzle."

Though reviewers for *Publishers Weekly* and *Kirkus Reviews* found some of Shay's material unconvincing, they acknowledged the validity of her information on various plans to save the Romanovs. *Russian Life* contributor Dorothy Sayers described *The Secret Plot to Save the Tsar* as a "compelling" work about a "true-life cloak-and-dagger mystery."

BIOGRAPHICAL AND CRITICAL SOURCES:

PERIODICALS

Contemporary Review, September 2001, review of *The Plot to Save the Tsar,* p. 188.

Kirkus Reviews, September 1, 2002, review of *The Secret Plot to Save the Tsar,* p. 1286.

Publishers Weekly, October 28, 2002, review of *The Secret Plot to Save the Tsar,* p. 62.

Russian Life, September-October, 2002, Dorothy L. Sayers, review of *The Secret Plot to Save the Tsar,* p. 46.

ONLINE

BookPage, http://www.bookpage.com/ (January 7, 2003), Alan Prince, review of *The Secret Plot to Save the Tsar.*

Shay McNeal Web site, http://www.shaymcneal.com (January 7, 2003).*

* * *

MEIER, Matt S(ebastian) 1917-2003

OBITUARY NOTICE—See index for *CA* sketch: Born June 4, 1917, in Covington, KY; died of complications from leukemia August 11, 2003, in Santa Clara, CA. Historian, educator, and author. Meier was a scholar of Latin American history who helped establish the field of Chicano history studies in the United States. His interest in Latin American history and culture began while attending the University of Miami, where he earned his bachelor's degree in 1948; the next year, he studied at Mexico City College, receiving a master's degree before taking his doctorate at the University of California at Berkeley in 1954. He then taught in Argentina for a year while on a Fulbright scholarship, returning to the United States to lecture at Bakersfield College from 1955 to 1963. Meier was also on the faculty of Fresno State College in the early 1960s; he joined Santa Clara University in 1966 as an associate professor, chairing the Latin American and Mexican American department from 1968 to 1971 and from 1976 to 1979, and retiring in 1989. Meier's enthusiasm for Latin American history and culture did much to help establish these subjects as areas of study in academia. As a writer, he was especially noted as the author, with Feliciano Rivera, of *The Chicanos: A History of Mexican Americans* (1972), which was later revised as *Mexican Americans/American Mexicans: From Conquistadors to Chicanos* (1993), and for his solo works *Bibliography of Mexican American History* (1984) and *Mexican American Biographies* (1988). Other works by Meier include *Notable Latino Americans* (1997) and *Encyclopedia of the Mexican-American Civil Rights Movement* (2000).

OBITUARIES AND OTHER SOURCES:

PERIODICALS

Los Angeles Times, August 17, 2003, p. B19.
San Francisco Chronicle, August 20, 2003, p. A18.

* * *

MEISSNER, Collin

PERSONAL: Male. *Education:* University of British Columbia, B.A., 1987; University of Notre Dame, Ph.D., 1995.

ADDRESSES: *Office*—Department of English, University of Notre Dame, Notre Dame, IN 46556; fax: 219-631-6897. *E-mail*—meissner.1@nd.edu.

CAREER: University of Notre Dame, Notre Dame, IN, assistant provost and associate director of doctoral program in literature.

WRITINGS:

Henry James and the Language of Experience, Cambridge University Press (New York, NY), 1999.

Contributor to periodicals, including *Studies in the Novel* and *HJR.*

WORK IN PROGRESS: A book on reading and the public sphere; a book on capital crimes in the work of Henry James.

BIOGRAPHICAL AND CRITICAL SOURCES:

PERIODICALS

Choice, January, 2000, D. Kirby, review of *Henry James and the Language of Experience,* p. 934.*

* * *

MEYER, Douglas K.

PERSONAL: Male. *Education:* Concordia Teachers College, B.S.Ed., 1960; Wayne State University, M.A., 1968; Michigan State University, Ph.D., 1970.

ADDRESSES: *Office*—Department of Geography, Eastern Illinois University, 600 Lincoln Ave., Charleston, IL 61920-3099.

CAREER: Eastern Illinois University, Charleston, professor of geography.

WRITINGS:

(With Nancy Easter Shick) *Pictorial Landscape History of Charleston, Illinois,* Rardin Graphics (Charleston, IL), 1985.

(With John A. Jakle and Robert W. Bastian) *Common Houses in America's Small Towns: The Atlantic Seaboard to the Mississippi Valley,* University of Georgia Press (Athens, GA), 1989.

Making the Heartland Quilt: A Geographical History of Settlement and Migration in Early-Nineteenth-Century Illinois, Southern Illinois University Press (Carbondale, IL), 2000.*

* * *

MEYERS, Richard
See HELL, Richard

MICHALSON, Karen 1960-

PERSONAL: Born 1960; married Bill Michalson (a professor of electrical engineering), May 27, 1983. *Education:* Framingham State College, B.A.; Boston College, M.A. (English); University of Massachusetts at Amherst, Ph.D. (English); attended Western New England College School of Law.

ADDRESSES: Home—Massachusetts. *Office*—Arula Records, P.O. Box 332, Southbridge, MA 01550. *Agent*—Jennie Dunham, Dunham Literary, 156 Fifth Ave., Suite 625, New York, NY 10010-7002. *E-mail*—arularec@aol.com.

CAREER: Writer and musician. Founder, lyricist, lead singer, keyboardist, and bass guitarist for the rock band Point of Ares; founder and head of record label Arula Records. University of Connecticut, Storrs, assistant professor of English, 1991-93.

AWARDS, HONORS: Prometheus Award finalist for best novel, 2002, for *Enemy Glory;* William L. Crawford Award finalist for best new fantasy writer, International Association for the Fantastic in the Arts, 2002.

WRITINGS:

Victorian Fantasy Literature: Literary Battles with Church and Empire (nonfiction), Edwin Mellen Press (Lewiston, NY), 1990.

Enemy Glory (fantasy novel), Tor Books (New York, NY), 2001.

Hecate's Glory (fantasy novel), Tor Books (New York, NY), 2003.

Also author of the short story "Of No Importance," released as a spoken-word album, Arula Records.

SONG LYRICS; SOUND RECORDINGS

Enemy Glory, Arula Records (Southbridge, MA), 1996.

The Sorrows of Young Apollo, Arula Records (Southbridge, MA), 1999.

Enemy Glory Darkly Blessed, Arula Records (Southbridge, MA), 2001.

WORK IN PROGRESS: The Maenad's God (novel), and an untitled fantasy novel.

SIDELIGHTS: If there is such a thing as an ordinary path to becoming a fantasy writer, Karen Michalson did not take it. She earned her Ph.D. in English with a dissertation on the conflict between British imperial aspirations and fantasy literature, and planned to become an English professor. She eventually took a job at the University of Connecticut, but in the meantime she developed two secondary careers that hardly comported with her chosen primary one.

The first was as bassist and lead vocalist for a rock trio, Point of Ares, and the second was as a fantasy writer. Though some forms of fiction-writing can and do coalesce well with the role of English professor, the writing of fantasy—as Michalson herself discussed in her dissertation, later published as *Victorian Fantasy Literature: Literary Battles with Church and Empire*—was long ago banished from the academy. Having completed *Enemy Glory,* Michalson left her job at the university to dedicate herself full time to writing fiction and music.

Michalson has said that her greatest influences as a child came from rock and roll and classic literature—including the few works of fantasy literature acknowledged as classics, such as Oscar Wilde's fantasy tales, Lord Dunsany's novels, and J. R. R. Tolkein's "Middle Earth" series. Studying under Charlotte Spivack, who, as Michalson later told the Worcester *Telegram and Gazette,* was "one of the very few legitimate scholars looking at fantasy as serious literature," she "became interested in finding out why fantasy became excluded from the literary canon and went in the direction of popular culture." The reasons, as she demonstrated in her dissertation, were political, governed by the fact that the British Empire sought to distinguish itself from the people it conquered, in India and elsewhere, by maintaining that whereas the natives believed in fairy tales, Englishmen subscribed only to hard, cold reality.

During the mid-1990s, Michalson taught herself how to play bass guitar and formed Point of Ares, which released three albums. The songs included on the first and third of these, *Enemy Glory* (1996) and *Enemy Glory, Darkly Blessed* (2001), explore the themes of her fantasy writing.

The writing itself began one Sunday afternoon when, as Michalson recalled for the *Telegram and Gazette,* "I was sitting in front of my computer, and I was just writing. And this voice seemed to come out, and this line: 'The first time I saw the old fisherman, I thought he was a compost heap.' And I wasn't even thinking about anything like this. I wondered what it could mean, but I just kept writing. When I was done, I looked at what I had [and] said, 'Oh my God, this is the first chapter of a novel. This isn't [literary] criticism.'"

The result was *Enemy Glory,* which Jackie Cassada in *Library Journal* described as a "grand-scale fantasy." As the story begins, the wizard Llewelyn has fallen ill as the result of a spell cast on him. He is revived by an old friend, the duke of Walworth, but clearly their relationship has changed: as soon as Llewelyn gains consciousness, Walworth draws his sword and accuses him of treason. This provides a frame for Llewelyn's life story, the subject of the trilogy that begins with the story of his early years.

A devotee of the evil goddess Hecate, Llewelyn spends his early years studying at a school of magic in the city of Sunnashiven. After escaping from Sunnashiven as it falls to outside forces, Llewelyn is led to another country, Threle, where he meets up with a group of rebels that includes Walworth and Walworth's sister, Caethne, as well as the scholar Mirand, who becomes Llewelyn's mentor. Believing that his new friends have betrayed him, Llewelyn then enters monastic training in the service of evil, vowing vengeance on his former comrades. Referring to the extremely popular fantasy series by J. K. Rowling, a reviewer in *Publishers Weekly* called *Enemy Glory* "a sort of Harry Potter on downers." The *Publishers Weekly* critic called *Enemy Glory* a "well-crafted first novel."

Michalson's literary career did not launch until several years after she left her position at the University of Connecticut. After publishing two successful novels, Michalson began dividing her time between writing, music, and studying law part time at Western New England College. Michalson told *CA* that her "interest in law was sparked by the legal themes in [my] novels." Before entering school, she completed *Hecate's Glory,* which continues the chronicle of Llewelyn's life. Leaving Threle, he winds up in the land of Gondal, where he has an opportunity to become king. He runs afoul of Hecate, however, who forces him to choose between destroying the beauteous kingdom or travelling north, where he will be captured and tried for treason. "Graceful story telling and a unique premise render this fantasy a good addition to most libraries," wrote Cassada in *Library Journal.*

Michason told *CA:* "In the worst moments of my life, books have been an oasis, a comfort to turn to when nobody else was there. I don't know who originally said that it's impossible to be lonely so long as you have a good book. I would like my books to make it impossible for readers to be lonely for a little while, to provide both an escape and intellectual stimulation. I would like my books to become part of my readers' mental landscapes."

BIOGRAPHICAL AND CRITICAL SOURCES:

PERIODICALS

Association of Libertarian Feminist News, winter, 1996, Joan Kennedy Taylor, interview with Michalson.

Library Journal, January 1, 2001, Jackie Cassada, review of *Enemy Glory,* p. 163; February 15, 2003, Jackie Cassada, review of *Hecate's Glory,* p. 173.

Publishers Weekly, January 8, 2001, review of *Enemy Glory;* January 20, 2003, Peter Cannon, review of *Hecate's Glory,* p. 62.

Telegram and Gazette (Worcester, MA), February 21, 2003, Nancy Sheehan, "Fantasy League: Fiction Author a Real Defender of Underappreciated Genre," p. C1.

ONLINE

Arula Records Web site, http://www.arularecords.com/ (September 17, 2003).

FantasticaDaily.com, http://www.fantasticadaily.com/ (February 2, 2001), Eva Wojcik-Obert, review of *Enemy Glory;* (February 5, 2001) Eva Wojcik-Obert, interview with Michalson; (December 14, 2001) Eva Wojcik-Obert, review of *Victorian Fantasy Literature: Literary Battles with Church and Empire;* (January 10, 2003) Eva Wojcik-Obert, review of *Hecate's Glory.*

MICHENER, Marian

PERSONAL: Female. *Education:* San Francisco State University, M.A. (creative writing).

ADDRESSES: *Home*—Seattle, WA. *Agent*—c/o Spinsters Ink, 32 East First St., #330, Duluth, MN 55802-2002.

CAREER: Writer and college administrator.

WRITINGS:

Three Glasses of Wine Have Been Removed from This Story: A Novel, Silverleaf Press (Seattle, WA), 1988, published as *Dreaming under a Ton of Lizards,* Spinsters Ink (Duluth, MN), 1999

SIDELIGHTS: In her novel *Dreaming under a Ton of Lizards,* originally published as *Three Glasses of Wine Have Been Removed from This Story,* Marian Michener tells the story of Olivia, a would-be writer whose dreams of success are foiled by her addiction to alcohol. She spends her days and nights obsessing about "Sister Wine," as well as her destructive relationship with her lover, Brooke. As Olivia realizes she must break her addiction, she takes the first steps toward sobriety and ends her relationship with Brooke. Olivia takes a job as caretaker of a remote cottage on the Oregon coast to concentrate and withdraw into her writing. By doing so, she manages to write about her path to addiction and how it has affected her life. Although she doesn't succeed as a writer, the process allows her to understand how her past contributed to both her addictions and new state of consciousness, which aids her in staying away from alcohol and beginning the long climb through life as a sober person. In *Publishers Weekly,* a reviewer praised Michener's "multifaceted and fresh" characters as well as her "down-to-earth details." In *Lambda Rising,* reviewer Debra Weinstein commented that although the book's structure, a series of flashbacks, is not as strong as it could be, "the strength of this book is in the [elegant] writing."

BIOGRAPHICAL AND CRITICAL SOURCES:

PERIODICALS

Booklist, September 15, 1999, Whitney Scott, review of *Dreaming under a Ton of Lizards,* p. 233.

Lambda Rising, December, 1999, Debra Weinstein, review of *Dreaming under a Ton of Lizards.*

Publishers Weekly, September 20, 1999, review of *Dreaming under a Ton of Lizards,* p. 76. *

* * *

MILGRIM, David

PERSONAL: Married: wife's name, Kyra; children: Wyatt.

ADDRESSES: *Home*—Petaluma, CA. *Agent*—c/o Author Mail, Atheneum/ Simon & Schuster, 1240 Avenue of the Americas, New York, NY 10020. *E-mail*—david@davidmilgrim.com.

CAREER: Writer and illustrator. Previously worked as a graphic designer.

WRITINGS:

SELF-ILLUSTRATED PICTURE BOOKS

Why Benny Barks, Random House (New York, NY), 1994.

Dog Brain, Viking (New York, NY), 1996.

Here in Space, Bridgewater Books (Mahwah, NJ), 1997.

Cows Can't Fly, Viking (New York, NY), 1998.

My Friend Lucky, Atheneum Books (New York, NY), 2002.

See Otto, Atheneum Books (New York, NY), 2002.

Ride Otto Ride!, Atheneum Books (New York, NY), 2002.

See Pip Point, Atheneum Books (New York, NY), 2003.

Thank You, Thanksgiving, Clarion Books (New York, NY), 2003.

Swing Otto Swing!, Atheneum Books (New York, NY), 2004.

ILLUSTRATOR

Patrick's Dinosaurs on the Internet, by Carol Carrick, Clarion Books (New York, NY), 1999.

Little Lamb's Christmas, by Josephine Page, Cartwheel Books (New York, NY), 2003.

SIDELIGHTS: In *My Friend Lucky,* writer and illustrator David Milgrim presents a series of opposites narrated by a little boy who uses his dog, Lucky, to demonstrate them. These opposites are enunciated in extremely simple couplets such as "I love Lucky / Lucky loves me," and illustrated by spare black line drawings on a field of white, with color reserved for the main characters themselves. In many cases, the demonstration of opposing concepts involves witty distinctions: for example, "Lucky's big" finds the dog looking down at a caterpillar, while "Lucky's small" shows him gazing up at a horse. For "Lucky's loud," the dog is barking while the narrator tries to do his homework, and though "Lucky's quiet" shows him still barking, now the narrator has on earmuffs.

"Though the interplay of text and illustration has more subtlety and wit than most books of opposites," wrote Carolyn Phelan in *Booklist,* "there's no mistaking the meanings of the paired images." Kay Bowes in *School Library Journal* called *My Friend Lucky* "a gentle concept book about opposites," and a reviewer in *Publishers Weekly* similarly described it as a "mild-mannered book." A critic in *Kirkus Reviews* characterized it both as "a splendid primer in the art of visual irony" and "a love story" of a boy and his dog. "A winner," the review concluded, "and not just for dog lovers."

See Otto and *Ride Otto Ride!* chronicle the adventures of a robot from another planet whose spaceship has run out of fuel, forcing him to land on Earth. Using a vocabulary of just twenty-one words, the first book follows the protagonist as he lands in a jungle and, after running afoul of a rhinoceros, makes friends with two cheerful monkeys. "Though the limited vocabulary imposes its own restraints," a commentator in *Kirkus Reviews* wrote of *See Otto,* "Milgrim uses visual humor with a touch of irony to craft a real story with enough action to appeal to new readers." Reviewing both works in *Booklist,* Phelan called the books "an appealing option for children just beginning to read and feeling as hopeful and adventurous as Otto."

BIOGRAPHICAL AND CRITICAL SOURCES:

PERIODICALS

Booklist, April 15, 2002, Carolyn Phelan, review of *My Friend Lucky,* p. 1408; September 15, 2002, Carolyn Phelan, review of *Ride Otto Ride!,* p. 241.

Kirkus Reviews, November 1, 2001, review of *My Friend Lucky,* p. 1553; August 1, 2002, review of *See Otto,* p. 1138.

Publishers Weekly, December 10, 2001, review of *My Friend Lucky,* p. 68.

School Library Journal, February, 2002, Kay Bowes, review of *My Friend Lucky,* p. 108; March, 2003, Nancy A. Gifford, review of *Ride Otto Ride!,* p. 199.

ONLINE

David Milgrim Web site, http://www.davidmilgrim.com (September 16, 2003).*

* * *

MILLER, Christopher L. 1953-

PERSONAL: Born 1953. *Education:* Boston University, B.A., 1975; studied at L'École Normale Supérieure (Paris, France), 1981-82; Yale University, Ph.D., 1983.

ADDRESSES: *Office*—Yale University, Department of French, New Haven, CT 06590. *E-mail*—christopher.miller@yale.edu.

CAREER: Peace Corps, Institut Bondoyi, Muene Ditu, Zaire, English instructor; Yale University, New Haven, CT, assistant professor, 1983-87, Charles B. G. Murphy Associate Professor of French and Afro-American Studies, 1987-90, professor, 1990-99, chair of French department, 1997—, Frederick Clifford Ford Professor of French and African American Studies, 1999—. National Endowment for the Humanities, member of review committee.

AWARDS, HONORS: Morse fellowship in the Humanities; Fulbright Africa research fellowship; Yale senior faculty fellowship; National Endowment for the Humanities fellowship and Guggenheim fellowship, both 2003-04.

WRITINGS:

Blank Darkness: Africanist Discourse in French, University of Chicago Press (Chicago, IL), 1985.

Theories of Africans: Francophone Literature and Anthropology in Africa, University of Chicago Press (Chicago, IL), 1990.

Nationalists and Nomads: Essays on Francophone African Literature and Culture, University of Chicago Press (Chicago, IL), 1998.

Contributor of scholarly articles to journals and books, including *The Encyclopedia of Sub-Saharan Africa, A New History of French Literature* and *Literary Theory and African Literature.*

SIDELIGHTS: Christopher L. Miller is a professor at Yale University and a scholar of Francophone (French-language) African literature who has written several books on the topic, including *Blank Darkness: Africanist Discourse in French, Theories of Africans: Francophone Literature and Anthropology in Africa,* and, more recently, *Nationalists and Nomads: Essays on Francophone African Literature and Culture.*

Nationalists and Nomads is a collection of six essays, four of which originated as articles Miller wrote for various journals. Taken together, the essays cover the history of Francophone African literature, which Miller argues began with the publication of Senegalese author Ahmadou Mapate Diagne's book *Les trois volontes de Malic* in 1920. In the second and third essays Miller discusses the relationship between France and its African colonies in the 1930s as reflected in the International Colonial Exposition held in 1931 and in a novel, *Mirages de Paris,* which was set at that exposition. The fourth essay covers the impact the emerging nationalist movements in Africa had upon the region's literature. *Journal of African History* contributor William B. Cohen commented particularly favorably upon this chapter, calling attention to Miller's "interesting and eye-opening discussion of Ferdinand Oyono's [novel] *Houseboy.*" In the final two essays Miller examines current debates in American academia over the proper ways of teaching African literature. "Miller's knowledge of theoretical and more pragmatic research on questions of curricular choice and on the evolution of critical theory itself is quite comprehensive," Louise M. Jefferson noted in *Criticism.* He added that Miller "builds his argument carefully and convincingly."

BIOGRAPHICAL AND CRITICAL SOURCES:

PERIODICALS

African Affairs, January, 1992, Richard D. E. Burton, review of *Theories of Africans: Francophone Literature and Anthropology in Africa,* pp. 161-163.

African Studies Review, September, 1992, Janice Spleth, review of *Theories of Africans,* pp. 104-106.

Bookwatch, April, 1999, review of *Nationalists and Nomads: Essays on Francophone African Literature and Culture,* p. 8.

Choice, July-August, 1999, S. R. Schulman, review of *Nationalists and Nomads,* p. 1952.

College Literature, October-February, 1992, Paul Stoller, review of *Theories of Africans,* pp. 242-245.

Comparative Literature, fall, 1989, Mildred Mortimer, review of *Blank Darkness: Africanist Discourse in French,* pp. 408-409.

Contemporary Literature, fall, 1992, Alan Isaacs, review of *Theories of Africans,* pp. 563-572.

Criticism, winter, 2002, Louise M. Jefferson, review of *Nationalists and Nomads,* pp. 90-96.

French Review, December, 2001, Janis L. Pallister, review of *Nationalists and Nomads,* p. 361.

International Affairs, April, 1992, Patrick Chabal, review of *Theories of Africans,* p. 383.

International Journal of African Historical Studies, summer, 1991, William B. Cohen, review of *Theories of Africans,* p. 646-648; winter, 2000, Isaac Bazie, review of *Nationalists and Nomads,* pp. 202-203.

Journal of African History, July, 2000, William B. Cohen, review of *Nationalists and Nomads,* p. 336.

Research in African Literature, fall, 2000, Ambroise Kom, review of *Nationalists and Nomads,* p. 175.

World Literature Today, autumn, 1991, Evelyn Uhrhan Irving, review of *Theories of Africans,* p. 753; autumn, 1999, Harold A. Waters, review of *Nationalists and Nomads,* p. 793.

ONLINE

Yale University Web site, http://www.yale.edu/ (November 14, 2003).

MILLER, James G(rier) 1916-2002

OBITUARY NOTICE—See index for *CA* sketch: Born July 17, 1916, in Pittsburgh, PA; died November 7, 2002, in La Jolla, CA. Psychiatrist, educator, administrator, and author. Miller, a former president of the University of Louisville at Kentucky, was at the forefront of the creation of a new discipline: behavioral science, a term he himself coined. Although he initially studied to be a minister at Columbia Bible College, his love of science caused him to switch majors and attend the University of South Carolina, the University of Michigan, and Harvard University, where he earned his medical degree in 1942 and his doctorate in psychiatry in 1943. During World War II Miller served in the Army Medical Corps as a captain and was involved in evaluating potential agents for the Office of Strategic Services, which later became the Central Intelligence Agency. After working for a year at the U.S. Veterans Administration, he joined academia as a professor of psychology and chair of the department at the University of Chicago. The late 1950s and most of the 1960s were spent at the University of Michigan in Ann Arbor, where he was a professor until 1967. From 1967 to 1971 Miller was a professor at Cleveland State University, where he was also vice president of academic affairs until 1970 and provost from 1970 to 1971. He then moved to the University of Louisville as vice president of academic educational development, becoming president in 1973 and leaving in 1980. As president of the university, Miller helped set up the nursing college and significantly increased enrollment while transitioning the school from a private to a public institution. While working as a university president, Miller's influention book *Living Systems* (1976) was published. This work thoroughly explains the discoveries in behavioral science up to that time, a discipline that he and others had been working on since the 1940s and that is intended to uncover common principles governing everything from the smallest living cell to complex organizational systems, such as political states and business corporations, as well as the organization of nonliving things. In 1980 Miller moved to California to become president of the Robert Maynard Hutchins Center for the Study of Democratic Institutions until 1983; and during the early 1980s he was also an adjunct professor at the Universities of California at Santa Barbara, San Diego, and Los Angeles. He worked as a psychiatrist at Brentwood V.A. Hospital from 1981 to 1988, and at the La Jolla V.A. Hospital in 1989. In addition to his teaching and psychiatry work, Miller was the founder of the journal *Behavioral Science* (now *Systems Research and Behavioral Science*), which he edited from 1956 to 1986, and created the online education network Educom, which later became part of Edunet. Miller's other publications include *Unconsciousness* (1942), the coauthored works *Assessment of Men* (1948), *Computers and Education* (1967), and *Measurement and Interpretation in Accounting: A Living Systems Theory Approach* (1989), as well as several edited works.

OBITUARIES AND OTHER SOURCES:

PERIODICALS

Los Angeles Times, November 15, 2002, p. B14.

* * *

MILLETT, Larry 1947-

PERSONAL: Born 1947.

ADDRESSES: *Agent*—c/o Author Mail, Penguin Putnam, 375 Hudson St., New York, NY 10014.

CAREER: Journalist and author. *St. Paul Pioneer Press,* St. Paul, MN, architecture columnist.

AWARDS, HONORS: International Architecture Book Award, American Institute of Architects, 1993, for *Lost Twin Cities.*

WRITINGS:

FICTION

Sherlock Holmes and the Red Demon, Viking (New York, NY), 1996.

Sherlock Holmes and the Ice Palace Murders: From the American Chronicles of John H. Watson, M.D., Viking (New York, NY), 1998.

Sherlock Holmes and the Rune Stone Mystery: From the American Chronicles of John H. Watson, M.D., Viking (New York, NY), 1999.

Sherlock Holmes and the Secret Alliance, Viking (New York, NY), 2001.

The Disappearance of Sherlock Holmes: A Mystery Featuring Shadwell Rafferty, Viking (New York, NY), 2002.

NONFICTION

The Curve of the Arch: The Story of Louis Sullivan's Owatonna Bank, Minnesota Historical Society Press (St. Paul, MN), 1985.

Lost Twin Cities, Minnesota Historical Society Press (St. Paul, MN), 1992.

Twin Cities Then and Now, contemporary photographs by Jerry Mathiason, Minnesota Historical Society Press (St. Paul, MN), 1996.

ADAPTATIONS: Books adapted for audio include *Sherlock Holmes and the Ice Palace Murders* (abridged; four cassettes), Penguin Audiobooks, 1998.

SIDELIGHTS: Larry Millett is a former architecture columnist and the author of several books on that subject, including *The Curve of the Arch: The Story of Louis Sullivan's Owatonna Bank,* called "an engaging, straightforward history of that small but majestic structure" by Martin Filler in a *New York Review of Books* article. Sullivan was hired by banker Carl Bennett to design a bank building in Owatonna, Minnesota, and Millett provides a history of its design, construction, and remodeling, and follows the ascent and decline of Sullivan's career.

Millett's award-winning *Lost Twin Cities* is a history of the change and urban renewal in Minneapolis and St. Paul, Minnesota over a century. He includes nearly 400 black-and-white photographs and profiles more than sixty churches, houses, theaters, office buildings, and other structures and includes a social history. A *Bloomsbury Review* contributor noted that Millett "has chosen not only the grand and distinguished places but also the ordinary, the humble, the poorly designed, and the downright peculiar." *Library Journal*'s H. Ward Jandl remarked that the study "makes us mourn for the richness that has been lost but also makes us appreciate how much has survived."

Millett followed up with *Twin Cities Then and Now,* which offers seventy-two historic photographs of streets, taken from the 1880s until the late 1950s, along with contemporary photographs for comparison. The volume also contains four detailed maps that identify significant buildings and locations.

Millett began a series of mysteries featuring Arthur Conan Doyle's fictional characters Sherlock Holmes and John Watson with *Sherlock Holmes and the Red Demon.* Doyle, a Scottish physician, penned the Holmes novels and short stories to supplement his income, but he did not hold them in high regard, feeling that he would be remembered for his serious historical novels, science fiction, and spiritualism. But writers like Millett have picked up where Doyle left off, rewriting the characters of Holmes and Watson and plopping them down in all manner of places far removed from Baker Street. Millett sets his stories primarily in Minnesota.

In the opener, Holmes and Watson arrive in Minnesota at the request of real-life railroad magnate James J. Hill, whose Great Northern Railway is being threatened by an arsonist. *January* online reviewer J. Kingston Pierce wrote, "Chock-full of colorfully wrought frontier characters, including puissant lumberjacks and high-spirited backwoods prostitutes, and incorporating actual events (most prominently the deadly and still-mysterious Hinckley, Minnesota fire of 1894), *Red Demon* was a careful tribute to Doyle and a welcome elaboration of the Holmes legend." *Armchair Detective*'s Ronald C. Miller felt Millett's first Holmes mystery to be the best since *The Hound of the Baskervilles.* Miller called *Sherlock Holmes and the Red Demon* "magnificent, with a wonderful and accurate turn-of-the-century setting, a labyrinthine plot, colorful characters, and the most diabolical and fiendish villain in recent memory."

Sherlock Holmes and the Ice Palace Murders: From the American Chronicles of John H. Watson, M.D. is set in 1896 St. Paul, home of the winter carnival. At the behest of Hill, Holmes and Watson search for clues to the disappearance of Jonathan Upton, son of prosperous merchant George Upton, who vanished as he was about to marry heiress Laura Forbes. They are joined by Shadwell Rafferty, an Irishman whose business card reads "bartending and discreet investigations," and who has been hired by the senior Upton. A *Publishers Weekly* reviewer commented that Rafferty "lights up each scene in which he appears, adding a distinctively American bounce to a solid, complex mystery distinguished by its vibrant portrayal of nineteenth-century St. Paul." The parents of F. Scott Fitzgerald, who lived in St. Paul during the 1890s, make a cameo appearance.

Pierce called this second Holmes novel by Millett "a satisfying yarn that generally moves at a breakneck clip, its plot buttressed by often-witty dialogue and a few scenes (including a nocturnal chase across the frozen Mississippi) that stay with you even after you turn the book's last page. Doyle would surely have hated *Sherlock Holmes and the Ice Palace Murders,* for it is destined to draw a whole new crop of fans to the character he came to resent."

Sherlock Holmes and the Rune Stone Mystery: From the American Chronicles of John H. Watson, M.D. begins in Sweden, with King Oskar II asking Holmes to verify the authenticity of a rune stone found on a farm in Minnesota, and which might prove that America was actually discovered by the Scandinavians. Just as they arrive, the farmer is killed, and the stone is stolen. Rafferty appears in this story, now becoming more of a partner than the rival he had been. A *Publishers Weekly* contributor felt that Millett "is in his comfort zone with Rafferty, a thoroughly engaging character."

Sherlock Holmes and the Secret Alliance is set in 1899 in the Twin Cities. On the eve of President McKinley's visit, union activist Michael O'Donnell is found hanging from a tree outside the family home of Mayor Arthur Adams. The sign hanging from the lynched man proclaims that he was murdered by the Citizens Alliance for the Maintenance of Order and the Freedom of Labor. Rafferty and O'Donnell's sister, Addie, become overwhelmed by the corruption, bribery, and continuing violence they face as they delve into O'Donnell's killing, and Rafferty finally calls on Holmes and Watson, who travel from New York to help. *Booklist*'s Connie Fletcher called the mystery "great fun."

The Disappearance of Sherlock Holmes: A Mystery Featuring Shadwell Rafferty begins with the disappearance of Elsie Cubitt, a woman Holmes had helped and become strongly attracted to while on another case. The chief suspect is Chicago mobster Abe Slaney, thought to have drowned in a prison escape. Holmes and Watson travel from England to New York City, and when Holmes disappears, himself now a hostage, Watson and Rafferty are left to rescue the pair. Fletcher commented that Millett "recreates the world of Holmes with uncanny precision."

BIOGRAPHICAL AND CRITICAL SOURCES:

PERIODICALS

AB Bookman's Weekly, September 9, 1985, review of *The Curve of the Arch: The Story of Louis Sullivan's Owatonna Bank,* p. 1643.

Armchair Detective, spring, 1997, Allen J. Hubin, review of *Sherlock Holmes and the Red Demon,* p. 149; winter, 1997, Ronald C. Miller, review of *Sherlock Holmes and the Red Demon,* p. 115.

Bloomsbury Review, December, 1992, review of *Lost Twin Cities,* p. 11.

Booklist, October 1, 2001, Connie Fletcher, review of *Sherlock Holmes and the Secret Alliance,* p. 302; October 1, 2002, Connie Fletcher, review of *The Disappearance of Sherlock Holmes: A Mystery Featuring Shadwell Rafferty,* p. 304.

Kirkus Reviews, August 1, 1996, review of *Sherlock Holmes and the Red Demon,* p. 1103; October 15, 1998, review of *Sherlock Holmes and the Ice Palace Murders: From the American Chronicles of John H. Watson, M.D.,* p. 1498; August 15, 2001, review of *Sherlock Holmes and the Secret Alliance,* p. 1170; September 1, 2002, review of *The Disappearance of Sherlock Holmes,* p. 1269.

Library Journal, December, 1992, H. Ward Jandl, review of *Lost Twin Cities,* p. 134; February 15, 1999, Theresa Connors, review of *Sherlock Holmes and the Ice Palace Murders,* p. 202; October 1, 1999, Rex E. Klett, review of *Sherlock Holmes and the Rune Stone Mystery: From the American Chronicles of John H. Watson, M.D.,* p. 137; October 1, 2001, Fred Gervat, review of *Sherlock Holmes and the Secret Alliance,* p. 146.

New York Review of Books, January 29, 1987, Martin Filler, review of *The Curve of the Arch,* pp. 30-34.

Publishers Weekly, August 5, 1996, review of *Sherlock Holmes and the Red Demon,* p. 434; October 12, 1998, review of *Sherlock Holmes and the Ice Palace Murders,* p. 61; September 27, 1999, review of *Sherlock Holmes and the Rune Stone Mystery,* p. 75; September 17, 2001, review of *Sherlock Holmes and the Secret Alliance,* p. 58; October 7, 2002, review of *The Disappearance of Sherlock Holmes,* p. 55.

Washington Post Book World, January 2, 2000, Guy Amirthanayagam, review of *Sherlock Holmes and the Rune Stone Mystery,* p. 7.

ONLINE

January, http://www.januarymagazine.com/ (May 5, 2003) J. Kingston Pierce, review of *Sherlock Holmes and the Ice Palace Murders.**

* * *

MILLUS, Donald (J.) 1939-
(Felix Anthony)

PERSONAL: Born June 11, 1939, in Brooklyn, NY; son of Felix (in real estate) and Margaret (a homemaker) Millus; married Patricia Sikora, August 21, 1967; children: Chris, Donald M., Sara T. *Ethnicity:* "Native American." *Education:* Fordham University, A.B. (cum laude), 1961; Yale University, Ph.D., 1973. *Politics:* "Yellow-dog Democrat." *Religion:* Roman Catholic. *Hobbies and other interests:* Fishing, golf, cooking.

ADDRESSES: Home—905 Lakeside Dr., Conway, SC 29526. *Office*—Coastal Carolina University, Conway, SC 29528-6054. *E-mail*—millus@coastal.edu.

CAREER: New Haven Journal Courier, New Haven, CT, editor, 1973-74; Coastal Carolina University, Conway, SC, professor, 1974—. *Military service:* U.S. Army, Special Services, 1969-71; became captain; received Bronze Star.

MEMBER: Golf Writers Association of America, Outdoor Writers Association of America, SCOPe.

AWARDS, HONORS: Shakespeare Big Game Writing Contest winner, 1978.

WRITINGS:

A Contemplative Fishing Guide, Sandlapper (Orangeburg, SC), 1977.

Fishing the Southeast Coast: Essays on Fish, Fishing, Fishermen, and Fishing Places, from Morehead City, North Carolina, through coastal South Carolina, to the Georgia Sea Islands, Sandlapper (Orangeburg, SC), 1989.

Wading South: Fishing the Twentieth Century, Part II, Atlantic Publishing (Tabor City, NC), 2001.

Author of weekly column, "Just Angling." Contributor to outdoor magazines and other periodicals, including *America, Charlotte Observer,* and *New York Times.* Editor of golf magazine, 1977-90. Some writings appear under pseudonym Felix Anthony.

WORK IN PROGRESS: A critical edition of *Exposition of I John,* by William Tyndale, publication by Catholic University of America Press (Washington, DC); *Praise of Golf, Praise of Folly; The Ebbets Field Knot Hole.*

SIDELIGHTS: Donald Millus told *CA:* "I love to expose myself, but not offend. I share my life experiences: growing up in Brooklyn, fishing, and golfing. I moved to South Carolina in 1974 to teach (Shakespeare, Chaucer, American literature), write, and fish. Unfortunately I also became a golf addict when I edited a golf magazine to put my children through college. My political and sports essays have appeared in numerous outdoor magazines. I get a high out of writing, whether I'm reviewing a new translation of *Utopia* or doing a column on throwing a cast net for shrimp in a tidal creek."

* * *

MIN, Pyong Gap 1942-

PERSONAL: Born February 19, 1942 in Choongnam, Korea; son of Hong Sik Min and Nam Hee Song; married Young Oak Kim, November 30, 2001; children: Jay, Michael, Tony. *Ethnicity:* "Korean; Asian American." *Education:* Seoul National University, B.A., 1970; Georgia State University, M.A., 1975, Ph.D. (education), 1979, Ph.D. (sociology), 1983. *Politics:* Democrat. *Hobbies and other interests:* Travel.

ADDRESSES: *Home*—205-14 50th Ave., Oakland Gardens, NY 11364. *Office*—Queens College, Department of Sociology, Flushing, NY 11367; fax: (718) 997-2810. *E-mail*—min@troll.soc.qc.edu

CAREER: Writer and professor. Georgia State University, instructor and research associate, 1983-86; Queens College, City University of New York, assistant professor, 1987-91, associate professor, 1992-95, Graduate Center faculty, 1993—, professor, 1996—. Korea *Herald,* Seoul, Korea, general reporter, 1969-70; Dongbook High School, Seoul, English teacher, 1970-72; Asian American Studies Center, University of California, Los Angeles, visiting professor, 1986; Institute for Far Eastern Studies, Kyung Nam University, Seoul, visiting professor, 1995; Seoul National University, Institute of Social Sciences, visiting professor, summer, 1997.

MEMBER: Korean Cultural Education Association (president, 1989-93), American Sociological Association, Korean Global Foundation (board member and award committee chair, 2000—).

AWARDS, HONORS: National Science Foundation grant, 1986; Professional Staff Congress of City University of New York research award, 1988, 1990, 1992-96, 1998, 2001-03; Korean Research Foundation grant through Queens College, 1989; Ford Foundation diversity grant, 1992, 1998; Korean Foundation fellowship, 1997; Association for Asian American Studies National Book Award in Social Science, 1997, and Asia and Asian America section of the American Sociological Association Outstanding Book Award, 1998, both for *Caught in the Middle: Korean Merchants in America's Multiethnic Cities;* Korean Association of New York Community Service through Research Award, 1997; Asian Americans for Equality grant, 1998.

WRITINGS:

Ethnic Business Enterprise: Korean Small Business in Atlanta, Center for Migration Studies (New York, NY), 1988.

Caught in the Middle: Korean Merchants in America's Multiethnic Cities, University of California Press (Berkeley, CA), 1996.

Changes and Conflicts: Korean Immigrant Families in New York, Allyn and Bacon (Boston, MA), 1998.

EDITOR

Asian Americans: Contemporary Trends and Issues, Sage Publications (Thousand Oaks, CA), 1995.

(With Rose Kim) *Struggle for Ethnic Identity: Narratives by Asian-American Professionals,* AltaMira Press (Walnut Creek, CA), 1999.

Mass Migration to the United States: Classical and Contemporary Periods, AltaMira Press (Walnut Creek, CA), 2002.

(With Jung Ha Kim) *Religions in Asian America: Building Faith Communities,* AltaMira Press (Walnut Creek, CA), 2002.

The Second Generation: Ethnic Identity among Asian Americans, AltaMira Press (Walnut Creek, CA), 2002.

Editorial board member, *Journal of American Ethnic History,* 1997—, *Amerasia Journal,* 1997—, *Monthly Korea Forum,* 1999—, and *International Migration Review,* 2001—; *Development and Society* international advisory committee member, 1997—.

Contributor to periodicals and journals, including *Ethnic and Racial Studies, International Migration Review, Journal of American Ethnic History, Academy Journal of Korean Studies, Sociological Quarterly, Sociological Forum, Gender and Society, Journal of Comparative Family Studies, Amerasia Journal, Journal of Urban Affairs,* and *Educational Theory.*

Contributor to books, including *Koreans in North America,* edited by Seung Hyong Lee, Kyung Nam Unversity Press (Masan, Korea), 1988; *The Present and the Future of the Korean American Community,* edited by Tae-Hwan Kwak and Seung Hyong Lee, Kyung Nam University Press, 1990; *Origins and Destinies: Immigration, Race, and Ethnicity in America,* edited by Sylvia Pedraza and Ruben Rumbaut, Wadsworth (Belmont, CA), 1996; *Women and Work: Exploring Race, Ethnicity, and Class,* edited by Elizabeth Higginbothom and Mary Romero, Sage Publications (Thousand Oaks, CA), 1997; *Ethnic Families in America: Patterns and Variations,* 4th edition, edited by Charles Mindel, Robert Habenstein, and Roosevelt Wright, Jr., Prentice Hall (Upper Saddle

River, NJ), 1998; *Korean American Women: From Tradition to Modern Feminism,* edited by Young Song and Ailee Moon, Prager (New York, NY), 1998; *New Immigrants in New York,* edited by Nancy Foner, Columbia University Press (New York, NY), 2001; and *The Handbook of Research on Multicultural Education,* 2nd edition, edited by James Banks and Cherry Banks, Wiley (New York, NY), 2003.

WORK IN PROGRESS: Encyclopedia of Racism in the United States, for Greenwood Press; *Religion and Ethnicity: Indian Hindus and Korean Protestants in New York; The Korean Victims of Japanese Military Sexual Slavery and the Redress Movement in South Korea.*

SIDELIGHTS: "Most sociologists write papers based on quantitative data to publish in sociology and other social science journals," Pyong Gap Min told *CA.* "In the early years of my career, I did the same thing: I usually used survey data for my research on Korean immigrants and published articles in social science journals. But as I grew older I became skeptical of the worth of publishing articles in scholarly journals. Since social science journals are very specialized, only a small number of scholars in a particular field reads articles published there. I realized that to communicate with more lay readers I needed to write books.

"To write a book oriented to lay readers as well as to scholars, I need to use a broad range of data sources, including my participant observation and tape-recorded personal interviews," Min told *CA.* "My book, *Caught in the Middle: Korean Communities in New York and Los Angeles,* published in 1996, is based on multiple data sources, including survey data, census data, my participant observation, and Korean newspaper articles. *Changes and Conflicts: Korean Immigrant Families in New York,* published in 1998, is mainly based on my participant observation and tape-recorded personal interviews with Korean immigrants. While *Caught in the Middle* examined the middleman economic role of Korean immigrants in New York and Los Angeles, *Changes and Conflicts* focused on the effects of Korean immigrant women's increased economic role in marital conflicts. Both books have been widely read by scholars, college students, and lay readers. They have been able to reach lay readers partly because of the practical significance of research issues examined and partly because of more humanistic data sources."

Caught in the Middle: Korean Merchants in America's Multiethnic Cities focuses on the lives of Korean merchants and retailers in often disadvantaged urban minority areas in New York, Los Angeles, and other large cities. With little opportunity for viable employment, many Korean immigrants have become business owners in poorer, ethnically diverse neighborhoods. Their role as middlemen in commerce has placed them in conflict with the predominantly white suppliers and wholesalers who provide them with goods to sell and with the black, Hispanic, and other minority customers who shop at their stores and sometimes feel taken advantage of and deprived of the possibility of owning such a business themselves. Min's book "refers in essence to a minority that engages in trading activities, distributing merchandise to subordinate groups on behalf of the dominant group," wrote Nazli Kibria in *Society.* "With solid empirical evidence, Min argues that ethnic solidarity among Korean Americans, which cannot be taken for granted, is promoted by their middleman minority role," Kibria remarked. The central idea of *Caught in the Middle,* wrote Joanne van der Luen in *Journal of Ethnic and Migration Studies,* is that "Koreans' role as middlemen has increased the conflicts with African Americans who have, in turn, enhanced their ethnic solidarity as they organize to protect themselves and their businesses." Min's account of the violent and destructive confrontations between Korean shop owners and African-American inner-city residents during riots in Los Angeles and New York "accords well with the buffer role played by middleman groups," van der Luen remarked.

In *Changes and Conflicts: Korean Immigrant Families in New York,* Min "provides a sensitive account of how migration to the United States has dramatically altered traditional Korean family life," wrote Mia Tuan in *International Migration Review.* In addition to the hard work required to survive in the United States, "few were likely prepared for the strained marital and parent-child relationships, disrupted gender roles and family patterns, cultural clashes, unrealistic expectations for themselves as well as their children, deferred dreams, status anxiety, and monotonous work lives," Tuan observed. Korean men face an especially difficult adjustment to a society where male dominance and filial piety are no longer commonplace. The book's greatest strength, Tuan wrote, "lies in Min's sobering account of the personal costs of immigration, costs which are entirely dismissed by the model minority stereotype."

"I have two major advantages for writing books focusing on Korean immigrants." Min told *CA.* "For one thing, as an insider I already know many things about them without formally collecting data. Moreover, my observations of the Korean immigrant community carry more credibility because I am an insider. Many people do not feel comfortable reading a book about their own group written by an outsider.

"While I have the aforementioned advantages for writing books on Korean Americans, scholarly works focusing on one immigrant group are very limited in the market. To reach a broad audience, we need to focus on research issues that are relevant to several different groups. Therefore, I have recently tried to publish books focusing on Asian Americans as a whole.

"It is not easy for me to write a book covering several different Asian groups because I do not have an insider's knowledge about other Asian communities. Moreover, regardless of how well I know other Asian communities, many readers tend to question the validity of observations made about their own ethnic community by a non-ethnic scholar. To solve these problems, I have tried to edit books in which I have arranged several Asian-American contributors to write about their own group with regard to particular research issues while I have written the introductory and theory chapters. Four of the five books I have edited or co-edited focus on Asian Americans and have taken this form."

Struggle for Ethnic Identity: Narratives by Asian-American Professionals, edited by Min, draws together the accounts of fifteen Asian Americans as professionals and as part of the culture of both Asia and America. Min himself is a first-generation Korean American, and his book "is a welcome and valuable resource that brings out the human dimensions of the Asian American experience that are too often obscured by homogenizing stereotypes," wrote Keith Osajima in *Journal of American Ethnic History.* The essays in the book "detail each contributor's struggles to come to terms with his or her own identity and negotiate with American society a way of being both Asian and American, none of which are completely resolved, and none are formulaic," wrote Allen Bartley in *Journal of Ethnic and Migration Studies.* Among the revelations in the book was that practically none of the 1.5 or second-generation professionals encountered discrimination in their careers, while those contributors who were considered "migrant" experienced discrimination directly and blatantly. In addition, female professionals in the book expressed displeasure with the patriarchal structure of the society they had left, but felt that those same types of patriarchal values continued to hinder them in the United States. Bartley concluded that *Struggle for Ethnic Identity* is "an excellent book for students, or for others who wish to introduce themselves to the key issues and concepts around migration and ethnic identity—particularly as they impact on recent migrants from both east and south Asia." The book received an honorable mention at the 2000 Gustavus Myers Outstanding Book awards.

Min told *CA:* "I am currently completing a book project that examines how Indian Hindus and Korean Protestants in New York use their religions in radically different ways to preserve their ethnicity. For this project, I have personally interviewed about 180 Indian Hindus and Korean Protestants (immigration and second-generation) in the New York area, closely observed worship services and other socio-cultural activities in a selected Indian Hindu temple and a Korean Protestant church in Queens, and conducted a survey of Indian Hindu and Korean Protestant immigrants in Queens. For *Encyclopedia of Racism in the United States,* which I am currently editing with Greenwood Press, I have created approximately 550 entries related to racism in the United States and I have invited thirty contributors to write the entries.

"Unlike creative writers, I do not write books based mainly on imagination. As a sociologist, I have to collect data and analyze them before I start writing a book. However, I have also used a lot of insights in selecting topics for research, designing questionnaires, analyzing data, and writing books. In this sense, social science research and writings involve a great deal of creativity. This creativity is the main reason I have chosen the academia and I have thoroughly enjoyed the creative component of conducting research and writing sociological books.

"Moreover, unlike scholars in the humanities, social scientists are supposed to tackle social issues and suggest policy recommendations to solve social problems," Min continued. "I pursued a Ph.D. program in sociology late in my life partly because of my social concern. I have enjoyed the practical side of sociological research and writing as much as the creative side. I have undertaken the racism encyclopedia project mainly to help to combat racism in the United States. I strongly believe that the availability of such an encyclopedia will contribute to more research on racism and thus help to moderate it.

"Finally, the major factor that has inspired me to conduct research and write on Korean/Asian Americans is my sense of mission to describe and interpret their experiences more objectively and more accurately. More than twenty years ago, as a graduate student, I read articles focusing on Korean immigrant businesses written by white American scholars. I thought I could better explain Korean businesses, and this is how I decided to specialize in Korean/Asian Americans. Many Korean/Asian Americans and media have approached me for shedding light on Korean/Asian American communities, which is the most rewarding experience to me in conducting research and writing on Korean/Asian Americans. Many Korean and non-Korean scholars, students, and media have approached me to say they enjoyed reading my publications. This is the most rewarding experience to me in conducting research and writing on Korean/Asian Americans."

BIOGRAPHICAL AND CRITICAL SOURCES:

PERIODICALS

American Journal of Sociology, July, 1997, In-Jin Yoon, review of *Caught in the Middle: Korean Merchants in America's Multiethnic Cities,* pp. 226-227.

Contemporary Sociology, July, 1997, Kwang Chung Kim, review of *Caught in the Middle,* p. 477.

Ethnic Conflict, October, 1999, Steven Gold, review of *Struggle for Ethnic Identity: Narratives by Asian American Professionals,* p. 44.

International Migration Review, fall, 1999, Mia Tuan, review of *Changes and Conflicts: Korean Immigrant Families in New York,* pp. 786-788.

Journal of American Ethnic History, summer, 1997, Nancy Abelmann, review of *Caught in the Middle,* pp. 98-100; summer, 2000, Keith Osajima, review of *Struggle for Ethnic Identity,* p. 104.

Journal of Ethnic and Migration Studies, January, 1998, Joanne van der Leun, review of *Caught in the Middle,* pp. 225-226; January, 2001, Allen Bartley, review of *Struggle for Ethnic Identity,* p. 175.

Los Angeles Times, January 2, 1997, K. W. Lee, review of *Caught in the Middle,* pp. 61-62.

Multicultural Review, December, 1999, Suping Lu, review of *Struggle for Ethnic Identity,* p. 77.

New York Newsday, September 11, 1996, Merle English, review of *Caught in the Middle.*

Society, September-October, 1998, Nazli Kibria, review of *Caught in the Middle,* pp. 85-88.

Village Voice, December, 1996, Edward Park, review of *Caught in the Middle,* pp. 61-62.

* * *

MINDELL, Arnold 1940-

PERSONAL: Born January 1, 1940, in Schenectady, NY; son of Max and Bianca (Gruenberg) Mindell; married Amy Kaplan (a psychologist), August, 1986. *Education:* Massachusetts Institute of Technology, M.S., 1962; Jung Institute (Zurich, Switzerland), diploma, 1969; Union Institute, Ph.D., 1972.

ADDRESSES: Office—Process Work Center of Portland, 2049 Northwest Hoyt St., Suite 1, Portland, OR 97209-1260. *E-mail*—arny@aamindell.net.

CAREER: Psychologist, author, lecturer, and teacher. In private practice of psychology in Portland, OR; Institute for Process-oriented Psychology, Portland, and Zurich, Switzerland, founder.

WRITINGS:

Dreambody: The Body's Role in Revealing the Self, edited by Sisa Sternback-Scott and Becky Goodman, Sigo Press (Santa Monica, CA), 1982.

River's Way: The Process Science of the Dreambody: Information and Channels in Dream and Bodywork, Psychology and Physics, Taoism and Alchemy, Routledge, Kegan Paul (Boston, MA), 1985.

Working with the Dreaming Body, Routledge, Kegan Paul (New York, NY), 1986, reprinted, Lao Tse Press (Portland, OR), 2001.

The Dreambody in Relationships, Routledge, Kegan Paul (New York, NY), 1987.

City Shadows: Psychological Interventions in Psychiatry, Routledge, Kegan Paul (New York, NY), 1988.

The Year and I: Global Process Work, Arkana (New York, NY), 1989.

Coma: Key to Awakening, Shambhala (Boston, MA), 1989.

Working on Yourself Alone: Inner Dreambody Work, Arkana (New York, NY), 1990, reprinted, Lao Tse Press (Portland, OR), 2001.

The Leader as Martial Artist: An Introduction to Deep Democracy, HarperSanFrancisco (San Francisco, CA), 1992, published as *The Leader as Martial Artist: Techniques and Strategies for Resolving Conflict and Creating Community,* Lao Tse Press (Portland, OR), 2000.

(With wife, Amy Mindell) *Riding the Horse Backwards: Process Work in Theory and Practice,* Arkana (New York, NY), 1992, reprinted ("Foundation" series), Lao Tse Press (Portland, OR), 2001.

The Shaman's Body: A New Shaminism for Transforming Health, Relationships, and Community, HarperSanFrancisco (San Francisco, CA), 1993.

Sitting in the Fire: Large Group Transformation Using Conflict and Diversity, Lao Tse Press (Portland, OR), 1995.

Dreaming While Awake: Techniques for Twenty-four-Hour Lucid Dreaming, Hampton Roads Publishing (Charlottesville, VA), 2000.

Quantum Mind: The Edge between Physics and Psychology, Lao Tse Press (Portland, OR), 2000.

The Dreambody in Relationships, Lao Tse Press (Portland, OR), 2001.

The Dreammaker's Apprentice: Using Heightened Awareness to Interpret the Waking Dream of Life, Hampton Roads Publishing (Charlottesville, VA), 2002.

The Deep Democracy of Open Forums: How to Transform Organizations into Communities, Hampton Roads Publishing (Charlottesville, VA), 2002.

Contributor to periodicals, including *Yoga Journal, Psychological Perspectives,* and *Psychology Today.*

ADAPTATIONS: Coma: Key to Awakening was adapted for the stage and produced in Edinburgh, Scotland, 1999.

WORK IN PROGRESS: Big Medicine, Quantum Dimensions of Symptoms; (with wife, Amy Mindell) *The Internal Holocausts: The Roots and Solution to Terrorism.*

SIDELIGHTS: Arnold Mindell is a Jungian-trained analyst and author of many books that have been translated into nearly twenty languages. He is the founder of the Institute for Process-oriented Psychology and maintains a private practice with his wife, Amy Mindell, with whom he conducts seminars around the world. Mindell is recognized for his dream work, bodywork, relationship work, and conflict resolution, and for his healing approach based on Taoism and physics in process work.

On his Web site, Mindell defines process work as "a cross-disciplinary approach to support individual and collective change. . . . Also known as process-oriented psychology (POP) or dreambody work, Process Work offers new ways of working with areas of life that are experienced as problematic or painful. Physical symptoms, relationship problems, group conflicts and social tensions, when approached with curiosity and respect, can lead to new information that is vital for personal and collective growth. With its roots in Jungian psychology, Taoism, and physics, Process Work believes that the solution to a problem is contained within the disturbance itself and provides a practical framework through which individuals, couples, families, and groups can connect with greater awareness and creativity."

Mindell's *Coma: Key to Awakening* contains case histories of patients he reached through patient communication techniques and who responded to Mindell's attentions. *Coma* was adapted for the stage by the Improbable Theatre Company of Edinburgh, Scotland. Thom Dibdin wrote in the Edinburgh *Evening News* that "it is on Mindell's alternative health approach to the near death experiences of people in comas that these 'stories from the edge of life' are based." The production included six performers and two cellists. Dibdin called the cello "the perfect instrument for this twilight subject." Stories were played out through actors, hand puppets, shadow puppetry, and interaction with the audience.

John-Paul Flintoff noted in Edinburgh's *Scotland on Sunday* that the show demonstrates that the people in Mindell's case studies "are not lost to a coma but going through potentially meaningful inner experiences. We are wrong, Mindell suggests, to think that the mind in a coma simply goes blank. The opposite could be true: in coma, the mind races faster than ever, processing ideas and emotions that elude us in ordinary states of consciousness. And, with the right methods, we can communicate with people even while they are comatose."

In *Coma,* Mindell writes about his communications with a patient, saying, "We screamed and shouted together for a long time, stretching the limits of the hospital's clinical regulations." "But Mindell avoids jargon," wrote Flintoff, "and it's precisely his humanity which is moving. When Peter [a patient] wakes to tell his wife he loves her, Mindell admits: 'I got embarrassed, and got up to leave.' (They asked him to stay)."

Richard Leviton wrote in *East West* that Mindell "doesn't rest his case until he's made one more point. Maybe coma isn't 'this dark hole of life,' as most M.D.s contend, he says. 'Coma and all these physical symptoms, all the dreadful pathological things that happen to us—they could all be a doorway. The stronger the symptom, the more powerful the enlightenment. Such cases lead me to the idea that awareness can also be located outside the physical body.'"

Whole Earth Review contributor Jean Gilbert Tucker called *The Leader as Martial Artist: An Introduction to Deep Democracy* "significant, passionate, important." The volume begins with Mindell's question, "Am I sufficiently developed to write this book?" Tucker wrote that "this spirit of humility suffuses a remarkable study of psychological and political insight addressing the growing problems of conflict and leadership. What follows is a provocative appraisal of an invigorated human spirit." Mindell proposes a new way to approach working with individuals and groups large and small to help them live and grow in harmony. His "worldwork" would draw together psychology, science, and spiritual traditions through dreamwork, bodywork, field theories, and relationship and transnational organizational work in uniting the peoples of the world.

BIOGRAPHICAL AND CRITICAL SOURCES:

PERIODICALS

Booklist, November 15, 1993, Pat Monaghan, review of *The Shaman's Body: A New Shamanism for Transforming Health, Relationships, and Community,* p. 583.

East West, September, 1990, Richard Leviton, "Mysteries of the Coma," p. 64.

Evening News (Edinburgh, Scotland), April 22, 1999, Thom Dibdin, "It's Surreal Thing . . . the Coma Company," p. 34.

International Journal of Social Psychiatry, summer, 1989, Shulamit Ramon, review of *City Shadows: Psychological Interventions in Psychiatry,* p. 210.

Library Journal, November 1, 1993, Carolyn Craft, review of *The Shaman's Body,* p. 100.

Scotland on Sunday, April 18, 1999, John-Paul Flintoff, "What Happens When People Fall into a Coma?," p. 6.

Whole Earth Review, winter, 1992, Jean Gilbert Tucker, review of *The Leader as Martial Artist: An Introduction to Deep Democracy,* p. 21.

ONLINE

Amy and Arnold Mindell Web site, http://www.aamindell.net (May 7, 2002).

Process Work Center Web site, http://www.processwork.org/ (May 7, 2002).*

* * *

MITCHELL, Wayne

PERSONAL: Born in St. Louis, MO; married; wife's name Tamara (a writer). *Education:* St. Louis University, A.B.; University of Iowa, teacher certification (English).

ADDRESSES: *Agent*—Lisa Miller, P.O. Box 964, Springfield, MO 65801. *E-mail*—lmiller@echowork.com.

CAREER: Author of nonfiction. *Military service:* U.S. Navy, 1967-70, became lieutenant junior grade.

WRITINGS:

(With wife, Tamara Mitchell) *Your Other Half,* Echo Work (Springfield, MO), 1998.

(With Tamara Mitchell) *Direct Answers,* Echo Work (Springfield, MO), 2000.

Also coauthor, with Tamara Mitchell, of syndicated relationship advice column, "Direct Answers from Wayne and Tamara."

SIDELIGHTS: Wayne Mitchell told *CA:* "Some people write because they 'want to write.' Others write to convey their experience. Tamara and I didn't set out to rewrite what has been written, to compile what others have said, or to make a living. We write because we experienced something which needs to be expressed."

* * *

MOERS, Walter 1957-

PERSONAL: Born 1957.

ADDRESSES: *Home*—Hamburg, Germany. *Agent*—c/o The Random House Group, 20 Vauxhall Bridge Road, London SWIV 2SA, England.

CAREER: Cartoonist, writer, painter, and sculptor.

WRITINGS:

ILLUSTRATOR

Adolf, the Nazi Pig, Eichborn (Frankfurt, Germany), 1999.

Die 13 1/2 Leben des Käpt'n Blaubär, Eichborn (Frankfurt, Germany), 1999, translation by John Brownjohn published as *The 13 1/2 Lives of Captain Bluebear,* Vintage UK (London, England), 2003.

A Wild Ride through the Night, Stecker & Warburg (London, England), 2003.

Author and illustrator of numerous comic books sold in Germany, including *Little Arsehole.*

ADAPTATIONS: Characters and stories have been adapted for German television.

SIDELIGHTS: Known for his farcical and often tasteless comics, German artist Walter Moers has been condemned by the Catholic Church for obscenity but is nonetheless immensely popular in Germany. Moers has also had English versions of his illustrated novels made available in the United States and Great Britain. His lengthy comic book about Adolf Hitler in modern times has garnered widespread attention, including recognition by several prestigious German publications that previously ignored the author's work as childish. The author's illustrated book about his immensely popular character Captain Bluebear is also available in English.

In *Adolf, the Nazi Pig,* Moers tells the story of Hitler surviving World War II and resurfacing in modern times. Hitler consults a mysterious psychiatrist, who at one point recommends as therapy that he start another war. He is also bewildered by modern advertising selling everything from McDonald's hamburgers to kosher food. Moers also has the infamous Nazi Hermann Göring surviving the war only to become an assassin for the Central Intelligence Agency (CIA). Göring's "hits" included President John F. Kennedy, Martin Luther King, Jr., and Malcolm X, until changing attitudes within the government halted his work for the CIA. Hitler and Göring meet, and Göring helps get Hitler hooked on crack cocaine. Other characters include the late Diana, Princess of Wales, and Mother Theresa, as well as aliens.

"In *Adolf,* Hitler is a pathetic figure and not even the most bone-headed neo-Nazi could find anything inspirational in the cartoons," wrote Roger Boyes in the London *Times.* "The book is offensive, full of smut and silliness, but that is largely the point." Writing in *Time International,* contributor Ursula Sautter noted, "At its best, the book is funny because of Moers' minimalistic style of caricature, the crazy plot, and the protagonist's idiosyncratic way of talking." The reviewer went on to note, "But the hitch is this: Adolf, the Nazi Pig is a farce—and nothing but. It never manages to do what the satirical comic art form should do." Although the work has been compared to *Maus,* am award-winning graphic novel about the Holocaust, many see little resemblance. Michel Friedmann of the Central Council of German Jewry was quoted by Boyes as saying, "It is difficult to call this work politically incorrect, if you accept the premise that Hitler can be a subject of satire in the manner of Art Spiegelman's *Maus,* raising a bitter laugh but also leaving something stuck in the throat."

Another issue surrounding the publication of *Adolf, the Nazi Pig* is the idea that there is a growing movement among the current German generation to address the taboos of World War II in an unconventional and satirical manner. However, many questioned whether it is right for Germans to make fun of Hitler. Moers was quoted in the London *Times* as saying he saw a Japanese Hitler comic book and believed that if they could satirize Hitler and the war, so could he. He is also quoted by Sautter in *Time International* as writing in the book's preface, "In reality I made this book because Adolf Hitler is so easy to draw." To prove his point, Moer shows the six basic parts of Hitler's face and urges readers to try drawing Hitler themselves. The book's popularity in Germany quickly led to three printings.

In *The 13 1/2 Lives of Captain Bluebear* Moers treads much safer ground in an epic tale of his immensely popular character that originated as a puppet on German television. The seventy-plus-page illustrated book tells the story of how Captain Bluebear expends thirteen-and-a-half of the twenty-seven lives he is allotted, as are all Bluebears. Rescued by Minipirates who find him floating in a walnut shell on the ocean, his subsequent adventures include being marooned on an island and travelling to exotic places. Throughout his adventure, Bluebear is aided by a copy of Professor Nightingale's *Encylopaedia,* a graduation gift from the professor's school. Moers combines a liberal use of childish humor with a narrative full of surprises, such as Captain Bluebear's travels into the past and future.

Writing in the London *Independent,* Martin Chalmers noted that the book is "inexplicably marketed" for an adult audience, although it is clearly a children's book. He commented that while this may have worked in Germany, where many grew up as enormous fans of Captain Bluebear, it is less likely to be a good marketing strategy in either England or the United States. Nevertheless, Chalmers called the book "fun" and noted, "There are plenty of occasions here for kids to cry out: 'Yeuch!'" He also noted that it was a good book to skim through because of the illustrations. In the London *Daily Telegraph* Bronwen Riley noted that, "Part science fiction, part fairy tale, part myth, part epic, the book is a satire on all these genres and constantly satirises itself." Riley also noted that he found the Bluebear character to often be "smug" but added, "Yet, within the first 15 pages I was carried away by the sheer craziness of it all."

BIOGRAPHICAL AND CRITICAL SOURCES:

PERIODICALS

Booklist, October 15, 2002, review of *The 13 1/2 Lives of Captain Bluebear,* p. 396.

Daily Telegraph (London, England), October 28, 2000, review of *The 13 1/2 Lives of Captain Bluebear.*

Independent (London, England), October 28, 2000, review of *The 13 1/2 Lives of Captain Bluebear,* p. 11.

Time International, August 17, 1998, Ursula Sautter, review of *Adolf, the Nazi Pig,* p. 48.

Times (London, England), August 1, 1998, Roger Boyes, review of *Adolf, the Nazi Pig,* p. 11.*

* * *

MOLODOWSKY, Kadia 1894-1975

PERSONAL: Born 1894, in Poland; immigrated to United States, 1935; died 1975; married 1921-74. *Education:* Trained as a kindergarten teacher. *Religion:* Jewish.

CAREER: Poet. Former kindergarten teacher.

AWARDS, HONORS: National Jewish Book Award, 1966.

WRITINGS:

Frevdke, 1935.

Afn Barg, "Yungvarg" Bibliotek bam Kooperativn Folks-Farlag fun Internatsyonaln Arbeter Ordn (New York, NY), 1938.

Yidishe Kinder, Tsentral-komitet fun di Yidishe folks-shuln in di Fareynikte Shtatn un Kanade (New York, NY), 1945.

A Shtub mit Zibn Fentater (title means "A House with Seven Windows"), Matone's (New York, NY), 1957.

Lider fun Hurbn: 700-705, Y. L. Perets (Tel Aviv, Israel), 1962.

Likht fun Dornboym: Lider, Kiem (Buenos Aires, Argentina), 1965.

Shire Yerushalavim, Ha-Kibuts ha-me'uhad (Tel Aviv, Israel), 1971.

Notsot Zahavj Sipurim Ba-harusim, Sifriyat po'alim (Tel Aviv, Israel), 1978.

Im Niv Li Munah: Shirim, Targume Shin Reshimot, Tel Aviv, Israel, 1982.

Paper Bridges: Selected Poems of Kadya Molodowsky, translated, edited, and introduced by Kathryn Hellerstein, Wayne State University Press (Detroit, MI), 1999.

SIDELIGHTS: One of the early Yiddish poets, Kadia Molodowsky actually began as a kindergarten teacher, writing children's stories and occasionally poetry for her students. When she was "discovered" by a group of Yiddish writers in Kiev in 1920, she decided to take on poetry as a full-time avocation. Yiddish poetry was still new enough that she developed her own standards and set about revising her work to meet them. Much of her work is only available in Yiddish, but in 1999 Kathryn Hellerstein translated and published a collection of Molodowsky's poems as *Paper Bridges: Selected Poems of Kadya Molodowsky.*

Reviewing *Paper Bridges* in the *New Republic,* Hillel Halkin wrote, "one finds in her verse the sometimes whimsical and sometimes melancholy suggestion that she is just an ordinary woman whom life, or some power beyond life, has seduced into a career of poetry." Whimsy and melancholy alternate throughout her long poetic career. From grimly urging God to "choose another people" in the wake of news of the Holocaust, to zany children's verse, all aspects of Molodowsky's varied poetry appear in *Paper Bridges.* "Her broad poetic range encompasses folkloric evocations, biblical allusions, realistic depictions of Shtetl life and immigrant experiences, and children's tales—all witnessed and rendered by a distinctive female sensibility," wrote a reviewer for *Choice.*

BIOGRAPHICAL AND CRITICAL SOURCES:

PERIODICALS

Choice, January, 2000, M. Butovsky, review of *Paper Bridges,* p. 927.

New Republic, October 18, 1999, Hillel Halkin, "Angels Arrive," p. 38.*

* * *

MORRISON, Dennis L(ewis) 1949-

PERSONAL: Born October 29, 1949, in Miami, FL; son of Buzz (in sales) and Bettie (a homemaker) Morrison; married August 2, 1991; wife's name Rebecca (divorced May 1, 1995). *Ethnicity:* "Caucasian (Irish-Albanian)." *Education:* Queens College of the City University of New York, B.A., 1975; University of Houston at Clear Lake City, M.A., 1989; University of Houston, Ed.D., 1993. *Politics:* Republican. *Religion:* Church of Christ. *Hobbies and other interests:* Boating, sky diving, scuba diving.

ADDRESSES: *Home*—2016 Main St., No. 2507, Houston, TX 77002. *Office*—San Jacinto College South, 13735 Beamer Rd., Houston, TX 77089; fax 713-650-0346. *E-mail*—dmorri@sjcd.cc.tx.us.

CAREER: San Jacinto College South, Houston, TX, professor, 1990—. University of Houston, adjunct professor, 1995—. Survey Publications, chief executive officer, 1997—. American Heart Association, member of board of directors; Chamber of Commerce, member; Salvation Army, volunteer.

MEMBER: Association of Pacific Coast Geographers, Phi Alpha Theta, Phi Kappa Phi, Pi Kappa Delta.

WRITINGS:

(With Mark Saka) *Woman of Conscience,* Brandywine Press (New York, NY), 1994.

(Editor with Mark Saka) *Silent No More: A Multicultural Reader,* Emancipation Press (Waterbury, CT), 1995.

(With Mark Saka) *Up, down, and Out,* Emancipation Press (Waterbury, CT), 1995.

(With Mark Saka) *Our Moral Duty,* Emancipation Press (Waterbury, CT), 1996.

(With Sara Mayfield) *World Geography,* Emancipation Press (Waterbury, CT), 1997.

Coeditor of four history anthologies. Contributor to periodicals.

WORK IN PROGRESS: *Our Moral Duty,* Volume II, *Still Silent No More,* with Mark Saka.

SIDELIGHTS: Dennis L. Morrison told *CA:* "As a specialist in multiculturalism, I am concerned that students learn more than just the 'great white man' part of history. My dual majors were black history and women's history. As a white man, I feel it is my duty to tell 'all of the story' when discussing the history of our great country."

MORROW, W(illiam) C(hambers) 1853-1923

PERSONAL: Born 1853, in AL; died April 3, 1923, in San Francisco, CA.

CAREER: Novelist and short story writer, c. 1879-1908. Also worked as a journalist in San Francisco.

WRITINGS:

Blood-Money, Walker (San Francisco, CA), 1882.
The Ape, the Idiot, and Other People (short stories), Lippincott (Philadelphia, PA), 1897.
A Man: His Mark, Lippincott (Philadelphia, PA), 1900.
Bohemian Paris of To-day, Lippincott (Philadelphia, PA), 1900.
Lentala of the South-Seas: The Romantic Tale of a Lost Colony, Stokes (New York, NY), 1908.
The Logic of Punctuation, for All Who Have to Do with It, H. Law (San Francisco, CA), 1926.

Also contributor to periodicals, including *San Francisco Examiner, Argonaut, Californian,* and *Overland Monthly.*

SIDELIGHTS: Author and journalist W. C. Morrow was perhaps best remembered for the short stories he wrote for turn-of-the-twentieth-century Californian periodicals, many of which were revised and republished in his 1897 collection *The Ape, the Idiot, and Other People.* Some of them were borderline science fiction, but others were fairly straightforward horror stories, and still others fell into the category of *contes cruel* (stories of cruelty), explained *St. James Guide to Horror, Ghost, and Gothic Writers* contributor Brian Stableford. This might help explain Morrow's relative neglect. Beginning in 1879 and continuing through the turn of the next century, he published fiction that concentrated mostly on violence and mayhem rather than the fantastic and the horrific. Morrow adopted the conte cruel for a reason, however—he saw himself as the American West's answer to European writers in the decadent genre, of whom the conte cruel was a favorite form. "Morrow was one of the West Coast Bohemians," Stableford stated, "who were as close as America ever came to a Decadent Movement. He was, in fact, the man who emphasized their cultural and ideological links with the French Decadent writers." Morrow's stories collected in *The Ape, the Idiot, and Other People* are perhaps the foremost example of this particular genre in the United States. His "name has been preserved," Stableford concluded, "because his stories continue to be reprinted in anthologies."

Most of the stories contained in *The Ape, the Idiot, and Other People* fall into the conte cruel category, including the revenge stories "His Unconquerable Enemy," "The Inmate of the Dungeon," and "An Original Revenge." Others, such as "The Resurrection of Little Wang Tai" and "Over an Absinthe Bottle," are, according to Stableford, "closer in spirit to the ironic Grand Guignol *contes* of Maurice Level." "'Two Singular Men' is a tale of carnival freaks, unapologetically relayed in the worst possible taste," Stableford concluded, "while 'The Faithful Amulet' is a gleefully violent black comedy of remarkable coincidences."

Perhaps the most famous of the stories in the collection, however, is "The Monster-Maker." This tale, originally published in *The Argonaut* on October 15, 1887, anticipates some of the work of more popular science-fiction and fantasy authors, like Edgar Rice Burroughs, while at the same time acknowledging the direct influence of Mary Shelley's *Frankenstein.* "The Monster-Maker" tells the story of an elderly physician-surgeon who is approached by a young man wanting to commit suicide. The doctor agrees to help him in exchange for the sum of $5,000. A number of years pass. Finally, after a number of complaints, the local police raid the doctor's residence. They find there "a gorilline creature of fantastic strength—but with a silver globe where its head ought to be," explained a contributor to Everett Bleiler's compendium *Science-Fiction: The Early Years.* "Read individually," Stableford concluded, "Morrow's tales are startling; read as a series they have a collective effect which is unequalled by any other volume."

BIOGRAPHICAL AND CRITICAL SOURCES:

BOOKS

Bleiler, Everett, *Science-Fiction: The Early Years,* Kent State University Press (Kent, OH), 1990.
St. James Guide to Horror, Ghost, and Gothic Writers, St. James Press (Detroit, MI), 1998.

Who's Who in Horror and Fantasy Fiction, Elm Tree Books (London, England), 1977.*

* * *

MOSLEY, Diana 1910-2003

OBITUARY NOTICE—See index for *CA* sketch: Born June 17, 1910, in London, England; died August 11, 2003, in Paris, France. Author. Mosley was one of the renowned sisters of the English Mitford family who became infamous in England for her marriage to the leader of the English fascist party and for her admiration for and friendship with Adolf Hitler. Born into a life of privilege, Mosley, whose sisters included novelist Nancy Mitford, was a young socialite in the 1930s who enchanted people with her wit and beauty. She married Bryan Guinness, the brewing company heir, at the age of eighteen, and seemed to be headed for a comfortable life among England's elite. However, she fell in love with Lord Oswald Mosley, a fascist, and left her first husband for him in 1932, creating a huge scandal. When the Mosleys married, their wedding guests included Hitler and Josef Göbbels, and she imagined that she could play a role in reconciling differences between England and Germany. However, she was quickly seen as a traitor, and in 1940 she was imprisoned, spending over two years at Holloway Prison during the war. After the war, she and her husband moved to Paris to live in exile, and she remained there even after his death in 1980. Forever unrepentant for admiring Hitler, she nevertheless acknowledged that he had been guilty of terrible things. She wrote about her feelings and experiences in her autobiography, *A Life of Contrasts* (1977), and was also the author of *The Duchess of Windsor* (1980).

OBITUARIES AND OTHER SOURCES:

PERIODICALS

Chicago Tribune, August 14, 2003, section 1, p. 11.
Los Angeles Times, August 14, 2003, p. B13.
New York Times, August 14, 2003, p. C14.
Times (London, England), August 13, 2003.
Washington Post, August 14, 2003, p. B6.

MURNION, Philip (Joseph) 1938-2003

OBITUARY NOTICE—See index for *CA* sketch: Born March 1, 1938, in Bronx, NY; died of colon cancer August 18, 2003, in Bronx, NY. Religious leader, educator, and author. Murnion was a monsignor in the Catholic Church who was founder of the National Pastoral Life Center in New York City. Earning his bachelor's degree at St. Joseph's Seminary and College in 1959, followed by a master's degree there in 1963, he was ordained a priest that year; he then continued his education at Columbia University, where he received his doctorate in 1971. During the 1960s Murnion was a high school religion teacher and pastor in Staten Island, becoming an associate pastor at St. Gregory the Great Roman Catholic Church in New York City from 1968 to 1974. He started teaching at the university level in 1971 as an adjunct professor at St. Joseph's, followed by positions at the University of Notre Dame and St. Peter's College. Beginning in 1981, he also taught at Fordham University, and he was also a professor at Boston College for a time. Murnion had a deep interest in sociology that led him to search for ways of improving relationships between the organized church and its laity, especially as more and more laypeople began to fulfill ministerial duties in the Catholic Church because of a shortage of priests. His work led him to found the National Pastoral Life Center and to establish, with Cardinal Joseph Bernardin, the Catholic Common Ground Initiative, which sought to reconcile differences between liberal and conservative factions in the church. Among his published works, he was the coauthor of two important sociological studies: *New Parish Ministers: Laity and Religion on Parish Staffs* (1992) and *Parishes and Parish Ministers: A Study of Parish Lay Ministry* (1999). During his career, Murnion was also director of the National Parish Project from 1978 to 1982 and chaired the Senate of Priests.

OBITUARIES AND OTHER SOURCES:

PERIODICALS

Los Angeles Times, August 23, 2003, p. B21.
New York Times, August 22, 2003, p. A23.
Washington Post, August 22, 2003, p. B7.

N-O

NICHOLSON, (Edward) Max 1904-2003

OBITUARY NOTICE—See index for *CA* sketch: Born July 12, 1904, in Kilternan, Ireland; died April 26, 2003, in London, England. Ornithologist, environmentalist, journalist, civil servant, and author. Nicholson is best remembered as a cofounder of the World Wildlife Fund and former director of the Nature Conservancy. He published his first book about birds, 1926's *Birds in England,* while he was still a student at Sedbergh and Hertford College, Oxford, and this was soon followed by *How Birds Live* (1927). The success of these books is credited by some with the revival of the hobby of bird watching in Britain during the 1920s and 1930s. Nicholson's first job outside of writing, though, was as a journalist for the *Saturday Review* and the *Weekend Review* during the early 1930s. He then founded a social science foundation called Political and Economic Planning, for which he served as general secretary from 1933 to 1939. When World War II began, he entered the British civil service and headed the supply department of the Ministry of War Transport, and from 1945 to 1952 was secretary of the office of the lord president of the council. He left government work in 1952 to become director general of the Nature Conservancy, which he led until 1966. He was a cofounder of the World Wildlife Fund in 1961 and was chair of Land Use Consultants from 1965 until 1989, the latter organization being a consulting firm that advised businesses on proper land management. Other involvements in environmental conservation activities included being founder and president of the New Renaissance Group, where he was chair from 1995 to 2000, and trustee and chair of Earthwatch Europe from 1989 to 1993. Among Nicholson's writings on birds and the environment are *Songs of Wild Birds* (1936), *More Songs of Wild Birds* (1937), *Birds and Men* (1951), *The Environmental Revolution* (1970), *The New Environmental Age* (1987), *Bird-watching in London* (1995), and the coauthored *Where Next?* (2000).

OBITUARIES AND OTHER SOURCES:

PERIODICALS

Independent (London, England), April 29, 2003, p. 18.
Times (London, England), April 30, 2003.

* * *

NOYES, Gary 1943-

PERSONAL: Born May 22, 1943, in St. Catharines, Ontario, Canada; son of Norman (a tool-and-die maker) and Hannah Mary (a homemaker) Noyes; married (divorced); children: Sherry Knott, Allan, Timothy, Marcus. *Education:* Houghton College, B.A., 1964; Asbury Theological Seminary, M.Div., 1966; Alfred Adler Institute of Minnesota, M.A. (Adlerian counseling and psychotherapy), 1993. *Hobbies and other interests:* Spirituality, fitness, travel, mountain backpacking, canoeing.

ADDRESSES: Home and office—P.O. Box 256, 40 Burgess St., Silver Creek, NY 14136. *E-mail*—noyes@utec.net.

CAREER: Minister, psychotherapist, and writer. Minister in Wesleyan and United Methodist denominations for twenty years; psychotherapist for ten years; Parchment Press, Silver Creek, NY, founder and publisher.

WRITINGS:

You Weigh What You Believe: Change Your Mistaken Life-style Beliefs and Lose Weight, Parchment Press (Silver Creek, NY), 2000.

WORK IN PROGRESS: More self-help books.

SIDELIGHTS: "My life has been centered on three major issues: spirituality, fitness, and psychology," Gary Noyes told *CA*. "After spending twenty years as a minister and ten years as a mental health psychotherapist, I have combined my three areas of interest in my first book, *You Weigh What You Believe.*

"What a privilege it was to have been a pastor of a number of churches across the Midwest. I learned so much about my spirituality beliefs. I realized that my relationship to the inner spiritual self was crucial to me.

"It was when I recognized that my mistaken life-style beliefs were keeping me from the success in my life that I began to learn how to change them. My own mental health improved. I was helping many others in their search for renewed mental health.

"A few years ago I realized that I was getting very sick with diabetes. I discovered that I had a number of mistaken life-style beliefs about weight loss and fitness that were allowing diabetes to attack me. As I discovered the mistaken life-style beliefs and learned how to change them, I defeated diabetes and lost eighty pounds of ugly fat in the process. I became more fit than I have ever been in my whole life.

"There is a fire in my bones to help others discover how to change their mistaken life-style beliefs and see more success in many areas of their lives."

* * *

OAKLEY, Violet 1874-1961

PERSONAL: Born June 10, 1874, in Bergen Heights, NJ; died February 25, 1961, in Philadelphia, PA; daughter of Arthur Edmund and Cornelia Swain Oakley. *Education:* Attended Art Students League, New York, NY, 1892; attended Académie Montparnasse, Paris, France, and Pennsylvania Academy of the Fine Arts; studied art in England with Charles Lazar; attended Drexel Institute (Philadelphia, PA). *Religion:* Christian Scientist.

CAREER: Artist, designer, and author. Illustrator, 1897-1902; stained-glass window and mural designer, 1899-1961; taught design and mural decoration, Pennsylvania Academy of the Fine Arts, 1913-17; self-appointed ambassador to League of Nations, 1927-30.

AWARDS, HONORS: Gold Medal and Silver Medal, St. Louis Exposition, 1904; Gold Medal of Honor, Pennsylvania Academy of the Fine Arts (PAFA), 1905; Medal of Honor, Panama-Pacific Exposition, 1915; Medal of Honor, Architectural League of New York, 1916; Philadelphia Prize, PAFA, 1922; Joseph Pennell Memorial Medal, Philadelphia Water Color Club, 1932; Walter Lippincott Prize, PAFA, 1940; Emily Drayton Taylor Medal, Society of Miniature Painters, 1941; Woodmere Prize, Woodmere Gallery, 1947; Gold Medal, Springside School, 1947; Mary Smith Prize, PAFA, 1948; honorary doctor of laws degree, Drexel Institute, 1948; Gold Medal as distinguished daughter of Pennsylvania, 1950.

WRITINGS:

Cathedral of Compassion: Dramatic Outline of the Life of Jane Addams, 1860-1935, Press of Lyon & Armor (Philadelphia, PA), 1915.

The Holy Experiment: A Message to the World from Pennsylvania, privately printed (Philadelphia, PA), 1922.

International Supplement and Key to the Holy Experiment in French, German, Italian, Spanish, and Japanese, privately printed (Philadelphia, PA), circa 1922.

Law Triumphant: Containing the Opening of the Book of the Law and the Miracle of Geneva, privately printed (Philadelphia, PA), 1933.

La présence divine a la société des nations, Kundig (Geneva, Switzerland), 1937.

Samuel F. B. Morse: A Dramatic Outline of the Life of the Father of Telegraphy and the Founder of the National Academy of Design, Cogslea Studio Publications (Philadelphia, PA), 1939.

Great Women of the Bible: A Series of Paintings in the Room of the Pastoral Aid Society: First Presbyterian Church, Germantown, Philadelphia, Eldon (Philadelphia, PA), 1949.

The Holy Experiment: Our Heritage from William Penn, Cogslea Studio Publications (Philadelphia, PA), 1950.

SELECTED BOOKS ILLUSTRATED:

(With Jessie Willcox Smith) Henry Wadsworth Longfellow, *Evangeline: A Tale of Acadie,* Houghton, Mifflin (Boston, MA), 1897.

Elizabeth Phipps Train, *A Marital Liability,* Lippincott (Philadelphia PA), 1897.

Amlie Rives Troubetzkoy, *A Damsel Errant,* Lippincott (Philadelphia, PA), 1898.

Charles King, *From School to Battle-field: A Story of the War Days,* Lippincott (Philadelphia, PA), 1899.

Charles Montgomery Skinner, *Do-nothing Days,* Lippincott (Philadelphia, PA), 1899.

Charled Montgomery Skinner, *With Feet to the Earth,* Lippincott (Philadelphia, PA), 1899.

Lucy Bethia Walford, *A Little Legacy, and Other Stories,* Herbert S. Stone (Chicago, IL), 1899.

Contributor to periodical publications including: *Ladies' Home Journal, McClure's, Harper's, Collier's, Woman's Home Companion, Philadelphia Press, Everybody's, Book Buyer, St. Nicholas, Century, Scribner's, Architectural League Yearbook, American Magazine of Art, International Studio, Mentor, Christian Science Monitor, New York Herald Tribune, National Geographic, Survey Graphic, Philadelphia Forum,* and *Philadelphia Inquirer.*

SIDELIGHTS: Violet Oakley, while best known for her religion-based murals and stained-glass designs, was also a quality magazine and book illustrator. Oakley's career began with illustrations for magazines such as *Everybody's Magazine, Collier's, Woman's Home Companion,* and *Harper's Weekly.* Critics were impressed with her draftsmanship and expression. Although Oakley's earnest religious themes eventually became outdated, she transcended fashion with her meticulous, imaginative work. As Susan Hamburger wrote in the *Dictionary of Literary Biography,* "Oakley—a versatile portraitist, illustrator, stained-glass artisan, and muralist—earned a reputation as the first American woman artist to succeed in the predominantly male architectural field of mural decoration. . . . Her strong commitment to her religion and world peace influenced her art as well as her life."

Oakley's grandfathers, George Oakley and William Swain, were members of the National Academy of Design, and several of her family members had studied art abroad. Oakley, in a newspaper interview, said she was drawn to book illustration in a former life. She explained: "The abbesses and sisters were too busy nursing the sick and doing fine needleworks. I never heard of them illuminating manuscripts. I am quite sure I was a monk."

Oakley received little formal education; her parents, worrying about her asthma and general fragility, thought college would be too exhausting. Still, Oakley began to study at the Art Students League in New York in 1892; three years later she traveled to Europe with her parents and studied in England and in Paris at the Académie Montparnasse. Upon returning home she continued to study at the Pennsylvania Academy of the Fine Arts in Philadelphia. It became a home base, providing Oakley with exhibitions, teaching appointments, and honors throughout her career.

While she was studying in Philadelphia, Oakley's father became ill and her family's income fell; she had to work as an illustrator to support herself. She began to sell drawings to *McClure's, Harper's,* and *Woman's Home Companion.* Oakley studied practical illustration with Howard Pyle at the Drexel Institute, where she learned to draw from ideas, research details, and imagine the emotional valences of each piece. Hamburger wrote: "Pyle's stylistic influence is readily apparent in Oakley's large, expressive figures in a shallow space; broad, flat areas; draftsmanship; and design sense." In many illustrations, she merged detail with a frieze-like design, giving viewers a sense of history in patterned, meaningful design.

Oakley also published much of her work in books, including drawings for Elizabeth Phipps Train's *A Marital Liability,* Henry Wadsworth Longfellow's *Evangeline: A Tale of Acadie,* and Charles King's *From School to Battle-field: A Story of the War Days.* Oakley used charcoal drawings, sometimes overlaying watercolors, and included detail—a specific pattern on a chair covering, for example—drawn into an overall design. Hamburger remarked, "Oakley's signature style, reminiscent of illuminated manuscripts, executed on a grand scale in her murals, appeared early in her book-illustration work."

During the late 1890s, Oakley began producing her trademark stained-glass windows. She also began to live with fellow artists Jessie H. Dowd, Jessie Willcox

Smith, and later Elizabeth Shippen Green. Eventually, the artists moved to the Red Rose Inn in Villanova, outside Philadelphia, seeking a quiet, rural area in which to paint. Having converted from the Episcopalian Church to Christian Science, she credited faith for her childhood asthma abating.

In 1902 architect Joseph Miller Huston commissioned Oakley to paint eighteen murals in the governor's reception room in the Pennsylvania State Capitol in Harrisburg. At the time, this was the largest public commission a woman artist in the United States had yet received. Other such commissions followed, and in all, Oakley painted forty-three murals for the capitol that expressed her hope for "world peace, equal rights, and faith in the work of unification of the Peoples of the Earth."

In Oakley's most famous works she conveys a divine pattern of physical realities. In "The Vision of William Penn," for example, she researched seventeenth-century textiles to "express the religious feeling behind the founding of Pennsylvania," as art critic Malcolm Vaughn put it. Other critics found Oakley powerful, though at times somewhat stiff; an *Art Digest* reviewer commented on her 1942 exhibit: "Always astonishing in its virtuosity and variety, her art has the great common denominator of an idealism that can be read into an army altar triptych defined for the battlefield a message of peace . . . If at times, her idealism of character robs it of personal punch, it also goes behind personality to what Miss Oakley herself believes—that there is a noble idealism in human nature."

Oakley, who died with projects unfinished, won awards as well as criticism from peers. But she kept designing the kinds of murals and stained-glass work that expressed her beliefs, and spent some time drawing members of the League of Nations as a self-appointed American delegate. She also created twenty-five portable triptychs for Army and Navy chapels during World War II. Oakley's work reflected her own beliefs and the sense that art could communicate the divine.

BIOGRAPHICAL AND CRITICAL SOURCES:

BOOKS

Catherine Connell Stryker, *The Studios at Cogslea, Delaware Art Museum, February 20-March 28, 1976,* Delaware Art Museum (Wilmington, DE), 1976.

Dictionary of Literary Biography, Volume 188: *American Book and Magazine Illustrators to 1920,* Gale (Detroit, MI), 1998, pp. 221-229.

PERIODICALS

Art Digest, March 15, 1942, "Woodmere Gallery Review."

Arts, February, 1930, Forbes Watson, "In the Galleries: 33 Moderns and Violet Oakley," p. 423; October, 1979, Helen Goodman, "Violet Oakley," p. 7.*

* * *

O'FARRELL, Maggie 1972-

PERSONAL: Born 1972, in Northern Ireland. *Education:* Attended Cambridge University.

ADDRESSES: *Agent*—c/o Author's Mail, Viking Press, 375 Hudson St., New York, NY 10014.

CAREER: Novelist, journalist, and freelance writer. Worked variously as a waitress, chambermaid, cycle courier, teacher, arts administrator for Poetry Society; former deputy literary editor for *Independent.*

AWARDS, HONORS: Betty Trask Award, Orange Prize for Fiction, and shortlisted for W. H. Smith's Thumping Good Read Award, all for *After You'd Gone.*

WRITINGS:

After You'd Gone, Viking Press (New York, NY), 2001.

My Lover's Lover, (London, England), 2002, Viking Press (New York, NY), 2003.

SIDELIGHTS: Maggie O'Farrell is a freelance writer and novelist who has lived in various parts of the United Kingdom, including Northern Ireland, Scotland, and Wales. She currently resides in London, which is the setting for her internationally acclaimed debut novel *After You'd Gone,* which received the Orange Prize for Fiction and the Betty Trask Award.

After You'd Gone tells the story of Alice Raikes, a London resident who travels to Scotland to visit her two sisters. After she disembarks from the train, Alice goes into the station's washroom and emerges from it quite upset due to something she has observed in the mirror. Alice is so distraught that she boards the next train for London, without explaining her distress to her siblings. A few hours later, as Alice attempts to cross a busy London street, she is hit by an oncoming car and is rushed to the hospital in a comatose state. Was it truly an accident, or a suicide attempt? The remainder of the novel unfolds as Alice's family gathers around her hospital bedside. During those agonizing, dark hours, many of Alice's personal memories and secrets, as well as those of her family, are revealed.

"O'Farrell performs a traditional, old-fashioned storytelling striptease . . . [by] artfully juxtaposing sections from the past and the present," noted *New York Times* book reviewer Maud Casey in her appraisal of *After You'd Gone.* Casey also said, "The novel is so finely put together that it would be criminal to divulge any of its hard-won plot turns." In a *Times Literary Supplement* review, Ruth Scurr commented, "This novel may serve as a poignant, unsettling reminder . . . of the fragility of human freedom." A *Publishers Weekly* writer praised O'Farrell for "sharply observed details of everyday life and language, original and telling figures of speech, and deftly handled plot twists." Francine Fialkoff of *Library Journal* thought it "hard to believe that such an assured work comes from a first novelist." "O'Farrell pulls off a warm and suspenseful novel," said Lisa Allardice in her *New Statesman* article.

O'Farrell's second book, *My Lover's Lover,* is also set in London. Lily, the chief protagonist, meets her future paramour, Marcus, when he lifts her to her feet after she has tripped over a curb. It is a case of love at first sight, and the two attend a party together that same evening. Their affair moves rapidly as Marcus suggests that Lily move into the spare bedroom of his warehouse flat. When Lily first enters the room, she finds vestiges of the former tenant: an unusual mark on the wall, an exotic trace of perfumed jasmine, a solitary dress hanging in the closet. Marcus is unwilling or unable to speak about his former lover, Sinead, which heightens Lily's sense of curiosity. As their affair deepens, Lily becomes convinced that she sees Sinead's ghost roaming throughout the house, causing her to wonder even more about Marcus and whether or not she is safe with him.

Some reviewers were disappointed when comparing *My Lover's Lover* with O'Farrell's first novel. *New Statesman* writer Rachel Cooke found the characters to be "motiveless pencil sketches" and the prose to be "sluggish," yet she also added that the author "is sure-footed when it comes to capturing the strangeness that comes with human intimacy." Noonie Minogue commented in a *Times Literary Supplement* review that "O'Farrell explores with great panache the gothic-horror potential of relationships . . . she exploits skillfully . . . the devices of the supernatural thriller."

BIOGRAPHICAL AND CRITICAL SOURCES:

PERIODICALS

Library Journal, January 1, 2001, Francine Fialkoff, review of *After You'd Gone,* p. 156.

New Statesman, May 29, 2000, Lisa Allardice, review of *After You'd Gone,* p. 57; March 25, 2002, Rachel Cooke, review of *My Lover's Lover,* pp. 51-52.

Publishers Weekly, January 15, 2001, review of *After You'd Gone,* p. 50.

Times Literary Supplement, March 31, 2000, Ruth Scurr, review of *After You'd Gone,* p. 22; March 29, 2002, Noonie Minogue, review of *My Lover's Lover,* p. 23.

ONLINE

Dymocks, http://www.dymocks.com/ (April, 2001), Todd Alexander, interview with Maggie O'Farrell.

New York Times on the Web, http://www.nytimes.com/ (April 22, 2001), Maud Casey, review of *After You'd Gone.*

Penguin Group (USA) Web site, http://www.penguinputnam.com/ (April 8, 2003).*

* * *

OGBU, John U(zor) 1939-2003

OBITUARY NOTICE—See index for *CA* sketch: Born May 9, 1939, in Onicha, Nigeria; died of a heart attack August 20, 2003, in Oakland, CA. Anthropologist, educator, and author. A highly respected professor at the University of California at Berkeley, Ogbu was interested in the anthropology of modern education and why some minority groups in America do worse than others at school. As a young student, he first studied teaching at the Methodist Teachers College in his homeland and taught Latin, geography, and math there for two years; he also studied at the Africa Writing Center in Zambia. Briefly considering a career in the ministry, he came to the United States in 1961 to study at the University of Princeton Theological Seminary before switching to anthropology and attending the University of California at Berkeley, where he eventually earned his doctorate in 1971. After working as an ethnographer for a year in Stockton, California, schools, he joined the faculty at Berkeley in 1970, becoming a full professor of anthropology in 1980. As a researcher, Ogbu was influential in his studies of minority student performance, and he formed a theory that "voluntary minorities"—those who had come to America of their own accord—did better than "involuntary minorities" such as African Americans and Latino Americans, because the latter saw school tests and other educational methods as ways in which mainstream white culture tried to oppress them and deny them their own cultural heritage. Consequently, he was also an advocate of using Ebonics to help teach African Americans. Ogbu was the author of several books about education, including *The Next Generation: An Ethnography of Education in an Urban Neighborhood* (1974), *Minority Education and Caste: The American System in Cross-cultural Perspective* (1978), and *Black American Students in an Affluent Suburb: A Study of Academic Engagement* (2003), the last of which gained him considerable attention in the media.

OBITUARIES AND OTHER SOURCES:

PERIODICALS

Los Angeles Times, August 30, 2003, p. B23.
San Francisco Chronicle, August 23, 2003, p. A21.

* * *

ONG, Water J(ackson) 1912-2003

*OBITUARY NOTICE—*See index for *CA* sketch: Born November 30, 1912, in Kansas City, MO; died August 12, 2003, in Richmond Heights, MO. Priest, educator, and author. Ong was an expert on Renaissance literature who was best known for his scholarly work on the development of oral and written communications. He studied Latin at Rockhurst College, where he graduated in 1933, and two years later he joined the Society of Jesus. Next, Ong earned a master's degree in English, a degree in philosophy, and a degree in sacred philosophy from St. Louis University; finally, in 1955, he received a Ph.D. in English from Harvard University. Ordained a priest in 1946, Ong spent his career in academia, although he considered himself a priest rather than an educator. He joined the faculty at St. Louis University in 1953 and remained there throughout his career, retiring as professor emeritus in 1984. Ong's interest in the history of language was greatly influenced by his famous mentor at St. Louis University, Marshall McLuhan, and his research and writings can be seen as an extension of McLuhan's work. He studied the differences in pre-literate and literate societies, as well as the more recent impacts of computerization, mass electronic media, and the Internet on people's language education. One of his conclusions was that societies exercising an oral tradition valued their elders as a link to their past and experienced stronger communal bonds, while in a literate society a community's members become more individualistic and isolated from the originators of written texts. The invention of the Internet, furthermore, has had the effect of making the boundaries between interior thought and external reality more indistinct. The author or editor of almost a dozen books, Ong received the most acclaim for his 1982 work, *Orality and Literacy: The Technologizing of the World.* Among his other books are *In the Human Grain: Further Explorations of Contemporary Culture* (1967), *Rhetoric, Romance, and Technology: Studies in the Interaction of Expression and Culture* (1971), *Hopkins, the Self, and God* (1986), and *An Ong Reader: Challenges for Further Inquiry* (2002).

OBITUARIES AND OTHER SOURCES:

PERIODICALS

Los Angeles Times, August 15, 2003, p. B11.
New York Times, August 25, 2003, p. A19.
Times (London, England), August 26, 2003.

* * *

O'SULLIVAN, Mark

PERSONAL: Married; children: daughters.

ADDRESSES: Agent—c/o Wolfhound Press, 86 Mountjoy Square, Dublin 1, Republic of Ireland.

CAREER: Environmental health officer, Cashel, County Tipperary, Ireland; writer.

AWARDS, HONORS: White Raven award, International Youth Library, for *Melody for Nora: One Girl's Story in the Civil War* and *White Lies;* Bisto Book Eills Dillon Memorial award, 1995, for *Melody for Nora.*

WRITINGS:

Melody for Nora: One Girl's Story in the Civil War, Wolfhound Press (Dublin, Ireland), 1994.

Wash-Basin Street Blues, Wolfhound Press (Dublin, Ireland), 1995.

Nora in New York, Wolfhound Press (Dublin, Ireland), 1995.

More than a Match, Wolfhound Press (Dublin, Ireland), 1996.

White Lies, Wolfhound Press (Dublin, Ireland), 1997.

Angels without Wings, Wolfhound Press (Dublin, Ireland), 1997.

Silent Stones, Wolfhound Press (Dublin, Ireland), 1999.

SIDELIGHTS: Mark O'Sullivan writes young-adult fiction set in the Ireland of the past and the present. His first book, *Melody for Nora: One Girl's Story in the Civil War,* is set in 1922 during the Irish civil conflict that followed the country's War of Independence. Fourteen-year-old Dublin girl Nora finds herself adrift when her mother dies and her alcoholic father disperses the children—Nora and her eight-year-old twin brothers—to relatives. The teen ends up in Tipperary with her aunt and uncle. The war comes home in this household, as Uncle Peter and his brother, Jack, take two different sides of the civil war. Bitter and resentful, Nora finds herself drawn into the hostilities "between the government force whom her uncle favors and the Irregulars for whom his younger brother fights," noted a reviewer for *Bulletin of the Center for Children's Books.* While Cyrisse Jaffee of *School Library Journal* found elements of the book melodramatic, the critic ultimately praised *Melody for Nora,* saying the setting "is well conveyed and the language is refreshingly reflective of the place and time."

In *Wash-Street Basin Blues,* the sequel to *Melody for Nora,* the heroine is now an aspiring pianist who visits 1920s New York. Now age sixteen, Nora is reunited with her brothers Denis and Ritchie, whom she has not seen since the breakup of her family in Dublin. "But the reunion is not as joyful as Nora imagined," wrote *Booklist*'s Laura Tillotson. She worries about Denis's involvement with a street gang; at the same time, a notorious mobster enters Nora's life, offering to pay her tuition to a prominent musical academy. Tillotson faulted the author for "stereotypical" gangster characters, but concluded that "overall this novel stands on its own."

Silent Stones explores the more recent issue of the Irish "troubles" in a story about two teenagers forced to confront their families' pasts. Robby lives with his uncle on a farm in Cloghercee. His father, Sean, was an Irish Republican Army soldier killed in an ambush before Robby was born. When Robby's mother marries a former IRA compatriot, the boy finds himself resentful of both the marriage and the politics involved. Meanwhile, Mayfly and her New Age parents—an upper-class Englishman called Bubbles and a California woman named Andy—have come to Cloghercee to visit the town's legendary circle of stones. Their hope is that the stones' power to heal will help Andy, who is suffering from cancer. The two teens meet when Mayfly uses herbal healing to save Robbie's dog, which has been poisoned. While the vastly different characters at first think they have little in common, Robby and Mayfly eventually form a bond that speaks of the beginnings of love.

Writing in the online *An Phoblacht/Republican News,* Aengus Ó Snodaigh said that even in a young-adult thriller-romance like *Silent Stones* "it is near impossible to avoid allowing the author's bias from manifesting itself in the text." A more welcoming notice, however, came from an *Interlink Books* reviewer, who thought O'Sullivan's work illustrates that "compassion is more important than blame and that love is stronger than all the mistakes people make."

BIOGRAPHICAL AND CRITICAL SOURCES:

PERIODICALS

Booklist, June 1, 1996, Laura Tillotson, review of *Wash-Basin Street Blues,* p. 1702.

Bulletin of the Center for Children's Books, November, 1995, review of *Melody for Nora: One Girl's Story in the Civil War,* pp. 101-102.

Junior Bookshelf, October, 1995, review of *Melody for Nora,* p. 190.

School Library Journal, August, 1995, Cyrisse Jaffee, review of *Melody for Nora,* p. 157.

ONLINE

An Phoblacht/Republican News, http://www.irlnet.com/ (June 24, 1999), Aengus Ó Snodaigh, review of *Silent Stones.*

InterlinkBooks.com, http://www.interlinkbooks.com/ (March 7, 2002), review of *Silent Stones.**

P

P., Sergie
See VOJNOVIK, Ivo

* * *

PAOLINI, Christopher 1984(?)-

PERSONAL: Born c. 1984.

ADDRESSES: *Home and office*—Paolini International, 52 Cascade La., Livingston, MT 59047.

CAREER: Writer.

WRITINGS:

Eragon (first volume in "Inheritance Trilogy"), Paolini International (Livingston, MT), 2002, second edition, Alfred A. Knopf (New York, NY), 2003.

WORK IN PROGRESS: *Eldest,* a sequel to *Eragon* and the second volume in the "Inheritance Trilogy."

SIDELIGHTS: Christopher Paolini achieved publishing success while still a teen when his *Eragon,* the first novel of a projected trilogy, topped the bestseller charts. Paolini, who was home schooled by his mother, began writing *Eragon* at the age of fifteen, after he earned his GED. He wasn't ready to begin college, and so he took the next year to write the first draft of the fantasy. The second draft consumed another year, and his parents, who own a small publishing company, helped with the editing and publishing. Paolini was offered a full scholarship to attend Reed College in Portland, Oregon, but instead, he and his parents took the book on the road. Paolini made appearances in schools, libraries, bookstores, and at fairs around the country, where he read from and signed copies of his book while dressed in medieval costume.

The Paolinis also placed some of the 10,000 copies they had printed in Montana book stores, and one of them was purchased by the stepson of novelist Carl Hiaasen, while the Hiaasen family was in Montana on a fly-fishing trip. Hiaason called his editor at Alfred E. Knopf and suggested that the publisher might want to look at *Eragon.* They did and published a second edition that is approximately 20,000 pages shorter. A new cover designed by John Jude Palencar replaced Paolini's own design. The agreement with Knopf freed Paolini to turn to *Eldest,* the second novel in the trilogy.

Paolini's Livingston, Montana home, nestled in the scenic Paradise Valley, was an inspiration for his story, described as a "solid, sweeping epic fantasy" by a *Kirkus Reviews* contributor. *Kliatt*'s Michele Winship reviewed *Eragon,* saying that Paolini "takes a little Tolkien, a little McCaffrey, a coming-of-age quest, and combines them with some wicked good storytelling in this first book."

The fantasy opens to a map of Alagaësua, Eragon's world, where the teen ekes out a living with his uncle and cousin on their farm. The story begins with the fifteen year old discovering a blue gemstone covered with white veins, that is, in fact, an egg. When a beautiful blue dragon emerges from it, Eragon names her Saphira. Over a hundred years, an evil king has destroyed the Dragon Riders, and in bonding with the mythical beast, Eragon becomes such a rider, and is pursued by King Galbatorix, who kills Eragon's family and charges his dark servants with capturing Eragon and Saphira. They become travelers, along with the old storyteller Brom, and Eragon matures over the year during which the story transpires. He gains an understanding of love, loss, and the evil that is present in his world as he is pulled into the struggle between the king and the resistance forces of the Varden. Together, the boy, dragon, and wise old man draw on a combination of magic and traditional methods to protect and defend themselves from humanoid warriors.

In a *Teenreads.com* interview Paolini said that he had "always been fascinated with the sources of most modern fantasy that lie in Teutonic, Scandinavian, and Old Norse history. This is disregarding a large chunk of writing devoted to the myths from the British Isles. Because of this, I used Old Norse as the basis of my Elven language in *Eragon,* as well as many names. All the Dwarf and Urgal words, however, are my own invention." Paolini provides a glossary of his invented language at the end of the book.

School Library Journal reviewer Susan L. Rogers felt that "sometimes the magic solutions are just too convenient for getting out of difficult situations," but felt that fans of the "Lord of the Rings" trilogy will find the characters and plot twists appealing. *New York Times Book Review* contributor Liz Rosenberg cited what she saw as faults, including cliches and "B-movie dialogue." Rosenberg wrote that Paolini's "plot stumbles and jerks along, with gaps in logic and characters dropped, then suddenly remembered, or new ones invented at the last minute. And yet, as Beatrix Potter wrote, 'Genius—like murder will out.' *Eragon,* for all its flaws, is an authentic work of great talent. The story is gripping; it may move awkwardly, but it moves with force. The power of *Eragon* lies in its overall effects—in the sweep of the story and the conviction of the storyteller. Here, Paolini is leagues ahead of most writers, and it is exactly here that his youth is on his side."

Booklist's Sally Estes wrote that Paolini's "lush tale is full of recognizable fantasy elements and conventions. But the telling remains constantly fresh and fluid." A *Publishers Weekly* reviewer noted Tolkien's influence on Paolini's writing, including similar naming of geography, the use of landscape as character, and the structure and scale of the story, but noted that, as to language, Paolini "dispenses with the floral, pastoral touch in favor of more direct prose." The reviewer called *Eragon* "an auspicious beginning to both career and series."

BIOGRAPHICAL AND CRITICAL SOURCES:

PERIODICALS

Booklist, August 15, 2003, Sally Estes, review of *Eragon,* p. 1981.

Christian Science Monitor, August 7, 2003, Yvonne Zipp, "Teen author wins readers book by book."

Kirkus Reviews, July 15, 2003, review of *Eragon,* p. 967.

Kliatt, September, 2003, Michele Winship, review of *Eragon,* p. 10.

New York Times Book Review, November 16, 2003, Liz Rosenberg, review of *Eragon.*

Publishers Weekly, July 21, 2003, review of *Eragon,* p. 196.

School Library Journal, September 1, 2003, Susan L. Rogers, review of *Eragon,* p. 218.

ONLINE

Teenreads.com, http://www.teenreads.com/ (September, 2003), interview with Paolini.*

* * *

PARSONS, Sara Mitchell 1912-

PERSONAL: Born April 18, 1912, in Canton, GA; daughter of Clarence A. (in the newspaper business) and Linda (a homemaker; maiden name, Bedell) Perry; married George Raymond Mitchell (deceased); married Thomas S. Parsons, December 18, 1968; children: (first marriage) George Raymond, Jr., Susan Mitchell Rogers, Perry. *Ethnicity:* "American." *Education:* Attended Humboldt State University, 1970. *Politics:* Democrat. *Religion:* Methodist. *Hobbies and other interests:* Politics.

ADDRESSES: Home—2091 Black Fox Dr., Atlanta, GA 30345; fax: 404-634-9594.

CAREER: Writer. Emory University, Atlanta, GA, teacher at Evening School, 1967; teacher at Redwood Junior College and in Humboldt County, CA. Humboldt County Board of Supervisors, member, 1977; KVIQ (radio station), public affairs commentator, 1981.

MEMBER: Humboldt Country Friends of the Library (president, 1975), Atlanta League of Women Voters (president, 1958-62).

AWARDS, HONORS: Good Neighbor of the Year Award, City of Atlanta, 1965; Friends of Education Award, Phi Delta Kappa (Atlanta chapter), 1988; Excellence in Service Environment Award, DeKalb County, GA, 1992; Role Model of the Year Award, Older Women's League of Atlanta, 1994.

WRITINGS:

From Southern Wrongs to Civil Rights, University of Alabama Press (Tuscaloosa, AL), 2000.

Contributor to periodicals, including *Atlanta Journal-Constitution.*

WORK IN PROGRESS: Research on politics.

SIDELIGHTS: Sara Mitchell Parsons told *CA:* "I wrote my book as an apology to blacks for three centuries of a segregated society. As a native southerner I lived through the second phase of our inhuman treatment of blacks, the first being slavery, the second the lie of 'separate but equal,' the third an improved 'laws with teeth' era. I hoped for black readers to sense my regrets and sorrow for our cruel treatment, and for white readers to understand and if needed to have a change of heart. I hoped my book would attract a wide readership. Don't all writers?"

* * *

PEACHEY, Paul 1918-

PERSONAL: Born October 10, 1918, in Elk Lick, PA; son of Shem (a farmer and minister) and Saloma (Bender) Peachey; married Ellen Shenk, June 10, 1945; children: Barbara Peachey Piekarski, Janet, Carl, George, James. *Ethnicity:* "Swiss/German." *Education:* Attended Eastern Mennonite College, 1945, University of Pennsylvania, 1945, University of Basel, 1948, University of Frankfurt, 1949, and Sorbonne, University of Paris, 1952; University of Zurich, Dr. Phil., 1954. *Politics:* Independent. *Religion:* Mennonite. *Hobbies and other interests:* Music, gardening, reading, travel.

ADDRESSES: Home—1285 Shank Dr., No. 212, Harrisonburg, VA 22802. *E-mail*—peacheype@planet.net.

CAREER: Mennonite Central Committee, Akron, PA, worked in Europe and Asia, 1945-60; Church Peace Mission, Washington, DC, executive secretary, 1961-67; Catholic University of America, Washington, DC, associate professor of sociology, 1967-87; Rolling Ridge Study Retreat Community, Harpers Ferry, WV, study director, 1981-91. Eastern Mennonite University, assistant professor, 1953-57; Washington Center for Metropolitan Studies, fellow, 1967-69. War-Nation-Church Study Group, Washington, DC, secretary, 1967-87; organizer of a research project in Vienna, Austria, 1975-83; Institute for Peace and Understanding, member and past chair. Citizens Planning Council for the Fort Lincoln New Town, member, 1968-69; Friendship Citizens Association, chair, 1979-81; Washington Hospital Center, member of institutional review board, 1985-88; FORUM for the Common Good, past member.

MEMBER: American Sociological Society, Society for Christian Ethics.

WRITINGS:

(Senior editor) *The Place of the Person in Social Life,* Council for Research in Values and Philosophy (Washington, DC), 1991.

Leaving and Clinging: The Human Significance of the Conjugal Union, University Press of America (Lanham, MD), 2001.

Contributor to books. Contributor to academic journals.

WORK IN PROGRESS: Editing his memoirs; a project on cosmology/soteriology.

SIDELIGHTS: Paul Peachey told *CA:* "Writing has been part and extension of a vocation in research and teaching in sociology and ethics. In later life my writing impulse has been strengthened by a growing sense of inter-generational accountability in life learning.

"I live and work as a Christian, a commitment which to me means both affirmation and sublation of our 'earthly' existence. I am indebted to the research and writing of countless others, both secular and religious, recognizing the potential for idolatry in all schemes and theories, including my own. Christian faith has to do with 'God in search of man,' as Rabbi Heschel wrote, thus with the teleology that the sciences eschew. Much of my work lies at the interface between the processes of nature and the life of faith; hence, also in the interplay of character with contingency in the life process.

"My writing process is hardly orderly. By the nature of the case—or just my makeup—my writing tends to be convoluted, though I wish it were otherwise. After struggling with an issue and immersing myself in the pertinent data and/or literature, I have to await an organizing inspiration whose emergence I cannot directly precipitate.

"My most recent work, *Leaving and Clinging: The Human Significance of the Conjugal Union,* emerged over many years. The problems of community in modernization and urbanization engaged me for decades, in both natural and religious perspectives. Eventually I discovered the seminal significance in human affairs of the 'leaving and clinging' formula that is stated archetypally in book of Genesis. Consanguinity/tribalism is sublated in this recurring human process, thus at once completing the human individual and engendering society. Accordingly, the *pro*duction of human reality in its own right is the warranty for human *repro*duction, contrary to the primacy traditionally accorded to the latter."

* * *

PEARSON, Ryne Douglas 1965(?)-

PERSONAL: Born c. 1965; married; wife's name Irene (a teacher).

ADDRESSES: *Home*—Huntington Beach, CA. *Agent*—c/o Kaplan-Perrone Entertainment, 10202 West Washington Blvd., Astaire Building, Suite #3003, Culver City, CA 90232.

CAREER: Writer of novels and screenplays. YMCA camp director.

WRITINGS:

Cloudburst (novel), W. Morrow (New York, NY), 1993.

October's Ghost (novel), W. Morrow (New York, NY), 1994.

Capitol Punishment (novel), W. Morrow (New York, NY), 1995.

Simple Simon (novel), W. Morrow (New York, NY), 1996.

(With Lawrence Konner and Mark Rosenthal) *Mercury Rising* (screenplay; based on Pearson's novel *Simple Simon*), Universal Pictures, 1998.

Top Ten (novel), G.P. Putnam's Sons (New York, NY), 1999.

ADAPTATIONS: *Simple Simon* was adapted for film and released as *Mercury Rising,* Universal Pictures, 1998.

WORK IN PROGRESS: Screenplay (with Richard Kelly) titled *Knowing,* released 2004; screenplay *Godspeed;* film adaptation of Ken Follet's *Code for Zero;* a novel titled *Class Action.*

SIDELIGHTS: Ryne Douglas Pearson's first novel, *Cloudburst,* was described as "a gripping blend of techno-thriller and detective story" by a *Publishers Weekly* reviewer. Set in the near future, the novel features a terrorist plot in which the U.S. president is assassinated and an American passenger jet is hijacked to Libya. When it returns to the United States, it is carrying a nuclear bomb, aimed at Washington, D.C. Ultimately, the military's Delta Force engages the terrorists in a tense conflict 20,000 feet over the Atlantic, as the plane hurtles toward the United States.

October's Ghost is based on the premise that, during the Cuban missile crisis, Cuban dictator Fidel Castro hid one of the missiles, believing he might need it for his future defense. Three decades later, the missile falls into the hands of anti-Castro revolutionaries, and both the United States and Russia are involved in defusing the tense situation. In *Booklist,* Denise Perry Donavin praised the book's detailed descriptions of weaponry and called it "suspenseful." A *Publishers Weekly* reviewer commented that conspiracy buffs and military historians would find "ample fodder" in the story.

In *Capitol Punishment,* Pearson tells the story of white supremacist John Barrish and his two sons, who obtain a deadly nerve gas, VZ, and plan to use it to attack both the Capitol building in Washington, D.C., and a Los Angeles office building during the president's State of the Union address. However, in a diabolical twist, Barrish contacts a black militant group, not telling them that he is a racist, and convinces them to plant the gas for him. Hints of this criminal conspiracy attract the attention of FBI agents Art Jefferson and Frankie Aguirre, who previously appeared in Pearson's *October's Ghost.* As the militants release the gas into the vents of the building in Los Angeles, the agents set out on a desperate mission to link Barrish to the crime and stop the final terrorist mission on the U.S. Capitol building. A *Kirkus Reviews* writer noted that, although the book lacks suspense overall, it "convincingly" explains the technology used in executing and preventing attacks; he also noted that it has some "riveting action scenes."

Simple Simon stars Simon, an autistic sixteen-year-old who is a prodigy at solving number puzzles. When he inadvertently cracks a secret National Security Agency code, the government sends an agent out to kill him. On Simon's side is Art Jefferson, an FBI agent who is also married to Simon's psychologist. In *Booklist,* Emily Melton called the book "cleverly crafted," and a *Publishers Weekly* reviewer wrote that "Every element seems crafted for maximum storytelling efficiency." In the *San Francisco Chronicle,* Mick LaSalle commented, "You'd think the government would offer. . . [Simon] a scholarship to MIT, but no. Instead, an assassin shows up with a gun and a silencer and kills the kid's parents." Pearson sold the film rights to the book for $1 million, and the novel was made into a film—written in part by Pearson—retitled *Mercury Rising,* and released in 1998 by Universal Pictures.

Pearson's novel *Top Ten* stars FBI agent Ariel Grace, who is withdrawn from her assignment to investigate the "Top Five Most Wanted" criminals and reassigned to the "Top Ten Most Wanted." Puzzled by her apparent demotion, she finds out she was removed because she was too close to catching one of the wanted men, Mills DeVane, who is, in reality, an undercover agent merely posing as a criminal. Grace's new assignment leads her to investigate serial killer Michelangelo, who creates macabre artwork from the bodies of his victims. When Michelangelo finds out that he's only number ten on the Top Ten list, he begins killing off the criminals who outrank him, gradually closing in on DeVane. Grace races against time to find both Michelangelo and DeVane. A *Publishers Weekly* reviewer noted that some readers might be repelled by the book's "excessive grotesqueries."

BIOGRAPHICAL AND CRITICAL SOURCES:

PERIODICALS

Booklist, June 1, 1994, Denise Perry Donavin, review of *October's Ghost,* p. 1772; July, 1996, Emily Melton, review of *Simple Simon,* p. 1809.

Chicago Sun-Times, April 3, 1998, Roger Ebert, review of *Mercury Rising,* p. 39.

Kirkus Reviews, April 15, 1994, review of *October's Ghost,* p. 501; May 1, 1995, review of *Capitol Punishment,* p. 580; April 15, 1996, review of *Simple Simon,* p. 555.

Library Journal, April 15, 1997, Jay Rozgonyi, review of *Simple Simon,* p. 138.

New York Times Book Review, July 25, 1993, Newgate Callender, review of *Cloudburst,* p. 19.

Publishers Weekly, June 7, 1993, review of *Cloudburst,* p. 52; May 9, 1994, review of *October's Ghost,* p. 62; May 27, 1996, review of *Simple Simon,* p. 66; September 27, 1999, review of *Top Ten,* p. 74.

San Francisco Chronicle, April 3, 1998, Mick LaSalle, review of *Mercury Rising,* p. C3.*

* * *

PELOSI, Olimpia 1957-

PERSONAL: Born August 27, 1957, in Serino, Italy; daughter of Carmine (an engineer) and Filomena (a teacher; maiden name, Verderame) Pelosi; married David M. Billmeyer (a biologist), September 1, 1994; children: Stanley Murphey. *Ethnicity:* "White." *Education:* University of Salerno, Ph.D. (Italian language and literature), 1978, Ph.D. (foreign modern languages), 1981; University of North Carolina at Chapel Hill, Ph.D. (Romance languages), 1990. *Politics:* Democrat. *Religion:* Roman Catholic. *Hobbies and other interests:* Painting.

ADDRESSES: Home—6079 East Old State Rd., Schenectady, NY 12303. *Office*—Department of Language, Literature, and Cultures, State University of New York at Albany, 1400 Washington Ave., Albany, NY 12222. *E-mail*—opelosi@csc.albany.edu.

CAREER: State University of New York at Albany, associate professor of Italian language and literature, 1990—.

MEMBER: Modern Language Association of America, American Association of Teachers of Italian, AISS, AISLLI.

WRITINGS:

Cinque saggi sul Polifilo, Edisud (Naples, Italy), 1987.

Satiroa barocca e teoriche sul genere dal cinque all'ottocento (criticism), Federico & Ardia (Naples, Italy), 1991.

Teseo e l'anima errante (criticism), Federico & Ardia (Naples, Italy), 1996.

Dal mio lato dell'ombra (poems; title means "On My Side of the Shadow"), Ibiskos (Florence, Italy), 2000.

WORK IN PROGRESS: A book of poems, with English translation; collecting material for a novel.

SIDELIGHTS: Olimpia Pelosi told *CA:* "I write because it is the only way I have to be completely happy and at peace with myself. There are two sides to my writing: the academic one, in which I have been more prolific until now, and the creative one, which I cherish the most in my heart. My academic writing is influenced by critical curiosity and intellectual challenges; my creative work is influenced by my feelings and emotions. My work is inspired by life, memories, dreams, the beautiful Italian and American landscapes that I love, and the intense desire to 'save' some dazzling or sad moments I have experienced."

* * *

PERDUE, Lewis 1949-
(Ian Ludlow)

PERSONAL: Born 1949, in Greenwood, MS; married; wife's name Megan; children: William, Katherine. *Education:* Attended University of Mississippi; Corning College, A.S. (biology; summa cum laude), 1970; Cornell University, B.S. (communications and biophysics; with distinction), 1972.

ADDRESSES: *Office*—462 West Napa St., Suite 201, Sonoma, CA 95476. *E-mail*—lperdue@ideaworx.com.

CAREER: Journalist, writer, entrepreneur, and educator. Wines West, founder; Manning, Selvage and Lee, managing director, 1985-86; Renaissance Communications, founder, 1986-90; Wine Business Publications, founder and publisher of *Wine Business Insider* and *Wine Business Monthly,* 1991-96; SmartWired, Inc., founder, chairman, CEO, and publisher of *Smart Wine,* 1996-97; IdeaWorx, principal and consultant, 1997—; Pocketpass.com, Inc., cofounder, CEO, CTO, and board member, 1999-2000. *Ithaca Star Journal,* Ithaca, NY, and *Elmira Star-Gazette,* Elmira, NY, reporter; taught journalism at UCLA and Cornell University; Ottoway, Dow-Jones, and States News Services, Washington, DC, White House and congressional correspondent; Gannet Newspapers, columnist; Internet technology, business, and finance journalist, 1997-2001. Served as a top aide to a U.S. senator and a state governor.

AWARDS, HONORS: Nominee, Pulitzer Prize for editorial writing; Los Angeles Press Club Award for business journalism; Clarion Award; Laurel Award, 1999, for column in *TheStreet.com*

WRITINGS:

FICTION

The Trinity Implosion, Manor (New York, NY), 1976.

The Delphi Betrayal, Pinnacle (New York, NY), 1981.

Queens Gate Reckoning Pinnacle (New York, NY), 1982.

The Da Vinci Legacy, Pinnacle (New York, NY), 1983.

The Tesla Bequest, Pinnacle (New York, NY), 1984.

The Linz Testament, Donald I. Fine (New York, NY), 1985.

Zaibatsu, Worldwide Library (New York, NY), 1988.

Daughter of God, Forge (New York, NY), 2000.

Slatewiper, Forge (New York, NY), 2003.

Also coauthor, writing as Ian Ludlow, with Lee Goldberg, of three books in ".357 Vigilante" series, Pinnacle (New York, NY), 1985. Wrote screenplays for *.357 Vigilante* for New World Pictures, and *The Delphi Betrayal.*

NONFICTION

(With Robin Moore and Nick Rowe) *The Washington Connection,* Condor (New York, NY), 1977.
The Country Inns of Maryland, Virginia, and West Virginia, Washingtonian Books (Washington, DC), 1977.
Supercharging Your PC: A Do-It-Yourself Guide to Expanding the PC, Osborn/McGraw Hill (Berkeley, CA), 1987
High Technology Editorial Stylebook, Dow-Jones/Irwin (Homewood, IL), 1991.
(With Keith Marton and Wells Shoemaker) *The French Paradox and Beyond: Living Longer with Wine and the Mediterranean Lifestyle,* Renaissance (Sonoma, CA), 1992.
The Wrath of Grapes: The Coming Wine Industry Shakeout and How to Take Advantage of It, HarperCollins (New York, NY), 1999.
EroticaBiz: How Sex Shaped the Internet, Writers Club Press (San Jose, CA), 2002.

Perdue's articles have appeared in newspapers, magazines, and online journals, including *Forbes, ASAP, Barron's, Wall Street Journal Online, CBS Marketwatch, TheStreet.com, California Business, California Magazine, Los Angeles Magazine, Los Angeles Times, Washington Post, Boston Globe, Washington Monthly, Nation, PC World, DigitalAge, Computer Currents, Smart Wine, VINOfile,* and *Travel and Leisure,* among others. Editor of *PC Management Letter.*

WORK IN PROGRESS: The Perfect Killer, a novel.

SIDELIGHTS: Lewis Perdue is a former investigative reporter, an entrepreneur, and a writer whose nonfiction books have explored topics as diverse as wine, technology, science, business, and travel, and whose novels deal with international intrigue and suspense. Perdue's 2000 novel *Daughter of God* posits the deeply kept secret of a female messiah, while his 2003 thriller *Slatewiper* looks at the malevolent side of gene therapy. As Perdue told Killian Melloy on *Wigglefish.com,* "I wrote my first thriller because I came up with some interesting stories that I couldn't prove [as a journalist], and I thought, well, heck, just go ahead and write a novel about it."

A fifth-generation Mississippian, Perdue left his native state and his family, tired of "having dead men run my life," as he noted on the *Slatewiper Web site.* He was referring to the ghosts in his own family: his great-grandfather was a senator from Mississippi and also a chief justice of that state's supreme court who was responsible for establishing Jim Crow laws perpetuating segregation of blacks and whites. Moving to New York, Perdue worked his way through Cornell University—where he studied biophysics—by working as a journalist. After graduating and working as a correspondent in Washington, D.C. for several news services, he helped break the Koreagate story in the 1970s that involved a highly placed person in the South Korean government who was bribing U.S. congressmen to vote for legislation that was favorable for his country. Perdue recorded this scandal in his first nonfiction title, *The Washington Connection.*

In his second novel, 1981's *The Delphi Betrayal,* Perdue established a trusted plot formula that would reoccur in his later work: two lovers uncover a powerful secret that puts them in jeopardy from those who want to discover the secret or who want it kept private. In this case, ex-police officer and attorney Beckett Snow becomes involved with Tracy Reynolds, who has found microfilm and a strange metal box in the briefcase of the man for whom she formerly worked—the recently assassinated U.S. vice president. Beckett and Tracy play a dangerous game of cat and mouse with the Delphi Commission, an international cartel anxious to retrieve these artifacts and thereby establish global financial hegemony. Barbara Bannon, reviewing the novel in *Publishers Weekly,* felt that Perdue "attempts a great deal in this complex thriller and, for the most part, succeeds." Bannon further noted that Perdue's novel had ample helpings of "surprises" and "graphically described bloodshed."

In his next thriller outing, *Queens Gate Reckoning,* Perdue turns to the world of espionage with his superpowered and well-born CIA operative Nathaniel Everett Lowell Worthington IV. Nat, as he is called, manages to mole his way into the KGB and work his way out of what seem impossible situations. His chief nemesis is an outsized, one-handed Arab. According to Sally A. Lodge, writing in *Publishers Weekly,* their "escalating strategies twist into plots and counterplots that boggle the mind."

Several further thrillers from Perdue employ the dangerous-secret motif. In *The Da Vinci Legacy* the secret is ecclesiastical and deals with the supposed illegitimate offspring of St. Peter. In *The Tesla Bequest* inventor Nikola Tesla has left behind a trove of research documents for development of a death ray. Powerful parties vie for control of these papers, and Jay Fleming and Alexandra Downing unwittingly get in their way in this "stolid, less than compelling thriller," as Sybil Steinberg described the work in *Publishers Weekly. The Linz Testament* once again turns to religion for its secret. In this take, Perdue postulates that the Nazis were able to blackmail the Vatican and Pope Pius to remain silent about the Holocaust or else they would reveal the shroud of a female messiah they had found. Again, a romantic couple is put in harm's way by discovering this secret. For Steinberg, again writing in *Publishers Weekly,* the novel began "slowly," but midway through "one is hooked." Steinberg also called Perdue "the master of the art of gruelingly violent suspense." *Library Journal*'s Barbara Conaty praised Perdue's "superb technical detail [and] . . . great sense of place."

The Delphi Commission is reprised as the villains in *Zaibatsu,* and they are again trying to control the global economy. Mark Stanton, a financial trader, aided by computer guru Coleen Davis, must stop them before it is too late. With *Daughter of God,* Perdue again looks at the idea of a church secret involving a female messiah and a Nazi plot to keep the Vatican quiet during World War II. In this plot incarnation, art historian Zoe Ridgeway is kidnapped in Switzerland after learning of the existence of a relic that could prove damning to the Catholic Church. During World War II the Nazis had found a shroud belonging to the female messiah, Sophia, who was later killed—along with her entire village—by Constantine, who was fearful that she would prove too dangerous to Christianity. Zoe's husband, Seth, an ex-cop and current religion professor, sets out on the hunt for his wife and the secret shroud in this thriller that is "spun around a religious coverup so devastating it could topple the Vatican and crush Western religion," according to a reviewer for *Publishers Weekly.* Budd Arthur, writing in *Booklist,* found the book an "outstanding thriller on every level." Perdue was not the only one reworking this religious idea, the author later felt. In 2003 he pointed out a string of similarities between his own *Daughter of God* and the then best-selling thriller by Dan Brown, *The Da Vinci Code.* "There are far too many parallels between the two books for it to be an accident," Perdue told Kathy McCormack of the *Chicago Sun-Times.*

Meanwhile, Perdue was busy bringing yet another title of his own to publication. *Slatewiper,* which initially was self-published electronically, was brought out in soft cover in 2003. It tells the story of bio-terrorism and the attempted eradication of unwanted elements of society. A mysterious disease hits Japan, killing off only its Korean inhabitants. When it turns out that this is the first testing of a bioweapon—a deadly gene that can be aimed at certain genetic groups—bidding begins internationally. The Saudis, for example, want it to be rid all the Jews in Israel. Genetic engineer Lara Blackwood must get to the bottom of the genetic weapon before time runs out for the entire world. *Booklist*'s David Pitt commended this bio-thriller, noting that it "deftly combines hard science and narrative panache." Similarly, Jeff Zaleski, writing in *Publishers Weekly,* felt the book delivered "rich research" and "science/action thrills."

Perdue's nonfiction has also been commended by critics. In addition to his book on Koreagate, he has written on personal computer upgrades and other high technology topics. His book on health and alcohol, *The French Paradox and Beyond: Living Longer with Wine and the Mediterranean Lifestyle,* was a best-selling title, while *The Wrath of Grapes: The Coming Wine Industry Shakeout and How to Take Advantage of It* was a "well-written, amusing and compelling list of the problems that beset the industry," according to Orley Ashenfelter in *Barron's.*

BIOGRAPHICAL AND CRITICAL SOURCES:

BOOKS

Reginald, Robert, *Science Fiction & Fantasy Literature, 1975-1991,* Gale (Detroit, MI), 1992, p. 759.

PERIODICALS

Barron's, October 4, 1999, Orley Ashenfelter, review of *The Wrath of Grapes: The Coming Wine Industry Shakeout and How to Take Advantage of It,* p. 57.

Booklist, March 1, 1992, review of *The High Technology Editorial Guide and Stylebook,* p. 1307; January 1, 2000, Budd Arthur, review of *Daughter of God,* p. 885; May 15, 2003, David Pitt, review of *Slatewiper,* p. 1649.

Chicago Sun-Times, June 12, 2003, Kathy McCormack, "Author Claims to Have Cracked Copycat 'Code,'" p. 47.

Inc., February, 1989, Hal Plotkin, "Chinese Checkers," p. 21.

Kirkus Reviews, June 1, 2003, review of *Slatewiper,* p. 776.

Library Journal, September 15, 1985, Barbara Conaty, review of *The Linz Testament,* p. 94.

M2 Best Books, June 17, 2003, "Author Claims Dan Brown's 'Da Vinci Code' Is Similar to His Own."

Magazine for Magazine Management, June 1, 1997, Jennifer Sucov, "A Web-ripened Launch from SmartWired."

National Catholic Reporter, May 5, 2000, Judith Bromberg, review of *Daughter of God,* p. 37.

Newsweek, June 9, 2003, Seth Mnookin, "Page-Turner: A Stolen 'Da Vinci'—or Just Weirdness?," p. 57.

PC Week, December 15, 1987, Bruce Brown, review of *Supercharging Your PC: A Do-It-Yourself Guide to Expanding the PC,* p. 85.

Publishers Weekly, May 8, 1981, Barbara Bannon, review of *The Delphi Betrayal,* pp. 250-251; June 4, 1982, Sally A. Lodge, review of *Queens Gate Reckoning,* p. 651; June 22, 1984, Sybil Steinberg, review of *The Tesla Bequest,* p. 97; July 26, 1985, Sybil Steinberg, review of *The Linz Testament,* p. 153; September 23, 1988, Sybil Steinberg, review of *Zaibatsu,* p. 67; January 10, 2000, review of *Daughter of God,* p. 47; June 23, 2003, Jeff Zaleski, review of *Slatewiper,* p. 48.

ONLINE

IdeaWorx, http://www.ideaworx.com/ (November 7, 2003).

Official Lewis Perdue Web site, http://www.lewisperdue.com (November 7, 2003).

Slatewiper Web site, http://www.slatewiper.com/ (November 7, 2003), "Lewis Perdue."

Wigglefish.com, http://www.stories.wigglefish.com/ (March 30, 2000), Killian Melloy, "Twenty Questions with Lewis Perdue."*

* * *

PETERSON del MAR, David
See del MAR, David Peterson

PHILIPSON, Ilene J. 1950-

PERSONAL: Born September 3, 1950, in Los Angeles, CA; married Jim Stockinger. *Education:* University of California, Ph.D. (sociology), 1981; Wright Institute, Ph.D. (clinical psychology), 1991.

ADDRESSES: *Home*—5478A College Ave., Oakland, CA 94618. *Office*—Northern California Behavioral Health, 3017 Telegraph Avenue, Suite 310, Berkeley, CA 94705. *E-mail*—iphillipson@earthlink.net.

CAREER: Clinical psychologist, sociologist, and author. Center for Working Families, University of California—Berkeley Center for the Study of Social Change, member of staff and former affiliate scholar of Beatrice M. Bain Research Group; former staff psychologist at Pacific Applied Psychology Associates. Has taught at University of California—Santa Cruz and New York University. Editor of *Socialist Review,* mid-1980s.

WRITINGS:

Ethel Rosenberg: Beyond the Myths, F. Watts (New York, NY), 1988.

(Editor, with Karen V. Hansen) *Women, Class, and the Feminist Imagination: A Socialist-Feminist Reader,* Temple University Press (Philadelphia, PA), 1990.

On the Shoulders of Women: The Feminization of Psychotherapy, Guilford Press (New York, NY), 1993.

Married to the Job: Why We Live to Work and What We Can Do about It, Free Press (New York, NY), 2002.

Work published in numerous periodicals, including *Fortune, Fast Company, San Francisco Chronicle,* and *Oakland Tribune.*

SIDELIGHTS: Ilene J. Philipson is a sociologist and licensed psychologist specializing in working with patients who suffer from work-related problems and issues. A former editor of the *Socialist Review,* she has written a biography of Ethel Rosenberg and co-edited an anthology of socialist-feminist writings. She has also contributed two books to the growing body of literature on women in the workforce: an exploration of the issues surrounding the rapid increase in the number of female psychotherapists, and a study on how people become too emotionally attached to their jobs.

Philipson's first book, *Ethel Rosenberg: Beyond the Myths,* is "a fascinating personal biography, using important information gathered from people who knew Ethel Rosenberg," according to *Choice* contributor P. W. McBride. A reviewer for *Booklist* noted that Philipson does not attempt to offer any definitive answers or judgments on the controversy surrounding her subject's life and death, but rather offers "a deeper understanding of her subject's personality, beliefs, and actions." Philipson tells the story of Rosenberg, who, along with her husband, Julius, was accused of being a communist spy and executed in 1953. Some critics commented that the thoroughness of Philipson's study is limited by its tendency toward speculation on Rosenberg's psychology, although others appreciated her interpretations of the family letters—which she was allowed only to read, and not reproduce or paraphrase. "The author has not arrived at conclusions about Ethel Rosenberg, but has posed multiple questions on her life," wrote Raymond E. Houser in a review for *Voice of Youth Advocates.*

Philipson coedited her next book, *Women, Class, and the Feminist Imagination: A Socialist-Feminist Reader,* with Karen V. Hansen, also a former editor of *Socialist Review.* In the mid-1980s the two had edited a series of articles with Vicki Smith titled "Socialist Feminism Today," and many of those articles appear in their 1990 anthology. L. A. Kauffman, writing for *Socialist Review,* called it "an authoritative compilation of U.S. socialist-feminist writings" that "portrays an ambitious exercise in grand theory-building that never quite succeeded, and an equally bold attempt at movement-building that all too frequently remained mired in the convoluted concerns of theory." Philipson and Hansen's book documents the intellectual history and political developments that evolved into second-wave socialist feminism, examining the growing ideological split between radical feminists and their socialist sisters, who had an uneasy relationship with the male-dominated New Left. *New York Review of Books*'s Helen Vendler noted that one of the tendencies of this split was that socialist feminism did not "make gender an overriding concept, as feminist literary criticism has done." Despite the ideological tension inherent in socialist feminism, *Women, Class, and the Feminist Imagination* carefully outlines its contributions to larger feminist debates, including reproductive rights and debates on the family. "Abandoning the notion of a unique and independent left feminism, those socialist feminists who remained activists came to engage more frequently, and more fruitfully, in broader feminist and left debates," noted Kauffman.

Shortly after the anthology was published, Philipson received her second doctoral degree; since then, her writing has focused more on psychology and psychotherapy. Her third book, *On the Shoulders of Women: The Feminization of Psychotherapy,* explores the influx of women practitioners into the field. *Contemporary Psychology*'s Marcy Plunkett called it "a timely intellectual and policy document" that is "an excellent example of feminist, interdisciplinary scholarship." In the book, Philipson questions the growing gender imbalance, the decrease in the occupation's status and pay, and the resulting effect on practitioners. Although Philipson admires the distinction women have received in the field, "she worries that its feminization is more reflective of a general devaluation of caregiving, and the cultural assignment of women to this arena, than a sign of progress," noted Frances L. Hoffman in *Women's Review of Books.* Tracing the development of psychotherapy from World War II onwards, Philipson's study documents the burgeoning field's success during the 1960s and its subsequent stymieing during the 1980s, when federal funds for mental health services began being cut. Despite the decreasing demand for psychotherapists, schools are churning out psychology graduates at a growing rate—and the majority of these newcomers are women. Philipson examines how this phenomenon has affected the field's intellectual and theoretical traditions. *Reading*'s Joan Laird and Ann Hartman appreciated Philipson's arguments, although they felt that she "failed to question elitist, antifeminist, classist, and self-serving stances within the psychotherapeutic professions themselves." Still, Laird and Hartman called the book "clear and well informed, displaying a command of rich sociological information," and, along with many other critics, felt that the text was a timely and provocative assessment of an important issue: "this volume should help to stimulate concerted action in redefining our professional goals and the nation's social agenda."

Diane Scharper, writing for *USA Today,* called Philipson's next book, *Married to the Job: Why We*

Live to Work and What We Can Do about It, "a well-researched book that asks why we are so enamored [with our jobs] and what that means for our futures." Drawing from many different case studies, Philipson examines how the workplace has become more and more important to workers' emotional lives, tracing the trend back to "the notion that emotional ties are a sign of weakness and that the workplace can substitute for the intimacy of the family," Scharper wrote. The notion is mistaken, Philipson explains, and goes on to illustrate the ways in which workers can feel let down, abandoned, and traumatized when the work environment fails them—a feeling of betrayal that occurs more frequently among women, Philipson says. Critics appreciated that Philipson dealt with the issue practically: "She shows readers how to see that there's more to life than work," a *Publishers Weekly* reviewer commented. *Library Journal* reviewer Stacey Marien, too, wrote positively of Philipson's remedial suggestions and called the book "an essential purchase for public and academic collections."

BIOGRAPHICAL AND CRITICAL SOURCES:

PERIODICALS

American Historical Review, February, 1990, Mark Naison, review of *Ethel Rosenberg: Beyond the Myths,* pp. 284-285.

Booklist, June 1, 1988, review of *Ethel Rosenberg,* p. 1631.

Choice, December, 1988, P. W. McBride, review of *Ethel Rosenberg,* p. 702.

Contemporary Psychology, January, 1995, Marcy Plunkett, review of *On the Shoulders of Women: The Feminization of Psychotherapy,* pp. 52-53.

Foreign Affairs, fall, 1988, Lucy Despard, review of *Ethel Rosenberg,* p. 188.

Journal of American History, June, 1989, Leslie Fishbein, review of *Ethel Rosenberg,* pp. 318-319.

Law and Social Inquiry, summer, 1988, review of *Ethel Rosenberg,* p. 654.

Library Journal, July, 1988, John Sillito, review of *Ethel Rosenberg,* p. 76; October 15, 2002, Stacey Marien, review of *Married to the Job: Why We Live to Work and What We Can Do about It,* p. 82.

Long Island Business News, October 4, 2002, review of *Married to the Job,* p. A25.

New York Review of Books, May 31, 1990, Helen Vendler, review of *Women, Class, and the Feminist Imagination: A Socialist-Feminist Reader,* pp. 19-25.

New York Times Book Review, August 21, 1988, John Patrick Diggins, review of *Ethel Rosenberg,* p. 17.

Publishers Weekly, April 8, 1988, Genevieve Stuttaford, review of *Ethel Rosenberg,* p. 81; June 17, 2002, review of *Married to the Job,* p. 56.

Readings, December, 1994, Joan Laird and Ann Hartman, review of *On the Shoulders of Women,* pp. 4-8.

Signs, winter, 1996, Janet Shibley Hyde, review of *On the Shoulders of Women,* pp. 488-490.

Socialist Review, April-June, 1990, L. A. Kauffman, review of *Women, Class, and the Feminist Imagination,* pp. 145-154.

Voice of Youth Advocates, February, 1989, Raymond E. Houser, review of *Ethel Rosenberg,* pp. 304-305.

Women's Review of Books, June, 1994, Frances L. Hoffman, review of *On the Shoulders of Women,* pp. 15-16.

ONLINE

Northern California Behavioral Health Web site, http://www.gpa-corp.com/ (June 1, 2003), "Ilene J. Philipson."

USA Today online, http://www.usatoday.com/ (September 15, 2002), Diane Scharper, "Book Examines Workers' Emotional Ties to Jobs."

* * *

PILIBOSIAN, Helene 1933-

PERSONAL: Born June 26, 1933, in Boston, MA; daughter of Khachadoor and Yeghsa Pilibosian; married Hagop Sarkissian (a photo-compositor), September 17, 1960; children: Sharon Sarkissian Hekimian, Robert. *Ethnicity:* "Armenian." *Education:* Harvard University, A.D.A., 1960. *Religion:* Armenian Apostolic. *Hobbies and other interests:* Travel, reading, attending concerts and museums.

ADDRESSES: Home—171 Maplewood St., Watertown, MA 02472-1324. *E-mail*—rsarkiss@ultranet.com.

CAREER: Editor, publisher, and author. *Armenian Mirror-Spectator,* Watertown, MA, editor, 1964-66 and 1975-81. Ohan Press, Watertown, MA, founder and publisher.

MEMBER: National Association for Armenian Studies and Research, Watertown Poetry Group.

AWARDS, HONORS: First prize, *Writer's Digest* Self-Published Book awards, 1998, for *At Quarter Past Reality.*

WRITINGS:

Carvings from an Heirloom: Oral History Poems, Ohan Press (Watertown, MA), 1983.

(With father, Khachadoor Pilibosian) *They Called Me Mustafa: Memoir of an Immigrant,* Ohan Press (Watertown, MA), 1992, 2nd edition, 1999.

(Editor) Hagop Sarkissian, *From Kessab to Watertown: A Modern Saga,* Ohan Press (Watertown, MA), 1996.

At Quarter Past Reality: New and Selected Poems, Ohan Press (Watertown, MA), 1998.

Contributor of poems to magazines.

WORK IN PROGRESS: Cinderella's Secret; The Everydream Theme: A Fantasy; and *Slices of Place,* all works of poetry.

SIDELIGHTS: Helene Pilibosian told *CA:* "I find writing necessary for self-expression and identity. Depending on publication or awards, I feel gratified by writing prose or poetry. Publication in many literary magazines and interested feedback from editors or readers keep the cycle of publishing and writing going.

"I have been influenced in prose writing and in subject matter by my work as editor at the *Armenian Mirror-Spectator,* an English-language Armenian newspaper for which I have written many articles and book reviews. I find the writing of poetry different and more emotional in nature. Thus it is influenced by people who inspire me and by the encouragement of publications and reviews.

"I write little prose these days, but when I do, I still take notes or make an outline, then write out the article on the computer. I have been steadily working at poetry for almost twenty years. As principal of Ohan Press, I published my first two books of poems, *Carvings from an Heirloom* and *At Quarter Past Reality.* I write when inspiration is high, then later revise or completely rewrite, sometimes in many versions.

"I have written about my family, place, and Armenian-American experiences because of strong family ties and my Armenian background. I wrote *They Called Me Mustafa: Memoir of an Immigrant* with my father Khachadoor, editing translations of his poems that were included in a second edition."

* * *

PLATTEN, David (P.)

PERSONAL: Male. *Education:* Leeds University, B.A., Ph.D., 1994. *Hobbies and other interests:* Coaching soccer; music.

ADDRESSES: *Office*—Department of French, University of Leeds, Leeds LS2 9JT, England; fax: 44-0-113-343-3477. *E-mail*—D.P.Platten@leeds.ac.uk.

CAREER: Educator and author. Leeds University, Leeds, England, lecturer in French, modern French literature, film, and liaison interpreting, 1989—.

WRITINGS:

Dijan: 37.2 le matin, University of Glasgow French & German Publications (Glasgow, Scotland), 1995.

Michel Tournier and the Metaphor of Fiction, St. Martin's Press (New York, NY), 1999.

WORK IN PROGRESS: A book on le roman noir; a book of essays on French popular culture.

SIDELIGHTS: David Platten, a British scholar of French language and literature, may be best known for his book *Michel Tournier and the Metaphor of Fiction.* This book was widely praised by *French Forum* contributor William Cloonan for its "sophisticated readings" of modern French novelist Tournier's works, and for the author's position regarding the place of literature in modern society. Platten opposes the post-structuralist trend in modern literary criticism that is rooted in the concept that texts can only be interpreted in relation to themselves; instead, he proposes a metaphorical reading of texts where works of fiction can be read for their commentaries on the real world. Platten's book "constitute[s] a more than modest contribution to the reintegration of literature and life," Cloonan commented, but Platten also "provides a fair-minded summary of the major critical approaches that have preceded this present one."

Journal of European Studies critic Michael Tilby also commented positively about Platten's grasp of critical history and his "resolute pursuit" of an original analysis."The result," Tilby continued, "is a fine piece of interpretative criticism, rich and mature in its insights, its intellectual pliancy complemented by the engaging manner in which the thesis is advanced."

BIOGRAPHICAL AND CRITICAL SOURCES:

PERIODICALS

Choice, June, 2000, A. Thiher, review of *Michel Tournier and the Metaphor of Fiction,* p. 1823.

French Forum, spring, 2002, William Cloonan, review of *Michel Tournier and the Metaphor of Fiction,* pp. 155-157.

French Studies, April, 1997, Stephen F. Noreiko, review of *Dijan: 37.2 le matin,* pp. 240-241; October, 2001, Colin Davis, review of *Michel Tournier and the Metaphor of Fiction,* p. 573.

Journal of European Studies, June, 2001, Michael Tilby, review of *Michel Tournier and the Metaphor of Fiction,* pp. 227-228.

Modern Language Review, January, 1997, Edmund J. Smyth, review of *Dijan: 37.2 le matin,* pp. 206-207.

ONLINE

University of Leeds Web site, http://www.leeds.ac.uk/ (October 29, 2003),"Dr. David Platten."*

PODRUG, Junius 1947-

PERSONAL: Born June 1, 1947, in Nevada City, CA; son of Mate (a miner) and Angela (a hotel maid) Podrug; married; wife's name Hildegard (a researcher). *Education:* California State University, Sacramento, B.A. (political science); McGeorge School of Law, J.D.

ADDRESSES: *Agent*—Carol McCleary, Wilshire Literary Agency, 20 Barristers Walk, Dennis, MA 02638.

CAREER: Author and lawyer.

AWARDS, HONORS: Rocky award for best first novel, *Rocky Mountain News* Unreal Worlds fantasy, science fiction, and horror awards.

WRITINGS:

Frost of Heaven, Dark Harvest Books (Arlington Heights, IL), 1992.

Presumed Guilty, Forge Books (New York, NY), 1997.

Stop Being a Victim, Tom Doherty Associates (New York, NY), 1998.

Dark Passage, Forge Books (New York, NY), 2002.

WORK IN PROGRESS: Sequel to *Dark Passage.*

SIDELIGHTS: Junius Podrug, a former Los Angeles attorney, is the author of several mystery and suspense novels. Each book is set in an exotic location, and, as Podrug told *CA,* "My books deal with ordinary people confronted with mystery and danger. The characters are unable to turn to the police for help, so must confront and solve the problem by their own wits." His books have been published in nine languages.

In Podrug's first novel, *Frost of Heaven,* Peter Nowak, an American reporter, travels to England, Tibet, and Calcutta in search of his father, a cold war spy pilot who mysteriously vanished while flying over the Himalayas. Peter is aided in his search by the mysterious and beautiful Tashi, who is pursuing her own quest. She protects the secret of Shambala that manifests in the golden rays of the sun piercing through a silvery mist of fog. This natural phenomenon, which is called "the frost of Heaven," is thought to be caused by the "bones of God." Before the end of the novel, Peter must confront some Chinese communists who are also pursuing the mysterious power source of these metaphysical bones.

"Podrug is a talented writer" whose book is filled with "captivating . . . descriptions," said a critic for *Kirkus Reviews.* Rex Klett in *Library Journal* felt that Podrug's novel is "uneven," yet found that it contains humorous moments. "The novel's a perfectly competent tale," commented Edward Bryant in a *Locus* article, although he added that "Podrug is still a writer learning his craft." A reviewer for *Publishers Weekly* called *Frost in Heaven* an "absorbing debut thriller" and mentioned that it "offers penetrating character studies along with colorful, nonstop action." The novel was awarded a Rocky award for best first novel by the fourth annual *Rocky Mountain News* Unreal Worlds fantasy, science fiction, and horror awards.

Lara Patrick, the heroine of *Presumed Guilty,* is a successful Russian-born lawyer who came to live in the United States at the age of seven following the death of her mother. She returns to her homeland, however, when she receives a photograph that confirms her long-held suspicion that her mother's death was not accidental. As Lara's investigation of her mother's death proceeds, more murders are committed. Lara herself becomes a suspect in the murder of a wealthy playboy's mistress and must prove her innocence under the severe conditions of a Moscow courtroom where a defendant is automatically presumed to be guilty of a crime.

A *Kirkus Reviews* contributor called *Presumed Guilty* "An interesting examination of alien jurisprudence." Nancy Pearl in *Library Journal* noted that the characters seem "one-dimensional," but added that "Podrug offers insights into the 'new' Russia." In a *Publishers Weekly* article, the reviewer considered the outcome of Podrug's novel to be "melodramatically predictable," although the author's description of the differences between the U.S. and Russian legal systems is "an interesting rumination."

Dark Passage, published in 2002, moves backward in time from present-day New Mexico to Galilee prior to the Crucifixion of Jesus. Some Islamic fundamentalists have used a time machine in a New Mexican laboratory to travel to the Israel of 30 B.C. in an attempt to change world history: they wish to assassinate the Son of God. In response to this, special government agents assemble an unusual party of four people who will follow the Zayvad brothers and insure that their murder attempt fails.

In *Library Journal,* Jackie Cassada called *Dark Passage* "a fast-paced, action-filled tale." She found the novel's characters to be "appealing." "Adventure, alternate-history, and historical fiction fans should find this an enjoyable read," wrote Michael Gannon in a *Booklist* review. A *Kirkus Reviews* critic remarked that *Dark Passage* is "another over-the-top but oddly effective adventure from Podrug."

BIOGRAPHICAL AND CRITICAL SOURCES:

PERIODICALS

Booklist, November 15, 2002, Michael Gannon, review of *Dark Passage,* p. 569.

Kirkus Reviews, May 15, 1992, review of *Frost of Heaven,* p. 633; July 15, 1997, review of *Presumed Guilty,* p. 1057; October 15, 2002, review of *Dark Passage,* p. 1500.

Library Journal, June 1, 1992, Rex Klett, review of *Frost of Heaven,* p. 186; August, 1997, Nancy Pearl, review of *Presumed Guilty,* p. 134; October 15, 2002, Jackie Cassada, review of *Dark Passage,* p. 98.

Locus, July, 1992, Edward Bryant, review of *Frost of Heaven,* pp. 19-21, 56.

Publishers Weekly, June 8, 1992, review of *Frost of Heaven,* p. 53; August 18, 1997, review of *Presumed Guilty,* pp. 69-70; October 12, 1998, review of *Stop Being a Victim,* p. 72.

ONLINE

Junius Podrug Home Page, http://www.juniuspodrug.com (January 28, 2003).

* * *

POHL, Frances K. 1952-

PERSONAL: Born April 6, 1952, in Kimberley, British Columbia, Canada; daughter of Frank and Caterina Regina Pohl. *Education:* University of British Columbia, B.A., 1977, M.A., 1980; University of California—Los Angeles, Ph.D, 1985.

ADDRESSES: Office—Pomona College, Room 212, Lebus Court, 333 North College Way, Claremont, CA 91711-4429. *E-mail*—FPohl@pomona.edu.

CAREER: Pomona College, Claremont, CA, professor, 1985—; author. Social and Public Art Resource Center, member of board of directors, 1997—; Jahrbuch der Guernica-Gesellschaft (Osnabruck, Germany, member of advisory board, 1999—.

MEMBER: College Art Association, National Women's Studies Association, American Studies Association.

AWARDS, HONORS: Social Sciences and Humanities Research Council of Canada fellowship, 1980-84; University of California, Los Angeles doctoral fellow; Smithsonian Institution postdoctoral fellow, 1988-89; National Endowment for the Humanities summer fellow, 1992; numerous research grants from Pomona College.

WRITINGS:

Ben Shahn: New Deal Artist in a Cold War Climate, 1947-1954, University of Texas Press (Austin, TX), 1989.

(With Ben Shahn) *Ben Shahn,* Pomegranate ArtBooks (San Francisco, CA), 1993.

In the Eye of the Storm: An Art of Conscience, 1930-1970, Pomegranate ArtBooks (San Francisco, CA), 1995.

Framing America: A Social History of American Art, Thames & Hudson (New York, NY), 2002.

Contributor to *Nineteenth-Century Art, A Critical History,* Thames & Hudson (New York, NY), 1993.

SIDELIGHTS: Frances K. Pohl strongly believes that art cannot be studied in isolation. Art is affected by the culture that surrounds the artist. Art is also not static as it is always evolving with the times. She studies, teaches, and writes about art with an interdisciplinary approach. In order to fully appreciate a work of art, Pohl believes, one must understand first how that creative piece functions within the particular era and in the particular place that the artist completed it, and to appreciate how the meaning of it has changed over time. She points out that what a specific artist might have wanted to express with his or her art is often used by others to convey different meanings, especially in the political arena.

Pohl is a Canadian living in the United States, close to the Mexican border. In her studies, she incorporates the works of artists in all three countries as well as works of different genres, such as paintings, furniture, sculpture, posters, needlework, and ceramics. Her works include two focused studies of artist Ben Shahn's pieces and the political messages of his work. Two other books offer comprehensive studies of art in North America.

Shahn, a social realist artist and photographer, is the subject of Pohl's first two books. The earlier one, *Ben Shahn: New Deal Artist in a Cold War Climate, 1947-1954,* narrows its topic to his work of the anti-Communism years in the United States following World War II. Shahn was a man who believed that art should be socially relevant and politically active. His own Jewish ethnicity often marked him as a target during the McCarthy years, and his works were blacklisted from time to time. He was able to find a political balance, however, and was equally supported by labor unions and big business. Pohl also points out how Shahn was able to create materials for the government, such as pro-war posters, as well as to produce works that depicted the deplorable working conditions that existed in the United States, particularly in the South. In demonstrating the nature and purpose of Shahn's dedication, as Paul Frosch reported in the *Library Journal,* Pohl shows how the artist can be "social critic" and his art, "social action." Although Pohl focuses on Shahn in this book, J. Barter, a reviewer for *Choice,* wrote that the real subject of her study "is the careful weaving of Cold War Politics, New Deal liberals, labor unions, and the changing art world of the 1950s."

Pohl's second book on Shahn, simply called *Ben Shahn,* is a collaboration of sorts, as Pohl works not only with Shahn's art and an historical perspective of his collective works but also with Shahn's own writings. With this book, Pohl outlines his history and demonstrates how his work changed over time. Patrick J. B. Flyn, writing for *Progressive* called Pohl's work, a "big, beautiful book" that "proves Ben Shahn was a master artist."

Shahn and his work have not been studied for many years. After the height of his career in the late fifties, most art historians ignored him. For this reason, Christopher Andreae, in the *Christian Science Monitor,* found Pohl's book "a welcome representation of Shahn, both of his art and his highly intelligent writing about art." Some of Shahn's most memorable works include one that represents his emotions about the famed trial of Nicola Sacco and Bartolomeo Vanzetti, Italian anarchists, whom many people believe were framed for murder—they were subsequently tried and sentenced to death. "Here was something to paint!" Shahn wrote, exposing how emotional he was about the trial. Shahn also worked with Mexican muralist Diego Rivera on the famous Rockefeller Center piece, "Man at the Crossroads," which was ultimately torn down almost immediately after it was finished because it contained a depiction of Vladimir Lenin, then-leader of the Soviet Union.

In 2002 Pohl published *Framing America: A Social History of American Art,* a book that is often referred to as the model for art-history text books. In this work, Pohl, according to Savannah Schroll for the *Library Journal,* "reaches further into history than previous surveys." She does this, for example, by pondering the influences of Native Americans on European explorers and their arts. She also covers objects that other art historians have neglected, such as articles usually defined as craft rather than art, and utilitarian implements. She includes works by Japanese-American internment camp inmates who tell the stories of their imprisonment through their art. Pohl's detailed observations of these often-overlooked pieces made a *Publishers Weekly* reviewer claim that Pohl's book "is determinedly and liberatingly inclusive." For instance, Pohl includes sketches made by survivors of the battle at Little Big Horn; art by spectators of the Haymarket riot; as well as diagrams of the construction of the Statue of Liberty. Also collected in the 560-page textbook is the art of everyday life of Native Americans, Hispanic Americans, and women, and other often underrepresented groups. In an online article for *Calendarlive,* Suzanne Muchnie quoted Pohl as stating that she wrote this book to examine "how the meaning of a work is a function not only of its content but also of where it is produced, where it is displayed, the identity of the artist and how this identity is affected by race, ethnicity, class, gender and sexuality." Schroll ended her review by calling *Framing America* the "most up-to-date American art textbook available."

BIOGRAPHICAL AND CRITICAL SOURCES:

PERIODICALS

American Historical Review, February, 1991, Maren Stange, review of *Ben Shahn: New Deal Artist in a Cold War Climate, 1947-1954,* p. 279.

Choice, December, 1989, J. Barter, review of *Ben Shahn: New Deal Artist in a Cold War Climate, 1947-1954,* p. 623.

Christian Science Monitor, February 2, 1994, Christopher Andreae, review of *Ben Shahn,* p. 21.

Library Journal, August, 1989, Paula Frosch, review of *Ben Shahn: New Deal Artist in a Cold War Climate, 1947-1954,* p. 132; October 1, 2002, Savannah Schroll, review of *Framing America,* p. 92.

Progressive, February, 1994, Patrick J. B. Flynn, review of *Ben Shahn,* pp. 38-41.

Publishers Weekly, August 26, 2002, review of *Framing America,* pp. 52-63.

ONLINE

Calendarlive, http://www.calendarlive.com (February 23, 2003), Suzanne Muchnie, review of *Framing American.* *

* * *

POLEN, Nehemia 193(?)-

PERSONAL: Born c. 1930s. *Education:* Johns Hopkins University, B.S.; Ner Israel Rabbinical College, ordination; Northeastern University, M.Ed.; Boston University, Ph.D., 1983. *Religion:* Jewish.

ADDRESSES: *Office*—Hebrew College, 160 Herrick Road, Newton Centre, MA 02459. *E-mail*—npolen@hebrewcollege.edu.

CAREER: Educator and ordained rabbi. Hebrew University in Jerusalem, visiting scholar; congregational rabbi for twenty-three years; Hebrew College, Boston, MA, professor of Jewish thought and director of Hasidic Text Institute.

AWARDS, HONORS: Harvard University Daniel Jeremy Silver fellow, 1994; National Endowment for the Humanities fellow, 1998-99; National Jewish Book Award for autobiography and memoir, 2002, for *The Rebbe's Daughter: Memoir of a Hasidic Childhood* by Malkah Shapiro.

WRITINGS:

(Compiler with Lauri Wolff-Polen) *A Blessing for the Sun: A Study of the Birkat ha-hammah from Early Times to the Present,* N. Polen (Everett, MA), 1981.

The Holy Fire: The Teachings of Rabbi Kalonymus Kalman Shapira, the Rebbe of the Warsaw Ghetto, J. Aronson (Northvale, NJ), 1994.

(Translator and editor) Malkah Shapiro, *The Rebbe's Daughter: Memoir of a Hasidic Childhood,* Jewish Publication Society (Philadelphia, PA), 2002.

SIDELIGHTS: An ordained rabbi and an educator, Nehemia Polen is considered a leading expert on Hasidism and Jewish mysticism and thought. Ordained at the Ner Israel Rabbinical College in Baltimore, Maryland, he served as a congregational rabbi for twenty-three years before entering the field of education, and now directs Hebrew College's Hasidic Text Institute in addition to his teaching duties.

Polen received his Ph.D. from Boston University in 1983, studying and serving as teaching fellow for Nobel laureate Elie Wiesel. While studying with Wiesel, Polen began work on his second book, *The Holy Fire: The Teachings of Rabbi Kalonymus Kalman Shapira, the Rebbe of the Warsaw Ghetto.* A well-known Hasidic educator, Shapira taught in the Warsaw Ghetto and compiled a manuscript of his teachings in the ghetto between 1939 to 1942. The work was buried at Shapira's death in 1943, along with a note that should it be found, his manuscript should be taken to Israel. After World War II the manuscript was discovered, sent to Israel, and published in Hebrew as *Eish Kodesh,* or "Holy Fire." The work achieves historical importance as the last work published by a Hasidic leader prior to the Holocaust. In his writings, Shapira ponders the purpose of Evil and searches for spiritual and mystical responses to the suffering and despair around him as the ghetto's Jews suffer under Nazi genocide. Reviewing *The Holy Fire* for *Cross Currents,* Rachel T. Sabath explained that "Shapira's response to the events engulfing him and his community demonstrates an attempt to transcend reality with Torah in new ways." "Polen suggests," Sabath added, "that Shapira's teachings can be applied to our own reality as well."

Writing in *Tikkun,* Lawrence Kushner commented of *The Holy Fire:* "The teachings of both Rabbi Shapira (and his disciple, Rabbi Polen) are so powerful and disturbing that the reader is quickly drawn into the inner workings of life and spiritual survival in the Warsaw Ghetto." Polen's Orthodox rabbinic education qualifies Polen to accomplish more than a mere historian, Kushner maintained: "He intuits that through the life teaching of Rabbi Shapira, he can teach us of a long-lost way to understand what seems to be gratuitous evil." Sabath concluded of *The Holy Fire* that "With careful attention to inconsistencies and the widest theological possibilities, Rabbi Polen is uniquely able to illuminate the unfolding of Shapira's theological responses to suffering."

It was while Polen was serving as a National Endowment for the Humanities fellow during the late 1990s that he became fascinated with the writings of Malkah Shapiro (1894-1971). The daughter of a noted Hasidic rabbi of Kozienice, Poland, Shapiro's memoirs examine women's spirituality during early twentieth-century pre-war Poland. Polen's research led to his translation of Shapiro's writings from the Hebrew and their publication as *The Rebbe's Daughter: Memoir of a Hasidic Childhood.*

Shapiro's autobiography focuses on her adolescence from age eleven to her marriage at age fourteen, and her curiosity about tradition, Hasidic spirituality, and Kabbalah. A contributor to *Publishers Weekly* commented of Polen's work in bringing Shapiro's writings to an English-speaking readership that he "masterfully translates Shapiro's lush descriptions, which offer an insider's view of a Hasidic master's family: the pungent smell of garlic and goose flesh; the fragrance of rose-scented soap; the taste of fresh raisin cakes; the sounds of chopping wood, quivering violins, and sacred singing; visions of cold blue air and snow sparkling on rooftops." Praised by critics, *The Rebbe's Daughter* won the 2002 National Jewish Book Award.

BIOGRAPHICAL AND CRITICAL SOURCES:

PERIODICALS

Cross Currents, spring, 1999, review of *The Holy Fire: The Teachings of Rabbi Kalonymus Kalman Shapira, the Rebbe of the Warsaw Ghetto,* p. 134.

Publishers Weekly, April 29, 2002, review of *The Rebbe's Daughter: Memoir of a Hasidic Childhood,* p. 61.
Tikkun, November-December, 1995, review of *The Holy Fire,* p. 86.

ONLINE

Hebrew College Web site, http://www.hebrewcollege.edu/ (July 15, 2003), "Nehemia Polen."*

* * *

PONTE, Antonio José 1964-

PERSONAL: Born 1964, in Matanzas, Cuba; *Education:* Received degree in hydraulic engineering from University of Havana.

ADDRESSES: Home—Havana, Cuba. *Agent*—c/o Author Mail, City Lights, 261 Columbus Ave., San Francisco, CA 94133.

CAREER: Author. Taught Cuban literature and creative writing at the University of Pennsylvania, c. 2001. Worked as an engineer for five years before becoming a screenwriter and author.

WRITINGS:

Asiento en las ruinas, Editorial Letras Cubanas (Havana, Cuba), 1997.
In the Cold of the Malecó & Other Stories, translated by Cola Franzen and Dick Cluster, City Lights Books (San Francisco, CA), c. 2000.
(With Méonica Bernabé and Marcela Zanin) *El abrigo de aire: ensayos sobre literature cubana,* B. Viterbo Editora (Rosario, Argentina), 2001.
Contrabando de sombras (novel, title means "Trafficking in Shadows"), Mondadori (Barcelona, Spain), 2002.
Cuentos de todas partes del imperio, translated by Cola Franzen as *Tales from the Cuban Empire,* City Lights Books (San Francisco, CA), 2002.

Also author of *Las comidas profundas* (satire; title means "Profound Meals"), Ediciones Deleatur.

Author's work has been translated and published in France and Spain.

SIDELIGHTS: Antonio José Ponte is a Cuban author with a growing reputation in Europe and North America as a deft writer and remarkably unrestrained critic of the Cuban government. His work includes screenplays, poetry, short stories, a novel, and essays. Two collections of his translated short stories, *In the Cold of the Malecó & Other Stories* and *Tales from the Cuban Empire,* have been published in the United States. These stories have been described as charming, playful, and subtle in their depiction of Cubans living in their homeland and abroad. Ponte is considered an important representative of a new generation of Cuban writers.

As a child growing up in Cuba, Ponte loved writing and briefly published a magazine for his friends. He became an engineer, a career he pursued for five years, because there was no equivalent training program for writers. Subsequently, he has created works that show the difficulties and hardships of life under Fidel Castro's dictatorship, but has escaped the obvious threat of censorship from the government. In 1997 he became the first Cuban writer to be featured at the Miami Book Fair International and in 2001 he was teaching Cuban literature and creative writing at the University of Pennsylvania on a temporary basis. At that time, Ponte planned to return to Havana before taking another teaching assignment in Iowa. In an interview with Fabiola Santiago for the *Miami Herald,* he would not conjecture about why he was allowed such freedoms, but did comment that "the fear of being arrested and the fear of a literary misstep" had in the past kept him from naming the Cuban Revolution or Castro in his fiction.

Ponte's first fiction to be translated into English was six short stories collected as *In the Cold of the Malecó & Other Stories.* Several of the tales share a theme of disconnection. In "Coming" Cuban students return from the Soviet Union to discover that their skills in the Russian language are not needed any more. In another, a historian and an astrologer fall in love; one has a fatal illness and they become vagabonds. A character in "Heart of Skitalietz" philosophizes that when the electricity is turned off in his neighborhood and turned on in another, someone else is doing things for him.

The stories were admired by critics for their literary value as well as for their insight into a hidden world. *Library Journal*'s Mary Margaret Benson described them as "stark ironic views of life in contemporary Cuba" and credited the author with creating "elegant prose." A reviewer for *Publishers Weekly* said the tales provide "a picture that will strike the U.S. reader as surreal in its simplicity." The reviewer concluded, "Cool, assured and quietly insightful, these tales provide rare glimpses into a Cuba often lost behind newspaper headlines."

With the translated collection *Tales from the Cuban Empire,* Ponte casts himself as a modern-day Scheherazade in the prologue. He hopes that the reader will not be bored by his account of a Cuban woman who hides in an airport bathroom, trying to escape all men in "Because of Men." In "Tears in the Congri," Cubans studying physics in the Soviet Union go to amazing lengths to make the rice and bean dish called congri. "At the Request of Ochon" is told by a Chinese butcher who is teaching a student how to gently guide his knife through the meat without dulling the blade, while also commenting on his life and how to butcher an elephant.

Reviewers of *Tales from the Cuban Empire* noted Ponte's vivacious style and comic touch. In *Kirkus Reviews* a critic said that the collection included "elusive, defiantly barogue tales" and called their combined effect a "virtuosic mingling of melodramatic intrigue, sociopolitical commentary, surrealism, and parody." In a review for the *Miami Herald,* Fabiola Santiago called Ponte "one of the most daring young intellectuals on the island" and reflected that both of his English translations "open a window into those hermetic spaces where suffering and joy often come hand-in-hand." Santiago advised that the stories merited re-reading, an opinion shared by Susan Salter Reynolds, who said in the *Los Angeles Times,* "Each story loops back upon itself, arrives at an inconclusive end, and should be read once more." According to Jonathan Kiefer in the *San Francisco Chronicle,* the collection shows Ponte to be "a compulsive storyteller" who makes good use of an "impish, conspiratorial tone." Kiefer found the stories to be refreshing and crisply written. He remarked that the opening of "At the Request of Ochon" is characteristic of "the nimble snap with which Ponte unfurls his written tapestries." Commenting on Ponte's audience, the critic said, "To call him under-appreciated misses the mark, because upon discovering him people often become as compulsive about reading his work as he is about writing it."

BIOGRAPHICAL AND CRITICAL SOURCES:

PERIODICALS

Kirkus Reviews, September 1, 2002, review of *Tales from the Cuban Empire,* p. 1265.

Library Journal, November 15, 2000, Mary Margaret Benson, review of *In the Cold of the Malecó & Other Stories,* p. 100.

Los Angeles Times December 29, 2002, Susan Salter Reynolds, review of *Tales from the Cuban Empire,* p. R11.

Miami Herald, March 12, 2001, Fabiola Santiago, "Cuban Author Antonio Jose Ponte Straddles Two Worlds"; January 15, 2003, Fabiola Santiago, review of *Tales from the Cuban Empire.*

Publishers Weekly, review of *In the Cold of the Malecó & Other Stories,* p. 59.

San Francisco Chronicle, September 15, 2002, Jonathan Kiefer, review of *Tales from the Cuban Empire.*

ONLINE

City Lights Web site, http://www.citylights.com/ (October 1, 2003), interview with Ponte.*

* * *

POON (ANDERSEN), Irene 1941-

PERSONAL: Born 1941, in San Francisco, CA; married Stanley Andersen (an English professor). *Education:* San Francisco State College, B.A. (art), 1964, M.A. (photography), 1967.

ADDRESSES: *Office*—Art Department, San Francisco State University, 1600 Holloway Avenue, San Francisco, CA 94132. *E-mail*—andersen@sfsu.edu.

CAREER: Photographer, educator, and author. Art Department, San Francisco State University, slide curator, 1965—; photographer. *Exhibitions:*Photographs have been displayed at Barrington Center for the Arts at Gordon College, Wenham, MA, M. H. de Young Memorial Museum, Oakland, CA, University of New Mexico, University of California-Davis, and E. B. Crocker Art Gallery, Sacramento, CA.

MEMBER: Chinese Historical Society of America.

WRITINGS:

Leading the Way: Asian-American Artists of the Older Generation, Gordon College (Wenham, MA), 2001.

SIDELIGHTS: Irene Poon was born in 1941 to first-generation Chinese immigrants in San Francisco's famed Chinatown. This community provided the thematic material for much of her later work. In 1995 she co-curated an exhibition at San Francisco State University titled "With New Eyes: Toward an Asian-American Art History in the West." The success of that show encouraged Poon to document these aging artists before they were gone. Ultimately an exhibit was created at the Barrington Center for the Arts at Gordon College, Wenham, Massachusetts, and a book, *Leading the Way: Asian-American Artists of the Older Generation,* followed.

Leading the Way features twenty-five pioneering Asian-American artists who worked from 1930 to 1970. Poon includes biographical sketches of each artist as well as her own photographs of them. All of these artists overcame cultural, social, and political obstacles to succeed as artists. Lucia S. Chen of *Library Journal* noted that "This book attempts to retrieve and capture an aspect of the American art scene that has traditionally been ignored by mainstream art historians." Praising Poon's photographs, *Choice* reviewer L. G. Kavaljian observed that "a full-page black-and-white portrait of each [artist], taken by the author, sensitively presents them intelligently located in settings that communicate their subjects." Among the gems Poon discovered while working on the book were artists Tyrus Wong, responsible for the paintings that inspired the Disney animated classics *Bambi* and *Fantasia,* as well as the Academy Award-winning special-effects artist Wah Ming Chang, whose credits include *The King and I, Star Trek,* and perhaps most surprisingly, the Pillsbury Doughboy advertising icon.

When asked by Roxana Botea in an interview posted on the *Arizona State University Web site* what she hoped to tell the world through her photography and what her message was, Poon responded that "I hope to convey what I see and feel at a particular moment in my life. My message is to be a human being and observe. . . believe and pursue your own vision."

BIOGRAPHICAL AND CRITICAL SOURCES:

PERIODICALS

Choice, October, 2002, L. G. Kavaljian, review of *Leading the Way,* p. 270.

Library Journal, November 1, 2002, Lucia S. Chen, review of *Leading the Way: Asian-American Artists of the Older Generation,* p. 86.

ONLINE

Arizona State University Web site, http://www.asu.edu/ (December 12, 2001), Roxana Botea, interview with Poon.

AsianWeek.com, http://asianweek.com/ (June 5, 2003).

San Francisco State University Art Department Web site, http://www.sfsu.edu/ (May 10, 2003).

* * *

PORTER, Andrew P. 1946-

PERSONAL: October 5, 1946, in Boston, MA; son of Phil, Jr. (a priest) and Joan (Peabody) Porter. *Education:* Harvard University, A.B., 1968; University of California—Davis, M.S., 1968, Ph.D. (applied science), 1976; Church Divinity School of the Pacific, M.Th., 1980; Graduate Theological Union, Ph.D. (philosophical theology), 1991. *Religion:* Roman Catholic.

ADDRESSES: *Home*—774 Joyce St., Livermore, CA 94550. *E-mail*—app@jedp.com.

CAREER: Lawrence Livermore National Laboratory, Livermore, CA, physicist in Special Studies Group, 1968-94, physicist in Physics and Space Sciences Division, 1994—. School for Deacons of the Episcopal Church, instructor, 1980-87; Los Medanos College, instructor, 1992; Las Positas College, instructor, 1996-98; Graduate Theological Union, adjunct member of theology faculty, 1998—; Dominican University, adjunct member of philosophy faculty, 2001—.

MEMBER: American Academy of Religion, Society of Christian Philosophers, Mathematical Association of America.

WRITINGS:

By the Waters of Naturalism: Theology Perplexed among the Sciences, Wipf & Stock Publishers (Eugene, OR), 2001.

Exposure, Limitation, and Need: Elementary Monotheism, University Press of America (Lanham, MD), 2001.

Contributor of articles and reviews to scholarly journals, including *Faith and Philosophy* and *Budhi.*

WORK IN PROGRESS: Unwelcome Good News, "a semi-popular exposition of the thesis that the heart of biblical religion consists in blessing human life in this world in full view of its pains, and in affirmation of the blessing in those pains"; a historical reflection on "how biblical religion came to its current perplexities"; a book on the theology in creation-evolution controversies; research on radical monotheism and historical religion.

SIDELIGHTS: Andrew P. Porter told *CA:* "My motive for writing is the pleasure of clear statement and a felt obligation to pass on what was given to me and is not already in the published literature. Who influenced my work? Teachers Jim Vendettuoli and Edward Hobbs; writers R. G. Collingwood, Ernst Troeltsch, H. Richard Niebuhr, and other who are cited in my bibliographies. Friends and neighbors? They are entitled to anonymity."

* * *

POWELL, Mark Allan 1953-

PERSONAL: Born 1953. *Education:* Texas Lutheran College, B.A., 1975; Trinity Lutheran Seminary (Columbus, OH), M.Div., 1980; Union Theological Seminary (Richmond, VA), Ph.D., 1987. *Religion:* Lutheran.

ADDRESSES: Office—Bible Department, Trinity Lutheran Seminary, 2199 East Main St., Columbus, OH 43209. *E-mail*—mapowell@trinitylutheranseminary.edu.

CAREER: Theologian. Trinity Lutheran Seminary, began as assistant professor of New Testament, 1987-92, became associate professor 1992—; also served as director of continuing education and postgraduate studies, 1989-92. Ordained minister, Evangelical Lutheran Church in America.

WRITINGS:

What Are They Saying about Luke?, Paulist Press (New York, NY), 1989.

What Is Narrative Criticism?, Fortress Press (Minneapolis, MN), 1990.

What Are They Saying about Acts?, Paulist Press (New York, NY), 1991.

(With Cecile G. Gray and Melissa C. Curtis) *The Bible and Modern Literary Criticism: A Critical Assessment and Annotated Bibliography,* Greenwood Press (Westport, CT), 1992.

God with Us: A Pastoral Theology of Matthew's Gospel, Fortress Press (Minneapolis, MN), 1995.

(Editor with David R. Bauer) *Treasures New and Old: Recent Contributions to Matthean Studies,* Scholars Press (Atlanta, GA), 1996.

Fortress Introduction to the Gospels, Fortress Press (Minneapolis, MN), 1998.

Jesus as a Figure in History: How Modern Historians View the Man from Galilee, Westminster John Knox (Louisville, KY), 1998.

(Editor) *The New Testament Today,* Westminster John Knox (Louisville, KY), 1999.

(Editor, with others) *Who Do You Say That I Am?: Essays on Christology,* Westminster John Knox Press (Louisville, KY), 1999.

Chasing the Eastern Star: Adventures in Biblical Reader-response Criticism, Westminster John Knox (Louisville, KY), 2001.

Encyclopedia of Contemporary Christian Music, Hendrickson (Peabody, MA), 2002.

Contributor of more than one hundred articles on theology and the Bible.

SIDELIGHTS: Mark Allan Powell is an ordained Lutheran minister and leading New Testament scholar with numerous books and articles to his credit. He joined the faculty of Trinity Lutheran Seminary in 1987, and has held the Leatherman Chair in New Testament since 1998. Powell has done significant research on the historical Jesus and has contributed a great deal to the study of the Bible as literature.

Jesus as a Figure in History: How Modern Historians View the Man from Galilee, summarizes past scholarship and explains and evaluates the most important recent work on the subject of the historical Jesus. In a review of the book for *Theological Studies,* Elliott C. Maloney commented that "It gives excellent analysis of recent historical inquiry into the life of Jesus," and "should be required reading for all seminarians." Critic Mark A. Matson suggested in *Interpretation* that "Powell has chosen the key scholars to review and has done an excellent job of describing their primary positions, giving enough of their arguments for one to appreciate the basis for their reconstructions," further noting that Powell remains "remarkably unbiased." Powell has done similar work on other New Testament topics, especially on the study of Matthew.

In a different vein, Powell has written *Encyclopedia of Contemporary Christian Music,* which *Library Journal* reviewer James E. Perone described as "an exhaustive opus on popular Christian music dating from the 1960s to the present." Having once worked as a rock journalist and critic, Powell has an informed appreciation for popular music. In an interview for *Christianity Today,* Powell explained that his early interest in music influenced his religious work. "As I became a professional theologian and I learned to think of things in what are supposed to be sophisticated and nuanced ways, I have never forgotten how much that music meant to me and how important it was to my faith development." *Encyclopedia of Contemporary Christian Music* includes entries not only on specifically religious music, but also on artists whose work, Powell believes, deals with more subtle aspects of Christianity. These include such artists as Sam Cook, Aretha Franklin, Marvin Gaye, Al Green, Creed, US, and Collective Soul. "What all these people have in common," he explained, "is an intersection of Christian faith and popular music that reveals something about the inter-relationships of religion and culture in the last thirty years in America." A reviewer for *Publishers Weekly* felt that "readers who appreciate Powell's assertion that contemporary Christian musicians are actually 'amateur theologians' whose perspectives are helping to shape Christian history will marvel at this book's stunning combination of breadth and depth."

BIOGRAPHICAL AND CRITICAL SOURCES:

PERIODICALS

America, February 9, 1991, review of *What Are They Saying about Luke?,* p. 133.

Booklist, December 15, 2002, review of *Encyclopedia of Contemporary Christian Music,* p. 778.

Catholic Biblical Quarterly, July, 1997, Robert Doran, review of *Treasures New and Old: Recent Contributions to Matthean Studies,* pp. 600-602.

Interpretation, July, 1991, Walter E. Pilgrim, review of *What Are They Saying about Luke?,* p. 312; July, 1992, Richard H. Hiers, review of *What Is Narrative Criticism?,* pp. 329-330; April, 1993, John T. Carroll, review of *What Are They Saying about Acts?,* p. 196; April, 1994, Elizabeth A. Castelli, review of *The Bible and Modern Literary Criticism: A Critical Assessment and Annotated Bibliography,* p. 218; January, 1997, John P. Meier, review of *God with Us: A Pastoral Theology of Matthew's Gospel,* p. 91; July, 1999, Mark A. Matson, review of *Jesus as a Figure in History: How Modern Historians View the Man from Galilee,* p. 309.

Library Journal, January, 1999, Graham Christian, review of *Jesus as a Figure in History,* p. 108; November 1, 2002, James E. Perone, review of *Encyclopedia of Contemporary Christian Music,* p. 82.

Publishers Weekly, February 15, 1999, review of *The New Testament Today,* p. 100; July 15, 2002, review of *Encyclopedia of Contemporary Christian Music,* p. 71.

Religious Studies Review, April, 1993, W. Lee Humphreys, review of *The Bible and Modern Literary Criticism,* p. 141; April, 1997, Fred W. Burnett, review of *God With Us,* p. 182; October, 1998, Fred W. Burnett, review of *Fortress Introduction to the Gospels April,* p. 417; 2002, Amos Yong, review of *Chasing the Eastern Star: Adventures in Biblical Reader-response Criticism,* p. 169.

Theological Studies, March, 2000, Elliott C. Maloney, review of *Jesus as a Figure in History,* p. 151.

Theology Today, July, 1996, A.K.M. Adam, review of *God with Us: A Pastoral Theology of Matthew's Gospel,* p. 278; July, 2000, Leander E. Keck, review of *Jesus as a Figure in History,* pp. 232-228.

Wilson Quarterly, winter, 2003, Randall Balmer, review of *Encyclopedia of Contemporary Christian Music,* p. 121.

ONLINE

Christianity Today online, http://www.christianitytoday.com/ (May 19, 2003), Todd Hertz, interview with Powell.
Trinity Lutheran Seminary Web site, http://www.trinity.capital.edu/ (May 19, 2003).*

* * *

POWER, Nani

PERSONAL: Female; children: two. *Education:* Attended Bennington College, Corcoran Art School, L'Ecole des Beaux-Arts Americaines (France), and Georgetown University.

ADDRESSES: *Home*—Lives in The Plains, VA. *Agent*—c/o Wendy Sherman, Wendy Sherman Associates, Inc., 450 Seventh Ave., Suite 3004, New York, NY 10123-0073.

CAREER: Writer. Worked variously as a caterer, nanny, nursing home aide, sandwich seller, and chef.

AWARDS, HONORS: Art Seidenbaum Award for First Fiction, *Los Angeles Times,* 2002, for *Crawling at Night.*

WRITINGS:

Crawling at Night, Atlantic Monthly Press (New York, NY), 2001.
The Good Remains, Grove Press (New York, NY), 2002.

Contributor to Salon.com.

SIDELIGHTS: Nani Power was a fine-arts major who worked at a number of unrelated jobs before taking a writing course that inspired her to write her first novel, *Crawling at Night.* Power's previous experience as a chef in a Japanese restaurant served her well, as one of the main characters, Ito, is a Japanese chef working in a sushi restaurant in lower Manhattan. A *Kirkus Reviews* contributor wrote that Power "is at her best when describing the selection, preparation, and serving of Asian food, something she does with visceral gusto and authority."

Ito, who is in his sixties, fled Japan after losing his wife to cancer, leaving behind a thirteen-year-old son. His possessions consist mainly of a pornography collection, and sex is always in his thoughts. Mariane, in her late thirties, is an alcoholic waitress who left behind a baby daughter who would now be in her teens. She sneaks sake for her coffee and sleeps with many men, including Yoshi, the owner of the restaurant. Both Mariane and Ito are despairing and self-destructive, and because of Mariane's raw sexuality and the fact that she reminds Ito of the prostitute he frequented when his wife was dying, he is drawn to her. The story takes place over two days and nights, and Power employs flashbacks and writing that is experimental as well as straightforward and literary. Secondary characters include Ling Yu, an erotic dancer Ito meets in a Chinese club, and Ton, her slow-witted Vietnamese boyfriend.

Reviewing *Crawling at Night* for *Salon.com,* Mary Gaitskill wrote, "Power has a gift for quick characterizations that layer oppositional qualities with subtlety and intensity; her portrayal of the prematurely experienced young girl's seduction of Ton is lovely, gentle, and deliciously crude."

The title of the novel comes from the Japanese term *yobai,* which Power told Gaitskill refers to a "Japanese farmer's tradition of accommodating large groups of overnight visitors on futons across the floor." If a man wishes to sleep with one of the women, he hides his face and crawls to her futon. If he is rejected, he can return to his own bed without having his identity known.

In a *New York Times Book Review* article, Dwight Garner wrote that "the story of Ito's and Mariane's slow-building relationship is interlarded with flashbacks to their own pasts, and Power busies herself with singling out a few too many 'Rosebud' moments. There is also a cacophony of other voices; she pops us in and out of the heads of many other characters here: a pork seller, a nasty yuppie, Ito's lounge singer, a young retarded boy. These sections tend to be accomplished but showy and a little staticky." Garner felt that *Crawling at Night* "would have been more potent if [Power] hadn't tried to cram so much in." "We're pretty certain this adventure is doomed from the start," wrote Garner. "That we're right doesn't make Power's ending—or her novel—any less caustic, or any less true."

Gaitskill wrote that *Crawling at Night* "isn't flawless. . . . But the novel's strength far outweighs its weaknesses. That strength is primarily in its sensate intelligence, its intuitive understanding of the irrational, the subtle moment-to-moment shifts of experience that give each life depth." *Library Journal*'s Joshua Cohen said Power "focuses on the dark picture of urban life, poignantly exploring the failure of people to build meaningful relationships." A *Publishers Weekly* contributor wrote that Power's "starkly realistic characters and terse, lyrical prose herald her as an exciting new voice."

BIOGRAPHICAL AND CRITICAL SOURCES:

PERIODICALS

Booklist, August, 2002, Carolyn Kubisz, review of *The Good Remains,* p. 1924.

Kirkus Reviews, February 1, 2001, review of *Crawling at Night,* p. 137; July 1, 2002, review of *The Good Remains,* p. 912.

Library Journal, April 1, 2001, Joshua Cohen, review of *Crawling at Night,* p. 134.

New York Times Book Review, April 29, 2001, Dwight Garner, review of *Crawling at Night.*

Publishers Weekly, March 5, 2001, review of *Crawling at Night,* p. 60; July 15, 2002, review of *The Good Remains,* p. 53.

Washington Post Book World, April 17, 2001, Jabari Asim, review of *Crawling at Night,* p. C02.

ONLINE

Salon.com, http://www.salon.com/ (April 4, 2001), Mary Gaitskill, review of *Crawling at Night.**

* * *

PRINCE, F(rank) T(empleton) 1912-2003

OBITUARY NOTICE—See index for *CA* sketch: Born September 13, 1912, in Kimberley, Cape Province, South Africa; died August 7, 2003, in Southampton, England. Educator and author. Prince was a prominent poet best known for his much-anthologized piece "Soldiers Bathing." He was a graduate of Balliol College, Oxford, receiving his B.A. there in 1934; he published his first collection, *Poems,* in 1938. The war found him serving in the British Intelligence Corps as a cryptographer for six years, and after returning home he had some difficulty publishing his works. He joined the University of Southampton as a lecturer in 1946, becoming a reader in 1955 and full professor of English in 1957; he also served as dean of the arts faculty from 1962 to 1967. The 1950s saw the release of his *Soldiers Bathing and Other Poems* (1954) and *The Stolen Heart* (1957). Syntactically complex, Prince's verses were usually free verse in form and were notable for their lyrical, often leisurely quality. Leaving Southampton in 1974, Prince became an English professor at the University of the West Indies in Jamaica from 1975 to 1978. It was around the 1970s, too, that his poems began to gain a larger audience, yet many of his later collections were released by small presses. One of his most acclaimed books at this time was *Drypoints of the Hasidim* (1975). His later career included two years at Brandeis University as Fannie Hurst Professor, and stints as a visiting professor at Washington University, Sana'a University in North Yemen, and Hollins College during the early 1980s. He retired in 1984. The recipient of an E. M. Forster award in 1982, Prince was the author of over a dozen poetry books, including *Memoirs in Oxford* (1970), *Afterword on Rupert Brooke* (1976), *Walks in Rome* (1987), and *Collected Poems, 1935-1992* (1993). He also edited several works by Shakespeare and Milton, and his book of literary criticism, *The Italian Element in Milton's Verse* (1954) is considered by some to be one of the most important works of literary scholarship of the twentieth century.

OBITUARIES AND OTHER SOURCES:

BOOKS

Contemporary Poets, 7th edition, St. James Press (Detroit, MI), 2001.

PERIODICALS

Independent (London, England), August 8, 2003, p. 18.

Times (London, England), August 8, 2003.

PROKHOROV, Vadim

PERSONAL: Born in Oslo, Norway; U.S. citizen; father, a diplomat; mother, an engineer. *Education:* Attended Gnesin Music Institute, Moscow, Russia.

ADDRESSES: *Agent*—c/o Author Mail, Scarecrow Press, Inc., 4720 Boston Way, Suite A, Lanham, MD 20706.

CAREER: Mosconcert, soloist and chamber music performer, 1969-87; composer and author, 1987—. Moscow Academy, assistant conductor of Stanislavsky Opera, 1969-77.

MEMBER: Authors Guild, Authors League of America, American Society of Composers, Authors, and Publishers.

WRITINGS:

Russian Folk Songs: Musical Genres and History, Scarecrow Press (Lanham, MD), 2002.

Composer of choral works published by Oxford University Press and Hal Leonard. Contributor to *Encyclopedia Americana.* Contributor to periodicals, including *Parade, Smithsonian, Air and Space,* and *Andante.com.*

WORK IN PROGRESS: An anthology of Russian folk songs, for Musica Russica.

* * *

PRUNTY, Morag 1964-

PERSONAL: Born 1964, in Scotland; married; children: one.

ADDRESSES: *Home*—Dublin, Ireland. *Agent*—c/o Pan Macmillan, 20 New Wharf Rd., London N1 9RR, England.

CAREER: Writer and journalist. Editor for magazines *Looks, More,* and *Just Seventeen,* London, England, and *Irish Tatler,* Dublin, Ireland.

WRITINGS:

Boys: A User's Guide, illustrated by Alison Everitt, Piccadilly (London, England), 1993.

Dancing with Mules (novel), Pan (London, England), 2001, published as *Wild Cats and Colleens,* HarperCollins (New York, NY), 2001.

Disco Daddy, Pan (London, England), 2002.

Poison Arrows, Pan (London, England), 2003.

SIDELIGHTS: Morag Prunty, born in Scotland of Irish parents, has been a magazine editor since the age of nineteen. After working in England at *Looks* (where she was the magazine's youngest editor), *More,* and *Just Seventeen,* she relocated to Ireland, where she worked as editor of *Irish Tatler.* Her first book, *Boys: A User's Guide,* is aimed at helping teenage girls understand the opposite sex. Prunty writes about the fears that go along with the first date and first kiss and about crushes, rejection, and other emotional issues. *School Librarian* reviewer Alison Hurst said all of these "are dealt with in a lighthearted but helpful way" and praised the accompanying cartoons by Alison Everitt, which Hurst felt help when addressing "such a sensitive subject."

Prunty's debut novel, *Dancing with Mules,* was published in the United States as *Wild Cats and Colleens.* A *Publishers Weekly* contributor wrote that one function of the book is "to blow away those blarney cobwebs from the Irish image and to show that the country is as up-to-date, materialistic and obsessed with glamour and trivia as much of the rest of the Western world." Prunty offers three heroines who include Lorna, a publicist who plays too hard; Gloria, whose life began in the slums but who now does Lorna's hair in her very successful salon; and Sandy, a journalist yet to get her first big story. *New York Times Book Review* contributor Fionn Meade felt that the Dublin-based characters "seem to be culled" from the HBO award-winning comedy *Sex and the City,* set in New York. Meade wrote that the book "is more like a polished sitcom than a searching work of fiction."

Xavier Power is an American billionaire, proud of his Irish heritage, who is looking for an Irish wife. What he has in mind is a sweet, preferably redheaded colleen, not the three wild women he meets when he travels to Ireland on his quest. He hires Lorna to plan the party at which he will meet prospects, and Lorna enlists Gloria's help. Sandy is hoping that her coverage of the event will result in her big story. *Booklist*'s Danise Hoover wrote, "The madcap situations that follow result in storybook-happy matchmakings for all concerned." "None of them marries the billionaire," noted Monica Collins in the *Boston Herald.* "Yet all three women find their pots of gold at the end of the rainbow." A *Kirkus Reviews* writer called *Wild Cats and Colleens* "an exuberantly absurd and intermittently amusing farce about three women looking for love and money in pop-culture-saturated contemporary Ireland."

BIOGRAPHICAL AND CRITICAL SOURCES:

PERIODICALS

Booklist, October 15, 2001, Danise Hoover, review of *Wild Cats and Colleens,* p. 383.

Boston Herald, December 2, 2001, Monica Collins, review of *Wild Cats and Colleens,* p. 50.

Kirkus Reviews, September 1, 2001, review of *Wild Cats and Colleens,* p. 1240.

New York Times Book Review, December 23, 2001, Fionn Meade, review of *Wild Cats and Colleens,* p. 17.

Publishers Weekly, September 10, 2001, review of *Wild Cats and Colleens,* p. 56.

School Librarian, August, 1993, review of *Boys: A User's Guide,* p. 127.*

* * *

PUNTER, John (V.)

PERSONAL: Born December 15, 1945. *Education:* University of Newcastle upon Tyne, graduated, 1967; University of Toronto, M.A., Ph.D., 1967-74. *Hobbies and other interests:* Travel, photography, mountain walking.

ADDRESSES: Office—Department of City and Regional Planning, University of Wales, Cardiff, P.O. Box 906, Cardiff, CF1 3YN, Wales, United Kingdom; fax: 01222 875845. *E-mail*—PunterJ@cardiff.ac.uk.

CAREER: Educator and author. York University, Toronto, Ontario, Canada, professor of urban studies, 1972-75; University of Reading, Reading, England, professor of land management and development, 1975-93; Strathclyde University, Glasgow, Scotland, professor of environmental planning, 1993-96, also head of the department of environmental planning; Cardiff University, Cardiff, Wales, professor of urban design, 1996—. Consultant for various groups, including the Organization for Economic Cooperation and Development (OECD), Paris, France; Reading Borough Council, Reading, England; Comedia; Urban Cultures; Hillier Parker; David Lock Associates; and the Welsh Development Agency, Cardiff, Wales. Research Assessment Exercise Panel for Town and Country Planning, panel member, 1996, panel chair, 2001.

MEMBER: Royal Town Planning Institute (expert member of urban design panel), Urban Design Group and Academy, Academy of Learned Societies for the Social Sciences (founding member), Cardiff Initiative (board member), Royal Society of Architects in Wales (honorary fellow).

AWARDS, HONORS: British Planning Education Award, 1992.

WRITINGS:

(With Matthew Carmona) *The Design Dimension of Planning: Theory, Content, and Best Practice for Design Policies,* E & FN Spon (New York, NY), 1997.

Design Guidelines in American Cities: A Review of Design Policies and Guidance in Five West Coast Cities, Liverpool University Press (Liverpool, England), 1999.

The Vancouver Achievement 1970-2000: Discretionary Zoning, Planning, and Urban Design, University of British Columbia Press (Vancouver, British Columbia), 2002.

Contributor to the book *British Planning: Fifty Years of Urban and Regional Policy,* edited by B. Cullingworth, Athlone, 1999. Contributor of articles to scholarly journals, including *Urban Studies, Urban Design International, Built Environment, Town Planning Review, Journal of Urban Design,* and *Journal of*

Environmental Planning and Management. Member of editorial boards of *Town Planning Review, Journal of Urban Design,* and *Urban Design International.*

SIDELIGHTS: John Punter is a scholar of urban planning and development who has influenced modern design, planning, and management. His books, including *Design Guidelines in American Cities: A Review of Design Policies and Guidance in Five West Coast Cities* and *The Vancouver Achievement 1970-2000: Discretionary Zoning, Planning, and Urban Design,* examine urban planning practices in various cities in an attempt to illustrate examples of the most effective way to design modern cities.

In *Design Guidelines in American Cities,* Punter looks at the urban planning process of Seattle, Washington; Portland, Oregon; San Francisco, California; Irvine, California; and San Diego, California. Every chapter reviews a particular city's development and design, including "substantial extracts" of original planning documents, Elizabeth MacDonald noted in *Journal of the American Planning Association.* "This gives a clear and direct sense of the issues each city is addressing and the design policy response," MacDonald continued.

The Vancouver Achievement 1970-2000 is a case study of the urban planning of the Canadian city of Vancouver, in British Columbia. Punter traces the development of the city and attempts to explain why Vancouver is often referred to as an example of success in urban design.

BIOGRAPHICAL AND CRITICAL SOURCES:

PERIODICALS

Journal of the American Planning Association, winter, 2000, Elizabeth MacDonald, review of *Design Guidelines in American Cities: A Review of Design Policies and Guidance in Five West Coast Cities,* p. 94.

Town and Country Planning, July, 1998, John Dalafons, review of *The Design Dimension of Planning: Theory, Content, and Best Practice for Design Policies,* pp. 234-235.

ONLINE

Cardiff University Web site, http://www.cf.ac.uk/ (November 26, 2001), "John Punter."

Resource for Urban Design Information Web site, http://rudi.herts.ac.uk/ (February 7, 2000), "John Punter."

University of British Columbia Press Web site, http://www.ubcpress.ca/ (October 27, 2003).

OTHER

Liverpool University Press Catalog, autumn, 1999, information about *Design Guidelines in American Cities.**

* * *

PUPIN, Michael (Idvorsky) 1858-1935

PERSONAL: Born October 4, 1858, in Idvor, Hungary (now Yugoslavia); naturalized U.S. citizen, 1993; died of kidney failure March 12, 1935, in New York, NY; married Sarah Katherine Jackson, 1888 (died 1897). *Education:* Columbia University, B.A., 1883; attended Cambridge University; University of Berlin, Ph.D., 1889. *Religion:* Serbian Orthodox.

CAREER: Physicist, educator, and author. Columbia University, New York, NY, instructor, 1890-92, adjunct professor of mechanics, 1892-1901, professor of electro-mechanics, 1901-31, then emeritus. Member of National Research Council and National Advisory Committee for Aeronautics. Scientific advisor to Yugoslavian delegation at Paris Peace Conference, 1919.

MEMBER: National Academy of Sciences, American Physical Society, American Mathematical Society, Engineering Foundation (former chair), American Association for the Advancement of Science (president, 1925-26), New York Academy of Sciences, American Philosophical Society, University Club (president, 1930-31), Sigma Xi.

AWARDS, HONORS: Elliot Cresson Medal, Franklin Institute, 1902; Herbert Prize, French Academy, 1916; Order of the White Eagle (Serbia); Order of the White Lion (Czechoslovakia); Edison Medal, American Institute of Electrical Engineers, 1920; Medal of Honor, Radio Institute of America; Gold Medal,

American Institute of Social Sciences; Gold Medal of Honor, Institute of Radio Engineers; Pulitzer Prize for autobiography, 1923, for *From Immigrant to Inventor;* Washington Medal for Engineering, Western Society of Engineers, 1928; named Councilor of National Industrial Conference Board, 1929; John Fritz Gold Medal, 1932. Honorary degrees include Doctor of Laws from New York University, University of California; D.H.L. from George Washington University; Doctor of Science from Princeton University, Columbia University, and Union College; L.L.P. from Johns Hopkins University and University of Rochester; and degrees from Muhlenberg College, Marietta College, Rutgers University, Delaware University, Kenyon College, Brown University, University of Rochester, Middlebury College, University of Belgrade, and University of Prague.

WRITINGS:

Max Osterberg, editor, *Thermodynamics of Reversible Cycles in Gases and Saturated Vapors: Full Synopsis of a Ten Weeks' Undergraduate Course of Lectures,* J. Wiley and Sons (New York, NY), 1894.

From Immigrant to Inventor, Scribner (New York, NY), 1923, reprinted, with foreword by Freeman J. Dyson, 1960.

The New Reformation: From Physical to Spiritual Realities, Scribner (New York, NY), 1927.

Romance of the Machine, Scribner (New York, NY), 1930.

Contributor to scientific journals and publications.

SIDELIGHTS: Physicist Michael Pupin remains highly regarded for his work in developing the circuitry that enabled the development of long-distance telephone service. His autobiography, *From Immigrant to Inventor,* which reflects the American dream in its profile of a self-made man and brilliant scientist and inventor in the early twentieth century, won the Pulitzer Prize for biography in 1923.

Pupin was born in 1858, in Idvor, a small Serbian village near Belgrade. Although illiterate, his parents were loving and deeply religious, and encouraged his education. After the sudden death of his father in 1874, sixteen-year-old Pupin immigrated to the United States and found employment in New York City. In addition to working at a series of jobs, he enrolled at Cooper Union, taking evening classes. Awarded a scholarship to Columbia University, he graduated from that school with honors in 1883. Pupin spent two years studying mathematics at Cambridge University before returning to Columbia as John Tyndall fellow in 1885. At the University of Berlin he studied and conducted research in experimental physics under Hermann Von Helmholtz, earning his Ph.D. in 1889.

Pupin returned to New York in 1889 to teach mathematical physics at Columbia, and remained there for the rest of his life, rising through the ranks to instructor become professor of electro-mechanics in 1901. In 1892 he began to experiment with electromagnetic phenomena, which experiments resulted in advances in radio technology when patents for Pupin's inventions were sold to the Marconi Company. His work in X-rays resulted in a way to greatly increase the speed of X-ray photography, as well as the first therapeutic application of X-rays to a woman with breast cancer. His discovery that atoms struck by X-rays emit secondary X-ray radiation made a lasting contribution to electron physics.

As a result of his work, Pupin applied for and received twenty-four patents, many of them in the area of communications transmission. The first to treat electrical transmission over artificial lines mathematically, Pupin developed a theory that served as the foundation for the development of the electrical filters used in all telephonic, telegraphic, and radio transmission. He also devised a way of extending the range of long-distance telephone communication through the use of wire loading coils; the patent for this system was purchased by American Telegraph and Telephone and remains in use today. Pupin also invented the tuned oscillating circuit that allows more than one message to be transmitted along a wire at the same time; Bell Telephone Company became the owner of this technology in 1901.

During World War I Pupin served on the National Research Council and worked to develop telephone communication between aircraft as well as to enhance electronic communications with submarines. Most important contributions was his discovery, under the direction of President Woodrow Wilson, of sonar, which allowed U.S. forces to detect the location of enemy submarines. Following the war, Pupin served as scientific advisor to the Yugoslavian delegation at the 1919 Paris Peace Conference. He also was elected to the National Academy of Sciences, contributed much of the funding for the American Mathematical Society, and was a founder of the American Physical Society and the National Research Council.

In his autobiography *From Immigrant to Inventor* Pupin not only recounts the events of his life, but also expresses his belief in science as a means to cure many of the world's ills. He writes: "I firmly believe that in the National Research Council we have an organization which represents the mobilized scientific intellect of the United States, and which in the pursuit of its lofty ideals will someday succeed in creating in our democracy a profound respect for the services of the highly trained intellect." Henry B. Fuller wrote in the *New York Times Book Review* that "Richness of temperament, and activity of imagination are evident throughout" Pupin's autobiography, the critic noting in particular Pupin's declaration "that scientific research will bring us closer to divinity than any theology invented by man."

Pupin retired from his teaching position at Columbia University in 1931, although he continued his scientific work with the help of an assistant. In recognition of Pupin's lengthy service, the university renamed the building housing his former laboratory the Pupin Physics Laboratory. Twenty-eight American scientists from this laboratory have gone on to receive the Nobel Prize, and the Pupin Laboratory is also noteworthy as the site of the preliminary scientific investigations for the first atomic bomb.

During his lifetime Pupin received numerous other honors in gratitude for his service to science, including five medals and eighteen honorary degrees. His influence in the field of science and technology extended well past his death in 1935: In 1958 the Pupin Medal was created by the Columbia Engineering School Alumni Association, and in 1979 Pupin was honored on a postage stamp issued in his native Yugoslavia.

BIOGRAPHICAL AND CRITICAL SOURCES:

BOOKS

Dictionary of American Biography, Supplement 1, Scribner (New York, NY), 1944.

Encyclopedia of World Biography, second edition, Gale (Detroit, MI), 1998.

Parkman, Mary R., *High Adventurers,* Century Co. (New York, NY), 1931.

Preston, Wheeler, *American Biographies,* Harper (New York, NY), 1940.

Pupin, Michael, *From Immigrant to Inventor,* Scribner (New York, NY), 1923.

PERIODICALS

New York Times Book Review, October 14, 1923, Henry B. Fuller, review of *From Immigrant to Inventor,* p. 2; October 21, 1923, pp. 3, 5; December 2, 1923, p. 4.*

ONLINE

Tesla Memorial Society of New York Web site, http://www.teslasociety.com/ (July 4, 2003), "Michael Idvorsky Pupin."

OBITUARIES:

PERIODICALS

New York Times, March 13, 1935, p. 19.*

Q-R

QI, Shouhua 1957-

PERSONAL: Born February 10, 1957, in Nanjing, China; son of Yingyao (a teacher) and Huilan (a farmer; maiden name, Ye) Qi; married Xiaohong Wang (a medical technologist), April 28, 1982; children: Frank Y. *Ethnicity:* "Chinese." *Education:* Nanjing Teachers' University, B.A., 1981, M.A., 1985; Illinois State University, Ph.D., 1993.

ADDRESSES: Home—6106 Ironwood Dr., Harrisburg, PA 17112. *Office*—Department of English, Harrisburg Area Community College, 1 HACC Dr., Harrisburg, PA 17110. *E-mail*—s9qi@hacc.edu.

CAREER: Educator and author. Harrisburg Area Community College, Harrisburg, PA, assistant professor of English, 1993—. Pennsylvania State University, Harrisburg, adjunct professor of humanities, 1997—. Central Pennsylvania Little Star Chinese Language School, cofounder and coordinator, 1998—.

MEMBER: Modern Language Association of America, National Council of Teachers of English, Central Pennsylvania Chinese Association (member of executive board; director of public relations, 1998-99).

WRITINGS:

Transcending the Pacific (essays; in Chinese; also see below), Henan People's Publishing House (China), 1999.

Bridging the Pacific: Searching for Cross-Cultural Understanding between the United States and China (essays and short stories; includes translation of *Transcending the Pacific*), China Books and Periodicals (San Francisco, CA), 2000.

The New Century Guide in Practical English Communication, Shanghai Foreign Language Education Press (Shanghai, China), 2000.

Western Writing Theories, Pedagogies, and Practices, Shanghai Foreign Language Education Press (Shanghai, China), 2000.

Success in Advanced English Writing: A Comprehensive Guide, Shanghai Foreign Language Education Press (Shanghai, China), 2000.

Contributor to periodicals.

TRANSLATOR INTO CHINESE

Thomas Hardy, *A Pair of Blue Eyes* (novel), Yiling/ Translators' Press (China), 1994.

Thomas Hardy, *The Well Beloved* (novel), Yiling/ Translators' Press (China), 1998.

WORK IN PROGRESS: Research on cross-cultural issues and on rhetoric and composition in American, English, and Chinese literature.

SIDELIGHTS: Shouhua Qi told *CA:* "It was early 1996. The skies over the Taiwan Strait were clouded with smoke from a recent, live missile exercise. Huge, stoic shadows of aircraft carriers loomed just miles away from the southern mouth of the strait that had been sealed off for war games. The specter of another major, bloody showdown hung in the air.

"As a Chinese scholar living and teaching in the United States, I felt called upon to help build a bridge of understanding across the muddy waters of the Pacific so that there would be peace, not only 'in our time,' but also in the twenty-first century, between two of the most important countries in the world. This self-assigned (and exaggerated, perhaps) mission resulted in many essays and op-ed pieces on U.S.-China relations and on cross-cultural (mis)understanding, published in various newspapers and magazines. Later, I translated and rewrote them into Chinese, put them in a collection titled *Transcending the Pacific,* and had the work published in China. The English edition, which includes other personal essays and short stories, is titled *Bridging the Pacific: Searching for Cross-Cultural Understanding between the United States and China.*

"Is an ocean as wide as the Pacific bridgeable? Can we find a happy mean between old and new, East and West, friend and foe? The quest (quixotic?) for understanding and for a peaceful relationship between two of the most important nations in the world today is what drives me to think and write in both English and Chinese. The efforts by many to build a bridge of understanding across the Pacific have encountered many setbacks, sometimes of Sisyphean proportions, but there is no reason to give up.

"The other book-length projects I have undertaken, whether translating classic English novels or introducing Western writing theories and pedagogies into the classrooms in China, are all part of this bridging project. I am a teacher, scholar, and writer, and I am also a self-appointed 'cultural ambassador' of some sort between China and the United States. Being bilingual and bicultural, I'm in a unique position to play this multi-faceted role."

* * *

RANDALL, Charlotte

PERSONAL: Born in Dunedin, New Zealand; married. *Education:* Attended University of Canterbury, New Zealand.

ADDRESSES: Home—Wellington, New Zealand. *Agent*—c/o Penguin Books, Penguin Putnam, 375 Hudson St., New York, NY 10014.

CAREER: Writer.

AWARDS, HONORS: Reed Fiction Award and Best First Book Award, Commonwealth Writers Prize, 1996, for *Dead Sea Fruit;* Victoria University of Wellington writing fellow, 2000.

WRITINGS:

Dead Sea Fruit, Secker & Warburg (London, England), 1995.

The Curative, Penguin Books (New York, NY), 2000.

Within the Kiss, Penguin Books (New York, NY), 2002.

WORK IN PROGRESS: Painting the World on the Wall, a novel.

SIDELIGHTS: Novelist Charlotte Randall won the Commonwealth Writers Prize's Reed Fiction Award and Best First Book award for *Dead Sea Fruit,* a novel about two families in Dunedin, New Zealand in the 1960s and 1970s. As Donald Matheson observed in the Wellington *Evening Post,* the book deals with the familiar theme of growing up in a stifling and conformist era, but does so with exceptional depth and skill. The novel has "huge emotional energy," Matheson wrote, and transcends the confines of its "heritage in New Zealand writing."

Randall followed this successful debut with *The Curative,* a novel set in Bedlam, London's notorious hospital for the insane. It is the Napoleonic era, and William Lonsdale, a middle-aged and once-successful theater critic, has been incarcerated in the madhouse, a victim, he insists, of an unfair plot against him. Chained to the wall, he tells his story to his cellmate and to a woman inmate with whom he rehearses a therapeutic play.

Critics found *The Curative* an ambitious and interesting, if not wholly successful, novel. In a review for *Landfall,* Patrick Evans raised questions about Randall's decision to limit her character's freedom of movement. Because the narrator cannot move, Evans wrote, the novel "highlights language" and ultimately subverts the conventions of fiction: "that novels have protagonists, that those protagonists have lives, wives, husbands, children, and environments, that these characters do things in the quotidian, and that in the good old days fiction used to be about something as well, something that was somehow larger than the sum of those events." In the end, Evans found *The Curative* an overly intellectual novel, lacking the emotional appeal and the authentic regional grounding of *Dead Sea Fruit.* Penelope Davie noted in the Brisbane *Courier-Mail* that Lonsdale is a "very unlikable" character whose story about the events that landed him in Bedlam is "convoluted and unpleasant." Even so, Davie added that this very unpleasantness is part of Randall's message: "being bad, or clever, or different, or even stark raving mad is no reason for the arbitrary evil of this sort of incarceration." The book, she went on to say, "has moments of genuine horror, and a clever, creative, and often humorous plot." *The Curative* was nominated for the 2001 Montana New Zealand Book Award.

In *Within the Kiss* Randall reimagines the Faust myth. Her Faust character is a New Zealand tennis-mom who aspires to literary fame but who has questionable talent. She agrees to sell her daughter's soul to the girl's seedy tennis coach, who promises to make the girl into a tennis star and the mother into a best-selling author. The process of writing itself, which Randall treats with humor, becomes a central theme. "I wanted it to be . . . humorous and whimsical," Randall explained in an online interview for *Book-Club.* "But always with this grain of truth about the true horrors of writing and the true horrors of competitive sport." Randall also pointed out that her Faust is not really a serious writer, but a "desperate scribbler. The person to whom writing itself means very little and publishing success means a lot. And they are always looking for the story, the one that's going to be the bestseller, and makes them whatever they think a writer is—rich, famous, and unemployed. I'm not that kind of writer. I'm going to write what I'm interested in and if no one else likes it, well I guess that means it's too bad."

Reviewing the novel for the *New Zealand Herald,* contributor Jenny Jones commented that "Reading Charlotte Randall is like being caught up in a lolly scramble. There's so much largesse bombarding you from her intellectual helicopter you haven't time to unwrap each individual sugarplum. It doesn't matter, you grab what you can. . . . You are immersed in a world of delight made exquisite by intellectual refraction." Randall, Jones concluded, is "an original and I'm glad she can't keep it simple."

BIOGRAPHICAL AND CRITICAL SOURCES:

PERIODICALS

Courier-Mail (Brisbane, Australia), December 8, 2001, Penelope Davie, review of *The Curative,* p. M05.

Evening Post (Wellington, New Zealand), March 3, 1995, Donald Matheson, review of *Dead Sea Fruit.*

Landfall, November, 2001, Patrick Evans, review of *The Curative,* pp. 173-177.

New Zealand Herald, September 6, 2002, Jenny Jones, review of *Within the Kiss.*

ONLINE

Book-Club, http://www.book-club.co.nz/ (September 9, 2002), interview with Randall.*

* * *

RANDOLPH, Georgiana Ann 1908-1957 (Craig Rice, Michael Venning)

PERSONAL: Born June 5, 1908, in Chicago, IL; died of an overdose of barbiturates and alcohol in Los Angeles, CA, 1957; daughter of Harry Moschiem (itinerant artist) and Mary (Randolph) Craig; married Arthur John Follows, Arthur Ferguson, H. W. DeMott Jr., and Lawrence Lipton; children: (fourth marriage) Nancy, Iris, David. *Hobbies and other interests:* Marksmanship, cooking, gardening.

CAREER: Worked variously as a crime reporter, radio and motion picture script writer, publicity manager, and freelance writer.

WRITINGS:

"MELVILLE FAIRR" SERIES, AS MICHAEL VENNING

Murder through the Looking Glass, Coward-McCann Inc. (New York, NY), 1943.

Jethro Hammer, Coward-McCann Inc. (New York, NY), 1944.

"JOHN J. MALONE" SERIES, AS CRAIG RICE

Eight Faces at Three, Simon and Schuster (New York, NY), 1939.
The Corpse Steps Out, Simon and Schuster (New York, NY), 1940.
The Wrong Murder, Simon and Schuster (New York, NY), 1940.
The Right Murder, Simon and Schuster (New York, NY), 1941.
Trial by Fury, Simon and Schuster (New York, NY), 1941.
Big Midget Murders, Simon and Schuster (New York, NY), 1942.
Having a Wonderful Crime, Simon and Schuster (New York, NY), 1943.
Lucky Stiff, Simon and Schuster (New York, NY) 1945.
The Fourth Postman, Simon and Schuster (New York, NY), 1948.
Knocked for a Loop, Simon and Schuster (New York, NY), 1957.
My Kingdom for a Hearse, Simon and Schuster (New York, NY), 1957.
The Name Is Malone, (short stories), Pyramid Book (New York, NY), 1958.
(With Stuart Palmer) *People vs. Withers and Malone: Six Inner Sanctum Mystery Novelettes,* Simon and Schuster (New York, NY), 1963.

"BINGO RIGGS AND HANDSOME KUSAK" SERIES, AS CRAIG RICE

Sunday Pigeon Murders, Simon and Schuster (New York, NY), 1942.
Thursday Turkey Murders, Simon and Schuster (New York, NY), 1943.
(Completed by Ed McBain) *April Robin Murders,* Random House (New York, NY), 1958.

OTHER

Telefair, the House on the Island, Bobbs-Merril (New York, NY), 1942.
To Catch a Thief, Dial Press (New York, NY), 1943.
Home Sweet Homicide, Simon and Schuster (New York, NY), 1944.
Innocent Bystander, Simon and Schuster (New York, NY), 1949.
Forty-five Murders: A Collection of True-Crime Stories (nonfiction), Simon and Schuster (New York, NY), 1952.

Also author of several short stories, many of which first appeared in the *Ellery Queen's Mystery Magazine.* Also wrote radio and television scripts, such as *The Amazing Mr. Malone.*

AS GHOST WRITER

(With Gypsy Rose Lee) *The G-String Murders,* Pocket Books (New York, NY), 1941.
(With Gypsy Rose Lee) *Mother Finds a Body,* Simon and Schuster (New York, NY), 1942.
(With George Sanders and Cleve Cartmill) *Crime on My Hands,* Simon and Schuster (New York, NY), 1944.

ADAPTATIONS: The following stories were made into films: *Lady of Burlesque* United Artists, 1943; *Having a Wonderful Crime,* RKO, 1945; *Home Sweet Homicide,* Twentieth Century-Fox, 1946; *Tenth Avenue Angel,* Metro-Goldwyn-Mayer, 1948; *The Lucky Stiff,* United Artists, 1994; *Mrs. O'Malley and Mr. Malone,* MGM, 1950; and *Underworld Story,* United Artists, 1950.

SIDELIGHTS: Georgiana Ann Randolph, who wrote most of her work under the pseudonym Craig Rice, turned mystery writing somewhat on its head when she created protagonists who solved crimes by finding courage in a bottle of alcohol. Drinking apparently played a significant part in Randolph's own life and, indeed, contributed to her death, which was caused by an overdose of barbiturates and alcohol. Yet her fiction is noted for what biographer Jeffrey A. Marks described as "screwball" humor rather than the hard-bitten realism so prevalent in the mystery genre of that era. As a contributor to the Web site *Thrilling Detective* noted, "Almost everything that happens in one of her witty, whacky novels is completely off the wall. To Rice, reality was truly just a concept; a weird and wonderful playground where her imagination could romp around unfettered."

Randolph grew up in Chicago and at one time was a crime reporter, a job that acquainted her with the subject of murder. Her first detective novel, *Eight Faces at Three,* took her almost two years to write, but when it was published it was such a crowd pleaser that she used the same protagonist, John J. Malone, in several succeeding books. Malone turned out to be one of her most memorable characters. An attorney-turned-sleuth, he was more often found at his favorite haunt, Joe the Angel's City Hall Bar, than in the courtroom. Malone made his debut in Randolph's novels, but he could also be found in some of her short stories, and finally, he became a movie star in *Mrs. O'Malley and Mr. Malone.* Mrs. O'Malley was based on a character created by fellow mystery writer Stuart Palmer, who often collaborated with Randolph. Malone also made appearances on radio and television.

Randolph once claimed that she never knew where her stories came from, insinuating that she sat down at the typewriter with a blank sheet of paper, having no clue as to what would develop next. She wrote from her intuition rather than from notes and outlines. Whatever method she used, she was one of the most popular authors of mystery novels of her time. She wrote novels, short stories, and radio and television scripts, as well as screenplays. She also wrote three books as a ghostwriter: two for the showgirl Gypsy Rose Lee and one for actor George Saunders. Some critics have suggested that Randolph employed ghostwriters to complete her own works, especially later in her career.

Though Randolph's readers loved her, some critics did not. *New York Times* reviewer Isaac Anderson suggested that one of her first books, *The Wrong Murder,* was so saturated with alcohol that it should be reported to the Internal Revenue Bureau. A year later, Anderson lightened his tone a little, referring to Randolph's *The Right Murder* as being funny, "if you like that sort of fun." When *Trial by Fury* was published, Anderson praised the book, but only conditionally. He warned that there is a lot of bad language present in Randolph's latest mystery. When Randolph published *Murder through the Looking Glass* under the pseudonym Michael Venning, she might have thrown Anderson off guard, because he ended his review of the book with the statement: "Keep your eye on Michael Venning. He has something on the ball." By the late 1940s Anderson appeared to be totally convinced of Randolph's merits, though, writing in a 1948 review: "Why can't all murders be as funny as those concocted by Craig Rice!" Will Cuppy, writing for *Books,* expressed more unqualified praise for Randolph's novels. He stated that her *Big Midget Murders* has plenty of "macabre fun," and described *Sunday Pigeon Murders* as a "killer-diller."

After Randolph's untimely death, several writers attempted to honor her legacy. In 1960 Laurence Mark Janifer wrote a story incorporating some of Randolph's main characters in *The Pickled Poodles: A Novel Based on the Characters Created by Craig Rice.* Stuart Palmer, who reportedly collaborated with Randolph on stories or used her ideas in his own works, put together a posthumous collection of her short stories, *People vs. Withers and Malone.* A novel Randolph left partially completed, *The April Robin Murders,* was finished by author Ed McBain and published in 1958.

In more recent years Randolph's writing has enjoying renewed attention. New editions of her work have been published, as well as Marks's comprehensive study *Who Was That Lady?: Craig Rice: The Queen of the Screwball Mystery.* Marks provides details of Randolph's life, including the fact that she was abandoned by her parents, had four unhappy marriages, and then pretty much ignored her own children. Her fans often compare her to Ellery Queen to Jonathan Latimer. Though they admit that she was no literary heavy-weight, they note that Randolph knew how to make readers laugh.

BIOGRAPHICAL AND CRITICAL SOURCES:

BOOKS

Bakerman, Jane S., *And Then There Were Nine—More Women of Mystery,* Bowling Green State University Popular Press (Bowling Green, OH), 1985.

Magill, Frank N., editor, *Critical Survey of Mystery and Detective Fiction,* Salem Press (Englewood Cliffs, NJ), 1988.

Marks, Jeffrey A., *Who Was That Lady?: Craig Rice: The Queen of the Screwball Mystery,* Delphi Books (Lee's Summit, MO), 2001.

PERIODICALS

Booklist, May 1, 1957, review of *My Kingdom for a Hearse,* p. 455.

Books, June 14, 1942, Will Cuppy, review of *Big Midget Murders,* p. 18; November 15, 1952, Will Cuppy, review of *Sunday Pigeon Murders,* p. 46.
Chicago Sun, April 22, 1949, review of *Innocent Bystander,*
Kirkus Reviews, October 1, 1952, review of *Forty-five Murderers,* p. 676.
New Yorker, February 12, 1944, review of *Home Sweet Homicide,* p. 88.
New York Herald Tribune, September 22, 1957, James Sandoe, review of *Knocked for a Loop,* p. 13.
New York Times, November 10, 1940, Isaac Anderson, review of *The Wrong Murder,* p. 18; March 23, 1941, Isaac Anderson, review of *The Right Murder,* p. 24; November 30, 1941, Isaac Anderson, review of *Trial by Fury,* p. 32; February 7, 1943, Isaac Anderson, review of *Murder through the Looking Glass,* p. 19; October 24, 1948, Isaac Anderson, review of *The Fourth Postman,* p. 37.
Time, January 28, 1946, "Mulled Murder, with Spice," pp. 84, 86, 88, 90.

ONLINE

ThrillingDetective.com, http://www.thrillingdetective.com/ (April 21, 2003), "Authors and Creators: Craig Rice*."

* * *

RANSOM, Ray A. 1957-

PERSONAL: Born December 29, 1957, in West Palm Beach, FL; son of Johnny Lee and Willie Mae Ransom; married Stephanie Cara, August 7, 1976 (divorced August, 1982); children: Renee, Ray II, Rosalind, Rhonda, Ashley. *Ethnicity:* "African-Native American." *Education:* Western Illinois University, B.A., 1995; California Coast University, Santa Ana, M.B.A., 1996, Ph.D (business administration), 1998; studies toward Ed.D.; California Coast University, Dominguez Hills, graduate study. *Religion:* Christian. *Hobbies and other interests:* Writing, higher education, motivational speaking.

ADDRESSES: Home—159 Saratoga Blvd. E., Royal Palm Beach, FL 33411. *Office*—Palm West Publishing, P.O. Box 18176, West Palm Beach, FL 33416.

CAREER: Entrepreneur and author. Ransom Realty, Inc., Riviera Beach, FL, broker and officer manager, 1979-86; Ray A. Ransom, Mortgage Broker, Riviera Beach, 1981-85; Rokee Dian Corp. (real estate investment company), West Palm Beach, FL, president, 1983-86; Raw Records (record company), West Palm Beach, president, 1986-88. Business consultant to Palm West Publishing; freelance distance education consultant; freelance writer. Civil Air Patrol, West Palm Beach, sergeant, 1984-85.

MEMBER: Western Illinois University Alumni Association, Alumni Association of California Coast University, Palm Beach County Minority Contractors Association (secretary, 1979-80).

WRITINGS:

College Degrees through Home Study: 137 Accredited Schools That Offer High School Diploma, Associates', Bachelor's, Master's, and Doctorate Degrees through Home Study, Palm West Publishing (West Palm Beach, FL), 2000.
Real Estate in the New Millennium, Palm West Publishing (West Palm Beach, FL), 2000.

WORK IN PROGRESS: Research for second edition of *College Degrees through Home Study.*

* * *

RAWET, Samuel 1929-1985

PERSONAL: Born 1929, near Warsaw, Poland; immigrated as a child to Brazil; died 1985, in Brazil. *Religion:* Jewish.

CAREER: Engineer and writer.

WRITINGS:

Contos do imigrante (title means "Tales of the Immigrant"), Livraria J. Olympio Editora (Rio de Janeiro, Brazil), 1956, Ediouro (Brooklyn, NY), 1998.

Diálogo: contos, Edições GRD (Rio de Janeiro, Brazil), 1963.

Abama: novela, Edições GRD (Rio de Janeiro, Brazil), 1964.

O Sete sonhos, Orfeu (Rio de Janeiro, Brazil), 1967.

Consciência e valor, Orfeu (Rio De Janeiro, Brazil), 1969.

O Terreno de uma Pplegada, quadrada: contos, Orfeu (Rio de Janeiro, Brazil), 1969.

Homossexualismo: sexualidade e valor, Olivé Editor (Rio de Janeiro, Brazil), 1970.

Alienação e realidade, Olivé Editor (Benfica, Brazil), 1970.

Viagens de Ahasverus à terra Alheia em busca de um passado que não existe porque é futuro e de um futuro que já passou porque sonhado: novela, Olivé Editor (Rio de Janeiro, Brazil), 1970.

Eu-tu-êle: análise eidética, Livraria J. Olympio Editora (Rio de Janeiro, Brazil), 1971.

Angústia e conhecimento, Vertente Editora (São Paulo, Brazil), 1978.

Que os mortos enterrem seus mortos: contos, Vertente Editora (São Paulo, Brazil), 1981.

Dez contos escolhidos, Horizonte Editora em convénio como Instituto Nacional do Livro (Brasilia, Brazil), 1982.

The Prophet, and Other Stories, translated and with an introduction by Nelson H. Vieira, University of New Mexico Press (Albuquerque, NM), 1998.

SIDELIGHTS: Hailed as a pioneer of modern Brazilian-Jewish literature, Samuel Rawet wrote short stories and novellas that explored themes of alienation and displacement. Born near Warsaw, Poland, Rawet made the Roman Catholic country of Brazil his adopted home, yet his writing reveals a strong sense of otherness within this larger society. As his English translator Nelson H. Vieira noted in an essay posted on the *Brown University Web site,* Rawet "questions the behavior shown toward some 'ethnic others,' who do not reflect Brazil's predominantly Christian culture and its traditional mores. In other words, on the deep structural level, Rawet's stories address the difficulties of reconciling Jewish beliefs and culture with Brazilian nationalist and cultural norms."

Rawet moved to Brazil at age seven. Trained as an engineer, he lived in Rio de Janeiro until 1957, when he moved to the new national capital, Brasilia, to help design and build its infrastructure. His life was isolated; the writer lived alone and rarely traveled. His first collection of stories, *Contos do imigrante,* is considered a landmark. Rawet's stories not only introduce themes of Jewish experience in Brazil, but also use those themes to challenge the common idea of Brazil, or even all of Latin America, as a single cultural entity.

The Prophet, and Other Stories, the first book to present English translations of Rawet's work, includes twelve stories published between 1956 and 1969. Critic Naomi Lindstrom in *World Literature Today* found the stories to contain "highly imaginative and occasionally playful elements," surprising given the context of Rawet's social isolation. Lindstrom pointed out that dream imagery and a "wild profusion of intermingled narrative fragments" in "The Seven Dreams" and mystical and fantastic elements in "Johnny Golem" contrast sharply with the more realistic works in the volume.

BIOGRAPHICAL AND CRITICAL SOURCES:

PERIODICALS

World Literature Today, spring, 1999, Naomi Lindstrom, review of *The Prophet, and Other Stories,* p. 318.

ONLINE

Brown University Web site, http://www.brown.edu/ (May 30, 2003), Nelson H. Vieira, "Ethnicity and Cultural Identity in Latin-American Literature."*

* * *

RHODES, John J(acob II) 1916-2003

OBITUARY NOTICE—See index for *CA* sketch: Born September 18, 1916, in Council Grove, KS; died of cancer August 24, 2003, in Mesa, AZ. Politician, attorney, and author. Rhodes, an Arizona Republican, served for several years as the minority leader of the U.S. House of Representatives and was one of the officials who convinced President Richard Nixon that he would have to resign office to avoid impeachment. He was educated at Kansas State University, where he received his B.S. in 1938 before earning his law degree from Harvard University in 1941. During World War II he was an officer stationed in Arizona, after which he was a partner in the law firm of Rhodes, Killian & Legg in Mesa, where he also was vice president of Farm and Home Life Insurance. Becoming active in politics, he ran for office in 1952 and became the first Republican candidate from Arizona to win a place in the House of Representatives. Rhodes successfully remained in office for the next fifteen terms. While in office, he served as minority leader from 1973 to 1981 and chaired the platform committee at the 1972 Republican National Convention that saw the re-election of Nixon; he also served as chair in 1976 and 1980. Rhodes was a conservative who favored reducing government regulations and increasing budgetary fiscal responsibility; he was an admirer of Nixon, and would later say that approaching the disgraced president to tell him that he should resign was the most difficult thing he ever did while in government. After retiring from office, Rhodes worked as an attorney for Hunton & Williams until 1997, and he also served as a member of the board of overseers at the Hoover Institution from 1984 to 1992. A recipient of the Congressional Distinguished Service Award in 2002, Rhodes was the author of *The Futile System: How to Unchain Congress and Make the System Work Again* (1976) and *John Rhodes: I Was There* (1995).

OBITUARIES AND OTHER SOURCES:

PERIODICALS

Chicago Tribune, August 27, 2003, section 1, p. 11.
Los Angeles Times, August 26, 2003, p. B11.
New York Times, August 26, 2003, p. A21.
Times (London, England), August 28, 2003.
Washington Post, August 26, 2003, p. B4.

* * *

RICE, Craig
See RANDOLPH, Georgiana Ann

* * *

RICHARDSON, Charles R(ay) 1935-

PERSONAL: Born September 19, 1935, in Gorman, TX; son of E. W. "Dub" (an oil and gas wholesaler) and Maxine Loyd (a teacher and food service worker; maiden name, Ketcham) Richardson; married Karin Kay Dean, July 24, 1964; children: Timothy Clark, Zachary Charles. *Ethnicity:* "Caucasian." *Education:* Howard Payne College (now University), B.S., 1958; Hardin-Simmons University, M.A., 1971; East Texas State University (now Texas A & M University, Commerce), M.S., 1977; Southern Baptist Seminaries, diploma (educational ministries), 1987; Golden Gate Baptist Theological Seminary, certificate (Christian studies), 1993. *Religion:* Baptist. *Hobbies and other interests:* The American presidency, photography, travel, inspirational and motivational books, family history.

ADDRESSES: *Home*—1465 Clinton St., Abilene, TX 79603. *Office*—Office of Media Relations, Hardin-Simmons University, Box 16212, Abilene, TX 79698. *E-mail*—crichard@hsutx.edu.

CAREER: Journalist, media director, and author. *Abilene Reporter-News,* Abilene, TX, reporter, 1961, state and Sunday editor, religion editor, and staff writer, 1962-65; Golden Gate Baptist Theological Seminary, Mill Valley, CA, editorial associate and director of news bureau, 1961-62; Hardin-Simmons University, Abilene, director of media relations, 1965-67, 1968-73; 1982—. Correspondent, *San Angelo Standard-Times,* 1957-58, and *Fort Worth Star Telegram,* 1969-71. Texas Baptist Executive Board, Dallas, press representative, 1967-68; Abilene Citizens for Better Government, vice chairperson, 1972; Baptist General Convention of Texas, Dallas, assistant editor, 1973-76; Baptist State Convention of North Carolina, Raleigh, assistant editor, 1976-82; vice president of Abilene Boys and Girls Club and Abilene Mental Health Association. *Military service:* U.S. Army, information specialist, 1958-1960; served in Japan.

MEMBER: Public Relations Society of America (chairperson of educational and cultural organizations section, 1994), Baptist Communications Association, Council for the Advancement and Support of Education, Abilene Southwest Rotary Club (president, 1996-97), Abilene Baptist Association (member of administrative council).

AWARDS, HONORS: Inducted into Hall of Fame, Texas Baptist Public Relations Association, 1990; president's citation, Public Relations Society of America, 1994; Paul Harris fellow, Rotary International, 2000; journalism awards from Texas Baptist Public Relations Association and Baptist Public Relations Association.

WRITINGS:

True Servant Leader: James H. Landes, Hardin-Simmons University (Abilene, TX), 2000.

Coeditor of *Civil War Memories of A. M. Curry,* 1988. Contributor to periodicals, including *Deacon, Christianity Today, Texas Outlook, California Southern Baptist, Sunday School Leadership,* and *Japan Times.* Assistant editor, *Baptist Standard,* 1973-76, and *Biblical Recorder,* 1976-82.

SIDELIGHTS: Charles R. Richardson told *CA:* "Writing is an expression of communication to those in my community and the world. I enjoy meeting all kinds of people and having the opportunity for interviews which in some cases have been published. As a journalist, I've had the opportunity to work with several outstanding editors and reporters who have inspired me to be more precise in my own writing. *True Servant Leader: James H. Landes* was written because of my admiration of a truly outstanding Christian gentleman and leader. His life inspired me and others to strive to be better myself in my own vocation."

* * *

RICHLAND, W(ilfred) Bernard 1909-2003

OBITUARY NOTICE—See index for *CA* sketch: Born March 25, 1909, in Liverpool, England; died August 14, 2003, in Brooklyn Heights, NY. Attorney, educator, and author. Richland is most often remembered as being the corporate counsel for New York City during the 1970s budget crisis there. He immigrated to America from England at age sixteen and found work as an office boy for Judge Samuel Seabury in New York City. While studying at New York University, he became a clerk for Seabury; he graduated in 1936 and passed the New York State Bar and the U.S. Supreme Court Bar in 1937. Richland left Seabury's office in 1943 to join the city's Law Department as corporate counsel, and the next year he was made chief of the Opinions and Legislation Division. During the 1960s and early 1970s he worked for the private law firms Baer Marks and O'Dwyer & Bernstein before becoming general counsel to the State Charter Revision Commission of New York City in 1973; from 1975 to 1977 he was corporate counsel, heading the Law Department and helping to preserve important landmarks in the city that were threatened by budget cuts and building developers. After leaving this city post, he served as counsel to Botein, Hays & Sklar for ten years and taught local government law at New York Law School. His last job was as special master for appeals for the Agent Orange Administration from 1988 to 1996. In addition to contributing to law journals and serving on the *New York Law Journal*'s editorial board, Richland was the author of one book, *You Can Beat City Hall* (1980).

OBITUARIES AND OTHER SOURCES:

PERIODICALS

New York Times, August 19, 2003, p. C13.

* * *

ROACH, Mary C. 1959-

PERSONAL: Born March 20, 1959, in New Hampshire; daughter of Walter (a professor) and Clare (a secretary; maiden name, Falkner) Roach; married Ed Rachles (a designer and illustrator). *Ethnicity:* "Caucasian." *Education:* Wesleyan University, B.A., 1981. *Politics:* Democrat.

ADDRESSES: Office—San Francisco Writers Grotto, 26 Fell St., San Francisco, CA 94102. *Agent*—Jay Mandel, William Morris Agency, 1325 Avenue of the Americas, New York, NY 10019. *E-mail*—roach@sfgrotto.org.

CAREER: Freelance writer.

AWARDS, HONORS: Editor's Choice Award, *Entertainment Weekly,* 2003, for *Stiff: The Curious Lives of Human Cadavers.*

WRITINGS:

Stiff: The Curious Lives of Human Cadavers, Norton (New York, NY), 2003.

Columnist for periodicals and online sites, including *Health, Inc., Reader's Digest,* and *Salon.com.* Contributor to magazines, including *Outside, Wired, New York Times Magazine, Vogue, Esquire, Believer, Islands,* and *Glamour.* Contributing editor, *Discover.*

WORK IN PROGRESS: Another book, publication by Norton (New York, NY) expected in 2005.

SIDELIGHTS: Mary C. Roach told *CA:* "I write because writing is the only thing I know how to do reasonably well! I enjoy it possibly too much, as I never seem to get around to doing much else. I gravitate to the unexplored fringes of a subject, the taboo areas."

* * *

RODARI, Gianni 1920-1980

PERSONAL: Born 1920, in Italy; died April 14, 1980, in Rome; son of a baker. *Education:* Teaching certificate (Varese, Italy), 1938.

CAREER: Children's author, poet, short-story writer, journalist, and editor. Il Pioniere (eftist political organization), director; L'Unita, Italy, political columnist.

AWARDS, HONORS: Premio Prato, 1960, for *Nursery Rhymes in Heaven and on Earth;* Premio Castello, 1963, for *Gip nel televisoze;* International Board on Books for Young People Honor List, 1964, 1968; named highly commended author for Hans Christian Andersen Award, 1966; Premio Europa Dralon, 1967, and Premio Castello, 1968, both for *La torta in cielo;* Premio Rubino, 1968, for *Il libro deqli errori;* Hans Christian Andersen Award, 1970.

WRITINGS:

Favole al telefone (title means "Telephone Tales"), 1965.
The Befana's Toyshop: A Twelfth Niqht Story, 1970.
La torta in cielo (title means "A Pie in the Sky"), 1971.
Turista in Cina, Il Rinnovamento (Rome, Italy), 1974.
Tales told by a Machine, Abelard-Schulman (New York, NY), 1976.
C'era due volte it barone Lamberto, ovvero: i misteri dell'isola di San Giulio, Einaudi (Turin, Italy), 1978.
Il teatro, ragazzi, la citta: la storia di tutte le storie: un'esperienza di incontro tra scuola e teatro, Emme (Milan, Italy), 1978.
Il gioco dei quattro cantoni, Einaudi (Turin, Italy), 1980.
Piccoli vagabondi: romanzo, with commentary by Lucio Lombardo Radice e Marcello Argilli, Editori Riuniti (Rome, Italy), 1981.
Atalanta: una fanciulla nella Grecia degli dei e degli eroi, Editori Riuniti (Rome, Italy), 1982.
Il cane di Magonza, Editori Riuniti (Rome, Italy), 1982.
Storie di re Mida, Einaudi (Turin, Italy), 1983.
Giochi nell'URSS, appunti di viaggio, Einaudi (Turin, Italy), 1984.
Il secondo libro delle filastrocche, Einaudi (Turin, Italy), 1985.
Filastrocche per tutto l'anno, illustrated by Emanuele Luzzati, Editori Riuniti (Rome, Italy), 1986.
The Grammar of Fantasy: An Introduction to the Art of Inventing Stories, translated with an introduction by Jack Zips, Teachers & Writers Collaborative (New York, NY), 1996.

SIDELIGHTS: Winner of the Hans Christian Andersen Award in 1970 for his substantial body of work, Gianni Rodari has been recognized as one of Italy's leading children's authors. His numerous books for juvenile readers earned him many of Italy's major prizes and many have been translated into other languages. Rodari, however, was also politically active, working as a columnist for *L'Unita* and serving as the director of Il Pioniere, an Italian organization for children of parents who belonged or sympathized with leftist parties.

A *Children's Literature Review* critic noted that Rodari has been "celebrated as an original, versatile, and especially creative author who is credited with changing the direction of Italian juvenile literature by blending elements of traditional fantasy into the realistic characteristics of modern society, especially those relating to technology." Several of Rodari's books have proven popular in English translation, including The *Befana's Toyshop: A Twelfth Niqht Story, A Pie in the Sky,* and *Tales Told by a Machine.* These titles reflect Rodari's belief that children's literature should treat serious social and political issues while simultaneously exercising the child's imagination and verbal skills.

The Befana's Toyshop tells the Christmas story of Francesco, an impoverished little boy who never receives presents on Twelfth Night. The Befana is a female Italian version of Father Christmas, and though ultimately benevolent, she is also a somewhat witchy old woman who rides a broomstick. The toys in the window of the Befana's toyshop see Francesco pressing his nose on the window and feel sympathy for him. As a result, they decide to escape to go cheer him up. Unfortunately, gangsters kidnap Francesco and force him to climb up into the Befana's shop. When Francesco refuses to let them in so they can rob the toyshop, the Befana rewards Francesco. The toys, after an assortment of adventures, find loving homes. Margery Fisher in *Growing Point* judged *The Befana's Toyshop* "a rambling tale, fanciful and strange, with the mysterious witch Befana as presiding genius of the Italian Christmas scene" and appreciated the story's "swingeing do-good point in the Pinocchio tradition."

La torta in cielo concerns a bumbling scientist who mistakenly creates a giant dessert instead of an atom-bomb explosion. The adults in the story do not recognize this wonderful error and the authorities believe the cake is an invading spaceship from Mars. Only the children can see the huge cake in the sky for what it is and rejoice at their good fortune. The scientist is at first ashamed of his failure, but then is infected by the children's enthusiasm and vows to make only cakes, turning his knowledge away from weapons research. Again, the social implications are obvious to adults, yet the plot is imaginative, the language colorful enough to hold a young reader's attention. Carla Poesia in *Bookbird* remarked that the story's "facts and characters are tightly bound to the atmosphere and to the problems of our time. Rodari never tries to evade reality though it may often appear arid and painful. On the contrary, he lets us see how to live in it without losing the charge of humanity which exists in each of us . . . This does not mean that Rodari wishes to indulge the easygoing taste of children: on the contrary, it means that the writer's poetic invention and creative strength is suited to the topography and the myths of the child's psyche." *La torta in cielo,* one of Rodari's most popular tales, won him two major Italian literary prizes, the Premio Europa Dralon and the Premio Castello.

Tales Told by a Machine contains seven short stories written in answer to the question, "What would happen if . . . ?" The resulting tales are wildly fantastic, and John Naughton in the *Listener* described them as "ponderous but strangely effective." In one story the canals of Venice drown the town and its citizens must learn to live under water. In another, a piano-playing cowboy rides and his piano follows him on horseback. "A Tinned World" tells the story of a picnicking family followed to Rome by the empty bottles, discarded cans, and other garbage it left behind. Eventually the bottles and tins are accepted into the household—the parents sleep inside bottles, while the children's room becomes a coffee can. The message of environmental awareness is undeniable. Yet, as Fisher noted, Rodari balances the story so skillfully as to keep "the nightmarish aspect of the story in check." Another story in the collection, "Off with the Cats" concerns a stationmaster named Signor Antonio who joins a sit-in with a bunch of cats who demand to be represented by a "Car Star" in the constellations. Most of the stories in *Tales Told by a Machine* share the theme of lost or changed identity. They are nonsensical on the surface with more serious undercurrents. Some reviewers have wondered whether Rodari's young audience could understand his complex humor and satirical style. The tales "sound like a kind of science fiction," remarked B. Clark in the *Junior Bookshelf,* "but as they increase in improbability, so the humour becomes semi-adult in style. All children may not appreciate this, but for those who do, the books will prove a feast of enjoyment."

Treating children with the serious attention they deserve and challenging children through an imaginative use of language and inclusion of "adult" social problems seemed to be a Rodari priority. He invented the disease "televisionitis"—caught by children who wasted too many hours in front of the television. He commented on the flaws of human nature and societal ills by imagining the peaceful planet of Christmas trees whose unnecessary government is named "Government-which-does-not-exist." He wrote nursery rhymes about underpaid workers and used the Italian color-coded grading system to emphasize that adults make more serious mistakes than do children. Yet, as Lucia Binder observed in *Bookbird,* "Rodari never becomes didactic . . . his stories are much too fantastic and playful." Rodari earned much praise and many awards, and his stories have been translated into English and Spanish. Tales such as *La torta in cielo* and "A Tinned World" from *Tales Told by a Machine* still resonate with young readers.

BIOGRAPHICAL AND CRITICAL SOURCES:

BOOKS

Berger, Laura Standley, editor, *Twentieth-Century Children's Writers,* St. James Press (Detroit, MI), 1995.

Children's Literature Review, Volume 24, Gale (Detroit, MI), 1991.

Pendergast, Sara, and Tom Pendergast, editors, *St. James Guide to Children's Literature,* St. James Press (Detroit, MI), 1999.

Rodari, Gianni, *Tales Told by a Machine,* translated by Sue Newson-Smith, illustrated by Fulvio Testa, Abelard-Schuman (New York, NY), 1976.

PERIODICALS

Bookbird, September 15, 1980, pp. 28-30.

Growing Point, January, 1976, pp. 2785-2786; December, 1976, pp. 3010-3011; September, 1981, p. 3957; January, 1971, p. 1658.

Junior Bookshelf, August, 1977, p. 226; February, 1976, p. 29.

Listener, November 11, 1976, pp. 626-627.

Times Literary Supplement, October 30, 1970, p. 1252.*

* * *

ROGERS, Warren (Joseph, Jr.) 1922-2003

OBITUARY NOTICE—See index for *CA* sketch: Born May 6, 1922, in New Orleans, LA; died of complications from a perforated ulcer August 31, 2003, in Washington, DC. Journalist and author. Rogers was a Washington insider whose friendship with Robert F. Kennedy led to several books about the Kennedy clan. He attended Tulane University, but left in 1941 to join the Marines; he fought in the Pacific theater during World War II and saw action at Guadalcanal. Returning home, he worked his way up from copy boy to cub reporter at the *New Orleans Item.* He next joined the Associated Press in 1947, where he worked as a reporter in Baton Rouge before being assigned to Washington, D.C. in 1951, and he became a diplomatic correspondent there from 1953 to 1959. He was hired by the *New York Herald Tribune* in 1959. Rogers covered military affairs and international news for the next four years, and it was while working for the *Herald Tribune* that he met and became friends with Bobby Kennedy. He then returned to Washington, D.C. as chief correspondent for Hearst Newspapers and then as editor for *Look* magazine. The 1960s were eventful years, and Rogers covered such high-profile news as the Vietnam War and the Cuban Missile Crisis. His friendship with Kennedy gave him inside access into the 1968 campaign, and when Kennedy was shot in Los Angeles, Rogers was there and rode with him in the ambulance. He left *Look* in 1970 to work briefly for the *Los Angeles Times* and then the Chicago Tribune-New York News Syndicate, all the while covering events in the nation's capital. During the mid-1970s Rogers left journalism for a time to be vice president of public affairs for the National Forest Products Association, but he returned to journalism as editor-in-chief of Plus Publications from 1977 to 1979, and then worked as editor of the newsletter *White House Weekly* from 1981 to 1989. He also ran the *Georgetown Courier* from 1991 to 1992, but from 1979 on Rogers mostly worked as a freelancer. He was the author of several books about the Kennedys, including *Ted Kennedy* (1980), *Hickory Hill: Bob Kennedy at Home* (1985), and *When I Think of Bobby: A Personal Memoir of the Kennedy Years* (1993), as well as other works such as *The Floating Revolution* (1962) and *Outpost of Freedom* (1965), written with Roger Donlon.

OBITUARIES AND OTHER SOURCES:

PERIODICALS

Los Angeles Times, September 3, 2003, p. B10.

Washington Post, September 2, 2003, p. B4.

* * *

ROSS, William B. 1915-2003

OBITUARY NOTICE—See index for *CA* sketch: Born January 29, 1915, in Spokane, WA; died of complications following surgery August 21, 2003, in Los Angeles, CA. Businessman and author. Ross was a public relations advisor who specialized in organizing political campaigns for such important figures as

President Richard M. Nixon and California Governor Pat Brown. His undergraduate degree was in journalism, which he earned at the University of Southern California in 1937. To help pay for his schooling, he started publishing small newspapers and thus learned about advertising; this inspired him, while still a college senior, to found his first company, W. B. Ross and Associates, an advertising copy firm. He ran this company until forming a partnership with Herbert M. Baus to form Baus & Ross Co., a public relations firm, in 1948. Ross and Baus made for a creative team that is credited by many with initiating such then-innovative practices as direct mailing and telephone polls for political candidates. In addition to working for such candidates as Nixon and Brown, they campaigned for Barry Goldwater and mayoral candidates in Los Angeles and San Francisco. The firm also formed publicity campaigns for political issues such as bond and land acquisition measures. After Baus retired in 1968 Ross continued to run the company for several years. Ross and Baus's public relations firm was admired for its efficiency and innovation—they boasted a ninety-percent success rate—and together they published a popular book on their methods titled *Politics Battle Plan* (1968). In addition to running his company, Baus was a member of the board of directors of Golden State Bank and Welfare Planning Council for over twenty years, and he served as vice president of the California Adoption Foundation.

OBITUARIES AND OTHER SOURCES:

PERIODICALS

Chicago Tribune, August 27, 2003, section 1, p. 11.
Los Angeles Times, August 26, 2003, p. B11.
Washington Post, August 27, 2003, p. B6.

* * *

ROTHE, Dietmar (E.) 1934-

PERSONAL: Born August 22, 1934, in Oppach, Germany; U.S. citizen; son of Herbert Paul (an engineer) and Ella Clara (Berndt) Rothe; married Gerda K. Mahlstedt, 1957 (divorced, 1979); married Rose Angela Roeser 1986; children: Eric Wayne, Frederic Terence. *Ethnicity:* "German." *Education:* McMaster University, B.Eng. (honors; engineering physics), 1961; University of Toronto, M.A.Sc. (applied science), 1962, Ph.D. (aerospace sciences), 1966. *Religion:* "Reared Lutheran; now New Consciousness." *Hobbies and other interests:* Philosophy, nature, astrophysics, poetry, hiking, painting, photography.

ADDRESSES: Home—Encinitas, CA. *Agent*—Avila Books, P.O. Box 418, Cardiff by the Sea, CA 92007. *E-mail*—rtr@sand.net.

CAREER: Engineer and author. General Electric Co., Guelph, Canada, designer and engineering assistant, 1953-59; Cornell Aeronautical Laboratory, Buffalo, NY, research aerodynamicist and plasma physicist, 1966-71; Lumonics Research Ltd., Ottawa, Canada, staff scientist, 1971-76; Northrop Research and Technology Center, Palos Verdes, CA, research scientist, 1976-80; Helionetics, Inc., San Diego, CA, manager, laser division, 1980-83; Rothe Technical Research, Encinitas, CA, scientific consultant, 1983-99; writer and translator, beginning 1996. Lasertechnics Marking Corporation, Albuquerque, NM, scientific advisory board member, 1995-2000; activist for Urban growth control, 1985—. Holds four patents in pulsed-power technology.

MEMBER: Sierra Club, Optical Society of America, Astronomical Society Pacific, Sigma Xi.

AWARDS, HONORS: NASA Tech Brief Award, 1970; Editor's Choice Awards, National Library of Poetry, 1995, 1996; more than a dozen research and development grants from various sources, including U.S. Navy, U.S. Army, and NASA.

WRITINGS:

(Translator and editor) Ella Rothe, *My Verses,* privately published, 1992.
In Search of Truth and Freedom: A Path from Ignorance to Awareness, Avila (Cardiff by the Sea, CA), 2000.
(Co-translator) *The Talmud of Immanuel,* third edition, Blue Water, 2001.

Contributor of poetry to *The Path Not Taken,* edited by Caroline Sullivan, and *Best Poems of the '90s,* edited by Howard Eli, both published by National Library of Poetry, 1996. Author of scientific research papers.

SIDELIGHTS: Dietmar Rothe told *CA:* "Only in the last few years have I been writing seriously for the purpose of conveying my philosophical thoughts to others who might benefit from my insights and discoveries to guide them in their own quest for truth and meaning. So, I have not considered myself a writer until quite recently. Previously, I identified with being an engineer, a scientist, and an amateur artist. Now, after decades of critically observing and analyzing reality and human behavior, I feel I have grown enough in knowledge and wisdom to offer something of value to the inquisitive reader.

"My viewpoints, opinions, and convictions have crystallized out of a lifelong study of the world's philosophies, sciences, and religions. I have taken ideas from many sources of knowledge and integrated these with my own experiences and with my professional knowledge of physics and engineering in order to construct a self-consistent world view. My personal philosophy has been influenced by early Eastern philosophy, by the idealism and romanticism of the eighteenth century, and by New Age thought. Other contributions have come from my knowledge of Western science, from my sense of logic, and through my intuitions. I have found many truths in the writings of Immanuel Kant, Friedrich Schelling, Johann Wolfgang von Goethe, Ralph Waldo Emerson, Henry David Thoreau, Carl Jung, Khalil Gibran, Bhagwan Shree Rajneesh, Stewart Emery, Terry Cole-Whittaker, and many others."

* * *

ROWLANDS, John (Kendall) 1931-

PERSONAL: Born September 18, 1931; son of Arthur and Margaret Rowlands; married Else A. H. Bachmann, 1957 (marriage ended, 1981); married Lorna Jane Lowe, 1982; children: (first marriage) one son and two daughters, (second marriage) one daughter. *Education:* Gonville and Caius College, Cambridge, B.A., M.A. *Hobbies and other interests:* Making music.

ADDRESSES: *Home*—Brant House, Brant Broughton, Lincolnshire LN5 0SL, England.

CAREER: Freelance writer and art consultant. Department of Prints and Drawings, British Museum, London, England, deputy keeper, 1974-81, keeper, 1981-91.

MEMBER: Beefsteak Club.

WRITINGS:

(With Mary Woodall) *Centenary Exhibition of the Works of David Cox, 1783-1859,* Arts Council of Great Britain (London, England), 1959.
Bosch, Phaidon Press (London, England), 1975.
Rubens: Drawings and Sketches, British Museum Press (London, England), 1977.
Hercules Segers, British Museum Press (London, England), 1979.
German Drawings from a Private Collection, British Museum Press (London, England), 1984.
Master Drawings and Watercolours in the British Museum, British Museum Press (London, England), 1984.
Holbein: The Paintings of Hans Holbein the Younger (monograph), Phaidon Press (Oxford, England), 1985.
The Age of Dürer and Holbein: German Drawings 1400-1550, British Museum Press (London, England), 1988.
Drawings by German Artists and Artists from German-Speaking Regions of Europe in the Department of Prints and Drawings in the British Museum: The Fifteenth Century and Sixteenth Century by Artists Born before 1530, British Museum Press (London, England), 1993.

SIDELIGHTS: Art historian John Rowlands has written extensively on the subject of early Renaissance Dutch and Germanic drawings and paintings. As deputy keeper and then keeper in the British Museum's Department of Prints and Drawings, Rowlands has written several exhibition catalogs, including *The Age of Dürer and Holbein: German Drawings 1400-1550,* which accompanied an exhibit he developed at the museum in 1988.

Keith Andrews, reviewing the 1988 exhibition for *Burlington,* observed that Rowlands "envisaged the exhibition as a survey of one hundred and fifty years of German draughtsmanship, not only from the Museum's own holdings, but also including loans from other public and private collections in Britain." Andrews considered the exhibition "impressive," and noted particularly that, in addition to its focus on the famous artists Dürer and Holbein, the exhibition also thoroughly explores "the riches, varieties, and curiosities that have survived—including many from earlier periods often hidden in unexpected places." Christopher S. Wood in *Speculum* hailed the exhibition as "magnificent" and observed that in the catalogue Rowlands "makes substantial contributions to old debates" concerning Dürer. In *Choice,* F. W. Robinson praised the catalogue as a "superb" work filled with excellent reproductions and informative entries.

Rowlands' monograph *Holbein: The Paintings of Hans Holbein the Younger* also attracted favorable reviews. *Burlington* contributor Lorne Campbell found the book a "considerable improvement" over earlier works on the artist, noting that Rowlands deals effectively with questions of attribution and "allows us to form a much clearer idea of Holbein's stylistic development." Campbell further noted, however, that Rowlands, who is an authority on drawings but not paintings, does not present a fully satisfying account of the painter's entire body of work. *Spectator* reviewer Peter Quennell, on the other hand, described *Holbein* as "a highly informative and visually delightful monograph" that provides insight not only into the painter's mature career but also "into his happily productive youth."

BIOGRAPHICAL AND CRITICAL SOURCES:

PERIODICALS

Apollo, March, 1977, Gregory Martin, review of *Bosch,* pp. 224-225; February, 1983, Christopher White, review of *Hercules Segers,* pp. 146-147.

Burlington, February, 1986, Lorne Campbell, review of *Holbein: The Paintings of Hans Holbein the Younger,* pp. 149-151; October, 1988, Keith Andrews, review of *The Age of Dürer and Holbein: German Drawings 1400-1550* (exhibition), pp. 785-787.

Choice, April, 1979, review of *Rubens: Drawings and Sketches,* p. 213; March, 1989, F. W. Robinson, review of *The Age of Dürer and Holbein: German Drawings 1400-1550,* pp. 1142-1143.

Christian Century, January 18, 1989, review of *The Age of Dürer and Holbein,* p. 59.

Library Journal, January 15, 1979, Robert Cahn, review of *Rubens,* p. 181.

New York Review of Books, March 9, 1978, E. H. Gombrich, "The Life-giving Touch," pp. 6, 8, 10.

New York Times Book Review, December 8, 1985, John Russell, review of *Holbein,* p. 14.

Spectator, January 25, 1986, Peter Quennell, review of *Holbein,* pp. 24-25.

Speculum, April, 1991, Christopher S. Wood, review of *The Age of Dürer and Holbein,* pp. 471-474.*

* * *

RUCKER, Brian R. 1961-

PERSONAL: Born May 22, 1961, in Pensacola, FL; son of William R. and Shirley (Fortune) Rucker; children: Noah David. *Ethnicity:* "White (Southern)." *Education:* Pensacola Junior College, A.A., 1981; University of West Florida, B.A. (history), 1983, M.A. (history), 1985; Florida State University, Ph.D. (history), 1990. *Religion:* Christian. *Hobbies and other interests:* History.

ADDRESSES: Home—P.O. Box 284, Bagdad, FL 32530.

CAREER: Pensacola Junior College, Pensacola, FL, adjunct professor of history, 1990-96, associate professor of history, 1996—. Patagonia Press, founder, 1990—; University of West Florida, Pensacola, adjunct professor of history, 1993-96; Florida National Register Review Board, member, 1994-96.

MEMBER: Florida Historical Society, Gulf South Historical Association, Pensacola Historical Society, Santa Rosa Historical Society, Society for Commercial Archeology.

AWARDS, HONORS: Academy of Teaching Excellence, 2000; Golden Apple Award, 2000.

WRITINGS:

Jackson Morton: West Florida's Soldier, Senator, and Secessionist, Patagonia Press (Milton, FL), 1990.

A Bagdad Christmas: A Fictional Story about the Old Mill Town of Bagdad, Patagonia Press (Bagdad, FL), 1990.

Brick Road to Boom Town: The Story of Santa Rosa County's "Old Brick Road," Patagonia Press (Bagdad, FL), 1993.

Encyclopedia of Education in Antebellum Pensacola, Patagonia Press (Bagdad, FL), 1999.

Also, author of *Exploring Florida Heritage: Panhandle/West Florida,* Florida Humanities Council, 1991. Contributor of scholarly articles and book reviews to the *Florida Historical Quarterly, Gulf South Historical Review, Pensacola History Illustrated,* and *Journal of Southern History.*

EDITOR, EXCEPT AS NOTED

(Compiler) *Index to Deaths and Marriages in Pensacola Newspapers, 1821-1865,* Patagonia Press (Bagdad, FL), 1990.

Henry M. Brackenridge, *A Topographical Description of Pensacola and Vicinity in 1821,* Patagonia Press (Bagdad, FL), 1991.

(With Nathan F. Woolsey) F. F. Bingham, *Log of the Peep O'Day: Summer Cruises in West Florida Waters, 1912-1915,* Patagonia Press (Bagdad, FL), 1991.

(With Williams S. Coker and Bobbye S. Wicke) Regina M. K. Mandrell, *Our Family: Facts and Fancies—The Crary and Related Families,* Patagonia Press (Bagdad, FL), 1993.

Leora M. Sutton, *The Excavation of Santa Rosa Pensacola: An Insider's Account,* Patagonia Press (Bagdad, FL), 1993.

F. F. Bingham, *From Pensacola to Belize: An American's Odyssey through Mexico in 1903; or, The Ransoming of the Richard A. Bingham,* Patagonia Press (Bagdad, FL), 1997.

WORK IN PROGRESS: Floridale: The Rise and Fall of a Florida Boom Community and *Blackwater and Yellow Pine: The Development of Santa Rosa County, 1821-1865.*

SIDELIGHTS: Brian R. Rucker told *CA:* "Even as a child I was interested in writing, and I composed numerous short stories and even created a neighborhood newspaper. But history and archeology was always my first love, and I eventually acquired my Ph.D. degree in history from Florida State University in 1990. When approaching university presses concerning the publishing of my dissertation, I realized that regional historical studies were slighted by major academic presses because of the costs and limited profits such books would entail. Thus, in 1990, on a shoe string budget, I began Patagonia Press, created as a small, mail-order publishing company that would focus on the rich but often neglected historical and cultural legacy of the Gulf Coast, especially West Florida. The aim was to produce affordable volumes of high academic quality that would rescue valuable monographs, documents, and essays from never seeing the light of day. In essence, I hoped to produce material of a high scholarly level that university presses were unwilling to tackle because of limited markets. I am very happy to break even every year, realizing that the true reward is producing works that will endure and be used by future scholars. Since 1990 Patagonia Press has published fourteen titles dealing with Gulf Coast history and culture.

"My first love is research and writing. There is a great fulfillment in seeing a project through from inception until it appears as a book in my hands. I credit my family for their wonderful support and encouragement over the years. My list of most influential authors includes O'Henry, Mark Twain, Immanuel Velikovsky, and Henry M. Morris."

* * *

RUOTOLO, Lucio P(eter) 1927-2003

OBITUARY NOTICE—See index for *CA* sketch: Born March 14, 1927, in New York, NY; died of complications from heart surgery July 4, 2003, in Stanford, CA. Educator and author. Ruotolo was a former Stanford University professor who was an acknowledged authority on Virginia Woolf. A U.S. Army Air Corps veteran, he was a graduate of Colgate University in 1951, and completed his master's degree in 1954 and doctorate in 1960 at Columbia University. Joining the faculty at Stanford in 1957 as an instructor, he remained there throughout his career, becoming a full professor of English in 1973 and retiring in 1994. The founder, president, and later trustee of the Virginia Woolf Society, Ruotolo made the books of the early twentieth-century novelist his primary interest, editing the *Virginia Woolf Miscellany* and Woolf's *Freshwater* (1976). He was also the author of *Six Existential Heroes: The Politics of Faith* (1972), which won the Wilson Prize in 1972, and *The Interrupted Moment: A View of Virginia Woolf's Novels* (1986).

OBITUARIES AND OTHER SOURCES:

PERIODICALS

San Francisco Chronicle, July 10, 2003, p. A21.

S

SABERHAGEN, Joan 1943-
(Joan Spicci)

PERSONAL: Born June 16, 1943, in Chicago, IL; daughter of Joseph and Theresa (Ribandt) Spicci; married Fred Saberhagen (an author), 1968; children: Jill, Eric, Tom. *Education:* Loyola University, B.S. (mathematics), 1964; DePaul University, M.Ed. (secondary mathematics education), 1968; attends University of New Mexico (Russian language and history).

ADDRESSES: Home and office—P.O. Box 11243, Albuquerque, NM 87192. *Agent*—Eleanor Wood, Spectrum Literary Agency, 320 Central Park W., Suite 1-D, New York, NY 10025. *E-mail*—joan@joanspicci.com; jsabe@berserker.com; jsabe@thuntek.net.

CAREER: Author, independent scholar, and author's assistant to Fred Saberhagen. Has worked as a high school mathematics teacher, database manager, and president of her own electronics game company.

MEMBER: Association for Women in Mathematics.

WRITINGS:

(As Joan Spicci) *Beyond the Limit: The Dream of Sofya Kovalevskaya,* Forge Books (New York, NY), 2002.

Contributor of short entries on mathematics to *Encyclopedia Britannica,* 1970s. Technical writer for computer game manuals. Contributor to *Personal Computing.* Coeditor, with Fred Saberhagen, of *Pawn to Infinity,* Ace, 1981; assistant editor of *Spadeful of Spacetime,* Ace, 1981. Translator of letters of Sofya Kovalevskaya.

WORK IN PROGRESS: Infinite Rotations: The Career of Sofya Kovaleskaya (tentative title), a sequel to *Beyond the Limit: The Dream of Sofya Kovaleskaya; Hypatia Newton: And Then There Was War,* an historical adventure.

SIDELIGHTS: Trained as a mathematics teacher, Joan Saberhagen, who writes under her maiden name Joan Spicci, brings professional expertise to *Beyond the Limit: The Dream of Sofya Kovalevskaya,* her fictionalized account of the life of the first woman to obtain a doctorate degree in mathematics. Kovalevskaya, who lived from 1850 to 1891, struggled against considerable odds to develop her talents. Though Russia teemed with revolutionary feeling in the 1860s, when Kovalevskaya was a teenager, women still had few rights and were barred from admission to universities. The novel describes how Sofya and her older sister, Anyuta, devised a bold solution: one of them would marry a sympathetic man, and the couple would then travel abroad so that they could sponsor their Russian feminist friends at European universities. Accordingly, Sofya married Vladimir Kovalevsky and moved with him to Austria and Germany. While sponsoring other ambitious women scholars, Sofya also completed her own doctoral work, studying with the leading mathematicians of the time.

Yet tension grew when Vladimir realized that he loved his wife and wished to consummate their platonic relationship. Sofya, however, worried that a pregnancy could derail her studies, and resisted his advances. Meanwhile, Anyuta moved to Paris with her French Socialist husband and became involved with revolutionary politics. Sofya arranged for her sister's safety, while also seeking a way to save her relationship with Kovalevsky.

A writer for *Kirkus Reviews* observed that Saberhagen "meticulously details the turbulent times" in which her subject lived, though Sofya herself is less fully portrayed. Still, the critic praised the book as "an intriguing . . . portrait of an unusual marriage."

Saberhagen told *CA:* "My interest in writing comes from a desire to communicate and share ideas and information that I find fascinating. The structure of story allows me to share and, with luck, to recreate in the reader those ideas and feelings.

"Research accounts for the majority of my time on a project. My work is influenced by a strong interest in the history of women in science and an interest in nineteenth-century Russian history. As might be expected, my husband is a tremendous influence on my life and work. His example of professionalism and his belief in my abilities have kept me writing.

"*Beyond the Limit* is my first published book. The personality of Kovalevskaya has fascinated me for many years. I hope my books provide an enjoyable, thought-provoking experience for the reader."

BIOGRAPHICAL AND CRITICAL SOURCES:

PERIODICALS

Kirkus Reviews, September 15, 2002, review of *Beyond the Limit: The Dream of Sofya Kovalevskaya,* pp. 1344-1345.

ONLINE

Joan Spicci Saberhagen Web site, http://www.joanspicci.com/ (April 9, 2003).

* * *

SAER, Juan José 1937-

PERSONAL: Born June 28, 1937, in Serodino, Santa Fé, Argentina; son of José and María (Anoch) Saer; married twice; children: two. *Education:* Attended Facultad de Filosofía y Letras, beginning 1958; studied law briefly.

ADDRESSES: Home—Paris, France. *Agent*—c/o Author Mail, Seix Barral, Buenos Aires, Argentina.

CAREER: Fiction writer and journalist. *El Litoral* (newspaper), Santa Fé, Argentina, reporter, 1958; Instituto de Cinematografía, Universidad Nacional del Litoral, Santa Fé, instructor, beginning 1962; worked as a door-to-door salesman, c. late 1950s; University of Rennes, Rennes, France, lecturer, then associate professor of Latin-American literature and maitre de conférences beginning 1983.

AWARDS, HONORS: Nadal prize (Spain), 1987; Prix Roger Calloix (France), 1999.

WRITINGS:

NOVELS

Responso, Jorge Alvarez (Buenos Aires, Argentina), 1964.

La vuelta completa, Bblioteca Popular Connstancio C. Vigil (Rosario, Argentina), 1966.

Cicatrices (title means "Scars"), Sudamericana (Buenos Aires, Argentina), 1969.

El limonero real (title means "The Royal Lemon Tree"), Planeta (Barcelona, Spain), 1974.

Nadie nada nunca, Sigio Ventiuno (Mexico City, Mexico), 1980, translated by Helen Lane as *Nobody Nothing Never,* Serpent's Tail (London, England), 1993.

El entenado, Folios (Mexico City, Mexico), 1983, translated by Margaret Jull Costa as *The Witness,* Serpent's Tail (London, England), 1990.

Glosa, Alianza (Buenos Aires, Argentina), 1986.

La ocasión, Destino (Barcelona, Argentina), 1988, translated by Helen Lane as *The Event,* Serpent's Tail (New York, NY), 1995.

Lo imborrable, Alianza (Buenos Aires, Argentina), 1993.

La pesquisa, Seix Barral (Buenos Aires, Argentina), 1994, translated by Helen Lane as *The Investigation,* Serpent's Tail (London, England), 1999.

Las nubes, Seix Barral (Buenos Aires, Argentina), 1997.

OTHER

En la zona, 1957-1960, Castellví (Santa Fé, Argentina), 1960.

Palo y hueso (short stories; title means "Wood and Bone"), Cameda Junior (Buenos Aires, Argentina), 1965.

Unidad de lugar (short stories), Galerna (Buenos Aires, Argentina), 1967.

El arte de narrar: Poemas, 1960-1975, Fundación para la Cultura y las Artes del Distrito Federal (Caracas, Venezuela), 1977, expanded as *El arte de narrar: Poemas, 1960-1987,* Seix Barral (Buenos Aires, Argentina), 2000.

La mayor (short stories), Centro Editor de América Latina (Buenos Aires, Argentina), 1982.

Narraciones (collected works), two volumes, Centro Editor de América Latina (Buenos Aires, Argentina), 1983.

Una literatura sin atributos (nonfiction), Universidad Nacional del Litoral (Santa Fé, Argentina), 1986.

Juan José Saer por Juan José Saer (collected works), Celtia (Buenos Aires, Argentina), 1986.

El arte de narrar, Universidad Nacional del Litoral (Santa Fé, Argentina), 1988.

Por un relato futuro: Diálogo—Ricardo Piglia, Juan José Saer, Universidad Nacional del Litoral (Santa Fé, Argentina), 1990, published as *Diálogo,* 1995.

El río sin orillas: tratado imaginario (nonfiction), Alianza (Madrid, Spain), 1991.

La selva espesa, Universidad Nacional Autónoma de México (Mexico City, Mexico), 1994.

El concepto de ficción (nonfiction), Ariel (Buenos Aires, Argentina), 1997.

La narración-objeto (nonfiction), Seix Barral (Buenos Aires, Argentina), 1999.

Lugar (short stories), Seix Barral (Buenos Aires, Argentina), 2000.

(With Hugo Gola and Hugo Padeletti) *La trama bajo las apariencias: la pintura de Fernando Espino* (criticism), Universidad Nacional del Litoral (Santa Fé, Argentina), 2000.

Cuentos completos, 1957-2000, Seix Barral (Buenos Aires, Argentina), 2001.

Author of movie scripts, c. 1960s.

Saer's works have been translated into several languages.

ADAPTATIONS: Films adapted from Saer's works include *Nadie nada nunca,* directed by Raúl Beceyro and produced by Instituto Nacional de Cinematografía, 1988, and *Cicatrices,* directed by Patricio Coll, produced 2001.

SIDELIGHTS: Although he left Argentina at the start of his writing career, in 1968, Juan José Saer remains a regionalist writer, "deeply rooted . . . in the part of the vast grasslands or pampas of the province of Santa Fé where he lived during his formative years," explained Nick Caistor in an essay for *Contemporary World Writers.* As a son of Syrian immigrants to South America living in his adopted France, Saer has gone on to write a group of novels that, inspired by and yet breaking with the traditions established by other Argentinian writers such as Jorge Luis Borges, have been "freed" due to their author's self-imposed exile, "from the narrowness of much of what has been written" in Argentina in the late twentieth century. According to Caistor, Saer has been free to experiment with his own literary style, and has become known for his "bold, probing use of the Spanish language." Calling Saer a "canonical figure" within Latin American literature, *Times Literary Supplement* contributor Martin Schifino hailed the Argentine-born writer as "among the most distinctive Spanish stylists" of the second half of the twentieth century.

Affiliated with the Grupo Adverbio formed by young Argentinian intellectuals during the 1950s, Saer wrote poems, short stories, and essays. As Evelia Romano explained in *Latin American Writers,* "In Saer's early work, the preference for marginal characters, countrymen, and urban workers; a fascination with rendering their spoken language; and minute descriptions of their daily activities to reveal psychological processes are among the techniques that reflect [Grupo Adverbio's] . . . neorealistic influence." Another influence was Saer's interest in cinema, particularly the films of Italian director Michelangelo Antonioni.

Saer's most widely read novel, published in English translation as *The Witness,* focuses on a young man named Juan Díaz de Solis, a fifteen-year-old cabin boy who becomes the sole survivor of a 1515 expedition to Argentina. Stranded among the native tribes for a decade, de Solis witnesses the cannibalism the natives practice during an annual ceremony, and on his return to Spain cannot wholly readjust to European civilization. As Amanda Hopkinson explained in her *Times Literary Supplement* review, de Solis "has lost all sense of his own reality" and during the "picaresque travels in love-life Spain" following his return, for de Solis "there is no sense of return, recognition or belonging. On the contrary, the former cabin-boy turned religious hermit then strolling actor retains an

Indian vocabulary that treats 'being' and 'seeming' as synonymous." The text of *The Witness* is written in the form of a life history of de Solis as an elderly man who has retired to a comfortable life in a Spanish monastery. According to Romano, characteristic of Saer's more mature works, *The Witness* is "distinguished by a more linear organization of the story and a noticeable reduction in the repetition of scenes and narrative sequences." Despite its lack of complexity, the novel succeeds as an "imaginative . . . and thought-provoking work" that *Choice* contributor J. Walker cited as both an examination of the nature of native Americans and an exploration of "philosophical concepts like existence, reality, time, memory, being, nothingness, and . . . otherness."

Other novels by Saer translated into English include *The Event,* a 1987 novel that focuses on a nineteenth-century English telepath who flees to the pampas of Argentina after being exposed as a fake. In *Nobody Nothing Never,* the English translation of Saer's 1980 novel *Nadie nada nunca,* the mysterious shooting of horses in the town of Rincon prompts Don Layo to send his prized animals to safety before the situation descends into political violence. Praising the book as a "rich and complex novel," *New York Times Book Review* contributor James Polk cited in particular the author's heady mix of "conflict, characters and symbols" and the "precise and lively" translation by Helen Lane. *Nobody Nothing Never* is "wonderfully evocative of imminent political violence, tension, fear, languor and the furtive excitement of illicit love," wrote M. Wynn Thomas in the *Times Literary Supplement,* while in the *Review of Contemporary Fiction* contributor Jack Byrne dubbed it "an antidote to the excesses of magic realism." Saer's *Cuentos completos, 1957-2000* were released to Spanish-speaking readers in 2001.

BIOGRAPHICAL AND CRITICAL SOURCES:

BOOKS

Contemporary World Writers, 2nd edition, St. James Press (Detroit, MI), 1993, p. 452.

Latin American Writers, Supplement One, edited by Carlos A. Solé, Scribner's (New York, NY), 2002, pp. 517-527.

PERIODICALS

Choice, January, 1992, J. Walker, review of *The Witness,* p. 750.

Kirkus Reviews, July 15, 1995, review of *The Event,* p. 979.

Latin American Literary Review, June, 1993, Rita De Grandis, "The First Colonial Encounter in *El entenado:* Paratextuality and History in Postmodern Fiction," pp. 30-38.

New Statesman & Society, November 30, 1990, Nick Caistor, review of *The Witness,* p. 39.

New York Times Book Review, July 17, 1994, James Polk, review of *Nobody Nothing Never,* p. 16.

Publishers Weekly, August 23, 1991, review of *The Witness,* p. 55; May 30, 1994, review of *Nobody Nothing Never,* p. 50.

Review of Contemporary Fiction, spring, 1995, Jack Byrne, review of *Nobody Nothing Never,* p. 170.

Revista Iberoamericana, October-December, 1983, pp. 965-981.

Times Literary Supplement, January 4, 1991, Amanda Hopkinson, review of *The Witness,* p. 16; March 25, 1994, M. Wynn Thomas, review of *Nobody Nothing Never,* p. 22; August 2, 2002, Martin Schifino, review of *Cuentos completos, 1957-2000,* p. 21.

Translation Review Supplement, December, 1999, review of *The Investigation,* p. 33.

Washington Post Book World, September 10, 1995, review of *The Event,* p. 12.

ONLINE

Literatura Argentina Contemporánea Web site, http://www.literatura.org/ (September, 1999), "Juan José Saer."*

* * *

SAFI, Omid

PERSONAL: U.S. citizen; married; children: one son. *Education:* Duke University, B.A. (religion), M.A. (history of religion), Ph.D. (Islamic studies), 2000.

ADDRESSES: *Office*—Department of Philosophy and Religion, Colgate University, Hamilton, NY 13346. *E-mail*—osafi@mail.colgate.edu.

CAREER: Colgate University, Hamilton, NY, assistant professor of Islamic studies, 1999—. Affiliated with Pluralism Project, Harvard University.

MEMBER: American Academy of Religion (cochair of steering committee for the study of Islam), Middle East Studies Association.

AWARDS, HONORS: American Research Center in Egypt grant, 2995; Colgate Faculty Development Council and Research Council grants, both 2000.

WRITINGS:

Bargaining with Baraka: Persian Sufis, "Mysticism," and Pre-Modern Politics, Muslim World, 2000.

(Editor and contributor) *Progressive Muslims: On Justice, Gender, and Pluralism,* OneWorld (Oxford, England), 2003.

Contributor of articles, reviews, and translations to periodicals, including *Journal of Scriptural Reading, Religious Studies News, Muslim World, Middle East Studies Association Bulletin, Islamic Studies,* and *Journal of Muhyiddin ibn Arabi Society.* Contributor to books, including *Taking Back Islam: American Muslims Reclaim Their Faith,* edited by Michael Wolfe, Rodale Press, 2002.

WORK IN PROGRESS: Translating *The Tamhidat of Ayn al-Quzat al-Hamadani: Preparations for the Path of Love,* for Paulist Press, 2004; a monograph on Ayn al-Quzat Hamadani's Sufi vision; a monograph on intellectual life in Saljuq Iran; research on Islamic mysticism, Persian literature, and Iranian history.

* * *

SALSITZ, Norman 1920-

PERSONAL: Born Naftali Saleschutz, 1920, in Kolbuszowa, Poland; immigrated to United States, 1947; son of Isak Saleschutz (a businessman); married Amalie Petranker (a Hebrew teacher), 1945; children: Esther Cylia Dezube. *Ethnicity:* Jewish. *Education:* Educated in Poland. *Politics:* Democrat. *Religion:* "Conservative Judaism." *Hobbies and other interests:* Stamp collecting, coin collecting, photography, antique collecting.

ADDRESSES: Home—Springfield, NJ. *Office*—c/o Author Correspondence, Syracuse University Press, 621 Skytop Rd., Suite 110, Syracuse, NJ 13244-5290.

CAREER: Worked as a builder in New Jersey; writer and photographer. *Military service:* Served in Polish army, 1942-45.

MEMBER: Magen David Adom, suburban chapter (president), Federation of Jewish Holocaust Survivors, Bnai Brith, Hazak, U.S. Holocaust Memorial Museum.

AWARDS, HONORS: Names Man of the Year by B'nai B'rith, and Israel Bonds.

WRITINGS:

(With wife, Amalie Petranker Salsitz) *Against All Odds: A Tale of Two Survivors,* Holocaust Library (New York, NY), 1990.

(With Richard Skolnik) *A Jewish Boyhood in Poland: Remembering Kolbuszowa,* Syracuse University Press (Syracuse, NY), 1992.

(With Petranker Salsitz, and Amy Hill Hearth) *In a World Gone Mad: A Heroic Story of Love, Faith, and Survival,* Abingdon Press (Nashville, TN), 2001.

(With Stanley Kaish) *Three Homelands: Memories of a Jewish Life in Poland, America, and Israel,* Syracuse University Press (Syracuse, NY), 2002.

WORK IN PROGRESS: They Deserved to Be Remembered: "You Are Still Alive? I Thought They Killed All of You."

SIDELIGHTS: When Norman Salsitz was given a camera during his boyhood in Poland, he could not have predicted that the pictures he took of his hometown and his Jewish friends and family there would be the only record of their existence by 1945. As his town, relatives, and friends were successively obliterated by the Holocaust, Salsitz survived by being physically hardy and by assuming a false identity smuggled to him by a sympathetic Polish citizen. He hid his precious photographs in the thatch on barn roofs so that, should he not escape the Nazis, his record of Jewish life might some day be found. Salsitz's wife, Amalie Petranker, suffered similar hardships and terror during the Holocaust years—they met when Salsitz was sent to retrieve top-secret information from her, and then shoot her. One of the most improbable stories of love and survival in the twentieth century, the saga of Norman and Amalie Salsitz provides important details of Jewish life in Poland before, during, and after the Holocaust.

Salsitz has donated his photographs to the Holocaust Museum in Washington, D.C. In Washington some of them appear in the memoirs he and his wife have written together and in books he has worked on with coauthors. Everything he writes is intended to keep alive the memory of the Holocaust and the heartless extermination not only of Jews themselves but of the physical evidence of their existence, including the very homes they lived in. "I tell and I tell and I write and I speak," Salsitz said in the *San Francisco Chronicle.* "We shouldn't let people forget."

In books such as *A Jewish Boyhood in Poland: Remembering Kolbuszowa, In a World Gone Mad: A Heroic Story of Love, Faith, and Survival,* and *Three Homelands: Memories of a Jewish Life in Poland,* Salsitz recalls the joys and sorrows of growing up Jewish in a small Polish town, the encroaching horrors of the Nazi occupation, the forcible relocation of Jews to ghettos and then concentration camps, and the desperate measures people took to save themselves and their families. In *AB Bookman's Weekly* Carl Simmons wrote: "Salsitz's story is one of both love and sadness toward the land he escaped in 1941—but not before he and other Jewish youths were forced by the Nazis to take his ghetto apart, brick by brick." *Slavic Review* contributor Marsha Rozenblit noted that in *A Jewish Boyhood in Poland,* Salsitz "movingly describes Jewish family life, education, economic activities and the inroads of modernity in a very traditional community." Rozenblit found the author's reflections to be "indispensable tools for understanding how ordinary human beings coped with the horrors of the Nazi attempt to annihilate European Jewry."

U.S. News and World Report correspondent Dan Gilgoff described how Salsitz collected photographs from homes in the Jewish ghetto and hid them away with those he had taken himself. Salsitz lived to retrieve the pictures after assuming a false identity and becoming an officer in the Polish army. Gilgoff declared: "Today, Salsitz's two albums of black-and-white photographs form a comprehensive depiction of Jewish life in his town from before the war through the first year in the ghetto." Salsitz's written histories help give the photographs more meaning in the context of the Holocaust. A *Publishers Weekly* reviewer concluded of *Three Homelands:* "What makes these vignettes worth reading is the sense of place." The same critic felt that Salsitz's "characters seem to spring off the pages." Salsitz himself told a writer for the Newark, New Jersey *Star-Ledger:* "The irony hasn't escaped me. Because I was sent to destroy the last remnants of Jewish life in the ghetto, I was able to preserve a major record of that life."

BIOGRAPHICAL AND CRITICAL SOURCES:

PERIODICALS

AB Bookman's Weekly, March 29, 1993, Carl Simmons, "America, the Holocaust, and the Jewish Identity," pp. 1334-1335.

Booklist, September 15, 1991, George Cohen, review of *Against All Odds: A Tale of Two Survivors,* p. 117; December 15, 2002, George Cohen, review of *Three Homelands: Memories of a Jewish Life in Poland, Israel, and America,* p. 729.

Kirkus Reviews, March 1, 1992, review of *A Jewish Boyhood in Poland: Remembering Kolbuszowa,* p. 309.

Library Journal, April 15, 1992, Gerda Haas, review of *A Jewish Boyhood in Poland,* p. 104.

Publishers Weekly, October 28, 2002, review of *Three Homelands,* p. 61.

San Francisco Chronicle, April 23, 1998, Amy Westfeldt, "Pair's Tale of Hiding, Survival," p. A8.

Slavic Review, summer, 1995, Marsha Rozenblit, review of *A Jewish Boyhood in Poland,* pp. 455-456.

Star-Ledger (Newark, NJ), November 21, 1996, "Jewish Record Spared from Axes," p. 1; "Woman Outwitted Nazi Murderers," p. 1; March 30, 1998, Bob Braun, "Pretzels, Plum Brandy, and a Thirst to Repay Generosity from Long Ago," p. 17.

U.S. News & World Report, July 9, 2001, Dan Gilgoff, "Gone, but Never to Be Forgotten," p. 44.

SANTIAGO, Silviano 1936-

PERSONAL: Born September 29, 1936, in Formiga, Minas Gerais, Brazil. *Education:* University of Minas Gerais, B.A., 1959; University of Rio Janeiro, Diploma of advanced study, 1961; Sorbonne, D.Univ., 1968.

ADDRESSES: *Home*—Brazil. *Agent*—c/o Author Mail, Duke University Press, P.O. Box 90660, Durham, NC 27708-0660.

CAREER: Poet, novelist, and literary critic. University of New Mexico, Albuquerque, lecturer; Rutgers University, Brunswick, NJ, lecturer; State University of New York—Buffalo, associate professor of French literature; Universidade Federal Fluminense, Niterói, Brazil, professor of Brazilian literature. Visiting professor at Catholic University, Rio de Janeiro, and University of Texas.

WRITINGS:

(With Ivan Angelo) *Duas faces,* Editôra Itatiaia, 1961.

Brasil prosa e poesia: Antologia, Las Americas (New York, NY), 1969.

O Banquete, Editôra Saga (Rio de Janeiro, Brazil), 1970.

Salto (poems), São Sebastião do Paraiso (Brazil), 1970.

Barroco, Universidade Federal de Minas Gerais (Brazil), 1971.

Latin American Literature: The Space in between, Council on International Studies, State University of New York-Buffalo (Buffalo, NY), 1973.

O Olhar, Edições Tendência (Brazil), 1974.

(Author of commentary) *Iracema,* José Martiniano de Alencar, Livraria F. Alves Editôra (Rio de Janeiro, Brazil), 1975.

Carlos Drummond de Andrade (criticism), Editôra Vozes (Petrópolis, Brazil), 1976.

Glossário de Derrida, Livraria F. Alves Editôra (Rio de Janeiro, Brazil), 1976.

A Bagaceira, Universidade Federal do Paraná (Curitiba, Brazil), 1976.

Crescendo durante a Guerra Numa Província Ultramarina, Livraria F. Alves Editôra (Rio de Janeiro, Brazil), 1978.

Uma literature nos Trópicos: ensaios sobre dependência cultural, Editôra Perspectiva (São Paulo, Brazil), 1978.

Em liberdade (fiction), Paz e Terra (Rio de Janeiro, Brazil), 1981.

Vale quanto pesa: ensaios sobre questões politico-culturais, Paz e Terra (Rio de Janeiro, Brazil), 1982.

Stella Manhattan (novel), Editôra Nova Fronteira (Rio de Janeiro, Brazil), 1985, translation by George Yudice, Duke University Press (Durham, NC), 1994.

(Translator) Jacques Prévert, *Poemas,* Editôra Nova Fronteira (Rio de Janeiro, Brazil), 1986.

Nas malhas da letra: ensaios (essays), Companhia das Letras (São Paulo, Brazil), 1989.

História de um livro, Universidade Federal do Rio de Janeiro (Rio de Janeiro, Brazil), 1989.

(With Oswald de Andrade and Mário da Silva Brito) *Ponta de lança,* Editôra Globo (Sao Paulo, Brazil), 1991.

Leitura e litensidades discursivas, Universidade Federal do Rio de Janeiro (Rio de Janeiro, Brazil), 1991.

(With Tania Barros Maciel) *O Ambiente inteiro: a contribuição crítica da universidade à questão ambiental,* Universidade Federal do Rio de Janeiro (Rio de Janeiro, Brazil), 1992.

Uma história de família (fiction), Rocco (Rio de Janeiro, Brazil), 1992.

(With Edilberto Coutinho) *Amor na boca do Túnel: antologia* (fiction), Tempo Brasileiro (Rio de Janeiro, Brazil), 1992.

Cheiro forte, Rocco (Rio de Janeiro, Brazil), 1995.

Viagem ao México, Rocco (Rio de Janeiro, Brazil), 1995.

Keith Jarrett No Blue Note: improvisos de jazz, Rocco (Rio de Janeiro, Brazil), 1996.

(With Eneida Maria de Souza and Wander Melo Miranda) *Navegar é preciso, viver: escritos para Silviano Santiago,* Editôra UFMG (Brazil), 1997.

Silviano Santiago: depoimento em 11/09/95, Fundacao Memorial da América Latina (São Paulo, Brazil), 1997.

Worldly Appeal: Local and Global Politics in the Shaping of Modern Brazilian Culture, University of Texas Press (Austin, TX), 1997.

De cócoras (fiction), Rocco (Rio de Janeiro, Brazil), 1999.

(With Wander Melo Miranda) *Narrativas da modernidade,* Autêntica (Belo Horizonte, Brazil), 1999.

(With Else Ribeiro Pires Vieira and Macdonald Daly) *Silviano Santiago in Conversation* (interviews), Zoilus Press (London, England), 1999.

Intérpretes do Brasil, Editôra Nova Aguilar (Rio de Janeiro, Brazil), 2000.

The Space In-between: Essays on Latin-American Culture, edited by Ana Lúcia Gazzola, Duke University Press (Durham, NC), 2001.

Also contributor, with others, to *Alexandre Eulálio,* Universidade Federal do Rio de Janeiro (Rio de Janeiro, Brazil), 1989.

SIDELIGHTS: Silviano Santiago taught for several years at universities in the United States, including University of New Mexico, State University of New York at Buffalo, and University of Texas. He is a professor of Brazilian literature at the Universidade Federal Fluminense in Niterói, Brazil. Best known to North American readers for *Stella Manhattan,* a novel, Santiago has produced a diverse body of work that includes poetry, fiction, criticism, and essays. He is considered to be one of the most important Brazilian authorities on French literature and criticism.

As critic Idelber Avelar explained in a *Modern Fiction Studies* article, Santiago rejected the prevalent Brazilian literary styles of the 1980s, which were based on modernism, and challenged the conventions of modernism by re-evaluating the canon of respected authors. He argued that the use of popular literary forms, hitherto dismissed by modernist critics, was a useful stylistic response to the threats contemporary writers face from the mass media. Santiago introduced post-structural theory to Brazil and made seminal contributions to postcolonial theory.

Santiago illustrates his critical ideas in his book *Em liberdade,* which he describes as an essay-novel. The book is structured as a fictional continuation of Graciliano Ramos's acclaimed work, *Memorias do carcere,* which purports to be Ramos's account of his imprisonment by the regime of Getulio Vargas in 1936. Santiago presents himself as the editor of Ramos's unpublished manuscript, and provides commentary and notes that pose questions regarding literature's use of the past. As Adolfo Marin-Minguillon put it in a *Latin American Literary Review* article, *Em liberdade* "questions cultural codes," whereas other postmodern Brazilian novels "pursue the exploitation of those codes."

Stella Manhattan, which *Américas* contributor Barbara Mujica described as "a riveting thriller," established Santiago's fame in the United States. The novel presents the story of a gay transvestite from Brazil whose father, through his old friend Colonel Valdevinos Vianna, gets him a job in the Brazilian consulate in New York City. Eduardo/Stella develops a strong bond with Vianna, who appears to be a respectable and charming married man. Vianna, however, has military links to the Brazilian junta and is a known torturer. He also enjoys a secret life within New York's sadomasochistic club scene. When a Brazilian communist group recruits Eduardo to help them trap Vianna, the dangers intensify, and Eduardo eventually finds himself suspected by both the FBI and Vianna.

Mujica praised the novel for its depiction of Eduardo's dual existence and for its "sense of New York's vibrant, chaotic Brazilian community in the sixties." *Booklist* reviewer Whitney Scott admired the book's unlikely combination of tragedy and farce, describing the novel as a "tumultuous circus of the surreal." In *Lambda Book Report,* however, Jaime Manrique faulted *Stella Manhattan* for "its inability to establish any kind of believable context and texture for the historical time it depicts." Suggesting that "Santiago is not at his best when writing political satire," Manrique complained that the book lacks narrative coherence and convincing characterizations. *Observer* contributor Adria Frizzi, on the other hand, commended the novel as a book "that transcends the 'gay novel' label as well as the purely literary to enter the larger realm of culture."

The novel *Uma história de família* examines the dynamics of a dysfunctional family. The story centers on Uncle Mario, a hapless black sheep who, according to Malcolm Silverman in *World Literature Today,* serves as the "allegorical personification of general misfortune" that surrounds the clan. Santiago uses a "low-keyed" approach in this novel, Silverman wrote, and combines autobiographical elements with bits of memoir, essays, and "suspenseful suggestions of the surreal." Santiago creates a world lacking in love and characterized by a "prevailing sadomasochistic and deterministic milieu," observed Silverman, who commended *Uma história de família* as a "disturbing and convincing account of the complexities of human interrelationships."

The Space In-Between: Essays on Latin American Culture includes pieces written over a thirty-year period, and presents the first English translation of some of Santiago's most important essays on critical theory. These explore such notions as original and copy, dominant and dominated cultures, and cultural dependency. Kenneth Maxwell in *Foreign Affairs* admired Santiago's insights regarding the "complex play between traditional theories of national cultural identities" and the new cultural dynamics that are emerging as a result of globalization.

BIOGRAPHICAL AND CRITICAL SOURCES:

PERIODICALS

Amerícas, July-August, 1996, Barbara Mujica, review of *Stella Manhattan,* p. 60.

Booklist, November 1, 1994, Whitney Scott, review of *Stella Manhattan,* p. 479.

Foreign Affairs, November-December, 2002, Kenneth Maxwell, review of *The Space In-Between: Essays on Latin American Culture.*

Lambda Book Report, March-April, 1995, Jaime Manrique, review of *Stella Manhattan,* p. 20.

Latin American Literary Review, January-June, 1990, Adolfo Marin-Minguillon, review of *Em liberdade,* pp. 18-31.

Library Journal, December, 1994, Brian Kenny, review of *Stella Manhattan,* p. 134.

Modern Fiction Studies, spring, 1998, Idelber Avelar, review of *Em liberdade,* pp. 184-214.

Observer, May 28, 1995, Adria Frizzi, review of *Stella Manhattan,* pp. 203-04.

World Literature Today, winter, 1980, W. Martins, review of *Uma literature nos trópicos: ensaios sobre dependência cultural,* p. 89; spring, 1993, Malcolm Silverman, review of *Uma história de família,* p. 346.*

* * *

SARKAR, Prabhat Ranjan
See ANANDAMURTI, Shrii Shrii

* * *

SAVOCA, Nancy 1959-

PERSONAL: Born 1959, in New York, NY; married Richard Guay (a writer and film producer), 1980; children: two. *Education:* Attended Queen's College of the City University of New York and New York University Film School.

ADDRESSES: Agent—United Talent Agency, 9560 Wilshire Blvd., Suite 500, Beverly Hills, CA 90212.

CAREER: Film writer and director. Directed the films *Renata,* 1982, *Bad Timing,* 1982, *True Love,* 1989, *Dogfight,* 1991, *Household Saints,* 1993, *The Twenty-four-Hour Woman* 1999, *Janis,* 1999, and *Reno: Rebel without a Pause,* 2002; television director of special *Dark Eyes,* 1995, series *Murder One,* 1995-96, and of first two segments of *If These Walls Could Talk* (movie), 1996. Has also worked as a production assistant and assistant auditor.

AWARDS, HONORS: Haig P. Manoogian Award, New York University Student Film Festival, 1984, for overall excellence; Grand Jury Prize for Drama, Sundance Film Festival, and Prize San Sebastian, San Sebastian International Film Festival, both 1989, and Independent Spirit Award nomination for best director, 1990, all for *True Love;* Independent Spirit Award nomination for best feature (with Richard Guay), 1993, for *Household Saints.*

WRITINGS:

SCREENPLAYS

Renata, 1982.

(Coauthor) *Bad Timing* (movie short), World Northal, 1982.

(Coauthor) *True Love,* Metro-Goldwyn-Mayer/United Artists, 1989.

(Coauthor) *Household Saints* (based on a novel by Francine Prose), Fine Line Features, 1993.

The Twenty-four-Hour Woman, Artisan Entertainment, 1999.

Janis, Redeemable Features, 1999.

(Coauthor) *If These Walls Could Talk* (television movie; includes "1952," "1974," and "1996"), HBO, 1996.

Dirt, 2003.

Contributor to periodicals, including *Vogue, Filmmaker,* and *Interview.*

SIDELIGHTS: Film director and writer Nancy Savoca began as an amused chronicler of the courtship and wedding rituals of the Italian-American culture of her upbringing. Like her senior male counterparts, Francis Ford Coppola in the "Godfather" saga and Martin Scorsese in *Mean Streets,* Savoca was inspired by the emotional volatility of such ferociously tight-knit communities. She works, however, on a more intimate cinematic scale, avoiding Coppola's expansive narratives and Scorsese's jittery manner in dramatizing how tribal life shapes, even deforms individual identity.

The social consciousness of Savoca's films extends beyond the confines of Italian-American culture, as *Dogfight* and her television work demonstrate. "I like to look at people who are looking to follow the rules," she once revealed, "looking desperately to get in." Savoca "is unsentimental, yet tactful in focusing on characters, usually of unexceptional looks, circumstances, and talents, who stand out in some small, but definitive way," according to Maria DiBattista in *Women Filmmakers and Their Films.* "The Group not only offers her characters a security that eludes them elsewhere, but promises them personal fulfillment in a socially sanctioned destiny—marriage in *True Love;* military camaraderie in *Dogfight. Household Saints* works a poignant reversal on this formula by giving us a heroine who takes the strictures of her Catholic upbringing so seriously that she aspires to sainthood, thus baffling the loving mother and tenderhearted, but secular father who want a less eccentric, self-denying life for her. Savoca's films observe a discrepancy between an established social consensus on the 'good life' and the actual experience of men and women hampered in their desire to realize such a life."

This discrepancy is presented with a comedic touch in Savoca's films. But her comedy, like her irony, is gentle, even fragile, and on rare occasions is supplanted by pathos—as in the suicide of Michael, the emotionally dislocated and disabled Italian-American son of *Household Saints,* hopelessly adrift in the Orientalist fantasies spawned by *Madame Butterfly.* "Still," according to DiBattista, "Savoca excels in revealing her characters not so much through their solitary moments as in their search for company or a night's diversion. Her films take on an invigorating satiric energy in representing boys on the town or hanging out at their favorite bar, women at a male strip club, or such ritual gatherings as family dinners and, of course, weddings."

True Love has the more contemporary feel than Savoca's other work, although it is set in a community whose traditionalism makes it less susceptible to the convulsive changes that periodically rock American culture. Edvige Giunta, writing in *Melus,* explained that in *True Love,* which follows the story of two Italian Americans about to be wed, Savoca "speaks an unusual language and tells an unusual story. The cozy kitchen of this Italian/American family functions as a claustrophobic setting that epitomizes women's entrapment within a pre-existing plot." The writer/director reveals marriage from both the man's and the woman's point of view: The man, Michael, sees it as a potential threat to his masculinity, while for his bride to be, Donna, "marriage represents the female odyssey." Neither side is able to fully appreciate or understand the other's viewpoint, a rift that is further complicated by the "central fictions of Italian/American mythology" of which they are both an inextricable part.

Savoca's second film, *Dogfight,* set in November 1963, ambitiously presents its story of a soldier on leave before being shipped off to Vietnam as an allegory of an America about to change its ways in the decade ahead. This film initially concerns a group of young soldiers who dub themselves "the four Bs," brought together primarily by the proximity of their names on the military rolls. On their last night Stateside, they stage a "dogfight," a party to which each soldier brings the ugliest girl—or dog—he can find, the winner to be determined by a panel of "judges" who rate the dogs as they take to the dance floor. It is a cruel game, but finally one that only boys, especially those uncertain about their future, would play with such stupid intensity. "Savoca seems to understand this," commented DiBattista, "so while not excusing the game, she shows that a woman can be appreciative as Fellini of unsightly females." The "dogs" she rounds up for the competition are not freaks, however, but plain young women unused to male attention, so that when it comes their way, they are too grateful or surprised to question its sincerity.

Spiritedly playing, then renouncing the game is Eddie Birdlace, played by River Phoenix, who settles on Rose. The second half of the film sweetly pursues the emotional adventures of this odd couple as they enjoy a "second" night on the town, having dinner at a restaurant they cannot afford, wandering through the romantic San Francisco streets until returning to her home to make awkward but fervent love. The film has two endings, both ambiguous. In the first Birdlace tears up Rose's address as he, reunited with his buddies, decides that his fate, if not his heart, is cast with the buddies on whom his life may one day depend. The second shows the war-scarred Vietnam vet, returning four years later to a transformed city and a transformed, but still recognizable Rose, who welcomes him back in a quiet embrace.

Household Saints, based on Francine Prose's novel of the same name, genially takes its tone from those entertaining family legends recounted with droll solemnity after a hearty meal—in this instance, the story of how "it happened by the grace of God, that Joseph Santangelo won his wife in a pinochle game." It took a perfect hand to win her, the first of many surreal occurrences that Savoca presents as co-existing imperturbably with commonplace happenings of everyday life. Tracey Ullman and Vincent D'Onofrio play the magically matched couple. Lili Taylor brings her talent for conveying spiritual insensitivity to the role as their daughter, whose religious ardor, denied any worldly outlet, surfaces as anorexia and culminates in a vision of a blond Christ who looks like a rock star and talks the King's English. Savoca never settles the question of whether Rose has suffered a mental breakdown—the official diagnosis—or has in fact been elected into a community of saints.

With *The Twenty-four-Hour Woman* Savoca puts the modern problem of balancing motherhood and work under the microscope as she simultaneously skewers the television industry in a story about a talk show producer named Grace who has a baby with her husband—the show's host. The event makes her a media darling, while it is also used to boost ratings and kick-start her husband Eddie's acting career. Grace soon finds all the attention from fans making her life impossible, and her husband, who is mostly absent as he pursues his career, is no help in easing her stress. Despite its well-meaning message, though, several critics were unimpressed by *The Twenty-four-Hour Woman,* saying that it is not particularly enlightening. *Variety* critic Dennis Harvey also complained about the movie's conclusion, which "culminates with a ridiculous face-off in which Grace—experiencing that only-in-the-movies type of lovably wacky nervous breakdown—chases Eddie . . . around the TV studio with a gun, ranting her domestic/career woes to a national audience." *People* contributor Marianne Jean-Baptiste further concluded, "One wants to like and keeps trying to like *The Twenty-four-Hour Woman* . . ., but the film never makes it easy. By the time [it] . . . comes to its limp, seemingly tacked-on ending, you've given up even trying. Although well-intentioned, the movie is a mess."

If These Walls Could Talk displays an unadorned, even harrowing realism that was only vaguely hinted at in Savoca's earlier work. Her direction of the segment set in 1952, featuring Demi Moore as a widow desperately seeking an abortionist, is unrelenting in showing us how a trained nurse might go about aborting herself. Nor does Savoca spare audiences the details of how an abortionist, making a house call with his seedy wares in hand, plies his trade on the kitchen table. The camera only pulls away in the final shot of Moore hemorrhaging and calling for help. Savoca does not pretend her audience can identify with such horror as easily as all that. "Whether the matter before her be comic or grave," asserted DiBattista, "Savoca never slips into condescension or sanctimonious irony. Her gift is for understatement, trusting as she does to the surfaces of life to indicate the depths in which her characters are in danger of losing their footing, perhaps even drowning." "Although Savoca may not be regarded as an avant-garde film director," concluded Giunta, "her work does raise questions about what makes a feminist film."

BIOGRAPHICAL AND CRITICAL SOURCES:

BOOKS

Contemporary Theatre, Film, and Television, Volume 25, Gale (Detroit, MI), 2000.

Women Filmmakers and Their Films, St. James (Detroit, MI), 1998.

PERIODICALS

Entertainment Weekly, October 11, 1996, Lisa Schwarzbaum, review of *If These Walls Could Talk,* p. 77.

Melus, summer, 1997, Edvige Giunta, "The Quest for True Love: Ethnicity in Nancy Savoca's Domestic Film Comedy," p. 75.

New York Times, December 28, 1997, Jennifer Steinhauer, "A Director Who Films What She Knows Best."

People, February 8, 1999, Marianne Jean-Baptiste, "Screen," p. 31.

Rolling Stone, September 21, 1989, Peter Travers, "Women on the Verge: Four Women Attempt to Infiltrate a Male Stronghold: The Director's Chair."

Time, March 1, 1999, Richard Corliss, review of *The Twenty-four-Hour Woman,* p. 81.

Variety, January 25, 1999, Dennis Harvey, review of *The Twenty-four-Hour Woman,* p. 75.*

* * *

SAWYER, Clyde Lynwood, Jr. 1951-
(Shiva Sawyer)

PERSONAL: Born December 11, 1951, in Danville, VA; son of Clyde Lynwood, Sr. (in sales) and Glenn (a certified public accountant) Sawyer; married Lisa Feigelis, July, 1974 (divorced, April, 1980); married Jill Irene Maddox, December, 1992. *Education:* New College, B.A., 1973; attended graduate school. *Religion:* "In the original sense." *Hobbies and other interests:* India.

ADDRESSES: *Home*—Brooklyn, NY. *Office*—c/o Author Mail, Memento Mori Mysteries/Avocet Press, 19 Paul Ct., Pearl River, NY 10965-1539; fax 914-735-6807. *E-mail*—uncertain@altavista.com.

CAREER: Screenwriter and novelist. Deutsche Bank, microsystems consultant, 1985—.

MEMBER: Mystery Writers of America, Association of Independent Video and Filmmakers, IFP.

AWARDS, HONORS: First Story award from *Ellery Queen's Mystery Magazine,* 1978.

WRITINGS:

(With Richard Haines) *Alien Space Avenger* (screenplay), American International Pictures, 1992.

(With Frances Witlin) *An Uncertain Currency* (mystery novel), Memento Mori Mystery (New York, NY), 1999.

Author of play *Pecos Diamond.* Contributor to periodicals, including *Ellery Queen's Mystery Magazine.* Some writings appear under the pseudonym Shiva Sawyer.

WORK IN PROGRESS: A suspense novel, *Windswept;* the screenplay *A Passion for Peace.*

SIDELIGHTS: Clyde Lynwood Sawyer, Jr. told *CA:* "Being raised the only listener in a Southern family of talkers, and blessed/cursed with the storytelling gene, one would think my writing would be inevitable. But not until 1973, when I was studying for organic chemistry qualifying exams, did Adi S. Irani (the brother of Meher Baba) point out that I was not a chemist, but a writer. I insisted that I was a chemist and went on to graduate school. In my class, there were twenty-seven introverts and one extrovert, twenty-seven thinkers and one emotional person, twenty-seven yes-no people and one who viewed the world in shades of gray. In each case I was the outlier. At that point I realized that the Old Man might have had a point, and I was not a chemist but indeed a writer.

"In terms of influences on my writing, when you mention Attar, Rumi, and Hafix, where else can you go? For my own material, I write stories that, for whatever reason, demand to be told. Fortunately my publishers at Avocet Press feel the same way and limit their list to books which, as they themselves say, 'speak to them.' For screenwriting, I love collaborating with visionary directors who feel passionately about a particular project, often a narrative that has been secretly nurtured for decades."

* * *

SAWYER, Shiva
See SAWYER, Clyde Lynwood, Jr.

* * *

SCHRAG, Myles 1969-

PERSONAL: Born November 11, 1969, in Topeka, KS; son of Joe (a teacher and track coach) and Joleen Schrag; married Shelley Smithson (a journalist), June 7, 1997. *Ethnicity:* "German." *Education:* Goshen College, B.A., 1992. *Religion:* Mennonite. *Hobbies and other interests:* Outdoor activities, including camping, hiking, running, and biking.

ADDRESSES: Home—611 West Beardsley Ave., Champaign, IL 61820. *Office*—Human Kinetics Publishers, P.O. Box 5076, Champaign, IL 61825-5076. *E-mail*—myless@hkusa.com.

CAREER: Journalist and sports editor, 1993-2000; Human Kinetics Publishers, Champaign, IL, developmental editor, beginning 2000; teacher in Champaign, 2000—.

MEMBER: Society for American Baseball Research.

AWARDS, HONORS: New Mexico state journalism awards for sports writing.

WRITINGS:

Diamond in the Desert: The Story of the Connie Mack World Series in Farmington, New Mexico, Adina Publishing (Farmington, NM), 2000.

Grand Junction's Juco World Series, Arcadia Publishing (Chicago, IL), 2004.

SIDELIGHTS: Myles Schrag told *CA:* "I have long written and read about sports, but it is only when sports reach emotions and issues beyond the playing field that they become a worthwhile topic. In the case of my book *Diamond in the Desert: The Story of the Connie Mack World Series in Farmington, New Mexico,* baseball provides this community with an identity and, as a result, the community treats the Great American Pastime in a way that is unique and heroic. I hope that books such as this not only showcase a deep love and respect for the game of baseball, but also encourage communities to be proud of their contributions to American society and encourage people to delve into the reasons why sports can be so special. Writers like Frank Deford, Roger Kahn, and Jim Murray long ago discovered those types of stories.

"The future project I am currently working on also uses sports and specific athletes to invite the reader to look at strong personalities and historical context. Of course, like most writers, I have a novel in my head and partially on paper that I hope to get out some day, but I believe the nonfiction disciplines and skills are best suited for me now. Writing allows me to discover, and I hope the result of that writing does the same for the readers."

* * *

SHACKLETON, Ernest Henry 1874-1922

PERSONAL: Born February 15, 1874, in Kilkea, County Kildare, Ireland; died of a heart attack January 5, 1922, near South Georgia Island; son of Henry (a doctor) and Henrietta Letitia (Gavin) Shackleton; married Emily Mary Dorman, 1904; children: Raymond, Cecily, Edward. *Education:* Dulwich College (later part of the University of London).

CAREER: Mariner, explorer, and author. In merchant service, 1890-98, master, 1898; Royal Naval Reserve, sub-lieutenant, 1901; crew member of *Discovery,* expedition to Antarctic, 1901-03; Royal Scottish Geographical Society, secretary, 1904-05; commanded *Nimrod,* expedition the Antarctic, 1907-09; commanded *Endurance* and *Aurora,* expedition across Antarctic, 1914-16; commanded *Quest,* expedition across Antarctic, 1921-22. *Military service:* British Army, North Russian expeditionary force; major, 1918-19.

AWARDS, HONORS: Knighthood, 1909; C.V.O. (Royal Victorian Order), 1909; Order of the British Empire, 1919.

WRITINGS:

Aurora Australis, Joyce and Wild, 1908, reprinted, Bay Books (Sydney, New South Wales, Australia), 1988.

The Heart of the Antarctic; Being the Story of the British Antarctic Expedition 1907-1909, Lippincott (Philadelphia, PA), 1909, reprinted, Carroll & Graf (New York, NY), 1999.

South: The Story of Shackleton's Last Expedition, 1914-1917, Heinemann (London, England), 1919, reprinted as *South: A Memoir of the Endurance Voyage,* Carroll & Graf (New York, NY), 1998.

Shackleton: His Antarctic Writings, edited by Christopher Ralling, Harper & Row (New York, NY), 1986.

Shackleton, the Polar Journeys, Collins Press (Cork, Ireland), 2002.

SIDELIGHTS: Famed explorer of Antarctica, Ernest Henry Shackleton began as a merchant mariner for various shipping lines, and in 1900 found himself assigned to a ship transporting British soldiers to the Boer War in South Africa. On this voyage, he befriended the son of a man helping to finance the National Antarctic Expedition. With this introduction, he returned to England and in short order became part of this expedition, led by Robert Scott, which managed to get within 400 miles of the South Pole. Back in England, he tried his hand at various jobs, including journalism and a stint with the Royal Geographical Society, but it was clear that reaching the South Pole had become Shackleton's true calling.

In 1907 Shackleton organized and led another expedition in which he came within ninety-seven miles of reaching his elusive goal. In *The Heart of the Antarctic: Being the Story of the British Antarctic Expedition, 1907-1909* Shackleton tells the story of this harrowing voyage, from the pack ice that prevented them from reaching their intended landing site through a year and a half of surviving bitterly cold temperatures, injuries, and the threat of starvation. According to a *Library Journal* reviewer, "Just reading this will make your toes fall off." Also on this expedition, Shackleton managed to put together the first book printed in the Polar regions, a collection of his journal entries and contributions by expedition members titled *Aurora Australis.*

In 1909 Shackleton returned to a hero's welcome in England, where he received a knighthood and went on a lecture tour to pay back the voyage's creditors. Before long, he was planning another attempt on the Pole. By August 1914, he was set to go just as World War I broke out. Although he offered to turn over his ship and his men to the British Admiralty, the government declined. However, the mood had changed somewhat. Originally a glorious adventure, Shackleton had begun to sell the journey as a patriotic part of the war effort, even referring to it as "white warfare" in a cable to London. Once again, Shackleton was his own chronicler, this time in *South: The Story of Shackleton's Last Expedition, 1914-1917.* In this memoir, with photographs from expedition member Frank Hurleyhe, Shackleton tells the story of the rough seas, the difficult landing, and the way the ice floes trapped and ultimately crushed the *Endurance,* forcing the expedition to make their way across the ice to Elephant Island, the nearest ice-free land. Leaving most of his party in this remote spot, in April 1916 Shackleton set off with five companions for South Georgia Island, a journey of 800 miles across rough and treacherous seas in a twenty-two-foot boat. Amazingly, the small force made it to South Georgia, and then crossed the unexplored interior to find a Norwegian whaling station on the north coast. After three failed attempts to make it back to Elephant Island, Shackleton finally succeeded in August, rescuing his entire party and bringing them safely to South America. As an *Observer* reviewer wrote, "It's a terrific yarn, and the original photographs are startlingly evocative." A *Washington Post* reviewer concluded, "Shackleton may have been a failed polar explorer, but, unlike [Robert F.] Scott, he was not also a failed leader." In 1922, on yet another Antarctic expedition, Shackleton suffered a heart attack and was buried at a whaling station on South Georgia Island.

Interest in Shackleton has longed survived him. In 1986 Christopher Ralling pulled together some of Shackleton's letters, diaries, and other pieces, including selections from *Heart of the Antarctic; Being the Story of the British Antarctic Expedition 1907-1909* and *South: The Story of Shackleton's Last Expedition, 1914-1917,* and published them as *Shackleton: His Antarctic Writings.* "Aside from the sheer adrenal interest in man-against-nature accounts, *Shackleton* happily boasts sublime passages of Antarctic description that make clear indeed why these explorers were lured back by the siren beauties of the ice world," concluded a *Kirkus Reviews* contributor.

BIOGRAPHICAL AND CRITICAL SOURCES:

BOOKS

Albert, Marvin H., *The Long White Road: Ernest Shackleton's Antarctic Adventures,* McKay (New York, NY), 1957.

Alexander, Caroline, *The Endurance: Shackleton's Legendary Antarctic Expedition,* Knopf (New York, NY), 1998.

Armstrong, Jennifer, *Shipwreck at the Bottom of the World: The Extraordinary True Story of Shackleton and the Endurance,* Crown (New York, NY), 1998.

Armstrong, Jennifer, *Spirit of Endurance,* Crown (New York, NY), 2000.

Baughman, T. H., *Shackleton of the Antarctic,* Eothen Press (Tallahassee, FL), 2002.

Begbie, Harold, *Shackleton, a Memory,* Mills and Boon (London, England), 1922.

Bickel, Lennard, *Shackleton's Forgotten Argonauts,* Macmillan (South Melbourne, Australia), 1982.

Bickel, Lennard, *Shackleton's Forgotten Men: The Untold Tragedy of the Endurance Epic,* Thunder's Mouth Press (New York, NY), 2000.

Bixby, William, *The Impossible Journey of Sir Ernest Shackleton,* Little, Brown (Boston, MA), 1960.

Brown, Michael, *Shackleton's Epic Voyage,* Coward-McCann (New York, NY), 1969.

Calvert, Patricia, *Sir Ernest Shackleton: By Endurance We Conquer,* Benchmark Books (New York, NY), 2003.

Dictionary of National Biography, 1922-1930, Oxford University Press (London, England), 1937.

Encyclopedia of World Biography, 2nd edition, Gale (Detroit, MI), 1998.

Explorers and Discoverers of the World, Gale (Detroit, MI), 1993.

Fisher, Margery Turner, *Shackleton and the Antarctic,* Houghton Mifflin (Boston, MA), 1958.

Great Britons, Oxford University Press (Oxford, England), 1985.

Grosvenor, Charles, *The Forgotten: Dick Richards and Shackleton's Trans-Antarctic Expedition, 1914-1917: A Narrative,* Otterden Press (Pasadena, CA), 2000.

Heacox, Kim, *Shackleton: The Antarctic Challenge,* National Geographic Society (Washington, DC), 1999.

Hooper, Meredith, *The Endurance: Shackleton's Perilous Expedition in Antarctica,* Abbeville Kids (New York, NY), 2001.

Hunford, Roland, *Shackleton,* Atheneum (New York, NY), 1985.

Hurley, Frank, *Shackleton's Argonauts, a Saga of the Antarctic Ice-Packs,* Angus and Robertson (Sydney, Australia), 1948.

Hurley, Frank, *South with Endurance: Shackleton's Antarctic Expedition 1914-1917: The Photographs of Frank Hurley,* Simon & Schuster (New York, NY), 2001.

Hussey, Leonard Duncan Albert, *South with Shackleton,* Low (London, England), 1949.

Kostyal, K. M., *Trial by Ice: A Photobiography of Sir Ernest Shackleton,* National Geographic Society (Washington, DC), 1999.

Kulling, Monica, *Sea of Ice: The Wreck of the Endurance,* Random House (New York, NY), 1999.

Lansing, Alfred, *Endurance: Shackleton's Incredible Voyage,* McGraw-Hill (New York, NY), 1959.

Lansing, Alfred, *Shackleton's Valiant Voyage,* Whittlesy House (New York, NY), 1960.

Marr, J. W. S., *Into the Frozen South,* Funk and Wagnalls (New York, NY), 1923.

Mill, Hugh Robert, *The Life of Sir Ernest Shackleton,* Heinemann (London, England), 1923.

Modern Irish Lives, St. Martin's Press (New York, NY), 1996.

Morrell, Margot, *Shackleton's Way: Leadership Lessons from the Great Antarctic Explorer,* Viking (New York, NY), 2001.

Perkins, Dennis N. T., *Leading at the Edge: Leadership Lessons from the Extraordinary Saga of Shackleton's Antarctic Expedition,* Amacom (New York, NY), 2000.

Shackleton, Jonathan, *Shackleton: An Irishman in Antarctica,* University of Wisconsin Press (Madison, WI), 2002.

Thomson, John, *Shackleton's Captain: A Biography of Frank Worsley,* Hazard Press (Christchurch, New Zealand), 1998.

White, Matt, *Endurance: Shipwreck and Survival on a Sea of Ice,* Capstone Curriculum (Mankato, MN), 2002.

Wild, Frank, *Shackleton's Last Voyage: The Story of the Quest,* Cassell (London, England; New York, NY), 1923.

Worsley, Frank Arthur, *Endurance: An Epic of Polar Adventure,* J. Cape and H. Smith (New York, NY), 1931.

PERIODICALS

Kirkus Reviews, November 1, 1986, review of *Shackleton: His Antarctic Writings,* pp. 1641-42.

Library Journal, November 1, 1999, review of *The Heart of Antarctica,* p. 130.

Observer (London, England), September 29, 1991, review of *South,* p. 61.

Washington Post, September 6, 1998, review of *South,* 12.*

SHEARMAN, John (Kinder Gowran) 1931-2003

OBITUARY NOTICE—See index for *CA* sketch: Born June 24, 1931, in Aldershot, England; died of a heart attack August 11, 2003, near Lethbridge, Alberta, Canada. Art historian, educator, and author. Shearman was a scholar of Renaissance art who helped in the restoration of the Sistine Chapel frescoes by Michelangelo. A graduate of the Courtauld Institute of Art at the University of London, where he received his Ph.D. in 1957, he joined the faculty there as a lecturer after graduation, becoming a professor of art history and director of the department in 1974. He moved on to Princeton in 1979, where he was chair of the Department of Art and Archaeology, and then to Harvard University in 1987, where he was Charles Adams University Professor from 1994 until his retirement in 2002. Shearman was an authority on the art of Michelangelo, da Vinci, Poussin, del Sarto, Raphael, and Bartolomeo. He was also an expert on art restoration, and traveled to Italy in 1966 after a flood in Florence to help repair the art that had been damaged; in the early 1990s, he also worked with the Pontifical Advisory Commission for the Restoration of the Sistine Chapel. As an author, Shearman completed a number of valuable texts about Renaissance art, including *Andrea del Sarto* (1965), *The Early Italian Pictures in the Collection of Her Majesty the Queen* (1983), *Funzione e illusione* (1983), *Only Connect: Art and the Spectator in the Italian Renaissance* (1992), and his last book, *Raphael in Early Modern Sources.*

OBITUARIES AND OTHER SOURCES:

PERIODICALS

Los Angeles Times, August 30, 2003, p. B23.
New York Times, August 29, 2003, p. A21.
Times (London, England), September 8, 2003.
Washington Post, August 30, 2003, p. B23.

* * *

SHERVEN, Judith 1943-

PERSONAL: Born 1943; married James Sniechowski (a therapist).

ADDRESSES: Home—Windham, NY. *Agent*—c/o Author Mail, 175 Fifth Avenue, New York, NY 10010. *E-mail*—jksjes@hotmail.com.

CAREER: Clinical psychologist and psychotherapist. Private practice in psychology, 1978—; Institute for Advanced Training in Experiential Psychotherapy, founder and director, beginning 1981; The Magic of Differences (relationship training and consulting firm), NY, cofounder with husband, James Sniechowski; Westside Gender Reconciliation Workgroup, cofounder. With Sniechowski, conductor of training seminars, workshops, lectures, and corporate consultations; cohost, with husband, of *Wisdom* radio show.

WRITINGS:

WITH HUSBAND, JAMES SNIECHOWSKI

The New Intimacy: Discovering the Magic at the Heart of Your Differences, Health Communications (Deerfield Beach, FL), 1997.
Opening to Love 365 Days a Year, Health Communications (Deerfield Beach, FL), 2000.
Be Loved for Who You Really Are, Renaissance Books (Los Angeles, CA), 2001, published as *Be Loved for Who You Really Are: How the Differences between Men and Women Can Be Turned into the Source of the Very Best Romance You'll Ever Know,* St. Martin's Griffin (New York, NY), 2003.

Coauthor, with Sniechowski, of audiobooks, including *Embracing Intimacy, Breaking through Resistance, Mothering the Girl Within, Fathering the Boy Within, Womanhood: Power, and Identity, Calling Men to Community, Sons and Fathers* (three-tape series), *You Are the Healer, The Healing Power of Relationships,* and *Preventing Domestic Violence.* Coauthor of online column for Wisdom Networks, and of articles for periodicals and Web sites, including *Chinese Women Today, Lightworks, Backlash!, Los Angeles Times,* and *Mensight.*

SIDELIGHTS: Judith Sherven, a clinical psychologist and psychotherapist, met her husband, James Sniechowksi, a doctorate in human behavior, on a blind date. They fell in love, married, and have gone on to rank among the most sought-after and respected husband-and-wife relationship counselors in the United

States. With Sniechowski, Sherven has written three books, produced several cassette tapes, and published numerous articles designed to improve romantic, family, and work-related relationships. She and Sniechowski travel nationally and internationally to hold seminars and workshops based on their published materials, and have been guest experts on hundreds of television and radio shows. "We have actively put ourselves out in the public arena," commented the authors in an online interview with Jenna Glatzer for *Absolute Write.* "We are critical of the relationship experts and books that espouse 'techniques' and 'manipulations' for getting along. Relationships are the building blocks of society. Men and women are all there is to create civilization. How we treat each other, so goes the world!"

The couple's first book, *The New Intimacy,* is based on the idea that "at the heart of the new intimacy is the capacity to consciously open yourself and take in more of who your partner truly is." In the book, Sherven and Sniechowski tell readers that "we live in very challenging times, so we need to have compassion for ourselves. But there is much we can learn to make loving and being loved more rewarding and deeply fulfilling."

Sherven and Sniechowski's second book, *Opening to Love 365 Days a Year,* expands on some of these concepts and promotes strengthening one's ability to accept love every day, no matter what else may be going on in life. "In this book we offer you a delightful daily reminder that love must be continually created and nourished," say the authors. "We cover topics as serious as conflict and finance, as engaging as love notes and surprises. Our central message is: true love can only grow and unfold in mutual respect and value for the differences between people." The book contains many daily affirmations for couples. "Thought-provoking, inspiring and wise, these affirmations are little one-page teachers," explained *PlanetPsych.com* contributor Mike Weaver. Sherven and Sniechowski recognize that, as they comment in *Opening to Love 365 Days a Year,* honest communication is the key: "most people never receive any meaningful training or preparation for enjoyable, effective dating, or for creating a healthy and vital marriage."

In their third book, *Be Loved for Who You Really Are,* Sherven and Sniechowski encourage couples to come to a deeper understanding of each other and to base their relationship on such findings. "When you understand, emotionally and spiritually, the very real and significant fact that the other person, your partner, is truly other-different and distinct from you, in a sense a whole other world—then your relationship is not only grounded in reality, but also has its roots deep into the truth of what love can be and what the two of you can create together," the authors explain in the book. "To be loved for who you really are means to be loved in your wholeness, to be loved for the one-of-a-kind that you truly are. And that is exactly what you must return to the one you love." Sherven and Sniechowski draw on stories from their own marriage to illustrate points throughout their writings, bringing the reader into a deeper understanding not only of what he or she should be doing in a relationship, but of the inner-workings of the authors' relationship. Noting the unique nature of the book, *Library Journal* contributor Margaret Cardwell noted that the book's "narrative tends to have a spiritual, New Age flavor. Love is often personified, and a higher power or spirit is referenced throughout, though no particular doctrine is espoused."

BIOGRAPHICAL AND CRITICAL SOURCES:

BOOKS

Sherven, Judith, and James Sniechowski, *The New Intimacy: Discovering the Magic at the Heart of Your Differences,* Health Communications (Deerfield Beach, FL), 1997.

Sherven, Judith, and James Sniechowski, *Opening to Love 365 Days a Year,* Health Communications (Deerfield Beach, FL), 2000.

Sherven, Judith, and James Sniechowski, *Be Loved for Who You Really Are: How the Differences between Men and Women Can Be Turned into the Source of the Very Best Romance You'll Ever Know,* St. Martin's Griffin (New York, NY), 2003.

PERIODICALS

Library Journal September 15, 2001, Margaret Cardwell, review of *Be Loved for Who You Really Are,* p. 99.

ONLINE

Absolute Write, http://www.absolutewrite.com/ (June 3, 2003), interview with Sherven and Sniechowski.

Book Review, http://www.bookreview.com/ (June 4, 2003), interview with Sherven and Sniechowski.
Lightworks http://www.lightworks.com/ (June 4, 2003), interview with Sherven and Sniechowski.
Mensight Online, http://mensightmagazine.com (June 5, 2003), J. Steven Svoboda, review of *Be Loved For Who You Really Are.*
New Intimacy: Sherven-Sniechowski Web site, http://www.thenewintimacy.com (November 16, 2003).
PlanetPsych.com, http://www.planetpsych.com/ (June 4, 2003), Mike Weaver, review of *Opening to Love 365 Days a Year.*
Wisdom, http://www.wisdomnetworks.com/ (June 3, 2003), column archive.*

* * *

SHERWOOD, Marika 1937-

PERSONAL: Born November 8, 1937, in Budapest, Hungary; British citizen; married Peter Sherwood (divorced); children: Craig. *Ethnicity:* "European." *Politics:* "Anti-racist socialist."

ADDRESSES: Home—Laurier Rd., London NW5 1SG, England. *Office*—University of London, ICS, 28 Russell Sq., London WC1B 5DS, England; fax: 02-07-862-8820. *E-mail*—marikas@sas.au.uk.

CAREER: Historian and writer.

MEMBER: Black and Asian Studies Association (secretary), Black and Asian Archives Working Party (secretary).

WRITINGS:

Many Struggles: West Indian Workers and Service Personnel in Britain, 1939-45, Karia Press (London, England), 1984.
Daniels Ekaste and the African Divides Mission, Savannah Press (Liverpool, England), 1994.
(With Hakim Adi) *The 1945 Manchester Pan-African Congress Revisited,* 3rd edition, New Beacon (London, England), 1995.
(With Bob Rees) *The Black Experience: In the Caribbean and the USA,* Peter Bedrick Books (New York, NY), 1995.
Kwame Nkrumah: The Years Abroad, 1935-1947, Freedom (Legon, Ghana), 1996.
Claudia Jones—A Life in Exile, Lawrence & Wishart (London, England), 2000.
(With Hakim Adi) *Pan-African History: Political Figures from Africa and the Diaspora since 1787,* Routledge (London, England), 2003.

WORK IN PROGRESS: Researching the history/biography of Henry Sylvester Williams.

* * *

SISTER SARAH CLARKE
See CLARKE, Sarah

* * *

SMITH, Danyel 1965?-

PERSONAL: Born c. 1965, in Oakland, CA.

ADDRESSES: Home—Brooklyn, NY. *Agent*—c/o Author Mail, Crown Publishing Group, 299 Park Ave, New York, NY 10171-0002. *E-mail*—me@danyelsmilth.com.

CAREER: Novelist, music critic, and editor. Time, Inc., New York, NY, former editor-at-large; *Vibe* (magazine), New York, NY, editor-in-chief. beginning 1997; New School University, New York, NY, member of adjunct faculty.

AWARDS, HONORS: Residency award, Millay Colony for the Arts, 2003.

WRITINGS:

More like Wrestling, Crown (New York, NY), 2003.

Contributor of music reviews to periodicals, including *Rolling Stone, Cosmopolitan, New York Times, San Francisco Guardian, Village Voice,* and *Spin.*

WORK IN PROGRESS: A second novel.

SIDELIGHTS: Music journalist Danyel Smith's first novel, *More like Wrestling,* focuses on two sisters growing up in Oakland, California, during the 1980s. High school freshman Paige and her younger sister

Pinch have moved away from their mother and their mother's abusive boyfriend, and are determined to make it on their own. Although the responsibility of work and school and being the oldest weighs heavily on Paige, she gains a few close friends, while Pinch remains more withdrawn and cautious about the changing face of their Oakland neighborhood. Taking place over several years and narrated in turn by each of the sisters, the novel follows Paige and Pinch as they learn to rely on each other's strengths and deal with their own weaknesses. Ultimately the drugs and violence that injure their friends and threaten their urban landscape force each of the young women to make the choice whether to succumb to their surroundings or take a risk and strike out on their own someplace new.

Writing in *Booklist,* Vanessa Bush praised *More like Wrestling,* noting that "Smith's poetic writing captures the rhythm and cadence" of the novel's urban setting. Although some critics faulted the novel for its sentimentality, a *Publishers Weekly* contributor praised it as a "rich, idiosyncratic, impressionistic first novel" of two young women coming of age. In an interview posted on the *Sistah Circle Book Club Web site,* Smith stated the message she hoped the novel would impart to readers: "That relationships between women, especially mothers and daughters, are difficult sometimes but ultimately rewarding. That love relationships between men and women are about that 'zing', but are mostly about dealing with someone, building on the partnership so it stays strong when the going is truly rough. Also that Oakland, California, is a wonderful place to grow up. Even when it's not."

In addition to fiction, Smith contributes music reviews to a number of newspapers and magazines, and also teaches a course at New York City's New School University. In the late 1990s she was appointed editor-in-chief of *Vibe,* a top urban-culture magazine founded by musician Quincy Jones in 1992. Raised in California like her fictional protagonists, she now makes her home in Brooklyn, New York.

BIOGRAPHICAL AND CRITICAL SOURCES:

PERIODICALS

Black Issues Book Review, March-April, 2003, Mondella S. Jones, review of *More like Wrestling,* p. 42.

Booklist, November 15, 2002, Vanessa Bush, review of *More like Wrestling,* p. 578.

Kirkus Reviews, October 15, 2002, review of *More like Wrestling,* p. 1501.

Library Journal, January, 2003, David A. Berona, review of *More like Wrestling,* p. 160.

Ms., July-August, 1998, Amy Aronson, interview with Smith, pp. 86-88.

Publishers Weekly, November 11, 2002, review of *More like Wrestling,* p. 40.

ONLINE

Morelikewrestling.com, http://www.morelikewrestling.com (January 29, 2003).

Sisah Circle Book Club Web site, http://www.thesistahcircle.com/ (January 29, 2003), interview with Smith.*

* * *

SOELLE, Dorothee 1929-2003

OBITUARY NOTICE—See index for *CA* sketch: Born September 30, 1929, in Cologne, Germany; died of a heart attack April 27, 2003, in Goppingen, Germany. Theologian, educator, and author. Soelle was a prominent left-wing, feminist theologian known for her stand against Western capitalism and for her books that bridge the gap between Christianity and atheism. After attending universities in Cologne and Freiburg, she earned her Ph.D. from the University of Göttingen in 1954. But because of her personal politics, she had a hard time gaining a university post in West Germany, so she taught religion and German at various schools for six years and then became a research assistant at the Technical University of Aachen. In 1964, she finally was hired into the University of Cologne faculty, where she taught until 1975. During the 1970s she also taught at the University of Main. But Soelle found that her ideas were better received in the United States, so, from 1975 to 1987, she spent six months every year teaching at the liberal Union Theological Seminary in New York City. Soelle, who grew up in a middle-class family during the Nazi era, became disillusioned with the conservative mainstream values that had failed to resist Hitler and embraced Communism

and the underclass instead. She became a popular lecturer and writer during the radical 1960s, railing against materialism and male-dominated churches—her influence is credited by some as making it possible for women to become bishops in Germany—and causing not a little consternation for the Lutheran church to which she belonged. Often making her voice heard on the political scene, she protested against the Vietnam war and made visits to North Vietnam and, later, Nicaragua, where she supported the Sandinistas. More recently, she protested the United States' wars against Afghanistan and Iran. Soelle's writings often focus on what she called the "theology after the death of God" and include such books as *Die Wahrheit ist Konkret* (1967; translated as *The Truth Is Concrete* in 1969), *Politische Theologie: Auseinandersetzung mit Rudolph Bultmann* (1971; translated as *Political Theology* in 1974), *Die Hinreise: Zur Religiösen Erfahrung—Teste und Überlegungen* (1976; translated as *Death by Bread Alone* in 1976), and *To Work and to Love: A Theology of Creation* (1984), which she cowrote with Shirley Cloyes. More recently, she completed the autobiography *Against the Wind* (1995) and *The Silent Cry: Mysticism and Resistance* (1997). She was also the author of several collections of poetry.

OBITUARIES AND OTHER SOURCES:

BOOKS

Encyclopedia of World Biography, second edition, Gale (Detroit, MI), 1998.

Hastings, Adrian, editor, *The Oxford Companion to Christian Thought,* Oxford University Press (New York, NY), 2000.

PERIODICALS

Guardian (London, England), May 10, 2003, p. 25.

Independent (London, England), May 26, 2003, p. 14.

Times (London, England), May 19, 2003.

* * *

SPICCI, Joan

See SABERHAGEN, Joan

SPINDLER, Erica 1957-

PERSONAL: Born 1957, in Rockford, IL; married Nathan Spindler (an advertising executive); children: two sons. *Education:* University of New Orleans, M.F.A.

ADDRESSES: *Office*—P.O. Box 8556, Mandeville, LA 70470. *E-mail*—comments@ericaspindler.com.

CAREER: Writer and artist. Southeastern Louisiana University, teacher in fine arts program.

MEMBER: Romance Writers of America, Mystery Writers of America.

AWARDS, HONORS: Listen-up Award, *Publishers Weekly,* 1999, for audio version of *Shocking Pink;* Daphne du Maurier Award, 2002, for *Stone Cold.*

WRITINGS:

"BLOSSOMS OF THE SOUTH" SERIES

A Winter's Rose, 1992.

Night Jasmine, 1993.

Magnolia Dawn, 1993.

OTHER

Heaven Sent, Silhouette (New York, NY), 1988.

Chances Are, Silhouette (New York, NY), 1989.

Read between the Lines, Silhouette (New York, NY), c. 1989.

Rhyme or Reason, Loveswept (New York, NY), 1990.

Wishing Moon, Loveswept (New York, NY), 1991.

Longer Than, Silhouette (New York, NY), 1991.

Baby Mine, Silhouette (New York, NY), 1992.

Tempting Chance, Loveswept (New York, NY), 1993.

Baby Come Back, Silhouette (New York, NY), 1994.

Slow Heat, Loveswept (New York, NY), 1995.

Red, Mira (New York, NY), 1995.

Forbidden Fruit, Mira (New York, NY), 1996.

Fortune, Mira (New York, NY), 1997.

Shocking Pink, Mira (New York, NY), 1998.

Cause for Alarm, Mira (New York, NY), 1999.

All Fall Down, Mira (New York, NY), 2000.
Bone Cold, Mira (New York, NY), 2001.
Dead Run, Mira (New York, NY), 2002.
In Silence, Mira (New York, NY), 2003.

ADAPTATIONS: Audio version of novels include *Shocking Pink,* read by Eliza Ross (abridged); *Red* was adapted as both a daytime drama and a cartoon strip in Japan.

WORK IN PROGRESS: See Jane Die, forthcoming.

SIDELIGHTS: Erica Spindler was intent on pursuing a career in art and teaching when a twist of fate intervened. In June 1982 she stopped at a drugstore to pick up cold tablets and tissues, and the cashier dropped a romance novel into her bag. Spindler curled up with the book when she arrived home and after six more months of reading romances, she began to write her first. Over the next two decades, Spindler's stories were published at a rate of more than one a year.

Spindler's novels evolved to include themes of abuse, obsession, and murder. *Cause for Alarm* is about a New Orleans couple who adopt the child of a CIA assassin and a teenage girl and the slightly deranged birth mother who intrudes on their life. *All Fall Down* is a psychological thriller in which abused triplet girls grow up to become dysfunctional women. *Bone Cold* takes place in New Orleans and features an abduction, a severed finger, and the murders of red-headed women in the French Quarter. *Romance Reader*'s Karen Lynch called it "a fast-paced psychological thriller with a strong romantic thread that will particularly please fans of romantic suspense." Key West, Florida, is the setting of *Dead Run,* in which one sister looks for another, the vanished pastor of a local church. The story involves a satanic cult, murder, and various evil influences. Spindler's 2003 effort, *In Silence,* is set in Cypress Springs, Louisiana, a small southern town that staunchly resists the cultural changes of the modern world. According to Thea Davis writing for *Romance Reader* online, "Spindler uses what appear to be her favorite themes—friendship, obsession, deviant behavior and murder, to construct a complicated mystery novel."

BIOGRAPHICAL AND CRITICAL SOURCES:

PERIODICALS

Books, autumn, 1999, "Love & Death in the Crescent City" (interview), p. 21.
Kliatt, November, 1998, Bette D. Ammon, review of *Shocking Pink* (audio version) p. 53.
Library Journal, May, 1995, review of *Red,* p. 62.
Publishers Weekly, May 22, 1995, review of *Red,* p. 54; February 17, 1997, review of *Fortune,* p. 217; December 22, 1997, review of *Shocking Pink,* p. 57; January 25, 1999, review of *Cause for Alarm,* p. 93; February 14, 2000, review of *All Fall Down,* p. 179; June 3, 2002, review of *Dead Run,* p. 65; June 2, 2003, review of *In Silence,* p. 34.

ONLINE

All about Romance, http://www.likesbooks.com/ (January 8, 2003), Claudia S. Terrones, review of *Dead Run.*
Erica Spindler Home Page, http://www.ericaspindler.com (April 22, 2003).
Romance Reader, http://www.theromancereader.com/ (November 16, 2003), Thea Davis, review of *Shocking Pink;* Karen Lynch, review of *Bone Cold;* Thea Davis, review of *In Silence.*

* * *

SPINK, Alfred H(enry) 1854(?)-1928

PERSONAL: Born August 24, 1854 (some sources say 1853), in Quebec, Canada; died May 27, 1928, in Chicago, IL; son of William amd Frances (Woodbury) Spink; married.

CAREER: Writer. Founder and editor, *The Sporting News,* 1886; also founder and editor, St. Louis *World;* former editor for Missouri *Chronicle* and St. Louis *Chronicle.* Involved in creation of the American Association baseball league, 1882; secretary and press agent for the St. Louis Browns.

WRITINGS:

The National Game: A History of Baseball, America's Leading Out-Door Sport, From the Time It Was First Played up to the Present Day, with Illustrations and Biographical Sketches of the Great Players Who Helped to Bring the Game into the Prominence It Now Enjoys, National Game Publishing (St. Louis, MO), 1910, 2nd edition, 1911, published as *The National Game,* Southern Illinois University Press (Carbondale, IL), 2000.

Spink Sport Stories: 1,000 Big and Little Ones, 1921.

SIDELIGHTS: Alfred H. Spink is perhaps best known as the founder of *Sporting News* magazine. In addition to his interests in sports journalism, Spink was also involved in the creation, in 1882, of the American Association, the rival to the existing National League baseball league, and he helped found the St. Louis Browns, the city's first major league baseball team.

The *Sporting News* is the oldest sports periodical in existence, and celebrated its centennial anniversary in 1986. It reports a weekly international circulation in excess of 700,000. "From 1886 to 1982 the Spinks—Alfred Henry, his brother Charles Claude, his nephew John George Taylor and his great nephew Charles Claude Johnson—were synonymous with sports publishing," commented Lowell Reidenbaugh in the *Sporting News.* "From a struggling, eight-page weekly in the late 19th century, they built an ever-widening publishing empire that includes *The Sporting Goods Dealer,* a trade monthly, plus numerous baseball, football, basketball and hockey annuals." The Spinks' dynasty ended in 1977 when Charles C. Spink sold the magazine to Times Mirror.

Spink's *The National Game* is among the first comprehensive histories of baseball. First published in 1910, but out of print after its second edition was published in 1911, it was reprinted in 2000 by Southern Illinois University Press. *The National Game* includes a history of the game before 1910, and biographical portraits of the major players who helped to bring the game to prominence in the early twentieth century. In addition to *The National Game,* Spink also published *Spink Sport Stories: 1,000 Big and Little Ones* in 1921. Spink died in 1928.

BIOGRAPHICAL AND CRITICAL SOURCES:

PERIODICALS

Sporting News, January 23, 1982, Lowell Reidenbaugh, "Saga of the Spink Family: A Rich Publishing Heritage," pp. 24-27, 31-32; February 28, 1986, Lowell Reidenbaugh, "A Boys Game and a Man's Dream," pp. 16-22, 26-30, 32, 34-36, 38, 40-48, 53.*

STELLA, Carmelo 1956-
(Charlie Stella)

PERSONAL: Born June 1, 1956, in New York, NY; married; wife's name Ann Marie; children: (first marriage) Nicole; (third marriage) Charles, Dustin. *Education:* Attended Minot State College and Hofstra University; Brooklyn College, B.A. (political science), 1982.

ADDRESSES: Home—New Jersey. *Agent*—c/o Carroll & Graf Publishers, 245 West 17th St., 11th Floor, New York, NY 10011-5300.

CAREER: Writer. Worked as a football coach, window cleaner, and word processor.

AWARDS, HONORS: Eugene Schneider Memorial Short-Story Award; Abraham Kraditor Memorial Award for Political Science, Brooklyn College, 1982.

WRITINGS:

Eddie's World, Carroll & Graf Publishers (New York, NY), 2001.

Jimmy Bench-Press, Carroll & Graf Publishers (New York, NY), 2002.

Charlie Opera, Carroll & Graf Publishers (New York, NY), 2003.

Author of several plays, including *Coffee Wagon, Mr. Ronnie's Confession,* and *Double or Nothing.*

SIDELIGHTS: Carmelo "Charlie" Stella grew up in Brooklyn, New York, and the city's street life serves as the milieu for his writings. Stella played football in high school and attended Minot State College in North Dakota on a football scholarship. His greatest influence at Minot, however, was Dave Gresham, the English teacher who sparked his interest in literature and writing. Stella also attended Hofstra University in New Jersey, where he won a short-story writing award, but did not earn a degree. It was not until later, while he was washing windows and coaching football, that he decided to return to school and ultimately graduated from Brooklyn College. He worked as a word processor and then became what he describes as a "street guy." It is from these nearly two decades of associating with small-time operators and gamblers that Stella draws in writing his fiction.

Library Journal's Craig L. Shufelt wrote that "despite a slow start, Stella's debut picks up enough steam to distinguish itself from the scores of other crime novels." In *Eddie's World* protagonist Eddie Senta, like Stella, works as a word processor and is the author of a book. Eddie is also a bookie with a history, and he is heading into a mid-life crisis. His much-younger wife wants to have a baby, and he is struggling in trying to parent his teenage son. He could buy a Corvette, but he decides instead to take part in one last burglary, for kicks and the quick score, but also to help his friend Tommy Gaetani. The supposedly easy job gets messy: Tommy winds up dead, and Eddie, who is suspected of a triple murder, is chased by the police, the real killer, and the FBI. "Stella throws in Russian mobsters, ex-cons, federal agents, Mafia figures, local cops and gangbangers, all of whom convulse Eddie's world," wrote a *Publishers Weekly* reviewer.

In reviewing the book for *Romantic Times* online, Toby Bromberg called it "a fast-paced novel peopled with quirky characters." A *Kirkus Reviews* contributor noted that *Eddie's World* is "fresh, fast, and darkly funny. A sure-footed debut from a writer with a spare, no-nonsense prose style who can make you like characters you think you shouldn't."

BIOGRAPHICAL AND CRITICAL SOURCES:

PERIODICALS

Kirkus Reviews, October 15, 2001, review of *Eddie's World,* p. 1458; September 15, 2002, review of *Jimmy Bench-Press,* p. 1357.

Library Journal, November 15, 2001, Craig L. Shufelt, review of *Eddie's World,* p. 98; November 15, 2002, Craig L. Shufelt, review of *Jimmy Bench-Press,* p. 103.

Publishers Weekly, November 5, 2001, review of *Eddie's World,* p. 43; October 28, 2002, review of *Jimmy Bench-Press,* p. 54.

ONLINE

Charlie Stella Web site, http://www.charliestella.com (April 27, 2002).

Romantic Times, http://www.romantictimes.com/ (April 27, 2002), Toby Bromberg, review of *Eddie's World.**

* * *

STELLA, Charlie
See STELLA, Carmelo

* * *

STEPANEK, Matthew J(oseph) T(haddeus) 1990-
(Mattie J. T. Stepanek)

PERSONAL: Born July 17, 1990, in Washington, DC; son of Gregory and Jeni Stepanek.

ADDRESSES: Agent—c/o VSP Books, P.O. Box 17011, Alexandria, VA 22302.

CAREER: Poet and illustrator.

AWARDS, HONORS: Melinda Lawrence International Book Award for inspirational written works, Children's Hospice International, 1999; Muscular Dystrophy Association, Maryland State Goodwill Ambassador, and 2002 National Goodwill Ambassador.

WRITINGS:

Heartsongs, VSP Books/Hyperion (New York, NY), 2001.

Journey through Heartsongs, VSP Books/Hyperion (New York, NY), 2001.

Hope through Heartsongs, VSP Books/Hyperion (New York, NY), 2002.

(And illustrator) *Celebrate through Heartsongs,* Hyperion (New York, NY), 2002.

(And illustrator) *Loving through Heartsongs,* VSP Books/Hyperion (New York, NY), 2003.

Also wrote lyrics for CD-ROM *Music through Heartsongs,* sung by Billy Gilman.

WORK IN PROGRESS: Believing through Heartsongs and *Heartsongs for All Seasons.*

SIDELIGHTS: Matthew "Mattie" J. T. Stepanek suffers from dysautonomic mitochondrial myopathy, a rare form of muscular dystrophy inherited from his mother that also took the lives of two brothers and a sister—all of whom died before they were four years old. His mother, who has the adult form of the disease, teaches him at home, and he was studying at a high-school level when he was eleven. Stepanek breathes with a tracheotomy tube and a ventilator that is attached to his wheelchair, and his prognosis is uncertain. What is certain is the impact he has made with his books of poetry.

Stepanek started writing at the age of three, after the death of his brother Jamie. At that time, he had three wishes—to meet his hero Jimmy Carter, to publish his poetry, and to appear on *The Oprah Winfrey Show*. He not only met Carter, but the former president wrote the foreword for his second collection, *Journey through Heartsongs.*

When he was in the Children's Hospital in Washington, D.C., Stepanek met volunteer Cheryl Barnes, who, with her husband, had begun VSP Books, a small press in Alexandria, Virginia, in 1992. Stepanek's second wish was granted through Barnes, who printed 200 copies of his first collection, *Heartsongs,* which consists of twenty-eight pages written when Stepanek was between three and six years old. In less than one hour, all of the copies were bought by friends, family, and supporters at a book party in the hospital. After a profile of Stepanek appeared in the *Washington Post* and Oprah Winfrey learned of his wish to meet her, sales of his books exceeded all expectations. Winfrey dedicated an entire show to Stepanek after the publication of his second book, *Journey through Heartsongs,* which contains poems Stepanek wrote from ages six through ten. Winfrey said, "If ever I had a book to recommend, it's Mattie's. If ever you were going to buy a book, I recommend it; this is the one, my friends." Stepanek has also been interviewed by *Good Morning America* and National Public Radio.

Publishers Weekly writer Charlotte Abbott quoted Stepanek's publisher, who commented that "people have been buying four and five copies of his book at signings, saying, 'this is my Christmas gift this year.' . . . It has to do with September 11. People are saying, 'if this child can have this type of spirit in the position he's in, we can get through this.'" A *People* contributor called Stepanek's poems "plaintive reflections on spirituality and mortality."

Sarah Baxter also referenced the September 11, 2001, attack on America in a London *Sunday Times* article, saying that, since then, "poetry has been a popular source of solace for Americans. . . . Stepanek's touching verse, with its optimistic self-help message, has captured the mood of the moment. He describes his life's philosophy as 'to play after every storm.'" Publisher Barnes was so swamped with orders for Stepanek's books that she had her printer ship them directly from the plant. In less than a year the first two volumes sold half a million copies and shot to the top of the bestseller lists. In December 2001, Barnes partnered with Hyperion in order to meet the demand.

Interviewing Stepanek for *U.S. News & World Report*, Holly J. Morris asked him his meaning of "heartsong," which is the title of his first collection and is contained in the titles of his others. He responded, "What God gives us as a purpose—we could some of us turn out to be president of an organization, some of us feel our purpose is to be a waitress—but no matter, we all have our heartsong, and what we choose to do with it." *Teen People*'s Andrea Sachs noted that "Mattie's health problems have given him a unique appreciation for life—and death—which is why he writes about angels and God and is a fierce champion of world peace." Kathryn Hoffman wrote in *Time for Kids* that "although much of what he writes about is sad, Mattie's message is one of hope."

BIOGRAPHICAL AND CRITICAL SOURCES:

PERIODICALS

New York Times, November 29, 2001, Martin Arnold, "Pluck and Publicity Elevate a Young Poet," p. E1; December 10, 2001, David D. Kirkpatrick, "Hyperion Signs a Best-Selling, if Young, Poet," p. C9.

O, November, 2002, Oprah Winfrey, interview with Stepanek, p. 188.

People, January 14, 2002, "Words of Courage: Mattie Stepanek, Eleven, Turns a Tragic Illness into Poetry—and Two Bestsellers," p. 105.

Publishers Weekly, November 19, 2001, Charlotte Abbott, "Three Wishes Make a Bestseller: With Two Books on the *Times* List, an Eleven-Year-Old Poet Puts VSP Books on the Map," p. 28; January 28, 2002, "Handsprings for *Heartsongs,*" p. 141.

School Library Journal, August, 2002, Karen Sokol, review of *Hope through Heartsongs,* p. 224.

Sunday Times (London, England), January 27, 2002, Sarah Baxter, "America Takes Poems of Tragic Child to Its Heart," p. 24.

Teen People, May 1, 2002, Andrea Sachs, "Hot Property: Mattie Stepanek's Deadly Illness Hasn't Stopped Him from Writing Best-selling Poetry Books," p. 132.

Time for Kids, January 25, 2002, Kathryn Hoffman, "Poems from the Heart: A Young Writer Offers Words of Hope," p. 7.

U.S. News & World Report, November 26, 2001, Holly J. Morris, "Remembering to Play after the Storm" (interview), p. 8.*

ONLINE

Mattie J.T. Stepanek Home Page, http://www.mattieonline.com (January, 2004).

* * *

STEPANEK, Mattie J. T.
See STEPANEK, Matthew J(oseph) T(haddeus)

* * *

STEPHENSON, Hugh 1938-

PERSONAL: Born July 18, 1938, in India; son of Sir Hugh and Lady Stephenson; married Auriol Stevens, 1962 (divorced, 1987); married Diana Eden, 1990; children: (first marriage) two sons, one daughter. *Education:* Attended Winchester College; New College, Oxford, B.A.; attended University of California, Berkeley.

ADDRESSES: *Office*—Department of Journalism, City University, Northampton Square, London EC1V 0HB, England. *E-mail*—h.stephenson@city.ac.uk.

CAREER: Journalist and educator. Oxford Union, president, 1962; served in diplomatic service, London, England, and Bonn, Germany, 1964-68; *Times,* London, 1969-81, editor of *Times Business News,* 1971-81; *New Statesman,* London, editor, 1982-86; City University, London, professor of journalism, 1986—. London Borough of Wandsworth, councillor, 1971-78; History Today, Ltd., director, 1981—.

WRITINGS:

The Coming Clash: The Impact of Multinational Corporations on the Nation State, Weidenfeld and Nicolson (London, England), 1972, published as *The Impact of Multinational Corporations on National States,* Saturday Review Press (New York, NY), 1973.

Mrs. Thatcher's First Year, J. Norman (London, England), 1980.

Claret and Chips: The Rise of the SDP, M. Joseph (London, England), 1982.

(With others) *Libel and the Media: The Chilling Effect,* Clarendon (Oxford, England), 1997.

(Editor, with Michael Bromley) *Sex, Lies, and Democracy: The Press and the Public,* Longman (New York, NY), 1998.

(Editor) *Media Voices: The James Cameron Memorial Lectures,* Politico's (London, England), 2001.

SIDELIGHTS: British journalist and professor of journalism Hugh Stephenson wrote his first book, a critique of globalism titled *The Coming Clash: The Impact of Multinational Corporations on the Nation State,* in the early 1970s, when he was a reporter for the London *Times.* A *Saturday Review* contributor, who called this a "carefully researched, objective book," noted Stephenson's prediction that unless international regulations are put in place to regulate banking, taxation, and antitrust matters, "individual nations may well lose their economic sovereignty, as well as control of other political and social changes that are bound to follow."

Claret and Chips: The Rise of the SDP is a study of the founding of the Social Democratic Party in 1981. Bernard Crick, who reviewed the book in the *Times Educational Supplement,* wrote that "the judgements of this book are balanced and shrewd, and it will be of use to future historians (limited only by its inability to disclose its sources)." Crick called Stephenson's tone one of "dry and respectful curiosity. It is good to see that an editor can be a true reporter, showing hard graft and self-restraint rather than the flash opinionating of the born columnist or sketch writer."

Stephenson is editor, with Michael Bromley, of *Sex, Lies, and Democracy: The Press and the Public,* a collection of commentary by authors from the United Kingdom, United States, France, and Germany on the state of British journalism. In reviewing the volume in *Contemporary Review,* George Evans wrote that "the national and international media academics who contribute to this critical wide-ranging study of the British press leave no room for doubt about the depth and extent of public resentment caused by press intrusion and the invasion of privacy, particularly Royal privacy. Though it lays most of the blame on the popular tabloid papers, the so-called qualities or broadsheets also earn their share of it for adopting tabloid values themselves." *Times Higher Education Supplement* reviewer Nick Couldry said that "this is clearly an area where debate is needed, and this collection will be of use to journalism students."

Media Voices: The James Cameron Memorial Lectures is a collection of lectures about the media arranged by the London *Guardian* as a memorial to journalist James Cameron, who died in 1985. Every lecture is here, with the exception of one given by Studs Terkel, who used no notes. *Times Literary Supplement* contributor Michael Davie commented that editor Stephenson "notes that one dominant theme coming out of the lectures is the running tension between the protection of privacy and the freedom of the press."

BIOGRAPHICAL AND CRITICAL SOURCES:

PERIODICALS

Contemporary Review, December, 1998, George Evans, review of *Sex, Lies, and Democracy: The Press and the Public,* p. 323.

London Review of Books, October 21, 1982, Peter Clarke, review of *Claret and Chips: The Rise of the SDP,* pp. 3-5.

Saturday Review, March 17, 1973, review of *The Coming Clash: The Impact of Multinational Corporations on the Nation State,* p. 86.

Spectator, August 26, 1972, Patrick Cosgrave, review of *The Coming Clash,* p. 324; September 25, 1982, Peter Paterson, review of *Claret and Chips,* p. 24.

Times Educational Supplement, November 12, 1982, Bernard Crick, review of *Claret and Chips,* p. 22.

Times Higher Education Supplement, November 5, 1999, Nick Couldry, review of *Sex, Lies, and Democracy,* p. 28.

Times Literary Supplement, May 24, 2002, Michael Davie, review of *Media Voices,* p. 27.*

* * *

STERN, Theresa
See HELL, Richard

* * *

STOCK, Francine 1958-

PERSONAL: Born 1958; married Robert Lance Hughes; children: Rebecca, Eleanor. *Education:* Jesus College, Oxford, B.A. (modern languages).

ADDRESSES: *Home*—London, England. *Agent*—c/o Author Mail, Chatto and Windus/Viking Penguin UK, 80 Strand, London WC2R ORL, England.

CAREER: Broadcaster and writer. *Petroleum Economist,* staff writer; BBC, London, England, producer, reporter, and presenter, 1983—.

WRITINGS:

A Foreign Country, Chatto & Windus (London, England), 1999.

Man-made Fibre, Chatto & Windus (London, England), 2002.

SIDELIGHTS: A veteran producer and reporter for the British Broadcasting Corporation (BBC), Francine Stock did not realize her ambition to write a novel until she was diagnosed with advanced breast cancer just five months after the birth of her second daughter. Her hospitalization and treatment forced her to decide what was really important to her—and it gave her time away from her broadcasting responsibilities to complete the novel she had always wanted to write. Abandoning the nonfiction book she had been working on for several months, she instead focused on her first novel, *A Foreign Country.*

The book interweaves the stories of seventy-four-year-old Daphne and her two adult sons, one of whom is working on a documentary about troubles in a former

Soviet republic. As a young woman during World War II, Daphne had worked for a government department responsible for interning Italian civilians in Britain. Daphne determined who among this group might pose security risks, and the unforeseen consequences of her decisions still trouble her. Ophelia Field in the *Times Literary Supplement* appreciated Stock's handling of this subject matter, pointing out that "the novel is not . . . a simple study of xenophobic alarmism" but a thoughtful exploration of the moral ambiguities created by war. These complexities, Field observed, have parallels in the television culture where Daphne's son works, where careers are made on the exploitation of human suffering.

Field hailed *A Foreign Country* as a "novel of rare moral intelligence" that "is, above all, a study of how far we can know other people, even those closest to us." Stock told *Guardian* interviewer Stephen Moss: "I don't think it's a brilliant book. But I think it's an interesting one. I surprised myself while I was writing it because I realized this was what I really liked doing." Stock added that she enjoys the ambiguity that fiction creates. "I don't like the way in journalism that you have to decide what you think about something immediately," she explained. "There are some things that just can't be expressed in terms of a string of abstract nouns, and there are some things that can only be expressed by describing the way someone moves their hands."

Stock's second novel is a satirical look at the newly suburbanizing culture of the 1950s. Its title, *Man-made Fibre,* refers to the perfect substance that industrial chemist Alan hopes to create at his new lab in America. Meanwhile, back in England, his wife Patsy is left with their three children and her own loneliness. As Alan entertains bizarre dreams of modern technological utopias, including robot workers, underwater hotels, and jet-powered taxis, Patsy is tempted into the arms of another man and becomes increasingly distressed by the course her life is taking. Eventually, she joins Alan in the States, but Alan has discovered that his miracle fiber retains an unpleasant human odor that he can't eliminate. *New Statesman* contributor Katie Owen concluded that "in the end, one wonders what the point is of venturing on to such well-trodden ground," but she enjoyed the novel's ironies and its light touch, and found the center of the book to be "quite compelling reading."

BIOGRAPHICAL AND CRITICAL SOURCES:

PERIODICALS

Guardian, March 8, 1999, Stephen Moss, "Francine Stock: Break in Transmission."

Independent, April 7, 1997, Ann Treneman, "Alive and Presenting," pp. M4-M5.

New Statesman, August 12, 2002, Katie Owen, review of *Man-made Fibre,* p. 39.

Observer (London, England), April 16, 2000, Claudia Pugh-Thomas, review of *A Foreign Country,* p. 14.

Times Literary Supplement, March 19, 1999, Ophelia Field, review of *A Foreign Country,* p. 23; July 26, 2002, Alex Clark, review of *Man-made Fibre,* p. 21.

ONLINE

BBC Web site, http://www.bbc.co.uk/ (April 9, 2003), "Francine Stock."*

* * *

STONE, Richard

PERSONAL: Male; married; wife's name Mutsumi. *Education:* Graduated from Cornell University.

ADDRESSES: Home—Washington, DC. *Agent*—Kerry Nugent-Wells, The Garamond Agency Inc., 12 Horton St., Newburyport, MA 01950. *E-mail*—rstone@science-int.co.uk.

CAREER: Science journalist. *Science* magazine, European news editor.

AWARDS, HONORS: Evert Clark Award for science journalism, 1995; Walter Sullivan Award, American Geophysical Union, 2001, for "Vostok: Looking for Life beneath an Antarctic Glacier."

WRITINGS:

Mammoth: The Resurrection of an Ice Age Giant, Perseus Publishing (Cambridge, MA), 2001.

Contributor to periodicals, including *Discover, Moscow Times, Smithsonian,* and *Washington Post.*

SIDELIGHTS: Two expeditions to Siberia to study the remains of a frozen woolly mammoth provide the basis for Richard Stone's book *Mammoth: The Resurrection of an Ice Age Giant.* Stone, an award-winning science journalist and European news editor of *Science,* accompanied researchers and a team from the Discovery Channel when they traveled to the Taimyr peninsula in 1999 and airlifted the carcass of a woolly mammoth, still encased in twenty-three tons of permafrost, to a special refrigerated facility. Workers with a second expedition focused on gradually thawing the animal's body so that tissue samples could be studied. One goal was the extraction of sperm cells that could be used to regenerate the species.

Stone told *Salon.com* interviewer Katharine Mieszkowski that he believes "we could see a cloned mammoth within a generation, within twenty years." The mammoth DNA scientists currently have is broken. With improvements in technology, however, it would be possible to repair the damaged DNA and "essentially stitch together an entire mammoth genome to clone." But Stone also explained that cloning a mammoth would pose significant risks. Mammoths may have been hosts for unknown diseases that could affect humans or other animals. Also, cloned animals may encounter serious medical problems. "You might create these really pathetic, miserable creatures," he added. "Talk about a denouement. All the excitement would really be gone. And all this dream of having mammoths roaming the earth would not happen."

Critics found the book exciting and thought-provoking. Catherine Badgley in *Quarterly Review of Biology* described it as "part travelogue, part history of Siberian mammoth discoveries going back 200 years, and part review of the theories about Late Pleistocene extinction." Yet Badgley also found that "adventure, novelty, fame, and fortune outweigh science" in Stone's account. *Times Literary Supplement* writer Ian Tattersall also noted the book's "heroic" appeal as a story of a "quixotic quest" against harsh elements, bureaucratic difficulties, political corruption, and tribal superstitions. A reviewer for *Publishers Weekly* considered *Mammoth* "sometimes digressive and overly detailed," but nevertheless a "provocative look at the world of today's mammoth hunters." In *Wilson Quarterly,* Ann Finkbeiner wrote, "The book's science is beautifully clear, the expedition leaders are obviously nuts, and those mammoths are lovely to think about."

BIOGRAPHICAL AND CRITICAL SOURCES:

PERIODICALS

Antiquity, December, 2001, N. James and Simon Stoddart, review of *Mammoth: The Resurrection of an Ice Age Giant,* p. 878.

Booklist, August, 2001, Nancy Bent, review of *Mammoth,* p. 2066.

Library Journal, September 1, 2001, Gloria Maxwell, review of *Mammoth,* p. 221.

Publishers Weekly, September 24, 2001, review of *Mammoth,* p. 82.

Quarterly Review of Biology, June, 2002, Catherine Badgley, review of *Mammoth,* pp. 192-193.

Science News, October 26, 2002, review of *Mammoth,* p. 271.

Times Literary Supplement, August 2, 2002, Ian Tattersall, review of *Mammoth,* p. 3.

Wilson Quarterly, autumn, 2001, Ann Finkbeiner, review of *Mammoth,* p. 154.

ONLINE

Book Sense, http://www.booksense.com/ (January 23, 2004), Richard Stone, "In Search of the Mammoth."

Mammoth Home Page, http://www.nasw.org/users/rstone (January 23, 2004).

Salon.com, http://www.salon.com/ (January 3, 2002), Katharine Mieszkowski, interview with Stone.*

* * *

STONE, Tom

PERSONAL: Male; divorced; children: Sara, Matt. *Education:* Yale University, graduated, 1958.

ADDRESSES: Home—Santa Monica, CA. *Agent*—c/o Author Mail, Simon & Schuster, 1230 Avenue of the Americas, New York, NY 10020. *E-mail*—tom@tomstonestaverna.com.

CAREER: Writer. Worked as a stage manager and assistant director on Broadway and as a screenwriter in Hollywood, CA.

WRITINGS:

Tom Stone's Greek Handbook: An A-Z Phrasal Guide to Almost Everything You Want to Know about Greece (and Are Sometimes Afraid to Ask), illustrated by Scotty Mitchell, Lycabettus Press (Athens, Greece), 1982.

Greek-English, English-Greek Dictionary and Phrasebook, Hippocrene Books (New York, NY), 1998.

Greece: An Illustrated History, Hippocrene Books (New York, NY), 2000.

The Summer of My Greek Taverna (memoir), Simon & Schuster (New York, NY), 2002.

ADAPTATIONS: The Summer of My Greek Taverna was adapted for audio, read by Lloyd James (unabridged; six cassettes), Blackstone Audiobooks, 2002.

SIDELIGHTS: Tom Stone traded Broadway for the Greek island of Patmos, where St. John is said to have received the Book of Revelation. Stone stayed for more than two decades to write, and to fall in love with a beautiful French artist he calls Danielle in his memoir, *The Summer of My Greek Taverna.* An *Authorlink* writer called it "as much a love story as it is the grand, humorous, and sometimes bittersweet adventure of an American pursuing his dreams in a foreign land, a modern-day innocent abroad."

Stone and his wife move to Crete, where he supports his family with a job as an English-language teacher. His chance to return to his beloved Patmos comes with an offer from Theo, owner of a seaside tavern called The Beautiful Helen. Stone is an accomplished amateur chef, and Theo offers him a split of the profits if he will make an investment in the business and do the cooking. His wife, who has reservations, reminds Stone that Theo's nickname means "the oily one."

And oily he is as he avoids doing any of the work, leaving Stone to not only cook, but wait tables, and work twenty-hour days during the busy tourist season when fisherman come in early and visitors stay late into the night. Word of Stone's fine cooking spreads, and yachts dock in the harbor so that their owners can sample his specialties. Although his financial return for all his hard work was to come in August, Theo was siphoning off the profits and Stone ultimately loses all of his investment.

Smithsonian reviewer Dan Akst wrote that "in the end, though, his loss is our gain. . . . The taverna may have cost him some cash and even more illusions, but the experience has yielded a colorful and richly observed memoir."

Stone includes some of his favorite recipes, including traditional tzatzika, moussaka, and his own chicken Retsina. Willard Manus reviewed *The Summer of My Greek Taverna* for *Lively Arts* online, saying that it "is a worthy book: beautifully written, vibrant with humor, humanity, and truth, one of the finest documents of Greek island life on the market today."

BIOGRAPHICAL AND CRITICAL SOURCES:

BOOKS

Stone, Tom, *The Summer of My Greek Taverna,* Simon & Schuster (New York, NY), 2002.

PERIODICALS

Booklist, July, 2002, Mark Knoblauch, review of *The Summer of My Greek Taverna,* p. 1816.

Kirkus Reviews, May 1, 2002, review of *The Summer of My Greek Taverna,* p. 643.

New York Times Book Review, August 18, 2002, Jillian Dunham, review of *The Summer of My Greek Taverna,* p. 21.

Publishers Weekly, June 3, 2002, review of *The Summer of My Greek Taverna,* p. 78; October 7, 2002, review of *The Summer of My Greek Taverna,* p. 37.

Smithsonian, September, 2002, Dan Akst, review of *The Summer of My Greek Taverna.*

ONLINE

Authorlink, http://www.authorlink.com/ (January 8, 2003), review of *The Summer of My Greek Taverna.*

Lively Arts, http://www.lively-arts.com/ (January 8, 2003), Willard Manus, review of *The Summer of My Greek Taverna.*

Sydney Morning Herald, http://www.smh.com.au/ (November 23, 2002), Judith Armstrong, review of *The Summer of My Greek Taverna.*

Tom Stone Taverna (author Web site), http://www.tomstonestaverna.com (November 16, 2003).*

* * *

STRAVITZ, David 1940-

PERSONAL: Born 1940.

ADDRESSES: *Home*—New York, NY. *Agent*—c/o Author Mail, Princeton Architectural Press, 37 East Seventh St., New York, NY 10003.

CAREER: Designer and product developer, photographer, and author.

WRITINGS:

The Chrysler Building: Creating a New York Icon, Day by Day, introduction by Christopher Gray, Princeton Architectural Press (New York, NY), 2002.

SIDELIGHTS: A designer and product developer who holds more than 100 patents and 400 copyrights, David Stravitz is also a photography aficionado. In 1979 Stravitz met with a retiring photographer who was selling all of his equipment. As he decided on what he wanted to buy, Stravitz came across a box in a corner of the studio. Full of eight-by-ten negatives that were being scrapped for their silver content, Stravitz held a few up to the light and discovered that they were a chronicle of the construction of one of New York City's most famous architectural landmarks, the Chrysler Building. Stravitz bought the entire box of negatives and then held on to them for the next twenty years before assembling many of them in his book *The Chrysler Building: Creating a New York Icon, Day by Day.*

Most of the photos that appear in *The Chrysler Building* were taken by Peyser & Patzig, a prominent commercial and industrial photographic firm of the time. The firm took the photos with a large-format camera like the ones used by Ansel Adams for many of his famous shots of national parks. "The detail is magnificent," Stravitz observed in the *Library Journal.* In fact, the photographs appear just as they were taken, cleaned up a bit for dust and fingerprints but without the use of computerized digital enhancement. In addition to providing a chronicle of the building's construction—starting with the destruction of the building that once stood on the lot—and interior design, the photographs also inadvertently capture the day-to-day life going on in the city's streets. The Chrysler Building, which many consider to be the epitome of the Art Deco architectural style, was completed in 1930. In addition to a preface and some brief descriptions of the photographs in the back pages, the book includes an introduction by *New York Times* architectural writer Christopher Gay.

Some reviewers, such as Carolyn Kuebler writing in the *Library Journal,* criticized the book's lack of text. "A more thorough text would have given the volume further value," said Kuebler. However, David Middleton noted in *January* online that "the book is mercifully free of pages and pages of uninterrupted text and the photographs are unencumbered by subtitles (except for those which appeared on the original negative). The reader gets to experience the erection of the building almost the way any New Yorker in 1929 would have."

For many reviewers, the highlight of the book was not the construction process itself or the first images of the building's marvelous Art Deco design. Rather, they found the glimpse of life in New York City eighty years ago amidst the Great Depression to be the collection's most intriguing aspect. Calling the "more 'architectural' photos . . . pretty dull," Rupert Loydell, writing in *Tangents,* noted that "it's the wider picture that intrigues." Martin Filler wrote in the *New York Times Book Review,* "Gritty street scenes straight out of Depression Era movies underscore the stark contrast between the dazzling new tower and the tough lives of those who pounded the pavements below."

BIOGRAPHICAL AND CRITICAL SOURCES:

PERIODICALS

Booklist, October 1, 2002, Donna Seaman, review of *The Chrysler Building: Creating a New York Icon, Day by Day,* p. 295.

Library Journal, September 1, 2002, p. 48; November 1, 2002, Carolyn Kuebler, review of *The Chrysler Building,* pp. 87-88.

New York Times Book Review, December 8, 2002, Martin Filler, review of *The Chrysler Building,* p. 40.

Publishers Weekly, October 21, 2002, review of *The Chrysler Building,* p. 66.

ONLINE

January, http://www.januarymagazine.com/ (January 29, 2003), David Middleton, review of *The Chrysler Building: Creating a New York Icon, Day by Day.*

Tangents, http://www.tangents.co.uk/ (January 29, 2003), Rupert Loydell, review of *The Chrysler Building.**

* * *

STROM, Dao 1973-

PERSONAL: Born 1973, in Saigon (now Ho Chi Mihn City), South Vietnam; daughter of a writer and journalist. *Education:* Attended Iowa Writers' Workshop.

ADDRESSES: *Home*—Austin, TX. *Agent*—c/o Author Mail, Houghton Mifflin, 222 Berkeley, Boston, MA 02116-3764.

CAREER: Novelist and author of short fiction.

AWARDS, HONORS: James Michener fellowship; *Chicago Tribune* Nelson Algren award; recipient of several grants.

WRITINGS:

Grass Roof, Tin Roof, Houghton Mifflin (Boston, MA), 2003.

Contributor of short fiction to *Chicago Tribune* and to literary magazines and anthologies.

SIDELIGHTS: First-time novelist Dao Strom was born in Saigon, South Vietnam, in 1973, but was taken to the United States two years later when her mother fled the country. Her father stayed in Vietnam and was later incarcerated by the communist regime. In Strom's 2003 novel *Grass Roof, Tin Roof,* she fictionalizes the experiences of her mother, a noted Vietnamese journalist who, forced to flee her native land, finds a new family and faces a new set of challenges in the United States. Praising the author for her "spare, matter-of-fact prose," a *Publishers Weekly* contributor noted that, despite a slowing in the novel's narrative pace and a confusing story line, "Strom shows promise."

Grass Roof, Tin Roof fictionalizes not only the life of Strom's mother, but its author's own experiences as a child of the Vietnam War coming of age in 1980s America. In the novel, Trinh Ahn Tran finds her outspoken newspaper columns soon attract the attention of the Vietnamese government, and she decides to leave her husband and job behind her when the chance to take her two young children on board a U.S. airlift is offered her. Although no longer threatened by the government, Trinh finds a new source of worry in her second husband, a cold-hearted Dane who marries her shortly after her arrival in Sacramento, California. Strom's novel incorporates multiple points of view, and the story eventually shifts from that of the mother to the experiences of the children, Thuy, Thien, and Beth, as they grow up in a new culture and deal with an abusive father who is left to raise the children on his own after Trinh's death from tuberculosis. Calling *Grass Roof, Tin Roof* "unusually fragmented . . . [but] always engrossing," a *Kirkus Reviews* commentator praised the novel for portraying the "aching sense of rootlessness" experienced by its young protagonists.

BIOGRAPHICAL AND CRITICAL SOURCES:

PERIODICALS

Kirkus Reviews, December 1, 2002, review of *Grass Roof, Tin Roof,* p. 1729.

Library Journal, November 1, 2002, Shirley N. Quan, review of *Grass Roof, Tin Roof,* p. 130.

Publishers Weekly, January 13, 2003, review of *Grass Roof, Tin Roof,* p. 41.*

STUCKEY-FRENCH, Elizabeth

PERSONAL: Female; married; children: two daughters. *Education:* Purdue University, B.A. (sociology and social work), M.A. (English); Iowa Writers Workshop, M.F.A., 1992.

ADDRESSES: *Home*—Tallahassee, FL. *Office*—Dept. of English, Florida State University, 325 Williams Bldg., Tallahassee, FL 32306-1580. *E-mail*—estuckey-french@english.fsu.edu.

CAREER: Writer and educator. Florida State University, Tallahassee, assistant professor of English. Worked as an elementary school teacher and a social worker.

AWARDS, HONORS: James Michener fellowship; Indiana Arts Commission grant.

WRITINGS:

The First Paper Girl in Red Oak, Iowa, and Other Stories, Doubleday (New York, NY), 2000.
Mermaids on the Moon (novel), Doubleday (New York, NY), 2002.

Contributor to periodicals and literary journals, including *Atlantic, Gettysburg Review, Southern Review,* and *Five Points;* work represented in anthologies, including *New Territory: Contemporary Indiana Fiction.*

WORK IN PROGRESS: *The Last Summer of Peace,* for Doubleday.

SIDELIGHTS: Elizabeth Stuckey-French's *The First Paper Girl in Red Oak, Iowa, and Other Stories* is a collection of twelve stories featuring a number of quirky characters, most of them Midwesterners and people who make bad choices. Among them are a woman who pays a gas station attendant to keep her and her children company on a cross-country road trip, a psychic who finds missing pets, and a scuba-diving female police officer who searches for dead bodies in the murky waters of polluted rivers.

In reviewing the collection for *Austin Chronicle Books,* Martin Wilson found "Electric Wizard" to be the "best story." A student commits suicide, and his parents come to his poetry teacher asking for his work as proof that he was driven by genius. The student never wrote any poems, however, and the teacher is torn between telling them the devastating truth or a lie that will preserve their vision of their son.

A *Publishers Weekly* reviewer noted that fiction writers are now forced to compete with bizarre situations and characters that populate daytime talk shows and concluded by saying that Stuckey-French "bests those spectacles of the everyday absurd, and does so with style and verve."

Mermaids on the Moon, Stuckey-French's debut novel, was called "wonderfully quirky" by a *Publishers Weekly* contributor. The novel centers on the mysterious disappearance of Grendy, a minister's wife and former performer in a synchronized swimming exhibition that was a tourist attraction in Florida many years ago. *Library Journal*'s Molly Gorman compared *Mermaids on the Moon* with the writing of Fannie Flagg and wrote, "as refreshing, crisp, and tangy as a summer drink, this is a beguiling read."

BIOGRAPHICAL AND CRITICAL SOURCES:

PERIODICALS

Kirkus Reviews, May 1, 2002, review of *Mermaids on the Moon,* p. 609.
Library Journal, June 15, 2002, Molly Gorman, review of *Mermaids on the Moon,* p. 96.
Publishers Weekly, April 24, 2000, review of *The First Paper Girl in Red Oak, Iowa, and Other Stories,* p. 64; June 3, 2002, review of *Mermaids on the Moon,* p. 61.
School Library Journal, December, 2000, Susanne Bardelson, review of *The First Paper Girl in Red Oak, Iowa,* p. 169.

ONLINE

Atlantic Unbound, http://www.theatlantic.com/ (June 11, 1998), Katie Bolick, "Wise Kids, Childish Adults: A Conversation with Elizabeth Stuckey-French."

Austin Chronicle online, http://www.austinchronicle.com/ (September 29, 2000), Martin Wilson, review of *The First Paper Girl in Red Oak, Iowa, and Other Stories.**

* * *

SUMMER, Jane 1954-

PERSONAL: Born June 30, 1954, in New York, NY. *Education:* Kirkland College, B.A.

ADDRESSES: *Agent*—Malaga Baldi Literary Agency, 204 West 84th St., New York, NY 10024.

CAREER: Writer. Reporter for *Women's Wear Daily;* grant proposal writer for Ms. Foundation for Women; editor/writer for Charles Scribner & Sons, United Nations Development Fund for Women, New Jersey Historical Society, New York State Historical Association, and *American Health.* Former waitress and Westchester Humane Society kennel cleaner.

AWARDS, HONORS: Watrous Writer's Prize, Kirkland College, 1973; CAPS/NYSCA grant for literature, 1978; first prize, American Poetry Academy, 1985; winner, *New York Times* Dining in/Dining out Essay Contest, Literal Latté Poetry Contest, and North American Open Poetry Contest, all 1998.

WRITINGS:

The Silk Road (novel), Alyson (Los Angeles, CA), 2000.

Contributor to books, including *The Women's Guide to Political Power, The Girl's Guide to Life, Ardis Anthology of New American Poetry,* and *Alone amid All This Noise;* contributor to periodicals, including *Biography, Literal Latte, Executive Female, McCall's, New Woman, Weight Watchers, Women's Sports Traveler,* and *YM.* Some writings appear under pseudonym Jane Character.

WORK IN PROGRESS: Poetry; a work of fiction about psychoanalysis.

SUNDARESAN, Indu

PERSONAL: Born in India; immigrated to the United States; daughter of a military pilot; married. *Education:* University of Delaware, graduate degrees in economics and operations research.

ADDRESSES: *Home*—Bellevue, WA. *Agent*—c/o Author Mail, Atria Books/Simon and Schuster, 1230 Avenue of the Americas, New York, NY 10020. *E-mail*—indu@indusundaresan.com.

CAREER: Writer. Encore Playhouse, Seattle, WA, writer and set builder.

AWARDS, HONORS: Washington State Book Award, 2003, for *The Twentieth Wife.*

WRITINGS:

The Twentieth Wife, Pocket Books (New York, NY), 2002.

The Feast of Roses, Atria Books (New York, NY), 2003.

Contributor to periodicals, including *Vincent Brothers Review.*

SIDELIGHTS: Indu Sundaresan was born in India and grew up on air force bases across the country, and as a child inherited a love of storytelling from her fighter-pilot father and her grandfather. After earning her undergraduate degree in India, she came to the United States to conduct graduate work in economics at the University of Delaware. She met her husband-to-be, and the couple eventually moved to Seattle, where Sundaresan made the decision to forego a career in economics in order to write.

Lucinda Dyer noted in *Publishers Weekly* that "to transport herself back to steamy seventeenth-century India in the midst of cold, rainy Washington winters, Sundaresan would crank up the thermostat in her home and settle in to write in shorts and a T-shirt—'but then the phone would ring and I would be back in Seattle.'"

Sundaresan's debut novel, *The Twentieth Wife,* is based on the true story of Mehrunnisa (the historical Empress Nur Jahan), called the Sun of Women. A *Publishers Weekly* contributor described the book as "a sweeping, carefully researched tale of desire, sexual mores, and political treachery." Born in a tent in 1577, the baby daughter of refugees fleeing persecution in Persia, Mehrunnisa comes to live in the palace of Mughal Emperor Akbar following her father's introduction to court. She first meets Prince Salim, who will later become Emperor Jahangir, on the day of the young heir's first marriage, when she is eight years old. At that moment, the beautiful young girl whose ambition far exceeds her station in life decides that one day she too will be Salim's wife. Harriet Klausner noted in a review for *BookBrowser* online that Sundaresan's descriptions of life in the Mughal court are "very illuminating. . . . However, the wealth of information . . . overwhelms the characters and thus undercuts the prime tale of Mehrunnisa's efforts to become the empress."

Salim later shares Mehrunnisa's passion, but they are forced to go their separate ways. She marries Ali Quli, a cruel soldier, and suffers several miscarriages and the hate of the emperor's primary wife, Jagat Gosini. Twenty-six years after Mehrunnisa first saw the emperor, she becomes his twentieth wife, and although she never has any children to carry on the line, she grows into one of the most powerful women of her time in the dynasty that built the Taj Mahal. She issues coins, gives orders, owns and trades property, and supports the arts. The book ends as Mehrunnisa reaches power. Elsa Gaztambide noted in *Booklist* that in the book Sundaresan explains the dynamics of the harem and provides a glossary of Indian words used throughout the text. "More than just a love story," wrote Gaztambide, "this novel offers a kaleidoscope of India's history and culture." *Library Journal*'s Michelle Reale wrote that Sundaresan "writes in the great tradition of the Indian epic, an art she carries forward with grace and brilliance." Sundaresan completed the epic in the sequel *The Feast of Roses,* published in 2003.

BIOGRAPHICAL AND CRITICAL SOURCES:

PERIODICALS

Booklist, January 1, 2002, Elsa Gaztambide, review of *The Twentieth Wife,* p. 14; May 15, 2003, Elsa Gaztambide, review of *The Feast of Roses,* p. 1640.

Library Journal, January, 2002, Michelle Reale, review of *The Twentieth Wife,* p. 155; June 15, 2003, Jeanine K. Raghunathan, review of *The Feast of Roses,* p. 102.

Publishers Weekly, August 6, 2001, Lucinda Dyer, review of *The Twentieth Wife,* p. 46; December 10, 2001, review of *The Twentieth Wife,* p. 49; May 19, 2003, review of *The Feast of Roses,* p. 53.

ONLINE

BookBrowser, http://www.bookbrowser.com/ (January 9, 2002), Harriet Klausner, review of *The Twentieth Wife.*

Indu Sundaresan Web site, http://www.indusundaresan.com (October 20, 2003).*

* * *

SUTHERLAND, Grant

PERSONAL: Born in Sydney, Australia; married; two children. *Education:* Attended United World College of Southeast Asia and London School of Economics.

ADDRESSES: *Home*—England. *Agent*—(literature) Simon Trewin, PFD, Drury House, 34-43 Russell St., London WC2B 5HA, England; fax: 020 7836 9544; (film and television) Charles Walker, PFD, Drury House, 34-43 Russell St., London WC2B 5HA, England; fax: 020 7836 9544.

CAREER: Writer. Previously worked in the financial services industry.

WRITINGS:

Due Dilligence, Headline Feature (London, England), 1997.

East of the City, Headline Feature (London, England), 1998.

Diplomatic Immunity, Bantam Books (New York, NY), 2001.

The Consignment, Bantam Books (New York, NY), 2003.

SIDELIGHTS: Grant Sutherland's international thrillers are informed by their author's experiences living in Australia, Southeast Asia, and the United Kingdom. Raised in western Australia, he studied at the United World College of Southeast Asia in Singapore, then at the London School of Economics before returning to Australia to work in finance. He eventually left the marketplace to pursue his interest in writing, publishing the novels *Due Diligence* and *East of the City* and settling with his wife and two children in England.

Diplomatic Immunity, Sutherland's first novel published in the United States, takes place in the world of the U.N. headquarters in New York City. When Toshio Hatanaka is murdered, his friend Sam Windrush, a legal affairs deputy, soon becomes involved in the investigation. An avowed pacifist, Hatanaka had worked as a hostage negotiator, and three years earlier, had tried unsuccessfully to secure the release of Windrush's wife from terrorists holding her in Pakistan. She was eventually killed, and after Hatanaka is murdered, Windrush suspects a tie with a bid to make Japan the sixth permanent member of the U.N. Security Council.

According to a reviewer commenting on *Diplomatic Immunity* in *Publishers Weekly,* "the author uses the rarified world of the U.N. to his advantage in a fast-paced novel that will keep readers engaged." Wrote David Pitt in *Booklist,* "This is an intelligent, well-constructed thriller that gives readers a behind-the-scenes look at the U.N. and international politics."

The murder of a colleague also occupies a central place in the plot of *The Consignment.* U.S. Army Ranger Ned Rourke bows to pressure from his wife, Fiona, and leaves the military for a job as a sales representative. But his is no ordinary sales job: working for Haplon Systems, he sells military equipment to clients who range from soldier-of-fortune wannabes to warlords operating in the Third World. When a rival salesman—Dmitri Spandos, who happens to have also been Ned's roommate at West Point—is killed, apparently by a stray bullet at a shooting range, Ned suspects that something sinister is afoot. Dmitri had been involved in an effort by the Department of Defense to investigate arms dealers such as Ned, and now Ned must go back into the military world to solve the mystery of Dmitri's death.

"Rourke, both hero and narrator, is a strong, likeable fellow," wrote Pitt in a review in *Booklist.* A commentator in *Kirkus Reviews* described *The Consignment* as "an interesting and complex tale informed with an oddly macho ethos: a little bit like putting Rambo into a [John] le Carre novel." Wrote Jeff Zaleski in *Publishers Weekly,* "A strong, cunning writer, Sutherland knows how to plant his characters in complex, threatening situations and then turn them loose as the action escalates."

BIOGRAPHICAL AND CRITICAL SOURCES:

PERIODICALS

Booklist, March 1, 2001, David Pitt, review of *Diplomatic Immunity,* p. 1231; October 1, 2001, Joyce Saricks, review of audio version of *Diplomatic Immunity,* p. 342; February 15, 2003, David Pitt, review of *The Consignment,* p. 1056.

Kirkus Reviews, December 15, 2002, review of *The Consignment,* p. 1800.

Publishers Weekly, March 12, 2001, Peter Cannon, review of *Diplomatic Immunity,* p. 248; March 24, 2003, Jeff Zaleski, review of *The Consignment,* p. 50.*

* * *

SVICH, Caridad 1963-

PERSONAL: Born July 30, 1963, in Philadelphia, PA; daughter of Emilio Dario and Aracely Besteiro. *Education:* University of North Carolina, B.F.A. (theatre); University of California, San Diego, M.F.A. (theatre). *Religion:* Catholic. *Hobbies and other interests:* Yoga, tennis, cycling, reading, singing.

ADDRESSES: Home—4601 Tweedy Blvd., Ste. H, SoGate, CA 90280; fax 520-569-9191. *E-mail*—csvich21@aol.com; csvich@hotmail.com.

CAREER: Playwright, editor, songwriter, teacher, and performer.

MEMBER: New Dramatists, Dramatists Guild, Playwrights' Center.

AWARDS, HONORS: Goucher College Open Circle Theatre Playwriting Award, 1983; Cincinnati Playhouse Rosenthal New Play Prize, 1993-94; first runner-up, Arizona Theatre Company National Hispanic Playwrights Award; first place, West Coast Ten-Minute Play Festival, 1999; first place, Perishable Theatre Annual Women's Theatre Festival, 2000; grants and additional awards from academic and private theatre and playwright organizations.

WRITINGS:

PLAYS

Waterfall, produced at University of North Carolina, 1983.

Winter in July (one-act text), produced at University of California—San Diego, 1986.

Proper Positions (one-act text), produced at University of California—San Diego, 1987.

Voice and Vision Play with Your Food, produced at University of California—San Diego, 1988, produced in New York, 1996.

Gleaning/Rebusca, produced in New York, 1989.

But There Are Fires (one-act text), produced in New York, 1991.

Shelter, produced in New York, 1991.

Any Place but Here (produced in California, 1992), published in *TCG Plays-in-process,* Volume 13, number 12, 1993.

Alchemy of Desire/Dead-Man's Blues (produced in Los Angeles, 1993), published in *Out of the Fringe: Contemporary Latina/o Theatre and Performance,* TCG Books, 2000.

Scar, produced in Cincinnati, then New York, NY, 1994.

Away down Dreaming, produced in San Francisco, 1995.

Pensacola, produced in California, 1997.

Prodigal Kiss, produced in California, 1997.

Twelve Short Prayers for Life When Dying, produced in California, then New York, NY, 1998.

Carnival (one-act text), produced in Los Angeles, 1998.

The Archaeology of Dreams, produced in California, 1999.

Torch, produced at Vanguard Theatre, California, 1999.

Finding Life (one act text; produced in Providence, RI), published in *Eighth Annual Women's Playwriting Festival Anthology of One-Act Plays,* Perishable Theatre, 2000.

Nightwood (one-act text), produced in Toronto, Ontario, Canada, 2000.

Steal Back Light from the Virtual, New Dramatists Fall Readings, 2000.

Iphigenia Crash Land Falls on the Neon Shell That Was Once Her Heart, produced in California, 2000.

Fugitive Pieces, produced in Chicago, IL, 2000.

(With others) *Stations of Desire: Saints, Sinners, and In-Between* (online text), produced in Minneapolis, MN, 2000.

Also author of *Brazo Gitano,* published in *Ollantay Theatre Magazine,* Volume VI, number 11.

OTHER

(Editor with Maria M. Delgado) *Conducting a Life: Reflections on the Theatre of Maria Irene Fornes,* Smith & Kraus (Lyme, NH), 1999.

(With Maria Teresa Marrero) *Out of the Fringe: Contemporary Latina/Latino Theatre and Performance,* Theatre Communications Group (New York, NY), 2000.

(Translator) Federico García Lorca, *Impossible Theatre: Five Plays and Thirteen Poems,* Smith & Kraus (Hanover, NH), 2000.

(Editor) *Trans-global Readings: Crossing Theatrical Boundaries,* Palgrave (New York, NY), 2003.

Author of articles and reviews in periodicals, including *Monologues for Women by Women, Contemporary Theatre Review, Dramatist, Theatre Today,* and *American Theatre.*

WORK IN PROGRESS: Transmission 05:00/To the Blue Peninsula, a play; *In the Upper Room,* a play; *Random Acts of Culture,* an online text collaboration with eleven playwrights.

SIDELIGHTS: Caridad Svich told *CA:* "Flux is at the core of my writing aesthetic. My work, although an outgrowth of a singular vision, reflects my interest in a variety of structural forms, styles, and tones.

"Born in the United States of Cuban-Argentine-Spanish-Croatian descent, I am a first-generation hybrid, a daughter of a hybrid sensibility which is neither fully Latina nor fully American, but rather an sensibility in flux: bilingual, multicultural, female. Although primarily a playwright, I am also an editor, songwriter, teacher, and performer.

"My plays are naturally built on the concept of collage, mixing poetry, songs, ritual, traditional Western dramatic scenes, movement, and images. They are character-based and rooted in a sense of place, be it emotional or geographic terrain, as well as rooted in the notion of giving voice to dispossessed voices.

"My play *Alchemy of Desire/Dead-Man's Blues* in particular stems from a desire to re-imagine the United States from within: to take apart familiar structures and reconfigure them in a way that will forge a new theatrical identity, one that is reflective of a multifaceted culture yet rooted in ancient, even primeval impulses and forms. The nature of my work is to always chart anew, building on what has gone before, seeking transcendence and spiritual transformation in a world not yet gone wrong.

"Plays like *Any Place but Here, Fugitive Pieces, Iphigenia Crash Land Falls on the Neon Shell That Was Once Her Heart,* and *Steal Back Light from the Virtual* explore the nature of violence, its randomness, and the inescapable hold of myth on contemporary life.

"The biggest influence on my work, besides my cultural lineage and the influence of having grown up bilingual—speaking Spanish in the home and English 'outside'—would have to be the rather nomadic existence I have lived. Between the ages of five and twenty-seven I lived in Pennsylvania, New Jersey, North Carolina, Florida, Utah, New York, and California, along with twice as many cross-U.S. trips in between.

"The process of seeing the country, being constantly uprooted and having to adapt to new circumstances, has left a marked imprint in the formation of my work and worldview. You can never really escape where you're from, but if you're from nowhere and everywhere, the source of the work is significantly changed. It has meant that I write both consciously and not about location, dislocation, about longing for home, and running away, about feeling like an exile and feeling like a native. The decidedly American obsession with wanderlust is both a topic of exploration and continual de-mythologization.

"I have a strong connection to various literary figures—Virginia Woolf, Federico García Lorca, Annie Dillard, Borges, Shakespeare—but also to the work of other artists in dance, music, and photography, including Velazquez, Ana Mendieta, Helen Levitt, Twyla Tharp, Charles Ives, and Patti Smith, to name a few. From Woolf's writings I especially learned about form, the role memory plays, and the necessity for experimentation and the vitality of a woman's voice. From one of my teachers, Maria Irene Fornes, with whom I studied for four years, I learned to not be afraid to speak the truth in my work.

"My commitment to theatre even in this technological age is strong and vital. Although I welcome the use of sophisticated technology in theatre, my primary concern is a poet's concern: voice and space, voice in space and time. My areas of experimentation are never far removed from this basic concern. The language of theatre with its ability to encompass literary, painterly and musical traditions is the language with which I currently feel most comfortable to address the public and private realms of experience which constitute the focus of my work."

* * *

SYMMES, Patrick 1964-

PERSONAL: Born July 12, 1964, in New Haven, CT; son of David (a research scientist) and Jean (a psychologist) Symmes. *Education:* Wesleyan University, B.A.

ADDRESSES: *Home*—45 West Tenth St., No. 2A, New York, NY 10011. *E-mail*—chasingche@aol.com.

CAREER: Writer, contributing editor and freelance foreign correspondent.

WRITINGS:

Chasing Che: A Motorcycle Journey in Search of the Guevara Legend, Vintage (New York, NY), 2000.

Contributing editor to *Harper's* magazine. Contributor to periodicals, including *Outside, GQ, Conde Nast Traveler, New York,* and *Wired.*

SIDELIGHTS: Patrick Symmes told *CA:* "Most of my articles are political travelogues, set in the troubled regions and on the cultural fault lines of our shrinking sphere. I've been to Cuba eight times, and have hobnobbed with guerilla groups in Peru, Columbia, and Cambodia. I've traveled New Zealand, Patagonia, the western deserts of China, the peaks of Wyoming and Montana, the Sinai desert, and much of the Andes. My articles are filled with peasants, refugees, and slum dwellers. My travels have only been possible thanks to them; I hope my work repays some of that generosity.

"I started as a file clerk at the *Washington Post,* went to boot camp at the *Middletown Press* (CT), passed briefly through the *Hartford Courant,* and—after a detour through college and a few walkabouts—washed up in the gutter of freelance journalism. Aside from five horrifying months at ABC News London and two years at *Washington City Paper* writing 8,000-word features every six seconds, I've been here ever since."

BIOGRAPHICAL AND CRITICAL SOURCES:

PERIODICALS

Booklist, February 15, 2000, Gilbert Taylor, review of *Chasing Che: A Motorcycle Journey in Search of the Guevara Legend,* p. 1075; September 15, 2000, Brad Hooper, review of *Chasing Che,* p. 209.

Library Journal, February 1, 2000, Mark L. Grover, review of *Chasing Che,* p. 108.

Publishers Weekly, January 24, 2000, review of *Chasing Che,* p. 304.

T

TAHER, Bahaa 1935-

PERSONAL: Born 1935, in Cairo, Egypt; *Education:* Graduated from the University of Cairo.

ADDRESSES: *Agent*—c/o Author Mail, American University in Cairo Press, 420 Fifth Avenue, New York, NY 10018-2729.

CAREER: Novelist. Worked for Radio 2 in Egypt after graduating from college; worked as a translator for the United Nations in Geneva, Switzerland.

AWARDS, HONORS: State Award of Merit in Literature, Egypt, 1998; Giuseppe Acerbi prize, 2000, for *Khalti Safiyya wal-Dayr.*

WRITINGS:

NOVELS

Sharq al-Nakhila (originally serialized in *Sabah al-Khayr,* 1983), Dar al-Mustaqbal al-'Arabi (Cairo, Egypt), 1985.

Qalat Duha (originally serialized in *al-Musawwir,* 1985), Dar al-Hilal (Cairo, Egypt), 1985.

Khalati Safiyya wal-Dayr, Dar al-Hilal (Cairo, Egypt), 1991, translation by Barbara Romaine published as *Aunt Safiyya and the Monastery,* University of California Press (Berkeley, CA), 1996.

Al-Hob fi al-Manfa, Dar al-Hilal (Cairo, Egypt), 1995, translation by Farouk Abdel-Wahab published as *Love in Exile,* American University in Cairo Press (New York, NY), 2002.

Nuqtat al-Nour (title means "The Point of Light"), al-Hilal Novels (Cairo, Egypt), 2001.

OTHER

Masrahiyyat Misriyya: 'Ard wa-Naqd/Analysis of Ten Egyptian Plays, Dar al-Hilal (Cairo, Egypt), 1985.

Collected works published by Dar al-Hilal, 1992. Also author of short story collection *Zahabtu ila Shallal* (title means "I Went to a Waterfall"). Contributor of short stories to anthologies, including *Egyptian Short Stories,* selected and translated by Denys Johnson-Davies, Three Continents Press (Washington, DC), 1978; *Arabic Short Stories,* selected and translated by Johnson-Davies, Quartet (New York, NY), 1983; *Egyptian Tales and Short Stories of the 1970s and 1980s,* edited by W. M. Hutchins, American University in Cairo Press (Cairo, Eqypt), 1987. Contributor of short stories to periodicals, *Mukhtarat Fusul* and *Matbu'at al-Jadid.*

SIDELIGHTS: A victim of state censorship during the 1970s, Bahaa Taher is now a prominent literary figure in his native Egypt and throughout the Arab world. He spent many years of self-exile in Geneva, Switzerland, where he worked as a translator for the United Nations. His writings became more widely known in the 1990s, when two of his novels were translated into English. *Aunt Safiyya and the Monastery* and *Love in Exile* indirectly address cultural and political troubles in Taher's homeland through stories that are geographically distant from Egypt's social and political centers. Both novels are dark depictions of personal crisis, but reflect on larger issues such as tensions between tradition and modernization, and the interplay between personal and political aspects of life.

After graduating from the University of Cairo, Taher started working on cultural programming for Egypt's Radio 2 and became a storyteller and commentator. He published his first short story in 1964 and was part of left-wing and avant-garde literary circles, including the Gallery 68 movement. During the mid-1970s, political repression under the Sadat administration ended Taher's broadcast career and his publishing opportunities in Egypt. He moved to Geneva in 1981 and did not return to Egypt until sometime after 1996. During the 1990s Taher received increased attention on an international scale as the subject of a 1995 film by Jamil 'At iyyat Ibrahim that focuses on Taher's activism in the 1960s, and as the recipient of Egypt's Award of Merit in Literature in 1998 and the Italian Giuseppe Acerbi prize in 2000.

The translation *Aunt Safiyya and the Monastery* furthered Taher's reputation with its graceful style and thoughtful exploration of religious conflict in the Middle East. In a review for *World Literature Today,* Issa Peters explained that, among contemporary Egyptian novelists, Taher "represents a competent voice of the new generation that came after the giants, Nobel laureate Naguib Mahfouz and Yusuf Idris." Other reviewers noted the timeliness of the story, which centers on the interactions between Muslims and Coptic Christians in a remote Egyptian village near the time of the 1967 Arab-Israeli war, in the wake of escalating violence between Israelis and Palestinians in 1996. The novel is a realistic portrayal of conflict within a remote village in Upper Egypt where Muslims and Christians have lived together for centuries. Aunt Safiyya is a Muslim woman who wants revenge for the death of her husband, following the ancient tradition of the blood feud. Her husband's killer, however, was himself an undeserving victim of torture who acted in self defense. The narrator's father, also a Muslim, and a monk from the local Coptic monastery devise a plan to protect the man behind its walls. Later, the narrator is brought to tears when he recognizes a man's mournful voice singing in the night.

The novel earned numerous positive reviews. One exception, however, appeared in *Choice,* in which K. I. Semaan dismissed it as having "no artistic or historical satisfaction." More often, the book has earned praise for its social significance and the author's quiet, non-judgmental approach. A reviewer for *Christian Century* advised that *Aunt Safiyya and the Monastery* is enriched by "a subtle, complex love story, three-dimensional characters and a fully realized social world." A *Publishers Weekly* reviewer noted the novel's "clear, beautiful and exotic" style and recommended it to readers interested in history, literature, and the pursuit of peace. *Boston Book Review* contributor Elizabeth Shostak described the book as an "enigmatic" work in which "the song of one broken man speaks the larger anguish of a diminished community." It is a "dramatic and horrifying story," according to Penelope Lively in the *New York Times Book Review.* She commented, "Simply told, without adornment or much authorial intrusion, this is a brief tragedy with resonances wider than its village setting."

The subject of displacement is central to *Love in Exile,* in which the protagonist, like Taher, has been forced out of Egypt because of his political views and comes to live and work in a European city. The unnamed man is a journalist who finds himself happy to be free from reminders of his divorce and the disappointments of being a socialist and supporter of former president Nasser. But he is also unhappily disconnected from his new surroundings and current political events. He finds some solace in an affair with a young Austrian woman and is stirred to protest the 1982 Israeli occupation of Lebanon. As the journalist prepares to write a story on the subject, however, a stroke incapacitates him and he is subsequently ordered to avoid anything, including the news, that will upset him.

The novel was received by critics as a compelling, if bleak look at the conjunction between personal and political identity. It was named as an international book of the year for 1995 by *Times Literary Supplement* contributor Ahdaf Soueif, who wrote that it "takes on the soul-searching sadness and bewilderment that being an Arab today means" and noted that the book poses important, if unanswerable questions. A *Kirkus Reviews* writer described the work as "brooding" and an "unusually intelligent and absorbing political tale." The translation was commended in *Middle East Times* by Tariq Hassan-Gordon, who noted that the recent Israeli occupation of Palestinian cities proved "the timelessness of Taher's literary effort." The critic remarked that the novel "will not only keep you up reading through the night, but will also leave you reflecting on your own personal experiences." In a review for *Al-Ahram,* Nur Elmessiri advised that in Arabic the novel is "a gripping, moving read" that had not been not diminished in translation. According to this critic, *Love in Exile* is "at once ruthlessly honest and compassionate in its exploration of the agonizingly fuzzy line separating 'exile' from 'escape.'"

BIOGRAPHICAL AND CRITICAL SOURCES:

PERIODICALS

Boston Book Review, June, 1996, Elizabeth Shostak, review of *Aunt Safiyya and the Monastery.*

Choice, December, 1996, K. I. Semann, review of *Aunt Safiyya and the Monastery,* p. 608.

Christian Century, November 20, 1996, review of *Aunt Safiyya and the Monastery,* p. 1169.

Kirkus Reviews, September 1, 2002, review of *Love in Exile,* p. 1265.

New York Times Book Review, June 30, 1996, Penelope Lively, "Family Feud," p. 18.

Publishers Weekly, April 8, 1996, review of *Aunt Safiyya and the Monastery,* p. 63.

Times Literary Supplement, December 1, 1995, Ahdaf Soueif, review of *Love in Exile,* p. 13.

World Literature Today, winter, 1997, Issa Peters, review of *Aunt Safiyya and the Monastery,* p. 216.

ONLINE

Al-Ahram Weekly online, http://weekly.ahram.org.eg/ (June 13-19, 2002), Nur Elmessiri, "Questions of Exile and Memory."

Arab World Books, http://www.arabworldbooks.com/authors/ (March 10, 2003).

Middle East Times online, http://www.metimes.com/ (March 11, 2003), Tariq Hassan-Gordon, review of *Love in Exile.**

* * *

TALBOTT, Lisa

PERSONAL: Female. *Education:* San Francisco State, B.S.; University of Washingtonm M.Ph.

ADDRESSES: Home—Seattle, WA. *Agent*—c/o Author Mail, St. Martins Press, 175 Fifth Ave., New York, NY 10010. *E-mail*—ltalbott@cancerlifeline.org.

CAREER: Fitness trainer and women's rehabilitation expert. Cofounder of Team Survivor (national non-profit organization aiding women cancer survivors), 1995; Cancer Lifeline, Seattle. WA, health promotions manager; Fred Hutchinson Cancer Research Center, consultant and support specialist.

WRITINGS:

(With Anne McTiernan and Julie Gralow) *Breast Fitness: An Optimal Exercise and Health Plan for Reducing Your Risk of Breast Cancer,* St. Martin's Press (New York, NY), 2000.

SIDELIGHTS: Lisa Talbott is a women's rehabilitation expert who has conducted research to prove that regular exercise reduces a woman's risk of developing breast cancer. Along with coauthors Anne McTiernan, a breast cancer specialist, and Julie Gralow, director of the University of Washington's Breast Cancer Genetics Clinics, Talbott published her findings in the book, *Breast Fitness: An Optimal Exercise and Health Plan for Reducing Your Risk of Breast Cancer.*

Talbott, McTiernan, and Gralow are not the first to make a connection between exercise and reduced cancer risk. Bette-Lee Fox in *Library Journal* noted that many books advise cutting calories and increasing exercise to reduce the risk of disease, "and this book is no different," explained the reviewer, "except that it specifically relates both concepts to the avoidance and recurrence of breast cancer."

According to *Breast Fitness,* a woman's weight plays a critical role in whether or not she develops breast cancer. If she does develop the disease, weight plays a significant role in recovery. The authors note that obese women are two times more likely to develop breast cancer than thin women, and overweight women are two times less likely to survive after diagnosis. The authors theorize that high-fat diets produce fat stores within the body. These fat stores raise hormone levels in the blood, which are related to tumor growth.

While critics in general praised the book, a reviewer in *Publishers Weekly* cautioned that "many of the authors' suggestions are based upon theories still undergoing testing (such as the idea that high estrogen levels increase breaks cancer risk)." However, the same reviewer added that the authors "clearly explicate their reasoning so readers can make educated guesses about how to prevent the disease."

BIOGRAPHICAL AND CRITICAL SOURCES:

PERIODICALS

Library Journal, September 15, 2000, Bette-Lee Fox, review of *Breast Fitness: An Optimal Exercise and Health Plan for Reducing Your Risk of Breast Cancer,* p. 108.

Publishers Weekly, September 4, 2000, review of *Breast Fitness,* p. 104.

ONLINE

Annie Appleseed Project, http://www.annieappleseedproject.org/ (October 1, 2003).*

* * *

TATLOCK, Ann 1959-

PERSONAL: Born December 8, 1959 in Parkersburg, WV; daughter of Edward L. (a retired chemical engineer) and Jane Tatlock (a registered nurse and homemaker) Shurts; married Robert Blank, October 9, 1992; children: Laura Jane Tatlock. *Ethnicity:* "White." *Education:* Oral Roberts University, B.A., 1981; Wheaton College Graduate School, M.A., 1987. *Politics:* Republican. *Religion:* Christian. *Hobbies and other interests:* Antiques, art museums, book collecting, voluntary English-as-a-second-language tutor for students from Afghanistan, Russia, and Bosnia.

ADDRESSES: Agent—Steve Laube, The Literary Group International, 270 Lafayette St., Suite 1505, New York, NY 10012. *E-mail*—anntatlock@yahoo.com.

CAREER: Novelist. *Decision* magazine, Minneapolis, MN, assistant editor, 1987-93.

AWARDS, HONORS: Silver Angel Award, Excellence in Media, 1999, for *A Room of My Own;* Midwest Independent Publishers Association, 2002 Midwest Book Awards, first place, adult fiction category, and Christy Award, contemporary fiction category, 2003, both for *All the Way Home.*

WRITINGS:

A Room of My Own, Bethany House Publishers (Minneapolis, MN), 1998.

A Place Called Morning, Bethany House Publishers (Minneapolis, MN), 1998.

All the Way Home, Bethany House Publishers (Minneapolis, MN), 2002.

I'll Watch the Moon, Bethany House Publishers (Minneapolis, MN), 2003.

ADAPTATIONS: A Room of My Own was adapted for audiocassette, read by Kate Forbes, Recorded Books, LLC, 1998, and by Northstar Audio Books, 2000; *A Place Called Morning* was adapted for audiocassette, read by Barbara Caruso, Recorded Books, LLC, 1998; *All the Way Home* was adapted for audiocassette, read by Christina Moore, Recorded Books, LLC, 2003.

WORK IN PROGRESS: Under the Aging Sun, a novel.

SIDELIGHTS: Ann Tatlock's first novel, *A Room of My Own,* chronicles the life of thirteen-year-old Virginia Eide in Depression-era Minnesota. A typical teenager, Virginia struggles with her own coming-of-age issues, yearns for her independence, giggles with her friends, and idolizes movie stars. But Virginia's comfortable family life begins to crumble when her laid-off uncle and his family are forced to move in and "a room of her own" becomes an impossibility. Her father, a doctor, begins treating the desperately poor residents of Soo City, a ramshackle shanty town outside the city limits. Virginia starts helping him bring aid to Soo City, where in contrast to her own life, she sees up-close the extreme poverty and despair of those most affected by the Depression. When her uncle is swept up in the violence surrounding his attempts to start a labor union, Virginia understands the sacrifices that many must make to survive, and realizes the profound effect of service to others. "*A Room of My Own* shines both for its content and the loving, sensitive way it is conveyed," wrote a reviewer in

Moody. A *Booklist* reviewer opined that it is "Perhaps the best Christian novel of the year." Critics Kristine Harley and Carolyn Petrie, writing in *Skyway News,* remarked that, "full of affectionate, bittersweet memories, this layered tale of one family's struggle and triumph is socially relevant without ever lapsing into preachiness," concluding that "*A Room of My Own* is a lovely first effort, infused with grace."

In *A Place Called Morning,* Tatlock's second novel, Mae Demaray finds her once-strong faith challenged when her young grandson is killed while she was taking care of him. She believes the accident was her fault, though no one else does. The lingering guilt and grief gradually erode her life until her only friend is Roy, a kindly but mentally disabled man who has been a part of Mae's life since their childhood. Though Mae and Roy are never romantically involved, they eventually do live together, ostensibly so that Mae can care for Roy. But Roy, in his own way, cares for Mae, and helps bring her out of her isolation and back into the world. "This quiet, offbeat love story, about forgiving oneself and preparing for death, is another fine effort from Tatlock," wrote John Mort in *Booklist.* With the book, Tatlock presents "an intelligent mix of domestic insight and Christian philosophy," wrote a *Library Journal* reviewer.

Tatlock addresses issues of racial and social injustice in *All the Way Home,* her third novel. As a young girl in the 1930s, Augusta "Augie" Schuler Callahan suffered the effects of an alcoholic and abusive family. She develops a close relationship with the Japanese-American Yamagata family, and an especially deep friendship with the Yamagata's daughter Sunny. But with the advent of World War II, the Yamagata family is sent to an internment camp, as were hundreds of other Asian Americans at the time. Augie loses contact with the family, but years later, as a prominent civil rights journalist, she is convinced by Sunny to cover the story of Sunny's attempts to secure voting rights for blacks in racially divided Mississippi. The two women must come to terms with what racism did to them years ago, and how it has changed their lives as adults. Tatlock "adeptly traces the girls' journey of faith with a light and sometimes humorous touch," wrote a *Publishers Weekly* reviewer. "She does an excellent job juxtaposing the horrors of Americans in Japanese hands and Japanese-Americans in the hands of their countrymen." *All the Way Home* is "a fine example of the progress" being made in Christian fiction, the reviewer observed. To Tracy Farmsworth, reviewing the book on the *Romance Reader's Connection* Web site, "there is no question as to why Ms. Tatlock is an award-winning novelist: the depth of emotion that is magically intertwined into her novel amply demonstrates her talent."

I'll Watch the Moon is a story seen through the eyes of nine-year-old Nova Tierney. The year is 1948, and St. Paul, Minnesota is in the midst of another outbreak of polio. Public swimming pools are closed and movie theaters are off-limits as parents try to keep their children close to the nest. The nest of Nova is a boarding house run by her Aunt Dortha and filled with an odd assortment of tenants. After Nova tries unsuccessfully to follow her revered older brother Dewey to a local lake for a swim with his friends, she becomes a horrified witness to the consequences: Dewey develops polio. Nova's mother, Catherine, sees this as one more proof as God's disfavor with her. But Catherine is about to learn something of God's mysterious ways from an unlikely source: boarding house resident Josef Karski, a survivor of the Auschwitz death camp. *I'll Watch the Moon* is a "beautiful story laced with hope, redemption and forgiveness," wrote a reviewer from *Publishers Weekly.* A reviewer for *Renown* online concluded by saying, "This is a moving and wonderfully encouraging novel . . . one of the most realistic and significant ones I've read; and one that leaves a great inspiration and message of trust in God for the outcome of all things."

Tatlock told *CA:* "From a very young age I knew I wanted to be a writer, but I had no idea I would end up a novelist. Magazine journalism was my main interest while in college and in the years directly afterward. I loved to read novels but had no interest at all in writing them. Until I was twenty-five, I would have said I had no talent for writing fiction. I was fairly adept at getting down on paper stories that had actually happened, but far be it from me to use my imagination to make something up!

"But my mid-twenties were a time of personal loss—including the loss of my mother to cancer. In the midst of it, I realized I needed a new way to express my grief. I turned to fiction, found it a powerful way to express feelings and ideas, and my whole style and writing and the goals for my work shifted at that time. My main focus has been novel-writing ever since.

"Thirteen years separated the moment I first decided to write a novel and the moment I saw my first novel in print. I wrote six or seven books (I've lost count) before I felt ready even to begin thinking about publishing. I had a long apprenticeship—years of simply learning *how* to write fiction. I never took a creative writing class; I learned by trial and error (writing and writing and writing some more) and by reading top-quality literature. Though I'm indebted to many writers, both past and present, I particularly appreciate the works and writing styles of Frederick Buechner and Ann Morrow Lindbergh.

"I love my work," Tatlock declared. "From the moment an idea comes into my mind, through the months of research and planning and plotting and *seeing* the book in my mind, through the many long months of writing and rewriting and rewriting yet again, I love every moment. My characters are the people I spend my days with, and they become very real to me. They even have minds of their own, and tell me what they are going to do! That, by the way, is undoubtedly the most surprising discovery I've made as a writer of fiction: I don't have as much control over the story as one might think. First of all, I find it's no use to consciously try to come up with a story idea. Whatever I come up with invariably doesn't work. The ideas that work are the ones that come to me, dropping into my mind at sometimes the oddest moments. From there, as I begin to do some initial research, the story unfolds as I listen to it. I actually spend much of my time simply listening, allowing the characters to tell me who they are and what they're doing.

"My books tend to deal with how the large events of history impact and influence the lives of individuals. Wars, epidemics, civil rights, economic depressions—I strive to give these abstract happenings a human face, the face of my characters. I want to show not only what happens, but what choices people are faced with in the midst of world events. Much of life is beyond our control; yet much of our individual life is under our control as well, depending on our choices. I like to examine how this delicate balance plays itself out in the lives of my characters. Ultimately, I'm a writer who believes in the triumph of good over evil, and will never write a story without hope in it.

"The wonderful thing about fiction is that it is the perfect vehicle for truth," Tatlock continued. "Every novelist, of course, writes from his or her own world view. What a writer believes, how a writer makes sense of the world—of life and death and life after death—will inevitably come through. The cumulative mass of the world's literature is an on-going theological/philosophical conversation, and it is exciting to have a voice in that."

BIOGRAPHICAL AND CRITICAL SOURCES:

PERIODICALS

Booklist, October 1, 1998, John Mort, review of *A Room of My Own,* p. 290; December 1, 1998, John Mort, review of *A Room of My Own,* p. 659; January 1, 1999, John Mort, review of *A Place Called Morning,* p. 830; October 1, 1999, John Mort, review of *A Place Called Morning,* p. 324.

Library Journal, November 1, 1997, Melissa Hudak, review of *A Room of My Own,* p. 66; November 1, 1998, Melissa Hudak, review of *A Place Called Morning,* p. 66; September 1, 2002, Shawna Saavedra Thorup, review of *All the Way Home,* p. 158; June 1, 2003, Tamara Butler, review of *I'll Watch the Moon,* p. 102.

Moody, March-April, 1998, review of *A Room of My Own,* p. 71.

Publishers Weekly, April 29, 2002, review of *All the Way Home,* pp. 38-39; May 5, 2003, review of *I'll Watch the Moon,* p. 197.

Skyway News, March 26-April 1, 1998, Kristine Harley and Carolyn Petrie, review of *A Room of My Own.*

ONLINE

Renown online, http://www.renownmagazine.com (November 11, 2003), review of *I'll Watch the Moon.*

Romance Reader's Connection, http://www.theromancereadersconnection.com/ (September 10, 2002) Tracy Farnsworth, review of *All the Way Home.*

* * *

TAYLOR, Don(ald) 1943-1999

PERSONAL: Born 1943, in Jamaica; died 1999; mother's name Vernal Kidd.

CAREER: Manager and writer.

WRITINGS:

Marley and Me: The Real Bob Marley Story, Barricade, 1995.

SIDELIGHTS: Don Taylor was reggae superstar Bob Marley's manager from 1975 until Marley's death from cancer in 1981. Taylor's memoir *Marley and Me: The Real Bob Marley Story* details this period, as well as Taylor's own life, which in many ways parallels Marley's. Taylor and Marley were both born in Jamaica, and both of their fathers were white. Taylor was the son of a thirteen-year-old mother, Vernal Kidd, but when he was born, his mother named him for her current lover, a Mr. Taylor. When baby Donald's skin remained light, Mr. Taylor questioned his fatherhood; Taylor's mother finally turned her son over to his natural father. Taylor lived as Donald Kidd in many homes where he was placed by his absentee father, and by the time he was thirteen, he lived alone in Kingston, surviving as a pimp and a hustler. When he was sixteen, singer Jackie Wilson, who had been performing in Jamaica, gave Taylor an opportunity to come to the United States.

In the book's acknowledgments Taylor expresses his appreciation for Wilson and others, including Ben E. King, Jerry Butler, Chuck Jackson, the Shirelles, the Drifters, Little Anthony, and Patti La Belle, and the Blue Belles. He managed other acts, such as Martha and the Vandellas, and more recently Soul II Soul. He was associated with nearly all the top black singers of the 1960s and 1970s, including Marvin Gaye and Sly Stone, as well as with top promoters and producers, such as Elvis's manager Colonel Tom Parker.

Herman Hall noted in *Everybody's* that many books about Marley have been written. "Unfortunately, most of them are by young, white writers who believe they know more about Jamaica than Jamaicans and more about reggae and Caribbean music than the people of the region." As Marley's manager, Taylor saw him as others could not. He waited fourteen years before writing the book, which Hall felt demonstrates that he was not doing it for money or publicity. "These factors make the book genuine and serious," wrote Hall, "though all the information may not necessarily be accurate, nor Taylor's view objective."

Hall said the book "is about the CIA, the Mafia, poverty and riches, hatred and kindness, sex, beautiful women, soccer, the Bible, Rastafarians, assassination attempts and execution, politics, fancy restaurants, the jet set, wit and tragedies, obeah, philanthropy, loyalty, and exploitation." Hall wrote that Taylor "creates two heroes in his book, Robert Nesta Marley and himself. Except for Marley's children, then pre-teenagers and early teens, in Taylor's eyes, all the rest of the cast . . . were mere cheaters, thieves, and exploiters."

The cast includes Marley's wife, Rita; his mother, Cedella Booker; the founder of Island Records, Chris Blackwell; Marley's best friend, Allan "Skill" Cole; Cindy Breakspeare, Miss World and the mother of a son with Marley; the Twelve Tribes of Israel; the Peoples' National Party; and the Jamaica Labour Party.

Taylor, Rita, and Marley were shot during a 1976 attempt on Marley's life, and Taylor offers proof that the failed assassination was plotted by the Central Intelligence Agency (CIA). Hall said there "is no reason to doubt his views given the political situation in Jamaica at that time, the growing influence of Bob Marley and his music on the youth in black nations, and his influence among young whites in America and elsewhere. It was a time when the CIA was most active in black countries as the Cold War was waged. Bob Marley was judged as a supporter, although he denied it, of Michael Manley, who was then prime minister of Jamaica and whom the CIA was actively trying to remove from power."

A *Publishers Weekly* reviewer wrote that Taylor captures Marley's "navigation of Jamaica's incendiary political landscape in the 1970s," and said "the story of the attempt on Marley's life is well told." David Szatmary wrote in *Library Journal* that Taylor offers an inside view of the music business, "including cutthroat financial dealings, political machinations, and the Mafia connection." *Booklist* reviewer Mike Tribby called *Marley and Me* "a must read for anyone who cares about the legacy of one of the most charismatic pop musicians ever."

BIOGRAPHICAL AND CRITICAL SOURCES:

PERIODICALS

Booklist, September 1, 1995, pp. 27, 51.
Everybody's, March 31, 1995.

Library Journal, August, 1995, p. 77.
Publishers Weekly, August 7, 1995, p. 457.*

* * *

TELLIS, Gerard J. 1950-

PERSONAL: Born March 27, 1950, in Bombay, India; immigrated to United States, 1979; son of Aloysius Louis and Lucy Tellis; married Cheryl Anne Evelyn, March 5, 1980; children: Neil, Viren, Kethan, Sonia. *Education:* University of Bombay (India), B.S. (chemistry), 1975; Xavier Institute of Management (Jamshedpur, India), PGDBM, 1977; University of Michigan, Ph.D., 1983.

ADDRESSES: Office—Marshall School of Business, University of Southern California, Los Angeles, CA 90089-1421. *E-mail*—tellis@usc.edu.

CAREER: Johnson & Johnson, Bombay, India, sales development manager, 1977-79; University of Iowa, Iowa City, associate professor of marketing, 1983-88; University of Southern California, Los Angeles, professor, 1989-95, Neely Professor of Marketing, 1996—.

MEMBER: American Academy of Advertising, American Marketing Association, Association for Consumer Research, Institute for Operations Research and the Management Sciences, American Youth Soccer Association, director of coaches, 1996-99, Hacienda Heights, CA tournament director, 1998-99.

AWARDS, HONORS: Best Paper Award, American Marketing Association Summer Educators' Conference, 1982; Chester B. Phillips Award for Outstanding Teaching as a professor, 1988; Best Paper Award, Marketing Science Institute's Working Paper Series, 1993; Donny Award for best cover art in marketing science, 1996; William F. Odell Award for best paper, *Journal of Marketing Research,* 1998; Harold D. Maynard Award for most significant contribution to marketing thought, *Journal of Marketing,* 2000, 2002; best business book citation, *Harvard Business Review,* 2001, for *Will and Vision;* AMA-Berry Award for best book in marketing, 2003; Distinguished Alumnus Award, University of Michigan, 2003; winner of research competition on global marketing, Marketing Science Institute and *International Journal of Research in Marketing,* 2003.

WRITINGS:

Advertising and Sales Promotion Strategy, Addison-Wesley (Reading, MA), 1998.

(With Peter N. Golder) *Will and Vision: How Latecomers Grow to Dominate Markets,* McGraw-Hill (New York, NY), 2002.

Effective Advertising: Understanding When, How, and Why Advertising Works, Sage Publications (Thousand Oaks, CA), 2004.

Contributor to periodicals, including *Journal of Marketing Research, Strategic Management Journal, Journal of Marketing,* and *Sloan Management Review.*

WORK IN PROGRESS: Cases in Advertising and Promotion, Sage Publications (Thousand Oaks, CA), forthcoming; research into innovation, market entry, new product growth, advertising, pricing, and promotion.

SIDELIGHTS: Gerard J. Tellis was born in India, where he was also educated before immigrating to the United States and earning a Ph.D. at the University of Michigan. Tellis worked for Johnson & Johnson in sales and marketing in India, and from 1983 he taught marketing, first at the University of Iowa and then at the University of Southern California, where he was named Neely Professor of Marketing. Tellis contributes articles to a long list of business journals and has written books that include *Will and Vision: How Latecomers Grow to Dominate the Market,* which he coauthored with Peter N. Golder, associate professor of marketing at New York University.

Tellis and Golder provide an historical analysis of the evolution of various markets over ten years. What they conclude is that rushing to be first with an idea or product does not guarantee success. Instead, the principles that ensure market leadership include vision, persistence, innovation, commitment, and asset leverage. "The real causes of enduring market leadership are vision and will," they write. "Enduring market leaders have a revolutionary and inspiring vision of the mass market, and they exhibit an indomitable will to realize that vision."

The authors offer case studies in sixty-six industries of companies that have become dominant but were not first. These include Gillette, which entered the safety razor market decades after it began; Microsoft, which has never pioneered; and Amazon, not the first Internet bookseller, but now the largest. Other companies discussed include Hewlett-Packard, Federal Express, Procter & Gamble, Charles Schwab, Xerox, Intel, and Matsushita.

BIOGRAPHICAL AND CRITICAL SOURCES:

PERIODICALS

Adweek, April 17, 1989, Nina Lentini, "'Stop Wasting Money,' Researcher Tells TV Advertisers," p. 40.

Sloan Management Review, winter, 1996, "First to Market, First to Fail? Real Causes of Enduring Market Leadership."*

* * *

TEMPLE-RASTON, Dina 1964-

PERSONAL: Born August 25, 1964, in Brussels, Belgium; daughter of John Clark and Sandra Hughes Temple Raston; married Frank S. Coleman, October 9, 1993. *Education:* Northwestern University, B.A. (with honors), 1986; Liaoning University, Shenyang, China, degree (Chinese language), 1989. *Religion:* Roman Catholic.

ADDRESSES: *Office*—Foreign Editor, *New York Sun,* 105 Chambers St., New York, NY 10025. *E-mail*—templeraston@aol.com.

CAREER: Liaoning Provincial Government, Shenyang, China, special foreign assistant, 1988-89; *Asiaweek,* Hong Kong, China correspondent, 1990-91; Bloomberg News, Hong Kong correspondent, 1991-93, White House correspondent, 1993-2000; *USA Today,* economics correspondence, 2000-01; CNNFN, producer, 2001-02; *New York Sun,* foreign editor, 2002—.

MEMBER: Counsel of Foreign Relations, White House Correspondent Association.

AWARDS, HONORS: Prize for Top Essay, Northwestern University, 1986; Discover Award, Barnes & Noble, 2002, for *A Death in Texas.*

WRITINGS:

A Death in Texas: A Story of Race, Murder, and a Small Town's Struggle for Redemption, H.Holt (New York, NY), 2002.

WORK IN PROGRESS: *Justice in the Grass,* a book about the 1994 genocide in Rwanda and the country's attempts to recover.

SIDELIGHTS: Dina Temple-Raston is a journalist and former foreign correspondent. In her first book, *A Death in Texas: A Story of Race, Murder, and a Small Town's Struggle for Redemption,* she draws heavily on her skills as a journalist.

In 1998, in the small town of Jasper, Texas, a black man was dragged to his death while chained behind a pickup truck. Three white supremacists were charged with the murder and later convicted. In this book, Temple-Raston chronicles what happened to the community in the aftermath of the murder.

Temple-Raston describes Jasper as an economically depressed and shockingly segregated community with a large number of white supremacists. However, the residents had developed a sort of tenuous truce with one another and lived relatively peacefully, until the murder of James Byrd. Temple-Raston writes about how the incident left the community in fragments, struggling to make sense of their way of life. A *Publishers Weekly* reviewer observed that the author "uses this basic crime narrative as the backdrop for a complex, multilayered portrait of a small town coming to grips with its own history of racial hatred." Using extensive interviews and observations during the trials, Temple-Raston "writes not only about the crime but also about the town, its casual segregation, and the terror of its black community," noted Deirdre Root in *Library Journal.* A *Kirkus Reviews* writer called the book a "grimly powerful chronicle of a hate crime."

BIOGRAPHICAL AND CRITICAL SOURCES:

PERIODICALS

Book, January-February, 2002, Ruth Lopez, review of *A Death in Texas: A Story of Race, Murder, and a Small Town's Struggle for Redemption,* p. 76.

Booklist, December 1, 2001, Vanessa Bush, review of *A Death in Texas,* p. 613.
Kirkus Reviews, October 15, 2001, review of *A Death in Texas,* p. 1473.
Library Journal, November 15, 2001, Deirdre Root, review of *A Death in Texas,* p. 85.
Publishers Weekly, October 22, 2001, review of *A Death in Texas,* p. 60.

ONLINE

Henry Holt and Company Web site, http://www.henryholt.com/ (March 6, 2003).

* * *

THARPS, Lori L. 1972-

PERSONAL: Born 1972. *Education:* Smith College, bachelor's degree; Columbia University Graduate School of Journalism, M.A.

ADDRESSES: *Agent*—c/o Author Mail, St. Martin's Press, 175 Fifth Avenue, New York, NY 10010.

CAREER: Journalist and author. *Vibe,* former fact-checker; *Entertainment Weekly,* correspondent.

WRITINGS:

(With Ayana D. Byrd) *Hair Story: Untangling the Roots of Black Hair in America,* St. Martin's Press (New York, NY), 2001.

SIDELIGHTS: Lori L. Tharps is a journalist who has traced the history of black women's emotional ties to their hair from 1400 to the present. She published her findings in the book *Hair Story: Untangling the Roots of Black Hair in America.*

Tharps began *Hair Story* as part of her master's thesis about the social, cultural, and political implications of hair. With the help of friend and coauthor Ayana D. Byrd, she expanded her findings into a full-length book in which the authors explore why hair is an integral part of a black woman's identity. They begin their chronological history in Africa during the slave trade, and note how African women in polygamous marriages styled their hair to annoy other wives, and how warriors preparing for battle braided their hair to show that they were ready to die. Continuing their history in the United States, Tharps and Byrd poke fun at the "mushrooms" of the 1960s and 1970s and black women's relentless attempts to straighten their hair. They also describe popular hairstyles of today. A reviewer in *Publishers Weekly* noted that while *Hair Story* is about African-American hair, the book has appeal for readers of all races: it explains "black hair culture to the uninformed, so readers who don't already know what 'the kitchen' refers to (hair at the nape of the neck, usually the 'nappiest') will soon find out."

While most critics praised *Hair Story* for its historical accuracy, some questioned its organization. Robin Givhan remarked in *Dread and Locks* that the book "meanders from one topic to another and often backtracks. And, ultimately . . . it devolves into a familiar lament about the woes of styling kinky hair in a culture that values straight hair." However, Patrik Henry Bass, who reviewed the book for *Essence,* recommended that the book "be at the top of everyone's must-read list."

BIOGRAPHICAL AND CRITICAL SOURCES:

PERIODICALS

Black Issues Book Review, July, 2001, Arlene McKanic, review of *Hair Story: Untangling the Roots of Black Hair in America,* p. 54.
Entertainment Weekly, March 9, 2001, James W. Seymore, Jr., review of *Hair Story,* p. 8.
Essence, February, 2001, Patrik Henry Bass, "Back to Our Roots," p. 66.
Plain Dealer (Cleveland, OH), March 11, 2001, "Black Women's Hair Hangup: Untangling an Emotional Complex," p. 9.
Publishers Weekly, December 11, 2000, review of *Hair Story,* p. 73.
Washington Post, May 30, 2001, Robin Givhan, "Dread and Locks," p. C10.*

THESIGER, Wilfred (Patrick) 1910-2003

OBITUARY NOTICE—See index for *CA* sketch: Born June 3, 1910, in Addis Ababa, Ethiopia; died August 24, 2003, in London, England. Explorer and author. Thesiger was a renowned adventurer who spent the majority of his life traveling uncharted areas of Africa and the Middle East. The son of a British minister stationed abroad, he spent his early years in Ethiopia—what was then Abyssinia—and India. His family returned to England in 1919, and he attended boarding school there, later attending Eton and completing a master's degree at Magdalen College, Oxford. An invitation to attend Haile Selassie's coronation in 1930 presented all the inspiration he needed to begin his life in exploration, and the next he joined a fishing crew off the coast of Iceland. Next, he returned to warmer climes to mount an expedition to find out where the Awash River ended its course. This first effort was unsuccessful, but a second expedition led Thesiger to find out that the river eventually drained into Abhebad Lake. From 1935 until 1940, he was employed in the Sudan Political Service, during which time he learned Arabic and the culture of Arabic tribes, gaining a great love and appreciation for the beauty of the desert and its people. When World War II began, he served in the Sudan Defense Force, fighting on the Ethiopian frontier, North Africa, and Syria, earning the rank of major, and being named to the Distinguished Service Order in 1941. With the war over, he returned to his traveling ways, mounting expeditions across the barren Empty Quarter of Saudi Arabia by camel and, in the 1950s, living with Madan Arabs in Iraq, where he gathered rare plant species for the British Museum. His other travels took him to Afghanistan, Kurdistan, Pakistan, and Kenya; in Kenya he lived with Samburu tribespeople, who adopted him into one of their families. He spent much of the rest of his life in Kenya, only moving back to England to stay in 1995. Thesiger's extraordinary life and travels, which also earned him titles of Commander of the British Empire in 1968 and Knight of the British Empire in 1995, are captured in his books, which include *Arabian Sands* (1959), *The Marsh Arabs* (1964), *Desert, Marsh and Mountain* (1979), *The Life of My Choice* (1987), *Visions of a Nomad* (1987), *My Kenya Days* (1994), *The Danakil Diary* (1996), *Among the Mountains* (1998), *Crossing the Sands* (1999), *A Vanished World* (2001), and *My Life and Travels* (2002).

OBITUARIES AND OTHER SOURCES:

BOOKS

Dictionary of Literary Biography, Volume 204: *British Travel Writers, 1940-1997,* Gale (Detroit, MI), 1999.

PERIODICALS

Independent (London, England), August 27, 2003, p. 16.
Los Angeles Times, August 28, 2003, p. B14.
New York Times, August 27, 2003, p. C14.
Times (London, England), August 26, 2003.
Washington Post, August 27, 2003, p. B6.

* * *

THIBODEAUX, Mark E. 1970-

PERSONAL: Born February 13, 1970, in Church Point, LA; son of Carroll J. (a farmer) and Shirley V. (a spiritual director) Thibodeaux. *Ethnicity:* "Cajun (French Canadian)." *Education:* Loyola University, B.S., 1993; Weston Jesuit School of Theology, M.Div., 2000, Th.M., 2001. *Hobbies and other interests:* Reading, running, cooking.

ADDRESSES: *Office*—Strake Jesuit College Preparatory, 8900 Bellaire Blvd., Houston, TX 77036. *E-mail*—thibodeaux_m@strakejesuit.org.

CAREER: Ordained Roman Catholic priest of the Society of Jesus (Jesuits; S.J.), 1988—, member of formation consultants for New Orleans Province, New Orleans, LA, 1996-97. Dallas Jesuit College Preparatory, Dallas, TX, teacher of theology and counselor, 1993-97; Strake Jesuit College Preparatory, Houston, TX, director of pastoral ministry and teacher of theology, 2001—. *Company* (magazine), member of board of directors, 2001—.

WRITINGS:

Armchair Mystic: Easing into Contemplation, St. Anthony Messenger Press (Cincinnati, OH), 2001.

Dear God, I'm Moody: Prayer Starters for Every Occasion (tentative title), St. Anthony Messenger Press (Cincinnati, OH), in press.

Contributor to books, including *A Shepherd for New Orleans,* New Orleans Province, Society of Jesus (New Orleans, LA).

WORK IN PROGRESS: Two children's books, *José and the Ants* and *The Apple Tree.*

SIDELIGHTS: Mark E. Thibodeaux told *CA:* "As a Jesuit and a Roman Catholic priest, my purpose in writing is to inspire and inform 'the people in the pew,' the everyday Christians who do not have a theological background. In my writing, I try to take difficult theological and spiritual concepts such as contemplation and discernment and make them easy for anyone to understand and to practice."

* * *

THOMAS, Trisha R. 1964-

PERSONAL: Born May 28, 1964, in San Diego, CA; married; three children. *Ethnicity:* "African American." *Education:* California State University, Los Angeles, B.S. (business administration), 1988.

ADDRESSES: *Home*—Seattle, WA. *Agent*—Marie D. Brown, Marie Brown Associates, 625 Broadway, New York, NY 10012.

CAREER: Novelist. Worked variously as a marketing consultant, bridal store owner, artist, designer, and teacher.

AWARDS, HONORS: Outstanding Literary Work in Fiction, National Association for the Advancement of Colored People Image Award, finalist, 2001, for *Nappily Ever After.*

WRITINGS:

Nappily Ever After, Crown Publishers (New York, NY), 2000.

Roadrunner: A Novel, Crown Publishers (New York, NY), 2002.

ADAPTATIONS: *Nappy Ever After* was optioned for a motion picture.

SIDELIGHTS: Tricia R. Thomas received thirty-five rejections for her first novel, an African-American mystery that Thomas later realized "wasn't what was supposed to happen." Thomas told reporter John Marshall, of her hometown newspaper the *Seattle Post-Intelligencer* that the success of other contemporary African-American authors "lit a fire" in her, and she tried again. Her second effort worked: the 2000 novel *Nappily Ever After* was sought after by literary agents and eventually won its author both a multi-book publishing contract and a nomination for the prestigious National Association for the Advancement of Colored People Image Award. Her best-selling debut was also optioned for a major motion picture planned for release in 2003.

Nappily Ever After is the story of Venus Johnson, an advertising executive who decides at the age of thirty-four to change her hair and change her life. She leaves her boyfriend, Clint Fairchild, a doctor who will not commit, and perhaps more significantly she cuts off her long, chemically straightened hair, leaving her with a close-cropped, "nappy" afro. In her newfound freedom she is forced to face the conventions of beauty, her own self-image, and her desire for security with a hard-to-find "good man." Venus also faces sexual harassment and racism at work, and a "black Barbie" who becomes her rival for love. Critics found that, if the basic plotline covers familiar territory, the book also offers surprises, insight, and wit. Reviewer Delorese Ambrose, for *Black Issues Book Review,* wrote that in *Nappily Ever After* "Thomas delivers up a powerful, funny and sensitive coming-of-age novel." *Booklist* reviewer Vanessa Bush said "Thomas offers painful but amusing insights" into relationships, beauty, and black culture itself. In the *Washington Post* Rhonda Stewart favorably compared Thomas's thoughts on beauty and self-acceptance to those of African-American feminist bell hooks. Stewart wrote, "Thomas deftly uses the premium placed on long and straight 'good' hair to tackle a host of sensitive issues in an honest and compelling way: the internecine politics of skin color, the dreaded 'good black man' shortage and the contortions that black women put themselves through hoping to measure up."

Nappily Ever After was a finalist for the NAACP Image Awards in 2001; finalists in other categories included African-American luminaries such as Denzel Washington, Oprah Winfrey, and Stevie Wonder.

Thomas's second novel, *Roadrunner,* tells the story of a professional athlete who loses his career due to an injury, which has also left him addicted to painkillers. Increasingly moody, Dell neglects his family and abuses his wife. The novel, described in *Kirkus Reviews* as "another solid drama" from Thomas, recounts the efforts of Dell and Leah to save their marriage while also coping with unwanted attention from outsiders. A writer for *Publishers Weekly* praised Thomas's narrative skill and observed that this novel "packs a punch."

Speaking of the role of writing in her life, Thomas told *CA:* "Writing is the personal truth of the author. I'm inspired by finding the truth."

BIOGRAPHICAL AND CRITICAL SOURCES:

PERIODICALS

Black Issues Book Review, January, 2001, Delorese Ambrose, review of *Nappily Ever After,* p. 17.

Booklist, November 15, 2000, Vanessa Bush, review of *Nappily Ever After,* p. 620; June 1, 2002, Vanessa Bush, review of *Roadrunner,* p. 1689.

Courier-Mail (Brisbane, Australia), February 4, 2002, Darrell Giles, "All Hail Oscar Favourite Halle," p. 20.

Essence, December, 2000, review of *Nappily Ever After.*

Kirkus Reviews, May 15, 2002, review of *Roadrunner,* p. 697.

Library Journal, November 1, 2000, Ann Burns and Emily Joy Jones, review of *Nappily Every After,* p. 102.

Publishers Weekly, November 6, 2000, review of *Nappily Ever After,* p. 71; June 17, 2002, p. 45.

Seattle Post-Intelligencer, February 15, 2001, John Marshall, "Double Exposure: Washington Writers in the Celebrity Spotlight for NAACP Image Award."

Washington Post, July 23, 2001, Rhonda Stewart, "The Tress Code," p. C3.

ONLINE

Book Remarks.com, http://www.book-remarks.com/ (December, 2000) interview with Thomas.

Zap 2 It, http://www.zap2it.com/ (January 29, 2002), "Halle Berry to Become 'Nappily Ever After.'"

* * *

THOMPSON, Mark 1956-

PERSONAL: Born January 24, 1956. *Education:* Graduated from Columbia University Law School. *Hobbies and other interests:* Urban backyard farmer.

ADDRESSES: *Home*—P.O. Box 4039, Culver City, CA 90231. *E-mail*—markthomp@yahoo.com.

CAREER: Journalist and author.

AWARDS, HONORS: Best Western Nonfiction: Biography, Spur Awards, 2002, for *American Character: The Curious Life of Charles Fletcher Lummis and the Rediscovery of the Southwest.*

WRITINGS:

American Character: The Curious Life of Charles Fletcher Lummis and the Rediscovery of the Southwest, Arcade Publishing (New York, NY), 2001.

Contributor of articles to several publications, including *Los Angeles Times, Atlantic, New Republic, Wall Street Journal, Economist,* and *In Season.*

SIDELIGHTS: Mark Thompson is a New York City law student who moved west and became a journalist. His topics range from genetic fingerprinting to paddlewheel steamers in Bangladesh, and he is also the author of *American Character: The Curious Life of Charles Fletcher Lummis and the Rediscovery of the Southwest,* a biography that won the 2002 Spur Award for best Western nonfiction.

Charles Lummis was born in New England and became a student at Harvard University. His academic studies did not particularly interest him, but he befriended a fellow member of his class, Theodore Roosevelt, a connection that would be renewed in his later years. When Lummis was twenty-five years old, he gained national attention by walking from Cincinnati, Ohio to Los Angeles, California during the fall and winter months between 1884 and 1885, in order to begin his journalistic career with the *Los Angeles Times.* Lummis, however, was not merely a journalist, but a man skilled in many areas, including anthropology, musicology, archaeology, and photojournalism. A man who did not even allow blindness or partial paralysis to deter his prodigious activities, he was an indefatigable activist, environmentalist, and defender of the rights of Native Americans. Due to Lummis's activism, President Roosevelt established a new approach to the relationship between the federal government and Native American tribes.

"This well-written and well-researched biography. . . . [captures] Lummis's bohemian and flamboyant lifestyle," as well as "the numerous facets of Lummis's life," remarked James J. Rawls and Doyce B. Nunis, Jr. in a *California History* review of *American Character.* In *Library Journal,* Stephen H. Peters commended Thompson for saving Lummis "from undeserved obscurity" and dubbed *American Character* "an important work." Thompson "paints an honest, vivid portrait of a man whose life was nothing short of cinematic," praised a *Publishers Weekly* writer.

BIOGRAPHICAL AND CRITICAL SOURCES:

PERIODICALS

California History, winter, 2002, James J. Rawls and Doyce B. Nunis, Jr., review of *American Character: The Curious Life of Charles Fletcher Lummis and the Rediscovery of the Southwest,* pp. 69-70.

Kirkus Reviews, February 1, 2001, review of *American Character,* p. 173.

Library Journal, March 1, 2001, Stephen H. Peters, review of *American Character,* p. 108.

Publishers Weekly, February 12, 2001, review of *American Character,* p. 195.

ONLINE

Arcade Publishing Web site, http://www.arcadepub.com/ (April 9, 2003).*

THRASHER, Travis 1971-

PERSONAL: Born 1971, in Knoxville, TN; married; wife's name Sharon (a teacher). *Education:* Trinity Christian College, B.A. (communications).

ADDRESSES: Office—Tyndale House Publishers, 351 Executive Dr., Carol Stream, IL 60188.

CAREER: Writer. Tyndale House Publishers, Carol Stream, IL, author relations manager, c. 1994—.

WRITINGS:

The Promise Remains, Tyndale House Publishers (Wheaton, IL), 2000.

The Watermark, Tyndale House Publishers (Wheaton, IL), 2001.

The Second Thief, Moody Publishers (Chicago, IL), 2003.

Three Roads Home: Stories of First Love and Second Chances, WaterBrook Press (Colorado Springs, CO), 2003.

WORK IN PROGRESS: A suspense novel with Moody Publishers titled *Gun Lake.*

SIDELIGHTS: Travis Thrasher works as an author liaison for a Christian publishing house and is himself the author of Christian romance novels, including *The Promise Remains,* called "a tender romance" by Roberta Blair in a review for *Romantic Times* online. Thrasher, who has lived in Australia, Germany, Florida, and New York, set the story in North Carolina, where he lived the longest. It depicts two lovers who have been separated for many years. Kindergarten teacher Sara Anthony is engaged to be married, but she cannot forget Ethan Ware, a writer she fell in love with long ago, but who did not share her religious beliefs. Ethan, who has been adrift and unable to write, has been offered a wonderful career opportunity, but before he can take it and move to Germany, he must discover what has happened to Sara. They find each other, and Sara's faith is accepted by Ethan. "But," said a *Publishers Weekly* contributor, "the book is driven by authentic, engaging characters, not its predictable action." A reviewer for *Marriage Partnership* called Thrasher "a promising new author."

The Watermark is about musical prodigy Sheridan Blake, whose past contains a tragic secret. Sheridan meets beautiful graduate student Genevie Liu at Covenant College where, seven years earlier, he was involved in an accident that has left him filled with remorse and guilt. His inability to open up and trust her nearly ends their relationship, but she gives him another chance, and he is ultimately able to forgive himself. In a *Library Journal* review, Melanie C. Duncan called *The Watermark* "a beautiful, sometimes whimsical journey to faith." *Romantic Times* reviewer Bev Huston considered the book "a personal journey-type novel rather than a romance." *Booklist*'s John Mort said Thrasher "writes engagingly."

BIOGRAPHICAL AND CRITICAL SOURCES:

PERIODICALS

Booklist, January 1, 2002, John Mort, review of *The Watermark,* p. 804; June 1, 2003, John Mort, review of *Three Roads Home,* p. 1740.

Library Journal, November 1, 2001, Melanie C. Duncan, review of *The Watermark,* p. 78.

Marriage Partnership, fall, 2000, review of *The Promise Remains,* p. S4, and "Birthplace of Love," p. S6.

Publishers Weekly, July 3, 2000, review of *The Promise Remains,* p. 50; December 2, 2002, review of *The Second Thief,* p. 32.

ONLINE

Evangelical Church Library Association Web site, http://www.eclalibraries.org/ (October 9, 2003), "Travis Thrasher."

Romantic Times, http://www.romantictimes.com/ (April 30, 2002), Roberta Blair, review of *The Promise Remains;* Bev Huston, review of *The Watermark.**

* * *

TINDAL, Mardi 1952-

PERSONAL: Born September 17, 1952 in Victoria Square, Ontario, Canada; married; husband's name Doug; children: two sons. *Education:* York University, B.A.; Ontario Institute for Studies in Education, M.A. *Religion:* United Church of Canada.

ADDRESSES: Home—Burlington, Ontario, Canada. *Office*—Five Oaks Centre, R.R. 3, Paris, Ontario, Canada N3L 3E3. *E-mail*—mardi.tindal@tindalgroup.com.

CAREER: Spirit Connection (television show), Ontario, Canada, co-host and story producer, 1988-97; host and producer of television shows for TV Ontario, 1997-99; Five Oaks Centre, Paris, Ontario, adult program coordinator; writer. Consultant with public, private, and voluntary organizations in Canada and the United States. Leader of adult spiritual retreats.

AWARDS, HONORS: Aurora Gold Awards for documentary, reporting, religious issues, and editing, all for video *Soul Maps.*

WRITINGS:

Soul Maps: A Guide to the Midlife Spirit, United Church Publishing House (Toronto, Ontario, Canada), 2000, Augsburg Books (Minneapolis, MN), 2003.

ADAPTATIONS: A half-hour video documentary, *Soul Maps,* has been produced in Canada.

SIDELIGHTS: Mardi Tindal is a former Canadian broadcaster who turned her own spiritual quest into a book for those who are facing midlife crises. *Soul Maps: A Guide to the Midlife Spirit* contains advice from people of varied faiths and walks of life who have managed to turn the middle years into a period of intellectual and emotional growth. Each chapter in the book contains questions to help the reader define and focus upon a spiritual search while redefining relationships with parents and children. In *Canadian Book Review Annual,* Sheila Martindale noted that while Tindal's message "may not be new or ground-breaking," it nevertheless "is packaged here in a readable and thought-provoking fashion." A *Publishers Weekly* reviewer likewise felt that the author's reflections "teach us that we're not alone in experiencing the bleak valleys of midlife."

In an interview on the *Soul Maps Web site,* Tindal said of *Soul Maps:* "I wrote this book because I needed to read it. At forty-six I was knee-deep in spiritual confusion as a person for whom spirit is critically important. I needed some mid-life wisdom so I went looking for wise, spiritually attuned mid-lifers and found them everywhere."

BIOGRAPHICAL AND CRITICAL SOURCES:

PERIODICALS

Canadian Book Review Annual, 2000, Sheila Martindale, review of *Soul Maps: A Guide to the Midlife Spirit,* p. 2147.

Publishers Weekly, October 28, 2002, review of *Soul Maps,* p. 65.

ONLINE

Augsburg Fortress Web site, http://www.augsburgfortress.org/ (January 29, 2003).

Ontario Women's Conference Web site, http://www.ontariowomensconference.ca/ (April 22, 2003).

Soul Maps Web site, http://www.soulmaps.com/ (January 29, 2003).

* * *

TODOROV, Nikolai (Todorov) 1921-2003

OBITUARY NOTICE—See index for *CA* sketch: Born June 21 (one source says June 6), 1921, in Varna, Bulgaria; died August 27, 2003. Historian, politician, educator, and author. Todorov was a former director of the Institute for Balkan Studies who was also active as a local politician and international diplomat. Originally taking a degree in medicine from Sofia University in 1947, his allegiance to Marxist principles led him to complete a history degree at the Kliment Ohrid University in 1951, and a doctorate in that subject from the Institute of Slavonic and Balkan Studies in 1972. Todorov's early academic career involved teaching at Sofia State University, where he was a reader in Balkan history from 1957 to 1970. After that he was director of the Institute of Foreign Policy at the Ministry of Foreign Affairs for a year. This was followed by several years as director of the United Center for Research and Training in History. Todorov earned a reputation as an outstanding scholar and was consequently made a senior researcher at the Bulgarian Academy of Sciences' Institute of History, and in 1964 he was named director of the Institute for Balkan Studies. As director from 1964 to 1989, Todorov made the institute an internationally recognized center of study, and from 1982 to 1989 he also served as vice president of the Academy of Sciences. A believer in the Communist Party, he was elected to the party's central committee in 1981 and 1986, though he never held a high office in Bulgaria's political system. He also became involved in international diplomacy, and his fluency in Greek made him a logical choice to be Bulgaria's ambassador to Greece in 1979. Other involvements in international organizations included serving as member of UNESCO's executive council in the early 1970s, and vice president of its International Commission on the History of Civilization in the 1980s. He was also president of UNESCO's general conference from 1985 to 1987. After the fall of the communist government in Bulgaria in 1989, Todorov still managed to be involved in politics and was chair of the Constituent Assembly of Bulgaria from 1990 to 1991. Despite his political and diplomatic work, Todorov is often best remembered as an historian, publishing several respected books, including *The Balkan City, 1400-1900* (1975), and *Sindomi istoria tis Voulgarias* (1983; "Short History of Bulgaria"); he was also the author of *The Ambassador as Historian: Bulgarian-Greek Relations during the Eighties* (1996). In recognition for his contributions to history he was made a member of the Soviet Academy of Sciences and in 1985 earned the Palmes Academiques, among other honors.

OBITUARIES AND OTHER SOURCES:

PERIODICALS

Herald (Glasgow, Scotland), August 30, 2003, p. 18.

Times (London, England), October 2, 2003.

* * *

TRINKLE, Dennis A. 1968-

PERSONAL: Born August 24, 1968, in Indianapolis, IN; son of John (an educator) and Gayle (an educator) Trinkle ; married; wife's name Kristina (an information scientist) *Ethnicity:* "White/AmerIndian" *Educa-*

tion: De Pauw University, B.A. (history; magna cum laude), 1991; University of Cincinnati, M.A. (history; with highest distinction), 1993, Ph.D. (history), 1998.

ADDRESSES: Home—1860 Bridgewater Dr., Indianapolis, IN 46123. *Office*—DePauw University, 713 South Locust St., Greencastle, IN 46135. *E-mail*—dtrinkle@depauw.edu.

CAREER: History professor and Internet research specialist. DePauw University, Greencastle, IN, associate technology coordinator and assistant professor (history), 1998—. American Association for History and Computing, executive director, 1997—; National Science Foundation, Information Technology Research Review Panel, member, 2000—; International Center for Computer Enhanced Learning, fellow, 2000—.

MEMBER: International Association for History and Computing, Society for French Historical Studies, Society for the History of Technology, American Historical Association, American Association for History and Computing, Educause, Phi Beta Kappa.

AWARDS, HONORS: Grants from University of Cincinnati, 1995; Charles Taft graduate fellow, 1995-96; Wake Forest University International Center for Computer-enhanced Learning fellow, 1999; Emory University Frye Leadership Institute fellow, 2000-01.

WRITINGS:

RESEARCH AND TECHNOLOGY

The History Highway: A Guide to Computer Resources for Historians, M. E. Sharpe (Armonk, NY), 1997.

Writing, Teaching, and Researching History in the Electronic Age, M. E. Sharpe (Armonk, NY), 1998.

(With Scott A. Merriman) *The History Highway 2000: A Guide to Internet Resources in History,* M. E. Sharpe (Armonk, NY), 2000.

(Editor, with Scott A. Merriman) *History.Edu: Essays on Teaching with Technology,* M. E. Sharpe (Armonk, NY), 2001.

(With Scott A. Merriman) *The European History Highway: A Guide to Internet Resources,* M. E. Sharpe (Armonk, NY), 2002.

(With Scott A. Merriman) *The History Highway 3.0: A Guide to Internet Resources,* M. E. Sharpe (Armonk, NY), 2002.

(With Scott A. Merriman) *The U.S. History Highway: A Guide to Internet Resources,* M. E. Sharpe (Armonk, NY), 2002.

(With Scott A. Merriman) *The World History Highway: A Guide to Internet Resources,* M. E. Sharpe (Armonk, NY), 2002.

HISTORY

The History of Computing and the Information Revolution, Bell & Howell (Ann Arbor, MI), 2001.

The Industrial Revolution, Bell & Howell (Ann Arbor, MI) 2001.

The Napoleonic Press: The Public Sphere and Oppositionary Journalism, Edwin Mellen Press (Lewiston, NY), 2002.

(Editor) *Red Computers: How the Soviet Union Lost the Cold War—The Memoirs of Dr. Boris Malinovsky,* M. E. Sharpe (Armonk, NY), 2002.

Contributor to journals, including *Journal for the Association of History and Computing, Studies on Voltaire and the Eighteenth Century,* and *Journal of Social Education.*

WORK IN PROGRESS: World History of the Information Revolution, for American Bibliographic Center-Clio.

SIDELIGHTS: Dennis A. Trinkle is an historian who has worked to push his profession into the future. Trinkle is the author and editor of multiple guides to history research on the Internet and using technology in the history classroom. With co-author Scott A. Merriman Trinkle has published an ongoing "History Highway" series addressing general history, U.S. history, European history, and world history. A professor at DePauw University, Trinkle has also been invited to participate in several national and international forums on the use of information technology in research and education.

The first of Trinkle's research guides, *The History Highway: A Guide to Internet Resources,* was published in 1997. Reviewing the book for *Historian,* critic Kevin E. Manzel wrote, "Publication of *The*

History Highway could not have come at a better time." *The History Highway* and later editions contain Web site addresses and brief descriptions of thousands of sites, organized by region, time period, or subject. Jacki L. Andre and Elizabeth Colwill, reviewing *The History Highway 2000* for *Canadian Journal of History,* said that "the excellent organization and concise descriptions made reading the book a breeze." *The History Highway 2000* also discusses Internet etiquette and the use of e-mail, news groups, and discussion lists.

Trinkle and Merriman also edited the 2001 book *History.edu: Essays on Teaching with Technology,* aimed at history teachers interested in incorporating new information technology in their classrooms. Trinkle and Merriman surveyed history professors to learn how they were using the Internet to make their courses more interactive, to teach research methods, and to enhance learning. John R. Moore reviewed the book for the journal *Teaching History: A Journal of Methods,* concluding, "*History.edu* provides a valuable service in describing what is being done to incorporate technology into the classroom." In addition to publishing on technology and education, Trinkle also works in the field of eighteenth-century French history. His works in this specialty include *The Napoleonic Press: The Public Sphere and Oppositionary Journalism.*

BIOGRAPHICAL AND CRITICAL SOURCES:

PERIODICALS

Booklist, February 15, 1997, George Eberhart, review of *The History Highway: A Guide to Internet Resources,* p. 974.

Canadian Journal of History, April, 2001, Jacki L. Andre and Elizabeth Colwill, review of *The History Highway 2000,* p. 201.

Historian, summer, 1999, *The History Highway,* p. 969.

Library Journal, November 1, 2000, Terry Christner, review of *History.edu: Essays on Teaching with Technology,* p. 94.

Teaching History, spring, 2002, John R. Moore, review of *History.edu,* pp. 33-34.

Times Higher Education Supplement, February 5, 1999, Mike Cosgrave, review of *The History Highway,* p. 13.

ONLINE

AskaHistorian.com, http://www.askahistorian.com/ (June 12, 2002), "Dennis A. Trinkle."

Dennis A. Trinkle Home Page, http://www.depauw.edu/acad/history/dtrinkle.htm/ (June 12, 2002).

U-V

URBINA, Nicasio 1958-

PERSONAL: Born July 12, 1958, in Buenos Aires, Argentina son of Guillermo (a lawyer) and Celia (a homemaker) Urbina; married Elaine Mott (a pediatric cardiologist), June 20, 1990; children: Francesca. *Ethnicity:* "White Hispanic." *Education:* Florida International University, B.A. and M.S.; Georgetown University, Ph.D.

ADDRESSES: *Home*—3406 State Street Dr., New Orleans, LA 70125. *Office*—Department of Spanish and Portuguese, Tulane University, New Orleans, LA 70118. *E-mail*—urbina@mailhost.tcs.tulane.edu.

CAREER: Tulane University, New Orleans, LA, associate professor of Spanish, c. 1990—. International Hospital for Children, secretary, 1998—.

MEMBER: Modern Language Association of America, Latin-American Studies Association, Nicaraguan Academy of Language.

AWARDS, HONORS: Ruben Dario Literary Award, 1995.

WRITINGS:

El libro de las palabras enajendas, Editorial Universitaria Centroamericana (Santa José, Costa Rica), 1991.

La significación del género: estudio semiótico de las novelas y ensayos de Ernesto Sabato, Ediciones Universal (Miami, FL), 1992.

Sintaxis de un signo, Editorial Decenio (Managua, Nicaragua), 1995.

La novela nicaraguense: analisis narratologico, Instituto Nicaraguense de Cultura (New Orleans, LA), 1995.

El ojo del cielo perdido, Centro Nicaraguanse de Escritores (Managua, Nicaragua), 1999, 2nd edition, Editorial Decenio (Managua, Nicaragua), 1999.

* * *

VAJDA, Edward (J.) 1958-

PERSONAL: Born Edward M. Johnson, September 10, 1958, in Camp Le Jeune, NC; changed name, 1981; son of Richard (a U.S. Marine Corps sergeant) and Elizabeth (a typist; maiden name, Vajda) Johnson; married Amy Logan, June 15, 1991; children: Michael, Derek, Kathryn. *Ethnicity:* "Carpatho-Rusyn, Hungarian." *Education:* Indiana University, B.A. (Russian language), 1980; University of Washington, M.A. (Slavic linguistics), 1984, Ph.D. (Slavic linguistics), 1987. *Politics:* Independent. *Religion:* Christian.

ADDRESSES: *Home*—2481 Pheasant Way, Ferndale, WA 98248. *Office*—Western Washington University, Modern Languages—9057, Bellingham, WA 98225. *E-mail*—vajda@cc.wwu.edu.

CAREER: Western Washington University, Bellingham, professor of Russian, East Asian studies, and linguistics, 1987—.

MEMBER: Linguistic Society of America, Society for the Study of the Indigenous Languages of the Americas, International Linguistics Association.

AWARDS, HONORS: Excellence in Teaching Award, Western Washington University, 1992.

WRITINGS:

(With Valentina Umanets) *Russian Punctuation and Related Symbols: A Guide for English Speakers,* Slavica (Bloomington, IN), 1999.

Yeniseian Peoples and Languages, Curzon (Surrey, England), 2000.

Ket ("Languages of the World" series), Lincom Europa (Munich, Germany), in press.

WORK IN PROGRESS: Tomam's Feathers: A History of Siberia's Kets; editor, "Current Issues in Siberian Studies" series.

SIDELIGHTS: Edward Vajda told *CA:* "Many indigenous languages and ethnic groups around the world today are under threat of extinction. For the past decade I have studied the native minority peoples of Siberia in an attempt to trace their ancient connections with native Americans. In many cases, my scholarly publications on the peoples and languages of North Asia represent the first substantial descriptions available in English. In 1998 I became the first American to travel to Central Siberia and study the Ket people of the Yenisei River region. The Kets number about 1,200 and speak a unique language unrelated to the other tongues of North Asia. I plan to continue to write scholarly articles and monographs on the Kets and their language to help acquaint the rest of the world with this fascinating group of people. My writing involves a great deal of preliminary research. My inspiration derives from the conviction that every ethnic group contributes an important piece of the story of human history."

* * *

VALGEIRSDÓTTIR, Sigríður 1919-

PERSONAL: Given name is sometimes transliterated as "Sigridur"; born November 16, 1919, in Reykjavik, Iceland. *Education:* College of Physical Education and Sport, graduated, 1942; University of California, Berkeley, M.A. and teaching credential, 1947; State University of New York, Buffalo, M.Ed., 1968, Ph.D., 1974.

ADDRESSES: Agent—c/o Menntamálaráðuneytið, Sölvhólsgötu 4, 150 Reykjavik, Iceland.

CAREER: Member of Orchesis dance group, beginning 1944; College of Physical Education and Sport, Iceland, teacher, 1949-51; Folk Dance Society of Reykjavik, Reykjavik, Iceland, founder, 1951, choreographer and director of Icelandic folk dance performances in Iceland and around the world, 1951-94. Teachers College of Iceland, professor of educational psychology and director of Institute of Educational Research of Iceland, 1982-91. National Theater of Iceland, choreographer of stage productions, 1954-67.

AWARDS, HONORS: Golden Pin, Icelandic Sport Union, 1950; award from Gymnastic Society of Reykjavik, 1956; German cultural awards for choreography, 1969; award from Folk Dance Society of Reykjavik, 1976; Order of the Falcon, President of Iceland, 1990.

WRITINGS:

Leikir (title means "Games"), Leiftur (Reykjavik, Iceland), 1958.

Pjó dansar I (title means "Folk Dances I"), Menntamálará uneyti (Reykjavik, Iceland), 1959.

Gömlu dansarnir (title means "Old-time Dances in Iceland"), Leiftur (Reykjavik, Iceland), 1986.

(With Mínerva Jónsdóttir) *Gömlu dansarnir í tv ær aldir: brot úr íslenskri menningarsögu* (Reykjavik, Iceland), 1994.

Kennari, skóli & læsi íslenskra barna, Menntamálaráðuneytið (Reykjavik, Iceland), 1996.

BIOGRAPHICAL AND CRITICAL SOURCES:

BOOKS

International Dictionary of Modern Dance, St. James Press (Detroit, MI), 1998.*

* * *

VANSTRUM, Glenn S.

PERSONAL: Born in MN; married; wife's name, Diane; children: Erik, Nicholas. *Education:* Grinnell College, B.A., 1974; University of California, San Diego, M.D. (anesthesiology and emergency medicine), 1980.

ADDRESSES: Home—La Jolla, CA. *Office*—c/o Vanstrum Nature Photography, Market Place Color, 1760 Tullie Circle NE, Atlanta, GA 30329.

CAREER: Physician, photographer, and journalist. Executive in Vanstrum Nature Photography, La Jolla, CA, and Atlanta, GA.

MEMBER: Phi Beta Kappa.

WRITINGS:

(Editor) *Anesthesia in Emergency Medicine,* Little Brown (Boston, MA), 1989.

The Saltwater Wilderness (nonfiction), Oxford University Press (New York, NY), 2003.

Contributor to books, including *American Nature Writing: 1999,* edited by John Murray, Oregon State University Press (Corvalis, OR), 1999; *American Nature Writing: 2001,* edited by Murray, Oregon State University Press, 2001; and *American Nature Writing: 2002,* edited by Murray, Fulcrum Publishing, 2002. Contributor to periodicals, including *California Wild, Ocean Realm, Sierra,* and *Los Angeles Times.*

WORK IN PROGRESS: A book on apex marine predators, a series of children's books, and a collection of short stories.

SIDELIGHTS: The arc of Glenn Vanstrum's life and career has taken him from Minnesota to California, and along the way he has acquired skills and talents in a number of areas—including anesthesiology and emergency medicine, his specialty as a medical doctor. But his "day job" is only one aspect of the body of work produced by Vanstrum, who first developed a love of the outdoors in the wild northern portion of his native state. He graduated from the National Outdoor Leadership School in the Wind River Range of Wyoming, and studied science and music at Grinnell College in Iowa before moving to California. There he discovered the largest wilderness on the planet: the ocean. Emblematic of the diversity in Vanstrum's pursuits are the titles of his first two published books: *Anesthesia in Emergency Medicine* and *The Saltwater Wilderness.* Margaret Rioux in *Library Journal* called the second of these a "collection of fascinating essays" that she recommended for any library where "there is, or should be, an interest in preserving the oceans." As Rioux noted, while Vanstrum uses as his point of departure in each chapter a specific locale or activity involved in surfing or diving, he eventually brings to bear a variety of topics relating to everything from ecology to history, and from marine biology to politics. "Whether he's riding the waves or diving below them," wrote Donna Seaman in *Booklist,* "Vanstrum is a well-informed and engagingly informative marine explorer and advocate."

BIOGRAPHICAL AND CRITICAL SOURCES:

PERIODICALS

Booklist, February 15, 2003, Donna Seaman, review of *The Saltwater Wilderness,* p. 1025.

Library Journal, February 15, 2003, Margaret Rioux, review of *The Saltwater Wilderness,* p. 166.

Nature Conservancy, spring, 2003, Cathy Asato, review of *The Saltwater Wilderness.*

ONLINE

Glenn Vanstrum Home Page, http://www.vanstrum.net (September 14, 2003).*

* * *

VARNEDOE, (John) Kirk (Train) 1946-2003

OBITUARY NOTICE—See index for *CA* sketch: Born January 18, 1946, in Savannah, GA; died of colon cancer August 14, 2003, in New York, NY. Art historian, educator, and author. Varnedoe is best remembered as the chief curator of painting and sculpture at New York City's Museum of Modern Art. He earned his undergraduate degree at Williams College in 1967, where he taught for a year before going on to graduate school and receiving his Ph.D. at Stanford in 1972. Varnedoe then taught at Stanford for a year and Columbia University for six years before joining the faculty at New York University. He rose from associate professor in 1980 to full professor in

1984. The next year, he also joined the Museum of Modern Art as an associate curator. In 1989, while retaining his position at New York University as an adjunct professor, he was promoted to chief curator of painting and sculpture at the museum. As curator, Varnedoe made significant contributions to the museum by opening it up more to modern artworks of the post-war era. Before Varnedoe's activities there, the museum had gained a reputation for being closed-minded about such pieces, but he brought in art for exhibits from the 1960s, 1970s, and beyond, while also opening up the galleries to artists from outside of France and America (the museum's previous main focus), as well as including more pieces by modern women artists. Thus, the name Museum of Modern Art became much more apropos under Varnedoe. In addition, however, Varnedoe did not neglect the earlier masters, and he added valuable pieces from artists such as Van Gogh and Matisse to the museum's collection. He also organized several important and popular exhibitions, including "Vienna 1900: Art, Architecture, and Design" and "High and Low: Modern Art and Popular Culture." Awarded the genius prize in 1984 from the MacArthur Foundation fellowship, among other honors, Varnedoe was the author of several art history books and exhibit catalogs, including *The Drawings of Rodin* (1971), written with Albert Elsen, *Gustave Caillebotte* (1987), *Nordic Light: Nordic Art at the Turn of the Century* (1988), *Cy Twombly: A Retrospective* (1994), and (with Pepe Karmel) *Jackson Pollock* (1998). He was writing a book about a van Gogh portrait of Joseph Roulin that the museum had recently acquired when he passed away.

OBITUARIES AND OTHER SOURCES:

PERIODICALS

Chicago Tribune, August 16, 2003, section 2, p. 11.
Los Angeles Times, August 16, 2003, p. B18.
New York Times, August 15, 2003, p. C12.

* * *

VELOSO, Caetano 1942-

PERSONAL: Born August 7, 1942, in Santo Amaro da Purificao, Bahia, Brazil; *Education:* Attended Federal University of Bahia (philosophy), 1963-66.

ADDRESSES: *Agent*—Nonesuch Records, c/o Debbie Ferraro, 75 Rockefeller Plaza., New York, NY 10019.

CAREER: Musician, composer, performer, writer, poet, and painter. Has recorded over thirty albums for labels including PolyGram, Warner, Phillips, and Nonesuch. As a performer, tours widely in Brazil and around the world.

WRITINGS:

Alegria, Alegria, P. Q. Ronca (Rio de Janeiro, Brazil), 1977.
A imagen do som de Caetano Veloso: 80 composicoes de Caetano Veloso, F. Alves (Rio de Janeiro Brazil), 1998.
Tropical Truth: A Story of Music and Revolution in Brazil, Knopf (New York, NY), 2002.

AUTHOR OF LYRICS; SOUND RECORDING

Domingo, PolyGram (Rio de Janeiro, Brazil), 1969.
Barra 69, PolyGram (Rio de Janeiro, Brazil), 1971.
Transa, PolyGram (Rio de Janeiro, Brazil), 1972.
Araca Azul, PolyGram (Rio de Janeiro, Brazil), 1973.
Temporada de Veraro, PolyGram (Rio de Janeiro, Brazil), 1974.
A arte de Caetano Veloso, Fontana (Rio de Janeiro, Brazil), 1975.
Historia da tropicalia, Philips (Rio de Janeiro, Brazil), 1985.
Caetano Veloso, Nonesuch (New York, NY), 1986.
(With Chico Buarque) *Melhores momentos de Chico e Caetano,* Som Livre (Rio de Janeiro, Brazil), 1986.
Sem lenco sem documento, PolyGram (Rio de Janeiro, Brazil), 1989.
Estrangeiro, Nonesuch (New York, NY), 1989.
Circulado, Nonesuch (New York, NY), 1991.
Os Cariocas, Warner (São Paulo, Brazil), 1992.
Fina Estampa, PolyGram, 1994.
(With Gilberto Gil) *Tropicalia 2,* Nonesuch (New York, NY), 1994.
Livro, Nonesuch (New York, NY), 1999.
Live in Bahia, Nonesuch (New York, NY), 2002.

SIDELIGHTS: Brazilian singer and songwriter Caetano Veloso came to prominence during the 1960s "tropicalia" movement, a fusion of folk, popular, and foreign musical influences. A musician of the stature of Bob Dylan or John Lennon in those men's respective countries, Veloso is "the elder statesman of Brazilian popular music," according to Larry Rohter in *New York Times.* "He has been an indelible cultural force in this country since the 1960's [and] many of the 325 or so songs he has written are now standards [in Brazil]," Rohter further noted. According to *Newsweek*'s Malcolm Jones, "Veloso elevates prankishness to an esthetic." Comfortable in musical idioms from jazz to pop to bossa nova, rap, funk, and Afro-Brazilian, Veloso is no mere musical chameleon. His music and the musical movement he helped found have been a vital feature of the Brazilian scene for almost four decades, and his influence on world music has greatly increased since the 1990s and the first original issuing of one of his recordings in the American market.

Born in a small town of the Bahian province in 1942, Veloso grew up listening to Caribbean, African, and even North American pop music. The bossa nova of João Gilberto of the 1950s were also a powerful influence. Veloso's family moved to Salvador in 1960 so he could attend high school there, and in 1963 he entered the Federal University of Bahia where he studied philosophy. He also began singing bossa nova in bars during these years, as well as penning articles for a local newspaper and acting in avant-garde theater. His sister, Maria Bethania, meanwhile was embarking on what would be a very successful singing career. In 1966, Veloso accompanied her to Rio de Janeiro, where she became involved in the theater. He was not only along for the ride, however; soon he had won a lyric-writing contest with his song "Um Dia," and was signed on the Phillips label. He competed in various music festivals and began to build a following for his music, still strongly influenced by bossa nova at this time.

Soon Veloso had joined forces with other young artists, such as Gal Costa and Gilbert Gil—with whom he had been friends since his Salvador days—to create a new wave in Brazilian music that blended such foreign elements as rock with more traditional forms of Brazilian music and began to blur the border between low and high music. His early singles hits, the 1967 "Alegria, Alegria" (Happiness, Happiness), and the 1968 "Tropicalia," as well as his first album, *Domingo,* helped to define the aesthetics of the new movement. "Arty and eclectic, Tropicalismo retained a bossa nova influence," wrote Laura Hightower in *Contemporary Musicians,* "but added elements of folk-rock and art-rock to a mixture of loud electric guitars, poetic spoken-work sections, and jazz-like dissonance."

Outspoken culturally as well as politically, Veloso and Gil soon came under the watchful eye of the military dictatorship that, by the mid-1960s, had been ruling Brazil for two decades. Censorship was a normal course of events on Brazilian television and the rest of the media, including the music industry. Arrested for supposed anti-government activity in 1968, they spent two months in prison and the following year Veloso was exiled. He spent nearly three years in London, until he was granted permission once again to live in Brazil in 1972. Since then, his reputation as a musician has grown, and this was added to by the publication of a book of articles, lyrics and poems titled *Alegria, Alegria* in 1977. His first U.S. appearance was in 1983, when he performed to sold-out crowds in New York City. In 1989 his first non-import release, *Estrangeiro,* helped further advance his popularity among U.S. audiences. The 1993 recording *Tropicalia 2* made it onto many top ten-lists in the United States; Veloso showed his versatility also with the Spanish-language recording *Fina Estampa,* celebrating the Latin American songs which he had enjoyed since a youth.

With growing popularity in the United States, Veloso mounted a large American tour in 1997, and two years later brought out the album *Livro,* voted one of the best albums of the year both by *New York Times* and *Rolling Stone.* Jones, writing in *Newsweek,* praised that album, commenting that "by the second song, in which books are extolled for their intellectual and their material benefits . . . you know you are in the presence of a master writer."

With *Tropical Truth: A Story of Music and Revolution,* Veloso once again surprised the public by turning to memoir and social history. Published in Brazil in 1997, and in English translation in 2002, the book is Veloso's testament, a "fascinating look into the world of one of the great creative forces in popular music, and indeed into the broader cultural life of Brazil," according to Tom Moore writing in *Notes.* The book traces Veloso's life journey from his Bahian beginnings to his love for bossa nova and to the formation of tropicalismo. His years in exile in London are also covered as well as his return to Brazil in 1972. "Veloso's book recaptures the turmoil and excitement of that time," according to

Rohter, "including an insider's account of a hilariously chaotic but historic performance at a song festival." Writing in the *New York Times Book Review,* Gerald Marzorati noted that Veloso "is likely to be remembered as one of the era's great composers," and one of the innovators of truly global music. "In that sense, he was a revolutionary for sure," concluded Marzorati. Moore dubbed the memoir "an important book," while *Booklist*'s Brad Hooper felt it is "not, strictly speaking, an autobiography but more a personal history of tropicalismo." For Hooper, however, the "wordy and indirect prose style" limits the book's popularity. Similarly, a contributor for *Publishers Weekly* called the book "rambling," but also praised it as an "extremely erudite memoir." James E. Perone voiced similar sentiments in *Library Journal,* noting that Veloso "exhibits a rare, vibrant erudition while tracing how in the 1960s he and his friends developed a post-bossa nova music and movement called tropicalismo."

Riding a crest of a wave of popularity, Veloso also released a double retrospective album in 2002, *Live in Bahia.* As Rohter noted, Veloso occupies a "curious" niche in Brazilian society: "His opinions on subjects from politics to race relations are constantly sought, valued and dissected, and the songs he has written over the years are heard everywhere." He even had his first million-selling hit in 1998. Ironically, it was not one of his own deeply felt compositions, but a cover he sang for a television soap opera.

BIOGRAPHICAL AND CRITICAL SOURCES:

BOOKS

Hightower, Laura, *Contemporary Musicians,* Gale (Detroit, MI), 2000, pp. 237-240.

PERIODICALS

Billboard, October 8, 1994, John Lannert, "Brazil's Veloso Makes Classic Songs His Own on New PolyGram Latino Set," p. 59.

Booklist, September 1, 2002, Brad Hooper, review of *Tropical Truth,* p. 39.

Diogenes, fall, 2000, Ariane Witkowski, "Caetano Veloso or the Taste for Hybrid Language," pp. 126-135.

Down Beat, October, 1999, Aaron Cohen, "Backstage with . . .Caetano Veloso," p. 14.

Granta, winter, 2001, John Ryle, "Translating Caetano," pp. 149-157.

Library Journal, October 15, 2002, James E. Perone, review of *Tropical Truth,* p. 76.

Newsweek, July 12, 1999, Malcolm Jones, "Troubadour with a Twist: Brazilian Musicians Are Out to Reinvent the Latin Sound, and Caetano Veloso Is Leading the Charge," p. 67.

New York Times, June 23, 1997, Peter Watrous, "Caetano Veloso," p. B3; June 29, 1999, Ben Ratliff, "Wily Mixer of Cool Jazz, Brazilian Pop and High Art," p. B1; May 20, 2002, Jon Pareles, "Pop Embracing Its Ancestors," p. AR34; November 17, 2002, Larry Rohter, "A Revolutionary Who's Still on the Move," p. L27.

New York Times Book Review, September 29, 2002, Gerald Marzorati, "Beyong the Bossa Nova," p. 19.

Notes, December, 1999, Tom Moore, review of *Verdade tropical,* pp. 429-430.

Publishers Weekly, September 2, 2002, review of *Tropical Truth,* p. 68.

Rolling Stone, June 25, 1992, Stephen Holder, review of *Circulado,* p. 45; December 19, 1992, Mark Coleman, review of *Circulado,* p. 182; August 11, 1994, Daisann McLane, review of *Tropicalia 2,* p. 69.

Spin, June, 1999, pp. 106-112.

ONLINE

Albertos.com, http://www.albertos.com/bands/ (April 9, 2003), "Caetano Veloso."

Borzoi Reader Online, http://www.randomhouse.com/ (April 9, 2003).

Cosmopolis.ch, http://www.cosmopolis.ch/ (June, 2000), "Caetano Veloso."

MetroActive Music Web site, http://www.metroactive.com/ (November 28, 2002), Greg Cahill, "Tropical Truth: Caetano Veloso Gets Long Deserved Nod."

NewsHour Online, http://www.pbs.org/newshour/ (April 9, 2003), Jason Manning, "Caetano Veloso—Biography."*

* * *

VENNING, Michael
See RANDOLPH, Georgiana Ann

VIGODA, David 1946-

PERSONAL: Born May 18, 1946, in Brooklyn, NY; son of William Vigoda (a comic book illustrator) and Anita (Rinzberg) Shapiro; married Elizabeth Eson (an artist), June 22, 1969; children: Benjamin William Hemingway. *Education:* University of Chicago, B.A., 1968. *Hobbies and other interests:* T'ai chi, foreign languages.

ADDRESSES: Home—21 Aviation Rd., Albany, NY 12205. *E-mail*—vigoda@whyitsgreat.com.

CAREER: David Vigoda Associates, Albany, NY, principal, 1983—. Why It's Great (writing workshop), director, 2003.

MEMBER: PEN American Center.

AWARDS, HONORS: Research fellow, University of Utah, 1972; creative writing fellow, National Endowment for the Arts, 1981.

WRITINGS:

Song of the Hunt (play), produced in Chicago, IL, 1969.
Unfinished (play), produced in London, England, 1970.
Nucleus (novel), Baronet Publishing (New York, NY), 1980.
The Samson Concerto (radio play), broadcast by National Public Radio, 1981.
Call Me by My Name (novel), 1981.
Exhalations of the Intellect (short stories), 1989.
Rebels Outlaws Spies Dreamers Prisoners Strangers (short stories), 1990.
The Innocent Alone Crave Justice (short stories), 1993.
Against Us, Tyranny (short stories), 1993.
Toward the Annihilation of Distance (short stories), 1994.
Family Values (play), produced in Chelsea, NY, 1998.
Plinth (novel), 1999.
Annihilating Distance: Selected Stories, Collioure Books (Albany, NY), 2003.

Author of additional short stories.

WORK IN PROGRESS: Re-enchanting Nature, a novel; *The Nature of Artifice: How Biotechnology Challenges Our Beliefs about the Natural and the Unnatural,* nonfiction; research on the relationship between science and the sacred, with emphasis on biotechnology and pre-modern philosophy and religion.

SIDELIGHTS: David Vigoda told *CA:* "Life is astonishing; writing is the best way I know how to ponder it. The primary theme or feeling that runs through my work is the experience of distance. Yet my fundamental belief is in the possibility of constructive change, and so I have sought to infuse my work with the counter-theme to distance, which is the struggle to overcome it. I can't help ruminating about what's wrong with the world and what might be done to make less of a mess of things. I don't recall when the phrase 'the annihilation of distance' first occurred to me, but it was many years ago, and it still encapsulates for me the essential human task. Not all my protagonists succeed, but most of them try."

* * *

VISCOUNT ECCLES, Mary
See HYDE, Mary (Morley Crapo)

* * *

VITALIEV, Vitali 1954-

PERSONAL: Born 1954, in Kharkov, Ukraine, USSR (now Kharkov, Ukraine); immigrated to England, January 31, 1990, immigrated to Australia, naturalized citizen; son of a nuclear physicist and a chemical engineer; married, third wife's name, Jacinta; children: Andrei, Anya, Alina. *Education:* Kharkov University, B.A.

ADDRESSES: Office—The Herald, 200 Renfield St., Glasgow G2 3QB, Scotland.

CAREER: Journalist in former USSR, 1981-90; print and television journalist in Australia and Great Britain; *Herald,* Glasgow, Scotland, writer-at-large, 2002—. Producer of television documentaries, including *My Friend Little Ben,* British Broadcasting Corporation

(BBC1), 1990, and *The Train to Freedom,* Channel 4 (London, England), 1994. Guest on television shows in England, including *Have I Got News for You,* BBC, *Saturday Night Clive,* and *Europe Direct,* BBC World. Radio reporter for *Breakaway,* Radio 4 (London, England).

AWARDS, HONORS: Golden Calf Literary Award (USSR); five *Krokodil* awards for journalism; Journalist of the Year honorary diploma (USSR), 1987; Ilf and Petrov prize for satirical journalism (USSR), 1989.

WRITINGS:

King of the Bar, Pravda Publishers (Moscow, USSR), 1987.
Investigating Perestroika, Arrow Books (New York, NY), 1990, published as *Special Correspondent: Investigating in the Soviet Union,* Hutchinson (London, England), 1990.
Dateline Freedom: Revelations of an Unwilling Exile, Hutchinson (London, England), 1991.
Vitali's Australia, Random House Australia (Milsons Point, New South Wales, Australia), 1991.
(With Derek Kartun) *The Third Trinity,* Hodder & Stoughton (London, England), 1993.
Little Is the Light: Nostalgic Travels in the Mini-States of Europe, Touchstone Books (New York, NY), 1995.
Dreams on Hitler's Couch, Richard Cohen Books (London, England), 1997.
Vitali Vitaliev, Vintage/Ebury (New York, NY), 1997.
Borders Up!: Eastern Europe through the Bottom of a Glass, Scribner (New York, NY), 1999.

Also author, with Kartun, of *Ikonen-Mafia.* Contributor to periodicals, including *Granta, Ogonyok, Age, Literaturnaya Gazeta, Nedelya, Krokodil, Punch, Guardian, Spectator, European,* and London *Daily Telegraph.*

SIDELIGHTS: Vitali Vitaliev defected from the former Soviet Union in 1990 after a decade of award-winning work as an investigative journalist in Moscow. Equipped with fluent English—learned during his college days when he wanted to be an interpreter—Vitaliev immigrated first to England and then to Australia, where he established himself as a reporter and essayist for English-language periodicals and newspapers. Although a citizen of Australia, Vitaliev has spent much of his recent career in the United Kingdom as a contributor to such periodicals as *Guardian, Punch,* and *Spectator* and as a writer-at-large for the Glasgow, *Herald.* He is well known for his travel writings, his on-air commentary for the British Broadcasting Corporation (BBC), and his regular appearances on the popular British television show *Saturday Night Clive.* Glasgow *Herald* correspondent Lorna Martin observed that Vitaliev's work in various media provides "a fresh, funny, and unique look at nationalism, cultural identity, and what it takes to create a country."

The son of a nuclear physicist and a chemical engineer, Vitaliev grew up in the Ukraine while it was still a state in the Soviet Union. He studied English and French in college and worked briefly as an interpreter and translator before turning to journalism in 1981. While still in the Soviet Union, his work appeared in the satirical magazine *Krokodil* as well as other periodicals, and he became known as a reporter who challenged the KGB and the Russian mafia. In 1990, fearing for his safety, he fled with his family to London. From there he traveled to Australia and began a new phase of his career.

In an interview with the Glasgow *Herald,* Vitaliev said that he had a hard time adjusting to "western liberties." He spent money lavishly, traveled nonstop, and bought more books, magazines, and newspapers than he could possibly read. "Unknowingly, I was suffering from freedom bulimia," he said. Fortunately, he was able to write vividly not only about his travels, but also about his life in the former Soviet Union and about political changes in that troubled country. He became something of a celebrity when host Clive James recruited him as Moscow correspondent for *Saturday Night Clive,* and since then has been productive as both a television and a print journalist.

Reviewers of his books have observed that Vitaliev can be humorous without resorting to cynicism. In a *Globe* magazine piece on the author's *Borders Up!: Eastern Europe through the Bottom of a Glass,* Andrew Varley wrote that Vitaliev "looks at humanity in all its splendour and vulnerability. . . . The strength and resilience of the human spirit in appalling or absurd circumstances shines through his invigorating prose." *Times Literary Supplement* contributor Anne Applebaum, in her review of the same title, maintained of Vitaliev, "There is a joyfulness in his writing that is hard to find elsewhere: the joy of a former citizen of the closed Soviet Union on the loose abroad, the joy of a non-English-speaker writing in English, the joy of a naturally humorous person confronted with endlessly amusing people and places." Martin concluded that Vitaliev "belongs to a rare group of people who can write with brilliance, humour, and style in a second language, to point out our foibles and idiosyncrasies and even enable us to laugh at ourselves in the process."

BIOGRAPHICAL AND CRITICAL SOURCES:

PERIODICALS

Birmingham Post (Birmingham, England), May 1, 1999, Charlie Hill, "Booze Cruise Goes East," p. 60.

Herald (Glasgow, Scotland), December 6, 2002, Lorna Martin, "The Vitali Spark in Search of a Storm," p. 14.

New Statesman & Society, August 16, 1991, Susan Richards, "Gangsters of Glasnost," p. 37.

Times Literary Supplement, October 29, 1999, Anne Applebaum, "Of Vines and Vodka."

ONLINE

Globe online, http://www.ias.org.uk/theglobe/ (1999), Andrew Varley, "Arise, Ye Starvelings, from Your Slumbers!"*

* * *

VOETEN, Teun 1961-

PERSONAL: Born 1961, in the Netherlands; *Education:* Studied photography at the School of Visual Arts, c. 1989; Leiden University, M.A., 1991.

ADDRESSES: Home—New York, NY. *Agent*—Panos Pictures, Studio 3B, 38 Southward St., London SE1 1UN, England. *E-mail*—teunvoeten@aol.com.

CAREER: Photojournalist and anthropologist. Provides photographs to relief organizations; appears regularly on talk shows in the Netherlands and Belgium. *Exhibitions:* Photographic exhibitions include "Former Yugoslavia," Université Libre de Bruxelles, Brussels, 1994; "Three Times Latin America: Images from Ecuador, Haiti, and Nicaragua," Leiden University, Leiden, Netherlands, 1994; "Tunnel People" and "The Forgotten Wars," Emerging Collector Gallery, New York, NY, 1996-97; "Tunnel People, Homeless in New York," Dr. Guislain Museum for Psychiatry, Gent, Belgium, 1998; "Afghanistan: End or Renewal?" Center for Contemporary Art, 1999; "A Ticket To," Leiden, Netherlands, 1999; "Sierre Leone: The Good, the Bad and the Ugly," Soros Foundation/Open Society Institute, New York, NY, 2001; "Human Crises in Afghanistan, Bosnia, Kosovo, and Rwanda," Columbia University School for International and Public Affairs, 2001; "Afghanistan: End or Renewal," Fort Mason Center, San Francisco, CA, 2001; "Our Grief is Not a Cry for War," Firepatrol Nr. 5, New York, NY, 2001; "Afghanistan 2001," Halfking Gallery, New York, NY, 2001; and "Afghanistan 2001 and Sudan 1997," Museum Ethnography, Leiden, 2002.

AWARDS, HONORS: Zelveren Camera/*Foreign News* Photo Journalistic Competition (Netherlands), winner, 1995, 1998, 1999; Sais Novartis Award, 2001, for "The Terror of Sierra Leone"; Laureate Natali Award for journalism and human rights, 2001.

WRITINGS:

Tunnelmensen (title means "Tunnel People"), Atlas (Amsterdam, Netherlands), 1996.

A Ticket To, Veenman Publishers (Leiden, Netherlands), 1999.

How de body?: Hoop en Horror in Sierra Leone, Meulenhoff (Amsterdam, Netherlands), 2000, translation by Roz Vatter-Buck published as *How de Body?: One Man's Terrifying Journey through an African War,* Thomas Dunne Books (New York, NY), 2002.

Contributor of photographs to *Vanity Fair, Granta, National Geographic, New Yorker, New York Times Magazine, World & I, High Times, Details, Village Voice, Vrij Nederland, NRC, De Standaard,* and *Frankfürter Algemeine.*

SIDELIGHTS: Teun Voeten was born in the Netherlands and has studied and worked around the world as a photojournalist and cultural anthropologist. The subject of his photographs has most often been human-rights violations amidst military conflict, which has taken him to places such as Haiti, Rwanda, Colombia, Afghanistan, and Sierra Leone. His photographic work has been exhibited in Europe and the United States, and he has published books in Dutch and English. Voeten has also published in many prominent magazines and supplies photographs to relief organizations. He has done anthropological studies among gold diggers in Ecuador and with the homeless in Manhattan. His most widely reviewed book is *How de Body? One Man's Terrifying Journey through an African War.*

Voeten's first book was *Tunnelmensen,* a Dutch-language book based on his experiences living with homeless people in a railroad tunnel in Manhattan. For five months, he lived with these "tunnel people," observing and photographing their efforts to maintain their dignity. Voeten's *A Ticket To* is comprised of an English/Dutch text that accompanies photographs taken during conflicts in Bosnia, Sudan, Rwanda, Sierra Leone, and Afghanistan.

One of Voeten's most harrowing war-time experiences took place in Sierra Leone, where he was documenting the use of child soldiers in an eight-year-long civil war. Amidst a failed cease-fire agreement, he became the target of rebel forces and was in hiding for two weeks before being rescued. He later returned to the country and developed a book relating his experiences and observations. *How de Body? One Man's Terrifying Journey through an Africa War* contains background on the mineral wealth that motivated the fighting and details the horrific means—including amputations—that rebels used to force children into service. In contrast to this violence, he also describes the courage and caring shown by those who helped save his life.

Reviewers commented on the relationship between Voeten's experiences and his account of the war in Sierra Leone. In *Publishers Weekly,* a writer who did not have access to the book's photographs said it was "dramatic but incomplete," given that the author "doesn't delve beneath the surface of his interest in Sierre Leone." *Library Journal*'s Edward G. McCormack called the book "a very interesting but depressing narrative" in which Voeten "exposes his own biases by using words such as natives, thick lips, bastards, fat, and the like." Conversely, Vernon Ford commented in *Booklist* that this is "an exciting adventure that educates the West to one of the many wars about which we cannot afford to be indifferent." And a *Kirkus Reviews* writer admired Voeten's "fresh punchy prose" and recommended the book as an "exhilarating" story about journalism and "a heroic portrayal of an overlooked, blood-soaked corner of the world."

BIOGRAPHICAL AND CRITICAL SOURCES:

PERIODICALS

Booklist, June 1, 2002, Vernon Ford, review of *How De Body?: One Man's Terrifying Journey through an African War,* p. 1674.

Kirkus Reviews, May 1, 2002, review of *How De Body?,* p. 634.

Library Journal, October 1, 2002, Edward G. McCormack, review of *How De Body?,* p. 117.

Publishers Weekly, May 6, 2002, review of *How De Body?,* p. 43.

ONLINE

Teun Voeten Home Page, http://www.teunvoeten.com (July 28, 2003).

* * *

VOJNOVIK, Ivo 1857-1929
(Sergie P.)

PERSONAL: Born October 9, 1857, in Dubrovnik, Austro-Hungary (now Croatia); died August 30, 1929, in Belgrade, Yugoslavia; son of Konstantin (Kosto) Vojnovik; married Maria Serragli, 1855. *Education:* Attended law school in Zagreb, 1878-80.

CAREER: Narodni list (People's Newspaper), Zadar, correspondent; in law practice, 1879-90; civil servant, 1890-1907; Zagreb National Theater, dramaturge, 1907-11.

WRITINGS:

(As Sergie P.) *Perom i olovkom* (title means "With Pen and Pencil"), Matica Hrvatska (Zagreb, Croatia), 1884.

Ksanta, Matica Hrvatska, 1886, published as *Stari grijesi* (title means "Old Sins"), Drustvo Hrvatskih Knjizevnika (Zagreb, Croatia), 1919.

Psyche, Matica Hrvatska (Zagreb, Croatia), 1889.

Ekvinocij (title means "The Equinox"), Matica Hrvatska (Zagreb, Croatia), 1895, published as *Ekvinocijo,* Srpska Knjizevna Zadruga (Belgrade, Yugoslavia), 1905.

Dubrovacka trilogija, Matica Hrvatska (Zagreb, Croatia), 1903 (includes *Suton,* translation by Fanny S. Copeland published as "The Dying Republic," in *Slavonic Review,* 1922-1923, translation by John Batistich and George R. Noyes published as "The Twilight," *Occident,* 1924), translation by Ada Broch published as *A Trilogy of Dubrovnik,* Leyham (Graz, Austria), 1921, translation by Batistich and Noyes published as *A Trilogy of Dubrovnik, Poet Lore,* 1951.

Smrt majke Jugovica, Dionicka Tiskara (Zagreb, Croatia), 1907.

Gospodja sa suncokretom, San mletacke noci, Triptyhon, Matica Hrvatska (Zagreb, Croatia), 1912.

Lazarevo vaskrsenje, Matica Srpska (Dubrovnik, Croatia), 1913, translation by John Batistich and George R. Noyes published as "The Resurrection of Lazarus," in *Poet Lore,* 1926.

Jakobina, Matica Hrvatska (Zagreb, Croatia), 1914.

Djela, 3 volumes, J. Toskovic (Dubrovnik, Yugoslavia), 1914-1922.

Akordi, Jug (Zagreb, Croatia), 1917.

Imperatrix, Knjizevni Jug (Zagreb, Croatia), 1918.

Maskarate ispodl kuplja, Zabavna biblioteka (Zagreb, Croatia), 1922.

Prolog nenapisane drame, Srpska Knjizevna zadruga (Belgrade, Yugoslavia), 1929.

Sabrana dela, 3 volumes, Geca Kon (Belgrade, Yugoslavia), 1939-1941.

PLAYS

Psyche, produced in Zagreb, Croatia, 1890.

Gundulicev san, produced in Dubrovnik, Croatia, 1893.

Ekvinocij, produced in Zagreb, Croatia, 1895.

Smrt majke Jugovica, produced in Belgrade, Yugoslavia, 1906.

Gospodja sa suncokretom, 1913.

SIDELIGHTS: Ivo Vojnovik was a late nineteenth-and early twentieth-century Yugoslav dramatist, short-story writer, and poet who wrote in Croatian. He published fourteen volumes and saw productions of five of his dramatic works. His best work is probably his first published novella, *Geranium,* which some critics believe began the Croatian realist movement. He is also known for his inventiveness as a playwright, his popularity peaking just before World War I. A contributor to the *Encyclopedia of World Literature* wrote that, "although his mediocre plays outnumber the truly outstanding ones, the latter secured for him a prominent place in Yugoslav dramatic literature." Thomas Eekman, writing in *Dictionary of Literary Biography,* noted that Vojnovik was interested in the symbolist movement and admired writers Edmond Rostand, Maurice Mäterlinck, and Henrik Ibsen, but, "on the other hand, in his prose of the mid-1880s a certain influence of the French realists can be established, including Alphonse Daudet, Emile Zola, and especially Gustave Flaubert." Vojnovik's prose, Eekman noted, features "a luxuriant, flamboyant style with an abundance of images, comparisons, metaphors, inversions, and other elegant stylistic features."

Vojnovik's father, Konstantin Vojnovik, a member of an old, noble, Serbian family, converted to Catholicism. His great-grandfather, Djordje, was a Russian army major. Within a year of Vojovik's birth, the family moved to Split and his father started a law practice, but the family continued to spend many summers in Dubrovnik, a city with which Vojnovik bonded. He was especially close to his mother, who taught him French, drawing, and painting. While in Split he attended the Italian high school. When he was seventeen, the family moved to Zagreb, where his father taught law at the new university and eventually became a member of Parliament. Vojnovik attended law school while in Zagreb from 1878 to 1880, and became a law school assistant. While still a student, he worked as a correspondent for the Zadar-based *Narodni list,* covering Zagreb's cultural life. After graduating, he practiced law.

During a tense political situation in Croatia, Hungarian governor Khuen-Hedevary, believing Vojnovik was a political opponent, exiled him to the town of Krizevci. During his five-year exile, Vojnovik wrote a series of four short stories collectively titled *Perom i olovkom,* the unfinished novel *Ksanta,* and his first drama, *Psyche,* which premiered in Zagreb in 1890. In 1889 he was transferred to Bjelovar and a few months later to Zadar, where he took a position in the governor's office. He was a civil servant, then a full-time writer, until 1914, when the Austro-Hungarian government imprisoned him in Dubrovnik as a Yugoslav nationalist. He transferred to Zagreb the following year due to a serious eye illness. From 1919 to 1922 he lived in France and then settled in Dubrovnik. In 1917 his birthday was nationally celebrated. Eekman wrote, "During the euphoria of 1918 due to the foreseeable end of the war and the fall of the Austro-Hungarian Empire, Vojnonik, as a staunch champion of Serbian-Croatian brotherhood and Yugoslav unity, was elevated to the height of a national hero and martyr." He was admitted to a Belgrade hospital in 1928 for eye treatment and died the following year.

Vojnovik's first published work of fiction, *Geranium,* appeared in installments in the periodical *Vijenac* ("Wreath") in 1880. Set in Split and bearing the subtitle "Romance of a Spinster," *Geranium* was widely popular. Sljivic-Simsic quoted Vojnovik as saying that the work focuses "on the anatomy of the heart of an unattractive woman." It tells of Mare, who lost the secret object of her affection to her beautiful, yet superficial sister. Mare redirects her unrequited love to a handicapped niece, whom she takes into her house, and experiences, for the first time, true happiness. Eekman asserted that the geranium is "a metaphor of the barren, unsatisfactory existence of a good but unattractive poor girl." He added, "The narrative structure is complex; its style shows influences of some of the authors he had read and admired, including George Sand, Alexandré Dumas, Charles Dickens, Alessandro Manzoni, and August Senoa."

In "U Magli" ("In the Fog"), the first of the four stories in *Perom i olovkom,* Vojnovik reveals his romantic sentimentalism in a story about a poor, blind organ grinder in Zagreb who grieves over his dead son. "Sirena" is a happier story that describes the playfulness of three girls enjoying the beaches of the Adriatic and features Vojnovik's own memories of his summers in Dubrovnik. "Rose Mery," set in Vienna, features the enigmatic title character and her doomed love affair with the young Count Marko Branski. Set in Rome, "Cemu?" ("Why?") involves a mysterious female who shows the demonic nature of love to a young violinist from Dubrovnik. Soon after the popular stories were published, they were translated into German and appeared in the *Agramer Zeitung.*

Vojnović, in his four-act play, *Ekvinocij,* attempts to dramatize *Ksanta.* He relates the story of Jela and her lover, who left her to go to America before their son's birth. He returns many years later, wealthy, and his selfishness endangers their son's happiness. Jela kills her ex-lover and then commits suicide so their son and his fiancée may go to America to enjoy the happy life she could never have. The *Encyclopedia of World Literature* essayist called this a play "in which realistic, symbolic, and lyrical elements are interlaced to create a moving drama of mother love and violent human passions against the background of rampaging equinoctial winds over the stormy Adriatic." It was made into the film *Nevjera* ("Infidelity"), and Vojnovik translated the work into Italian. Eekman found similarities to the myth of Oedipus and to Anton Chekhov's *The Cherry Orchard* (1904).

In 1902 Vojnovik joined three short plays together to form the triptych *Dubrovacka trilogija.* The plays, usually performed and printed together, are: *Suton,* a one-act play finished in 1889-1890; *Allons enfants,* a one-act play finished in 1901; and *Na taraci,* a play finished in 1902. Eekman wrote, "The title 'Twilight' would be appropriate for the whole cycle, as the period of decay of old Dubrovnik is at the core of each drama." The first play, set in 1806, centers on Napoleon's troops entering Dubrovnik. The *Encyclopedia of World Literature* essayist noted that the other two plays "depict the further deterioration of the old aristocratic social order and the transformation of the proud and independent republic into an ordinary coastal town and a future sea resort. Aware of the inevitability of changes brought about by modern times, [Vojnovik] nevertheless looks with sadness and nostalgia at the decline of Dubrovnik and at the disappearance of his own aristocratic class." Eekman added, "*Dubrovacka trilogija* has been called the apogee of Vojnovik's dramatic work. There was criticism as well: he was a sentimental-romantic author who constantly looked back at the past of one city and used patriotic rhetoric, decorative melodramatic effects, and a fashionable symbolism but lacked in great, new ideas and personalities."

Vojnovik was a strong contemporary voice for Croatian and Yugoslav literature and politics. His passion for and identification with Dubrovnik led to some literary works depicting the nineteenth-century socioeconomic decline of the city-republic. Eekman wrote, "He has been rightfully called a precursor of the Moderna movement of the early twentieth century, both with his prose, in which the expressive, picturesque element takes precedence over the plot, and his dramatic works, which elevated Croatian drama to a European level." The *Encyclopedia of World Literature* contributor concluded that Vojnovik's "omnipresent lyricism, his sensitivity to music and color, his theatrical craftsmanship and readiness to experiment on the stage, his creation of a gallery of three-dimensional female characters, the detailed and explicit instructions for staging his plays (often longer than the actual dramatic text and an integral part of it), the local dialect saturated with Italianisms, and his nostalgic love for Dubrovnik and its patricians" are among the hallmarks of his work.

BIOGRAPHICAL AND CRITICAL SOURCES:

BOOKS

Dictionary of Literary Biography, Volume 147: *South Slavic Writers before World War II,* Gale (Detroit, MI), 1995.

Encyclopedia of World Literature, third edition, St. James Press (Detroit, MI), 1999.

PERIODICALS

Canadian Review of Comparative Literature, Volume 2, 1975.*

W

WARREN, Charles 1868-1954

PERSONAL: Born 1868, in Boston, MA; died 1954, in Washington, DC; son of Winslow and Mary (Tinkham) Warren; married Annie Louise Bliss, January 6, 1904. *Education:* Harvard University, A.B., 1889; Harvard Law School, 1892. *Politics:* Democrat.

CAREER: Attorney, educator, author, and civil servant. Admitted to the Bar of the State of Massachusetts, 1887; Moorfield Story (law firm), Boston, MA, associate; private secretary to Massachusetts Governor William E. Russell, 1893; assistant U.S. Attorney General, 1914-17; special adviser to U.S. State Department; appointed special master by U.S. Supreme Court, 1924, 1929, 1938. Lecturer in history and law in various colleges and universities, including Princeton University, Boston University Law School, Johns Hopkins University, Cornell University, and College of William and Mary, 1924-40. Massachusetts Civil Service Commission, chairman, 1905-11; Trail Smelter Arbitral Tribunal, member, 1937; member of Conciliation International Committee during treaty between United States and Hungry, 1939; President's War Relief Control Board, member, 1943-46; Harvard University board of overseers, member; New England Conservatory of Music, trustee.

MEMBER: American Society of International Law (honorary vice president), National Institute of Arts and Letters, American Academy of Arts and Letters, American Philosophical Society, Harvard Alumni Association (president, 1941-42), Metropolitan Club and Cosmos Club (Washington, DC), Harvard Club and St. Botolph Club (Boston, MA), Century Club and Harvard Club (New York, NY).

AWARDS, HONORS: Pulitzer Prize for History, 1923, for *The Supreme Court in United States History;* honorary L.L.D. from Columbia University, 1933.

WRITINGS:

The Girl and the Governor, Scribner (New York, NY), 1900.

(With others) *Politics,* McClure, Phillips (New York, NY), 1901.

History of the Harvard Law School and of Early Legal Conditions in America, 3 volumes, Lewis Publishing Co. (New York, NY), 1908, volumes 1 and 2 reprinted, Da Capo Press (New York, NY), 1970, 3 volumes reprinted, Lawbook Exchange (Union, NJ), 1999.

A History of the American Bar, Little, Brown (Boston, MA), 1911, reprinted, Longwood Press (Boston, MA), 1980, revised edition, H. Fertig (New York, NY), 1939, reprinted, 1978.

The Supreme Court in United States History, 3 volumes, Little, Brown (Boston, MA), 1922, revised edition, 1926, reprinted, F. B. Rothman (Littleton, CO), 1987.

The Supreme Court and Sovereign States (Stafford lectures), Princeton University Press (Princeton, NJ), 1924, reprinted, W. S. Hein (Buffalo, NY), 2001.

Congress, the Constitution, and the Supreme Court, Little, Brown (Boston, MA), 1925, revised edition, 1935, reprinted, W. S. Hein (Buffalo, NY), 1994.

The Making of the Constitution, Little, Brown (Boston, MA), 1928, reprinted, F. B. Rothman (Littleton, CO), 1993.

Congress as Santa Claus; or, National Donations and the General Welfare Clause of the Constitution, Michie (Charlottesville, VA), 1932, reprinted, Arno Press (New York, NY), 1978.

Troubles of a Neutral (bound with *The Post-War Development of International Law and Some Contributions by the United States of America* by Manley O. Hudson, and *Soviet Foreign Policy,* by Michael T. Florinsky), Carnegie Endowment for International Peace, Division of Intercourse and Education (Worcester, MA), 1934.

Bankruptcy in United States History, Harvard University Press (Cambridge, MA), 1935, reprinted, W. S. Hein (Buffalo, NY), 1994.

(Editor) *The Story-Marshall Correspondence 1819-1831,* New York University School of Law (New York, NY), 1942.

Odd Byways in American History, Harvard University Press (Cambridge, MA), 1942.

Jacobin and Junto; or, Early American Politics as Viewed in the Diary of Dr. Nathaniel Ames, 1758-1822, Blom (New York, NY), 1931, reprinted, AMS Press (New York, NY), 1970.

Contributor to periodicals, including *Foreign Affairs.*

Warren's works have been translated into Spanish.

SIDELIGHTS: Attorney, author, educator, and civil servant Charles Warren was extremely influential as a constitutional authority and historian. As much interested in writing as in politics, Warren penned and published a number of works, from short stories to articles in law journals. His important works include the now-classic three-volume *History of the Harvard Law School,* first published in 1908, as well as *Early Legal Conditions in America* (1909), and *History of the American Bar, Colonial and Federal, to 1860* (1911), the last one of the earliest works on this area of legal history.

Born in Boston in 1868, Warren graduated from Harvard University in 1889, then taught there for a year before entering Harvard Law School. Following an interest in politics, Warren became private secretary to Massachusetts Governor William E. Russell in 1893, and eventually served as Russell's law partner. In 1905 Warren was appointed chairman of the Massachusetts State Civil Service Commission, serving there until 1911 and honing the commission into a more effective instrument. In 1914 President Woodrow Wilson appointed Warren, a Democrat, assistant attorney general of the United States. By August of that year the United States was becoming involved in World War I, putting Warren in charge of legal matters relating to the war for the Department of Justice. Warren began to focus on problems associated with neutrality and international law, and eventually became a leading expert in the field. He implemented several important wartime measures, including the Espionage and Trading with the Enemy acts of 1917. He briefed or argued thirty-nine cases before the U.S. Supreme Court before resigning in 1918 and returning to private practice.

Due to his experience and reputation in international law, after the end of World War I the Supreme Court named Warren special master in several cases. He later served as American representative on international conciliation and arbitration commissions involving disputes surrounding U.S. territorial rights, and was much sought after as a lecturer. His lectures were often transcribed and bound in book form.

Warren's primary contribution was made through his most important publication, the three-volume *The Supreme Court in United States History,* which won the Pulitzer Prize for history in 1923. "Unlike earlier books which have been, in the main, histories of the Supreme Court as such, and therefore have been of interest chiefly to members of the legal profession, this elaborate work by Mr. Warren is a narrative of United States history as affected by the Supreme Court, and was written for laymen and lawyers alike," reported a contributor to the *American Review of Reviews.* One of Warren's major themes was his contention that after the 1880s the Court's intervention in state and national legislative powers increased significantly. He maintained that the resulting "judicial law," though not constitutionally final, is a necessary stage in the evolving process of law. According to Edward S. Corwin in the *American Historical Review,* "The two principle criticisms of Warren's book are, first, that it is too long; and, secondly, that it is not long enough. . . . Warren's attempts to correct accepted historical verdicts are not always convincingly successful, but otherwise the work is singularly free of statements to which the informed reader will be apt to take exception. . . . But these, after all, are very minor blemishes of a highly valuable work." In perhaps the most telling testament to Warren's book, the U.S. Supreme Court has been known to cite *The*

Supreme Court in United States History when establishing historical precedents.

Warren's second important work was 1925's *Congress, the Constitution, and the Supreme Court.* William McDonald, reviewing the book in the *New York Times,* summarized: "Warren . . . appears in the main to think and speak of the Constitution as comprised in a document framed by a convention in 1787, and put into operation in 1789, and since that time variously amended by joint action of the Congress and states. . . . When, as sometimes happens, a decision of the Supreme Court runs counter to what a respectable number of people want . . . we have writers like Mr. Warren hastening to steady the ark of the covenant lest it fall." Warren's *The Making of the Constitution* followed in 1928 and was written in a similar vein.

Warren remained influential during the 1930s, and worked as a consultant to the Department of State on matters of neutrality and the problems of neutral nations. Many of his suggestions, especially those dealing with contraband and war materials, were incorporated into the Neutrality Acts of 1935, 1936, and 1937. He was also influential within the legal profession; in 1938 his research was specifically sited by Justice Brandeis in the Supreme Court's reversal of a nearly century-old decision based on Joseph Story's interpretation of the Judiciary Act of 1789. Similarly, Presidents Roosevelt, Truman, and Eisenhower cited Warren on presidential prerogatives in justifying some of their more controversial executive orders.

Although he retired from public affairs after World War I, during World War II Warren served on the War Relief Control Board, where he contributed to the debate over the fate of Axis leaders after the war. Beginning in 1943, he wrote many speeches and articles in which he argued against holding postwar trials under conventional rules of criminal justice. He advocated instead military tribunals, citing numerous precedents for trying the vanquished as part of normal military proceedings. This reasoning and process continued to be followed in the twenty-first century. He died in 1954, in Washington, D.C.

BIOGRAPHICAL AND CRITICAL SOURCES:

PERIODICALS

American Historical Review, October, 1922, review of *The Supreme Court in United States History,* p. 134; January, 1932, review of *Jacobin and Junto; or, Early American Politics as Viewed in the Diary of Dr. Nathaniel Ames, 1758-1822,* p. 354.

American Political Science Review, November, 1929, review of *Making of the Constitution,* p. 1044; June, 1933, review of *Congress as Santa Claus; or, National Donations and the General Welfare Clause of Constitution,* p. 497.

American Review of Reviews, July, 1922, review of *The Supreme Court in United States History,* p. 110; January, 1926, review of *Congress, the Constitution, and the Supreme Court,* p. 109; February, 1929, p. 24.

Booklist, January, 1923, p. 110; February, 1929, p. 195; January, 1936, p. 146.

Boston Transcript, September 24, 1922, p. 7; December 19, 1925, p. 3; November 17, 1928, p. 4; January 14, 1933, p. 1.

Columbia Law Review, February, 1933, p. 392.

Harvard Law Review, November, 1931, p. 204; January, 1936, p. 514.

Nation, January 24, 1925, review of *The Supreme Court in United States History,* p. 98; December 23, 1925, p. 736.

New York Times, January 10, 1926, review of *Congress, the Constitution, and the Supreme Court,* p. 12; November 25, 1928, review of *Making of the Constitution,* p. 13.

Saturday Review of Literature, April 6, 1929, p. 97.

OBITUARIES:

PERIODICALS

New York Times, August 17, 1954, p. 21.*

* * *

WARREN, Clay 1946-

PERSONAL: Born August 11, 1946, in Lexington Park, MD; son of Cassius Clay (a farmer and business person) and Dorothy (a homemaker; maiden name, Christiansen) Warren; married Gitte Kolind (an artist), May 1, 1985; children: Laura, Daniel Clay. *Ethnicity:* "Caucasian." *Education:* Attended Michigan State University, 1963; U.S. Naval Academy, B.S., 1968;

University of Colorado at Boulder, M.A., 1973, Ph.D. (communications), 1976. *Hobbies and other interests:* Contemporary piano, creative writing, travel.

ADDRESSES: Home—4703 Langdrum Lane, Chevy Chase, MD 20815. *Office*—Communication Program, George Washington University, 2130 H St. N.W., Suite 707, Washington, DC 20052; fax 202-994-4555. *E-mail*—claywar@gwu.edu.

CAREER: University of Colorado at Boulder, instructor in communication, 1973-76; Institute for Shipboard Education, Laguna Hills, CA, assistant professor of communication on voyage around the world, 1977; University College of Cape Breton, Sydney, Nova Scotia, visiting assistant professor of communication, 1978; Shepherd College, Shepherdstown, WV, assistant professor of communication, 1978-79; University of Hawaii at Manoa, Honolulu, assistant professor of speech, 1979-82; International People's College, Elsinore, Denmark, senior lecturer in communication and psychology, 1982-84; University College of Cape Breton, associate professor of communication, 1984-90, Tompkins Institute for Human Values and Technology research fellow, 1987-89; George Washington University, Washington, DC, associate professor, 1990-91, Chauncey M. Depew Professor of Communication, 1991—, and department chair. M J Solutions, Inc., consulting associate, 1986-98; Warren Consulting, director, 1988—. Pepperdine University, adjunct faculty member, 1978-81; International Masonry Institute, member of core faculty of communication, 1997-99. American Council on Education, member of Military Installation Voluntary Education Review Project team, 1992—, national coordinator of College Credit Recommendation Service, 1996—. *Military service:* U.S. Navy, 1968-71; became lieutenant.

MEMBER: North American Society of Adlerian Psychology, National Communication Association, Folk Education Association of America (member of executive council, Euro-North American Folk Education Resource Exchange Network, 1992—), American Association of University Professors.

AWARDS, HONORS: Grants from Social Sciences and Humanities Research Council of Canada, 1985, 1987, 1988, 1989, 1990; Rudolf Dreikurs Memorial scholar in Chios, Greece, International Committee for Adlerian Summer Schools and Institutes, 1988; first prize in short-story category, Annual Atlantic Writing Competition, Writers' Federation of Nova Scotia, 1990, for "Soren Sorensen"; ACS Seminarian, Princeton University Academy of Consciousness Studies, 1994; grants from International Consciousness Research Laboratories, 1995, and Grundtvig Foundation, 1995, 1996, 1997; Direct Marketing Institute for Professors fellow, 1996; Morton T. Bender Award, George Washington University Center for Excellence and Teaching, 2000.

WRITINGS:

(Coauthor) *Once upon an Island* (musical play), first produced in Glace Bay, Nova Scotia, 1978.

Minnesota Megvar (novel), Mora/Kozmosz (Budapest, Hungary), 1986.

(Editor) *Inner Visions, Outer Voices: An Anthology of Cape Breton Poetry,* University College of Cape Breton Press (Sydney, Nova Scotia), 1988.

(Editor and contributor) *Democracy Is Born in Conversations: Recreating N. F. S. Grundtvig for Lifelong Learners around the World,* Circumstantial Productions Publishing (Nyack, NY), 1998.

Contributor to books, including M. Davis-Finck and T. Gilmore-Finck, editors, *Viktor Frankl and Logotherapy: Everything to Gain,* Institute of Logotherapy Press (Berkeley, CA), 1993; and T. J. Socha and G. Stamp, editors, *Parents, Children, and Communication: Frontiers of Theory and Research,* Lawrence Erlbaum (Hillsdale, NJ), 1995. Contributor to academic journals, including *National Issues in Higher Education, Option: Journal of the Folk Education Association of America, Health Communication, Individual Psychology, Adult Education Quarterly,* and *East European Quarterly.* Member of editorial board, *Journal of Communication Therapy,* 1988-91.

WORK IN PROGRESS: Beds of Strange, a novel and film treatment.

SIDELIGHTS: Clay Warren told *CA:* "A Scandinavian writer by the name of Knud Faldbakken once wrote, 'I refuse to be a mascot for others' misunderstandings of themselves.' This comment speaks to me. Life is full of misunderstandings. The writing I do, whether fiction or nonfiction, seeks to clarify the conditions of life."

BIOGRAPHICAL AND CRITICAL SOURCES:

ONLINE

George Washington University Web site, http://www.gwu.edu/ (December 15, 2003), "Clay Warren."

* * *

WELCH, James (Phillip) 1940-2003

OBITUARY NOTICE—See index for *CA* sketch: Born 1940, in Browning, MT; died of a heart attack August 4, 2003, in Missoula, MT. Author. Welch was a poet and novelist who wrote books that drew on his Native-American background and concern for native culture and history. Educated at the University of Montana, he received his bachelor's degree in English there and also attended graduate courses at Northern Montana College. His first book was a poetry collection, *Riding the Earthboy Forty* (1971), and though he later switched to prose, critics would comment that his writing maintained a poetic quality. Welch went on to write several more books, which, though critically praised in America, were even more popular in Europe, where they were frequently published in translation. These works include *Winter in the Blood* (1974), *Fools Crow* (1986), which won the *Los Angeles Times* Book Prize and the Pacific Northwest Booksellers Association book award, *The Indian Lawyer* (1990), and *The Heartsong of Charging Elk* (2000). He also wrote the nonfiction title *Killing Custer: The Battle of the Little Bighorn and the Fate of the Plains Indians* (1994), which he penned after working on a PBS documentary on the subject. After establishing himself as an author, Welch became a popular lecturer and was a visiting professor at Cornell University and the University of Washington.

OBITUARIES AND OTHER SOURCES:

PERIODICALS

Chicago Tribune, August 8, 2003, section 1, p. 11.
Los Angeles Times, August 7, 2003, p. B12.
New York Times, August 9, 2003, p. A12.
Washington Post, August 8, 2003, p. B6.

WELLER, George (Anthony) 1907-2002

OBITUARY NOTICE—See index for *CA* sketch: Born July 13, 1907, in Boston, MA; died December 19, 2002, in San Felice Circeo, Italy. Journalist and author. Weller was a Pulitzer Prize-winning journalist famous for his war reporting. He completed his bachelor's degree at Harvard University in 1929 and did additional graduate study at the University of Vienna and the Max Reinhardt School of Theater in 1930 and 1931. His first journalism job was with the *New York Times* for which he was a correspondent in Greece and the Balkans in the early 1930s. From 1937 to 1940 he was director of the Homeland Foundation in New York City before returning to journalism as part of the *Chicago Daily News* staff. During World War II he became famous for reporting on the first undersea surgery, which happened on the submarine *Seadragon* when, on September 11, 1942, a crew member suffering from appendicitis was operated on by untrained comrades guided only by a medical manual; the surgery was a success, and Weller won the 1943 Pulitzer for his story on the event. Weller also was present at several other important stories of World War II, including the 1941 fall of Saigon and the nuclear aftermath at Nagasaki. After the war, he returned to the United States briefly on a Nieman fellowship at Harvard University before heading back to Europe. His series of stories about Turkey earned him a George Polk Memorial Award in 1955; Weller mostly reported from Rome—he was president of the Foreign Press Association in Italy in 1954—during his last years with the *Chicago Daily News,* from which he retired in 1972. He was the author of several historical books, including *Singapore Is Silent* (1943) and *Story of Submarines* (1962), and of the novels *Not to Eat, Not for Love* (1933), *Clutch and Differential* (1936), and *The Crack in the Column* (1949). His last published work was *Walking Time* (1965).

OBITUARIES AND OTHER SOURCES:

BOOKS

Roth, Mitchel P., *Historical Dictionary of War Journalism,* Greenwood Press (Westport, CT), 1997.

PERIODICALS

Chicago Tribune, December 21, 2002, section 2, p. 11.
Los Angeles Times, December 24, 2002, p. B11.

New York Times, December 29, 2002, p. A26.
Washington Post, December 22, 2002, p. C11.

* * *

WEST, Naida

PERSONAL: Born in ID; married; children: three. *Education:* University of California at Berkeley, B.A., 1963; California State University at Sacramento, M.A.; University of California at Davis, Ph.D., 1979. *Hobbies and other interests:* Tennis.

ADDRESSES: *Home*—CA. *Agent*—c/o Author Mail, Bridge House Books, P.O. Box 809, Rancho Murieta, CA 95683. *E-mail*—west@bridgehousebooks.com.

CAREER: Worked variously as a potato picker, babysitter, house cleaner, waitress, seamstress, secretary, interpreter, telephone operator, researcher, teacher, and lobbyist.

AWARDS, HONORS: Best Fiction/Drama, Small Publishers Association award, 2000, for *Eye of the Bear.*

WRITINGS:

Leadership with a Feminine Cast, R and E Research Associates (San Francisco, CA), 1976.
River of Red Gold, Bridge House Books (Rancho Murieta, CA), 1996.
Eye of the Bear: A History Novel of Early California, Bridge House Books (Rancho Murieta, CA), 2000.

SIDELIGHTS: Naida West has won acclaim for her historical novels based during the California gold rush. Her first novel, *River of Red Gold,* was heavily researched and based on actual events and historical figures from California during the gold rush, 1844 through 1853. The story's primary figure is an Indian woman named Howchia, a member of the Miwok tribe that lived in the Sacramento River Valley until miners came to destroy the land. *Western American Literature* reviewer Barbara Howard Meldrum wrote that *River of Red Gold* is a "fascinating, gripping story that is firmly rooted in historical research." Roger Voight of the *Bloomsbury Review* agreed and called *River of Red Gold* a "superb novel" that only uses fiction when historical documents are unavailable. Voight wrote that *River of Red Gold* tells the story of the "American holocaust" where tribes were killed to extinction and their land was brutally destroyed. Meldrum referred to the novel as a "multicultural, multiethnic" story. Although the novel follows several historical figures, some white, Indian, and Spanish, ultimately, *River of Red Gold* is a "devestating, wrenchingly tragic story" about the extermination of the Miwok Indians of the Sacramento River Valley, according to Meldrum.

West's second novel to be based on California history is *Eye of the Bear,* which won the Small Publisher's Award for Best Fiction/Drama.

BIOGRAPHICAL AND CRITICAL SOURCES:

PERIODICALS

Bloomsbury Review, July-August, 1999, review of *River of Red Gold,* p. 12.
Western American Literature, summer, 1999, review of *River of Red Gold,* p. 255.

ONLINE

Bridge House Books Web site, http://www.bridgehousebooks.com/ (May 16, 2003), "Naida West."
Sacramento Publishers and Authors Web site, http:www.sacpublishers.org/ (May 16, 2003).*

* * *

WHITEHEAD, James (T.) 1936-2003

OBITUARY NOTICE—See index for *CA* sketch: Born March 15, 1936, in St. Louis, MO; died of a ruptured aortic aneurysm August 15, 2003, in Fayetteville, AK. Educator and author. Whitehead was a poet and novelist who was also recognized for helping to establish the master of fine arts program at the University of Arkansas. He attended Vanderbilt University on a football scholarship, but his hopes of becoming a professional athlete were dashed by an injury. Completing his master's degree at Vanderbilt in 1960, he taught at Millsaps College in Jackson, Mississippi for three years and then completed his M.F.A. at the renowned University of Iowa program. After finishing his second degree, he was hired at the University of Arkansas, where he and friend and fellow writer William Harrison established a nationally respected writing program. He retired from teaching in 1999. Whitehead was the author of the poetry collections *Domains* (1966), *Local Men* (1979), *Actual Size* (1985), and *Near at Hand* (1993), as well as one novel, *Joiner* (1971).

OBITUARIES AND OTHER SOURCES:

BOOKS

Contemporary Poets, fourth edition, Gale (Detroit, MI), 1985.

PERIODICALS

Los Angeles Times, August 22, 2003, p. B12.
New York Times, August 19, 2003, p. C13.
Washington Post, August 20, 2003, p. B6.

* * *

WHITTEMORE, (Edward) Reed (Jr.) 1919-

Reed Whittemore

PERSONAL: Born September 11, 1919, in New Haven CT; son of Edward Reed (a doctor) and Margaret (Carr) Whittemore; married Helen Lundeen, October 3, 1952; children: Catherine, Edward, John, Margaret. *Education:* Yale University, B.A., 1941; Princeton University, additional study, 1945-46.

ADDRESSES: *Home*—4526 Albion Rd., College Park, MD 20740. *Office*—English Department, University of Maryland, College Park, MD 20740.

CAREER: Poet, literary critic, biographer, essayist, and short story writer. *Furioso* (literary quarterly), editor, 1939-53; Carleton College, Northfield, MN, professor of English, 1947-66, chair of department, 1962-64, editor, *Carleton Miscellany* (literary quarterly), 1960-64; University of Maryland, College Park, professor of English, 1967-84, professor emeritus, 1984—. *New Republic,* Washington, DC, literary editor, 1969-73; *Delos* (magazine), College Park, MD, editor, 1988-92. Library of Congress, consultant in poetry, 1964-65, honorary consultant in American letters, 1968-71, interim consultant, 1984-85; Bain-Swiggett lecturer, Princeton University, 1967. Former judge, National Book Awards. Program associate for National Institute of Public Affairs, 1966-68; member of National Academy of Arts and Sciences through 1991; director of Association of Literary Magazines of America. *Military service:* U.S. Army Air Force, 1941-45; became major; awarded Bronze star.

AWARDS, HONORS: Harriet Monroe Memorial Prize, *Poetry* magazine, 1954; Emily Clark Balch Prize, *Virginia Quarterly Review,* 1962, for "The Music of Driftwood"; National Endowment for the Arts grant, 1968-69; National Council on the Arts Award, 1969, for lifelong contribution to American letters; American Academy of Arts and Letters Award of Merit Medal, 1970; Litt.D., Carleton College, 1971; Poet Laureate of Maryland, 1985-88.

WRITINGS:

POETRY

Heroes and Heroines, Reynal (New York, NY), 1946.
An American Takes a Walk, University of Minnesota Press (Minneapolis, MN), 1956.
The Self-made Man, and Other Poems, Macmillan (New York, NY), 1959.
The Boy from Iowa, Macmillan (New York, NY), 1962.
Return, Alpheus: A Poem for the Literary Elders of Phi Beta Kappa, King & Queen Press (Williamsburg, VA), 1965.
Poems, New and Selected, University of Minnesota Press (Minneapolis, MN), 1968.

Fifty Poems Fifty, University of Minnesota Press (Minneapolis, MN), 1970.

The Mother's Breast and the Father's House, Houghton (New York, NY), 1974.

The Feel of Rock: Poems of Three Decades, Dryad Press (Washington, DC), 1982.

The Past, the Future, the Present: Poems Selected and New, University of Arkansas Press (Fayetteville, AK), 1990.

OTHER

(Editor) *Robert Browning,* Dell (New York, NY), 1960.

The Fascination of the Abomination (poems, stories, and essays), Macmillan (New York, NY), 1963.

Little Magazines (pamphlet), University of Minnesota Press (Minneapolis, MN), 1963.

Ways of Misunderstanding Poetry (lecture), Library of Congress (Washington, DC), 1965.

From Zero to the Absolute (essays), Crown (New York, NY), 1968.

William Carlos Williams: Poet from New Jersey (biography), Houghton (New York, NY), 1975.

The Poet as Journalist: Life at the New Republic, New Republic Book (Washington, DC), 1976.

A Whittemore Miscellany (sound recording), Watershed Intermedia (Washington, DC), 1977.

Pure Lives: The Early Biographers, Johns Hopkins University Press (Baltimore, MD), 1988.

Whole Lives: Shapers of Modern Biography, Johns Hopkins University Press (Baltimore, MD), 1989.

Six Literary Lives: The Shared Impiety of Adams, London, Sinclair, Williams, Dos Passos, and Tate, University of Missouri Press (Columbia, MO), 1993.

Also contributor to periodicals, including *New Republic, Nation, New Yorker, Saturday Review, Kenyon Review, Esquire,* and *Yale Review.*

SIDELIGHTS: Saturday Review critic Lewis Turco stated that Reed Whittemore "has been one of the more influential poets of his generation. . . . Early in his career he began to prove . . . that the best qualities of prose may be a fit vehicle for a new poetry." Expressing his opinion of Whittemore's talents, James Dickey wrote in *Poetry* that, "as a poet with certain very obvious and amusing gifts, Reed Whittemore is almost everyone's favorite. Certainly he is one of mine. Yet there are dangerous favorites and inconsequential favorites and favorites like pleasant diseases. What of Whittemore? He is as wittily cultural as they come, he has read more than any . . . man anybody knows, has been all kinds of places, yet shuffles along in an old pair of tennis shoes and khaki pants, with his hands in his pockets."

Apart from his work as a poet, Whittemore has been influential as an editor of literary magazines and as a proponent of poetry through his teaching, his association with the Library of Congress, and as the poet laureate of Maryland, among many other positions. Whittemore grew up in New England and though his family's fortune disappeared in the depression, he attended prep school and Yale University. During World War II he served in the U.S. Air Force and rose to the rank of major. Upon his return to the United States, he enrolled at Princeton University but left shortly thereafter for a teaching position at Carleton College in Minnesota. There he revived the literary journal *Furioso,* which eventually became the *Carleton Miscellany.* The position led to his association with the editors of other notable literary journals and ultimately to the formation of the Association of Literary Magazines of America, with which he was involved for many years. This path led to Washington, D.C., where he served a year-long term as the poetry consultant for the Library of Congress, a position in which he attempted to meld politics to an awareness of poetry. He then went back to teaching at Carleton for three years before obtaining a position as the *New Republic*'s literary editor. After four years with the *New Republic,* Whittemore became a professor at the University of Maryland. He retired in 1985 but went on to serve a second term at the Library of Congress. Apart from his poetry publications, Whittemore's most well-known work is his biography *Six Literary Lives: The Shared Impiety of Adams, London, Sinclair, Williams, Dos Passos, and Tate.*

In regards to Whittemore's poetry, a *Choice* reviewer suggested two reasons for its popularity: A free-flowing style and a sense of humor. Whittemore's poetry is marked by "end and internal rhyme . . . with highly amusing and often subtle results," the critic wrote. "He skillfully organizes and structures his poems on the basis of line length, yet he avoids relying on visuality for understanding." The writer further compared his work to that of Denise Levertov, Edward Dorn, and Ted Hughes, noting that "his skill in truly humorous verse sets him apart." J. T. Demos similarly commented in *Library Journal* that "Whittemore has the saving face of humor. . . . Being middle-aged and academic, Whittemore fights both labels as best he can, and then succumbs. When he is at least experimental and most aware of himself he can be charming as so few middle-aged academic poets really are."

Whittemore expresses his own feelings on poetry in his essay in *Poets on Poetry.* As he once commented, "I think of poetry as a thing of the mind and tend to judge it, at least in part, by the qualities of mind it displays. . . . The properties of mind I most admire are the daytime properties—those that get us to the store or shop and back, and put us on the radio discussing poetry or arguing about communism and democracy. Most of my poems, therefore, tend to deal primarily with the daytime part of the mind, that is, the prosaic part; only occasionally do they deal directly with the nighttime self."

On the subject of the length of his poetry, Whittemore once stated: "I have been impressed by the insufficiencies of the short-poem art for about twenty-five years; yet I have gone on writing short poems, and I suspect that my reputation as a poet, if I have any, is almost entirely based on a few short poems. I find the genre a congenial one in which to deal with my own insufficiencies, among which is my own rational incapacity to work things out, order them logically, on a big scale."

Reed Whittemore contributed the following autobiographical essay to *CA:*

AUTOBIOGRAPHICAL ESSAY:

He is in his crib and the crib is in a wallpapered corner. It is nap time but he is not napping. He is standing in his crib, wetting his fingers on his tongue, and rubbing the fingers on the wallpaper. Bits of wallpaper are beginning to come off in little rolls. He is rubbing harder, and now there is a blank place where there is no wallpaper. But Mother is coming. He hears her, lies down in the little rolls, and pretends to sleep.

And now he is in his high chair in the kitchen. His porridge is in his porridge bowl before him. He eats his porridge with his little silver spoon. He picks up the porridge bowl, shouts, "All gone," and throws the bowl over his shoulder.

And now he is in his high chair not eating but reading. He has a large book in front of him and is turning the pages slowly, saying, "Bararum bararum bararum." Lottie the cook is watching and listening. She says, "Look, Reed is reading."

Do I remember these events? The memories I am sure of come later; what I can vouch for is in the yellowing snapshots. I was chubby and round-faced. I was overdressed, and in winter I was invisible behind coats, caps, mittens, blankets. There was often a dog beside me, a white Samoyede. Once there were two half-brothers—twins—beside me, in knickers, with their slicked-back hair. And there was always Mother holding me, smiling at me, Mother in a cloche standing, looking down at me, perhaps beside a Wills Sainte Claire with a metal goose flying on the radiator.

But now I think I remember the Wills Sainte Claire directly. I am in the backseat alone. Mother is in the front, driving and talking endlessly with a friend. I am bored. I am bouncing on the backseat. I am fooling with the door handle. And now, surprise, I am out on the dirt road with scuffed knees watching the car drive on without me. I am running after it, crying.

Where was Father in all this? He could have been at the office for all the early years, except for one day when he had his picture taken holding me on his shoulder. Those years were at 175 East Rock Road in New Haven. The house was an ugly stucco affair with a square, pillared porch sitting in front of a square, two-story facade, but sometime before school began in earnest we moved from that house to Grandmother's more elegant one, up the street at One-ninety-three.

Grandmother was Nangma. She was long silk and velvet dresses. She was an old, stiff body sealed to the chin with "chokers." She was white hair with a bun, a tortoise comb, and pince-nez glasses with a silver chain. She was wrinkled hands with ringed fingers that stroked heads and gave electric shocks. And she was an inhabitant of two rooms, upstairs front, that were off-limits. There is no more of her except the hearsay, the bad words about her from Mother.

And Lottie? Lottie was round and black, dressed in blue with a white apron and black, patent-leather shoes with one strap across the instep. She was at the big black stove, or sitting in the kitchen rocking chair. She laughed, she scolded.

The author at nine months old

And sometimes John, tall and black in a white coat, was in the kitchen with her. Or he was in the pantry cleaning silverware with paste in a copper sink. Or he was outside sweeping the front walk. Or he was smoking in the cellar. He told me about railroads and winning at the numbers.

So Nangma and Lottie and John were at 193 with Mother and Father and me, and there was Cat too, and Bulldog Bobbie, who had asthma. Brothers Frank and Dick were not there, but at school. Their empty rooms had banners on the walls: Taft, Choate, Lehigh (which was taken down), and For God, for Country, and for Yale.

It was a large house with rhododendrons under the front windows and a heavy brass doorknocker that John made shine. Beyond the doorknocker was a front hall with a tall blue Chinese vase on a long dark table with a silver tray. To the right of the hall was the dining room, with a heavy sideboard and another dark table with a silver tray. To the left of the hall was the living room, with a gas-heater fireplace, bookcases holding uncut books, two stiff couches, and a big blue leather rocking chair next to a table covered with *Saturday Evening Posts*. In a corner was a grand piano with a player mechanism hidden in a drawer under the keyboard. Next to the piano was a case for piano rolls. "The Blue Danube" had a small, neatly pencilled circle on it, as guide for a prereader.

To the rear of the hall the staircase rose to a landing with a grandfather clock. When I climbed the fourteen stairs, passed the slow pendulum, and walked around the landing, I came to my room, three more steps up, front right. In the hall I did nothing except stroke Cat, who slept on the heat register under the silver tray. In the dining room I ate quietly, though I once dropped a butterball on the floor, and many times tried to refuse Bartlett pears. When I had finished my meal and the others were still gabbing, I was to say, "Ihavehadagreatsufficiencymaylbeexcused." I did. Then in the living room I lay on my neck in the leather chair looking at *Posts*, or perhaps sat at the piano pretending to play "The Blue Danube." But it was in my own room—with clocks, tools, gadgets, and Japanese waltzing mice—that I lived.

My brother gave me the mice for Christmas. They waltzed in a goldfish bowl. In the middle of the bowl was a square cardboard house filled with cotton. During the day the mice slept in the cotton, with just their little red noses showing, and perhaps a skinny tail. At night they waltzed. They spun around chasing their tails for hours, or they raced around the bowl for hours, higher and higher on its banked side. They seemed to go faster in the dark than when the light was on, and when they were really on the move they sounded like heavy beasts, until they squeaked. They were white and clean. My mother hated them, which must have been why Dick bought them for me.

There were radios in the room too. First there was one that Father, who had as a hobby actually making radios, helped me put together. He drew a plan and gave me the parts to fit it. I found a board, screwed the parts into the board, and attached a hard-rubber panel, with holes for knobs, to the front of the board. I strung striped copper wire to each of the parts, put pronged vacuum tubes into the four sockets, fitted tuning knobs, a rheostat knob, and a toggle switch to the panel, hooked up to big round "C" batteries, plugged in earphones. I turned the radio on and the tubes lit up.

But the radio did not play, not even static, and Father was at his office. I jiggled and punched, punched and jiggled. Nothing. Then, looking for the plan that Father had drawn (though it would have done me no good), I lifted one end of the radio perhaps an inch. Lo, static!

I put a screwdriver under that end of the radio, and soon I had WTIC, Hartford.

Father never found out why the radio only worked with a screwdriver under it, so soon he bought me a Philco.

Resume (part I)

(Edward) Reed Whittemore (Jr)

1919-

Father. Edward Reed Whittemore, physician, New Haven

Mother. Margaret Carr, North Adams

Schooling: Mrs. Weiss's kindergarten, Canner Street Elementary, Hopkins Grammar School, Phillips Academy Andover, Yale

Events and hobbies: white mice, radios, electric trains, jigsaw puzzles, and finally a black 1937 Ford V8 Roadster, followed by Furioso *and World War II*

First book: Heroes and Heroines, *1946*

*

At a political party in Washington when I was fifty-five, a young sociologist tricked me into talking about the past in *her* terms. She led me to say that my past had been an ordinary middle-class business, at which point she averred it had not been. Had not father been a prominent New Haven medico from a prominent "old" family up there? Was I not a Yale man from a stable of same?—then I had not been a middle-class business, but something patrician.

I spent the rest of the party drinking and trying to be admitted to my class. To be an old New England WASP is to be driven into the role of last Puritan, and does not stop with remarks about what snobs and racists Puritans are. It goes to the quick, saying what the *first* last Puritan, Henry Adams, said of himself long ago in his *Education.* He described himself as an eighteenth-century relic, unable to keep up with the raw immigrant blood around him. He said he had an energy deficiency, and was afraid of it. He kept walking up to the new forces around him, then backing away.

And thirty years later George Santayana described *his* last Puritan similarly, as a spent force in a changed world.

And fifty years after that?

My own writings have shown plenty of spent force, and as if the writings themselves were not enough, I contracted, at age fifty, a muscle disease that made me unable to close fist, lift arm, even walk. It plagued me intermittently for several years, and is even now only in remission. One can easily see a connection between last Puritans and myasthenia.

Yet young social-science persons who tell last Puritans that they are what they are should at least be told how complicated they can be. There may still exist old Puritan families in the country whose hormones have not been eroded, but mostly the last Puritans have been *forced* into ordinary middle-class business. Not many have been rich enough to fade away ideologically like Adams and Santayana; myasthenia remains a rarity. Usually eating has come first.

Eating came first, even in Nangma's big house, and surrounded by big houses filled with professors (*those* were the professorial days with private incomes). The Great Depression hit, and soon the hall with the Chinese vase was replaced by a hall-less, two-bedroom apartment into which the player piano fit poorly, so was disposed of, like everything else except the sideboard, the blue leather chair, and three beds. A young sociologist might be driven to compare my father and me with the impoverished lesser nobility in Spain and Poland in the eighteenth century, the ones who starved rather than soil their hands by labour, but she would be wrong. We were quite willing to soil our hands with labour; we simply had strange patrician notions about what to labour *at*. Father, a stiff Republican reading the *New York Herald Tribune* and cursing Franklin Roosevelt, knew in his bones that we should never be "in trade," yet making money in the stock market was permissible labour, so he lost our money there.

Thereby making Mother's role in Nangma's house even less tenable.

Mother was a little unmonied girl who had been teaching school in the Palisades across from Manhattan when Father met her, after the death of his first wife. The first wife had died of ptomaine poisoning from lobster at a fashionable dinner party on St. Ronan Street, died while the party was still in progress, in an upstairs room with Father beside her. The death was so scandalous that I was in the dark about it until after both Mother and Father were long dead and I was told the tale by an old family friend. Father married Mother within a year of the poisoning, and Mother entered Whittemore-land as an outsider under suspicion. The sad move to Nangma's house had been made because Nangma said she needed to be taken care of, but of course after the move Nangma had asserted her rule there to her last breath. She allowed Mother to order the meals but little else. Lottie and John were Nangma's servants, the dead living room was Nangma's living room, the Chinese vase her vase, the house her house. Mother's domain became two and a half bedrooms on the second floor—one was mine—plus a small room called the den in the rear on the first floor where bridge was played once or twice a week with just two other couples. When Father lost his capital in a radio stock, Nangma knew what to do. She set up a trust for *her* money that bypassed Father and Mother, leaving, after her own losses in the Crash, and after several years of gifts to Frank and Dick as they finished college (and Frank law school), a small amount to be divided among Frank, Dick, and myself. Mother went to drinking.

Father lived with her drinking for fifteen years. She died in 1943 when I was overseas in the war; and when Father died in 1946 I found in his papers a long letter to me about drinking. It was a hard letter to live with, a letter about his love for Mother, and about "the complete loyalty of her affections," followed by a close account of what and how much "dear Margaret" drank, followed by reassertions of love. Of course the letter was meant as a warning, but included with it, among his papers, was a pencilled statement by Mother, an informal will, in which she made *her* position clear:

> *In case my husband should not be living at the time of my death, all my possessions* [she had few] *will go to my own son—E. Reed Whittemore Jr. The twins have been given from time to time a great many things and have had the advantage of money which rightly belonged to their father; so I am sure they will not feel slighted if their younger brother is left the remainder. He—ERW Jr—was deliberately left out of his grandmother's will.*

What did Father talk about in all those young years? He had words of wisdom on jigsaws and radios, and occasionally he would take me to his office to look at one-celled life under his brass microscope, and to learn how to focus the microscope and keep eyelashes clear. Also, on a long trip to camp he once lectured me, literally, about the birds and the bees, blushing to the tops of his prominent ears when he arrived at humans.

But we were both New England. In New England there is never much to say, or if there is it is not much that is searchingly intimate. Father could recite lovingly the name of a twenty-syllabled lake in New Hampshire (it began "Chugaugugaug, munchaugagaug"). He could also talk about the universe like a Deist, believing that the whole thing was a large Erector Set, but he could not talk about sex, birth, and death except as a medico, and he could not talk of himself, the sadness of his own lost life, what had happened to it, and why the fine medical practice that had been *his* father's had dwindled to nothing. (I still don't know.) He let his feelings show about matters off in the distance like FDR, not about 193 East Rock Road.

Yet he was affectionate, dependable, unswerving, whole in his New Englandness. And in *my* own New Englandness I was closer to him than to Mother, who had, though from North Adams, a streak of anti-New England in her. The streak was partly just anti-

Whittemore, but anyway she would say to Father, "You are just like your mother," or, "You won't face up to things." And Father wouldn't.

So I was sent off to Andover at age fifteen to develop my New Englandness while escaping some of its gloom. It must have been Mother's hope that at Andover I would turn into a rare bloom that would dazzle East Rock Road, but I didn't dazzle. I listened to my now illegal Philco hate at night (keeping it locked in the day in a strongbox). I also listened, on a windup phonograph, to records of Louis Armstrong, Bing Crosby, Ray Noble, Glen Gray, Fred Waring, Red Nichols, Jimmy Lunceford, and, at the end, Benny Goodman.

In my first year I was billeted in the attic of an old frame house with two other boys, each of us with a separate low-ceilinged room. The housemaster was a little moustached man who tried to catch us smoking or listening to the radio, but since he didn't catch us he may have been more on our side than we knew. On weekends that year it always rained, and we were always disconsolate in our crow's nest. One of the boys, Dave Jones, was a good tennis player, but in our rooms there was no room for tennis. When we bounced a ball against the wall the noise brought the little moustache upstairs, so we resigned ourselves just to bouncing the ball up a foot or two from the racket. We did the same thing with Ping-Pong balls and paddles, our scores soaring into the thousands. Eventually the year was over.

In the second year we were all moved to a dormitory where I had a fat chemist-roommate whom I seldom saw. Dave roomed alone, and that year both of us learned to drink. I would go to Boston on Saturday afternoons, consume beer in dives near North Station, then come back to school with a pint of whiskey. One Saturday night Dave drank about half a bottle in the sudden way that the young begin by doing. He was giggly at midnight when our new housemaster, the school chaplain, knocked. I shoved Dave in my closet with the laundry, told him to shut up, closed the door, and we passed inspection. When the chaplain was clearly gone I opened the closet door and found Dave asleep in the dirty shirts. It was a good night, but there were few others.

Nangma died in my last and worst Andover year, which was also perhaps the first year of my education. What did I learn? (At this point *The Education of Henry Adams* enters my brain and I am tempted to switch to the third person.) During the dismal fall I went AWOL to New York on an overnight bus, thinking to join the world, but learning that joining the world was not easy. Two days later I came back to school, via home, in embarrassment, and learned, as a further part of education, to finish the Andover year. The unexpected reward for my misery was that I wrote two chapters of a novel about being miserable, then destroyed them and switched to writing poems of misery. The poems somehow arranged for me to be put in a seminar conducted by Alan Blackmur in an elegant, leathery room in Bulfinch Hall, and it was there that I had sudden dim insights into my future. Blackmur was the first teacher in my experience to try a bit of positive reinforcement.

> Travel is a trick I learned
> From my betters
> For trifling with the troubles that attend
> All that matters.
>
> The pains, the wear and tear
> Of living in the closenesses and loving
> By the year I forswear
> By simply leaving.
>
> The regions in the distance are my homelands.
> The cities with the shimmering walls and steeples
> House my gibbering friends,
> My peoples.
>
> The whole world I inhabit except the bit
> Where I at the moment sit.

The author of that eccentric sonnet (who was then more than a decade out of Andover, but his "travel trick" had started at Andover) is mixed up. The words are and are not speaking for him. He does not mean "betters" except ironically (and the irony is wasted), nor does he believe what he says, that staying home is all that matters. He flogs himself for fourteen lines for his love of homelessness, his failure to settle down, but in the process he shows himself rather pleased about the failure. He is thematically mixed up, for all his irony, but he is aesthetically very very neat. He must have written every line ten times, and been bowled over by such technical triumphs as his *tr* tetralogy in stanza one, and his long line-short line balancings throughout. For weeks, he remembers, he lacerated himself deciding whether or not to put "chosen" before "peoples" in stanza three. The poem has finish if not wisdom, and is one of the few poems of his own that he has been able to recite without a trot for thirty years. Why?

A little late-life psychoanalysis suggests that though he professed to be scornful of his escapism he really loved it. He learned early the joys of loner projects like cutting an intricate, thousand-piece jigsaw puzzle (he produced several of these before he was shipped to Andover) or a well-made poem. The genre didn't matter as much as the solitude, so that when a disliked godfather amazingly provided $760 for a car, he was sure he had reached maturity (he was sixteen) and heaven too. The car was a mobile one-man workshop. He could travel anywhere in it, yet be more at home in it than at home. He could be a genius with a pencil and pad of paper on top of East Rock.

Aside from my sweet escapism I had, starting at Andover but blossoming at Yale, something of a social conscience. I grew into it naturally with the Depression, the money troubles at home, the Spanish War, the Moscow trials, the Russo-German Pact, Archibald MacLeish's attack on the "irresponsibles," and much else, including the *Daily Worker* (to which I subscribed for some months) and all the crosscurrents between Stalinists, Trotskyites, and homegrown hawks and isolationists. Four years at Yale helped me into literature and little magazines—especially the magazine *Furioso,* which I will describe later—but they were issue-ridden years too, ending with the grand graduation-present issue, in 1941, of World War II—together with my 1-A draft card. World War II often provided exotically lonely places to park in a jeep and write, but other times it provided engagement, whether one liked it or not. In Sicily, where we stayed only two wild months, it provided so much that I went up to my colonel one afternoon and told him I couldn't hack it any more and was resigning from our honorable and distinguished Twelfth Air Force Service Command. The colonel was amused but I was not. I hadn't slept for a couple of days and could see that I was personally losing the war for everybody. Out with me.

Ah, but when the war proved not to be lost, our honorable XII AFSC regularized its pace and moved into the sort of quarters that supply officers normally find for themselves, an apartment in Naples with marble tables and a grand piano. For a year I could ignore

Reed Whittemore as a young man

100-octane gasoline two or three afternoons a week, and sit in the sun on a sixth-floor balcony looking out over the great bay and Vesuvius, as if I were not only a genuine but a well-paid poet. I wrote several escapist travel poems on that balcony but I also wrote the skeptical lines printed below about the Isle of Capri. (Capri had become an air-force rest camp immediately after our occupation of Naples, and I visited it several times.) Note my heavy suspicion that all is not well in the world's Capris:

Capri

There are hells under every mountain, hill
and rock, and under every plain and valley.

—Emanuel Swedenborg

It is good you are here as you are
And will stay for only a day or two, and will
see
Only the worthwhile sights, olives and grapes
And a lovely old *Mare.* Ships

And clouds and stars in the close of an eye
Will beckon as far and as deep as you'd best
wander.
For were you to linger and let the elegant vision
Work, as it were, of a garden scene,
You of a sameness season on season
Fathoms would fathom there sown,
And plumb not so much as a honeycomb hewn
Out of alien stone.

Travel was not, though, my main topic while the war went on. Except for the Naples year the XII AFSC travelled too much for me to like travel, so much that when I couldn't sleep at night I was in the habit of conjuring up all the beds or floors or grounds I had slept on since leaving New Haven—and counting them over and over. So instead of travel I became busy writing about the heroic. Not in *my* war, mostly, but in all the literary wars. I had in my barracks bag, or could pick up when the culture shipments from the States came in, all that anybody needed in the way of heroic models, ancient and modern. I read novels mostly, and wrote poems about their heroes and heroines. Then I mailed the results to my most resilient teacher at Yale, Arthur Mizener.

I had bothered Arthur steadily for my last two college years, especially on Sunday mornings when he was trying to be alone in his Pearson College office. After the war came and I left the country (he had to leave Yale, but he kept teaching), he was officially liberated from me but continued to accept my intrusions by mail and cope with them. He not only wrote back (he and my father were my chief correspondents for three years overseas) but sometimes he even wrote back to say he liked the stuff.

I had despised much that was Yale, but Arthur had been there to make it habitable, as well as Andrews Wanning and a couple of other instructors who taught me what a teacher was for. (The ones I was indebted to were kicked out by Yale my graduation year.) Arthur and I could argue endlessly about a single word in a young sonnet without thinking the "issue" trivial. Precisions of tone and feeling were our game, with Arthur, about ten years older, backing off from his days as an ideological Trotskyite, and with me struggling to establish, on paper, some connection or other with the world that seemed worldly. Partly because of Arthur the time overseas became for me one of constant mental shuffling, while I physically shuffled air-force supplies. Especially I shuffled between the great big war and the little, but indecently noisy, me.

I suppose that in any memorable private experience there is always a kind of San Andreas Fault lying underneath, to the presence of which the young learner must accustom himself as the Fault intermittently shakes him up, telling him, Watch it, kid, the ground you walk on is not yours. I know that in my own wartime life, even on sunny days on the Neapolitan balcony, the Fault kept speaking to the frivolity of my being where I was, doing what I was doing. And in retrospect it seems clear that if there was one subject that Arthur and I were really working at in our many long letters, it *was* the Fault: what it did, what it meant, how one reckoned with it. What the War and the Fault kept telling us was that though our correspondence was in some ways ridiculous—who cared about an infelicitous word in the first line of a tiny tiny sonnet?—still, the word was what we had and what we *could* intelligently care about. Furthermore it was *good* to care so long as we didn't care too much.

With Arthur's help I scribbled myself through many useful carings. And Arthur? He wasted more time on his ex-student than he could sometimes afford, but perhaps the correspondence helped him live with that larger talent, but not larger ego, than mine, Scott Fitzgerald. He took on a biography of Fitzgerald right after the war, and when he did he brought to the job our wartime assumptions about the self and the Fault underneath. He did not abide by the rising fashions of psychobiography, but moved as diligently *out* from Fitzgerald as he bored *in*.

Probably what I chiefly learned as soldier-scribbler was a little about the *deceptions* of self. For instance I learned that just settling in to study self-deception needs to be a core subject, in our time, in any curriculum devoted to understanding rather than doing. A tangled subject it is. Thus, in the sciences the professional focus is on the obstacles keeping an experimenter's self from making experimental objectivity possible. In psychobiography the focus is on how a biographee leads himself and his disciples astray by mythologizing his own being. And in literary criticism the focus is on the slipperiness of textual meaning, with much heavy argument proceeding out of those who tell us that no literary text has meaning independent of its readers' meaning for it. Tell away. I feel lucky that as a young critic I wrestled with the deceptions of self not in academia but by V-letter, and in the sun in Naples.

Not that I was so lucky as to be an undeceived self. My mind was a smorgasbord of amateurish speculations—a bit of my father's Darwinism, a bit of Marxism, a bit of Mizener, and a large bit of New England me. The me learned to disapprove of American self-glorification generally, but remained a me through all the disapproval, yearning, as a me always does, for glorification.

At least my confusion made me an amateur scholar of self-understanding. Most of my war poems were little studies of it. In a series of sonnets, for instance, I summarized what Emma Woodhouse, Hester Prynne, Lady Ashley, and a number of other well-known fictions learned, or failed to learn, about themselves as they progressed through the lives that their authors had provided. My analyst, if I had one, might tell me that I was not escaping *my* self by summarizing theirs, but while he wouldn't be wrong, there was more, I think, to the poems than that. All in all they were little verse tentacles reaching out for general truths from their self-cave, doing so in the long tradition of such reaching in poetry (though I did work hard to keep from sounding like Arthur Hugh Clough). I wanted to express the general rather than, or in addition to, the local and private, and being in the war helped; the military is not to be scorned as a self-chastener. I accommodated to it well, and it taught me duties, loyalty. It taught living for something beside a dollar (except when playing poker on payday). And it brought me the difficulties of democracy at a new, telling angle, starting with the first lineup, nude, at the reception center in Fort Devens, Massachusetts, for short-arm inspection. The army had great educational merit, and was cheap too.

But of all the lessons in self-understanding that I had, none was more critical than that of coming home to my lonely father *after* the war. Sharply I can remember, as I entered, his old bathrobe, his old voice, his telling me to sit in the old leather rocker amid the neat clutter (the neatness was his, the clutter had been Mother's). And as in a deep dream I can remember discovering that *his* self was no longer a depth to reach for. Four years earlier he had had "interests," but in the leather chair I learned he was now someone else. So there he

The author with his wife Helen and daughter Cate, Christmas, 1955

was, and there I was, and as we sat together producing long silences I could see that I was the only full self in the room.

Now I can say, as if with wisdom, that I was in the process of finding myself, while Father was in the process of losing his self; but that is glibness. So is saying that I had to make decisions, that he did not, and that I had to go on with my life, while he had no further imperatives. What is cleanest to say is that neither of us seems to have been greatly deceived by our respective states. He lay in bed much of the time doing crossword puzzles and reading detective stories. I sat in my room or up on East Rock with books and pads, becoming intense. We both knew we were as we were.

My intensities were indiscriminate but made a kind of sense, at least on paper. In the first few months at home I moved (tentatively) from sonnets to several verse dramas, none of which advanced past a scene or two. I was a nut about Joseph Conrad at the time, and as I struggled to revive, single-handedly, verse drama (I had decided that Eliot had simply been routed by the genre), my main efforts were aimed at converting *Heart of Darkness* and *Lord Jim* to the stage. I even became scholarly and wandered off to Sterling Library to see how Conrad (and Henry James too) had fared when they attempted conversion. I found that they had both been routed too by the process, neither being able to do anything, even in prose, but butcher stage dialogue. I marched on undeterred for about a month, but then my labors on *Heart of Darkness* suddenly emerged as merely more sonnets, and my *Lord Jim* added up to just a few unrelated soliloquies.

So the experiment did not work but was a useful failure. Half a century later I still know the immensities involved. And aside from the virtue of trying, there was the wisdom gained from simply reckoning with Conrad's characters' complicated selves, especially Jim's.

Two fragments of my work with Jim crept into my first book, one being a sonnet soliloquy by Jim, in which I had ship officer Jim talking tensely about the nasty little fix he had put himself into by abandoning his ship, the sinking *Patna,* in the middle of the Gulf of Aden (only to find out later that it *didn't,* with its boatload of Mecca-bound pilgrims, sink). I had personally abandoned no ship, had not even been able to abandon the XII AFSC, yet the heroic chatter I supplied Jim with in the sonnet must have had *something* to do with me, a modest supply-officer hero from the war who now lay abed, unshaven, feeling like a comic-strip derelict. The sonnet began with Jim crying, "Why this?" and came back to the same tough question at the end. "Why this? / Why are all my bravest plans amiss?"

But the other, longer monologue went further than to have its speaker fret. The speaker was a narrator like Conrad's narrator, Marlow, and he told Jim at some length to stop moping around and *do* something. Do what? Do something escapist, but do it. Do what Conrad's Jim did in the last half of the novel: go to Patusan (a remote, primitive, Eastern country in the novel, where Jim recovered his self-respect and became the head man). The connection with me seems to have been that I was arranging to go to a Patusan of my own at the time. My Patusan was the Princeton Graduate College, behind the golf course and flanked by bankers. The poem began like this:

Jim, there's a land within this land
(Of parakeets and palms)
Where a man may partly live;
Live and partly die; a land of whispers.
Jungles of greenest wonder crowd the clouds.
Creatures of zoos, flowers for fabulous gardens
Creep to a lush and lazy end. A man,
A man of garden talents
(Looking for long-tailed monkeys, flying frogs)
Might, might, might there, at last
Find peace.

That poem doesn't sound much like Princeton, though the golf course—like the poem—is lush. Anyway I went to Princeton, and went history. For a year and a half I sat on an inflated rubber pillow (the graduate student's balm) in the history-seminar room of the old Witherspoon Library (the Firestone Library was being built next door). Princeton and history were not nearly as educational as the war, but I did learn about the French Revolution, the Haymarket riot in Chicago, and drinking in Colonial New England. Also, from the chairman of the history department, Joseph Strayer, I learned how to read a scholarly book without reading it, a necessity for graduate students and a dubious luxury for reviewers. Princeton was good, in the sense of useful at the time, but its role in my life was pretty well destroyed by the news, after I'd been there three months, of my father's death.

He had wanted me to go, or had said he did. He knew I had to do something. But there it was.

After the funeral and the settlements (my two married brothers and I dealt with the burial of our past with customary New England familial frigidity and communed little), and after sitting in the New Haven apartment (now to be abandoned) for a few days feeling like an empty burlap sack, I went back to Princeton and was instantly invited to lunch, at the old French restaurant just off Nassau Street, by an apparently sane editor, and asked for the manuscript of my first book. It was like a children's game I think I remember called upsy downsy.

The editor's name I forget. The publisher's name was Reynal and Hitchcock, a firm briefly in chips from a best-seller during the war. The name of my book was *Heroes and Heroines,* and it had in it all the poems that Arthur and I had argued about. I dedicated it to Arthur. Meanwhile he had been called west to be chairman of the English department at Carleton College in Northfield, Minnesota, and fate was arranging for me to fill in for an ailing teacher out there, for one term only. Way out there in nowhere.

Resume (continued)

Schooling: One and a half years Princeton Graduate School, interrupted by Carleton offer. Moved to Minnesota. Stayed nineteen years.

Events: Furioso *continued. Learned to fly. Married Helen Lundeen of Fergus Falls, Minnesota. Stopped flying. Taught, wrote. Family grew to three children (and to four in the late sixties when we moved to Washington).* Furioso *was replaced by the* Carleton Miscellany.

Books: Two more volumes of poems: An American Takes a Walk, The Self-made Man. *They were followed by two books mixing poetry and prose:* The Boy from Iowa, The Fascination of the Abomination. *There was also a pamphlet on little magazines.*

*

The war was one kind of education, teaching another, adjusting to the open spaces of Minnesota another, and magazining still another. And marrying, the education I delayed longest, was the most important other, as well as the one I had most trouble with. Helen was younger, and from the Minnesota I didn't know. She was, and is, fine. She had to put up with what she thought of as a colossal ego, but what she didn't understand was that he was trying to put up with the ego too, busily hating the strident complaints and false impieties he kept trapping himself with. Much later in life he discovered of himself, while seriously ill, that he was really a simpler organism than he had led himself to believe, and could naively struggle for simple survival. But he didn't, then, feel illuminated. He was no D. H. Lawrence, and spent much of his creative breath protesting the easy illuminators. As a poet he had, of course, a steady, sneaky feeling that he *ought* to be an illuminator, and as a family man he had feelings like that too, but mostly he would sit quiet in his study until the feelings went away. He was a New Englander, and when, once, he wrote the beginnings of a rather "straight" novel of family life, they were rotten.

Still, the family was there, and he knew they were there, and Helen knew that he knew. From Helen—and then from Cate, Ned, Jack, and Daisy—he learned something bigger than the war and the writing, and he is grateful for the learning. But will not report on it.

Northfield, Minnesota, was where Jesse James had his comeuppance, and where all the Jesse James movies came first, to be jeered at by the students of Northfield's two colleges. I learned more about English departments there, and higher education there, than I ever wanted to know, yet the place was a good place and, for me, a good choice, ending the gap that had been Princeton. Princeton was useful but Northfield was a commitment.

It certainly didn't seem so, first term. I taught one course (Arthur told me I shouted in class so that I was heard in neighboring offices) and made six hundred dollars. I was full of the French Revolution when I should have been teaching Wordsworth—cool it, said my elders—and I was most melancholy in the presence of student themes. But I settled in, and cooled it. Soon academia, together with student themes, became my home.

The Whittemore children on the shore of Ottertail Lake, Minnesota: Ned, Jack, Daisy, and Cate

And little magazines became my home too. At Yale *Furioso*—which my roomate Jim Angleton and I started as sophomores—had been a bright idea full of surprises, like playing host to Ezra Pound in my parents' apartment for a night, and paying E. E. Cummings off in neckties. After the war Jim, who had joined the OSS while I squandered 100-octane in Africa and Italy, stayed with the "Agency," so *Furioso* fell to me; but certainly the original impulse was heavily his. He had searched out Pound in Rapallo, had played tennis with him, taken pictures of him, and talked Dante with him. Pound in return, in his grand cultural way, had decided that Jim was one of those who were going to save American literature. So Pound visited us in New Haven for twenty-four hours, (this was during EP's short 1939 visit to America, when he tried to persuade several senators in Washington to keep America out of the war) and then let us print in our first issue—Summer, 1939—a one-page economics textbook he had composed consisting of four quotations opposing usury—from John Adams, Thomas Jefferson, Abraham Lincoln, and George Washington (could there have been better evidence that he was, though eccentrically, a patriot?), followed by a bibliographical Pound note telling the reader what to read on the subject. Then, for later issues, he let us have a few light poems, plus a fine prose obituary for Ford Madox Ford.

With Pound came, as part of our earlier-generation stable, William Carlos Williams (who let us print an elegy of his to Ford in the same issue), Cummings, Archibald MacLeish, Wallace Stevens, Marianne Moore, and a number of others who were uncommonly kind in letting two undergraduates publish them. Little magazines were different then, partly because there were not so many, and partly because a mystique hovered about them that the contributors in our stable—especially Pound himself—believed in and helped promote.

There have been other magazines, but absolutely none as good as *Furioso*. Yes indeed, there never was . . . but as I say this I feel my nose growing longer, for I remember that sometime after the war we *Furioso* editors, now numbering about a dozen, actually received in the mail somebody else's *Furioso*. From Australia. An inferior product. Jim, with his partly Italian upbringing, originally chose the name, and Jim was the main driving force behind the early issues. Also, if Jim had not stayed in intelligence he might have made a far better magazine of it, after the war, than we did (though it almost certainly would not have come out regularly). Yet even without Jim it was good, and it certainly was an education. Every poet should have his own magazine. (Perhaps I should withdraw that remark. Too many have!)

In starting the magazine up again in 1947, without Jim (one intervening wartime issue had been turned out by Jim's sister Carmen in 1942), I changed the magazine's focus from our elders to my contemporaries and me. The shift was natural enough, since by then we had a few credentials other than having passed Shakespeare and the Romantics. The shift was also necessary psychologically—for me anyway. I wanted to be *in* the magazine, and have the other editors in it. We printed our own work mercilessly. (The "we" consisted of two complete sets of editors—this was 1946 to 1953. The roll call: Howard Nemerov, John Pauker, William R. Johnson, Ambrose Gordon, Jr., Irwin Touster [art editor], Scott Elledge, John Lucas, Arthur Mizener, Rosemary Mizener, Charles Sham, Edwin Peuet, Liane Elledge.) But we also became more portentously editorial, and with our large, loose, unpaid staff tried to be objective and judicious about what should be accepted, what not. We passed manuscripts around in grocery-store bags, and argued, and took votes, and argued more. Sometimes we agreed, but what impressed us most was how much disagreement we could arrive at. Put an innocent poem in front of us and we would come up with three yes's, three no's, and a maybe. A wilful mind like Pound's may move in and start a culture-saving movement, and may write angry letters to opponents, and make fine critical copy for scholars, but he won't live long with an editorial board. The mystique of little magazines that bred *Furioso* in Jim's head and mine originally could not survive editorial boards long in any culture or country, and in *Furioso's* case the mystique did slowly fade into the light of common day. Probably a good change, all in all.

I gave the magazine up in 1953, partly because of the fading but partly also because of money, and when in 1960 Carleton saw its way to backing it—the earlier money had been mine—we started it up again as the *Carleton Miscellany*. By then I had clearly become an old institutional type, being forty-one and a professor and *not* represented in an anthology of the *new* American poetry; and the magazine's new name signalled the shift. Still, we at least managed to be noisy in its pages. We attacked the *New York Times Book Review*, we had a feminist issue, we bombed the atom bomb, and we printed a socialist-realist diatribe that provoked more diatribes. Perhaps the project most indicative of what my own little magazining had come to by then was an attempt to form a combine, a collective, a *harmonious* association of little magazines. (The new board was smaller, less cumbersome, consisting of Wayne Carver, Erling Larsen, and myself, with help from Wayne Booth in Chicago, and Helen Lundeen [my wife] and Ruth MacKenzie [her sister]—but many of the projects were group projects.) "Wrong from the start," Pound would certainly have said of it, but fifteen years later it even became something of a success. It was an organizational event, a money event, something of a non-little-magazine event, but, as the first meeting to organize it showed, it was still spiritually attuned to the old mystique.

The project began at a two-week writers' conference in Salt Lake City, where my teacher-colleagues were two other editors, Andrew Lytle of the *Sewanee Review* and Robie Macauley of the *Kenyon Review*. For me the Utah conference was a fine extended editorial meeting, and the immediate result was the promoting of a gathering of editors in St. Paul the following winter. Twenty or so magazines sent representatives, about half aged and half fiery. The gathering became formalized as the proceedings of the Association of

Literary Magazines of America (ALMA), and the extensive minutes were soon printed in the *Miscellany.* (Later, after several more meetings in New York and Washington, ALMA changed its name and became an official nonprofit corporation known as the Coordinating Council of Literary Magazines: CCLM.) With the snow piling up around us in St. Paul, Allen Tate chaired the two-day event, during which we made speeches to each other that steadily invoked the wonders of the little-magazine tradition. Then we put on paper, aside from minutes and bylaws, a mighty preamble to the bylaws in which the wonders were again flaunted. In effect we said that *no* great living American writers would have gone *any*where or been anything if they hadn't first been printed in some *Blast* or *Little Review* or *Furioso.*

After loud arguments the assemblage approved the extravagance, and since we approved little else it seemed to have been written in gold. Yet I can remember the cynical hours or so that the preamble committee—Tate, Whit Burnett, and I—spent in a hotel room away from the general meeting, putting it together. Sentence by sentence we found ourselves hovering on the edge where principle becomes propaganda. Worse, the principle itself kept turning sour. At least for me the trouble with the preamble was that there was nothing in it touching on all those honesties that Arthur and I had wrestled with, nothing, for instance, about how the geniuses created by little magazines coped with the great Fault, what they did with their talents except show them, literarily, off. More and more my own talent, such as it was, had been battling for some time the phenomenon of "self-expression," as so fashionably promoted for health, education, and welfare, or just for its own lovely sake, yet there I was in a hotel room promoting it. There was further confusion to come.

Resume (continued)

Events: Poetry Consultantship at Library of Congress. Permanent move to Washington, DC. Humanities consultant in urban affairs think tank. Professorship at University of Maryland. Back-pages editor of New Republic. *Then the call to be a biographer. Retirement and more biography.*

Books: Four more books of poems: Poems, New and Selected, Fifty Poems Fifty, The Mother's Breast and the Father's House, *and* The Feel of Rock. *Also a book of lectures,* From Zero to the Absolute; *writings from the* New Republic, The Poet as Journalist; *and* William Carlos Williams: Poet From Jersey.

*

From its infancy in the early 1940s the poetry consultantship at the Library of Congress partook of the early little-magazine mystique, but because the library was not little, and was a public institution, it did so in a suitably complicated way. In effect it mixed the notion of a poet's responsibility to his society, as announced by Archibald MacLeish in *The Irresponsibles,* and the notion of his private responsibility, as announced by Allen Tate, "to his conscience, in the French sense of the word: the joint action of knowledge and judgment" (in "To Whom Is the Poet Responsible?"). It mixed them as I think no other conspicuous literary appointment in our country does, but the mixture may have been inevitable at the library, with both MacLeish and Tate originally behind the consultantship's conception.

Before MacLeish became the librarian of Congress (in 1939), there had been a less loftily principled poetry consultant on the library's regular staff, a working consultant looking up quotations and sources for congressmen. But when MacLeish came to his duties the time was wartime, MacLeish had been damning the social irresponsibility of American writers and scholars across the board, and was anxious to persuade the literary community of which he had been a part to become engaged. Meanwhile Tate, who had been engagé about being désengagé, decided to disagree publicly with MacLeish in the quarterlies, with the result that they made excellent combatants, seemingly opposed but actually "leaners," each in the direction of the other. It was they who concocted the nonworking, privately funded consultantship we still have (in the last few years it has merely been *supplemented* by the laureateship role). And it was they too who stirred up the private money for it, and put Allen himself in as the first consultant of the new dispensation.

The dispensation gave the poetry consultant the right to continue to be irresponsible in the way that Tate insisted a responsible poet sometimes had to be, but it also put him in the middle of our whole federal machine. Tate, being full of the engagement principle despite himself, delighted in the position, or, rather, in the problems of the position, the challenges of having for a poetic office an elegant third-floor room with a balcony looking straight at the Capitol across the street. The poets who came after him varied in their opinions of those delights, but when the appointment came to me I agreed with Tate.

I got the appointment because Howard Nemerov was my predecessor, and probably because Tate put in a plug too. I trafficked in public poetry that year—poetry from platforms, poetry saying social things—and I also pushed ALMA hard, gathering together eighty editors for two days of mayhem in the Coolidge Auditorium. Also I became absorbed by the MacLeishian issue of a poet's role in a big bureaucracy, if he had one. One noon in the cafeteria of the Department of Agriculture, for instance, I fired a few salvos at that helpless, hopeless target, bureaucratic prose, to the applause of about fifty paper-pushers. And I had similar, short-lived success at the Department of Interior when I rewrote (and was allowed to sign—a big issue) a government pamphlet describing, for tourists, the Jefferson Memorial. These were indeed delights, and the year at the library was a delight, but as far as my relationship to the literary community was concerned a dangerous one. Soon, serving on literary committees and writing magazine pieces, I began to look like an enemy of *all* that confused dissidence to which the literary community was committed, or like the unqualified enemy of self-expression, or perhaps like the unqualified enemy of just forgetting social affairs. I wasn't an enemy of that magnitude, but I was certainly becoming an enemy of the inward, isolate, Neapolitan-balcony excesses of the poetry being published around me, so much so that I even wrote a piece that Tate himself delighted in refuting, just as he had MacLeish. It was called "The Poet in the Bank" and made reference to T. S. Eliot's early position in a London bank, one that Pound started a one-man fund-raising campaign just to spring him from. In it I said that a bank might even be good for a poet, which, aside from being heresy, was almost as bad as saying that Washington might be good for a poet. And I believed what I said, mostly. And soon my family and I—having already enjoyed a year of Washington's bright lights and returned for a year of Northfield's dim ones—took the big step of leaving Minnesota permanently.

The step was especially big because when we did it I had only a temporary job to make the switch possible, and the job was in Princeton at that. For one term I commuted to Princeton weekly for a visiting professorship. Then I settled into Washington as a temporary thinker about bureaucracy in a temporarily well-endowed entity called the National Institute of Public Affairs. There, for more than a year, I concocted wild educational proposals, and told visiting mayors and other urban officials how the humanities would help them at their trade, though I was not sure they would. Soon the University of Maryland came along and I was able to go back to ordinary teaching again—but this time near the bright lights.

I thought the College Park campus would be a good place to play my socially dutiful role, it being a big, sprawling phenomenon supported by state money and in need of reform. But what mattered most about it for me was that I was coming on fifty and needed something permanent. The English department there was not as a whole respectful of my reformist ambitions for it (many colleagues thought I was becoming unhealthily interdisciplinary), but it had enough other problems not to be bothered by me, as did Maryland's diffuse faculty generally. An open institution collecting, loosely, many good minds, it had no center at all, no sense of community; it could hardly get quorums for small committee meetings. So I could see plenty before my eyes to reform, and I suppose that I might well have become more of a campus disturbance than I proved to be if I had not, my very first year, contracted myasthenia gravis: an excellently symbolic disease.

First there was double vision and droopy eyelids, then muscular weakness in hands and feet, then lung trouble—so it added up to no-see, then no-write, then no-walk, then no-breathe: a thorough no-can-do syndrome. I was spread too thin. Everything was becoming too much, financially, parentally, professionally, so the disease came along to diagnose my ailment.

Several years of hospitals and futile experiments followed, out of which finally came an unexpected cure in the form of the common hormone drug prednisone, which had been "contraindicated." I emerged nearly whole, and am still on prednisone (every *other* day), but there were psychic scars that naturally showed up in my poetry. I was led away from the platform poems that the Washington experience, not to mention my dramatic efforts, had encouraged, though the poems of my own that I like best still include some of those—a few narrative poems, a few polemics (especially "Ode

The author

to New York"), and a number of fables. But the long-term effect of the disease—or perhaps of aging itself—was to drive me back toward quieter, more introspective verse, like this one reaching back to the darknesses in my father.

When Father Left in the Morning

When father left in the morning
He had the mark of evening
On him, and at evening the evening
Was wholly evening.
He lay with forever
After supper.

Mother watched him
From the other bed,
Brushing her hair back, looking for slippers,
Smoking.
Somewhere out in the hall
Were the living. She was ill.

The moon revolved
Over East Rock Road.
The Packard sat by the curb.
I lay in my bed in the next room
Listening,
Waiting for news.

But the news in the evening
Was always the same news,
And in the morning
The drift was to evening.
I was grown
Before morning came.

In the early stages of the disease I crazily took on a second job, a marvelous job, as editor of the back pages of the *New Republic.* Nancy and Gilbert Harrison were our neighbors in Cleveland Park, and Gil was an extraordinarily kind employer as I became erratically incapacitated. The *New Republic* was a fine antidote to the casualness of little quarterlies, for though it had been going so long that we could joke about its coming out by itself every week even if we all went elsewhere, it was basically relentless in its weekly discipline, differing from any other writing-editing role I had ever played. Then too, in running the reviews and writing a good many myself, I found it relentless as a maker, for me, of enemies—but at least enmity can be broadening.

And as a dividend, being in hospitals and at the same time trying to function as an editor, I picked up a new profession while just pushing buttons. I lay in bed staring at the tube, and became *NR's* TV critic. Gil gave me an alias: Sedulus.

Where would the world now be if Sedulus had persisted? Could his reformism have taken hold of the media as a whole, and moved them sullenly away from inanity and Alka-Seltzer? Would they have *been,* suddenly, a new message? Ho ho. But Sedulus did not persist; he got better.

He also received at that time a different kind of opportunity. He was sitting at home minding his business when a publishing-house editor he did not know called him, and within a week he had a contract to write a biography of William Carlos Williams. The contract loosely coincided with the end of Gil's ownership and editing of NR, and it was also the kind of assignment the Guggenheim people liked. Soon Sedulus was not only not Sedulus any more, but he was not an editor and, for a year, not a teacher either. He was an explorer in the unknown seas of a new genre.

If ever there was a genre in which a practitioner needs to display professional and personal modesty, it is biography. Its obligations are only incidentally to the forms and graces native to other literary struggles, and only minimally to the art of self-expression and salesmanship. Always there is the biographee to reckon with, and even if the biographee is Attila the Hun, he comes first. Nor is he apt to *be* Attila the Hun. Biographees who are deserving victims of a biographer's scorn are not many; the tradition of biography is largely commemorative, and though our age is one of muckrakers looking for muck, a biographee is not usually chosen if he does not have a few qualities worth honoring. Ignorant though I was, I knew this about biography before I entered upon it, and I also knew that I would not have been approached to "do" Williams if I had looked unfriendly.

Soon I learned that I was an approved or authorized biographer. Williams's widow, Flossie, had blessed me via James Laughlin, who had been Williams's publisher, with the result that the Williams private papers were open to me, as well as the resources, memories, and friendship of the Williams family. Assets, obligations. I was aware of both when I settled in, and thought I understood both my freedoms, which the Williamses insisted on, and the limits to the freedoms. Now, long after the event, I can say that I misjudged those limits, and I sometimes wish I'd been commissioned to write a biography of someone *long* dead.

Yet I say that, oddly, without reference to the Williams clan itself. The clan itself was fine. It was not the clan but the literary community with a professional stake in Williams that went after me when the book appeared. The community was, I think, wrong, but from Allen Tate (who had never much liked Williams) I at least learned how I had erred, tactically. Tate wrote me a postcard with the simple, courteous intent of praising the book. So he said he liked it, and that was good news, but then he added that the trouble with Williams was that he had no brains. That was, inadvertently on his part, the bad news. The trouble with Williams. I had not meant to describe a trouble so much as a quality. I had meant to reinforce Ezra Pound's comic comment about him that he was the most incoherent bloke who ever gargled. I had thought that if *Pound* could dwell on the impressionistic urgencies of the man's writings and speech, while still respecting him, *I* could. I was wrong. For the professionals it was clear I had not shown respect: their kind. So: lesson number one about biography came my way expensively. The book was praised but in the places without clout. It did not make it to paperback.

So I was ready for biography lesson number two, and received that quickly in the form of rejections from several publishers of a partly completed manuscript of six short biographies. What was wrong with *it?* Everything. In the first place *nobody* was doing short biographies, they hadn't been done since Plutarch. In the second place my scheme for tying the six biographees together was ridiculous; I was working on social rather than literary connections between them, and was not suitably attuned to the critical infelicity of putting Henry Adams and Jack London in the same room (along with Upton Sinclair, John Dos Passos, Allen Tate, and of course Williams). And thirdly the focus of the biographies was wrong. In them I kept worrying about what my subjects were saying and thinking about their times, their world, their culture, when anybody with half a brain knew that literary people and literary biographers had more important private things to worry about. In other words lesson number two was that biography, though probably the fuzziest of literary genres, was not fuzzy for its merchandisers. *They* knew its dimensions and purpose.

So with my six-subject manuscript in a drawer I was ready for lesson number three.

But I was also ready to retire from teaching, and did so at age sixty-five, a financial error (there are no golden parachutes in academia, despite all the complaints about tenure). Retirement was also, however, an educational opportunity, since by putting aside my forty English-department years I was an instant free intellect. And by now I was even relatively free of family obligations, with all the children out of the nest and doing strange adult things. Nor was I yet, so far as I could determine, senile. So I entered retirement in 1984 and managed to tie myself up all over again.

Tying myself up seems to be my fate, though the first tying after retirement was not my doing. In June of 1984 Robert Fitzgerald had been asked to be poetry consultant at the Library of Congress, and having accepted had almost instantly learned he had cancer. I was asked to fill in—he died during the year—and so renewed my affair with the library and the Consultantship. Neither, I found, had changed much in twenty years, except that in the interval the *Washington Post,* that sole arbiter of Washington thought and culture, seemed to have decided that neither existed. My second stint at the library was quieter, but still rewarding, and it was followed by lesson number three, a happier one, in biography.

Reed Whittemore

Lesson number three involved becoming a student of the history of the genre and discovering, among many other things, that my manuscript in the drawer was not intellectually alien to it. Lesson number three also involved writing yet another book, *Pure Lives,* which is now out in the world and waiting to be accompanied by its sequel, *Whole Lives. Pure Lives* rushed the history of biography up to Johnson and Boswell. *Whole Lives* takes the genre up to the here and now. Both books are small. At age seventy one favors small books, especially when tied up with still other affairs.

Yes, in 1987—as if I had not had enough editing—I started another magazine: *Delos.* Why? I believe that Chaucer's Nun's Priest explained its appearance in my life precisely a few centuries before I existed, when, describing Chanticleer's foolishness in flying down from the beam, he cried, "O Destinee, that mayst not be eschewed!"

POSTSCRIPT: Reed Whittemore contributed the following update to *CA* in 2004:

To continue, briefly, after a long lapse.

The name *Delos* had first been settled on, by scholarly editors in Texas, as suitable for a translation magazine. My own colleagues and I appropriated it—with acknowledgments—and tried to show, for ten issues, that we knew what we were about. Thought we might simply put the quarrelsome world back together as, a while back, the Greeks had tried to do on the island of Delos where several cultures mingled. If there was any fault to our enterprise it was perhaps merely this futile integrative purpose, rather than the one of righteously tearing the world apart in the sensible tradition of little mags like those I had grown up with. If *Delos* had persisted it might even have become (God forbid) a regular establishment magazine—and in fact it seems to have been taken over anew for that purpose, after my aged friends and I tired, by a gentleman at the University of Florida. I know not how long the project lasted there, but a noble one it was and I will not complain about it, only pointing out that in our hands it was not a publication of properly indignant youth.

Yes, like most of my fellow editors I was aging by then though I kept my weight down, exercised regularly, and drank just two vodkas before supper. I kept working at poems plus a few stories and a small collection of fables. And as I write this I am even dreaming of putting together a miscellany of all such labor, perhaps headed by a long poem, *Job's Impiety,* that had been provoked by the loss of Helen's and my third child, Jack, to an insidious disease at age thirty-seven. Jack and I had even visited Israel healthily together before his trouble set in, and he had started a fine restaurant in Minneapolis where justice—if only it existed—would have prevailed and he would be with us now. The death of children does bring parents into Job's world despite any theoretically Godly compensations later.

For some years after retirement from the University of Maryland I took on informal teaching jobs, mostly inoffensive affairs putting me at a long table in a small room with retired folk like myself who, unlike myself, had not suffered at "Creative Writing" for decades and thought that creation might be fun. I didn't try consciously to discourage them but I'm sure I often did—decades of moping about with pen and ink can greatly reduce the trade's romance, especially when the romance is commercialized (as our country regularly manages to make it). I even tried a couple of informal sessions of discussion about the 1930s, reading (with more retired folk) angry books and magazines of the Depression time and noting how remote, literarily, from our own posh era it was. In that period—filled in my memory with my Republican father's anger at FDR—there was also of course leftist anger of what I thought of as the *right* kind—futile though it proved to be—anger at the money folk, anger that actually emerged in the period's literature, making that emotion a basic part of, rather than separate from, the labors of pen and ink. Many earnest scribbles then were trying to be a part of the messy world—that is, *furioso* about it—rather than a best-selling profiteer in it.

But teaching the Depression thirties from the distance of more than half a century proved to be in itself depressing, since so much had happened in between—not just World War II and Vietnam but also the rise of the social sciences in ways that managed, perhaps innocently, to drive the individualism historically practiced in the humanities toward social irrelevance. Poet Kenneth Fearing, poor chap, was one of the last talents in his trade to confront the new condition whereby masses rather than single minds do all the thinking, but one penetrating social-science volume of the 1950s also went at the problem, Whyte's *The Organization Man.* There the depressing rise of mass, Gallup-poll thinking was complained about, that *before* his complaint ceased to be a complaint and became accepted as simply a basic social condition. Three decades later in my old age I found myself even serving on a committee where a "social engineer" rose to inform us that an individual could not be complex. So much for the humanities.

While this demotion was occurring, I of course retired from teaching. Helen and I came to live quietly in College Park in a small house overlooking a fine woods that had somehow been preserved by Washington's Metro. There I walked regularly thinking of Thoreau until I fell in a hole and suffered a minor shin fracture. The fracture kept me—though the world did too—from imagining with Thoreau that I could achieve complex independence in my own private cabin. (I can't even stop a leak in the toilet, and our last water bill was frightful). So now we live here as weary old marrieds, sometimes wondering why the people on the trains we can hear tooting in the distance—as Thoreau did—want to go anywhere anyhow. Unlike Thoreau, however, we do of course have TV and the morning paper to tell us what is happening out beyond the woods in places like Baghdad.

Before the Iraq invasion I participated futilely in an anti-war event by writing an anti-war poem (see below), but before even that I sat down (as a hopefully complex individual) to put together one more biographical book describing the "shared impiety" of *Six Literary Lives.* For it I chose individuals who had been—in their primitive times—impious about the state of the collectively thoughtful world around them when each thought that he was doing the thinking. First there was rich worldly Henry Adams, worried that by 1921 the human mind would not be able to cope with *anything* any more (he just didn't know about Gallup). Then came Jack London, wandering for a day or two through the slums of London in the 1920s and discovering (a bit sociologically I admit) that the lot of people in general was in need of improvement. Then came his friend Upton Sinclair, who was a solid leftist, hence more businesslike as a problem-solver, but he was followed by a miscellany of persistently complex individuals—William Carlos Williams, John Dos Passos and Allen Tate—who obviously didn't really know what the world had come to be about. Looking back now, ten years after the book, I can't say that I knew what it was about either. I can't, that is, say with any confidence that I know, now, of what "impiety" consists, after all, in a world governed by polls rather than individuals. At least, however, I casually took on, in an appendix to the volume, a short history of "naturalists" in which I compared Thoreau with Darwin (among many others, like the mighty Humboldt, who wrote a complete history of the *Kosmos*), and had individualist Thoreau come out ahead! I proved this by simply providing his private response to a sunset rather than trying to put the helpless sunset in a universal historical context. Unfortunately Thoreau was, as any sociologist knows, quite wrong in imagining that he could keep the context (or the pollsters) out.

Oh well, a simplistically caged condition is what one lives with in old age, with or without TV. The condition is magnified, however, by the helplessness one feels when the outside comes crashing in, because it is deemed to be a wicked outside by the Gallupized forces of freedom at home, forces like those that flew American forces to Iraq in 2003. I therefore became a peacenik for our Iraq invasion and wrote the attached blast. And now, unfortunately, at the caged moment of this writing (with the forces of freedom well mired in their conquered country), I have no angry, *Furioso,* I-told-you-so editorial to present about our current national condition, but am instead merely depressed by how far the "free" world as a whole has moved away from Thoreau's (and archaic little mag editors') complaints about that world. The archaic condition known as individualism—by which one could at least profess to be, if not alone, at least an entity living quietly outside the monstrous human cage—such a condition no longer exists even when one is living quietly in retirement next to a quiet woods (owned by the Washington Metro).

So I now lie awake at night listening to the distant rumbling and tooting of old-fashioned earthy CSX trains but knowing more than Thoreau—lucky chap—seems to have. I now visit the Maryland campus just to go its fine library and get a helpful librarian to look up a book for me in its incomprehensible new filing machinery. The old books are at least still there, and I can take them home and lie down in my cage as if I were not there at all, but still able to wander about as if free and complex.

*Weapons of Mass Destruction**

Oh!
You should know
That Weapons M.D., Weapons M.D.,
Threatening all mortal beings with instant catastrophe,
Are now being made in more than one evil foreign country,
Foreign country,

But oh! oh!
Lucky we are to be making our very own Weapons M.D.
Weapons M.D.,
That are bigger and better and much more democratic
Weapons M.D.
Than any weapons M.D.
Made by any evil foreign country,

And oh! oh! oh!
We have our morality,
Our lovely sweet American morality
To fight off catastrophe
Brought on by any bad evil arrogant foreign country
With their weapons M.D.,
Weapons M.D.

**Written before the invasion of Iraq*

BIOGRAPHICAL AND CRITICAL SOURCES:

BOOKS

Contemporary Literary Criticism, Volume 4, Gale (Detroit, MI), 1975.
Contemporary Poets, seventh edition, St. James Press (Detroit, MI), 2001.
Dictionary of Literary Biography, Volume 5: *American Poets since World War II, First Series,* Gale (Detroit, MI), 1980, pp. 372-378.
Modern American Literature, fifth edition, St. James Press (Detroit, MI), 1999.
Nemerov, Howard, editor, *Poets on Poetry,* Basic Books, 1966.

PERIODICALS

Choice, May, 1975.
Library Journal, June 1, 1970.
New Leader, December 4, 1967.
New York Times Book Review, June 2, 1963.
Poetry, November, 1956.
Saturday Review, June 8, 1963; October 14, 1967.
Sewanee Review, Volume 71, 1963, Roger Hecht, "A Note on Reed Whittemore."
Yale Review, winter, 1968.

* * *

WORSLEY, F(rank) A(rthur) 1872-1943

PERSONAL: Born 1872, in Akaroa, New Zealand; died February 1, 1943.

CAREER: Explorer, navigator, and ship's captain. *Military service:* Commander, Royal Navy Reserve; ship captain for Ernest Shackleton on two polar expeditions.

WRITINGS:

Under Sail in the Frozen North, S. Paul and Co. Ltd. (London, England), 1927.
Endurance: An Epic Polar Adventure, P. Allan and Co. (London, England), 1931, Norton (New York, NY), 1999.

The Romance of Lloyd's: From Coffee-house to Palace, Hutchinson and Co. (London, England), 1932, Hillman-Curl (New York, NY), 1936.

First Voyage in a Square-rigged Ship, G. Bles (London, England), 1938.

The Great Antarctic Rescue: Shackleton's Boat Journey, introduction by Sir Edmund Hillary, Times Books (London, England), 1977, published as *Shackleton's Boat Journey,* Norton (New York, NY), 1977.

SIDELIGHTS: Born in 1872 during a time when the world's geographical extremes had still only been explored in a limited way, F. A. Worsley grew up to be a polar explorer and ship captain for Sir Ernest Shackleton on two expeditions to Antarctica. He was the joint leader of the British Arctic Expedition of 1925 as well as a commander in the Royal Navy Reserve.

Worsley first wrote of his polar excursions in *Under the Sail in the Frozen North* in 1927. In this volume he recounts the sixteen-day journey of the ship the *James Caird* to South Georgia under the navigation of Worsley, and the crew's rescue of people marooned on Elephant Island. In 1938 Worsley wrote *First Voyage in a Square-rigged Ship.*

Worsley is best known for his books *Shackleton's Boat Journey* and *Endurance: An Epic Polar Adventure,* both of which provide his account of the heroic and ill-fated transarctic expedition to the Weddell Sea from 1914 to 1916. Alfred Stephenson, a reviewer in the *Times Literary Supplement* called *Shackleton's Boat Journey* an account of "extraordinary hardship borne with unbelievable stoicism, as well as a thrilling story of the sea, and it is told with considerable descriptive ability and humor." Margery Fisher, a reviewer in *Growing Point,* described the book as "the book of a sailor, full of practical descriptions of storm, navigation, weather, but it is also the narrative of an incurable optimist and a shrewd student of human nature." Albert H. Johnston in *Publishers Weekly,* called the story one of the "world's great adventures," and "a stunning story of survival told by a captain who watched his ship's slow icy death in the Antarctic." A reviewer in the *New Yorker* was impressed with the way Worsley draws the reader's attention to such vivid details that they can "feel to [their] marrow the sub-zero cold, the endless soaking wet, the hunger and thirst, the stink and misery, the winds that ranged from gale to hurricane, the constant danger that the party endured before all hands were rescued."

BIOGRAPHICAL AND CRITICAL SOURCES:

BOOKS

Oxford Companion to Ships and the Seas, Oxford University Press (New York, NY), 1976, p. 944.

PERIODICALS

Growing Point, April, 1978, pp. 3302-3303.

New Yorker, March 28, 1977, pp. 126-127.

New York Times, December 27, 1998, p. 10.

Publishers Weekly, December 27, 1976, pp. 51-52.

Times Literary Supplement, August 25, 1978, p. 957.

Washington Post Book Review, February 15, 1987, p. 12.*

* * *

WRIGHT, Esmond 1915-2003

OBITUARY NOTICE—See index for *CA* sketch: Born November 5, 1915, in Newcastle on Tyne, England; died August 9, 2003, in Masham, North Yorkshire, England. Educator, politician, and author. Wright was a historian and former president of Swinton Conservative College, who gained national attention as a "television don" for his educational broadcasts and for winning a seat in Parliament as a Tory representing Glasgow. Specializing in American history—especially the American Revolutionary period—he was a graduate of the University of Durham, where he earned a B.A. in 1937 and an M.A. in 1948, and the University of Virginia, where he also received a master's degree in 1940. During World War II he enlisted in the Intelligence Corps and Education Corps and served in North Africa and the Middle East. He eventually achieved the rank of lieutenant colonel and returned to the United Kingdom to teach at the University of Glasgow in 1946. Becoming a professor of modern history there in 1957, he began using television to host television programs about history on the British Broadcasting Corp., and he also contributed regularly to newspapers. In 1967, much to the surprise of his colleagues, he ran for and won the Glasgow, Pollok seat in Parliament as a Conservative, a seat that had long been held by the Labour Party. However, political office did not suit him, and he left Parliament after only one term. Nevertheless, his status as a Conservative was established, and he was offered the position of principal of Swinton Conservative College, a job he held until 1976, when the college closed due to financial problems. Wright was not out of work, however, because since 1971 he had also been teaching American history and directing the Institute of U.S. Studies at the University of London, where he remained until his retirement in 1983. As a scholar, Wright was widely respected for his writings on American history, completing some twenty books during his career. These publications include *Fabric of Freedom: 1763-1800* (1961; revised edition, 1978), *The Causes and Consequences of the American Revolution* (1966), *Franklin of Philadelphia* (1986), *The Search for Liberty* (1994), and *The American Dream: From Reconstruction to Reagan* (1996).

OBITUARIES AND OTHER SOURCES:

PERIODICALS

Daily Telegraph (London, England), September 1, 2003.

Guardian (London, England), August 19, 2003, p. 23.

Times (London, England), August 19, 2003.